second edition

the AMERICAN FOUNDING

FRANK W. FOX

HISTORY DEPARTMENT
BRIGHAM YOUNG UNIVERSITY

Pearson
Custom
Publishing

Cover art: *The Spirit of Our Forefathers* by Jessica Hewlett-Ridd.

Printed in the United States of America

20 19 18 17 16 15 14 13 12

Please visit our web site at www.pearsoncustom.com

ISBN 0–536–68063–9

BA 995117

PEARSON CUSTOM PUBLISHING
75 Arlington Street, Suite 300, Boston, MA 02116
A Pearson Education Company

This book is dedicated
to the memory of my grandfather,
Frank M. Openshaw,
who cared deeply about
the American Founding.

CONTENTS

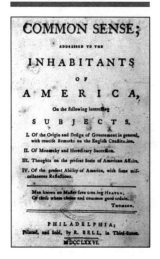

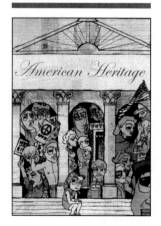

12

From the Constitution to the Republic   **336**

13

Expounding the Constitution   **372**

14

A Republican People   **408**

Conclusion **546**

Appendices **559**

Message from a former student and T.A.

One of the meanings of the word "heritage" is a gift passed down from one generation to another. This course is about a gift most people who have lived on the earth have never received—the gift of living in a stable, orderly, free society. We have been given that heritage from our nation's Founders. This class will help you better appreciate and understand America's heritage. But more important, if this class "works," you will be motivated to preserve it.

You will be rewarded for your hard work in this course. As you study America's story you will sense the reality that the future of America is whatever the American people want it to be. If America is to have a bright future we must make it happen. The material you study here will help you see how.

As a former student and teaching assistant I can tell you that no matter what your major or year in college, you can do very well in this class. You will have an excellent instructor. I predict that you will enjoy the lectures in this class as much as those in any other. While the class size is large, you will have a teaching assistant—a fellow student who has done well in the course—to review the material with you.

Now, a fair number of students do not earn a good grade in this class. You cannot simply attend most of the lectures, take casual notes, go to half of your review labs, do a little of the reading and get an "A." I have never seen it happen. This is not a fluff class. The students I have seen succeed have taken careful notes in lectures, read the assigned material and come to their review labs ready to discuss and examine the material. Anyone can do it. The students who don't "get" the material probably haven't paid the price to understand it. Paying the price now will be a very rewarding experience.

Good luck!

ACKNOWLEDGMENTS

This book evolved over a period of some twenty years in the teaching of a course titled "American Heritage" at Brigham Young University. The course seeks to combine insights and methodologies from history, political science and economics in order to give students a way of understanding their own past and, more especially, their own institutions. Because the course is interdisciplinary, it has drawn on an extended group of faculty in its design and pedagogy. The following constitute only the primary contributions.

In the history department, James B. Allen and Thomas G. Alexander pioneered course development. They were joined later on by Mark Grandstaff, Gary Daynes and Susan Rugh. In political science, Martin B. Hickman, Noel B. Reynolds and Louis Midgley led the way, to be followed by Ralph Hancock, Richard Vetterli, Brett Latimer and Matthew Holland. In economics, Clayne L. Pope and Larry Wimmer took part in the early discussions and helped establish American Heritage at the core of the university's general education curriculum.

Graphics were developed by Instructional Graphics at Brigham Young University, from ideas developed by Brett Hugh Latimer. The latter, a descendent of Bishop Hugh Latimer who was burned at the stake by Mary I in her attempt to return England to Catholicism, has been a valued collaborator in the entire project.

Several teaching assistants have also borne a hand, as the exercises found at the end of each chapter will indicate. A team consisting of Rebecca Johnston, Bryan Norton and Christopher Karpowitz developed a host of teaching materials early on, and their work was recently enhanced by another team consisting of Karen Reeder, Ben Ramsey and Tom Lufkin. Their efforts were ably directed by Joseph Darowski.

Virginia Rush conducted a competition among BYU art students which resulted in the cover art and several other visuals. Adam Darowski wrote the review questions found at the end of each chapter.

Joseph and Kay Darowski undertook meticulous copy editing and assisted in virtually every detail of preparing the manuscript for publication, and Neil L. York read through it to spot errors of fact and make valuable suggestions. Without the help of these three individuals, the project would never have come to fruition.

Introduction

A View of New Orleans by Boqueto de Woiserie (1803). (Courtesy of the Chicago Historical Society.)

One of the most curious aspects of the American Founding—a story filled with curious aspects—is the lack of interest it commonly merits from American college students. Even the most patriotic of them often fails to find the subject riveting. I suspect the reason for this is either that they accept the Founding as a given—like the Rocky Mountains or the Mississippi River—or else that they regard it as an impenetrable mystery. Either way, why try to figure it out?

Accordingly, the purpose of this book is twofold. First, we want to see if we can shed some light on the mystery. And second, we want to show that there was nothing "given" about it. Real people had to take chances, make tough decisions and try to come to grips with enormously difficult issues in order to make the Founding work. It was a dicey business all around, and for that reason alone an interesting one.

For it is the Founding, at bottom, that makes *America* interesting. Everything American, from Hollywood movies to computer software, seems to merit fascination in the world of the twenty-first century, but a rather special place is reserved for American constitutional forms. They were, after all, the first of their kind in the modern age, and beyond that they have proven to be the most stable and longest lasting. With the fall of communism in Europe, the interest in American institutions has increased. Peoples struggling toward nationhood in various parts of the world are asking anew questions about "founding" and are not infrequently looking to the United States for answers.

The Human Predicament

The story does not begin in 1776 with the ringing of the Liberty Bell. Indeed, it is as old as the human story—another reason it is so interesting—for it addresses a problem we can trace back to the very beginning. The Greeks knew the problem. So did the Romans. The Turks, the Chinese, the ancient inhabitants of the Americas, all of them ran up against it in one way or another and could give us an eloquent introduction to it. So, let's have one of them do so.

When the historian Thucydides looked back upon his world, the world of the ancient Greek republics, the sight he saw was little short of horrifying:

During the few days that Eurymedon, with his troops, continued at Corcyra, the people of that city extended the massacre to all whom they judged their enemies. The crime alleged was their attempt to overturn the democracy. Some perished merely through private enmity; some, for the money they had lent, by the hands of the borrower. Every kind of death, every dreadful act, was perpetrated. Fathers slew their children; some were dragged from altars, some were butchered at them; numbers, immersed in temples, were starved. The contagion spread through the whole extent of Greece. . . .

Thucydides' observations in this quotation are paraphrased by none other than John Adams, who was combing through the ancient record for lessons he could apply to his own time and place. As he read Thucydides and many others, Adams concluded that humankind has had to put up with a good deal of such pain and suffering. History strongly suggests, in fact, that the overwhelming majority of human beings have had to choose between two exceptionally unhappy alternatives—tyranny and anarchy:

Tyranny. We often think of tyrants as cruel despots, and many of them have certainly lived up to the reputation. But the truly essential feature of tyranny is neither cruelty nor despotism—it is simple human will. *Tyranny is the rule of will*. It is possible to imagine a "benevolent tyrant" such as Louis XIV, who does what he can to improve his people's lot, but even here it is the tyrant's will and that alone which determines life and death outcomes. With the rule of will, those who are ruled have to *hope* for benevolence on the part of the tyrant, for they literally have no other safeguards.

Anarchy. If tyranny is the rule of will, *anarchy is the rule of chaos*. Where the tyrant gathers all power unto himself, anarchy disperses it among the multitude, with the effect that every individual can exercise his *own* will. For a picture of the result, think of any good movie you have seen about the French Revolution, or the Russian, or the Chinese. Mobs roam the streets, burning and pillaging. Private armies crisscross the land with swaths of destruction. It is Thucydides' description of Corcyra over and over again.

Tyranny and anarchy often have a circular relationship, each leading around to the other. A tyrant, let us say, becomes so detested by the people he rules that they begin to plot his destruction. Sooner or later a revolt breaks out and, after a few thousand partisans have lost their lives, the tyrant is overthrown. But then, who will replace him? His opponents resolve themselves into various factions, each based on a separate creed or interest or ethnic identity, and the factions commence a bloody free-for-all. If none of the contenders proves capable of dominating its rivals, the anarchy goes on and on. And if one does manage to gain a whip hand, its leader becomes the new tyrant.

And so we come to what might be called the *human predicament*. It is not universal nor entirely without exceptions, but most human beings throughout most of history have essentially had to make a choice between tyranny, on the one hand, and anarchy, on the other. They have suffered under kings, lords, sultans, Caesars, pharaohs, moguls, satraps, chieftains, dictators, masters and a hundred other designations for tyrant, taking what comfort they could in the fact that they at least had order in their lives; or they have thrown in with rebels, insurrectos, renegades, rogues, adventurers, dissidents, freedom fighters, private armies and plotters of palace coups, hoping against hope that they could somehow ride the tiger.

The Good Society

With the human predicament in mind, we might note with small wonder that the longing for a "Good Society" has an equally long history. *The Good Society is one that escapes the human predicament.* It has had many different names over the centuries. Plato referred to it as a republic. In John Locke's day it was known as a commonwealth. John Adams used the term free government. We would probably call it a liberal democracy today. And as the terms are all different, so too are the various conceptions of the Good Society that political philosophers have advanced. Still, most of them have the following three attributes in common. The Good Society:

- Extends the benefits of social interaction beyond a single favored group or class to society as a whole.

- Strives for a reasonable balance between liberty—defined as the right of individuals to seek their own happiness in their own way—and order.

- Offers its citizens a variety of "goods of the soul"—including such things as political participation, a sense of individual empowerment and a sense of human dignity.

In sum, the Good Society gestures toward human good in meaningful ways. We acknowledge it whenever we talk about "truth" or "justice" in public affairs, or conversely whenever we point up "wrongs" and demand they be righted. In our own history, the Good Society was under discussion in Boston when the tea ships landed; and in Lincoln's Cabinet when he pondered freeing the slaves; and on Omaha Beach in Normandy when thousands laid down their lives for a just cause. On the other side, our recollections of Indian wars, or race riots, or the incarceration of Japanese Americans during World War II often give us a contrary feeling. Like the judge's famous definition of obscenity, we know the Good Society when we see it.

The ideal of the Good Society has been enshrined in Plato's *Republic*, in Locke's *Second Treatise on Government*, in Rousseau's *Social Contract*, in Montesquieu's *Spirit of the Laws* and in many other works of political philosophy. Indeed, whenever mortals have faced the horrors of the human predicament, the thoughtful among them have supposed that somehow there must be a better way.

USA

It is not the purpose of this book to argue that the United States of America is the world's first, best or only Good Society. Patriots, of course, have maintained that it is all of the above, while critics have denied that it is a Good Society at all. Our purpose is to study the American Founding as a way of understanding America itself, and from that perspective I would like to submit that America—and I use that term throughout as a reference to the United States of America—is the world's most self-conscious Good Society. That is to say, Americans, probably more than any other people, think of their nation-state in relation to the rest of the world, to universal truth and to the experience of mankind.

The American Founders themselves are a good illustration. If the center of their world was a point on the map somewhere between London and Paris, they were living on the far-flung periphery of that world, socially, politically, economically and culturally. They had every reason to regard themselves as the most provincial of provincials. Yet as we read through their correspondence, the records of their deliberations, their explanations to the world and most of all the founding documents themselves, we don't see them behaving like provincials at all—on the contrary, they spoke and acted as if they were the children of the ages. They laced their discussions with references to classical antiquity. They discoursed on their relationship to **Nature** (with a capital "N") and first principles. They spoke of their land in terms that reflected Eden and their hopes for the future in terms that reflected utopia. They discussed the European Enlightenment as though its real purpose had been to provide background for their own undertaking. Something seems to have convinced them of their own surpassing specialness—which may be one reason why we look back on them and see demigods.

There was, however, another side to their experience, and the two are often difficult to reconcile. If the Founders had one foot in the realm of theory, the other foot was in the realm of practice. Virtually every one of them were practical men of affairs, not cloud-bound philosophers, and throughout the events this book describes, they were harried, overworked, caught up in events which seemed anything but clear and wondering what on earth to try next. The consequence of this double-sidedness couldn't be more striking. Yes, the American Founders really were thinking about the Good Society and their own providential role in bringing it forth, and, yes, at the same time they were thinking about the nuts and bolts of actually building one.

Accordingly, what we will look for in the story of the American Founding are two interwoven strands. In one of them we will catch glimpses of an ideal world, the sort that Plato wrote about in the *Republic*, a world of truth and justice and human dignity. In the other we will see something more like, for want of a better term, "Peoria, Illinois." Politicos used to express doubt by saying: "Fine, but how will it play with the little old lady in Peoria?"—meaning how will it work in the real world as we know it? In the real world as we know it, it may not be possible to bring forth perfect justice, sublime happiness, total freedom and unbounded prosperity for everyone—the best to hope for is considerable justice, a chance for happiness, conditional freedom and a growing prosperity for most. Keep an eye on Utopia, in other words, but keep an eye on Peoria too.

The American Founding, then, was at once a stroke of extraordinary brilliance, approaching the very sublime of human achievement, and at the same time what a group of politicians was willing to settle for under the circumstances. Probe it as we may, it will partly remain a mystery. No single individual, no single point of view can be credited with the final accomplishment. There was a broad variety of contributions, some reflecting one idea and some another, some representing bold flights of theory and some meek acknowledgments of experience, often joined together in surprising ways. The resulting congruities and incongruities make the study of this exceptional phenomenon worthy of our attention. And as we sort through the tangle, it may help us to grapple with the deepest mystery of all—why the American Founding worked.

The Art and Science of Founding

(Courtesy of the Philadelphia Convention and Tourist Bureau.)

Not every political society can look back to a "founding" as such. Most, in fact, came into being as a result of military conquest, historical happenstance, or likeliest of all, some process of gradual evolution. But most attempts to establish a Good Society have included a founding, for the very idea of a Good Society implies conscious human intention.

This is not to say that there must always be a dramatic "founding moment"—a point in time when a document is signed and the bells are rung. Americans in particular like to celebrate such moments. There was July 4, 1776, when the Declaration of Independence was signed and, yes, the bells did ring. Many scholars would prefer September 17, 1787, when the Constitution was signed, or possibly June 21, 1788, when the ninth state ratified it. Thomas Jefferson thought of his election as President in 1800 as the founding moment—the "Second American Revolution"—and a number of his supporters agreed. Still other Americans pointed out that the United States as we know it today was essentially a product of the Civil War. It could be argued, in other words, that the American Founding is an episodic *re*founding.

Even so, we can still step back and visualize a founding moment. At some point in time the crucial elements really did come together and the political society we know as the United States of America experienced its birth. To discover when that moment actually occurred, and what actually transpired, might be to discover what the United States actually is.

Elements of a Founding

Most foundings include several elements. First, there is usually a specific name of the polity in question and perhaps a rough description of its geography. Second, there is generally a system of fundamental laws together with a sketch (at the very least) of an essential political order. Of the laws we will have more to say further on. The political order sets up a governmental structure of some kind and may also describe its operation. We use the word *constitution* to refer to either or both of the above, sometimes rather loosely. A constitution can exist

Founding: See study aid.

9

as a set of unspoken agreements—a broad understanding of the rules of the game—or it can be meticulously spelled out in writing like a legal document.

The third element of a founding concerns citizenship. *Who rules?* is the way the ancients used to put the question, and the answers were never simple. In the modern world we generally resolve *who rules* into two separate questions:

Who participates in the political process and why?

Who is excluded and why?

The answers can be quite revealing. For example, Aristotle argued that women, children and slaves could never take part in the political process because they were by nature the "ruled part" of humanity rather than the "ruling part"—made to take orders. In our own time, we have denied participation to African Americans for reasons less straightforward. Asking the citizenship question is a way of asking what a given society is all about.

Polity: A group of people who organize themselves into a political society.

The fourth element of a founding is what we might call a sense of "**polity**" or "nationhood." That is, citizens feel themselves to be part of a people, an organic whole, not just a political organization. As a people, they will probably have distinguishing manners and mores, a "cultural identity," which may affect their political life in subtle ways. They might also have some sort of moral consensus—a fundamental agreement about right and wrong—binding them together.

Finally, most foundings are rooted in a "**founding myth**." The myth may be as romantic as an ancient hero pulling a sword from a stone, or as prosaic as a group of founders praying over some burdensome issue before resolving it. In either case, the people need to feel that the founding is somehow sanctioned by the gods, by nature, by truth and justice, or by history. The founding myth imparts a sense of legitimacy.

One might ask how all of these elements are supposed to come together. How does a group of people suddenly begin to see themselves as *a* people, find that they share widespread agreement on fundamentals, work out a system of laws and a structure of government, resolve the question of citizenship, and come to believe that all of this is the result of divine purpose? Or in other words, why do foundings happen at all? To pose the question, and to think carefully about the answer, is to conclude that foundings, and especially foundings aiming at a Good Society, must be among the strangest and most improbable of human achievements.

Ancient Foundings

The foundings of ancient polities suggest that, in the old days at least, the mythical element was the key. For once the gods had made their determination, all else fell into place. Thus, Yahweh wrote Israel's law on stone tablets and entrusted them to Moses. Jupiter dictated the laws of Crete to his own sons, Minos and Rhadamanthus, who went on to found Minoan civilization. The laws of Lacedaemon were given to Lycurgus by Apollo. And the ancient Romans could thank Numa Pompilius and the nymph Egeria for their ceremonial laws and religious rites.

These cases also illustrate the crucial role of law in the founding process. The fact that the law was handed down by the gods themselves took care of the legitimacy problem. The structure and operation of government were implied in the law if not openly stated in it. And those who recognized and obeyed the law automatically became *the people*.

Equally crucial was the role of the "Lawgiver." When he was recognized as a divine or supernatural figure, that fact alone endowed the law with a special sanctity. In time, the Lawgiver became both mortalized and pluralized. He was ever less likely to be a mythical hero and ever more likely to be a statesman, a jurist, occasionally even a philosopher. And the edicts of a single individual were gradually replaced by the deliberations of a small body reasoning together. The "Lawgiver" became the "Founder."

As the founding process became humanized, founders tried to account for such ineffable things as moral truth, human dignity, even public happiness. They drew upon past experience, future possibility, custom and tradition, public values, religious perceptions and the unique genius of the people. With the ever greater importance of law, foundings became less a matter of fire and blood and more a matter of "justice." The idea of power associated with tyranny was gradually replaced by the idea of authority. In the very concept of a founding, we begin to see outlines of the Good Society.

> Examples of a **Lawgiver:** Moses for the Israelites, Hammurabi for Babylon, Solon for ancient Athens.

Revolution and Founding

Foundings rarely just happen. They usually result from some sort of political upheaval, such as a revolution, and the consequent need to rethink fundamentals.

Revolutions occur because large numbers in a given society become fed up. It has happened to relatively old peoples—the French, the English, the Russians, the Chinese—and relatively new ones. Revolution can also bring a people into being and give them a sense of themselves *as* a people.

Not infrequently, revolution takes the form of a cathartic "rebirth." A society suffering under tyrannical oppression builds steadily in its discontent until eventually something blows. Then, in a burst of energy, the people come together and throw off their shackles, tasting freedom for the first time. In the heady atmosphere of success, the revolutionists often consider making extreme changes. They may seek:

A return to "Eden." That is, they remember (or perhaps imagine) some earlier condition of happiness to which they now wish to return. In England's Glorious Revolution, for instance, many of the revolutionists looked back to what they fondly recalled as the lost Saxon democracy.

An advance toward Utopia. Perhaps the past was never that good—but the chance has come to right all wrongs, eradicate injustice and create the world as it ought to be. Thomas More's *Utopia* painted an alluring picture of such a world, and it became the theme of the Bolshevik Revolution in Russia, among others.

> **Utopia:** Book by Sir Thomas More published in 1516 describing an imaginary perfect society.

> **Thomas More/Utopia:** www.orst.edu/instruct/ phl302/philosophers/more .html

Just as there are alternative ways to see revolutions, there are alternatives ways to see foundings. Revolutionists who seek a return to Eden will regard the act of founding conservatively, drawing upon the inspiration of the past. This was the way the world used to be, they will say, and we liked it a lot better. They will value experience, tradition, established institutions, even though these may be flawed or may have been perverted of late. Conversely, revolutionists who look to an ultimate Utopia will regard their founding radically, seeking to establish a new and unprecedented order. They will tend to invoke reason rather than experience, will rely on the human imagination, and may advance a bold new revolutionary doctrine, such as "Marxism-Leninism."

There is a third possibility too. A founding could also be rooted in the "laws of nature." Belief in such laws goes way back. They are understood to be the moral equivalent of physical laws, such as the law of gravity. By nature, one might say, it is wrong for one person to steal property from another or to harm another without justifiable cause. Philosophers who have emphasized natural law, such as Cicero or Thomas Aquinas, argue that it is accessible to all human beings through common intuition, or "natural reason," and thus that it inspires many of the black-letter laws passed by legislatures. A political society founded on natural law principles might be neither radical nor conservative in the ways we have described—and yet it might also be both.

While revolutions typically precede foundings and make them possible, all revolutions do not lead to foundings, certainly not to successful ones. Indeed, most revolutions lead to the episodic chaos and tyranny described above. In his study of the ancient republics, John Adams listed massacre after massacre (and gave the death toll for each) resulting from revolutionary disturbances. Any reader of the newspapers today could more or less do the same.

Accordingly, one of the intriguing questions of human history is why some revolutions "succeed"—that is, lead to a successful founding—while others fail. Those committed to establishing a Good Society have been especially interested in this question. But they have found few hard answers. In the course of the 1600s, England experienced two revolutions: one of them resulted in a bloody civil war with an inconclusive outcome, and the other led to a successful founding. Here is another puzzler. The American and French Revolutions occurred within a few years of each other and were propelled by many of the same ideas. The French Revolution resulted in years of confusion, then the Terror, then Napoleon, then the restoration of the monarchy, then two more revolutions, another empire, several rocky attempts at establishing a stable democracy, and finally a world war. The American Revolution resulted in the USA.

The Durable Founding

While many lessons can be drawn from such comparisons, one stands out. For a revolution to result in a successful founding, the people themselves have to be generally satisfied with its outcome. If the satisfied include only a small group or a single class, everyone else will continue to perceive injustice and sooner or later there will be more turmoil.

Skulls of Khmers from Cambodian Killing Fields, circa 1980. Not all revolutions lead to the founding of a Good Society. (By Brian Eades, *The Observer*, courtesy of Getty Images.)

Epistemology

With the broad mass of the people in mind, we can think of foundings in one of two ways:

> *Universal.* As the term suggests, a *universal* founding is correct for all people at all times and in all situations—"what ought to be everywhere," in the words of Condorcet. Universalism implies that the human animal is of a common type, and if the right means are employed, we could take a random sampling of that type and work them into a successful political society. So thought the Russian revolutionists, in any case. After what appeared to be the triumphant founding of the Soviet Union in 1917, they confidently predicted that Europe, Asia, the Americas and eventually the entire world must follow suit.

> *Particular.* Here the assumptions are just opposite. A *particular* founding is correct only at a given time, in a given place and for a given people. It might not be right for any other. When we say, in common speech, that something "works for me," we are using the particularistic mode of

Universal/Particular:
See study aid.

Condorcet (1753–1794):
French mathematician, philosopher and politician; corresponded with John Adams.

thinking. A particularist would point out that Soviet Communism did not take the world by storm after all. It was adopted by others only at gunpoint and not very successfully at that.

Each of these alternatives requires—in the words of political scientist Bradley Thompson—its own "constitutional epistemology." This formidable phrase simply means that the kind of reasoning employed by the founders will be very different in the two cases. Universalism will emphasize abstract, deductive, *a priori* reasoning. The founders will say, in effect: *The human animal being thus and such will accordingly require this, that and the other to live in a successful political society*. We can see how the ancient lawgivers were regarded as prophets, for they spoke with enormous confidence and seemed to have all the right answers beforehand.

Particularism, on the other hand, will emphasize empirical, inductive, *a posteriori* reasoning. In other words, the founders will examine the established facts of a particular political situation, possibly of other similar situations, and will ask empirical rather than logical questions:

What has worked best for us?

What seems to work for those most like us?

What specific conclusions can we draw from this information?

There will be little abstract reasoning here and very little self-certainty. Conclusions will be limited and partial, often based on past mistakes, and made only after a great deal of discussion. Particularism, moreover, will emphasize things like "the character of the people" and will assume that such character is at least as important to a founding as any formal political arrangements.

Both types participate in most foundings, including the American. But in the American case it is the particularists who prevail. True, some of the American Founders liked to make blank assertions about politics and humanity, and their *Novus Ordo Seclorum* (New Order of the Ages), which is still visible on the dollar bill, was sweepingly universal. In the main, though, the Americans combed back over their English constitutional heritage and asked each other how this or that feature had worked (or perhaps failed to work) in actual practice. They were adapting traditional verities to new circumstances.

Stability

A durable founding also requires a stable polity. Two societies founded on similar ideals may have very different political arrangements, and one of them might turn out to be inherently more stable than the other. For a simple analogy, think about one pretty girl and two good-looking guys on a date—an inherently *un*stable arrangement. Under the Articles of Confederation, the American states had much in common and much to bind them together, but they had not achieved a stable political order, and as a result they experienced a good deal of grief. They had a founding of sorts but not a durable one.

Aristotle was especially interested in the durability problem, which is a very old one. He undertook a comparative analysis of the constitutional arrangements common in ancient Greece, noting what factors seemed to promote stability or instability in each. He had essentially three models to choose from:

Monarchy. The powers of government are concentrated in the person of a hereditary ruler. Aristotle called it "the rule of one."

Aristocracy. The powers of government are concentrated in the elite of society, the wisest, best educated and most virtuous. For Aristotle, "the rule of the few."

Democracy. The powers of government are exercised by all citizens. "The rule of the many."

Aristotle noted the tendency of each general model toward its own kind of instability and its own form of corruption. Monarchy often degenerated into **despotism**. Aristocracy could turn into **oligarchy**. And democracy easily fell into plain chaos. Yet there were strategies for strengthening each of the three so as to promote stability and integrity. Any of them, suitably modified, could become the foundation of a *republic*—the ancient world's term for a Good Society.

In the early 1700s, Aristotle's study was updated by a French political scientist named Montesquieu. His compendium, titled *Spirit of the Laws*, examined the structure and operation of governments all over the world, comparing and contrasting a variety of features. Montesquieu claimed to have no special favorites, but it was clear enough from reading between the lines that he admired many features of the English constitution. England had always had *government*, perhaps, but after the Glorious Revolution of 1688 and the established supremacy of Parliament, it had something that went deeper than government—a true *founding*.

America's two principal lawgivers, John Adams and James Madison, made studies of their own. Adams began his during the American Revolution. He examined no fewer than fifty republics, ancient and modern, asking himself over and over what it was that made them tick. Why did a few of them—a *precious few*—prove to be relatively durable, while the rest more or less self-destructed? he wondered. James Madison conducted his search through history when it became apparent to him that the American Confederation was foundering. Why did some constitutions work so well, he asked, while others, outwardly similar, failed so badly? Madison had an additional spur to his curiosity. He found himself in a veritable laboratory of comparative government, observing thirteen different republics in action, and once again he could see marked differences in their performance: some of the state governments appeared to be sailing along serenely, while others were heading toward the shoals. Why?

All of these observers, ancient and modern, drew some general conclusions. The first was that the durable constitution needed to be "mixed" or "balanced" in some way, so that the various orders in a given society might each have a say in public discourse, might each defend itself against the others, and above all might each check the drift of power into dangerous places. For it was when power began to drift that the difficulties occurred.

Ancient Greece:
http://eawc.evansville.edu/grpage.htm

See study aid.

Despotism: Oppressive rule by a single individual.

Oligarchy: Oppressive rule by an elite few.

Montesquieu:
www.fordham.edu/halsall/mod/monstesquieu-spirit.html

Glorious Revolution:
www.bartleby.com/65/gl/Glorious.html

Their second conclusion was that the durable constitution needed to pay careful attention to the question of *who rules*. Given that all groups had a certain voice in public affairs, whose voice ought to be loudest and heard most clearly? For Aristotle it was the middle classes. For they, he argued, were the most accountable of all the contenders and the least likely to go to extremes. As property owners and taxpayers, the middle classes had a stake in society. They also embraced cohesive institutions such as family and local community, and had a deeper regard for religion and morality. Both Adams and Madison reached similar conclusions. They distrusted the very poor for their lack of personal independence and the very rich for their "aristocratical passions"—love of gold, love of praise, love of power—and the influence these must have on politics.

Rule of Law: See study aid.

The third conclusion was that the "**rule of law**" was all-important. We will learn later on precisely what was meant by those three simple-sounding words. For now, it suffices to repeat a phrase often used by the American Founders— "government of laws and not men"—which meant that people must be governed by general rules, not particular directives. It also meant that citizens had to revere the law as they would revere something sacred.

In time there would emerge an entire science of creating durable constitutions. It would include some very subtle considerations:

> How much power can a government safely be given? How much is too much? How much is not enough?

> How to apportion that power so that its possessors will tend to respond appropriately? What conditions would prompt a public official to behave better than he otherwise might? Or worse?

> How flexible should a constitution be? Who should be able to change it and under what circumstances?

> How to create a sense of legitimacy in the constitution? How to endow it with the mysterium of those ancient mythical foundings?

All of this was important. However, the single *most* important factor in creating the durable constitution was to base it on a correct understanding of human nature. A government of angels, for angels, would be easy to contrive, Madison noted dryly—the trick was devising a government for men.

Foundings and Human Nature

For the ancients, there was a close tie between human nature and politics. The *polis*, which was the primary political unit of the ancient world, was thought to be much like an individual person, with strengths and weaknesses, likes and dislikes, an inclination toward certain kinds of endeavor and a disinclination toward others. In a manner of speaking, the soul of the *polis* was the individual soul writ large.

This belief had two implications. First, any given *polis* would presumably reflect the moral and spiritual qualities of its citizens. Thus Sparta, which was often aggressive and warlike, was inhabited by aggressive and warlike people, and its constitution bore the markings of a military dictatorship; while Athens, a lover of the muses, not only sponsored a wide variety of activities, it favored the inclusiveness of democracy.

Second, a good political order—as opposed to a bad one—might have the capacity not only to *reflect* human nature but to *improve* it. The argument goes something like this. The human animal is what it is by virtue of learned behavior. If children are exposed only to positive influences, they will develop accordingly. So in a society focused on truth, justice, honor, dignity and concern for one's fellow-man, we are much more likely to see those qualities reproduced. Plato went so far as to suggest that the ideal republic be guided solely by philosophers like himself.

These assumptions led to a level of political involvement we would hardly recognize today. In some of the ancient republics, citizens found highest meaning in political activity, the sort of meaning we might look for in professional careers or family life or even religion. The active shaping of one's own world—and thus one's own character—by means of the political process, with open horizons of possibility, we would associate with the most utopian of revolutionaries. It was what led Aristotle to observe that man was an "animal made for political activity"—a *zoon politikon*.

In what specific ways did the *zoon politikon* (political animal) link politics to human nature? The question is as relevant to our own time as it was to antiquity, and the American Founders pored over it as thoughtfully as the ancients did:

Tribalism

Human nature is "tribal" in the sense that *Homo sapiens* apparently want to live among their own kind. Within limits, we wish to act alike, dress alike, talk alike and see whatever movie is drawing the biggest crowds. The same (except for the movie) was true for the ancients. Societies have always been knit together by culture.

Tribalism creates a sense of community and common purpose—a sense of "we." It is the taproot of what we call patriotism. But it divides as well as unites. Those who cannot be a part of *our* tribe must necessarily be of some other, and this fact points up one of the fundamental problems of political society. How is the "other," the outsider, to be regarded? There were essentially only two answers for the ancients. Outsiders must either be excluded altogether or else included only as servants or slaves.

The problem of otherness would not be made easier in the modern world, especially in America. The bringing of various peoples together would create language differences, religious differences, ethnic differences and racial differences to deal with. No political society, apparently, could escape the homogenizing tendency of tribalism, nor could a political founding contemplate the inclusion of outsiders. Yet could a Good Society include only insiders?

Reason

All human beings had a capacity to reason, the ancients observed, but some had more than others. Accordingly, philosophers of antiquity often focused on "the rational element" in society. Who were they? How could they be identified? How could their numbers and quality be increased? How could their influence best be brought to bear on public issues?

Closely tied to reason was education. The assumption was that learning made a vast difference in the promotion of rationality. Give human beings the best possible education and you will make them into the best possible citizens. It was for this reason, broadly considered, that Plato established his Academy and Aristotle his Lyceum, and that Socrates posed his mind-bending interrogatives.

Also tied to reason was something we might call "creativity." Educated men, employing reason, could surely create their own political world, it was thought, not just inherit one from the past. Why remain content with the *polis* as it was when human creativity might be able to improve it, pare away its flaws and enhance its ability to perfect human nature? Platonic ideals such as truth, justice and the good often came into play when creativity was under discussion, and politics itself became a kind of spiritual undertaking.

Some of the ancients trusted reason more than others. Aristotle, who ranked among the doubters, pointed out that pure reason, disconnected from everyday realities, could lead political theory down some dangerous paths. In the modern world we have come to appreciate Aristotle's skepticism. Viable foundings have rarely been based solely on reason. Still, who would consider eliminating reason altogether?

Passions

The ancients concluded that "passions" such as greed, lust, jealousy, anger, fear and hatred arose from a different part of the mind than reason did. And just as some elements in society were more given to rational behavior, others were more given to emotionalism. The passions led people to do unpredictable things— things they might later regret. Moreover, passion was contagious. A rousing orator could stir up a crowd and soon have it ready to do something rash.

In politics, passion often led to turmoil. The peaceful life of the *polis* could be thrown into confusion by impassioned behavior, and war between friendly states could precipitate the same way. The lesson seemed to be that the passions must be held in check at all cost. But if they were truly a part of human nature, what, precisely, could be used to check them?

The most troubling of the passions, as the ancients saw it, was "desire." Human beings, it seemed, had a covetous affection for exotic foods, rare wines, fine cloth and glittering jewelry. They sought wealth not only for its own sake but for the prestige it often conferred. And they certainly preferred a life of ease to one of dull drudgery. The very leisure to engage in politics was often a product of fortune.

But desire had harmful effects. For one thing, it drew citizens away from public life and into private enjoyment. For another, it had a caustic influence on the political virtues. How could a person develop a true sense of justice, for example, if his own appetites got in the way? Desire often exacerbated the other passions too. Fear, envy, jealousy, suspicion were all made worse by the unequal distribution of wealth.

The most disturbing effect of man's incessant desiring was factional behavior. The "haves" of society often tended to form a political faction according to their common interest, and the "have-nots" would respond in kind. Since the latter always outnumbered the former, some form of chaos or tyranny was often not far to seek.

Honor

For the ancients, courage was among the most important virtues. One found it on the battlefield, of course, but one also found it in the political world in the form of moral courage—the courage of one's convictions. We acknowledge it today whenever we salute patriotism. The term used by the ancients to describe this quality was *honor*.

Deeds of honor have often been rewarded with political power—think of Julius Caesar or Napoleon. Plato coined the term *timocracy* to describe government by the glorious, and it was not a rare phenomenon. Public figures still seek reputations for heroism, and when no battlefield presents itself, they might gain their laurels through acts of political bravery. The powerful, it seems, are given to boldness.

John Adams referred to this tendency as the *spectemur agendo*—the "desire to be seen"—and he came to regard it as the single greatest peril to the Good Society. Adams' argument went something like this. Virtually all political persons seek a reputation more glittering than that of their rivals. Each wishes to be better known and more admired among the people, and as a result, each will reach for ever more power and resort to ever more brazen demonstrations of it. Too much, alas, is never quite enough.

Adams puzzled long and hard over the *spectemur agendo*. If a Good Society were to survive, he reasoned, this dark propensity must be dealt with. Since it couldn't be banished from the human heart, it would have to be transformed in some way, so that instead of tearing republics apart, as it had done throughout history, it somehow held them together instead. Was it possible, Adams wondered, to design a constitution in such a way as to make human nature in general, and the *spectemur agendo* in particular, a cohesive rather than corrosive influence?

Rule-Mindedness

Experiments have demonstrated that human beings almost instinctively search out rules for ordering their behavior. For example, young children on the playground, when presented with the idea of a new game, will quickly devise a set

Timocracy: Form of government led by those who have proven themselves heroic.

Theodore Roosevelt's well-advertised exploits in the Spanish-American War propelled his political career. After being elected governor of New York in 1898, he received the Republican nomination for vice president in 1900 and often seemed to overshadow President McKinley. (From The Verdict, *courtesy of the Harvard College Library, Theodore Roosevelt Collection, Cambridge, Massachusetts.)*

of rules for playing it. And we often find ourselves asking what the "rule" is for dealing with some new situation. A sense of "**rule-mindedness**" seems to arise from within.

What we call law is simply rules backed by ultimate sanction. History suggests a variety of ways law can come into being. It can be passed by a legislative body. It can be pronounced by magisterial decree. It can arise from custom or convention. It can be "discovered" in the natural order of things. It can be devised by a judge for the settlement of a specific dispute and then applied to similar disputes later on. It can be handed down by the gods.

Some legal theorists have argued that the source of law, and even its moral content, are relatively unimportant. What counts, according to this point of view, is the law itself and its recognition as such. In other words, the human need for rules is so great that virtually *any* rule, even a harsh or mindless one, can serve the required purpose. As long as the rule in question is truly a *rule*—a standing precept generally applied—and not just an arbitrary edict against some individual, it has the almost magical property of ordering human expectations.

On the other hand, something else in human nature prompts us to desire that the laws also be "just." Justice is a difficult term. For what seems just to one person may not seem so to another. (Is it "just," for example, to use indigent patients as guinea pigs in medical research?) As a result, human beings often disagree about the moral content of the laws they must depend on.

Habits of the Heart

Every society is set apart from all others by its customs and traditions. These "habits of the heart," as they have been called, have a life of their own. They are not in anyone's particular custody, nor are they subject to anyone's manipulation. And very often they make little rational sense. In England, for example, the institution of monarchy became so beloved that its color and pageantry were preserved for centuries after the monarch was essentially dethroned.

Precisely because custom and tradition cannot rationally be accounted for, they are not subject to ordinary scrutiny. Forms can become empty and meaningless, like the symbols attending college commencement ceremonies. Corruptions can creep in unnoticed, so that tipping the waiter for a job well done gradually turns into a compulsory "gratuity" added onto the check. Even so, our customs and traditions tell a lot about who we really are and how we really deal with the world. American colonists remained Englishmen for all intents and purposes, even with a revolution coming on, because they still maintained English habits of the heart.

Any significant political change, and certainly any founding, will have custom and tradition to reckon with. There will be cherished institutions (like the English monarchy) that make little sense but have enormous staying power. There will be assumptions about the world which are regarded as unchallengeable, but which in fact are only traditional beliefs. And there will be instances where reason points to a given course of action but custom makes it impossible to follow. More than one ardent reformer has denounced "the dead hand of the past." "What is established already," said David Hume, "is as important as what ought to be established."

Spiritual Sense

Even the most rational of the ancients acknowledged the gods' supervision of temporal affairs. If the ancient Athenians had not believed that Pallas Athena was smiling down on them, no constitution imaginable could have made their *polis* sound, for people have but scant faith in purely human contrivance. This helps us to understand why, in the American Founding, references to deity were insisted upon by some less-than-active churchgoers.

In God We Trust

Man's spiritual sense is relevant to the Good Society in other ways. For one thing, the citizens of a Good Society need to agree about what is in fact good, and such consensus often reflects spiritual values. For another, political actions are often based on a sense of the sacred. Some religions take eternal rewards and punishments into account in making this-world decisions, while others acknowledge the spiritual realm more indirectly. Finally, there are those "goods of the soul" the Good Society promises, many of which are spiritual in nature. The whole point of the Good Society is to create a life worth living.

Most foundings have been sacred in character, as we have seen, for they have required supernatural legitimation. And most political societies, until fairly recently, have been accompanied by the equivalent of a state church, the assumption being that secular authority needs all the help it can get. Even so, the spiritual sense poses dangers. It has driven human beings toward brittle dogmatism, seething prejudice, and with sad regularity, holy war. Ironically, no aspect of human nature has done more to thwart the Good Society.

Two Approaches to the Problem of the Ages

See study aid.

Given these and other aspects of human nature, what strategies could be employed in the design of a Good Society? Here are the brief outlines of two, one of them ancient and one modern.

Areté

Areté—a Greek term we usually translate as "virtue"—was an abiding preoccupation of the ancients. It referred not so much to moral virtue as to the quest for

Areté: Greek form of virtue; the selfless pursuit of excellence.

excellence in all things. Thus, there was the *areté* of the athlete, all about strength and timing, the *areté* of the soldier, all about battlefield courage, and so on. The sculptor, the poet, the artist, the musician—each had his own *areté*. Each called upon different resources of the body or mind. All had to do with perfection.

Areté proposed that the elements of human nature, once they were rightly understood, could be mobilized to resolve the human predicament and form the basis of a Good Society. To put the argument in simplest terms, the Good Society could be founded on virtue. In other words, if all elements of a political society could be persuaded to behave according to their highest human potential, the pieces of the age-old puzzle would finally fall into place.

Consider the role of the statesman, for example. In a regime inspired by *areté*, the statesman would constantly seek to improve in wisdom, in prudence, in courage, in personal integrity, in a sense of justice. He would also strive to perfect the rhetorical skill of the orator, the sophistication of the jurist and the shrewdness of the diplomat. Above all—and this was where *areté* became truly challenging—the statesman must come to hold the public good above any sort of private advantage.

The *areté* of the ordinary citizen, or "public virtue," was equally important. Like their leaders, citizens were expected to cultivate wisdom, prudence and the like, and they must also place the public good above their own self-interest. But the virtue of the citizen had its own dimensions too. One of these was to participate willingly in the political process regardless of any partisan concerns. Another was to abide the decision of the electorate no matter who won or lost. A third was to revere the law above all else—whether or not there was a cop on the corner.

Areté tended to draw people into public life and make political activity an end in itself. Many of the ancient regimes were aristocratic, for the *aristoi*—a Greek term literally meaning "the best"—were those most devoted to the pursuit of excellence. But democratic regimes emerged as well when the *demos* (ordinary citizens) caught the spirit of politics as self-expression.

Any *polis* that diligently practiced political virtue stood a good chance of becoming a Good Society. And thus *areté* was stressed by the ancients with an almost fanatical zeal. It was taught in the schools, preached in the temples, defended with eloquence in the symposia. If statesmen and citizens were but virtuous *enough*, it was argued, the destructive urges of humankind could be overcome and the constructive urges find fullest expression. Yet there was a troubling question below the surface, a question made all the more insistent by the actual experience (as opposed to the professed theory) of the Greek *polis*, and the American Founders would still be wrestling with it two thousand years later. Did human nature—*areté* or no *areté*—support a level of public-spiritedness *that* high?

Self-Interest

Let us fast-forward from the world of the ancient Greeks to the world of the European Enlightenment around the middle of the 1700s. Political thinkers continued to extol the importance of virtue—which they still referred to as

High Noon

On the very day that Marshall Will Kane turned in his badge, word arrived in Hadleyville that the notorious Frank Miller, whom the Marshall had sent to prison five years ago, had inexplicably been pardoned and was on his way back. "I'll kill you, Will Kane," he had vowed. "I swear I'll come back and kill you!" He was due to arrive in an hour and twenty minutes, on the high noon train. Three members of his old gang were already waiting at the station.

For a western movie, the plot of Stanley Kramer's 1952 classic, *High Noon*, started out ordinarily enough. Viewers expected to see plenty of action, a fisticuff or two, some fancy gunplay, and in the end, the unambiguous triumph of right. What they saw instead was a psychological drama that left many of them shaken. *High Noon* did not seem like a western at all. Rather, in a vague and indefinable way, it seemed to be about the viewers' own lives.

Hadleyville owed a lot to Marshall Kane. Before he came it had been a two-fisted frontier hell, ruled by the Miller bunch. Now, thanks to the law and order Kane had established, Hadleyville was peaceful and prosperous. "You cleaned up the town," says an admirer, "Made it fit for women and children to live in."

But had peace and prosperity been good for Hadleyville? The viewer began to wonder. As Marshall Kane pinned his star back on and attempted to recruit his old posse, it became clear that all was not well. Those who had helped to break the Miller gang five years earlier were not willing to break it again. Their reasons were a study in political psychology.

The deputy, Howard Pell, for instance, merely wants to play politics. He will strap on his gun and help the marshall out if the latter will make him his successor. Otherwise, Kane can go to hell.

The marshall's friend, Sam Fuller, cravenly hides in his bedroom and orders his wife to lie. "You want me to get killed?" he shrieks to her. "You want to be a widow?" The boys at the saloon are more subtle in their cowardice. "Things were different then, Kane," one of them explains of the earlier time. "You had six steady deputies to start off with, every one a top gun. You ain't got but two now."

Gradually it becomes clear that certain elements in the town are not upset about the return of Frank Miller. Business has been off at the local saloon; gambling is in a slump; prostitution has declined. Explains a resentful hotel clerk: "There's plenty of people around who think he's got a comeuppance coming."

The broader significance of this remark is established by the town judge, while packing his bags to clear out. "No time for a lesson in civics, my boy," he says but delivers one anyway. "In the fifth century B.C. the citizens of Athens, having suffered grievously under a tyrant, managed to depose and banish him. However, when he returned some years later with an army of mercenaries, those same citizens not only opened the gates for him but stood by while he executed members of the legal government."

So much for the corrupt elements of Hadleyville. What about the law-and-order people—those whose way of life Kane is defending? Their reasons for bailing out appropriately given at a church meeting are even more convoluted. Why should we get involved in a personal feud between Kane and Miller? Whose problem is this, anyway, but the politicians up north who turned Miller loose? Why should we fight Miller when we pay taxes for law enforcement?

Kane's staunchest supporter then delivers this speech: "People up north are thinking about this town. Thinking about sending money down here to build stores and factories. It'll mean a lot to this town, an awful lot. But if they're going to read about shooting and killing in the streets, what're they going to think then? If Will isn't here when Miller gets into town, my hunch is there won't be any trouble. Not one bit."

The last, and most devastating, defection is Will's best friend and fellow lawman, Mart. "Yeah," he says, "been a lawman all my life. It's a great life. You risk your skin catching killers, and the juries turn 'em loose so they can come back and shoot at you again. If you're honest, you're poor your whole life. And in the end you wind up dyin' all alone on some dirty street. For what? For nothin'. For a tin star."

Kane, however, refuses to buy any of this. He will stay and fight at whatever cost. "I've never run from anybody before" is the sum and substance of his explanation. As the townspeople, in their corruption and cowardice, make ever more rational sense, Will Kane makes ever less. All he seems to know is that he stands for the right—come what may. If need be he will face the Miller gang alone.

Which is, of course, precisely what he has to do. As the last deputy quits—"There's a limit how much you can ask of a man. I got a wife and kids"—the marshall loads his guns, makes out his will and heads through the deserted streets to meet the high noon train.

What was it that made *High Noon* so relevant to its American viewers? Without using the terms themselves, the film was exploring two fundamental concepts—virtue and self-interest. And it was asking which of the two was more important to the survival of the Good Society. It was a question that Americans had asked before.

Marshall Will Kane (Gary Cooper) at a church meeting in 1952's High Noon. (Courtesy of Corbis Images.)

areté—but their emphasis was beginning to shift toward a different approach to the Good Society. Human nature might not answer *areté*'s demand for selfless and unwavering public devotion, they reasoned, and even when it did so there were corollary difficulties, as we shall see further on. A more reliable understanding of mankind would place its stress not on the quest for perfection but on the tendency toward self-interest.

Someone noticed that there was a central theme running through almost all observations about human nature. Whether it was appetites and aversions under discussion or something exotic like the *spectemur agendo*, human beings displayed a marked tendency to consider themselves first. This appeared to be the case in spite of any spiritual sensitivity, any desire for excellence, or any inborn love of truth and justice they might have. And there was a cogent explanation for it. If human beings had a strong social sense bringing them together into communities, they could only feel pleasure or pain *as solitary individuals*. Accordingly, while I might sympathize with my neighbor whose house has burned down, I really can't share his sense of loss because I can't feel the chill of night as he can. While self-interest did not say much for the dignity of mankind in the way *areté* did, it had the redeeming value of being wholly reliable. People could be counted on to act in their own interest as surely as the winds blew and the tides surged. Individuals, on occasion, might behave generously, even altruistically, especially regarding close friends or family members, but behavior as a whole was almost mathematically predictable.

Enlightenment thinkers, no less than the ancients, understood the downside of self-interest. It could make people cold and uncaring. It could draw them away from community life. It could run to excess and lapse into corrupt, irresponsible, even criminal behavior. But several of the Enlightenment's best minds—Thomas Hobbes, John Locke, David Hume, Adam Smith—saw a side to self-interest that had escaped the ancients (Aristotle notably excepted). For one thing, it could lead to cooperative as well as destructive behavior, especially in economic life. For another, it was amenable to a certain type of control mechanism called *counterpoise*. That is, it was possible to structure political situations so as to balance, or "counterpose," the self-interest of one individual or group against that of another, each holding the other under control. And if self-interest drew hearts away from politics, that wasn't always such a bad thing. People who had what we call "a life" also had something to lose. They were less apt to go for wild experiments or easy utopias—and they did not make good fanatics.

It was less obvious how self-interest might lay a steadier groundwork for the Good Society than *areté* had. A great deal of analysis and experimentation would be required before political thinkers could really place full confidence in it. But we can guess at some of their main ideas. They would emphasize the structure of government rather than any guiding spirit, and hope to achieve as much counterpoise as possible. They would emphasize the limitation of government too, so that government was less likely to intrude upon the private lives of its citizens. And they would emphasize participation in the political process, not for *areté*'s sake, but for acknowledging and serving as many interests as possible.

Colonel and Mrs. James A. Whiteside, son Charles and Servants, *by James Cameron (c. 1858–59). An affluent life of ease—the modern "Good Society"?* (Courtesy of the Hunter Museum of Art, Chattanooga, Tennessee. Gift of Mr. and Mrs. Thomas B. Whiteside.)

And the modern Good Society? It would be calmer than its classical predecessor, more private in outlook, more materialistic and comfort-driven, and much more interested in individual freedom. It would be less inclined to deeds of honor and thus less inclined to war. And it would constantly work against tribalism and toward an ever broader sense of inclusiveness. It would be a convoluted, multi-layered society and it would need a government to match. Where the governments of antiquity had required *arête* and not much else, a government in the modern world, capable of sustaining a Good Society, would have to be crafted like a fine watch.

This is why the story of the American Founding is a story, not simply an event. Among its characters would be some who looked back to the English past, some who looked forward to utopia, several apostles of natural law, and quite a few of the practical sort focused on the here and now. The narrative would wind among every facet of human nature, from rule-mindedness to the *spectemur agendo*, and touch on every idea for building a stable foundation. There would be as much discussion of *areté*—using the modern term *virtue*—as there had been in ancient Athens, together with every means the Enlightenment had come up with for cashing in on self-interest. The story would tell of founding myths, of a conclave of lawgivers, of a written constitution (virtually without precedent), of an accountable political system, and of an emerging national character. Monarchy would play a role in it—rather larger than most Americans appreciate—but so would aristocracy and democracy, the three joined together in a unique way. And from the ancient world, which would furnish much of the vocabulary and not a few of the plot ideas, there would come a description of the whole as a *republic*.

Suggestions for Further Reading

Michael Crawford, *The Roman Republic* (1993).

Michael Gagarin and Paul Woodruff, *Early Greek Political Thought from Homer to the Sophists* (1995).

Michael Grant and Rachel Kitzinger, eds., *Civilization of the Ancient Mediterranean* (1987).

J. G. A. Pocock, *Politics, Language, and Time; Essays on Political Thought and History* (1971).

Sarah B. Pomeroy, Stanley M. Burstein, Walter Donlan, and Jennifer Tolbert Roberts, *Ancient Greece: A Political, Social, and Cultural History* (1999).

Paul A. Rahe, *Republics Ancient and Modern: Classical Republicanism and the American Revolution* (1992).

H.W.F. Saggs, *Civilization Before Greece and Rome* (1989).

Chester G. Starr, *The Roman Empire, 27 B.C.–A.D. 476: A Study in Survival* (1982).

Kenneth S. Templeton, *The Politicization of Society: Essays by Herbert Butterfield et al.* (1979).

Carol G. Thomas, *Myth Becomes History: Pre-Classical Greece* (1993).

CHAPTER 1 STUDY AID

(This aid is not all-inclusive and is not intended to be a substitute for thorough study of the material presented in the textbook.)

The Art and Science of Founding

I. **Elements of a Founding**

1. Identity:
   - Name
   - Geographic boundary
2. Constitution:
   - Fundamental law
   - Political order and governmental structure
   - Source of authority
3. Citizenship:
   - Who rules?
   - Participation—who is in?
   - Exclusion—who is out?
4. Polity:
   - Sense of nationhood
   - Cultural identity
5. Founding Myth:
   - Legitimacy

II. **Monarchy, Aristocracy and Democracy**

MAD (Monarchy, Aristocracy and Democracy)

GENERAL MODEL	PRO	CON
Monarchy the King (rule of one)	• Strong • Decisive leadership • Figurehead symbol • Can act quickly	• Despotism • Tyranny • Abuse of power • One man, even a good man, makes mistakes
Aristocracy the Nobles (rule of the few)	• Admirable, can be looked up to, can be aspired to • Advances the arts and learning • Best educated • Most virtuous	• Oligarchy • Snobbery • Self-interest • Ignores the poor • Does not seek the general welfare

| **Democracy** the People (rule of the many) | • Greater equality
• Civic involvement
• Welfare of the poor sought | • Chaos
• Slow to make decisions
• Much bickering
• Low opinion of arts and learning
• Susceptible to following a demagogue
• Base desires |

(Note: The negative tendencies of each estate can be remedied if the interests of all three estates are balanced in a mixed government under a rule of law.)

III. Constitutional Epistemology (Founding Archetypes)

Universalist Founding

- General and Inclusive
- All people
- All times
- All places

A Priori

- Abstract
- Deductive
- Based on self-evident "first" principles

What ought to be possible?

- Associated with Plato
- Theoretical
- Philosophical
- Idealistic
- Utopian

Revolutionary

- Virtue can be learned
- Self-interest can be suppressed
- Attitude dominates
- Human nature malleable, it can be made to change
- Virtuous elites should rule

Particularist Founding

- Limited or Exclusive
- Specific people
- Specific time
- Specific place

A Posteriori

- Empirical
- Inductive
- Based on "facts" and experience

What is possible?

- Associated with Aristotle
- Practical
- Scientific
- Pragmatic
- Temperate

Evolutionary

- Virtue not dependable
- Self-interest innate, but can be channeled into positive end
- Behavior dominates and must be controlled by institutions
- Human nature not malleable, but it can evolve

IV. Human Nature, Politics, and the Zoon Politikon

(Note: Anciently, the *polis*, or "political society" was thought to reflect the moral and spiritual qualities of a people. Moreover, it was thought that the political order did not just reflect human nature, but that it could actually alter human nature, for better or worse. Thus, political activity was seen as an imperative and man was seen as a **zoon politikon**, or "political animal.")

    1. Elements influencing political activity:

- Tribalism
- Reason
- Passions
- Honor
- Rule-mindedness
- Habits of the heart
- Spiritual sense

V. Two Approaches

The Ancient Greeks (Areté/Virtue)

- *Areté* = Virtue = Excellence
- A "Good Society" could be founded on virtue
- Statesmen seek public good
- Citizens willingly participate for the good of all
- Virtue could overcome excesses of human nature
- Upside—pursuit of excellence
- Downside—human nature unpredictable and a system built on the principle of *areté* susceptible to foibles of that nature

The Enlightenment (Self-interest)

- Self-interest not innately negative, could produce a "Good Society"
- Most people do not act nobly, but out of self-interest
- Self-interest is reliable, predictable
- Self-interest could be regulated through mechanisms that created structural counterpoise
- Upside—cooperation and improvement and caution
- Downside—exploitation

CHAPTER 1 REVIEW QUESTIONS ━━━━━

Key Terms

The Good Society

Laws of Nature

Monarchy

Aristocracy

Democracy

Zoon Politikon

Areté

Self-Interest

Multiple Choice Questions

1. Which of the following example best exemplifies the Greek notion of *areté*?
   a. A student writes her congressman about an important issue.
   b. A disgruntled worker does not vote because he does not like
      the candidates.
   c. A man obeys the law so that he will not be thrown in jail.
   d. A group of activists participates in a violent protest.

2. The text suggests that self-interest makes peoples' actions:
   a. Corrupt.
   b. Honorable.
   c. Predictable.
   d. Unpredictable.

3. All of the following are elements of a founding except:
   a. A unifying name for the country or people.
   b. Common agreement on basic laws and governing structures.
   c. A "founding myth."
   d. Recognition of nationhood by other countries.

4. Revolutions:
   a. Often precede foundings.
   b. Are a part of the Human Predicament Cycle.
   c. Can lead to further social turmoil.
   d. All of the above.

Review Questions

1. According to the text, how do most foundings occur?

   _____

   _____

   _____

   _____

2. Why have some scholars argued that the American Founding was actually an "episodic *re*founding"?

   _____

   _____

   _____

   _____

3. What are some causes of revolutions? What impacts do revolutions have on societies?

   _____

   _____

   _____

   _____

4. Why must a durable constitution be based upon a correct understanding of human nature?

   _____

   _____

   _____

   _____

5. In what ways has religion contributed to the Good Society? In what ways has it detracted?

   _____

   _____

   _____

   _____

Review Exercises

1. In your own words, describe the five elements of a founding listed in the text.

   _____

   _____

   _____

   _____

2. The text describes revolutionaries who seek either a "return to Eden" or an "advance toward Utopia." Explain the similarities and differences between these two approaches. Into which model does the American Founding best fit?

_____

_____

_____

_____

3. Explain the concepts of *areté* and self-interest. Which attribute do you think is more constant in human nature? Can the two coexist? Why or why not?

_____

_____

_____

_____

Big Essay Question

Suppose you were an American diplomat in Paris at the height of the French Revolution. Based on your understanding of the Human Predicament and other course concepts, what would you teach the revolutionary leaders to help them establish a Good Society?

Puritanism and the Founding

(Courtesy of the Vermont Agency of Development.)

Aboard the Arbella *A Modell of Christian Charity*

Wee shall finde that the God of Israell is among us, when tenn of us shall be able to resist a thousand of our enemies; when he shall make us a prayse and glory that men shall say of succeeding plantations, "The lord make like that of NEW ENGLAND." For wee must Consider that wee shall be as a Citty upon a hill. The eies of all people are upon Us, soe that if we shall deale falsely with our god in this worke we have undertaken, and soe cause him to withdrawe his present help from us, wee shall be made a story and a by-word through the world. . . . Therefore lett us choose life, that wee and our seede may live by obeying his voyce and cleaving to him, for he is our life and our prosperity.

—John Winthrop (1630)

It has been observed, sometimes ironically, that the English Puritans were the "real" founders of America. This is because so many American traits seem to have a whiff of the Puritan about them. But there are better reasons for beginning our story with **Puritanism**. The Puritan experience created many elements of a founding—and created them specifically in America. Moreover Puritan values, Puritan habits of thought, Puritan self-confidence, and an abiding sense of purpose that also merits the Puritan label have found their way into the American psyche, and Puritan institutions have had a way of metamorphosing into American institutions. Finally, the Puritans may have conceived the very *idea* of America. It is not wide of the mark to think of them as America's "first founders."

The English Puritans

Puritanism arose in seventeenth-century England. It was a complex phenomenon, and its roots tapped into a wide variety of social and economic causes. But Puritan self-understanding was the work of theologians, Protestant theologians, well outside the mainstream of Christian thought. The most important of these was **John Calvin**.

Calvin's *Institutes of the Christian Religion* (1536) still ranks among the most influential theological works of all time. Its tightly reasoned arguments seemed most relevant to those who took their religion deadly in earnest and sought perfectionist standards of Christian conduct. Calvin's general message was that Christianity had become encumbered with all manner of things for which there was no scriptural authority. These ought to be done away with, Calvin argued, and the church "purified."

Puritanism wasn't solely about religion. In England, it played a prominent role in the social and political turmoil of the time. Puritans in Parliament formed the backbone of resistance to the Stuart monarchy, and when the Civil War broke out in 1642, they swelled the ranks of Cromwell's army. That was only the beginning. Puritans spearheaded the rise of liberalism later on. Many prominent Whigs were Puritans, and echoes of their stern piety reverberated through the Glorious Revolution.

While the term "Puritan" encompasses several different things, on the most basic level the Puritans were those who sought to purify the Church of England of accumulated doctrinal and liturgical "corruptions," returning worship to a

John Calvin: See study aid.

John Calvin:
www.wsu.edu/~dee/REFORM/
CALVIN.HTM

state of original simplicity. Most Puritans were content to work within the Church as a proactive minority. Some, however, found the Church to be hopeless. These radicals, or "separatists" as they were usually called, formed their own congregations and cut all ties to the Anglican establishment. The Stuart monarchs regarded the Puritans as a political threat and often persecuted them in one way or another. Archbishop William Laud threatened to "harry them out of the land," and on occasion he did precisely that.

North America, which had been more or less familiar to the English for a century, provided the Puritans with sanctuary. At the same time, it offered an array of economic opportunities for them, for the Puritans, like many cutting-edge Protestants, were aggressively this-worldly in certain ways. The colonizing of New England—Plymouth Plantation, Massachusetts Bay, Connecticut, Rhode Island, New Hampshire—was largely the work of a large Puritan migration in the early 1630s. But Puritans settled elsewhere as well. Eventually, there were substantial Puritan minorities in most of the American colonies.

Numbers do not tell the whole story of Puritan influence. New England settlers pushed westward into the Ohio Valley and actively shaped the culture of the "heartland." Other dissenting religious groups—and even mainstream groups such as the Presbyterians—came to resonate with Puritan ideas. And Puritan institutions had an impact throughout the colonies, as we shall see.

Puritan Ideas: See study aid.

English Background:
www.wsu.edu/~dee/ENLIGHT/
ENGLAND.HTM

Puritan Ideas and Their Impact

Puritan ideas glowed like embers long after the fire of the movement had burned itself out. And many of them warmed the Founding in one way or another.

Human Nature

To begin with, Puritanism had a lot to do with the American understanding of human nature. Calvin had pondered long and hard about the problem of evil in the world, and had concluded that it originated not with God but with Satan—and was ushered forth by human agency. Thus, the fall of Adam recounted in Genesis represented far more than a simple act of disobedience. In disregarding divine instructions, Adam *and all his progeny* had sinned against God and isolated themselves from His influence. No wonder evil abounded.

This explanation made sense of the world's general wretchedness. It accounted for the corruption, depravity and vice so notable in the human experience. The more difficult thing to explain was why *all* men weren't lost. The answer, said Calvin, must be that God Himself had intervened and bestowed divine grace on a precious few. For everyone else, alas, there was only damnation in store—"**predestined**" damnation.

It was by means of this belief that the Puritans acquired their dour and grim-faced image—the haunting fear, as H.L. Mencken put it, that someone somewhere might be happy. Yet predestination had its optimistic side. Calvinists did not see themselves among the damned—*they* were the saved.

Predestination: The theological doctrine that all events have been willed by God; denies free will.

The notion of God's elect—or "saints" as they called themselves—supplies a basic theme of American history and some important implications for American politics. One implication might be called the assumption of guilt. In the godly community, Puritans reasoned, there would always be some, perhaps many, unregenerate persons. So there would always be jealousy, avarice, lust, contention, pride and other marks of damnation. Corruption might literally be found anywhere.

But there was a second, contrary assumption, the assumption of innocence. For, in the same godly community there would also be those whom God had saved. These saints were not subject to the ordinary frailties of mankind—they were significantly stronger and wiser than their fellows and were clothed with an undauntable righteousness. They could be counted on to provide the community with spiritual guidance and moral backbone no matter what it might have to face.

This "schizoid" view of human nature made it possible to have coldly realistic assumptions about political conduct, and at the same time to be capable of a certain warm idealism.

Confidence

Armed with divine grace, the Puritans had an almost legendary sense of confidence. Nothing seemed too difficult for them to tackle. Their courage in facing the wilderness on a far Atlantic shore was only one of the many benefits of that confidence. There were several others.

To begin with, the Puritans were so convinced of the soundness of their orthodoxy that they wasted little time debating or defending it—as they had had to do in England—and turned their main attention to practical tasks. Their "errand into the wilderness," as they put it, was to show by example what God could really do when it came to community building. This purpose gave rise to a metaphor that would come to define not only Puritan America but America as a whole. "We shall be as a city upon a hill," **John Winthrop** prophesied. "The eyes of all people are upon us."

Their confidence made it possible for the Puritans to do whatever they deemed necessary in order to accomplish this mission. They rarely had qualms about double-dealing with Native Americans, about launching wars of extermination, or later on, about participating in the slave trade. But they also rarely had qualms about clearing the wilderness, laying out towns and cities, founding colleges, setting up libraries, or doing the thousand other things necessary to build a society from the ground up.

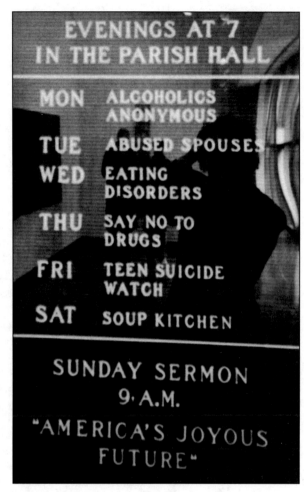

Idealism and Realism: still found close together in American life. (Courtesy of Louise Turner Arnold.)

John Winthrop
(1588–1649): A founder and governor of Massachusetts Bay Colony.

City upon a hill:
www.mtholyoke.edu/acad/
intrel/winthrop.htm

Although the Puritans' initial perceptions of America were fraught with images of the "howling wilderness," that would eventually change. They came to see America, graced by their presence, as nothing less than the Promised Land and their city upon a hill as the New Jerusalem. The imagery of blessedness and bounty began to replace that of the wasteland.

Several traits of the American character can be traced to Puritan self-confidence. Our reputed narcissism, smug superiority and evangelical enthusiasm (complaints lodged by early visitors) would appear to arise from Puritan beginnings. But so would the assurance necessary to face down the British Empire and found a successful republic.

Newness

Although the Puritans' response to the New World was backward looking in some ways—in the design of houses, for example, or the layout of villages—it was often forward looking in others. In building their city upon a hill, the Puritans proposed to make all things *new* again, re-creating the world by dint of first principles.

New lands are seedbeds for new ideas. With something like that fact in mind, John Adams would call the United States "the nation of futurity." By the time of the Revolution, Yankee tinkerers were already becoming known for their inventive skills, and in the years following they would create an astonishing array of new mechanical contrivances. As for new political ideas, the American Founding would either create or make use of dozens of them, and some would be directly traceable to the Puritan experience, as we shall see.

Newness also made it possible to "invent" oneself. Just as the Puritans came to America and began calling themselves "Americans," the re-creation of self became an American theme. Fiction writer Horatio Alger Jr. would one day tell engaging tales of immigrant paupers who declared themselves to be tradesmen, accountants and entrepreneurs—and went on to become precisely what they declared. "Rags to riches" would become one of America's founding myths.

Finally, newness laid the groundwork for an attitude historians have called "**American exceptionalism**." Americans would come to believe that they were quite unlike any people, any political society or any national state in the world's experience. America, they would say, breaks the rules.

Learning

Scholasticism: A philosophical and theological movement from the Middle Ages which argued that reason and faith are compatible.

The founders of English Puritanism had great respect for learning. Many of them were academics themselves, mostly affiliated with the university at Cambridge, and they were well versed in **Scholasticism**, a highly rationalistic mode of inquiry taught at the time. The scholastic investigator began from certain premises, usually taken from the Scriptures, and worked his way through a maze of careful deductions to final conclusions. It required a sharp mind and rigorous training.

One result of this heritage was a high regard for human reason. The Puritan ministers in New England were among the most learned men of their time, and their sermons were models of careful thought and wide reading. Having worked through the Scriptures by the light of Scholasticism, they saw little or no conflict between religious faith and secular knowledge, and therefore they saw nothing to fear from scientific investigation. American Puritans were among the first to embrace the new psychology of John Locke and the new physics of Isaac Newton. In Massachusetts Bay, they tried out inoculation for smallpox, based on the available data supporting it—the very cutting edge of applied science. Later on, the children and grandchildren of the Puritans would find it easy to modernize their faith with transfusions from the European Enlightenment.

Another result was that the American Puritans promoted learning at all levels. The alternative, as they saw it, to perishing in ignorance on the Atlantic frontier was to pursue knowledge with heroic single-mindedness. Thus, at a time when education in most colonies was virtually nonexistent, Puritan New England was an educational pioneer. Town and village schools taught the classics along with the three Rs, and turned out generations of exceptionally well-schooled children. And in order to maintain high standards in the ministry, they founded both Harvard and Yale.

In the famous Scopes trial in 1925, Christian fundamentalists challenged the teaching of evolution as a scientific theory. Would the Puritans have understood such a conflict? (Courtesy of AP/Wide World Photos.)

Many of the American Founders would be heirs of Puritan learning. Their wide reading in the classics, their interest in science, their ready acceptance of Enlightenment ideas, and on a deeper level their assumption that knowledge served the moral and spiritual purposes of mankind were all outgrowths of the Puritan heritage.

Paranoia

There was a dark side to the city upon a hill. For if the Puritans were squarely on the Lord's side, they were squarely in opposition to Satan and his minions. As a result, they tended to see forces of darkness all around them.

Satan, they believed, had a special advantage in his ability to exploit man's fallen nature. Almost anyone might be a target. In the most pious congregation, one might find those who were under the devil's influence. This fact posed a delicate problem. The Puritans believed God's judgments to be swift and sure. If the godly community tolerated sin in its midst, it might expect fire, flood, pestilence, even earthquake, not in the remote future but here and now. It was up to the elect to take stern measures when such were called for.

Occasionally, this mindset led to tragedy, as in the infamous Salem witchcraft trials. More often it simply created wariness. The enemy was at the gates in Puritan consciousness—but the enemy might also be within. Awareness of this possibility gave the Puritans a peculiar way of understanding change, especially social change. What a sociologist might see as the stresses and strains of a developing society a colonial Puritan would likely attribute to plain wickedness. And wickedness was never to be tolerated.

No wonder Puritanism erupted in periodic bursts of religious revivalism such as the Great Awakening. Spiritual healing, taught the ministers, could only be brought about by recognizing sin, crying repentance, purging the soul of its accumulated corruptions—chief among which were luxury and vice—and taking a stand for the Lord. This habit of mind gave the Puritans a high potential for reform. They had an urge to root out every iniquity, right every wrong, and when the occasion presented itself, they rarely hung back. It also gave them a high potential for revolution.

Calling and Community

John Calvin had little patience with the attempts of many Christians to rise above the human condition. Man, born in sin, should be content to live a mortal life, he argued. Rather than seeking to emulate God through self-denial or spiritual exertion, man ought to concentrate on worshipping God and glorifying His name.

One did not glorify God by singing hosannas, Calvin said, but by showing forth God's work among men—well-tended farms, busy shops, merchantmen plying the seas. If this was a European vision, it was all the more an American one, for America offered a blank slate on which the godly could write to best effect. We begin to see what Winthrop's city upon a hill was really about.

The Puritans' means for building that city was the Christian "calling." The calling was a worldly pursuit—banking, say, or shipbuilding—but it was also a religious pursuit. It was the manner in which a finite human being could glorify God. President Calvin Coolidge, a descendant of the Puritans, stated the theory of the calling in a nutshell. "One who builds a factory builds a temple," he said, "and one who works there worships there."

The calling mandated righteous behavior in the workplace. The godly merchant could not be a swindler, nor the godly wheelwright a shoddy craftsman. And all were expected to perform their labors with honesty and diligence. They must rise early, work soberly, save frugally, spend wisely, live modestly and impart a portion of their substance to the poor.

In this picture of things, prosperity had a special meaning too: that God was pleased with the community's worship. Prosperous individuals were very likely to be counted among the elect (we still believe that today), and there was nothing wrong with a little tasteful display of their wealth. There was a line, however, and one crossed it at one's peril, for real extravagance paved the way to hell. The point was that the entire *community* prospered, not just a few individuals. Businesses made good profits, artisans made good wages and the poor were decently cared for.

This vision of the American community would cast a long shadow. The small town, celebrated in hundreds of novels and plays, would become a keystone of Americana. When things seemed well on Main Street, they would seem well with the world. And when the community was beset by crime, vice, grinding poverty, politicians on the take, it would be a problem for everyone's concern.

Later on, we will see how Calvin's ideas helped get the American Founders around a difficult problem. For the time being, we need only note that for the Puritans, there was no necessary choice to be made between virtue and self-interest in the godly community. The two could fit together seamlessly.

Calling: A Puritan belief that by pursuing worldly careers virtuously, a person was in effect glorifying God.

Calling and community: virtuous self-interest benefits all. (Copperplate engravings from *The Book of Trades*, courtesy of the American Antiquarian Society, Worcester, Massachusetts.)

Puritan Constitutionalism

In much of the foregoing we see the dim outlines of things American. In their baggage, the Puritans brought myths and images, concepts and attitudes we would recognize today. But did they also bring the building blocks of a founding? Probably so. We might pay special attention to the following three:

Puritan Law

As educated Englishmen, Puritan magistrates were versed in the English common law, and they often made appropriate use of it. For most Puritans, however, the "real" law was God's law, as revealed in the Holy Scriptures. They paid particular attention to the commandments they found in the Old Testament, those given to Moses most of all. God's law—as opposed to man's law—must necessarily be coherent, consistent and in keeping with the truths of nature. A society could not go wrong by obeying it.

We have seen that all foundings require fundamental law of some kind. And if the law in question is divine—that is, given directly by the gods—then men do

A Quirk of the American Mind

This experiment, mind you, was not performed at a secular university but a religious and specifically Christian one. It could have been Notre Dame, or Southern Methodist, or Loma Linda, or Baylor. (And at any of them, I suspect, the outcome would be the same.)

A professor, addressing a large class, asked this question: "How many of you consider yourselves to be deeply and truly religious?" A majority of the hands went up. He then asked: "How many of you find it consistent with your religion to be rich—not just comfortable or well off, but rich?" Again, a majority of the hands went up. Indeed, they were the same hands.

The professor then singled out individuals who had raised their hands and asked them specific questions:

What about the wealthy young man who wanted to be Jesus' disciple, and was told to sell all he had and give it to the poor?

What about the scripture that says: "It is easier for a camel to go through the eye of a needle, than for a rich man to enter the kingdom of God?"

What about those early Christians who gave up private ownership of property and shared their goods with each other? What about those vows of poverty that carried tens of thousands into monasteries and convents? What about priests in the Third World today who decry the evils of wealth?

The students had answers for all these questions and more. When the discussion ended, the professor asked if any had changed their mind. None had.

It may not have gone this way anywhere else in the world. For what the professor was dealing with was not an abstract question of morals so much as a quirk of the American mind. As a matter of national character, Americans believe that wealth and spirituality easily and comfortably fit together—despite considerable evidence to the contrary. That unique synthesis of virtue and self-interest, in a nutshell, is John Calvin's legacy to modern America.

Jesus and the rich young man: would you *give it away?* By Heinrich Hoffman. (Photo by Hal Conroy, C. Harrison Conroy Co., Charlotte, North Carolina.)

not have to spend time and energy debating its merits. The law forms a reference that is beyond the wit of man.

In many societies of the time, the laws were uncertain. Kings could claim divine sanction for their edicts but so could legislatures, and in seventeenth-century England those two authorities were battling it out. The American Puritans were troubled by no such ambiguity. In their political affairs, which were at times very lively, they could scrap over particular applications or interpretations of divine law but the law itself remained inviolable. It became a kind of constitution.

Puritan Politics

The Puritans were not republicans, liberals, or democrats, as we understand these terms today. (The terms themselves will be explored in greater detail in the next chapter.) Yet there were elements of all three in the Puritan makeup.

Republicanism. The English Puritans steadfastly opposed the Stuart monarchs, as we have seen, and raised their voices against the so-called "divine right of kings." The king, they insisted, did not rule by God's pleasure and did not stand above the law. This was only one of their republican ideas; they embraced several others. And when civil war finally broke out in 1642 and the king was eventually executed, the Puritans pioneered England's first experiment in republican government known as the Commonwealth and Protectorate. Their dark view of human nature and their distrust of arbitrary power were engines that drove them on.

Driven by those same engines, the Puritan colonies in New England essentially became republics in their own right. In theory, of course, they were under the sovereignty of the English crown. But in fact they were based on corporate charters that granted them powers of self-government, and as a practical matter the crown could supervise them precious little. They were autonomous political societies in effect, and they behaved like it.

Liberalism. It was the belief of English liberals that government belonged to the substantial elements of society, the owning classes, and that its main purpose was to protect the rights of property. Most Puritans agreed. They believed that God intended the earth for the earnest and the toiling, and whatever property a man could accumulate, it was a sign of God's pleasure.

Liberals also favored religious toleration. Freedom, to them, meant freedom from established churches quite as much as from heavy-handed magistrates. The Puritans certainly agreed with part of that—being out from under the Church of England. However, when *they* became the established church, as they did in the colonies, they were no more tolerant of dissenters than the London episcopate had been. But in America the dissenters could do precisely as the Puritans had done—go somewhere else. Soon there were congregations of schismatics here and there, feuding and bickering with one another and causing the authorities to ponder the costs of enforced religious orthodoxy. Almost in spite of themselves, the Puritans were led toward toleration.

Other seeds of liberalism seemed to sprout among the American Puritans. Take the idea of "natural liberty." Liberals held that human beings were born free, not captives of the social order, and accepted government in their lives because they freely chose to. Puritans found themselves making exactly the same argument against the Church of England—that is, God required men to choose the correct path for themselves, not have it thrust upon them. Or take "natural equality." While the Puritans were not exactly levelers, they acknowledged that all souls were equal in the sight of God, and hence that all members of a given congregation deserved to participate. These ideas would someday spur on the American Revolution—and they would come straight out of Puritan New England.

Democracy. Just as the Puritans did not think of themselves as republicans or liberals, they did not think of themselves as democrats. Theirs was not a world in which ordinary people held the reins of power. Still, there were democratic strands in Puritan life, and in the American colonies they became more visible. Consider, for example, the role of the "**covenant**" in Puritan society. It was laden with democratic implications.

Covenant: A formal agreement among the members of a Puritan congregation which functioned as a founding document.

The covenant was a formal agreement worked out among every Puritan congregation. As a given congregation came together, its members would draw up and sign a compact among themselves making their congregational status official. This covenant, as it was called, was itself a kind of founding. (It foreshadowed both the Declaration of Independence—"we mutually pledge to each other our lives, our fortunes, and our sacred honor"—and the Constitution—"We the people of the United States . . . do ordain and establish this Constitution. . . .") In its text, each male head of household covenanted with God to live the commandments and walk uprightly. Each then covenanted with all the others to effect the same end. Everyone was in it together, for better or worse—their brother's keeper indeed.

Once established, the congregation proceeded to hire its own minister and arrange its own affairs. It answered to no external authority imposing uniformity of worship or orthodoxy of belief. For all intents and purposes, the congregants had formed themselves by covenant into an autonomous political society—a striking instance of people creating their own government. And "government" it truly was, for upon migration to America, each congregation became an independent town or village in one of the New England colonies. The members generally lived in close proximity to one another, with adjacent town lots and a village commons—this in order that they might "bear one another's burdens," as the scriptures commanded—and thus protected the integrity of the community. Outsiders were not welcome.

Town or village selectmen—those who actually ran things—were chosen in annual elections. Virtually all male heads of household were allowed to vote. Beyond that, there was a good deal of grass-roots participation in the political process, and town meetings became famous for blunt outspokenness. Colony leaders may have found the mince-no-words style a little troubling. One of them, John Winthrop, in his well-remembered "little speech on liberty," had to remind the people that Massachusetts wasn't a complete democracy. The magistrates might be chosen by the people, he admitted, but once they were chosen, their authority came from God.

All the same, "chosen by the people" took on real meaning in Puritan New England. If all church members had an equal right to participate in community affairs, the machinery of democracy—if not precisely the theory of it—was in place and operating.

Governance of the Self

In Winthrop's "little speech on liberty," he argued that there were two kinds of liberty, which he termed "natural" and "civil." **Natural liberty**, he explained, was the liberty to do whatever came into a person's mind, and this was the kind often favored by the unregenerate of mankind. **Civil liberty**, by contrast, was the liberty to do only that which was right—the unerring choice of God's elect. Puritan society had but scant means to enforce Winthrop's civil liberty. The institutions of police power were few and rudimentary. People could be hauled before the magistrates, but beyond expulsion or public humiliation, there was little of practical consequence to coerce them.

Instead, individuals were expected to govern their own lives. They might get encouragement from their neighbors, and even from the congregation assembled, but the most important source of rectitude was the self. To "walk uprightly before the Lord," a person was required to be honest, hard working, sober, thrifty, temperate and visibly respectable. Much stress was laid on appearances, to be sure, but appearances were assumed to reveal the actual condition of the soul.

Such a belief system assumed universal standards of right and wrong. The Puritans, in other words, looked to an unwritten law of moral behavior, and the individual conscience was expected to hold to that law unswervingly. There were important implications here. Aristotle had pointed out that in order for a Good Society to exist, there must be general agreement about what was "good." The Puritans had such agreement and they took it seriously.

Puritan freedom, then, might be called *freedom as self-governance*. Individuals governed their own actions according to the moral law. Families and communities did the same. The principle was easily extended, right up to the colony itself, as long as discipline remained strong and the moral law could be assumed. Moreover, self-governance was what made it possible for politics to become so democratic. Those who could govern their own behavior could be trusted to participate politically, and the decisions they made were more likely to win general approval. There was a final benefit. Those who had a hand in making their own laws were more likely to respect and obey them.

All of this was according to theory, of course. In the real world of colonial life, there were any number of gaps between theory and practice. All the same, Puritanism performed well enough in the real world to create a tough and resilient society, able to hold its own in the wilderness.

Little speech on liberty: http://www.law.du.edu/russell/lh/alh/docs/winthrop.html

Natural Liberty: Freedom to do whatever one wants.

Civil Liberty: Also known as moral self-governance; the freedom to do what is right.

The First Founding of America

Puritan New England provided a sort of "first founding," a rough draft of what the United States was to become. And the first founding would prove to be an important precursor to the second.

As a religious experience, Puritanism was simply too intense to last. Less than fifty years after the first ships had dropped anchor off the Massachusetts coast, the signs of its decline were everywhere. Yet burnout did not bring an end to the Puritan influence. On the contrary, that influence transformed itself in ways that would amplify its long-term effect. The intellectual side of Puritanism became even more intellectual, soaking up both the European and **English Enlightenment** like a sponge and providing the generation of John Adams (one of its great-grandsons) with much of its curiosity and learnedness. The emotional side of Puritanism gave rise to periodic bursts of religious revivalism, still evident in the American experience, and imparted a certain intensity to the American character.

Puritan political ideas, such as their deep distrust of power, and Puritan economic ideas, such as the calling, seeped into the American consciousness. So did their preoccupation with community, with self-governance, and with that hands-on style of political behavior. And so did their belief in moral law. The notion of a fundamental right and wrong permeating the universe would give coherence to American family life and shape the content of American education.

Our perception of selfishness (not to say sinfulness) as a basic human trait is undoubtedly of Puritan origin, and so is the restless, guilt-ridden and sometimes self-tortured American conscience. The events leading up to the American Revolution were but one example of how the political world might take on a startling new appearance when viewed through Puritan spectacles. Was Eng-

America as Promised Land.
(*American Progress (Manifest Destiny)*, by John Gast, courtesy of The Granger Collection, New York.)

lish society hopelessly corrupt? Were the lords of empire plotting to destroy American liberty and sully American virtue? Were the Americans themselves in peril of losing their souls by succumbing to temptation? Credit John Calvin.

The Puritans' unique view of the world would also provide the basis of an American political consensus. Americans could agree on essentials—and thus disagree only on *non*essentials—because Puritanism gave them a more or less common way of seeing life. Another kind of social cement was provided by the Puritans' assumption that religion mattered. For them, all sorts of ideas and institutions that we would think of as secular were permeated by spiritual significance. It has been observed of our own time that "the screws holding the world together often seem dangerously loose." In Puritan America the screws were all tight.

Finally, the Puritan worldview provided an elementary sense of nationhood. Winthrop's vision of a city upon a hill—prosperous, righteous, envied—would in large measure become America's vision of itself. And Puritan metaphors like the Promised Land and the New Jerusalem would eventually be transformed into America's founding myths. For there was something thrilling, indeed mythic, about the elect of God sorting themselves out of a depraved world and migrating westward, something to fire the mind and make the spirit soar. Nothing is more central to the American psyche than that feeling of chosenness.

Suggestions for Further Reading

Virginia DeJohn Anderson, *New England's Generation: The Great Migration and the Formation of Society and Culture in the Seventeenth Century* (1991).

Carl Bridenbaugh, *Vexed and Troubled Englishmen, 1590-1642* (1968).

Alfred A. Cave, *The Pequot War* (1996).

John Demos, *A Little Commonwealth: Family Life in Plymouth Colony* (1970).

David D. Hall, *Worlds of Wonder, Days of Judgment: Popular Religious Belief in Early New England* (1995).

Stephen Innes, *Creating the Commonwealth: The Economic Culture of Puritan New England* (1995).

Edmund S. Morgan, *Puritan Dilemma: The Story of John Winthrop* (1958).

Morison, Samuel Eliot. *Builders of the Bay Colony* (1958).

Neal Salisbury, *Manitou and Providence: Indians, Europeans, and the Making of New England* (1982).

Michael Walzer, *The Revolution of the Saints: A Study in the Origins of Radical Politics* (1965).

CHAPTER 2 STUDY AID

(This aid is not all-inclusive and is not intended to be a substitute for thorough study of the material presented in the textbook.)

Puritanism and the Founding

I. **John Calvin (1509-1564)**

1. Calvin:
   - Born Jean Chauvin or Chaulvin, a 16th-century French theologian and religious reformer
   - Author of *Institutes of Christian Religion* (1536)

2. Calvin's theology:
   - God is inscrutable and unknowable; man is degenerate and depraved due to the fall of Adam
   - All men are justifiably damned; God in his inscrutable wisdom chooses to save some portion of mankind at His own pleasure—the elect
   - The power of the atonement is limited to the elect
   - Only the elect can perform works which please God
   - Those who are among the elect cannot fall from grace
   - One might suspect one's election but never know with certainty
   - Man should not seek to become like God; that is blasphemy
   - Regardless of whether one is among the elect or not, all should worship and glorify God
   - All need to accept rather than evade the human condition by marrying, raising families, being educated and working at one's calling in life
   - One glorifies God by doing the best one can in any endeavor
   - If blessed with success and prosperity it is alright since it is but a by-product of glorifying and worshiping God
   - Consequently, one can live a virtuous live while pursuing what is in one's self-interest in life if it is done worshipfully and for the glory of God

3. Some "reasonable" deductions based on Calvin's theology:
   - Though one cannot know this with absolute certainty, it seems reasonable to assume that those who prosper the most are among the elect
   - Only the elect can perform work that is truly pleasing to God
   - Why would God prosper someone who was not among the elect?

- Thus, if one did lead a virtuous life, seeking to worship and glorify God, and in doing so prospered, was it not probable that one was among the elect?
- Therefore, it is in one's self-interest to be virtuous, industrious, and prosperous since this would imply that one is most likely among the elect

II. Puritanism

1. Puritan ideas and their impact:
   - Human nature
   - Confidence
   - Newness
   - Learning
   - Paranoia
   - Calling and Community

2. Puritan Constitution:
   - Puritan Law—"Real" law is God's law. There is nothing ambiguous about this. It provides a constitution for the community. One may disagree about how precisely to apply the law, but not about the law itself
   - Puritan politics—
     - ▸ Republican element—The king is not above the law; communities can be self-governing
     - ▸ Liberal element—Property is a sign of God's pleasure; the propertied class should lead out. Dissent is not to be tolerated, but in America dissenters could leave and set up their own communities. Men enjoy a "natural equality" and must choose the correct path themselves, not have it thrust upon them
     - ▸ Democratic element—Communities are governed by covenant; the community makes decisions for itself. All the elect can participate in regulating the community

3. Governance of the Self:
   - Natural liberty is the liberty to do whatever one wishes
   - Civil liberty is the liberty to do what is right
   - Individuals must govern themselves for the community to succeed. They must act with virtuous self-interest to worship and glorify God
   - Everyone knows what is right and wrong—God's law is clear

CHAPTER 2 REVIEW QUESTIONS

Key Terms

Puritanism

John Calvin

John Winthrop

Confidence

Newness

American Exceptionalism

Learning

Paranoia

Christian Calling

Covenant Communities

Multiple Choice Questions

1. Which of the following best exemplifies the idea of a Christian calling?
   a. "A life of poverty is a godly life."
   b. "By working hard and gaining wealth, I glorify God."
   c. "Wealth and fortune are evil vices."
   d. "Church service is the only service acceptable to God."

2. Puritans derived their name from their desire to:
   a. Cleanse the inner vessel.
   b. Purify the Catholic Church.
   c. Correct doctrinal corruptions in the Church of England.
   d. Purify England by gaining political power.

3. Puritans contributed all of the following to the American character except:
   a. A quest for knowledge.
   b. A robust sense of self-confidence.
   c. A fear that outsiders may ruin the City upon a Hill.
   d. Willful abandonment of self-interest.

4. Puritans defined freedom as:
   a. Moral self-governance.
   b. Lack of outside restraint.
   c. Freedom of religion.
   d. The right to bear arms.

Review Questions

1. Why have some observed that the Puritans were the "real" founders of America?

   _____

   _____

   _____

   _____

2. Why did the Puritans consider the New World to be a City upon a Hill? How did this belief affect their efforts in settling America?

   _____

   _____

   _____

   _____

3. What did the idea of American Exceptionalism mean to the Puritans? What does it mean now?

   _____

   _____

   _____

   _____

4. How did the Puritan trait of learning impact the Founding Fathers?

   _____

   _____

   _____

   _____

5. What were the underlying causes of the Puritan sense of paranoia?

   _____

   _____

   _____

   _____

Review Exercises

1. Explain the Puritan understanding of human nature, especially as it relates to the fall of Adam.

   _____

   _____

   _____

   _____

2. Explain how the Puritans reconciled the contradictory traits of virtue and self-interest. How does this understanding relate to the Puritan notion of a Christian Calling?

   _____

   _____

   _____

   _____

3. Explain the differences between the Puritan notions of natural liberty and civil liberty.

   _____

   _____

   _____

   _____

Big Essay Question

Think about your views of prosperity or modest living. Do you agree with the Puritan notion of a Christian Calling? Explain your opinion on the matter while showing an understanding of the opposing view.

American Republicanism

Freedom of Speech *by Norman Rockwell (1943).* (Printed by permission of the Norman Rockwell Family Trust. Copyright © 1943 the Norman Rockwell Family Trust.)

The American Revolution was of far more than local significance. Indeed, from the perspective of the present, it was a seismic, world-changing event, nothing less than a turning point in human history. Yet it was also among history's great surprises. Why, historians ask, did it occur when and where it did, not at the center of Western culture but out on the Atlantic frontier? Why did a colonial rebellion metamorphose into a true revolution and begin delving into new conceptions of the human experience? And why did its leaders insist that they were not revolutionizing anything, only restoring some prior condition of happiness? It was all very puzzling.

One clue must be that the Revolution began at a time when new ideas were in the air and, like the genie out of the bottle, they took on a life of their own. But why did the new ideas flourish in America? What made the English mainland colonies fertile ground for classical republicanism, or Whiggish liberalism, or political democracy? How did fishermen and tradesmen and tobacco farmers become interested in cutting-edge philosophical issues? Those who have spent their lives studying the American Revolution still feel a sense of wonder about it. On the one hand it seems vaguely inevitable, and on the other it seems like the most improbable thing that could have happened.

Ideas and Experience

The ideas in question came from the European Enlightenment. It was called that because it broke with the past in significant ways and prompted a feeling that the "light" had dawned at last. After centuries of Christian orthodoxy and the turmoil of the Reformation, there were new ideas about religion. After centuries of monarchy and feudalism, there were new ideas about society and government. After centuries of knowledge based on authority, there were new ideas about learning and discovering. And after centuries of looking to the medieval world for inspiration, there was a breathtaking rediscovery of antiquity.

The latter was especially important. For the texts of classical antiquity, many of which had reposed in musty vaults for two millennia, opened a world of new significance for the West. There was Plato's *Republic* and Aristotle's *Politics* to reckon with once again. There was Cicero on the law of nature, Polybius on politics and Livy on jurisprudence. There was Herodotus and Thucydides with their searing tales of tyranny versus liberty. Not least there was Cato, a moral hero of the Roman Republic, who would inspire, among others, the American Founders.

New ideas may take root more easily in new lands. America certainly was that. Yet there were other new lands in which Enlightenment ideas had scarcely any impact at all. To be sure, these were not colonized by England—which gives us one important clue. England was admired by intellectuals across Europe not only for the quality of its thought but also for the character of its practice. It became a kind of working model of Enlightenment political philosophy. Still, the American colonies didn't just replicate the English experience either; they went far beyond it and in the end broke away from it entirely.

So the puzzle comes down to this. Some remarkable, dynamic process appears to have taken place in the North American colonies of Great Britain. Some rare and potent mix of environment, circumstance and English culture seems to have made the soil of the New World especially fertile to Enlightenment ideas. We have seen the process hinted at in the previous chapter, where the American Puritans responded to New World conditions in highly significant ways, but the process existed beyond New England and with other groups besides the Puritans. Accordingly, what we want to focus on in this chapter is the relationship between ideas and experience in the American colonial setting. How did each affect the other? How did each cause the other to be modified, developing new ideas and altering experience? And how did ideas and experience together create the American Republic?

The term *republic* is elusive. Like other powerful words—*freedom, democracy, equality*—it means different things to different people. Thus, the American Republic isn't remotely similar to ancient Athens or Renaissance Florence, even while it does share a few of their characteristics. In order to understand what the American Republic is, we must explore three different strands of republican thought—three somewhat similar, yet also somewhat different conceptions of what the ideal republic should be.

For each of the three we must make the central concept as clear as possible. We must then see how each became manifest in the American colonial experience. Each would have a shaping influence on the United States, as we will see later on, yet the three reflected different political ideas, worked from different assumptions about human nature, and proffered different visions of the Good Society. Small wonder the American Founding is complex.

Classical Republicanism

Classical Republicanism:
See study aid.

The classical republics originated in Greece and Rome, as we have seen. Their history was generally troubled and their reach toward the good often short. The republics of Greece typically flared into tyranny or anarchy, while that of Rome swelled into an empire. But the ideal of the Good Society continued to glow within the ashes of experience. The rediscovery of classical texts in the Renaissance and a growing awareness of the ancients' wisdom and sophistication combined to keep those embers burning.

Renaissance political thought saw itself as taking up where the ancients had left off. And by the time of the Enlightenment in the latter 1600s, conceptions of the Good Society took Plato's *Republic* and Aristotle's *Politics* as their starting point. This was particularly true in England, where an education in the classics was *de rigueur* for a gentleman. In the great public schools (which were actually *private* schools), wellborn young Englishmen were required to memorize long passages of Herodotus, Thucydides, Plutarch, Cicero, Polybius, Livy—all of them committed republicans. Perhaps they absorbed the ancient politics unawares, along with the ancient literature.

Classical Republicanism looked to antiquity as a source of inspiration. (*The Course of Empire: Consummation of Empire*, by Thomas Cole, courtesy of the New-York Historical Society.)

In Stuart England, moreover, republican ideas had a uniquely romantic appeal. English writers often imagined their own society, in a mythic past before the Norman Conquest, to have been a republic in its own right. The "olde commonwealth," as they called it, had supposedly existed without feudal land tenure, without a standing army, without an established church and best of all, without a swaggering and disdainful nobility. Its monarch, so the belief went, had been elective, not hereditary, and his power had been shared with a democratic parliament. There had even been an ancient "constitution" to guarantee the rule of law.

Civil War and Revolution

The lost "Saxon democracy" was made all the more poignant by the bitter controversy between king and Parliament that ensued in the 1600s. Beginning with James I, who assumed the throne in 1603, the Stuart monarchs advanced a claim to rule Great Britain by a theory known as "divine right of kings." As the theory was expounded, it held that the king inherited the authority given by God to Adam—an authority without limitations. Those who resisted that authority were in violation of the Fifth Commandment. They were also liable to be drawn and quartered.

It is important to note—with the American experience in view—that the controversy centered on taxation. King James claimed the power to levy a variety of imposts—ship money, tunnage and poundage—more or less at his pleasure, along with a prerogative right to dun wealthy subjects for forced loans whenever it suited him. Parliament counterclaimed that as the voice of the people, it alone had the right to assess taxes, and that such right was well settled in the English constitutional experience.

Many of the king's parliamentary opponents gave voice to classical republican ideas. They pointed to the rule of law and argued that the king must obey the laws like anyone else. They pointed to the public good and argued that society didn't exist for the benefit of kings and nobles alone. They pointed to classical virtue and argued that the king's "evil" ministers—Buckingham, Strafford, Laud—were sources of moral decay.

Civil war broke out in 1642 and for the remainder of that decade England was torn with conflict. In the end, Charles I was beheaded by the victorious parliamentary forces and England was proclaimed a "Commonwealth and Protectorate." But the Commonwealth, under Oliver Cromwell, seemed more like Caesar's Rome than Arthur's Camelot—a bitter disappointment to the classical republicans. Cromwell ruled in despotic fashion throughout the 1650s, and there were enough abuses growing out of his dictatorship to unsettle the stoutest supporter. Upon his death in 1658, the English reluctantly restored the Stuarts to the throne. For England, as for so many others, revolution failed to bring about the Good Society.

Even so, republican ideas continued to flourish after the Restoration. They took on new relevance when Charles II returned to some of the same practices as his father. In 1679, opponents of the restored monarchy formed England's first political party. The Whigs, as they were called, would become both an inspiration and a model for American republicanism later on. For in their railings against the king, the Whigs made repeated reference to England's "ancient constitution," to the traditional rights and liberties of the people, and to a dozen other republican concepts. And these gained an ever wider influence.

The Whigs' greatest achievement—and one of the great achievements of all time—was the Glorious Revolution of 1688. James II, yet another Stuart despot, was driven from the throne in a bloodless uprising and this time there was real change. Parliament made it clear—indeed, spelled it out in writing—that when the next heir was invited to assume the throne, the monarchy was to be constitutionally limited. That is, the king of England was no longer "sovereign" in and of himself. For all intents and purposes, Parliament became the real sovereign power—which meant that England was now a kind of republic. It would take many years to work through the implications, both in England and America, but to the extent that Parliament represented the people as a whole, a true revolution had taken place.

The Commonwealth Ideology

Now the Whigs, who dominated Parliament, had to figure out how to make a constitutional monarchy work. For answers, they drew upon Aristotle's political science, exploring such ideas as the rule of law, the fragmentation of power and Aristotle's notion of intermixing monarchy, aristocracy and democracy. But their main focus, indeed their preoccupation, was that of the classical republicans—virtue. What is it, they asked, that maintains a high moral tone and sense of integrity in the body politic? What keeps a Good Society from going bad?

In response, Whig political thinkers began to develop a modern version of *areté*, which we recall from chapter 1 as the foundation of the classical republics. Historians refer to this as the "commonwealth" or "country" ideology. It was manifest most clearly in a series of newspaper essays by John Trenchard and Thomas Gordon, published in book form as *Cato's Letters*. By 1730 the commonwealth ideology had diffused to all parts of the British Empire. It was especially popular in the North American colonies, where it gave rise to dozens of

Commonwealth to Glorious Revolution:
http://www.britannia.com/history/narrefhist5.html

http://www.britannia.com/history/naremphist.html

Oliver Cromwell:
http://www.britannia.com/history/monarchs/mon48.html

Constitutional Monarchy:
Form of government in which the monarch is held in check by a written constitution.

Commonwealth Ideology:
See study aid.

pamphlets, broadsides and newspaper articles. If there was a single intellectual taproot of the American Revolution some forty years hence, this was it.

As a coherent view of the political world, the commonwealth ideology went something like this. Man is inherently evil, blind and foolish. Government must arrest his fallen tendencies by checking and balancing itself against the insidious wiles of the few. Yet in spite of the best efforts, there is a tendency for those close to the center of power (the "court") to usurp authority and corrupt the constitutional system. The rot can be impeded by only one thing—the voice of the truly virtuous in Parliament, the "country."

"Court" and "country" were highly charged terms in this dramatic interplay. The court party was the affiliation of those evil counselors of the king, of whom history had told much, but it was also the affiliation of a few Whigs themselves, stout republicans, indeed *reformers*, who nevertheless proved Lord Acton's dictum that "power corrupts." For those who got too close to the center of things, the "court," could not resist its beguiling influence, and eventually they were mired in depravity. The country party possessed all the opposite qualities—at least the way the story was told. It consisted of gentlemen farmers living out in the country, close to the soil, far from power's temptations, still in touch with the verities of life and above all graced with independence. They and they alone, it was held, could stem the tide of corruption.

The commonwealth ideology led to a fierce preoccupation with independence. Everything depended on it. The true patriot must think his own thoughts, chart his own course and be beholden to no one. Furthermore, he must be a man of property, for property alone could guarantee his personal autonomy. This explained why the commonwealthmen were so distrustful of taxes. The power to tax was the power to take property away—the power to destroy independence. Parliament alone should exercise that power because Parliament alone represented those who would have to pay. Finally, every stalwart of the country party must be constantly at vigil lest he fall prey to the court's machinations and forfeit his precious integrity.

Just as they had their own ideology, the commonwealthmen had their own style. They were all landed gentlemen, well off for the most part but not given to extravagant display. They valued sober conduct. Their schooling covered both classical and modern learning, and often included an enthusiasm for science. Since they didn't "work" for a living—relying on the income of their estates—they had no "interests" as such and thus possessed the detachment thought necessary for public service. They also possessed a strong sense of honor and were capable of great personal sacrifice.

This romantic ideal, which traced all the way back to Cicero, made an important contribution to the American Republic. For it provided the setting in which the American elite, including the Founders themselves, came of age. Even more to the point, it provided the conception of patriotism that would lie at the heart of American republicanism. The patriot is the person whose virtue operates as a bulwark against political corruption and moral decline. He is the backbone of the constitution.

Classical Republicanism in America

There is a legend to the effect that many of the gentry described above settled in the American colonies and shaped their political development. In fact, most early

Cato's Letters:
http://www.constitution.org/cl/cato_000.htm

The Lord of the Rings: The Temptation of Power

The psychology of tyranny has often been explored in literature. One problem, certainly, has been to explain why it is that ordinary people can become tyrants. Lord Acton offered a clue when he observed that "power tends to corrupt, and absolute power corrupts absolutely." For most of us the "something more" required by human beings is unquestionably good. We want love, companionship, beauty and grace in our lives. But what happens when chance presents us with power—a lot of power? Does the "something more" remain good? Or is it soon corrupted?

In J.R.R. Tolkien's *The Lord of the Rings* (1954), familiar throughout the western world, power exerts precisely the effect that Lord Acton attributed to it. For in the book the Ring of Power—which is something like possessing your very own nuclear arsenal—sorely tempts anyone who comes in contact with it. Staunch and faithful Boromir turns into a madman when he thinks the ring might be his; the once-fair Gollum degenerates into a loathsome reptile; and even the book's hero, Frodo, experiences moments of dark temptation. But the Ring's most unusual transformation is wrought upon Samwise Gamgee, Frodo's honest, humble, self-effacing manservant, who unexpectedly finds the ring in his custody:

> As Sam stood there, even though the Ring was not on him but hanging by its chain around his neck, he felt himself enlarged, as if he were robed in a huge distorted shadow of himself. . . . Already the ring tempted him, gnawing at his will and reason. Wild fantasies arose in his mind; and he saw Samwise the Strong, Hero of the Age, striding with a flaming sword across the darkened land, and armies flocking to his call as he marched to the overthrow of Baraddor. And then all the clouds rolled away, and the white sun shone, and at his command the vale of Gorgoroth became a garden of flowers and trees and brought forth fruit. He had only to put on the Ring and claim it for his own, and this could be.

At this rate, it is remarkable that anyone has courage enough to cast the ring to its destruction. And, indeed, no one does. At the critical moment, Frodo can't bring himself to pull the thing off his finger, and only the greed of Gollum, making a last desperate grab for it, plummets it into the fiery Crack of Doom.

colonists were of the more humble yeoman class. Owning their own land and running their own lives, they were not the poorest of the poor, to be sure, but they were far from the rank of gentleman. In any event, political matters were not uppermost on their minds. Survival was their immediate goal, and then simply making a go of it.

But America did work a change in many of them. Their lives had been modest in England. In the colonies they beheld a breathtaking expanse of available land and began to contemplate the opportunity that must surely go along with it. Depending on how the cards fell, a small stake in Virginia or the Carolinas could be sizably increased in a generation or two. And after the introduction of slavery in the 1620s and the development of tobacco, rice and indigo farming in the South, truly substantial gains became possible. Gov. William Berkeley of Virginia made a concerted effort to induce gentlemen to immigrate to his colony and take up large grants. In his eyes, and in those of other colonial overlords, America might well come to boast of a dazzling Old World gentry.

That didn't happen—exactly. But in the latter half of the 1600s, thousands of yeomen farmers increased the size of their holdings so dramatically that they could begin to put on gentlemanly airs, as it were, with imposing country houses, imported furnishings, fancy equipage and much else. These self-made squires were joined by another group similarly on the rise. Successful merchants in New England and the Middle Colonies often secured their own rural estates and adopted the same general lifestyle—such was the power of the gentlemanly ideal.

The rising colonial elite has been criticized for its artificiality and want of refinement. However, as historian Wesley Frank Craven points out, it was no less "real" for all that. Indeed, an up-by-the-bootstraps gentleman, while he may lack the essentials of etiquette, might rather outdo his European counterpart in some ways. In the eagerness with which the American upstarts assumed the country squire's political leadership role, for instance, they were marked by a positive zeal. In Virginia alone there were some 1,600 justices of the peace exercising both executive and judicial functions in local government—and most of them were regarded as gentlemen.

There was an even stranger sort of mirroring. The political institutions evolving in the colonies came to bear a marked resemblance to those of the mother country. The governor, for example, became not only the king's representative in a given colony but often the king's stand-in as well. And the governor's council, where sat the most distinguished members of the local elite, occasionally behaved like the House of Lords, demanding an outsize voice in the conduct of affairs.

The most striking parallel development was that of the colonial assemblies, which came to regard themselves as local "parliaments." Probably no one intended this result or even foresaw it clearly. Assemblies began as convocations of landowners discussing common problems. But consider how the participants might come to see themselves. Here is a governor and his "court," most of them powerful and well connected, sitting at Williamsburg or some other colonial seat. What keeps them from becoming a power unto themselves and running roughshod over the people? Why, those independent men of property and accountability, of course, who live out in the country and raise their voices in "parliament." Perhaps it was not a good description of reality but, as Bernard Bailyn has pointed out, it certainly provided Americans with a potent self-understanding.

No wonder they were so taken with the commonwealth ideology. And taken they were. Pamphlets extolling the "country" and warning against the "court" saturated the colonies, as did more ambitious works such as *Cato's Letters*. By its very nature, the colonial situation framed the commonwealth drama in such a way as to flatter American sensibilities. After all, those farmers-turned-gentlemen were undeniably the good guys.

The commonwealth ideology imparted a slightly spooky cast to colonial politics. Governors and other crown-appointed officials could not conduct affairs the way they did back in England, for their authority, so far from home, was much weaker. Accordingly, they were often forced to govern by means of under-the-table bargains. Besides, graft, bribery and other forms of chicanery were only too common among the kind of individuals often appointed to such posts. Imagine how all this looked to American Puritans, who were convinced of their own rectitude, skeptical of human nature—and always on the lookout for conspiracy. Small wonder that the men of the "country" had to be on their guard.

Here in embryo, then, was the essence of American republicanism. It was based on what Jefferson would call "the aristocracy of virtue and talent"—an aristocracy quite unlike any other. For its places of honor were not reserved for the highborn few, as in the Old World, but were open to all, or at least to most, on the basis of intelligence, drive, fortitude and other bootstrap qualities. The style of this squirarchy was one of relative simplicity, which Americans equated with purity, and in some way its members felt sanctified by the land they lived on, by the communities of which they were a part, and by Nature itself—a word they often capitalized—which in America seemed close at hand. They saw themselves as a bit more righteous than their English cousins—and a lot more righteous than their English administrators—and for that reason they tended to view politics in terms of good and evil. Aristocracy means "rule by the best." In America, it could be argued, the best really was the best.

Classical republicanism explains many of the issues that arose between England and the colonies. It explains a great deal about the American Revolution. It explains what many Americans had in mind when they declared independence and reconstituted their provinces as "republics," and what the delegates to the Constitutional Convention had in mind when they explored republican concepts and devised republican mechanisms. Most important, it explains why the conception of America as a "republic of virtue" would become a central founding myth.

Liberal Republicanism

Liberal Rupublicanism:
See study aid.

Growing alongside classical republicanism was a second set of ideas which we will call *liberal republicanism*. Many of the same people who embraced the one also embraced the other, yet not without certain difficulties. Liberalism was not necessarily "republican" in all respects and republicanism was not necessarily "liberal." For example, classical republicanism preached restraint of trade, the "just price" doctrine and a variety of sumptuary laws—and it held commercial prosperity to be the high road to perdition. Liberal republicanism embraced all the opposite points. Yet somehow the Founding had to straddle them both.

The term *liberal* is used here to designate personal freedom—the freedom of the individual against society. We take it to mean the freedom to go one's own way, think one's own thoughts and live one's own life. Where classical republicanism offers the citizen freedom *in* government—that is, freedom to participate in the political process—liberal republicanism offers him freedom *from* government. The two are rather different propositions and yet they are connected by an important tie. What sort of government would respect the citizen enough to keep out of his personal affairs *except* a government in which the citizen himself was powerful?

Personal freedom played virtually no part in the ancient republics. There the citizen found meaning in politics, not private life. The very idea of such freedom would have seemed odd to the ancients. How could a person be virtuous,

Just Price Doctrine:
The "just" price at which every good should be sold.

Sumptuary Laws:
Laws regulating personal behavior on moral or religious grounds; everyone must "toe the mark."

New York City in 1880: Liberal Republicanism promoted commercial activity.
(*Broadway, North from Cortlandt Street*, by J.J. Fogerty, courtesy of the New-York Historical Society.)

they would ask, if virtue's great projects were of no interest to him? (Imagine, say, the citizens of Athens convened to discuss an urgent political matter, when someone notices that a key figure is missing—he had stayed home to paint his house.) However, personal freedom did become important in seventeenth-century England, and even more important in the American colonies.

John Locke and English Liberalism

John Locke:
http://www.orst.edu/instruct/
phl302/philosophers/locke
.html

The importance began with the rise of English commerce in the 1500s. England's had been a sleepy subsistence economy. Now, rather suddenly, common land was fenced off for the grazing of sheep, and the woolen industry opened the way to expansive commercial development. Foreign trade turned the inward-looking English outward and gave rise to a new class of merchants, artisans and functionaries, whose way of life would be considerably different from that of the countryside.

A new outlook followed. Where Englishmen had once thought of their society as an organic whole, some now came to see it as diverse and divergent groups, each with different requirements. While the older groups preferred the status quo, the newer ones stood to gain by innovations such as religious toleration and the free expression of ideas. They would also benefit from the abatement of aristocratic influence, of course, and from enhancements in the rule of law. Theirs was a world of property, not privilege, and property required them to rethink almost everything.

In one way or another, the new middle class worked for these ends through political activity in the House of Commons, and they played into the great controversy between king and Parliament described above. Whiggism, too, embraced the new politics, for many Whigs were merchants or manufacturers themselves. It remained only for someone to put liberalism all together in a single coherent package. That person was **John Locke**.

As secretary to the Earl of Shaftsbury, the founder of the Whigs, Locke saw liberalism close at hand. Indeed, he was in exile for political activism when his most influential work was written. What Locke set about to do in his *Two Treatises on Civil Government* (1690) was take issue with the Stuart monarchs' claims that English subjects owed their king an absolute and unqualified obedience because of his "divine right" to govern. Such claims, Locke argued, missed the whole purpose of government as originally constituted. Government was not about *ruling* the governed so much as *protecting* them.

Locke's Five Principles:
See study aid.

In the *Second Treatise*, Locke carefully reasoned his way through five principles, which together spelled out the liberal case. They are important to us, all five, because they were to be echoed so clearly in the American Founding.

To begin with, said Locke, in the original "state of nature"—a hypothetical condition assumed to exist in the absence of government—human beings must have lived in perfect freedom and a rough equality. In such a world, moreover, all had the same rights, for "rights" were granted not by man but by Nature. All had the right to live their lives, enjoy their liberty and make the most of their property. As long as they did not disturb the rights of others, things promised to be well with them.

Some few, however, did disturb the rights of others, and beyond that there inevitably arose disputes. So the need was manifest for law of some kind and for a common judge. Accordingly, groups of people came together and agreed to form political society and establish government. There was no divine mandate for this "social compact," Locke asserted, only a simple and straightforward need. Government was a human invention and made to serve a human purpose.

The nature of that purpose was Locke's third principle. Government could have but a single end in view, he argued, and that was to protect the rights of its citizens. (After all, why else had they created it?) Those rights could never be surrendered, as the Stuart monarchs maintained, for they had been granted by Nature, but they could be disregarded by persons ill disposed. Government's job— its *only* job—was to make sure that didn't happen.

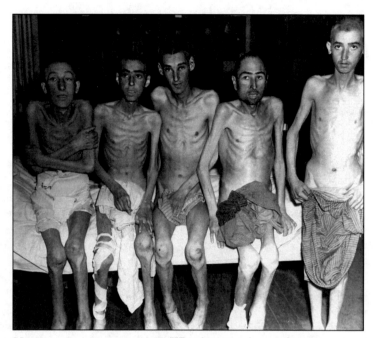

Nazi concentration camp, 1945. What happens when we forget human rights? (Courtesy of the Library of Congress.)

Government, then, existed by the *consent* of the governed and that alone— Locke's fourth principle. It meant that government was beholden to the people for its legitimacy. It could not presume to govern in God's name and the people be damned. There had to be elections, not democratic elections necessarily but "popular" elections nonetheless, where those who paid the bills had a chance to have their say.

Finally, if government violated the terms of consent, if it lost track of what it was supposed to do and whom it was supposed to serve, the people had the right, indeed the duty, to alter or abolish it, even if that meant revolution. The Glorious Revolution took place after the *Second Treatise* was written but before it was published. Nothing could have dramatized its argument more effectively. For here was the king, James II, accused of violating the trust of his people, and here was the result for all the world to see.

Of all the implications of Locke's philosophy, the most important was personal freedom. For if government stuck to securing the rights of its citizens, the citizens were bound to enjoy such freedom in wide measure. They could do what they wanted with their lives. They could enjoy their liberty to the fullest. And most of all, they could buy and own and improve and sell their property. They had, as humorist P.J. O'Rourke insightfully put it, "Life, Liberty, and Ka-ching!, Ka-ching!, Ka-ching!"

One other implication is worth noting. Like the classical republicans, Locke often bowed to the importance of virtue. But for Locke, virtue was significant only in its milder bourgeois forms, such as obeying the law and conducting

Natural Rights and the Uniqueness of Man

The appointment of [Peter Singer] to a tenured professorship of bioethics was unanimously recommended by a Princeton search committee and was approved by President Harold Shapiro, who chairs the National Bioethics Advisory Commission.

Peter Singer comes to campus to teach that truly ethical behavior will not flourish until humanity abandons the fallacy . . . of "the sanctity of life." He rejects "the particular moral order" which supposes that human beings are extraordinarily precious because God made them so. He also rejects secular philosophies that depict human beings as possessing a unique and exalted dignity that sharply distinguishes them from, and justifies their "tyranny" over, other species of animals.

Singer subscribes to utilitarianism, which holds that there is a single goal for human conduct— satisfaction of preferences and avoidance of suffering. Singer believes that . . . one pleasure is as good as another. Regarding humans, he says that assigning intrinsic moral significance to birth is arbitrary and logically indefensible. Birth is morally insignificant because a newborn, like a fetus, is incapable of regarding itself as "a distinct entity with a life of its own to lead." Because there are, he says, degrees of personhood, the intrinsic moral significance of the taking of the life of an individual gradually increases, like the physical being of the individual, from near nothingness in infancy.

He does not deny that killing a fetus or a baby involves killing a human being. Singer says infanticide is not necessarily more morally important than abortion, which is morally negligible. In fact, some infanticide is not even as important as, say, killing a happy cat. Killing an infant is never killing a person and is morally permissible in at least two kinds of situations. One is when a handicapped baby faces a life in which suffering will predominate. Another situation when infanticide is justified is when parents with a handicapped baby . . . will, if relieved of the burden of the baby, have another baby which will be happier than the handicapped baby would be, and will bring the parents more happiness. The logic of his position is that until a baby is capable of self-awareness, there is no controlling reason not to kill it to serve any preference of the parents.

From "Life and Death at Princeton" *by George F. Will*, Newsweek, *September 12, 1999, pp. 80 & 82.*

oneself civilly; it was not like the two-fisted *areté* of old. The people Locke was writing about were middle-class Englishmen. They weren't driven by a quest for honor on the battlefield or distinction in the halls of government so much as garden-variety comfort and prosperity. In other words, Locke's assumptions about human nature were different from those of the classical republicans, and his approach to the Good Society was not ancient at all but modern.

American Liberalism

Just as classical republicanism worked itself out in the American colonies, so too did liberal republicanism. Indeed, the American experience of building political societies seemed to reflect the very world Locke had described.

To begin with, Americans were far more equal than their European counterparts. They were not equal by present-day standards, of course, for there were property-owning requirements for the right to vote, and some groups—women, blacks, Native Americans—could not vote at all. But there was no formal aristocracy—it couldn't take root in a land made for hard work—and that fact was immensely important. It meant no titles of nobility, no special legal privileges, no feudal rents or dues. Consequently, where legal equality was an ideal to be striven for in Locke's England, it was a working reality across the Atlantic.

With available land, high wages and burgeoning opportunity, American society was also much more mobile than in England. Fortunes were made and lost. Wealth circulated. One never knew from year to year who one's betters really were, for the social register changed so rapidly. People gradually stopped thinking in the deferential terms typical of aristocratic societies. Instead of wondering where their place was in the social hierarchy, they dreamed of scrambling to the top themselves. A few went into politics, too, for in most of the colonies yeomen could easily meet the property requirements for political participation. Here was yet another striking contrast to the English case.

Second, if Americans were more equal than their European counterparts, they were also more free. Colonial governments were small and understaffed by English standards, and they often lacked the capacity to be meddlesome. Besides, settlers were dispersed over a vast terrain—Virginia alone was larger than England—and those in the backcountry were effectively out of range. Where a household in England would be under the constant watch of the parish authorities, for example, their cousins on the American frontier might never see a state-supported clergyman in their whole lives. Americans carried firearms too and knew how to use them. The local militia, out drilling on leafy afternoons, added to the sense of rugged self-sufficiency.

This fact pointed to still another Lockean feature of the American scene. The real government for most colonials, that of the township or county, was a government in which the local citizens were likely to have a good deal of influence. Indeed, it was a government they might well have created themselves. John Locke would have been impressed. He never supposed that the "state of nature" he described had actually existed, or that its inhabitants had actually executed a "social compact"—these were more in the way of theoretical constructs. In America, however, there actually were places where people lived without government, and there were any number of instances in which settlers had devised their own.

Legal Privileges:
For example, some had the legal privilege of wearing powdered wigs and some did not.

Feudal Rents or Dues:
Yearly rents and other obligations owed to titled noblemen or the crown by landholders and tenants.

Proprietary Colonies:
Royal grants of land to individuals or groups who then retained discretionary authority over the designated region, e.g. Maryland and Pennsylvania.

Entire colonies had been created that way. Several of them had begun as corporate enterprises, and the officials of the company in question had drawn up the charter of government for royal approval. Other colonies had begun as proprietary grants to an individual or a group, and here again the ground rules had been worked out by those who would have to live under them. In a few of the colonies the settlers themselves had literally sat around a table and worked up their own charter agreements. They took the idea of a church covenant, as described in the preceding chapter, and applied it to civil society, each signatory pledging to obey the laws and abide by the majority will.

In none of these cases was there anything mysterious about the origin of the government or the source of its sovereignty. These governments, at least, were clearly creatures of practical utility, not divine mandate, and they clearly drew their authority from the consent of the governed, just as Locke said. Their charters, moreover, were drafted by men who knew their Aristotle, and they included provisions for mixing and balancing the various social orders. Americans were not only creating their own governments, they were attempting to create them thoughtfully.

American colonials also experienced "rights" in a different way. Since legal equality was the rule, everyone (excepting the aforementioned women and minorities) had more or less the same rights as everyone else. It is true that symbolic activities such as horse racing or wearing a powdered wig were frowned upon if one was not a bona fide gentleman. But honest-to-goodness privilege, which affected the English in so many ways, did not really exist in America. In a world that favored concrete ability and practical results, it was difficult to maintain, for instance, that any individual ought to have the hereditary privilege of bringing his neighbors to trial and passing judgment on them. Locke would be impressed once again. Where his "natural rights" were largely theoretical in England, in the colonies they were a working reality. And when the colonists boasted of their traditional "rights of Englishmen," they had more to boast of than most Englishmen did.

American liberalism existed not only in the conditions of society but in its institutions as well. We have seen how colonial assemblies came to play a role similar to Parliament's. These bodies vigorously represented the interests of the propertied—a fundamental aspect of the liberal worldview. ("Ka-ching!, Ka-ching!, Ka-ching!") And as colonial leaders gained ever more experience, they were better and better able to hold their own against imperial administrations. The royal governor found himself confronting precisely the same go-easy-on-the-taxes opposition as the king was facing in Parliament.

The assemblies operated on the basis of an important principle, also borrowed from England, called *representation*. As practiced in the ancient republics, representation played an aristocratic role in government, according to Aristotle's idea of the "mixed regime." Since the people would likely choose their representatives from the wisest and most virtuous elements, an assembly of representatives would consciously reflect *areté*. But there was a liberal aspect to representation as well, and it was especially evident in the colonies. Representatives were regarded as spokesmen for specific, definable interests—Boston shipping, Philadelphia banking, tobacco planting on the lower James. It was only when such interests had an audible voice in government that the liberal society worked.

In England, liberalism and republicanism jostled each other uneasily. After all, one of them was all about virtue and honor and the public good, and the other was all about personal freedom and material self-interest. In America they got along pretty well together. The secret of their friendship lay in the relaxed, apolitical attitude of most Americans. As long as they felt free, the colonial middle classes were content to leave the governing process to their betters. They did participate in politics, but only in limited and deferential ways. There were plenty of other things of more interest to them—expanding the farm, adding onto the house, investing in a voyage to the Gold Coast. Let the truly virtuous worry about governance, they said.

The governing classes, in turn, knew their countrymen. They knew that the liberal society was an accomplished fact, and that most Americans had a vested interest in it. They were willing to live in a world that was fundamentally ambiguous—part classical, part liberal—and broad enough for both.

The quarrel with England in the 1760s imperiled liberal interest as well as republican virtue. New rules and regulations for the empire raised the specter of busybody government. New taxes laid by a "foreign" Parliament undermined the security of property. And new judicial procedures, such as trial without a jury, threatened the rule of law. In a liberal society, jeopardizing the "natural rights" of citizens was the unpardonable sin, according to John Locke. Indeed, it was grounds for revolution.

Democratic Republicanism

In the ancient world, there was a good deal of suspicion against rule by the *demos*. The many, as Aristotle called them, had their own behavioral style and it was not considered good. They could be shortsighted and self-serving. They were easily divided into competing interests. They were often willing to buy the flatteries of **demagogues** and fall in with their ambitious designs. All too frequently, it seemed, government by the many led to some sort of factional anarchy, and that in turn led to tyranny.

Yet Aristotle also noted an inherent drift in republican politics toward that very thing, the rule of the *demos*, owing to the fact that the many, tugging and pulling against the few, would always find a way to win in the end. This explained why Aristotelian political science sought to refine democracy with checks and balances. The hope was that a proper constitution might at least slow the inevitable decay into chaos.

Democracy was nothing to be feared in Georgian England. For the glittering titled "few" of that world not only monopolized political and social power, they monopolized the English mind itself with their ancient names, sprawling estates and ever so graceful manners. Liberalism was hardly more democratic itself. In theory, liberals held that all men were created equal. In practice, they represented a propertied elite almost as small as the aristocracy. In England, in other words, there simply weren't enough franchised individuals to pose a credible democratic threat.

In the colonies, however, things were different.

American Democracy

To begin with, owing to the absence of a formal aristocracy, the democratic element was necessarily stronger in the American mix. Moreover, with the exception of a few urban areas, most Americans were of at least modest means, so there was no large desperately poor class, as in Europe. Equally important was the feeling of equality that most Americans shared, blurring class lines and making success seem more achievable.

Politics adapted to these New World realities. We have seen that most freehold farmers were able to meet the property requirements for voting, and even in the cities many were well enough off to participate. There were steady pressures to expand the franchise even further and to represent an ever greater variety of interests, for freedom included the desire to use public power for one's own ends. For example, small farmers, seeking to expand their holdings, behaved like any other interest by seeking loans on favorable terms and supporting laws favorable to debtors.

There were democratic implications in American Puritanism, as we have seen, and even more pronounced ones in Puritanism's successors. In the Baptist movement, for example, the Puritan doctrine that souls were equal in the sight of God came to occupy a central place in worship. Even more central was the Baptist idea that souls must be free to choose the right.

Classical republicanism did not mix well with democracy at first, for many commonwealthmen, following Aristotle, doubted the virtue of ordinary people. Here again, however, the American experience began to suggest otherwise. Ordinary people had to bear a great deal in the travail of the Revolution. The embargo movement, for example, called upon them to forgo imported luxuries in order to send the British authorities a strong message. Overwhelming numbers complied. And their valor on the battlefield was tested time and again, to say nothing of their willingness to endure hardship in the unspeakable British prisons. There was nothing soft about democratic virtue.

Even so, democratic virtue was appreciably different from classical *areté*. Ordinary farmers lacked the passionate identification with politics that typified landed gentlemen. Urban tradesmen lacked the "stake" in society that property conferred, not to mention any mystical connection to the land. And the have-nots of the world, wherever found, were the needful elements, those who by definition lacked independence.

For these and other reasons, democracy was held in deep suspicion by most of the American Founders. Indeed, when they saw mobs in the streets at the time of the Stamp Act, they thought of the Athenian democrats crying for the blood of their rivals. But the Founders had no difficulty with a second cousin they referred to as "**popular government**," a mixed and balanced form in which some democratic elements were allowed. With popular government the common people would have their own role to play even if it was limited. Their lot would be to uphold the law, yield to proper authority, chose wise and virtuous leaders and lead quiet, sober lives. The democratic genie must be kept in its bottle.

And yet there were signs that the genie escaped anyway, in the turmoil of the Revolution. For if the Revolution was partly a republican movement and partly a liberal one, it was partly a democratic movement too.

We have seen above how both classical and liberal republican developments in America appeared to be thwarted by British imperial policy. The same was true of democratic republicanism. For several historians of the period have concluded that there were widespread fears that Britain's contemplated administrative reforms would threaten the democratic gains already made. Driven by such fears, artisans and laborers in the colonies became intensely active politically, and in key cities created the roughhouse that brought the Revolution to a flash point.

There were other evidences of democracy at work. In several states the electorate widened dramatically after the war was over. And lower houses of assembly, reflecting the democratic influence most directly, were given sweeping powers in some of the new state constitutions. The tone of politics became democratic too. In fact, much of the clamoring of special interests that James Madison found so objectionable in Virginia—and that led him to think about a new federal constitution—was simply what we would call politics as usual.

Threading its way among these changes was an outline theory of democratic government. Radicals like Samuel Adams and Thomas Paine searched for it in the writings of Jean Jacques Rousseau, a figure of the French Enlightenment who had stressed the role of the common people in political morality. Others looked to influential Scotsmen of the day such as Lord Kames and Thomas Ferguson. In Kames they found the concept of society as an organic whole in which all classes have legitimate roles to play. In Ferguson they found the concept of "common sense"—holding that truth was accessible not just to philosophers but to everyone.

In time, Americans would expand on these ideas. They would borrow from Puritan notions of grace and their own feeling of chosenness, and argue that the common people of the New World, unlike those of the old, were endowed with a practical wisdom they called "horse sense," with a form of virtue more relevant than *areté*, and with an uncorrupted sense of right and wrong. They would believe in regenerate human nature—that is, Calvinism flip-flopped—which political empowerment might further improve. They would have a liberal's dislike of government together with a romantic's enthusiasm for volunteer service and humanitarian causes. They would often be detained by questions of justice, and once in a while preoccupied with reform. They would disparage privilege, frown at pretentiousness and eventually conceive a violent dislike of slavery.

Democratic republicanism would create its own hero figure, too. This character would begin as the "minuteman" of the Revolution and wind up as the Hollywood "cowboy." He would lack the burnish of aristocracy, perhaps, but everything else about him would call ancient Greek virtue to mind. He would

Jean Jacques Rousseau:
http://www.utm.edu/research/iep/r/rousseau.htm

http://www.wsu.edu:8000/~dee/ENLIGHT/ROUSSEAU.HTM

Jean Jacques Rousseau:
(1712–1778) Swiss-French philosopher and political theorist. Celebrated for his theories of the "natural man" and "social contract."

Thomas Paine:
http://www.bartleby.com/133/index.html

Democratic Republicanism created a series of hero figures that included the mythical American cowboy. (Courtesy of PhotoDisc, Inc.)

be inflexibly moral and unflinchingly brave. He would live close to Nature out on the wide prairie and play hunches to catch the bad guys. And he would save the widow's ranch from the shady railroad lawyer for no better reason than it was the right thing to do.

Thomas Jefferson was to become the new democracy's patron saint. In his supple mind he connected the idea of opportunity with the idea of the common people—and both of those with the idea of a regenerate America. Jefferson was a classical republican who truly believed in rule by the best. But his aristocracy of talent and virtue would eventually be open to anyone, not just a privileged elite. He would, as he said, comb through each new generation for the best and the brightest, and provide them with a good education. If their parents were hardscrabble farmers, so much the better.

Jefferson's vision of America was not unlike John Winthrop's city upon a hill. In such a place, the Virginian thought, human nature might shed its acquired dysfunctions and find its way back to first principles. Wealth would lose its odor of decadence, liberalism would become generous and civic minded, and the common people would cease to behave like an Athenian mob. For Jefferson, the American Founding might be a triumph for the whole human race.

Everyone's Good Society

We can see all three conceptions of republicanism in the lives of the American Founders. Some of them were rising merchants. Some were entrepreneurs. Some were members of that budding American gentry. A few were lowborn and self-made.

A small but significant number of the Founders truly were figures out of ancient Greece. These "marble men," as Christopher and James Lincoln Collier called them in their study of the Founding, took classical *areté* as their guiding principle. They made patient and systematic efforts in the pursuit of excellence, achieving a kind of secular sainthood in the eyes of their contemporaries. George Washington certainly belongs in that category. But there were others as well.

Virtually all of the Founders resonated with some version of the republican ideal and frequently with more than one. There were gentlemen with an entrepreneurial flair. There were members of the elite who inclined toward democracy. There were town-bred merchants saving up for a rural estate and the life of a country squire. There were scholars proficient in practical politics, and vice versa.

For all of them, republicanism had given rise to some uniquely American conception of the Good Society. Its main elements included:

The Good Society: See study aid under **American Synthesis.**

John Wayne: American

(Excerpts from *Reagan Eulogy for John Wayne*)

In 1979 Ronald Reagan was gearing up for his successful 1980 campaign for the presidency. He took the occasion of John Wayne's death to sound some of the patriotic themes that would serve him so well in 1980 and 1984.

We called him Duke, and he was every bit the giant off screen he was on. Everything about him—his stature, his style, his convictions conveyed enduring strength. In this country and around the world, he was the most popular box-office star of all time. For an incredible twenty-five years he was rated at or around the top in box-office appeal. Yet John Wayne was more than an actor; he was a force around which films were made. As Elizabeth Taylor stated last May when testifying in favor of the special gold medal Congress struck for him: "He gave the whole world the image of what an American should be."

He was born Marion Michael Morrison in Winterset, Iowa. [After] his family moved to California . . . he picked up the nickname Duke. He rose at 4 A.M. to deliver newspapers, and after school and football practice he made deliveries for local stores. He was an A student, president of the Latin Society, head of his senior class and an all-state guard on a championship football team.

He accepted a full scholarship to play football at the University of Southern California. There Coach Howard Jones, who often found summer jobs in the movie industry for his players, got Duke work in the summer of 1926 as an assistant prop man on the set of a movie directed by John Ford.

From his job in props, Duke worked his way into roles on the screen. During the Depression he played in grade-B westerns until John Ford finally convinced United Artists to give him the role of the Ringo Kid in his classic film *Stagecoach*. John Wayne was on the road to stardom. He quickly established his versatility in a variety of major roles.

When war broke out, Duke tried to enlist but was rejected because of an old football injury, his age (34), and his status as a married father. He flew to Washington to plead that he be allowed to join the Navy but was turned down. So he poured himself into the war effort by making inspirational war films. To those back home and others around the world he became a symbol of the determined American fighting man.

Duke could not be kept from the front lines. In 1944 he spent three months touring forward positions in the Pacific theater. Appropriately, it was a wartime film, *Sands of Iwo Jima*, which turned him into a superstar.

As one of the true innovators of the film industry, Duke tossed aside the model of the white-suited cowboy/good guy, creating instead a tougher, deeper dimensioned western hero. He discovered Monument Valley, the film setting in the Arizona-Utah desert where a host of movie classics were filmed. He perfected the choreographic techniques and stuntman tricks which brought realism to screen fighting. At the same time he decried pornography, and blood and gore in films. "That's not sex and violence," he would say. "It's filth and bad taste."

Duke went to Vietnam in the early days of the war. He scorned VIP treatment, insisting that he visit the troops in the field. Once he even had his helicopter land in the midst of a battle. When he returned, he vowed to make a film about the heroism of Special Forces soldiers. The public jammed theaters to see the resulting film, *The Green Berets*.

I never once saw Duke display hatred toward those who scorned him. His work habits were legendary in Hollywood—he was virtually always the first to arrive on the set and the last to leave. To him, a handshake was a binding contract. Duke's generosity and loyalty stood out in a city rarely known for either. When a friend needed work, that person went on his payroll. When a friend needed help, Duke's wallet was open. He was also loyal to his fans.

Like any good John Wayne film, Duke's career had a gratifying ending. In the 1970s a new era of critics began to recognize the unique quality of his acting. The turning point had been the film *True Grit*. When the Academy gave him an Oscar for best actor in 1969, many said it was based on the accomplishments of his entire career. Others said it was Hollywood's way of admitting that it had been wrong to deny him Academy Awards for a host of previous films. There is truth, I think, to both these views.

Yet who can forget the climax of the film? The grizzled old marshal confronts the four outlaws and calls out: "I mean to kill you or see you hanged at Judge Parker's convenience. Which will it be?"

"Bold talk for a one-eyed fat man," their leader sneers.

Then Duke cries, "Fill your hand, you sonofabitch!" and, reins in his teeth, charges at them firing with both guns. Four villains did not live to menace another day.

"Foolishness?" wrote *Chicago Sun-Times* columnist Mike Royko, describing the thrill this scene gave him. "Maybe. But I hope we never become so programmed that nobody has the damn-the-risk spirit."

Earlier this year, when doctors told Duke there was no hope, he urged them to use his body for experimental medical research, to further the search for a cure. He refused painkillers so he could be alert as he spent his last days with his children.

When he died on June 11, a Tokyo newspaper ran the headline, "Mr. America passes on."

"There's right and there's wrong," Duke said in the *The Alamo*. "You gotta do one or the other. You do the one and you're living. You do the other and you may be walking around but in reality you're dead."

Duke Wayne symbolized just this, the force of the American will to do what is right in the world. He could have left no greater legacy.

Government for the benefit of the people, not the rulers.

Real and practical freedom for the individual.

Expanding economic opportunity.

A virtuous citizenry.

The rule of law.

Not all of these elements fit together comfortably, as we have seen. Moreover, each of them grew out of a different understanding of human nature. Before the Founding was completed, a great deal would have to be sorted out, and even then ambiguities and inconsistencies would permeate the final result. Was the US Constitution addressed to classical republicanism, liberal republicanism or democratic republicanism? critics asked. The answer: all three.

Perhaps this was a sign of strength rather than weakness. If there was an intellectual fuzziness to the American Republic, there was also a plastic, protean quality. America really could be different things to different people—which certainly helps to make it interesting.

Unifying all three conceptions was the assumption that an Everyone's Good Society was truly possible. Some idea of America as a promised land, a place apart, a historical exception, a *Novus Ordo Seclorum*—some founding myth, in other words—worked to fuse the disparate parts into a whole.

Suggestions for Further Reading

Bernard Bailyn, *The Origins of American Politics* (1968).

Robert E. Brown, *Middle-Class Democracy and the Revolution in Massachusetts, 1691–1780* (1969).

Richard Bushman, *King and People in Provincial Massachusetts* (1985).

John William Eadie, ed., *Classical Traditions in Early America: Essays by Meyer Reinhold, et al* (1976).

Jack P. Greene, *The Quest for Power: The Lower Houses of Assembly in the Southern Royal Colonies, 1689–1776* (1963).

Michael Kammen, *Empire and Interest: The American Colonies and the Politics of Mercantilism* (1970).

Henry May, *The Enlightenment in America* (1976).

Edmund S. Morgan, *Inventing the People: The Rise of Popular Sovereignty in England and America* (1988).

Caroline Robbins, *The Eighteenth-Century Commonwealthman: Studies in the Transmission, Development and Circumstance of English Liberal Thought from the Restoration of Charles II until the War with the Thirteen Colonies* (1968).

Charles S. Sydnor, *American Revolutionaries in the Making: Political Practices in Washington's Virginia* (1965).

Gary M. Walton and James F Shepherd, *The Economic Rise of Early America* (1979).

Michael P. Zuckert, *Natural Rights and the New Republicanism* (1994).

CHAPTER 3 STUDY AID

(This aid is not all-inclusive and is not intended to be a substitute for thorough study of the material presented in the textbook.)

American Republicanism

I. Enlightenment

1. Calvinism:
   - Theological solution to human predicament
   - American Puritans and the "New England Way"

2. European Enlightenment:
   - Secular solution to human predicament
   - Discounted virtue in favor of self-interest as prime motive force in human interactions
   - Reason represented by "science"
   - Practical and pragmatic—*a posterori* rather than *a priori*
   - Self-interest seen as predictable and reliable
   - Self-interest led to practical advances and cooperative behavior
   - Self-interest controllable structurally (counterpoise)

3. North America and the Enlightenment:
   - Filtered or refracted through English experience
   - Interpreted by the light of colonial experience
   - Source of several indigenous strains of republican reasoning that suggested how a good society might be established

II. Classical Republicanism

1. Freedom within government:
   - Rule of law
   - Common good
   - Virtue and honor
   - Constitutional protection of rights and liberties

2. Property (land):
   - Source of personal independence

3. Glorious Revolution of 1688:
   - Established constitutional monarchy
   - Patronage led to concentration of power at the "court"
   - The court perceived as seat of corruption

4. Commonwealth or "country" faction:
   - Opposition to perceived corruption at court became identified as the commonwealth or "country" position

- Country perspective opposed taxation of property
- Such taxation seen as attempt to limit personal independence
- Sought virtuous (disinterested) participation rather than self-interest

5. American variant of the commonwealth ideology:
- Yeoman farmers as landed gentry
- Aristocracy of talent and merit
- Virtue
- Simplicity

III. Liberal Republicanism

1. Freedom from government:
- "Middle class" politics
- Merchants and entrepreneurs
- Rule of law
- Toleration
- Protection of all forms of property
- Anti-patronage
- Sought abatement of privilege, restrictions and regulations that impeded commerce
- Emphasized need for the consent of the governed

2. John Locke (1632-1704):
- State of nature
- Social contract and creation of political society—both society and government were inventions
- Government was instituted to protect "natural rights" such as liberty, equality, and property
- Legitimate authority derived from the consent of the governed
- Sovereignty vested in the people not the government

3. Virtue and self-interest:
- Civic virtue
- Obey laws
- Act civilly

IV. Democratic Republicanism:

1. Colonial American society:
- No formal aristocracy
- Large "middle" class
- Social, economic and physical mobility
- Relative equality
- General prosperity

- Franchise for most male property holders

2. Democratic precedents and practice:
   - Puritan experience
   - Property ownership
   - Representative government
3. The working class:
   - Unrepressed
   - Aspirations
4. Common people:
   - Purity
   - Common sense
   - Trustworthy
   - Heroic virtue
   - Distracted by mundane aspects of life yet able to participate in government indirectly
   - Opportunity for advancement through virtue and merit
   - Pool of talent

V. American Synthesis:

1. Blending the three republican styles:
   - Open society
   - Differences among the three styles were not forced into a confrontation with each other
   - Classical republicanism (propertied class) = virtuous (disinterested) representatives
   - Liberal republicanism (merchant and entrepreneurs) = civic virtue and enlightened self-interest.
   - Democratic republicanism (working class) = inexhaustible pool of talent, heroic virtue and commons sense when called upon
2. The Good Society in colonial America:
   - Republicanism—for the people and by the people
   - Liberty—individual freedom
   - Opportunity—equality, mobility and prosperity
   - Order—virtue (classical, civic and heroic), the rule of law and natural rights
3. American exceptionalism:
   - Unique constellation of political, social and economic possibilities

CHAPTER 3 REVIEW QUESTIONS ━━━━━━

Key Terms

Republic

Classical Republicanism

Commonwealth Ideology

Liberal Republicanism

John Locke

Representation

Democratic Republicanism

Thomas Jefferson

Multiple Choice Questions

1. In the commonwealth ideology the corrupted center of authority is referred to as the:
   a. Gentry.
   b. Court.
   c. Tyrant.
   d. Country.

2. The term "liberal" in liberal republicanism means:
   a. Lack of traditional moral restraint.
   b. Leftward political leanings.
   c. Individual freedom from the government.
   d. A progressive approach to society.

3. Which colonial economic group did liberal republicanism most agree with?
   a. Middle class merchants.
   b. Colonial statesmen.
   c. Poor yeoman farmers.
   d. Wealthy gentlemen.

4. Which colonial leader extolled the virtue of democratic republicanism?
   a. John Adams.
   b. James Madison.
   c. Alexander Hamilton.
   d. Thomas Jefferson.

Review Questions

1. How did the European Enlightenment bring the ideas of classical thinkers to the American Founders?

   _____

   _____

   _____

   _____

2. How did Jefferson's proposed "aristocracy of virtue and talent" differ from traditional notions of aristocracy?

   _____

   _____

   _____

   _____

3. Why did liberal republicanism become so popular in colonial America?

   _____

   _____

   _____

   _____

4. Why were classical thinkers like Aristotle so leery about democracy?

   _____

   _____

   _____

   _____

5. What factors led to the rise of democratic republicanism in America?

   _____

   _____

   _____

   _____

Review Exercises

1. Explain the commonwealth ideology. To the Founders, who was the court and who was the country?

   _____

   _____

   _____

   _____

2. John Locke made reference to the "state of nature" in his writings. Explain this concept. How would idealists and realists view life in the state of nature?

_____

_____

_____

_____

3. Name a character from a movie or television show who embodies each of the three republicanisms discussed. Briefly state why each character embodies the particular republicanism.

_____

_____

_____

_____

Big Essay Question

The text outlines a five-step pattern of reasoning John Locke used in explaining the nature and role of government. Explain Locke's ideas. Then read the first two paragraphs of the Declaration of Independence. Find and write down a sentence or phrase from the Declaration that directly matches each of Locke's points.

The American Revolution

COMMON SENSE;

ADDRESSED TO THE

INHABITANTS

OF

AMERICA,

On the following interesting

SUBJECTS.

I. Of the Origin and Design of Government in general, with concise Remarks on the English Constitution.

II. Of Monarchy and Hereditary Succession.

III. Thoughts on the present State of American Affairs.

IV. Of the present Ability of America, with some miscellaneous Reflections.

Man knows no Master save creating HEAVEN,
Or those whom choice and common good ordain.
THOMSON.

PHILADELPHIA;

Printed, and Sold, by R. BELL, in Third-Street.

MDCCLXXVI.

(*Common Sense*, by Thomas Paine, courtesy of the Library of Congress.)

The American Revolution was more than just a glorified colonial rebellion. It was a true revolution—the first of several in the modern world. It inspired a wave of republican upheavals throughout Europe and the Americas, and made people rethink politics from the ground up. Arguably, in fact, it effected a turning point in human history.

The Revolution was also the premier event of the American Founding. At its beginning there were thirteen British colonies with little in common and few bonds of sympathy. At its end there was a United States of America. It is easy in the light of subsequent history to miss the epoch-marking significance of that transformation. But consider it. An entirely original polity, of continental size and global influence, emerges from a world of monarchy and aristocracy and religious establishment, proclaiming new doctrines, advancing new principles, relying on new mechanisms, and describing the whole as "self-evident truth." Strangest of all, it works.

The Coming of the Revolution

As schoolchildren, Americans learn all about the events leading to the outbreak of hostilities in April of 1775. These events—like Paul Revere's ride—have long since taken on the hyperrealism of myth.

Yet they were by no means inevitable. It is true that American and British institutions had been on divergent courses of development from the beginning. It is also true that political maturity in the American colonies pointed toward eventual home rule. But American institutions were as English as England's, growing out of the same historical experience and the same seedbed of ideas. And if the two societies were on divergent courses in some ways, they were on parallel courses in others. We could easily imagine American nationhood coming about by *evolution* rather than *revolution*, as it did in Canada or Australia. Virtually on the eve of hostilities, Americans were still toasting the king's health and celebrating his birthday, picturing themselves the most loyal of subjects. The first thing we must explain, then, is what happened to this particular corner of the British Empire—what made it mysteriously self-destruct?

In the beginning there was no empire as such, only colonies. These had been established in a variety of ways and for a variety of purposes. The colonies

Mercantilism:
http://www.westga.edu/
~cscott/history/mercan
.html

sometimes doubled as religious havens, as we have seen, but they also came to play a broader role described by the term *mercantilism*. That role was to strengthen the British economy by providing crucial products—such as tobacco, rice or naval stores—and by extending the British market for manufactured goods. The governing idea of the mercantilists was to achieve complete economic self-sufficiency.

Accordingly, toward the close of the 1600s, Britain organized the colonies into an empire. The subordinate relation of "chicks" to "hen," as the authorities sometimes put it, was codified into a series of laws known as the Navigation Acts, designed to insure that the colonies continued to advance English commerce generally and certain political interests in particular. All trade was to be carried in English ships. Certain colonial exports must go directly to London before being transshipped elsewhere. And virtually all colonial imports must come through London as well. In theory, the empire was supposed to benefit the colonies as well as the mother country. Some historians argue that it essentially did so, at least in the beginning, while others maintain that the benefits went mostly to London merchants. Either way, the colonies enjoyed a cartel monopoly in supplying important products, along with assorted franchises, bounties and other incentives. They were by no means cynically exploited.

The colonies also had the international situation to consider. Other empires were established in North America, and when relations among them grew tense in Europe—or erupted into actual war—their colonies played the role of proxies and pawns. Between 1689 and 1763 a series of four major conflicts was fought between Great Britain and France, and in all of them colonial militias saw action, colonial cargoes were confiscated on the high seas, and colonial settlements became targets of attack. As long as the world remained so perilous, the colonies had no choice but to seek protection from the British.

This situation changed dramatically in 1763. The last of the Anglo-French Wars came to an end, and a defeated France handed Canada over to its British foe. All over North America, the scales of power shifted. Suddenly the colonies had much less need of British protection. Conversely, the British had much less need of imperial solidarity in the face of a common enemy. Indeed, the lords of empire considered that the time had come to undertake some long overdue reforms.

Imperial Reform

The chief problem requiring reform was the growing political maturity of the colonies. By 1763 Virginia had been established for more than a century and a half—there were residents of the Old Dominion whose great-great-grandparents had been born on American soil—and the other colonies weren't much younger. Between 1670 and 1730 colonial leadership had quietly passed from English to American hands. In the process, "colonies" had become "provinces."

At the same time, American institutions of government had also come of age. We saw in the previous chapter how assemblies had come to view themselves not as local administrative units but as Westminster-like parliaments. The leaders of these bodies had gained in sophistication accordingly. They had learned to organize committees in order to get things done, to circumvent obstacles with parliamentary maneuvers, to use structure and procedure to their advantage. Most important, they had learned to manage strong-willed royal governors by such expedients as funding the governor's salary.

The lords of empire were also uneasy with American prosperity. Colonial merchants were among the most successful in the world, not excepting their London counterparts, and growers of tobacco, rice and other subsidized crops were doing equally well. American fishing and furring operations, American shipbuilding, American ironmongering and liquor distilling were all thriving industries, while ordinary farmers were selling their surplus foodstuff around the hemisphere. The famous "triangular trade" in sugar, molasses, rum, horses, ivory, gold dust and African slaves was reaping fabulous profits and personal fortunes were on the rise.

Americans, moreover, paid few taxes. They were taxed by their own assemblies for the support of local government, of course, and their trade was subjected to regulatory imposts. But when it came to, say, supporting the British armies that had come to *their* defense in the last French war, they had laid out very little. Their British cousins, meanwhile, had been taxed to the limit.

At the war's end in 1763, all of this would abruptly change. In what seemed like a series of lightning strokes, Parliament laid new duties on sugar and other commodities, tightened up restrictions on colonial trade, and blocked off further settlement in the West. Then, before the Americans could catch their breath, it followed with the notorious Stamp Act. This was not an impost or trade restriction but an internal tax—the sort of thing colonial assemblies had always been in charge of—and it was clearly meant to be enforced. By its provisions, revenue stamps were required for just about everything from legal documents to college diplomas. The colonists could well afford to pay such taxes, Parliament reasoned, and it was high time they did so.

Nothing could have better aroused American ire. For it was the old issue of taxation—the one that had driven the Stuarts from the throne—in new guise. When James I had demanded tunnage and poundage without his subjects' consent, Englishmen had wondered what protection was afforded *any* of their property. Americans now wondered the same thing. How could Parliament tax *them*? they asked. *They* had no voice in Parliament.

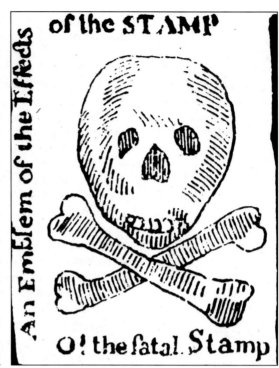

An American parody of the revenue stamps required by the Stamp Act. How could Parliament tax us? (Reprinted from the *Pennsylvania Journal and Weekly Advertiser*, October 31, 1765, courtesy of The Granger Collection, New York.)

Ordeal of the Empire

There ensued a decade of tumult. Colonial spokesmen penned angry remonstrances to Parliament, explaining why the Stamp Act violated the British constitution. Then mobs gathered in the streets and harassed the would-be stamp vendors. Shouting "No taxation without representation," the rowdies hurled both stones and epithets. They were not above resorting to tar and feathers either, and occasionally even worse. And pamphleteers had a field day. They cast British intentions in the darkest hues possible and harked back to the commonwealth ideology. This wasn't about funding imperial services, they accused; it was about corruption and tyranny.

The British Constitution was unwritten, consisting of traditional understandings about the origin of government and the distribution of its power.

In the Declaratory Act (1766) Parliament reasserted its right to govern the colonies "in all cases whatsoever," even though the Stamp Act was repealed for political reasons.

Eventually the Stamp Act was withdrawn, grudgingly, only to be replaced by a new series of imposts called the Townshend Duties. Colonial resistance to these was equally intransigent. Such "duties" were not trade regulations at all, the Americans cried, but Parliamentary taxes in disguise—clear evidence of deception.

Trans-Atlantic communication made things worse. Policy makers in England had to rely on American envoys, such as Benjamin Franklin and James Duane, to explain to them why the colonials found the measures so odious, and some explanations only confused matters the more. To many Britons, it appeared that the Americans were either bad citizens or free riders, and that their arguments were mere hypocrisy.

At the same time, Parliament overhauled the customs service and appointed a Board of American Commissioners to supervise rigorous enforcement of the Navigation Acts. (A number of colonial merchants were free traders even then—the usual term was smugglers—and they evaded the commerce laws when they could.) Unfortunately, the new officialdom was no more aboveboard than the old, which many knew to be corrupt. Officers took bribes as a matter of course, and some even practiced a sort of customs racketeering, condemning entire cargoes through legal technicalities and gaining handsome bounties for themselves.

The imperial reformers were on a roll nonetheless. In order to curb smuggling further, they gave the customs inspectors broader legal options, some of which circumvented the notoriously lenient local juries, and made use of high-powered search warrants. These writs of assistance, as they were called, gave the inspectors a much wider latitude of discretion in their investigations. In the hands of corrupt officials, such warrants could be used to raid colonial warehouses on the flimsiest of pretexts—and create further opportunities for racketeering.

Americans complained that these measures abridged their historic English rights. Jury trial was sanctioned by centuries of practice. And the invasion of property by snoopy government agents violated an equally long-standing tradition of privacy. Indeed, in arguing against writs of assistance, Boston attorney James Otis held them to violate the very law of nature. Such objections honestly puzzled the imperial authorities. If Americans were the law-abiding subjects they claimed to be, then why would they protect smugglers, and why all this fuss about rights and procedures?

Matters continued to escalate on both sides. Boston became so disorderly that the British government brought in troops from Nova Scotia and stationed them on call. This raised yet another specter of Stuart tyranny—standing armies. It was inevitable that soldiers and citizenry would come to blows sooner or later. They did so on the evening of March 5, 1770 in the infamous Boston Massacre.

"You know, the idea of taxation with representation doesn't appeal to me very much, either."
(By J. B. Handelsman, courtesy of the Cartoon Bank.)

Revolution of the Mind and Heart

In the afteryears, John Adams remarked that the real revolution had taken place long before the outbreak of hostilities in

1775—"in the minds and hearts of the people." It was this quiet revolution, he said, that made separation from the British Empire inevitable.

While the American colonists thought of themselves as loyal Englishmen, they had also begun to think of themselves as Englishmen with a difference—and to recognize the things they shared in common. Their lack of a collective identity was proverbial back in the days when Benjamin Franklin had attempted to unite them in a defensive alliance against the French. Once the Stamp Act was passed, however, they commenced a vigorous dialogue with one another. Committees of correspondence shared analysis and strategy with their counterparts in the nearby towns—and eventually the nearby colonies. The appearance of a "tyrant" accomplished more than a foreign enemy could in drawing them together.

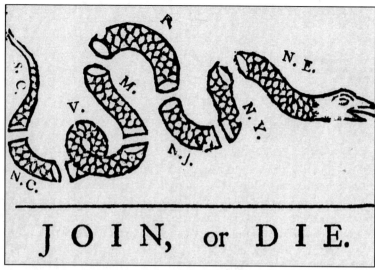

As early as the 1750s some colonial leaders sensed that a union of the North American colonies would be essential to their political survival. Benjamin Franklin created this political cartoon in 1754, appealing for colonial unity. (Courtesy of The Granger Collection, New York.)

It might be argued that the idiom used by Americans to explain the imperial controversy was the language of Puritanism. For even though Puritanism had long since cooled as an active force, its perspective and assumptions were still much a part of the American psyche. Adams himself may have been a case in point.

Consider, for example, how the lingering Calvinist mind-set reshaped the commonwealth ideology and gave it new meaning. For the commonwealthmen, there were essentially two character types: the corrupt official (the court party) and the virtuous patriot (the country party). These happened to correspond to two Calvinist counterparts: unregenerate humanity and God's elect. We begin to see how British and American spokesmen could talk past one another with such regularity.

But the parallels went further. The virtuous patriot of commonwealth lore possessed two essential qualities: personal independence and a sense of civic duty. There were Puritan analogies for both. Personal independence could also mean independence from the Tempter's snares—from the vice and debauchery he used to entrap the unwary. And civic duty could also mean responsibility for the community's moral well-being, as we saw in chapter 2.

To understand why these analogies were dangerous, we must examine a style of human relations prevalent in Great Britain at the time, a style generally known as *patronage*. In a patronage society—which was always markedly hierarchical—each person was obliged to reckon with a "patron," someone higher up on the totem pole, for the day-to-day advantages of life. In everything from getting a job to finding a spouse to locating a suitable school for the children, you had to cultivate your patron assiduously: pay him little visits, write letters of appreciation, bestow small gifts—and sometimes large ones. Patronage, with its never-ending "favors," oiled the world's machinery—the classic case of who you know, not what you know, that counts.

Life Under Patronage

What life could be like in a patronage society was illustrated by colonial New Hampshire under Gov. Benning Wentworth. Assuming the governorship in 1741, Wentworth immediately packed the Council with friends and relatives. He then subverted the elected Assembly by blackmailing new communities into electing pro-Wentworth representatives. Next, the governor began to make free with civil commissions, appointing so many of his followers justice of the peace that the office became a standing joke. As for military commissions, the governor's faithful supporters instantly became full colonels in the militia, while his two adolescent sons and a ten-year-old nephew had to be satisfied as captains.

Having passed around the favors, Wentworth now exacted his price. Every new township in the province had to reserve eight hundred acres as the governor's personal property. The New Hampshire mast industry—the mainstay of its economy—gave him a cut on every mast shipped to England. Smuggling operations also fell under Wentworth's control, and he skimmed his percentage off of every keg of molasses and every barrel of rum sneaked past the royal customs. The list went on. New Hampshire was compared to a "field of battle" and the governor's minions to "the vultures and ravens glutting on the carnage."

In vain did the Assembly try to fight back. It withheld Wentworth's salary—but he seemed to need none. It hauled his friends into court—but the governor controlled the courts too. It refused to seat his handpicked representatives—but Wentworth executed a deft maneuver and neatly tied its proceedings into knots. Finally, in desperation, the Assembly appealed over the governor's head to the British lords of trade. Unfortunately, the man they appealed to, John Tomlinson, happened to be a Wentworth crony himself, and he politely told them to take a hike.

On and on the saga went, a study in the politics of patronage. In his old age, Benning Wentworth could sit back on the veranda of his fifty-two-room mansion and look out happily on the bustling panorama of Portsmouth Harbor below him—master of all he surveyed.

In the commonwealth ideology, patronage spelled dependence, as we have seen. In the Puritan mind, it spelled something even worse. All the flattery and kowtowing that patronage made necessary seemed to Calvinists but a step from outright bribery. And in the administration of the colonies, it had often *become* outright bribery, for if a person wanted to get along with the powers that be, he had to perform his share of "favors." In other words, what seemed like politics as usual to the British authorities appeared far more ominous to Americans tinged with Puritanism. To them, the issue was nothing less than their own moral integrity. Were they to be corrupted by the landwaiters and tidewaiters of the customs office, by the royal governor and his minions, by the Board of Trade and its multitude of lackeys? Or were they, before God, to be their own men?

There were Puritan implications in the rhetoric of taxation as well. A person whose taxes supported a corrupt officialdom was helping to accomplish the Devil's work, or so it could be argued. And such a work it was. British officials were waxing proud and engrossing upon the fat of the land—all good biblical metaphors. They lived in sumptuous houses, rode the streets in gleaming carriages and fairly wallowed in moral delinquency. And, worse, Americans were following suit. Honest toil was giving way to idleness. Simplicity in dress and manners was being eclipsed by frippery. A tea-drinking, hand-kissing, Old World effeteness was seeping into the American soul.

If this picture seems overdrawn, we must remember that a streak of paranoia lay embedded in the Puritan mind. Just as Winthrop's generation had believed in the Devil's war against them, so too did descendants see their own dark shadows, and these were not irrelevant to the present situation. If they refused to drink the tea of iniquity freely, some supposed, Satan might employ any means at hand to force them—including the might of the British Empire.

In the five years between the Stamp Act and the Boston Massacre, then, American colonists reacted to Britain's reform measures in a way that defied normal logic. They flooded the streets with an accusatory pamphlet literature. They turned out in mobs to prevent the execution of parliamentary laws. They boycotted British goods, preferring homespun to silk and West Indian coffee to English tea. They argued confusedly that Parliament had no right to tax them "internally," then no right to tax them "externally," and finally no right even to regulate their trade. And all the while they alleged a demonic conspiracy to enslave them.

The Crisis

Two years of comparative calm followed the Boston Massacre, the result of steady hands on the tiller and forbearance on both sides. But nothing had really changed. British authorities were still determined to consolidate their power and reform their ramshackle empire. Another opportunity to do so arrived in 1773 with the ill fortunes of the British East India Company. In order to bail out the nearly bankrupt—and politically influential—corporation, the Board of

Boston Tea Party:
http://odur.let.rug.nl/~usa/
E/teaparty/bostonxx.htm

Boston Tea Party
(December 16, 1773):
Destruction of large
quantity of British tea in
response to the Tea Act
resulted in the Coercive
Acts, stationing of
British troops, closing of
Boston Harbor and thus
indirectly to Lexington
and Concord (1775).

Trade hatched a bold plan. The entire inventory of tea in company warehouses would be shipped to the colonies and sold at a bargain price, which ought to please the Americans, and the resulting revenues would boost company profits. But there was a pill within the sweetener. When the Townshend Duties had been repealed five years earlier, the tax on tea had been left standing—a reminder that Parliament truly did have the power to tax the colonies if it desired. The Americans had responded by virtuously forgoing tea. The new cut-rate price surely ought to tempt them into submission.

It didn't. It only confirmed their suspicions that conspiracy was afoot. Mobs prevented the landing of the tea in New York and Philadelphia. In Boston there was a standoff. The tea ships stood at anchor in the harbor while British authorities played a game of cat and mouse with colonial representatives. Then, when the former attempted an eleventh-hour landing, the Boston Tea Party ensued.

After that, as far as the British were concerned, all games were over. When Bostonians refused to pay for the tea they had dumped overboard, Lord North, who was then in charge of imperial policy, opted for a showdown. He asked Parliament to close the port to all shipping—assuming that rivals would eagerly snatch at Boston's commerce—and followed up with a series of kill-or-cure measures to end the disturbances. It was either this, reasoned North, or else it was to see the empire dissolve in tatters.

Harsh treatment for the worst offender while all others went free was a policy calculated to divide the Americans. It had the opposite effect. What happened to Boston today could happen to New York tomorrow and Philadelphia the day after, the colonists reasoned. Tyranny was attempting to conquer them piecemeal.

Both sides jockeyed for time and tactical advantage. Colonial militias began rounding up arms and ammunition, readying themselves for some sort of face-off. On the other side, General Gage, in command of the troops stationed in Boston, sent for reinforcements. The British now assumed that blood would have to be spilled, perhaps in quantity, before the rebellion fever subsided.

The question Americans now faced was whether or not to swerve from their course. There was still time to do so. Many of them, indeed most, regarded themselves as law-abiding British subjects—no more rebels than pirates or bandits. But the crisis had unlocked several doors, each of them opening upon some aspect of republicanism. Slowly, haltingly, Americans began to peer inside.

The first was the door of democracy. While issues flew back and forth in the pamphlet literature and were loudly debated on street corners, many normally apolitical elements—mechanics, tradesmen, country farmers—had taken an ever more active part. And for good reason. Corruption, subversion, conspiracy, tyranny— these were issues that concerned not just the political classes but everyone.

Equally clearly, the *demos* had its own stake in the outcome. Most institutions of local government were already strongly democratic by English standards, as we have seen, and by threatening these, the British government was in effect threatening democracy itself. After shutting down the port of Boston, for example, the North ministry went on to reorganize the Massachusetts government so as to minimize the democratic influence. The result was not to get the people out of the streets, as hoped, but to commit them all the more to revolution.

The second was the door of liberty. The cry was on everyone's lips. There were liberty poles and liberty trees and liberty bonfires. Orators like Patrick

Henry knew they could always score by inserting the word into their speeches. And parliamentary friends of the American cause, such as Edmund Burke, urged colleagues not to misapprehend the colonists' sincerity. When Americans said they loved freedom, they meant it.

But freedom from what? Americans were arguably the freest people on earth. They had the most power over their own lives, faced the least officious government, and paid the lowest taxes in the western world. So why did they sound like so many prisoners clanging on the bars? Because they had truly come to believe, reasonably or otherwise, that their freedom was about to be snuffed out. It might be argued that by its very nature, liberty tends to beget more liberty and becomes ever more suspicious of restraint. Like democracy, in other words, liberty was a kind of genie out of the bottle.

The third was the door of virtue. For the same events that appeared to endanger democracy and liberty also placed republican *areté* at risk. If the world was truly divided between a "court party" given to vice and corruption and a "country party" cherishing virtue and independence, what could the presence of the king's troops in Boston mean other than a showdown between the two? And could Americans really back away from that?

Virtually all colonial leaders belonged to that untitled aristocracy for whom the commonwealth ideology made greatest sense. They were steeped in a sense of personal *areté* and confirmed in political self-righteousness. America *was* the "country," as far as they were concerned, and it *must* hold out against the "court" no matter what. And if the court manipulators could not achieve their ends by the usual means—such as that come-hither offer of low-priced tea—of course they would use force.

Democracy, liberty and virtue—the three strains of republicanism we examined in chapter 3—and all were under challenge by Lord North. All three, moreover, tapped into the colonies' latent Puritanism. Weren't God's elect the people of extraordinary virtue? Weren't all souls equal in the sight of God? Wasn't there a spiritual liberty that accompanied political liberty, where the individual soul needed to freely choose the path of righteousness?

Old-time predestinarians questioned that last point, of course, but they were rapidly losing ground to believers in free will—another of those Puritan flip-flops. Indeed, the Protestant clergy in New England came to lead the crusade for American liberty, so important did they see the tie between political and spiritual freedom. While some colonial ministers were politically indifferent, those of the Congregational and Presbyterian churches—whom Loyalist Peter Oliver called "the Black Regiment"—were in the fray from the beginning. They inserted political messages into their special sermons on election days, fast days or thanksgiving days, many of them remarkably direct.

Even more direct was a sermon called the *jeremiad*, a formal call to repentance that generally preached industriousness, frugality and simplicity of manners—all good republican themes. As the trouble with Britain worsened, jeremiads began to thunder against passive obedience to wicked rulers, too, reminding worshippers that the profligacy of a people might provoke God's wrathful judgment. Repentance and revolution, as historian Perry Miller points out, were coming to be thought of as one.

Jeremiad: Term derived from Old Testament prophet Jeremiah, noted for prophecies lamenting the present and the future.

Given the Puritan conscience of New England, it was little wonder that on that April night in 1775 when Paul Revere made his historic ride, there were more than just a few who came in answer.

Forging the Bonds of Nationhood

It has been said that the United States of America was "invented" in a single day—July 2, 1776, when Richard Henry Lee's resolution for independence passed the Continental Congress. The actual genesis took much longer, of course, but a lot of it was accomplished between the night of Paul Revere's ride and the ringing of the Liberty Bell some fifteen months later.

With the outbreak of open warfare, the die of independence was essentially cast. There had been a flurry of backstage negotiations, peace proposals and the like, but when that memorable British expedition to Lexington and Concord limped back with 273 casualties, the war was clearly on and reconciliation clearly off.

Shared experiences, burdens and vision helped knit the American colonists into a new nation.
(*Lexington*, engraved from a painting by Alonzo Chappell, courtesy of the Library of Congress.)

American nationhood was another matter. Thirteen separate colonies had entered the war, and most Americans assumed that thirteen separate states would emerge from it. What these observers missed was the tendency of war to forge bonds of nationhood. What were those bonds, exactly?

Sovereign Government

What were loosely termed "continental congresses" had been called in the past in time of crisis. The one that came together in May of 1775, after the bloodshed outside Boston, became the de facto government of America. Its charter lay in public opinion, not the stroke of a royal pen, and not all Americans acknowledged its authority. Even so, it managed to raise an army, commission officers, plot strategy, supply and arm military forces, conduct diplomacy, coordinate the efforts of thirteen quarreling sovereignties, fund its own operations and by hook or crook fight a war.

For an extralegal body, Congress was remarkably orderly. Its delegates, chosen by self-called provincial conventions, quickly organized themselves, elected their own officers and established parliamentary procedures. Its politics was as bumpy as one might suppose under the circumstances, yet somehow it carried on with its job. It was a striking instance of people coming together in a "state of nature" and creating their own government—straight out of Locke's *Second Treatise*.

A National Military Force

After Lexington and Concord, General Gage's troops were essentially under siege in Boston. The besiegers were a motley consortium of local and regional militias, indifferently organized and poorly led. Congress lost no time in appointing George Washington to general command. The selection of a Virginian to take charge of New England forces showed a good deal of political acumen: this was not to be New England's fight alone.

In time and with the approach of independence, a national army would grow out of this unlikely beginning. While most of the officers serving in it were not without some military experience, the enlisted men were for the most part only armed civilians, and they lacked the vaguest idea of discipline. When Washington told one man to fetch him a shovel, he was answered with a crisp "Git it yerself. I'm busy." Before the war was over, the army would profit from the services of European drillmasters, spit-and-polish sergeants, artillery experts, battlefield tacticians and fortification engineers. And it would learn to hold its own.

Service in a national army imparted a national point of view. While the activities of Congress required only a few dozen to reach beyond colonial borders, the activities of the military required thousands. Later on, a lopsided number of Continental Army veterans would back the Federal Constitution.

Demystified Monarchy

Throughout their quarrel with Parliament, the colonists had continued to hold the king in high regard. As the sovereign, he was supposed to stand above the fray of politics and in some mystical way embody the idea of *patria*. George III, however, could never quite keep above the fray.

MPs: Members of British Parliament.

The cause of the problem was patronage. While in theory king and Parliament were supposed to be independent authorities, in fact the king, through the bestowal of titles, honors, appointments, pensions and assorted other munificences, had brought a considerable number of MPs under his control, making them in a sense members of his "party." Americans had turned a blind eye to this fact and blamed their troubles on the king's "evil counselors" instead. Bute, Mansfield, Grenville, Townshend, North—there was a long and growing list.

But the king's actions after the shooting started brought blindness to an end. Indeed, his employment of Hessian mercenaries—famous for their ruthlessness—was both a shock and rude awakening to the Americans. The king, they gasped, was as evil as his counselors! We must remember that the mystique of monarchy had provided a good deal of the glue holding the empire together. When George III "betrayed" his own subjects, it not only made them fighting mad, it demystified royal governance.

The demystification process was speeded up considerably by an elegant piece of rhetoric titled *Common Sense*. In this pamphlet to end all pamphlets, Thomas Paine said nothing new, perhaps, but he cast it into such mellifluous rolling cadences that readers were swept along. Monarchy, Paine argued, was washed up in the modern world. A king was a ridiculous figure—part sponger and part brigand—who had no claim to anyone's allegiance, least of all that of virtuous Americans. The indictment was so devastating that it amounted to a kind of symbolic regicide, according to social scientist Max Lerner, a killing of the European father that cleared the way for "natural-born republicans" to address the world on their own.

Bunker Hill

The fourth bond of nationhood was an old-fashioned military victory, at the Battle of Bunker Hill. On June 17, 1775 a patriot force of 1,200 under William Prescott was sent to fortify the high ground on Boston's Charlestown peninsula, overlooking the British encampment. Desperately needing to break the siege, the British opened fire on the American works, and later in the afternoon some 3,000 infantry prepared to attack. Two ferocious assaults were repulsed by withering fire from the defenders. The third British charge carried the hill, but only because the Americans lacked ammunition. There was stubborn hand-to-hand combat at the summit. And when the smoke cleared, the British had suffered 1,150 casualties, more than one-third of their total number.

While technically a defeat, the battle and its outcome caused American spirits to soar, for soldiers dismissed as "rag, tag and bobtail" had stood their ground against the best the British could muster.

Common Suffering

While it is hard to calculate the effect of common suffering, it may well have been substantial. Americans—*as* Americans—were being shot and killed, and given the realities of insurrectionary warfare, few could doubt what lay ahead. Cannonballs would soon rip through their towns. Men-of-war would cruise their harbors. Raiding parties would descend on their frontier settlements. Lives and fortunes would be torn asunder, and no group or class would be above risk. The common people would be in the thick of battle, facing professional soldiers armed with Brown Bess muskets and fourteen-inch bayonets. The gentry would see their country homes plundered, their plantations burned, their families persecuted and their own names placed on a wanted list. Furthermore, because there were plenty of loyalists, it would be a civil war, with all the bitterness and atrocity such wars commonly bring.

Working in and among these bonds of nationhood was the republican idea, whose effect was to remind Americans of the things that set them apart. What Rousseau referred to as a sense of "we," that mysterious togetherness which defines a people, grew not only out of the events of the Revolution but out of the feelings produced by those events when Americans stopped to think who they were, what they stood for, and what they stood to lose.

The Declaration of Independence

In the spring of 1776, the military situation took a turn. The British had given up the idea of holding Boston and had withdrawn to Nova Scotia to regroup. With the passing of winter's chill, they now launched a major thrust at New York. The Middle Colonies were appreciably calmer than New England: establishing an overwhelming presence there would divide the Americans geographically and isolate the New England firebrands—or so the British hoped.

The force they landed under Gen. William Howe truly was overwhelming. Howe defeated the Americans at the Battle of Brooklyn Heights, then again at the Battle of White Plains, and finally drove them deep into New Jersey. By the end of the year, Washington's original command of 20,000 had been reduced to a bedraggled 4,000. Nevertheless, they retreated without panic, for the most part, and even displayed moments of real soldiering. It was not the rout the British had expected.

This fact foreshadowed the faintest possibility of an eventual American victory. For time and circumstance were on their side. The territory of the colonies was very large, thinly populated and surrounded by wilderness. The British had to pin their hopes on a European-style "great battle" whose outcome might prompt the rebels to throw in the towel. Yet, clearly, a different scenario was possible. The American army might fight smaller engagements, skirmish a bit and then slip away as it had in New York. This could go on almost indefinitely.

Moreover, if the patriot army was not crushed soon, it stood to gain increasing moral ascendancy. People might come to believe that it couldn't be crushed at all. Accordingly, every day that Washington held out would tilt the balance a little more in his favor.

And finally, France had an interest in the outcome. After all, here was a chance to break the power of its English archrival once and for all, and at a bargain price. Who knew, the French might even be induced to enter the conflict themselves—*if* they were assured of a favorable outcome.

While these facts were only dimly glimpsed that spring, Americans did begin to glimpse them. And they pointed convincingly toward declaring independence. But how to do the job effectively? The powers of Europe, who were looking on with great interest, must be persuaded that American intentions were genuine and that this was not just a passing family quarrel. The American people were looking on too. Most of them were still lukewarm to the patriot cause and many were openly hostile. They wondered what sort of cause it was, and where it might ultimately lead.

A committee of Congress was put in charge of drafting a formal declaration. Thomas Jefferson became the designated draftsman. His task was to present the case for American independence in terms which all could understand and which the "right thinking" would be inclined to approve. Although still a youthful thirty-three, Jefferson was intelligent and sophisticated, and his reputation for a facile pen marched ahead of him. He knew the words of the document in question must be simple and lucid, their tone dignified, their logic unstrained and their effect utterly convincing. This couldn't be a disquisition in political philosophy or a rambling insurrectionary tirade. And it must communicate on several different levels at once.

On the surface level, the declaration had to be a legal brief, arguing an ironclad case against the British. It was they, not the Americans, who were the revolutionaries, Jefferson contended, for they had taken it upon themselves to abridge historic rights. Jefferson had to aim his barbs at the king, not Parliament, for the colonists had argued that Parliament had no place at all in the colonial scheme.

On a deeper level, the Declaration was bound to play a role in the American Founding—though few guessed how important that role would be. Jefferson, accordingly, set forth his idea of what the colonies were now to become and what their fundamental principles were to be. The prose here soared toward poetry and packed broad swatches of meaning into simple household words. In the crucial second paragraph, it offered a concise but eloquent theory of American nationhood:

Unalienable: Inalienable, incapable of being separated or transferred from an individual or a polity.

> We hold these truths to be self-evident, That all men are created equal, that they are endowed by their Creator with certain unalienable Rights, that among these are life, liberty, and the pursuit of Happiness. That to secure these rights, Governments are instituted among Men, deriving their just powers from the consent of the governed, That whenever any form of Government becomes destructive of these ends, it is the Right of the people to alter or to abolish it, and to institute new Government, laying its foundation on such principles and organizing its powers in such form, as to them shall seem most likely to effect their Safety and Happiness.

These words are often taken to be a digest of Locke's *Second Treatise*, and indeed, they did encapsulate Locke rather nicely. It has been pointed out, however, that they might also reflect Jefferson's acquaintance with the Scottish Enlightenment, whose philosophy differed with Locke on crucial issues. The point is, Jefferson may not have "voted" for a single conception of republicanism—he may have sought to encompass all three.

Whatever the intent, Jefferson's prose poem articulated a vision of nationhood that was enormously appealing to ordinary Americans and capable of being read open-endedly. Historian Joseph J. Ellis has underscored the seductiveness and inclusiveness of that vision:

Two monumental claims are being made here. The explicit claim is that the individual is the sovereign unit in society; his natural state is freedom from and equality with all other individuals; this is the natural order of things. The implicit claim is that all restrictions on this natural order are immoral transgressions, violations of what God intended; individuals liberated from such restrictions will interact with their fellows in a harmonious scheme requiring no external discipline and producing maximum human happiness.

Matters of equal significance lie buried in Jefferson's first paragraph, where he appealed to "the Laws of Nature and of Nature's God." On the surface level, once again, he was arguing his case for American independence (as opposed to mere resistance) on grounds that Britain had violated the very laws of the universe. Deeper down, it was a way of recognizing an authority that lay beyond the participants themselves. What they were doing was not simply in accordance with their own desires but in accordance with Nature and Providence. Jefferson was acknowledging universal moral truth, in other words, of which the Puritans had often spoken. It was this "self-evident" truth, more than anything else in the Declaration, that established the parameters of American nationhood.

For, whatever else the American nation must do, Jefferson was saying, it must recognize the legal equality of its citizens, protect their natural rights, and govern by consent. There was the shadowy form of a constitution here. The Declaration of Independence ruled out both enlightened despotism, which some Americans might have favored, as well as popular but oppressive regimes. A legitimate government, it said, had to reflect the will of the people broadly considered while at the same time protecting the rights of everyone, including unpopular minorities—a decidedly tricky business.

Jefferson's arguments were given added weight by their grounding in everyday reality. In the summer of 1776 there was no power on earth above the Continental Congress except Nature and God. Americans had come together as free beings and worked this out among themselves. The Declaration was living proof of its own principles.

The War of the Revolution

It might be argued that the war itself, and the way it was fought, contributed as much to the American Founding as the Declaration of Independence did. A different war fought in a different way might have led to a different political society.

The Politics of War Making

Historian John Shy applied insights gained from a study of the Vietnam War to understand the military history of the American Revolution. For the two experiences were by no means unrelated. In both, a formidable power attempted to suppress outmanned and outgunned insurrectionary forces—and lost. In both situations, moreover, it was political rather than military factors that made the difference.

But Is It True?

In his freshman seminar on American politics, Professor Charles R. Kesler, at Claremont McKenna College, asks his students a question they have trouble answering. Is the Declaration of Independence true?

"Invariably," he reports, "there are loads of bright freshman who know all about it and who can discourse plausibly on the Declaration's roots in the Enlightenment, John Locke's influence on its authors, the economic interests that actuated its signers, and so forth." But then comes the question about truth. "*Are* men created equal and endowed with certain unalienable rights?"

The question never fails to floor them. What does he mean? they ask one another. What is he talking about? They look at each other and grin sheepishly. For in the world of the college freshman of the 1990s, things are never true or false; they are useful, or handy, or relevant or the opposite of those three. "In *their* [the Founders'] opinion, it was true," a freshman will finally volunteer. That is about as far as a discussion of truth can go these days.

So, we might stop and consider the same question ourselves. *Is* the Declaration of Independence true? Or is it only one of those expressions of belief which have their little niche in history? And if the latter, what is it, exactly, that we stand for as a people—and why do we think it is so wonderful that Communism is falling apart?

In the American Revolution, Great Britain possessed not only a world-class fighting machine but also the economic strength and the political will to make it run. The British had seasoned officers, professional soldiers, the finest hardware available, undisputed control of the seas and a handful of truly gifted generals. On the battlefield, they quickly proved what every colonial already knew—that in a conventional encounter they could defeat any force the Americans could bring against them.

But the British were far less effective politically. They did not understand Americans very well, and as a result they routinely misassessed the political situations they encountered. In this kind of war, that was a serious liability.

To begin with, they failed to gauge the depth of American feeling. The colonists, they supposed, already had more liberty than was good for them, and it was absurd to bewail its threatened loss. Conversely, all the talk about conspiracy and slavery sounded like so much paranoid raving. To the British, in short, the American case seemed weak and muddled—the work of a few rabble-rousers.

As a result of these misperceptions, British commanders invariably overestimated the support they could count on from "good Americans" and underestimated support for the rebels. For some officers, in fact, this was not even a real war, only an insurrectionary disturbance, and the proper way to deal with it was through police action.

So conceived, British strategy passed through several phases. The first reflected a police-action mentality and sought only to isolate and punish. This approach fizzled, as we have seen, for the Americans perceived it as an attempt to divide and conquer. The British next pressed their advantage in conventional warfare and endeavored to fight textbook-style engagements. But the Americans would rarely go along. Occasionally they might take on the redcoats openly—as on that memorable Christmas night in Trenton, New Jersey when they dealt Colonel Rall's Hessians a stunning blow—but mostly they settled for rearguard harassment actions and the like. The British couldn't lose this way, but they couldn't really win either.

And so a third change of strategy, to that of comprehensive pacification. The concept was to move into strategically important areas with a convincing presence and try to get the machinery of government up and running again. Here was where the British were the most effective. And here was where the crucial issue of the Revolution came to the fore. For the Revolution, as Adams said, became a contest for the minds and hearts of the ordinary people, people who were essentially apolitical and uninvolved, who were mainly interested in getting on with their lives. Without the active commitment of this majority, it was not possible for the patriot side to win—much less to found a successful republic.

In some areas, especially in the South, the pacification strategy worked well enough. Still there were difficulties. In the first place, the British had to operate everywhere, while the rebels could pick and chose, and this stretched their forces thin. And in the second, they were obliged to operate with great sensitivity, luring the undecided to their side. Of this task they seemed almost utterly incapable.

For virtually everything the British did was wrong. If they were lenient with rebel sympathizers, they embittered the loyalists. If they were harsh and vindictive, they angered the very people they were trying to win over. If they dug in, the enemy would operate with impunity all around them. If they headed off in

American Revolution:
http://www.historyplace
.com/unitedstates/
revolution/index.html

pursuit, their friends were abandoned to reprisals. And try as they might, they couldn't seem to teach their own soldiers the difference between "rebels" and "noncombatants"—who were sadly treated alike.

Militias and the Continental Army

American Revolution:
http://www.fordham.edu/
halsall/mod/modsbook12
.html#American Independence

Where the British got the politics of the war all wrong, the patriots got important things right. And what they got most right was the militia.

Colonial militias, as every schoolchild knows, were regarded as a joke on the battlefield. Yet they often proved to be an effective military force, especially at providing timely reinforcements. The militia presented something that most British officers had never dealt with: a great spongy mass that could be driven from the field but could never be isolated or decapitated. It was, in Shy's words, "a people numerous and armed."

The militia was also a political educator. For where the Continental Army was professionally staffed, military in tone, always a bit foreign to the local scene and not infrequently on the run, militias were unprofessional, down home, filled with neighborhood good old boys and never far away—a sort of military version of the little red schoolhouse.

And their schooling was in appropriate community behavior. The problem for neutrals—and this included a large segment of the population—was how to behave prudently with a revolution going on. One could cozy up to the British army and gain protection that way, but what if its commander suddenly marched his troops out of town? It was more prudent to be on terms with the local militia. But the militia was likely to require something. Aid and comfort. Supplies and equipment. The affiliation of male family members. With the militia around, in other words, it was almost impossible to continue sitting on the fence.

The British did their own part to keep the fence clear by persecuting any and all who joined a militia, even if only for prudence's sake. So, for better or worse, neutrals did have to choose. And once they chose the militia, they were enfolded in its camaraderie and anointed with its esprit de corps. They were also treated to serial sermons about virtue, honor and patriotism. If their group saw action—and most of them did—these words took on a meaning they might otherwise lack, for nothing wins converts like bloodshed.

It would be hard to imagine a better way to politicize the populace. Hundreds of thousands of Americans who hadn't cared one way or the other about taxation or jury trial not only found themselves enlisted in battle groups but drinking in the revolutionary spirit. Their turbocharged tenure in the militia laid the foundations of the American Republic.

Something similar could be said for the Continental Army. In its ranks, young men from all over the colonies rubbed elbows with their contemporaries and got to know one another. Regional stereotypes often melted away. The loyalty of the men to one another and to their common cause was repeatedly tested under fire. Privation, sacrifice, defeat, betrayal all had psychological effects. Many leaders of the new republic gained their American sense of patria right here.

The Revolution's dreadful cost was manifest in privations suffered by the Continental Army at Valley Forge, Pennsylvania during the winter of 1777–78. (Courtesy of the Library of Congress.)

The Yankee Doodle memories enshrined in popular culture have obscured the dark side of the Revolution. Most of it was exceedingly grim. The revolutionary armies were on short rations and dwindling supplies much of the time. Physical privation was made more poignant by the willingness of some Americans to engage in profiteering or take advantage of flexible loyalty. Desertion and turncoatism were common. So were corollary misbehaviors ranging from alcoholism to psychosis. Battlefield medical services were poor to nonexistent, and care of the sick and wounded was often simply appalling.

Prisoners of war commonly suffered an unspeakable fate. Since rebellion enjoyed no legal protection in the British Empire, there were no rules governing the treatment of combatants. Many of those who were captured were summarily tossed into prison compounds, the holds of ships or damp stone cellars and left to rot. They were fed irregularly and given no other attention whatever. Conditions in several of the "prisons" were little short of horrifying.

Out of the suffering and sacrifice came an unusual kind of heroism. Some of the indifferently committed easily fell by the wayside. Others found inner sources of strength and a new access of meaning. The language of the Revolution and the significance of its cause were seared into their souls.

Nailing Jelly

In the end, the patriots won the day. With no victory in sight after seven years of conflict, the British finally despaired of their pacification strategy and switched back to conventional warfare. They continued to win major battles, but they could not seem to win the war. One disgruntled officer likened the American quagmire to "nailing jelly to the wall."

Just when the jelly seemed to stick, the bedraggled insurrectionists would rise above themselves and deliver a crushing counterblow. One such coup fell in October of 1777. A British plan to slice the colonies in two by driving one force up the Hudson Valley and another down from Canada went completely awry. Gen. John Burgoyne and his entire army were forced to surrender after the resulting Saratoga campaign. Even worse for the British, France was so impressed by Saratoga that it decided to come into the war.

And it was French participation that made Yorktown possible and brought the war to an end. Lord Cornwallis, one of the most successful of the British commanders, allowed his army to become trapped on a narrow spit of land between the York and James rivers in Virginia, on the assumption that the British fleet would arrive in Chesapeake Bay to relieve him. But it was Admiral de Grasse's battle squadron that got there first—George Washington literally jumped for joy when he saw the French flag fluttering from the frigates. Cornwallis held out under siege for a few days and decided to surrender.

The effort might have continued but to no good purpose. Great Britain, as it turned out, had been fighting on the strength of a false belief about the empire—a belief holding that the American colonies were essentially British and therefore that the points at issue were resolvable. They were not resolvable. They had grown and festered into a full-scale revolution. And the colonies of almost two-centuries standing had struggled free.

The Revolution as a Revolution

Historians have long debated the revolutionary nature of the American Revolution. What precisely was "revolutionized?" some have asked. J. Franklin Jameson and others began compiling a list. Several items on that list are of relevance to the Founding of the American Republic.

Social and Economic Changes

Quitrents: Money substitute for produce or labor owed to a landowner; held over from feudalism and still practiced in colonial America.

In the first place, a way of life that had focused on patronage relationships and psychological dependence was undermined by the revolutionary experience. In time the old mode of thinking would give way to a new one, and Americans would speak ever more insistently of independence and self-reliance.

Land ownership, already broad, was broadened still further by the Revolution. Loyalist lands were confiscated, some of them in expansive tracts, and distributed to veterans, small farmers and postwar immigrants. Aristocratic patterns of landholding were further weakened by the abolition of quitrents, primogeniture and entail.

Official churches were disestablished in several of the new states, notably Virginia, where the Anglican establishment had provided the Revolution with a few extra bones of contention. Americans became accustomed to the extraordinary idea of separating church and state altogether.

Slaves were freed throughout most of the North—the practice seemed wholly unrepublican—and there was a marked decline in indentured servitude. The democratic feeling spread elsewhere. New colleges were founded. New voices were heard in literature and journalism. New ideas began to circulate about the education of women and their role in society.

Even in the economic realm there were changes. Credit expanded. Capital started to accumulate. New manufactures were set up and new patterns of trade established. Farmers began to feel the effect of systematic agricultural improvements. And a host of new businesses sprouted along Main Street.

Political and Constitutional Changes

The elimination of the king and exile of the loyalists—many of an aristocratic bent—altered the complexion of American politics. The "popular element" was now without rivals. While that element still did not grasp for the reins of power, voting privileges were further broadened and legislatures came to represent a wider array of interests.

Not only the structure of politics but its conduct became more democratic. For example, the argument of no taxation without representation cut against American, as well as British, practice: if people were to be taxed by their legislatures, they wanted to be represented. Soon there were voter instructions and other forms of accountability, even public galleries for the onlookers. Those who ran for office were asked deeper and more difficult questions than ever before, and once elected they began hearing a lot more from their constituents.

As with democracy, so too with liberty. The word, which was heard so often, could be applied to everything from the freeing of slaves to the discarding of outworn contentions. Liberty, for many, became liberation: cutting away from a European past and forging into an American future. There was something breathlessly exhilarating about it.

All said and done, the most truly revolutionary thing about the American Revolution was its creation of successful republican government—which is getting a little ahead of the story.

Revolutionary Symbols of Nationhood

In the mythology of the Revolution, incidents were transformed into legends, objects into symbols and men into monuments. Any schoolchild could supply

Primogeniture: The eldest son's exclusive right of inheritance.

Entail: To restrict inheritance to landowner's lineal descendants; kept colonial estates from being divided and sold in smaller parcels.

a list. "Indians" throwing tea into Boston Harbor. Paul Revere's midnight ride. Lexington Green. Concord Bridge. A bell cracked from joyous ringing. The winter encampment at Valley Forge—those bloody footprints in the snow. Nathan Hale's last words: "I only regret that I have but one life to lose for my country!"

None of these exactly encapsulates the Revolution as a founding event, but one comes close. The image of the "minutemen" responding to the call of duty, turning out of warm beds and into the dark night, expresses much about the way Americans have come to see themselves and their national birth. The inspiration, of course, is classical antiquity once again—Cincinnatus, the farmer who left his plow in the field and took charge of the army that would save the Roman Republic, only to resign his command afterward and return to farming. It is a nice synthesis of all three republican ideals—classical, liberal and democratic.

After the war, Washington's officers formed themselves into the Society of the Cincinnati for the purpose of getting together and remembering the old times. While any of them might have resembled the Roman warrior in some way, it was their commander, George Washington, who fit Cincinnatus to a tee. And it was George Washington who came to symbolize the entire Revolution. As *the* Founding Father, Washington's importance could hardly be overstated.

Lacking Jefferson's intellect or Lincoln's common touch, Washington was once thought to require image enhancement. Accordingly, in successive editions of his biography, Mason Locke Weems added such humanizing touches as the story of the cherry tree. Weems needn't have bothered: the real George Washington was well up to the mark. After all, he held the Continental Army together by the sheer force of his personality, kept it in the field as a power to be reckoned with, bucked staggering odds, endured a thousand setbacks, brooked all kinds of intermeddling, won enough battles to keep the American people hanging onto hope, and in the end cornered the redoubtable Cornwallis at Yorktown.

The Protestant clergy, who had done so much to suffuse the conflict with meaning, had no trouble picturing Washington as a demigod. Nor was it difficult to find supporting imagery. Washington crossing the Delaware on a foggy Christmas night. Washington kneeling in the snow at Valley Forge. Washington groping for his spectacles at the great mutiny—"Gentlemen, I fear I have gone blind as well as gray in the service of my country." Washington refusing the laurels of a Caesar and the offer of a crown.

Americans cherish these images to good purpose. For they depict George Washington as the very soul of classical virtue. If the liberated colonists were truly to believe in such virtue and base their own republic on it, they needed to have at least one shining exemplar before their eyes. Washington was that. He was one of the few to take virtue so seriously as to deliberately cultivate it. As a young man, he made lists of desirable attributes and systematically worked to perfect them one at a time. He wanted to be a successful planter, a daring innovator, an imaginative entrepreneur, a graceful horseman, a winning poker player, a loving husband, an inspired leader, a victorious general and a wise statesman. Small wonder that our idea of him has become marbleized.

George Washington:
http://odur.let.rug.nl/~usa/
P/gw1/about/washington
.htm

George Washington, the great Founder, as Americans had come to see him. (*Washington Ascending into Heaven,* courtesy of the Winterthur Museum, Winterthur, Delaware.)

The Revolution and the Founding

Seldom in history had an entire populace transferred its allegiance from one sovereign to another. An enormous infusion of energy—indeed a full-scale shooting war—was required to accomplish it. The American Revolution made the inhabitants of thirteen separate colonies ask themselves who they were and what they were all about. It forced the American people, as a people, into being.

As denizens of an empire, Americans had taken many things for granted. Now they must think for themselves. They had to assess the relative merits of peace, security, freedom, prosperity, dignity, power and nationhood. And important questions underlay the choice making. Were the Americans *a* people? Did they have a common purpose? A common identity? A common destiny? Given the difficulties faced by nation-states in the modern world, was an American nation as such really feasible? If so, what sort of entity ought it be? A loose confederation of sovereign states? A single unity? Some sort of compromise between the two? Since any American nation must in some sense be "invented"—something rare in human history—what were the possible materials of its composition, and how could they best be brought together?

While the Revolution provided no answers as yet, it had provided a new set of realities. The colonies were independent of Great Britain. They could more or less govern themselves. They were recognized by the European powers as a bona fide nation-state. They had a place on the map and by European standards one of breathtaking size. They possessed a loose-jointed confederal government that had proved it could at least make war. And they had a founding document committing them to life, liberty and the pursuit of happiness.

America was off to a reasonably good start.

Suggestions for Further Reading

Bernard Bailyn, *The Ideological Origins of the American Revolution* (1992).

Paul U. Bonomi, *Under the Cope of Heaven: Religion, Society, and Politics in Colonial America* (1986).

H. Trevor Colbourn, *The Lamp of Experience: Whig History and the Intellectual Origins of the American Revolution* (1965).

Stephen Conway, *The War of American Independence, 1775–1783* (1995).

David Hackett Fischer, *Paul Revere's Ride* (1994).

Pauline Maier, *From Resistance to Revolution: Colonial Radicals and the Development of American Opposition to Britain, 1765–1776* (1972).

Edmund S. Morgan and Helen M. Morgan, *The Stamp Act Crisis: Prologue to Revolution* (1995).

Richard B. Morris, *The American Revolution Reconsidered* (1968).

Jack N. Rakove, *The Beginnings of National Politics: An Interpretive History of the Continental Congress* (1979).

Willard Sterne Randall, *George Washington: A Life* (1997).

Charles Royster, *A Revolutionary People at War: The Comtinental Army and American Character, 1775–1783* (1979).

John Shy, *A People Numerous and Armed: Reflections on the Military Struggle for American Independence* (1990).

Garry Wills, *Inventing America: Jefferson's Declaration of Independence* (1979).

Gordon Wood, *The Radicalism of the American Revolution* (1992).

CHAPTER 4 STUDY AID

(This aid is not all-inclusive and is not intended to be a substitute for thorough study of the material presented in the textbook.)

The American Revolution

I. Mercantilism

1. Centers and peripheries:
   - Closed economic network consisting of a dominant "center" and subordinate "peripheral markets and producers"
2. Regulation of trade:
   - Trade between the "peripheries" and foreign markets restricted
   - Production of finished products in peripheries proscribed
   - Guaranteed market for peripheries' raw products at the center
   - Limited trade among peripheries may be permitted
   - Center bears the cost and responsibility of administration, regulation, enforcement and protection
   - Concentration of wealth at the center provides incentive for the center to refine and maximize efficiency of the system
   - Ideally a mutually beneficial system is created

II. The Course of British Mercantilism in North America

1. Accumulation of wealth at the center
2. Military protection for North American colonies:
   - French and Indian War
3. Reforms:
   - Parliamentary and administrative attempts to increase revenue and control trade as well as eliminate smuggling
   - Ill-timed and ill-devised
   - Britain misinterpreted colonial response
   - Colonies misinterpreted British intentions
   - General failure of communication
4. British failure to recognize political, social and economic maturation of North American colonies

III. Hearts and Minds

1. A new people:
   - Development of distinctive consciousness and identity
2. Court and Country:
   - Court = corruption; England = Court
   - Country = virtue; America = Country
   - Puritan antecedents—regenerate saints versus unregenerate world

3. Colonial response to reform:
   - Evasions
   - Argument
   - Confrontation
   - Defiance
   - "Constitutional liberties"
4. Myopia at the center:
   - Continuation of efforts to centralize power
   - Continuation of efforts to enhance revenues
5. Transformation:
   - Escalation from crisis to confrontation to conflict
   - Rights and privileges; virtue and liberty
   - New habits and new aspirations

IV. Forging a Nation

1. Nationhood:
   - Identity—Thomas Paine's Common Sense
   - Recognizing boundaries—geographical, social, economic, political and cultural
   - Authority—colonial assemblies and continental congresses
   - Legitimacy—indigenous institutions, organizations and social structure
   - Sovereignty—foreign alliances and creation of an army, currency and functional confederal government
2. Declaration of Independence:
   - Vision
   - Laws of nature
   - Life, liberty and pursuit of happiness
   - Consent
   - Slavery unresolved
   - Republican synthesis
3. War:
   - The ultimate act of self-government
   - British response—from punishment to confrontation to pacification
   - Colonial militias and political education
   - Continental Army—shared experiences, suffering and vision
   - Political nature of the war—"Continentals" win by persevering even if losing on the battlefield
4. Consequences of revolution and nationhood:
   - Tangible social and economic changes
   - Political and constitutional changes
   - Archetypal national myths and symbols created

CHAPTER 4 REVIEW QUESTIONS ███████

NAME: _____   SECTION: _____

Key Terms

Mercantilism

The Stamp Act

Patronage

Boston Tea Party

Common Sense

Bunker Hill

Declaration of Independence

Colonial Militias

Multiple Choice Questions

1. Which of the following phrases best represents the idea of patronage?
   a. "Pull yourself up by your bootstraps."
   b. "It's not what you know, it's who you know."
   c. "Work hard and you can get ahead."
   d. "The best things come to those who wait."

2. The text lists three "doors" the crisis with Britain opened before the war. Which of the following was not one of those doors?
   a. Democracy.
   b. Liberty.
   c. Virtue.
   d. Equality.

3. Which of the following was not a bond of nationhood mentioned in the text?
   a. Unity of purpose.
   b. Sovereign government.
   c. Demystified monarchy.
   d. Common suffering.

4. The Revolutionary War has been compared to which other American war?
   a. Vietnam.
   b. Korea.
   c. World War I.
   d. The Gulf War.

Review Questions

1. Why have some argued that American independence came by evolution instead of revolution?

_____

_____

_____

_____

2. Why did British interests and actions change in America in 1763? What were some of those changes?

_____

_____

_____

_____

3. How did the Revolutionary War affect the colonies economically?

_____

_____

_____

_____

4. How did the creation of a national military force forge a bond of nationhood?

_____

_____

_____

_____

5. Why did the British exclaim that fighting the Americans was "like nailing jelly to the wall"?

_____

_____

_____

_____

Review Exercises

1. Explain how the Battle of Bunker Hill affected the American psyche at the start of the war.

_____

_____

_____

_____

2. Briefly explain the role the Declaration of Independence played within the war itself.

_____

_____

_____

_____

3. The text mentions the minuteman as a lasting symbol of the revolution. What does the minuteman symbolize?

_____

_____

_____

_____

Big Essay Question

Think about the key reasons why the colonists won the Revolutionary War. Come up with a list of your top three reasons and explain them, in descending order, in a one-page essay. Feel free to use material in the text or in other sources.

CHAPTER 5

The Confederation and the Rule of Law

Map of the early United States of America. (Courtesy of the National Archives.)

With the defeat of Cornwallis' army at Yorktown, Americans could turn attention to the fact of their independence, not just the idea, and begin to think about an American republic.

Or was it republics, plural? There were reasons for supposing the latter. Indeed, by the war's end, the colonies-turned-states had had republican governments up and running for more than five years. They had their historic names, of course, and other marks of individuality. Each had its own government, its own constitution. And while their citizens loosely spoke of being "Americans" or "continentals," they very much regarded themselves as separate and self-contained polities.

All of these entities—including the blurry "America"—saw themselves as Good Societies. From the discussion given in the introduction, we recall that a Good Society:

- Extends the benefits of social interaction beyond a single favored group or class to society as a whole.

- Strives for a reasonable balance between liberty—defined as the right of individuals to seek their own happiness in their own way—and order.

- Offers its citizens "goods of the soul"—such things as political participation, a sense of individual empowerment and a sense of human dignity.

Borrowing from antiquity, the American states used the term *republic* to designate the type of Good Society they had in mind. It came from the Latin *res publica*, "the public thing." And although the concept was a bit amorphous, most versions of it included a unifying moral code, a strong sense of public good, a reliance upon reason, a concern for justice and a notion that such things were possible because of human virtue.

Within these parameters there was plenty of room for variety, and the American republics had no certain course marked out for them. Would they evolve into modernized classical republics, Lockean liberal republics or some other unglimpsed form? Would their governments lean toward Aristotle's rule of the one (monarchy), rule of the few (aristocracy) or rule of the many (democracy)? What role would religion play in their political life? What role would commerce and industry play? How would they relate to one another and to the rest of the world? Would the feeling of nationhood come to reside in the whole or the parts—or both? And most important, would they rely upon virtue, as had the ancient republics, or upon more modern ideas as the key to their happiness? It all had to be worked out.

Virtue Versus Structure

While the new states already possessed working governments, some of those were only hastily revised colonial governments, and most Americans realized they must begin thinking about governance in a new way. The design of a truly republican regime ought to reflect human intentionality, they supposed, not just historical circumstances. Indeed, in some of the states constitution making inspired a heady enthusiasm.

The Failure of Civic Virtue

A beginning assumption held that virtue was the crucial element in constitutional design, far more important than anything else. There were solid reasons why. Americans often attributed their miraculous victory over Great Britain to God on the one hand and virtue on the other. Furthermore, history had convinced them that virtue must be the foundation of *any* republic. And "Jean Jacques," as they called him, did his part. For Rousseau's widely read *Social Contract* argued that modern equivalents of classical civic virtue were both possible and vitally necessary.

Some believed there were stronger claims for virtue in the New World than the old. After all, several of the colonies had been founded for specifically religious purposes, suggesting a high moral tone in the people. Life in the wilderness had required dogged determination and enormous strength of character. And during the Revolution, as we have seen, there were many acts of courage on the battlefield and much old-fashioned patriotism at home. Besides, virtue *had* to work. Americans had burned their ships, politically speaking, and there was no turning back. They had better be as virtuous as they claimed to be—or the future looked grim.

What did a republic of virtue look like in the modern world? How did it run? What set it apart? Americans weren't sure. They knew only that its life would be marked by simplicity and austerity—as different from London's Mayfair as they could make it. It would be governed by "aristocrats," to be sure, but they would be *natural* aristocrats, men of talent and virtue, not those whose only asset was a title. Small, simple, ascetic governments had to reflect virtue, Americans believed, and they had to respect freedom.

During the Confederation period this faith eroded considerably. Even before the war ended, there had been numerous stories of profiteering and disloyalty, but these were usually chalked up to *la guerre*. Harder to dismiss were instances of corruption, jobbery and other forms of misbehavior in high places—and they didn't end with Yorktown. Postwar America was a place of disillusionment, even cynicism, and it showed.

Of particular repugnance, at least to James Madison, was the interest-driven, me-first politics of state legislatures. The discourse there was all about power and advantage, he fumed, and no one so much as mentioned the public good. Worse, legislators were logrolling and horse trading with scant regard for justice, and when it came time to vote they could never see beyond their own little factions. Human nature, it seemed, had put on an altogether different face.

Shays Rebellion in Massachusetts was a kind of last straw. Disquiet among farmers in the western part of the state became so intense that angry bands began mustering in the townships and shutting down the local courts. In the winter of 1787, an "army" of these malcontents, many of them veterans, marched on the arsenal at Springfield and dispersed only after cannon fire had left four of them dead in the snow. Some Americans began wondering if the Revolution had been fought in vain.

Shays Rebellion:
http://www.sjchs-history
.org/shays.html

The Failure of Structure

At the same time, there was a growing interest in the use of political structure as a corrective to such difficulties. Aristotle, we recall, had taught that civic virtue was not constant in human affairs and could be influenced by a variety of institutional and situational factors. For example, citizens were more orderly and more mindful of the public good in a mixed regime, where the aims of one group were balanced against those of another, than in, say, a simple democracy. Hence, the intriguing idea of "**structure.**"

If virtue was the mainstay of the ancient republics, structure came to be that of the modern ones, as we saw in chapter 1. If the right structure could be found, that is. For all structures did not work equally well. The much-admired English monarchy, though it mixed and balanced Aristotle's one, few and many in a dozen ways, had proven itself only too capable of tyranny. Americans had to try to do better.

In field testing the effects of structure, the new state governments presented thirteen experimental laboratories, for each of them had different structural features in its constitution. One could observe, among other things, how virtue and structure worked together—or perhaps failed to work together—and hazard some guesses as to the cause.

While some state constitutions were merely revised colonial charters, others had been written from scratch and with great care. The latter were the more interesting. For in several of them, owing to the strong faith in civic virtue, the framers had thrown caution to the wind and shaped the constitution solely to accommodate the will of the people. If the voice of the people was the crucial element in a republic, they had concluded, by all means let us hear that voice loud and clear.

Pennsylvania was the best example. Here the framers designed the constitution around a strong, democratic, unicameral (one-house) legislature. They made the executive office weak, for they feared the inclination of executives to work mischief, and even placed the judicial system under the legislature's control. There ought to be no authority, they believed, to challenge that of the people's elected assembly.

Structure Undermining Virtue

Shrewd observers began to see that certain kinds of structural weakness played directly into the lapses of civic virtue. Take Pennsylvania again. The omnipotent assembly may have represented the people, all right, but it also represented the clash of competing interests among them. Large and vocal interest groups found that it was not too difficult to muster a legislative majority, and when they did so they could pass self-serving laws with impunity. The outcome was democratic, perhaps, but it was not conducive to political morality. For, as James Madison had noted, there were only winners and losers in such a game and it was hard for either of them to think about the public good.

In the postwar world, moreover, depression and dislocation added sharp urgency to the assembly's actions. Legislators saw themselves as fighting for their constituents' very survival, and a no-holds-barred mentality gripped the state house. There was another problem. Civic virtue turned out to be far less restraining on organized groups than on isolated individuals. For the dynamics of group interaction tended to nullify the role of conscience and convince everyone they were doing the right thing.

When other branches of the Pennsylvania government dissented, the assembly demonstrated another weakness of the structural situation. It could often find means, both legal and extralegal, to undercut competing authority. There was no executive to speak of, and the judiciary could be brought to heel by simply firing the judges and appointing new ones. John Adams pointed out that Pennsylvania was not really being "governed" at all. The strongest faction in the state was simply ruling according to its will—much in the way that tyrants in the ancient world had done.

Pennsylvania was the worst case, but many other states experienced similar difficulties. The tendency was for power to drift toward the newly democratized assemblies and there to be misused. The pattern went something like this. Indebted farmers, facing closed markets and other postwar adjustments, pushed hard for paper currency, legal tender laws, stay laws and the like, the practical effect of which was to cancel the debts they had incurred before the war. The farmers were strong enough as a political interest to get their way. Indeed, they were so strong they could roll right over the constitution, as in Pennsylvania, and those who failed to cooperate found themselves at risk. Their authority could be redefined. Their power could be emasculated. Their very offices could be wiped out. And constitutional prohibitions proved to be scant protection for them—mere "parchment barriers."

Legal Tender Laws: Legislation which declared that US currency must be accepted at face value for the payment of all debts and obligations.

Stay Laws: Prevented foreclosure of mortgages, etc.

Ex Post Facto Laws: Laws retroactively applied.

There were troubling implications in all this, and some Americans began groping to define them. "Majority tyranny," in Madison's phrase, was certainly one of them but there were others. The legislation the farmers typically demanded was both special interest and *ex post facto* in character. The laws singled out specific groups—such as moneylenders—and basically defrauded them of their property. The targets could not know in advance that this might happen to them, of course, so they were not only being punished, they were being punished after the fact.

Similar issues had had much to do with bringing on the Revolution. The security of property, for instance, had been a primary bone of contention between the colonies and Great Britain. Oddly enough, Americans were begin-

The French Revolution demonstrated how tyrannical an unchecked majority could be.
(*Taking of the Bastille*, courtesy of Hulton-Getty.)

ning to see that their own legislatures were now doing more or less what the British Parliament had done earlier, and for much the same reason.

Equally troubling was the question of expectations. All business—indeed, all affairs of society—must be conducted in a climate of certainty. A banker who places depositors' savings out on loan has to have some expectation that the money will be coming back with interest—or there will be no banks, no loans and no business. Without the stability of settled expectations, the American experiment would be in dire straits.

Many of those who found this situation alarming were among the revolutionary leaders themselves. They had fought a terrible war to secure the Good Society. The idea of property being wrested from one faction by another, more numerous and rowdy, was not the earmark of any Good Society—it was more like ancient Athens run amok.

The problem was not that virtue had failed, precisely, though in some ways it certainly had. It was that virtue and structure were not working together. A legislature structured in such a way as to allow one interest to run roughshod over another was simply not an inducement to civic morality. The structure, let us say, was pushing the wrong buttons in human nature.

Americans were not ready to despair, however, at least not yet. Analysis of the problems convinced many of them that the difficulties were not beyond resolving. But much thinking and rethinking were clearly in order.

The Confederation

According to the eighteenth-century doctrine of *sovereignty*, only a single sovereign authority could exist in any given political society. We can think of sovereignty as the place where the buck stops—the ultimate, complete and final authority to make political decisions. In a monarchy it is the king who is sovereign. In a democracy it is the people as a whole. And so on.

By such thinking, the political society now calling itself the United States of America had to ground its sovereignty *either* in the states *or* in the Confederation as a whole—there was no middle ground. Given that choice, it was a foregone conclusion that sovereignty lay in the states. After all, each state had its own separate identity and historical experience. Relations among them (as colonies) had always been difficult, sometimes even troubled, and a sort of rugged individualism had come to be the rule. And until the passage of the Stamp Act, all attempts to unite the colonies in some sort of larger dominion had dismally failed—even in the face of dire necessity.

Republican theory supported this state of affairs. For it strongly submitted that modern republics must be as small, local and separate as their ancient ancestors had been. Only in such a setting, as the argument went, could citizens exercise proper vigilance and could civic virtue operate as it should. By its very nature, a republic required political intimacy.

We have forgotten how appealing this idea was to many Americans—probably most. Small republics, each in command of its own affairs; popular participation in the political process; a town-meeting style of interaction with one's own friends and neighbors; sensitivity to local needs and problems; respect for the distinctive culture of a given locale; the ennobling aspects of a hands-on democracy—these and other benefits were assumed to derive from this modern rendition of the classical republic.

In consequence, the Confederation could hardly be imagined as anything but what it was—a loose-jointed alliance of sovereign republics for the purpose of common defense. Its organization and powers sufficed only to that end. It had a unicameral legislature in which all states were represented equally. (The equal voice bespoke state sovereignty more than anything else, for it represented states as individual entities, not the people as a whole.) There was no executive as such, nor was there a national judiciary. And the government lacked the all-important authority to raise revenue, the very hallmark of sovereignty, relying instead on humble requisitions to pay its bills. This meant that any other powers the Confederation had were largely illusory.

The Confederation was particularly hobbled by its inability to regulate interstate commerce. This was another sovereign power, for nation-states of the time commonly used trade regulation as a weapon against their neighbors. By taxing strategic imports, forbidding strategic exports and either subsidizing or monopolizing key industries, governments attempted to promote their own national well-being at the expense of others, and not rarely, such behavior led to actual war. This situation had characterized Europe for hundreds of years—and now it characterized America.

For these and other reasons, thoughtful Americans were deeply concerned about the Confederation's prospects. Yet few supposed that this league or any other could advance much further toward true sovereignty. Its constitution, called the **Articles of Confederation**, had been written by a committee of the Continental Congress during the Revolutionary War. The work of drafting and revising the document had begun in 1777 and had dragged on for nearly four years before final approval. And even then John Dickinson, who had played a central role in the process, regarded the adoption of the Articles as miraculous. This tells us much about the reluctance of American states to part with the meagerest scraps of their sovereignty.

The problem wasn't merely one of sibling rivalry. It was centered in the republican idea itself. For any powers given to a supergovernment like the Confederation were by definition "imperial" rather than "republican" in character. *Empire* was the only word in Thomas Jefferson's dictionary to describe an entity larger and more extensive than an individual state. Did they want to create an "empire"? To verify the answer, the framers of the Articles drove a final nail in its coffin. They stipulated that there could be no amendment of the document's provisions except by the approval of *all* members.

The behavior of the states was entirely consistent with their muscle-flexing sovereignty. They slammed tariffs on each others' goods, levied huge transit fees and wielded monopolistic assets—such as port facilities like a bludgeon. They sent their own ministers to foreign capitals and conducted their own diplomacy with the Indians. They went around the Confederation at every turn and subverted it whenever expedient.

Several of the states maintained their own military establishments—quite apart from the Confederation's anemic forces—and made use of them in settling interstate disputes. Indeed, in the six years between the cease-fire at Yorktown and the Convention in Philadelphia, there were no fewer than four separate brushfire conflicts involving state militias. The worst of these was between Pennsylvania and Connecticut over rival claims on the western frontier. The Pennamite War, as it was called, racked up scores of casualties and dramatized the high cost of state sovereignty. For in the absence of a national court system, there was no other way for states to settle their differences.

Foreign governments also took advantage of the Confederation and played off one state against another. Great Britain was the worst offender. Its diplomats maneuvered fast and loose among the Americans precisely because there was no central government to rein them in. They pressed the advantage of their own merchants and drove merciless trade bargains. They continued to occupy their forts in the Northwest, too, and conspired with the Indians to harass the American frontier. When the US Minister in London complained that this was in explicit violation of the peace treaty just signed, the British replied that American states violated the treaty every day, especially in the matter of repaying English debts. But, then, most borrowers couldn't repay the debts for a good reason: the British wouldn't grant them trade privileges. It was all a hopeless tangle.

Articles of Confederation:
http://www.earlyamerica
.com/earlyamerica/milestones/
articles//text.html

Nationalists came to depict this state of affairs as confused, dangerous, self-defeating and bordering on outright crisis. Their concern may have been overstated, perhaps, but the Confederation clearly did lack the power to deal with significant difficulties, and its impotence cast a long shadow.

To begin with, given the essential anarchy among them, states could never be sure of the good faith or ultimate intentions of their neighbors. Thus, they had no choice but to adopt strategic behavior, pressing the advantage when they could and seeking defensive measures when they must. A vague sense of hostility came to suffuse their world.

Clusters of states began to consider regional confederacies as an alternative to going it alone. New England, for example, comprised a rough-and-ready unit with its Calvinist background and common interest in trade. In the South there was a common interest in staple agriculture and the pervasive practice of slavery. The Middle States—New York, Pennsylvania, the Jerseys—had less in common than New England or the South, but they were beginning to share a growing cosmopolitanism. And beyond the Appalachians there was the West, already vibrant with distinctiveness. Might the future lie in such groupings?

Thoughtful Americans discussed the possibility. Since regional confederacies would be stronger than solitary states, and since they would also be faced with strong rivals, each would have to think about defending itself against the others. This might lead to standing armies, military budgets, high taxes and an imperial style of leadership. Parallels for this situation could be found in places like the Balkans: rival principalities, well armed, often at war with one another, living in constant uncertainty. None could exist as a republic.

The problem, once again, was not simply a failure of virtue. Indeed, virtue of a certain kind might make *this* situation worse. For remember that virtue's classical ancestor, *areté*, had a lot to do with deeds of honor on the battlefield and aggressive leadership at home—precisely what could (and in ancient Greece did) lead to a free-for-all. The problem, rather, was that virtue and structure were not working together toward a Good Society.

The Jerseys: Colonial New Jersey was once divided by its two proprietors into East and West Jersey.

John Adams and the Rule of Law

Like many of the Founders, John Adams was a perceptive observer of these events. He was also—and not coincidentally—widely read in history and political thought. Adams had trained as a lawyer and was an accomplished practicing attorney. It was the law, he often observed, that might well resolve America's present difficulties. In order to take in his full meaning, we need to examine a connection of crucial importance to the doughty New Englander—the connection between law and liberty.

The connecting argument was set forth in Adams' well-thumbed copy of Locke's *Second Treatise*. "Freedom is this," Locke had written,

> freedom of men under government, to have a standing rule to live by, common to every one of that society and made by the legislative power erected in it, a liberty to follow my own will in all things where the rule proscribes not, and not to be subjected to the inconstant, uncertain, unknown, arbitrary will of another man.

There was, Adams knew, a long and tortuous history behind those words.

In the early days of the *common law*, as the English legal system would be called, the king heard and decided controversies himself, judging them according to custom, reason or whatever rules might seem to apply. Eventually, when the "caseload" became too heavy, the king delegated his judicial function to others, and these became the first common law judges. If a dispute required some new principle, or "precept," for its resolution, the judges carefully spelled it out so that all future cases involving similar questions could be resolved the same way. Precedent embodied precept and became binding.

A few common law precepts had political implications. One of these, evolving through the mists of time, was called *habeas corpus*. It held that a person ought not be arrested and detained unless there were grounds for believing that he or she had violated some specific law. If the individual in question was merely, say, a political undesirable who had been arrested in order to be silenced, he could request a writ of *habeas corpus* from a judge, and armed with that he could require the arresting authority to show that he had actually broken the law. If no such evidence could be shown, the accused had to be set free.

John Adams understood the essential role the rule of law would need to play in the emerging American Republic.
(Courtesy of the White House Historical Association.)

The important feature of *habeas corpus* and similar devices was that in theory at least they applied to *everyone* in the realm—the king and his ministers not excepted. That was often a tough point to make, especially in the face of royal prerogative, but the judges kept hammering away. They argued over and over that for law to have meaning, the king himself must be bound by it.

When the point was finally made, centuries hence, a subtle transformation came about in English life. The government became obliged to *govern* the people, not just *rule* them. That is, the king could no longer order his subjects around and make them submit to his will. The existence of known, standing laws and their application to *all* members of society changed everything. England had achieved the *rule of law*.

Of the rule of law's many benefits, one of the most important was stable expectations. For wherever the law truly ruled, the laws of society became in a sense like the laws of nature—steady and reliable. Just as one could count on the law of gravity to propel water through an aqueduct, one could count on the law of contracts to insure the repayment of loans. And in both cases, predictability made society work better.

But the rule of law's greatest benefit was liberty. That was Locke's point. For knowing in advance what the law would or would not condone, people could calculate their situation to best advantage—precisely as athletes do when playing by the rules—and make the most of it. And when they could do so, what a change in the atmosphere. Citizens could get on with their lives unafraid.

Libel: Publication of knowingly false or malicious statements.

Sedition: Acts that incite rebellion against established government.

They could discuss public issues with candor. They could even stand up and criticize the government. A member of Parliament, for example, could make a hard-hitting speech against the ministry, and as long as he avoided libel or sedition—there were laws governing both—he could say whatever he pleased. It was the rule of law, more than anything, that made the English feel free.

Understandably, then, John Adams, who prized liberty, equally prized the rule of law. To him it represented the cardinal principle of a Good Society. If the rule of law existed, other things tended to fall into place: freedom, order, benefits for everyone and not just the few. And if it did not exist, nothing else seemed to work well either.

In 1770, some five years before the Revolution, Adams encountered a dramatic opportunity to demonstrate his commitment. After the so-called Boston Massacre, the soldiers accused of perpetrating it were arrested by the local authorities and charged with murder. After all, they had loaded their muskets and fired into a crowd—never mind what the crowd was about to do to them. What patriot leaders had in mind was a "show trial" aimed at discrediting the royal government. They wanted to use the law, in other words, to "get" a political adversary, precisely as the law was often used to get *them*.

Adams wanted none of that. He was as patriotic as the next person and certainly no friend of the royal government, but he knew the law of homicide, and knowing that knew that "murder" had not been committed on King's Street by the accused. He agreed to defend the soldiers in court—outraging fellow patriots in the process—and see to it they were given a fair trial. For he knew the rule of law was on the line. If lives and liberty could be made pawns in a political chess match, the law would be finished.

Now, a decade later, Adams became convinced that the rule of law was the key to unlock present difficulties. The governments of the American states were republican in a technical sense, perhaps, but many of them had failed to establish the rule of law. The government of the Confederation had a similar failing, though for a different reason. In both cases, to be sure, laws were being passed by legitimate legislative authorities. But in the one case, the laws were perceived as unjust and their effect inclined toward tyranny. And in the other, the laws were perceived as unenforceable and their effect inclined toward anarchy. Uncertainty was the bottom line in both situations: people never knew what to expect because the law was not steady and reliable.

Later on, when Adams spoke of the American Republic, he often used the phrase "empire of laws." In time, many of his colleagues came to see the Founding that same way. The notion that began to take shape in the early 1780s was to make the empire of laws not just a hopeful ideal but a working reality.

Five Principles of the Rule of Law

In John Adams' day the rule of law was more often felt than understood. For when applied to specific cases, the concept could abruptly dissolve into puzzling

The Trial of the Accused Soldiers

All Boston was scandalized. The soldiers accused of murder in the Boston Massacre were to be defended in court, not by the king's attorneys—there was not a one of them who would touch the case— but by native Yankees: Robert Auchmuty, Josiah Quincy and, most astonishingly, John Adams himself. None of the three had volunteered. Adams, for one, took the job only because of a dramatic personal appeal by one of the soldiers' friends.

Adams' soft-heartedness cost him dearly. His cousin, Sam, leader of the Liberty party, suddenly turned cool toward him. Rocks were thrown through his windows and a mudball splattered his cheek. There were whistles and catcalls wherever he went, and a voice behind a fence asked him why he left his red coat at home. He found solace in a passage from Beccaria: "If, by supporting the rights of mankind and of invincible truth, I shall contribute to save from the agonies of death one unfortunate victim of tyranny . . . his blessings and tears of transport will be sufficient consolation to me for the contempt of mankind."

The defense attorneys prepared their case well. Of the three, Adams was best versed in the English common law, and he grilled his colleagues for days on the distinctions between homicide justifiable, homicide excusable and homicide felonious. To many Bostonians such distinctions seemed irrelevant. They sided with the *Boston Gazette* when it piously thundered: "Whoso sheddeth Man's blood, by Man shall his blood be shed!"

That was tommyrot, and John Adams knew it. The soldiers had been cornered by a wild mob spoiling for their blood. One of the casualties himself, lingering before death, forgave the soldiers and confessed that the fault had been on his side. But to go too far into that, as John Adams also knew, would be to put the town of Boston on trial and harm the cause of liberty. So the defense strategy would be to stick to the law, and to the law's venerable distinctions. They would argue that this was a case of homicide justifiable.

The trial itself was the event of the decade. People drove in from the countryside and picnicked on the common while awaiting it. The courtroom was packed to overflowing and the spillover thronged the steps outside. The defense began with lengthy interviews of prospective jurors, throwing out one after another, and including in the final roster not a single Bostonian. Then the charge was read, the pleas entered and the trial formally commenced.

Auchmuty and Quincy acquitted themselves well. The latter's impassioned rhetoric on the soldiers' behalf made the jurors stop and think. But John Adams was the trial's real hero. Standing before the court in his barrister's wig and gown, he seemed to personify the law and its ancient traditions.

He stepped near to the jury and addressed it earnestly as he spoke. "Place yourselves in the situation of Killroy or the sentry, with the bells ringing—and you know well there is no fire—the people shouting, huzzahing and making the mob whistle as they call it. The people are crying, Kill them! kill them! knock them down!—and heaving snow balls, oyster shells, clubs, white birch sticks three and a half inches in diameter. . . . Consider yourselves in this situation and them judge if a reasonable man would not consider they were going to kill him." The law, said Adams, did not require a man to stand still for that. The law allowed him the right of self-defense—even if the result was homicide.

In the closing arguments, the defense appealed to good, hard, common sense. That and the law. Adams quoted Algernon Sidney that "The law no passion can disturb. 'Tis void of desire and fear, lust and anger. 'Tis written reason, retaining some measure of the divine perfection. 'Tis deaf, inexorable, inflexible." Them he added his own wisdom. "The law," he said, "on the one hand is inexorable to cries and lamentations of the prisoners. On the other it is deaf, deaf as an adder to the clamors of the populace."

The jury considered the matter for two-and-a-half hours and returned a verdict of not guilty for six of the soldiers, guilty of manslaughter (a lesser charge) for the remaining two. The punishment was a mere branding on the thumb. Then and there, with jurors and spectators alike craning there necks to see, an iron was heated, the two soldiers stretched out there hands, and the requirements of justice were met.

As Adams walked over to the prisoners, they seized his hand in gratitude. "God bless you. Mr. Adams!" they said. "We owe our lives to you and Mr. Quincy." Matthew Killroy, reputedly the toughest of the eight, sat weeping in his chair. Montgomery, the other brandee, held up his thumb as one might exhibit a trophy. "A small price to pay for our lives, Sir," he said with a smile.

ambiguity—and even today we often grasp it imperfectly. But people *felt* that something was wrong when the rule of law was violated. The words "unjust," "unfair," "unreasonable" or "arbitrary" were used to convey their displeasure. We have all been in situations described by these terms. They usually occur when we find ourselves confronting authority. If we perceive that a parent is being heartless, a bureaucrat mindless or a boss soulless, it is often because the rule of law is being shorted.

The rule of law is not law itself. It is an abstract ideal, a set of philosophical principles, guiding the way we think about law and make use of it. Accordingly, the rule of law can never be passed by a legislature or encoded into specific language—it truly must be "felt" in the hearts of the people. And, like any ideal, it can never be perfectly realized.

We have seen that an instinct for law is embedded in the human personality. Still, in some societies, there is an exceptional sensitivity to the principles we are discussing here, and when those principles are violated, the people cry out. Colonial America happened to be such a society. When Parliament passed the Stamp Act or the Townshend Duties, many Americans could not explain why they found those measures so odious. They heard all the reasonable arguments about paying their own way, enjoying relative prosperity, being "virtually" seated in Parliament—and came back all the louder with "No taxation without representation!" They were voicing a rule of law objection without fully realizing it.

Conversely, in other societies, there may be very little appreciation for the rule of law, and when its principles are violated, people are easily mollified with explanations. Hitler's Germany is a case in point. Although technologically proficient and highly civilized, Germans nevertheless failed to apprehend transgressions of the rule of law that became more or less systematic with the Nazis. If a given edict was "official," they supposed, it must be okay.

This fact tells us something else about the rule of law. It exists quite independently of the visible machinery of government. Nazi Germany had a legislature, a legal code, a court system and many other appliances of the law. All it lacked were those philosophical principles.

If John Adams had made a list of such principles, it would probably look something like this:

1. *Generality*

John Locke railed against the fact that in Stuart England there was one legal code for somebodies and another for nobodies. The laws, he said, are "not to be varied in particular cases, but to have one rule for rich and poor, for the

Hitler and followers: "Official" edicts must be okay.
(Courtesy of the National Archives.)

favorite at court and the countryman at the plow." In modern-day terms, this means that the laws must apply to broad categories of people. They must not single out specific individuals or groups for special treatment. If there is any singling out, it should be done by people themselves *after* the laws are passed. That is, I place *myself* in the category of "drivers" when I climb into my car and start the engine.

We would sense there was something wrong with a law addressed to the drivers of red Toyotas, for such an ordinance could also single out Mormons or Southerners or liberals. Those who make the laws should never know in advance to whom they apply. Lamentably, the British Parliament lacked that sort of blindness when it passed laws expressly for Americans and then began laying special taxes on them.

But in practice we too create exceptions. Some of these truly violate the principle of generality and ought to be viewed with extreme mistrust. Others are a practical necessity. And there is no hard and fast way to tell which is which.

A few categories of singling out, however, have become absolutely taboo in democratic polities. These involve ethnicity, gender, religion, political affiliation and increasingly, sexual preference. Above all, we abominate separate laws for the rich and the poor—somebodies and nobodies—knowing these could throttle a Good Society. "Equality under the law" has become a watchword.

Birmingham, Alabama police break up a 1963 civil rights demonstration. How many violations of the rule of law?
(By Bill Hudson, courtesy of AP/Wide World Photos.)

2. *Prospectivity*

This means that the laws must apply to future action, not past. We would feel as uneasy with a law punishing those who presently drink soda pop as with the singling out of red Toyotas. For the potential violator must always be able to decide *in advance* whether or not to obey.

Tyranny, of course, disagrees. For the tyrant wants to say in effect "I don't like what you did," and punish accordingly. The last thing a Hitler or Stalin would desire is for intended victims to evade sanctions by altering their behavior.

In practice, most violations of generality also violate prospectivity and vice versa. Together, in fact, these two abridgements of the rule of law account for most of the tyranny the world has known.

3. *Publicity*

This means that the laws must be both known and certain. They must be well publicized, and their enforcement must be reasonably reliable. Laws that are capriciously enforced—or else not enforced at all—do no favors for the rule of law. On the contrary, they sow public contempt.

But police apparatus is expensive. So governments occasionally trim back by funding a mere token enforcement of the laws, hoping that the possibility of punishment, no matter how remote, will suffice to deter lawbreakers. Many people will accept such gambles and bet they won't be caught. If government isn't serious about the laws, citizens won't be serious either.

Capricious enforcement was an aspect of British policy before the Revolution. It led to widespread smuggling on the part of colonials and to customs racketeering on the part of the authorities. Later on, when the British sought to reform the system and enforce the Navigation Acts rigorously, Americans were outraged.

4. *Consent*

In a single catchphrase, consent comes down to "No taxation without representation!" It means that the laws must be generally acceptable to those who must live by them. Electing the lawmakers and upholding the constitutional system are examples of the way we give consent.

Yet not all law making is subject to this sort of approval. Customary law, judge-made law and natural law are not usually submitted to the voters for endorsement. What counts, however, is that the people, if they truly *dis*like a certain law, have the means at their disposal to wipe it off the books, as they did with the Jim Crow laws of the South or the Volstead Act. For the theory of consent holds that the people as a whole would never consent to injustice—because they themselves would be its victims. The theory only works, of course, when the laws are *also* general and prospective.

Where consent becomes absolutely mandatory is in the matter of taxation. Once the people themselves consent to the amount they will be taxed, government undergoes a seismic transformation, and the distinction between rulers, on the one hand, and the ruled, on the other, virtually disappears. Put another way, if lawmakers themselves have to come up with the taxes *they* determine, all incentives to be unfair go out the window.

Jim Crow Laws: Segregation laws which were widespread in the South in the 1890s.

Volstead Act: A 1920 law enforcing Prohibition.

It was the absence of consent that sent the British Empire to its doom in 1776. For where one group, Parliament, is allowed to make laws for another group, Americans, and is not accountable to those laws itself, there is nothing whatever to restrain it. Why *not* pass a Stamp Act? asked the MPs. *They* didn't have to buy the stamps.

5. Due Process

The phrase *due process of law* simply means that the laws must be administered impartially. Justice, as the saying goes, has to be blind. It must consider nothing but guilt or innocence. If the accused person is black, or poor, or a communist or a Christian Scientist, the law must say: so what? And there must be an established set of procedures to insure that everyone before the bar is given a fair trial, an adequate defense, and if guilty an appropriate punishment.

Due process accounted for yet another sore spot in imperial relations. For the British authorities had few qualms about revoking jury trial and other traditional rights in the interest of tighter law enforcement. If Americans were a bad risk, they said, then by all means close up those procedural loopholes. We often say the same thing about "bad risks" today.

We have come to take these five principles so much for granted that they seem no more than simple common sense. Yet they have been willfully ignored by those we would least expect. For example, back in the days of the Stuart monarchy, not only did the king breach the rule of law, so did Parliament. In the notorious bills of attainder, a political offender—usually one of the king's henchmen—was singled out by name in a parliamentary act, accused of a crime and pronounced guilty. Think how many of the five principles such a law violated.

Bill of Attainder:
Legislative act in which an individual is simultaneously charged with a crime and found guilty.

Subtler abridgements of the rule of law are still committed almost everywhere. For governments with the worthiest of motives see a problem and take action to solve it, unmindful that they may be aiming legislation toward a specific group, penalizing past action or ignoring the rights of possible violators. In so doing, they come close to "administering" the lives of their citizens the way they administer park maintenance or road repair.

The same could be said about the controversy leading up to the American Revolution. Americans viewed British violations of the rule of law as darkly conspiratorial, as we have seen. But records show that the policy makers simply thought they were solving problems.

During the Confederation period, similar violations were common. Either the law was being used for political purposes—to advance one group's agenda at another group's expense—or else the law was simply incapable of enforcement. There was often no conscious thought of tyranny or anarchy, but the damage was the same as if there had been.

Virtue and the Rule of Law

While John Adams often alluded to civic virtue, he was one of the Founders who privately expressed doubts. "You will be very sensible," he wrote to James

Warren on the eve of the Constitutional Convention, "that our Countrymen have never merited the Character of very exalted Virtue. It is not to be expected that they should have grown much better."

Many of the Founders had reason for such skepticism. Their own hard experience, their reading of history and their acquaintance with the latest theories of psychology had convinced them that virtue was highly problematic. Unquestionably, some individuals *were* capable of the *areté* described by Plato. They could place public good ahead of private advantage. They could face stark sacrifice. They could find deep meaning and high purpose in politics. And they could love their country with a profound and selfless patriotism. The Founders themselves answered this description, and it broadly bespoke their aristocratic world.

But the day-to-day reality of a commercial society was simply otherwise. Most Americans were less motivated by high idealism than by old-fashioned self-interest. Comfort and convenience counted a great deal with them, and they measured life in dollars and cents. Accordingly, they weren't overmuch concerned with most public issues, especially the abstract or remote ones, and whenever they became so, it was usually with an eye to private advantage. The psychology of the day—notably that of David Hume—questioned whether the human mind was even capable of the moral thinking virtue required. What people took to be morality, Hume contended, was often just custom in disguise.

There were other problems in basing the Good Society on virtue. As the ancients had defined it, virtue appeared to be both unstable and situational. Soldiers were capable of great sacrifice in time of war—yet as veterans they thought nothing of engrossing themselves at public expense. A Benedict Arnold could be a national hero one minute and an archtraitor the next.

Virtue had a frightening side as well. Deeds of honor were one thing when the colonies were fighting for their lives—they were something else when the new states began jostling one another over rival claims. And empire wasn't the only danger Americans faced. *Areté* also stoked the fires of fanaticism, as history plainly showed, and while Stalin's gulags and Hitler's storm troopers were still far in the future, the French Revolution was just around the corner.

Gulag: The labor camp penal system of the USSR.

In pondering such matters, the Founders were grappling with one of philosophy's most elusive problems—the fundamental nature of man. They didn't claim to have final answers. At the same time, it was critically important that they get certain things "right," and human nature was one of them.

Wisdom and Virtue

As the Founders revised estimates of American virtue downward, the word *virtue* continued to appear in their correspondence—but it was increasingly connected to the word *wisdom*.

Wisdom was also a kind of code word. It represented an array of values, attitudes and specific insights which taken together meant that life was not simple. When *wisdom* and *virtue* were linked together, the republican picture that Plato had painted in broad strokes and blazing colors took on depth and shadow, and for the Founders it began to look something like this. A modern republic, even in America, could not be based on Spartan-style civic virtue, for liberal individualism simply couldn't deliver such an intense and single-minded public-spiritedness. Yet Americans did have their own forms of virtue—and clearly *some* forms were essential to *any* republic.

The questions posed by wisdom, then, were these. What kind of virtue *could* human nature deliver? What kind could liberal individualism deliver? What kind was necessary for a modern republic? And finally, how much virtue was "enough?"

We might think of the rule of law as representing a new approach to such questions. Probably none of the Founders, including John Adams, worked out the relationship between law and virtue in so many words, but Adams seemed to grasp the main idea. The rule of law offered a different way of focusing moral energy. Instead of asking citizens to put the good of society ahead of their own personal interest or to perform great and lofty deeds, they are asked instead to do two things:

> *Cherish the law.* People must commit themselves to observe the law with an almost religious devotion. Indeed, the law takes the place of the king as the symbol of nationhood and gains its own sense of mysterium. Obeying the law is not about fearing to get caught—but desiring to live virtuously.

> *Cherish the rule of law as an ideal.* This is a bit trickier, for it requires a sophisticated understanding of what law is and how it works. To revere the *rule of law*, rather than just law itself, one must know something of politics, something of life, something of philosophy perhaps, and assuredly something of wisdom. One must know, for example, how the rule of law is often undermined by seductive political temptations.

Alexis de Tocqueville (1805–1859): French observer of American life.

The rule of law required its own kind of virtue, to be sure, but it was a virtue within human reach. Indeed, it was the *kind* of virtue—orderliness, accountability, self-restraint—that a liberal society might well be able to deliver. (Insightfully, **Alexis de Tocqueville** dubbed it "enlightened self-interest.") The rule of law also required its own kind of wisdom, that of both the wise leader and the wise electorate. Shrewdness, cunning, the Machiavellian traits so often associated with politics, did not work well in a rule of law society, nor did go-for-broke activism or flashy charisma. What the rule of law society called for, rather, was statesmanship.

Machiavelli (1459–1527): Italian philosopher best known for his treatise on the attainment of political power through any means.

The Rule of Law and Constitutional Design

Virtue could not establish the rule of law by itself; it was also a matter of constitutional design. But what were the specific design principles involved? Why did some constitutions do a much better job of it than others?

Separation of Powers

One clue—and it would turn out to be an immensely important one—came out of the English constitutional experience. Once the king, the Parliament and the

The Noble Experiment

What happens to respect for the law when masses of citizens cannot bring themselves to obey it? Before the days of Prohibition, no one thought to ask. After all, among a law-abiding people, laws were supposed to be respected automatically. As Prohibition Commissioner John F. Kramer said of the Volstead Act: "This law will be obeyed, and where it is not obeyed it will be enforced." But it turned out that Prohibition was neither obeyed nor enforced, for American drinkers simply continued their drinking.

At home in their basement, they brewed hard cider, cheap wine and makeshift brandy, and in their bathtubs they literally concocted bathtub gin. For the making of high octane beverages, they rigged up their own distilleries, some of them fairly sophisticated. One still, steaming away in a New York cemetery, had produced fifty-one barrels of moonshine by the time Prohibition agents got onto it.

Most people, however, simply bought their bootleg ready-made. This could be done at the local speakeasy, a club or café with a secret back room, or at a variety of other establishments. Near Cornell University it was soda fountain. In lower Manhattan it was store that sold "sacramental wine." In Baltimore it was a sidewalk fish market, with tiny bottles of booze in the cash register drawer. In Atlanta it was a confectionary, and in New Orleans it was a taxi—*any* taxi. One woman bought a milk shake in New York's Van Cortlandt Park and wrote indignantly that by mistake it was filled with gin. (Bad gin, too, she reported.) Another complained that in a grocery store in Harlem, a clerk "charged me two dollars for a can of tomatoes, and when I got home I found there was nothing in it but a lot of nasty-smelling water." And nosing around in Brooklyn pawn shops, agents uncovered then-one-thousand-dollars' worth of liquor wrapped in the clothing left as pledges.

Nor was the illicit trade in alcohol confined to lowbrow establishments. In New York's tony Half Past Nine Club, a large stock of contraband was found in a stuffed grizzly bear. In a fashionable Madison Avenue delicatessen, the beribboned baskets of fruit concealed small bottles of rye. Before the "noble experiment" was over, Manhattan lost some of its most exclusive nightspots: Jack's, Shanley's, the Beaus Arts, Reisenweber's.

People regarded the mass evasion as good, clean fun. At the football game, they pulled flasks out of hip pockets, garter belts and raccoon coats, and had a wonderful time. Only dimly were they aware of names like Johnny Torrio, Frankie Yale and Al Capone; and the connection between big-time gangsters and the good, clean fun seemed tenuous. Then, on St. Valentine's Day of 1929, two carloads of Al Capone's hit men battered their way into a Chicago warehouse and gunned down seven members of "Bugs" Moran's gang. Americans were puzzled to learn that the massacre took place in a bootleg distillery. Somehow, the country was becoming downright lawless.

court system had accepted one another as fully legitimate entities, there was a division between the rule-making and the rule-enforcing authorities of the realm. The rule maker was Parliament. The rule enforcer was the king and the court system working together, royal officers bringing suspects to trial and the courts deciding their guilt or innocence.

It was only a rough-and-ready division, to be sure, and sometimes it broke down, but in the main it worked. As long as the rule makers couldn't directly enforce the rules, they had to make them blind, as it were, and general. And as long as the rule enforcers couldn't make the rules, they too had to operate on a general basis. The law couldn't be used for extracurricular purposes—to "get" someone—because it was under no *single* authority's control.

Enlightenment thinkers had expanded the theory of these mechanisms somewhat, positing that there were three functions with respect to the law, not just two. The legislative branch made the law. The executive branch implemented the law. And the judicial branch applied the law to specific cases. But it still came down to a structural separation between rule making and rule enforcement, and that separation worked to keep the law "blind."

It is also instructive to note what had happened to this system in the early 1700s. With Parliament on a roll after the Glorious Revolution, it took over some of the executive operations of government. Parliamentary officers did not arrest lawbreakers or decide their cases in court, to be sure, but with the emergence of the ministerial system (which is still in use today), these officers did acquire certain enforcement responsibilities. The separation between rule maker and rule enforcer grew blurry—and opened golden opportunities for political jobbery. Indeed, much of the "corruption" alluded to in the commonwealth ideology had its origins here. Powerful ministers and their friends could identify specific goals, marshal support for these in the House of Commons, secure the measures needed to further them along and implement them in the precise way they had in mind. No one had to operate "blind" any longer—for the powers got along with each other only too well.

Several of the American Founders began to grasp the difficulty. From their reading of Montesquieu, they had picked up the idea that there was something to be gained by keeping the powers apart. For when rule making, rule implementing and rule applying were all in different hands, officials were more likely to be aboveboard, or at least so held the growing belief. The idea—it was not yet a full-fledged theory—had gained enough currency to find its way into a few state constitutions. "The legislative, executive, and judicial powers of government ought to be forever separate and distinct from each other," was the way it was generally put—a sort of little sermon in their preambles.

The trouble was, this strategy had almost never worked. The powers of government did *not* remain separate and distinct, as we have seen: the moment a muscle-flexing legislature set out to solve a problem, it regarded the rest of the government as an impediment to overcome—and the little sermon as a mere nuisance. James Madison shook his head at such developments. Constitutional prohibitions, he said, posed but a "parchment barrier."

But there might be ways of designing the structure so that the powers really would force each other apart in the course of their routine operation. The question was, how?

Sir Thomas More and the Law

Nowhere was the power of the law to thwart tyranny depicted more clearly than in the struggle between Henry VIII and Sir Thomas More. King Henry, having married his late brother's wife, Catherine of Aragon, found himself with no son and, more important, no heir. He thus determined to divorce Catherine and try again with someone else—someone more comely. But there was a hitch: the king was Catholic, and the pope would not sanction his divorce. Henry plunged ahead anyway. He went through with the divorce, married Anne Boleyn and repudiated the authority of Rome.

Sir Thomas More was the king's chancellor, a high officer in this government. He was a wise, a saintly man, devoutly religious, and respected all over the realm. Had he ratified the king's bold actions, it would have gone far toward making them acceptable. But this his conscience would not permit. Of course, he would not renounce the divorce either, nor condemn the king's break with Rome, for that would amount to treason. He simply said nothing. A master of English jurisprudence, More knew exactly what the law would and would not condone. He also knew that English respect for the law was such that the king himself feared to break it.

Just where that left him was aptly illustrated by his trial in 1535, imaginatively recreated in *A Man For All Seasons*:

Thomas Cromwell (the prosecutor): "Let us consider now the circumstances of the prisoner's silence. The oath was put to loyal subjects up and down the country and they all declared his grace's title to be just and good. But when it came to the prisoner, he refused. He calls this 'silence.' Yet is there a man in this court, is there a man in this country who does not know Sir Thomas More's opinion of this title? Yet how can this be? Because this silence betokened, nay this silence was not silence at all but most eloquent denial."

More: "Not so. Not so, Master Secretary. The maxim is 'qui tacet cosentire videtur.' The maxim of the law is 'Silence gives consent.' If therefore you wish to construe what my silence betokens, you must construe that I consented, not that I denied."

Cromwell: "Is that in fact what the world construes from it? Do you pretend that is what you wish the world to construe from it?

More: "The world must construe according to its wits. This court must construe according to the law."

In the end, tragically, More was condemned and executed anyway, but only because his enemies found a witness willing to testify against him falsely. Short of such outright skullduggery, the law of England steadfastly shielded him, even from the wrath of a tyrannical king. It was an example that was not lost on the authors of the American Constitution.

Constitution of Massachusetts (1780):
http://vi.uh.edu/pages/alhmat/masscons.html

The Model Constitution

John Adams was one of those who thought he might have an answer. On the basis of his own wide reading in political theory and the recent experience of the several states, Adams wrote a landmark booklet titled *Thoughts on Government*. Although he wasn't thinking precisely about separation of powers, he hit upon an important idea. The antidote to too much power in the legislature, he submitted, was to strengthen the power of the executive.

To some, this seemed wrongheaded. Americans had fought a revolution because of, among other things, too much power in the hands of executives—the king's appointed governors. Were they now to return to that selfsame abuse? Yet there were arguments for doing just that. Strong executives were dangerous only when there was nothing to counterbalance them, Adams argued. Strong legislatures were dangerous for the same reason. But when *both* were strong, it might be a whole new situation.

The new situation became manifest in 1780 with the Massachusetts "Model Constitution." The original Massachusetts Constitution, drafted in 1775 at the beginning of the Revolution, had been as problematic as any. In the Model Constitution, the Massachusetts fathers hoped to learn from their mistakes—and from the best thought and reflection available. Many of Adams' ideas found their way into it.

To begin with, the office of the executive was strengthened in several ways. His term of office was lengthened. His appointment power was increased. And he was given a conditional veto over acts of the legislature. He could strike down any law he didn't like, but by a two-thirds vote his negative could be overridden.

The veto was the hardest innovation to abide. After all, it was by means of the "negative," as it was called, that the British governors had done their worst damage. Detractors envisioned a dark future with the veto back in place, everything from executive blackmail to governmental gridlock. Besides, political theorists—and especially those who liked separated powers—pointed out that the conditional veto in effect made the governor a legislator, at least in the negative sense, and thus *compromised* the separation of powers.

In operation, however, the Model Constitution had none of the predicted ill effects. On the contrary, it altered the psychology of power among the branches and promoted a new interactive spirit. We recall that the main defect in state constitutions was their vulnerability to a legislative power grab. Once the governor was re-armed with the veto, he could ward off attempts of the assembly to usurp power from the other branches (including his own). Conversely, when the legislature was counterarmed with the override—which colonial legislatures had never had—it could similarly protect itself from the governor. Each branch continued to eye the other warily, of course, but each knew it was safe from a truly tyrannical purpose. Both could relax and cooperate.

Above all, the Model Constitution performed wonders for the rule of law. By forcing the powers of government to work independently (without working at cross-purposes), it posed a real obstacle to those special-interest measures and cozy inside deals for which state regimes were becoming sadly famous. Bills lucky enough to be approved by both the legislature *and* the governor passed the rule of law test, as it were, with significantly higher marks. For no governor could make the legislature do his bidding—or vice versa.

The general lesson might be stated this way. In designing the structure of government, anything that could be done to insure that the laws were general, prospective, public and so on was good for the republican cause. The separation of powers did just that.

The Rule of Law and the Good Society

At the beginning of the chapter, we suggested that there were many possible visions of the Good Society. Here is the vision suggested by the rule of law.

In a rule of law society, the government must restrict itself to governance—the creation and enforcement of general rules—not solving problems and certainly not administering citizens' lives. It could promote the *general* welfare by providing defense or building highways, but it couldn't fret about the welfare of farmers who had borrowed money—or bankers who had loaned it to them. This

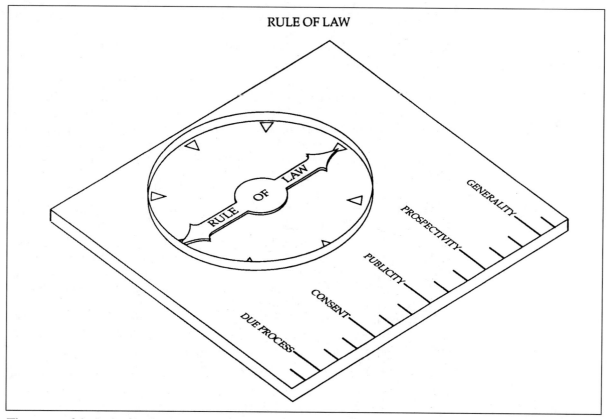

The concept of the "rule of law" represents the philosophical ideal that government may not act except in the impartial enforcement of a known general rule. The actions of such a government are predictable, much like the laws of nature. Those living under the rule of law can chart the course of their destiny in predictable self-determination.

is a far more restrained role than government played in the ancient republics. It is also far less interesting. When government is not conceived as the answer to every problem, it is no longer uppermost on everyone's mind.

Similarly, the rule of law society would be little inclined to save the world. The grand revolutionary schemes of modern times wouldn't appeal very much to the citizens. For they wouldn't be able to work up the turbocharged "virtue" such schemes require—theirs would be more along the lines of ordinary human decency. The citizens would not be the *zoons politikons* described by Aristotle either. The meaning of life for most of them would be found elsewhere than politics—in the home, in business, in the trades and professions, in leisure-time activities. Politics might be engaging at certain points, even exciting at election time, and yes, there would always be "professional politicians," but the consuming intensity of ancient public life simply wouldn't be there.

In a rule of law society much of the problem solving would take place outside of government. There would be more in the way of private initiatives, community efforts and voluntary organizations (churches, service organizations, lodges, clubs) to address social needs. Where government did become involved, it would tend to be on the local level.

The moral sense of the people might need to adapt somewhat to a rule of law society. What the ancients called virtue, for example, might have to trade public venues for private ones—fewer John F. Kennedys, let us say, and more Martin Luther Kings. And the individual pursuit of happiness might need to become a little less concerned with the condo in Malibu and a little more concerned with the plight of the homeless.

There would be a role for schools and churches in the society of law, but it would not be the role they played in the ancient republics. There the school and the church, like almost everything else, had been part of the government and in charge of promoting civic virtue. In a rule of law society, religion, like all personal matters, would be outside of public scrutiny, and learning would be only slightly less so. Ironically, however, if schools and churches failed to promote moral sensitivity and ethical standards, the Good Society might well turn bad.

In theory at least, the rule of law provided a way of bringing classical, liberal and democratic republics together. By transferring initiative from the public sphere to the private individual and the local community, it might redefine and redirect classical civic virtue. By requiring citizens to play by the rules in their pursuit of happiness, it might use that pursuit to benefit the whole of society. And by presupposing an entire populace committed to high (though not impossibly high) ideals, it might base its foundation on the *demos*.

But *only* in theory. In reality, there was no rule of law society anywhere in the world, and especially among the fledgling American republics. There were only a few ideas, a few experiments, a few significant intellectual correspondences—and a whole raft of practical difficulties.

Suggestions for Further Reading

Willi Paul Adams, *The First American Constitutions: Republican Ideology and the Making of the State Constitutions* (1980).

Richard Beeman, Stephen Botein, and Edward C. Carter III, eds., *Beyond Confederation: Origins of the Constitution and American National Identity* (1987).

Roger II. Brown, *Redeeming the Republic: Federalists, Taxation, and the Origins of the Constitution* (1993).

Merrill Jensen, *The New Nation: A History of the United States during the Confederation, 1781–1787* (1948).

Donald S. Lutz, *Popular Consent and Popular Control: Whig Political Theory in the Early State Constitutions* (1980).

Jackson Turner Main, *Political Parties before the Constitution* (1973).

Jackson Turner Main, *The Sovereign States, 1775–1789* (1973).

Frederick W. Marks III, *Independence on Trial: Foreign Affairs and the Making of the Constitution* (1973).

Gordon Wood, *The Creation of the American Republic, 1776–1789* (1969).

CHAPTER 5 STUDY AID

(This aid is not all-inclusive and is not intended to be a substitute for thorough study of the material presented in the textbook.)

The Confederation and the Rule of Law

I. Proto-Nation—The Articles of Confederation

1. Alliance:
   - Protection
   - Allegiance to one's state
2. Dimensions of republicanism:
   - Virtue and structure
3. Sovereignty:
   - Vested in states
4. Authority:
   - States retain effective power and ultimate authority

II. Is Virtue Enough?

1. Civic virtue:
   - In decline
2. Corruption:
   - In high places
3. Interests:
   - Factionalism
   - Partisanship
4. Shays Rebellion:
   - Limitations of the Confederation

III. Problems of Structure

1. Structure:
   - Counterpoint to civic virtue
   - Thirteen experiments in political structure
2. The example of Pennsylvania:
   - Weak executive
   - Susceptible judiciary
   - Strong unicameral legislature
   - Majority tyranny
   - Elective despotism
   - Special interests
   - *Ex post facto*
   - Uncertainty

IV. An Unsovereign Confederation?

1. States:
   - Jealous of their sovereignty

- Jealous of each other
- Mistrust of motives

2. Republican theory:
- Small is better

3. Decentralization of power—a toothless Confederation
- Revenue—no power to tax
- Commerce—no power to regulate
- Adjudication—no judicial power
- Diplomacy—no authority to conclude treaties

V. The Rule of Law

1. John Adams:
- Identifying the problem
- Providing the solution
- No rule of will
- Predictable laws
- Reliable enforcement
- Predictable laws and reliable enforcement = liberty

2. Antecedents:
- English common law
- *Habeas corpus*

3. Core principles:
- Generality
- Prospectivity
- Publicity
- Consent
- Due Process

4. Virtue and the rule of law:
- Exercise of wisdom and enlightened self-interest
- Cherish the law
- Observe the law
- Exercise self-restraint

5. Constitutional design:
- Separation of powers
- Rule making separate from rule enforcing
- Model Constitution—Massachusetts

VI. The Rule of Law and the Good Society

1. Government:
- Governs
- Enforces general laws

2. Private sector:
- Problem solving

CHAPTER 5 REVIEW QUESTIONS ——————

Key Terms

Majority Tyranny

Sovereignty

Articles of Confederation

Rule of Law

Generality

Prospectivity

Publicity

Consent

Due Process

Multiple Choice Questions

1. Which of the following was not an aspect of the Pennsylvania state government, as discussed in the text?
   a. Unicameral legislature.
   b. Weak executive office.
   c. Legislative control over the judiciary.
   d. A two-party system.

2. The main purpose of the Articles of Confederation was to:
   a. Regulate trade.
   b. Negotiate with foreign countries.
   c. Provide national defense.
   d. Create a national monetary system.

3. Racial profiling by law enforcement officers is a violation of which rule of law principle:
   a. Generality.
   b. Consent.
   c. Prospectivity.
   d. Due Process.

4. Which of the following mind-sets best illustrates the concepts of enlightened self-interest?
   a. I will not steal this car because stealing is wrong.
   b. I will not steal this car because the folks who parked it probably still want it.
   c. I will not steal this car because I don't want to get caught and thrown in jail.
   d. I will not steal this car because I would not want someone to steal my car.

Review Questions

1. How did the Founders benefit from the problems in early state governments?

   _____

   _____

   _____

   _____

2. What were the main provisions of the Articles of Confederation?

   _____

   _____

   _____

   _____

3. How did foreign countries use Confederation weakness to their own advantage?

   _____

   _____

   _____

   _____

4. How might have life under the Articles of Confederation led America into the Human Predicament Cycle?

   _____

   _____

   _____

   _____

5. Was John Adams an idealist or a realist? Explain your answer.

   _____

   _____

   _____

   _____

Review Exercises

1. Explain the relationship between the Boston Massacre and the rule of law. Why did John Adams defend the British soldiers?

   _____

   _____

   _____

   _____

2. Explain, using examples, the text's notion that the rule of law is something felt rather than understood.

   _____

   _____

   _____

   _____

3. Briefly explain the difference between governing and administering.

   _____

   _____

   _____

   _____

Big Essay Question

List and define the five principles of the rule of law. Then devise a separate scenario for each principle illustrating a violation. Be as creative as you wish. Include an explanation of why your example is a violation of the principle in question.

The Constitutional Convention I
The Framers

(*Against All Odds*, by Karin Draper, reprinted by permission of the artist.)

The Confederation experience underscored the difficulty of creating successful republican governments—a difficulty stretching back to the ancient world. But the Founders took heart from the Enlightenment notion of the social contract, free men coming together and creating their own government through conscious deliberation. That element—conscious deliberation—had often been missing heretofore. The Founders believed that it was possible to do much better. Through "wisdom and reflection," as Hamilton put it in *Federalist* 1, they trusted that the difficulties before them could somehow be resolved.

In a way, it was not a new challenge. Americans had been tinkering with constitutions of one kind or another for almost two centuries. They had learned that certain mechanisms in a colonial charter inclined in a rough way toward certain outcomes in the colony's life. There was a kind of "science" there—dim and shadowy though it was.

The trick was to bring the right people together, first of all, and then get them to deliberate as carefully and creatively as possible. It was not, alas, an easy trick to perform.

The Idea of an American Nation

The story begins with a small group of Americans generally referred to as "nationalists." Most of them were personally acquainted with one another, although they came from distant parts of the continent, and they tended to have a common background in the Revolutionary War.

Nationalists: Supporters of strong central government.

The important quality the nationalists shared was a vision of America as a unified nation. In their eyes, the America of possibility somewhat resembled the ancient Roman Republic—large, powerful, stable and "honorable to mankind." It would be respected in the world and capable of performing great works of public benefit. Not least, it would provide a veritable cornucopia of prosperity. For the nationalists, the very meaning of the Revolution required such a polity as its outcome.

Alexander Hamilton of New York was probably the best known of the nationalists. Certainly he was the most energetic. He had been urging a national constitutional convention ever since the guns had fallen silent. Eventually, others had taken up the cry, and by 1785 they were corresponding enthusiastically with one another. For with each passing month there was fresh evidence that the Confederation simply wasn't working.

Even so, it required the interest of George Washington to move matters off dead center. Like Hamilton, Washington had been a nationalist from the beginning. As commander in chief of the Continental Army, he had known firsthand the impotence and frustrations of the Confederation, but he also shared Hamilton's vision of American nationhood. Washington had once had a strong personal friendship with Hamilton, who had been his aide-de-camp during the war, and they had mutually reinforced one another's nationalist sentiments. Indeed, it was Washington rather than Hamilton who took the first step.

The place, appropriately, was Washington's backyard. His home, Mount Vernon, was on the Virginia side of the Potomac River, looking across the water toward Maryland. Friction between the two states had made navigation of the river difficult, and Washington was eager for a settlement that would please both parties. Accordingly, at the suggestion of fellow Virginian James Madison, he decided to host a conference at Mount Vernon in March of 1785 for the purpose of talking things out.

The Mount Vernon Conference succeeded well enough to prompt a wider effort. The Maryland legislature suggested inviting Pennsylvania and Delaware to a trade convention at Annapolis the following year. Once again, Madison became involved, and the invitations were expanded to include all the states. The Annapolis Convention did not lay commercial issues to rest—delegates from only five states appeared—but it accomplished a broader purpose. The nationalists spent several days reinforcing one another's convictions and lamenting the state of affairs. In the end, the delegates adopted a report by Alexander Hamilton calling for yet another convention, to meet in Philadelphia in May of 1787. The subject was no longer trade. It was the impotence of the Confederation.

If these developments confirmed the leadership of Hamilton, they also pointed to the emergence of his friend and fellow nationalist James Madison. Occasionally called the Father of the Constitution, Madison was known to his contemporaries as a Virginian's Virginian. He was the scion of a tidewater family whose fortune stretched back for generations, and his plantation, Montpelier, radiated patrician charm. Yet Madison felt uneasy about his wealth and even uneasier about the slaves who wrung it from the soil. He compensated by approaching life with a volcanic energy that belied his slight stature and tinsely voice. After deciding, reluctantly, against the priesthood, Madison read law at Princeton and buttressed his learning with a wide study of history, the classics and contemporary thought.

Madison was a nationalist for essentially two reasons. First, his service in the Continental Congress had given him that vision of American nationhood that so many of the nationalists shared; and second, his experience in the Virginia House of Burgesses had convinced him of the perfidy, duplicity and "mutability" of state governments. Up close, republican politics hadn't been about the public good at all, Madison concluded, but about rabid partisanship and factional interest. The cure for the disease, as he gradually came to see it, was to find constitutional means of bringing virtue to bear more effectively. A strong, energetic, national sovereignty, led by the wisest and most talented in the nation, was for Madison the only solution.

Madison the politician had an intuitive grasp of the situation. He realized that if any convention were to succeed, it would do so only with the active support of George Washington. Madison the scholar understood that a knowledge of political theory and historical precedent might come in equally handy. Both personae swung into action. The politician wrote to Washington and began clarifying the issues for him. The scholar wrote to his friend Thomas Jefferson, then serving as minister to France, and asked him to round up whatever books he could find on relevant topics and send them with dispatch. A hefty crate of volumes arrived shortly before Madison left for Philadelphia. He studied them literally night and day.

However serious the nationalists' preparations, much depended on factors beyond their control. How would the Confederation government respond to this call for a convention? And how would the *states* respond? (After all, no matter how bad things might be, some vested interests would prefer to leave well enough alone.) The most worrisome question was that of Washington's attendance. He was presently enjoying his retirement to the full and seemed little inclined to rejoin the political fray. Besides, it might be risky to commit his prestige to a project that might prove abortive. As March turned to April, letters from Mount Vernon appeared to banish all hope that the general would be on hand. Madison set out for Philadelphia on May 1 in a spirit of deep misgiving.

The Convention and Its Delegates

In the spring of 1787, Philadelphia was America's largest and most prosperous municipality. With a population of 45,000, it was larger than any city in England except London. At the intersection of Broad and High Streets, on the town square, stood the State House, "Independence Hall," an imposing brick edifice with Palladian windows and a towering cupola—although this had recently been taken down for repair. Philadelphia was the home of eight newspapers, several magazines, a dozen libraries and at least one authentic museum. Among its narrow cobbled streets were to be found more than a hundred inns at which travelers could rest and patrons could drink and dine. Several of these would become central to our story.

James Madison was the first delegate to arrive, nearly two weeks in advance of the scheduled opening on May 14. He took a room in a small pension on Market Street, tucked among the red brick townhouses, and returned to his heroic reading schedule. By the time the Convention gathered, he had become a walking disquisition on government.

On Sunday, May 13, Madison caught the first inkling that his hopes had not been in vain. To the boom of cannon and the rattle of musketry, General Washington had arrived in Philadelphia—the Convention had a chance! In the days following, as coach after coach rattled in with distant passengers, Madison's excitement grew. Almost all the states had sent delegates, and from appearances they had sent the very best.

Father of the Constitution

Delegates to the Constitutional Convention who did not know James Madison could not understand how such a small, quite unimposing man could wield so much influence. The secret, if there was one, was preparation; he always did his homework. Preparation, in fact, remained the key to Madison throughout his long and highly accomplished life. He was the epitome of the scholar in politics.

Both his mother and father came from established Virginia families, and the Madison estate, Montpelier, might be mistaken today for a well-endowed college. James himself was uneasy about his wealth—always playing it down—and doubly uneasy about the nearly two hundred slaves who produced it. (When his trusted valet ran away and was recaptured, Madison, instead of selling him off into the West Indies, set him free and then hired him.) It was, in fact, "to depend as little as possible on the labor of slaves" that the young man took up the study of law.

And when James Madison took up anything, he did so with single-minded devotion. Under Donald Robertson, his first tutor; under Reverend Martin, with him he later studied the classics; and finally under John Witherspoon at Princeton,

Madison worked so diligently that he seriously endangered his health. More than once he confided that he did not expect to live long.

Once settled in such habits, Madison was loath to alter them. Whether it was working on a problem in the Virginia House of Burgesses, guiding the Revolution in the Continental Congress or hammering out the new Federal Constitution, he addressed his tasks with a fearsome intensity. Much of his subsequent career was foreshadowed by his first term in Congress where he did not utter a single speech for six months. When he finally did take the floor, however, he was so well prepared that he immediately rose to leadership.

Curiously, though, everything about him belied his volcanic drive. His delicate stature, his reserved manner, his thin, tinsely voice combined to put adversaries off their guard. It was only upon looking closely that one noticed the exquisite tailoring, the finely powdered wig, the bright, scintillating eyes, the confident, bouncy step. "In the affairs of the United States," wrote one of the delegates, "he perhaps has the most correct knowledge of any Man in the Union." It was true. He was prepared on everything and for everything. Every argument, every objection,

every wrinkle in the tapestry of ideas he knew with loving intimacy and could address the same with cogency and conviction.

Madison reached the great watershed in his life with his work in Revolutionary Virginia. A passionate believer in virtue, he lost his bid for reelection because he refused to canvass actively or ply the voters with rum. But virtue, he found, didn't count for much in state politics. Indeed, after battling the factions and their special interests through the long years of the war, he gradually concluded that republicanism could never survive without a strong—and virtuous—central government. "The advice nearest to my heart and deepest in my convictions," he wrote, "is that the Union of the states be cherished and perpetuated."

There were ideas besides Madison's in Philadelphia, of course, and many of them found their way into the Constitution. But the heart of the document was his: it represented the strong and virtuous national republic that had shimmered before his eyes. When all else was said and done in the constitutional debates, there was just no gainsaying the boyish little Virginian with the amazing store of knowledge.

Madison the politician was as interested in the delegates as Madison the scholar was in theories of republican governance. The small Virginian undoubtedly assessed his colleagues from every possible angle as they bundled their luggage into various lodgings.

Collective Portrait

Altogether, seventy-four delegates had been appointed by twelve of the thirteen states. (Rhode Island, always the maverick, remained aloof.) Fifty-five of them actually showed up. Most of those who failed to appear "smelt a rat," as Patrick Henry put it, and chose not to affiliate with "consolidationists."

In background if not in temperament, the fifty-five were remarkably similar. Thirty-four of them were lawyers. Eight were judges. And literally all of them had held high public office. Some were governors or former governors of their respective states, and most had been members of Congress. Even so, their public careers were coterminous with private careers in the law, mercantile enterprise or agriculture. A quarter of them owned commercial plantations. They were men of practical affairs and counted themselves as such. If they had private libraries and well-thumbed books, they also made decisions and expected to abide by them.

James Madison has been called the Architect of the Constitution. (Courtesy of The Granger Collection, New York.)

Virtually to a man, they were representatives of the American elite. Some came replete with Honorables and Esquires by their names, and several were much at home in London drawing rooms. Still, a fair number were lowborn and self-made, often by means of commercial enterprise and occasionally by means of the right marriage. One delegate, Roger Sherman of Connecticut, had grown up in a hardscrabble farmhouse in which there were three beds for a family of nine. Self-creation was an American theme, and its representation here was significant.

Something else of significance was the instability of the delegates' fortunes. Robert Morris could boast that he had superintended the finances of the Revolution, but his reach often exceeded his grasp and his financial empire would eventually come crashing down. James Wilson would suffer a similar fate. George Washington, who was one of the wealthiest men in Virginia, was perennially hard-pressed for cash, as was his Virginia colleague George Mason. Many of the delegates were involved in some way with land speculation or with government securities, both of which were gamblers' games, and they were used to living life on the edge.

If they were not stuffy, neither were they doddering. A list of fifteen key participants at the Convention ranges in age from twenty-nine for Charles

The Founding Fathers: http://www.nara.gov/exhall/ charters/constitution/ confath.html

Pinckney to sixty-six for Roger Sherman. Their average age was forty-seven. Benjamin Franklin at eighty-one was by far the oldest in attendance. So debilitating was his gout, he was carried to the State House every morning on a sedan chair borne by four prisoners from the Walnut Street jail, and he favored the group with an endless stream of jokes about it.

Finally, the delegates were men of the Revolution. Eight of them had signed the Declaration of Independence. Thirty had served in the army, and roughly half of those had seen action. Several were authentic battlefield heroes. They had not convened here to undo 1776, as historians have occasionally imagined. On the contrary, what brought them together was an almost mystical sense that something more was needed, something elusive perhaps yet crucial, to bring the Revolution to full fruition.

Intellectual Influences

Several of the delegates were true scholars. James Madison certainly was that, and so was his friend and ally James Wilson. Wilson was a Scot, recently immigrated, and he still spoke with a lowlands burr. He had a razor-sharp legal mind and an encyclopedic store of knowledge. Only a cut below the two Jameses were the two Georges, Wythe and Mason, both from Virginia and both of a studious, scholarly bent; and along with them William Samuel Johnson of Connecticut, soon to take his father's place as president of Columbia College. Elbridge Gerry of Massachusetts had advanced degrees from Harvard and an interest in political philosophy. Alexander Hamilton had been a child prodigy in New York, writing sophisticated political tracts while still a teenager, and he enjoyed awing people with his facile brilliance. Yet he had nothing over Gouverneur Morris, a stout Pennsylvanian with a peg leg and a curmudgeon's temperament, who was one of the most learned and accomplished men in America. The scholars had an advantage at the Convention, especially when the voting was close, and they made the most of it. It was one of the few occasions in American politics when the central players were willing to heed the voice of learning.

Most of the delegates had some semblance of a classical education. In the process of reading their Greek and Latin, they had been exposed to the experience of the ancients, and to the doleful, cautionary lessons that experience seemed to convey. They were also schooled in the European Enlightenment. They had read their Hobbes and Locke, their Voltaire and Rousseau, and most of them had at least a passing acquaintance with Montesquieu's *Spirit of the Laws*, which impinged directly on their work in Philadelphia. Grotius, Vattel, Burlamaqui, Puffendorf all popped up from time to time in their discourse, and there were repeated references to Blackstone and English constitutionalism.

A number of the delegates had some exposure to the **Scottish Enlightenment** as well. They knew the works of Adam Smith, Francis Hutchinson and Lord Kames. Of particular significance were the writings of Thomas Reid and the so-called "common sense" school. Reid had argued that abstruse philosophy was not the means by which mankind apprehended moral truth—but rather by simple, everyday common sense. That point of view squared well with Americans.

One more Scot is worth mentioning. A few of the delegates—an important few as it turned out—were familiar with the writings of David Hume. His work had ruffled feathers throughout Europe, for it came down on the skeptical side of every question from human nature to divine miracles. But it was hard to question Hume's logic, especially when it came to understanding political society. Hume brimmed with ideas for controlling human behavior, reining in power and turning the dark side of man to moral profit. To the seekers of utopia he offered a trenchant piece of wisdom. What *is* established, he said, is just as important as what *ought* to be established. A dynamic interrelation of the "is" and the "ought" was to become a subtext of the US Constitution.

Still, philosophy as such would play but a minor role at the Convention. There was only a single discourse upon Enlightenment political theory—and it fell flat. For the delegates generally believed that truth was learned through observation, not speculation. "Experience must be our only guide," said John Dickinson, adding "Reason may mislead us."

It has occasionally been said that the American Founders were irreligious. A few may well have been **Deists**. Gouverneur Morris was a secular humanist and unabashed skeptic. Most, however, were more or less committed churchmen. The vast majority were mainstream Protestants. Two were Catholic. A few were Quakers. Some form of Calvinism lay in the background—or described the behavior—of several central players: William Paterson, George Mason, Elbridge Gerry, Roger Sherman. And the Convention's truly central players, James Madison and James Wilson, had both pondered careers in the ministry.

Deism: An 18th-century movement denying interference of the Creator with the laws of the universe.

Ideology and Interest

According to Karl Marx, there is a close relationship between "ideology" and "interest" in human affairs. In any given society, so the argument goes, there will always be a certain group in control of things, and the specific interests of that group will always be expressed in a system of governing ideas. Thus, for example, if religion is revered in a society, look for priests to be the "master class" in question. And so on.

The American Founding is sometimes presented as a showcase for the Marxian point of view. After all, the Framers of the US Constitution came together in a dramatic way, and they were white, Protestant males representing a well-defined social elite. Half of them held government securities bought up at bargain prices and roughly a third of them owned slaves. What else could they write but a constitution that protected property, acknowledged slavery and required the government to redeem its securities at par?

So, why isn't this a good explanation? Because it is too simple. It is true that the Framers made no bones about interest—they constantly discussed it in their deliberations. However, interest came in an assortment of forms and cut in many different directions. The interests of the various states prompted one course of action—highly conflicted—while the interests of the regions prompted quite

At Par: Redeemed for value stamped on face of note.

another. If there was a class interest among the Framers, it was at odds with both of the above, for the rank and file of Americans had no titles by their names and knew only a farming life. There was a commercial interest that favored low tariffs, an agrarian interest that favored high tariffs, a city and town interest, a backcountry interest, a debtor interest, a creditor interest, a large-scale plantation interest, a small-scale family farm interest, pro- and anti-slavery interests, pro- and anti-British interests, even a western interest whose main theme was suspicion of the East. These were all represented at the Convention. It was virtually impossible to bring them together in a single "controlling interest"—as we will soon see.

Ideology needs a closer look as well. As men of affairs, the Framers distrusted systems of ideas as such. Still, they had at least three broad commitments that could in some sense be called "ideological."

First of all, they distrusted power. It was dangerous by its very nature, they believed. All power tended to engross itself and invade other domains. All power inclined to curtail freedom. And all power disposed toward corruption. The Framers talked endlessly of ways to restrict it, tame it, civilize it and render it responsible.

Second, they upheld property. When they used that term, however, it was not quite in the way we would today. *Property*, for the Framers, was a kind of freedom—as it had been for the commonwealthmen of England. Ownership gave meaning and dignity to life. It made it possible to stand on one's own feet and be responsible for one's own actions. Fear of power and respect for property went hand in hand.

Third, they were committed republicans. A few of them leaned toward classical republicanism. William Paterson, for instance, had a great deal to say about the waning virtues of old, and George Mason wanted the Constitution to restrain private luxury. The vast majority were liberal republicans, however, and it was liberty rather than virtue that focused their concern. And an important few were democratic republicans. Benjamin Franklin, Charles Pinckney and one or two others belonged in this camp, along with James Wilson, its leader. Perhaps the most interesting of the "democrats" was Madison himself. He viewed the political world in terms of popular sovereignty, and sought practical means for breathing that sovereignty to life.

In a word, then, ideology and interest didn't jibe. For time and again the Framers demonstrated they would vote against their "interests"—state, regional, class, personal—in the name of some transcendent higher good.

Interesting facts about Constitution:
http://www.nara.gov/exhall/charters/constitution/conqa.html

http://www.nara.gov/exhall/charters/constitution/conmain.html

Getting Started

As the delegates greeted one another, there was a whiff of apprehension in the air. This was a risky business, they knew, and it might well result in failure. And high reputations were on the line.

At least the symbolism felt right. They were convened in "Independence Hall" and seated in the selfsame room in which the vote for separation had been taken. It was a spacious chamber, done up with Georgian flourishes and yet quietly dignified. At one end, before a classical pediment, stood an elevated dais on which the presiding officer sat at an imposing walnut table. The rest of the seating was at smaller circular tables covered with green baize cloth. Delegates sat grouped together by states, so they could confer with one another before casting their state's vote.

The hall was cool in the mornings, but as sunlight poured through the slatted blinds, the air grew fetid and stale. With the windows closed and locked to protect privacy, it was not long before beads of sweat began to stand out on foreheads or trickle beneath woolen waistcoats. It was, said the old-timers, an exceptionally hot summer, the worst in half a century.

Independence Hall in Philadelphia was the site of the Grand Convention. (Courtesy of the Library of Congress.)

As credentials were read out and special instructions voiced, the precarious nature of the Convention's mandate became clear. The delegates had been sent not to create a new government but to strengthen the existing one. Thus, their project must always be referred to as "the Convention," or perhaps "the Grand Convention," never "the *Constitutional* Convention." For similar reasons, the nationalists had to bury their intentions in cryptic phrases and speak only of creating "a more perfect union." *Innovation* was not a happy word in the 1700s, especially when applied to politics.

On May 25, George Washington was officially elected president of the Convention and solemnly escorted to the dais. He made a short speech of acceptance, notable for its humility, and took his place in the president's chair, which was carved with a gilded sunburst. Washington had an air of magic about him, variously described as personal charisma, deep strength of character or a sense of spiritual wholeness, and placing him at the head of a proceeding that promised to be fractious made practical good sense.

The first of the Convention's committees set to work on a list of operating procedures. Among the rules to be followed were:

Rise to speak, addressing the president.

Refrain from conversing, reading, et cetera while a member is speaking.

Refrain from walking in front of a speaker.

Some of the rules seemed legalistic and nitpicky. Yet on at least two occasions critical votes would have gone the other way but for the invocation of one small rule or another.

Benjamin Franklin and the Ambiguous Sun

Ben Franklin seemed to view the world in similes. The comment in his *Autobiography* that "Keimer stared like a pig poisoned" was just the sort of thing he would come out with, and similes filled *Poor Richard's Almanac* from beginning to end. So it was only natural that the old diplomat was thinking in similes during the long, hot summer of 1787.

Franklin knew that settling the sovereignty issue would be monumentally difficult. As it happened, he had tried to settle it himself some thirty years earlier, at the time of the French and Indian War. Then, the much younger and less experienced diplomat had conceived a plan for uniting the colonies in a common defense. The need for such unity had been real enough—almost critical—but the plan had been scuttled by the colonies' legendary jealousies and rivalries. Americans, it seemed, would literally rather face their enemies alone than join themselves together.

Why was that? Franklin asked himself. He supposed it was because as colonies they had all been so very different. They had been founded at different times by different groups and for different purposes. They had come of age individually, proud of their self-reliance and more than a little snooty toward one another. A New Englander traveling in Virginia remarked that the reputation of that place for hospitality was grossly exaggerated. A Virginian had the same idea about Pennsylvania, adding that its women were "remarkably homely, hard-favored, and sour." And, to complete the circle, Pennsylvanians lost no love on New England, a place, said one, of "low craft and cunning." It was that way all over.

It was not a happy condition, Franklin admitted, but it did explain some things. It explained why the states so cherished their independence. It explained why they sent their own diplomats abroad and why nine of them now boasted of having their own navies. New York was presently engaged in a shooting war with Vermont, as was Pennsylvania with Connecticut. No wonder the British had failed to take the "United States" seriously.

It was with such gloomy thoughts in mind that Franklin, sitting in the infernal heat, swatting flies, fanning himself with a sheaf of papers, began to ponder the sun disk painted on the back of General Washington's chair. It was a stylized sun, with rays fanning outward, a decorative motif often used. The painter, thought Franklin, wasn't very good. He had failed to make it clear whether the sun was rising or setting.

Franklin's own sun was setting. At eighty-one he was far and away the oldest man here, and though he was revered as the elder statesman, the tough issues were being tackled by younger and more vigorous men. He had seen a great deal in his lifetime. He had seen America grow from colonies to provinces to independent nations. Would he live to see it become a single nation—one capable of holding its head up in the world? He wondered.

And suddenly there was the perfect simile. Was that sun on the chair back rising or setting? Was it casting its rays over the beginning of something important or the end? What did the American Revolution mean, after all, a mere colonial rebellion that happened to succeed— or a new epoch in human history?

Ah, yes, that was it, the ambiguous sun. Rising or setting?

Beyond formal procedure, there was a great deal of old-fashioned courtliness. It was always *Colonel* Mason, *General* Pinckney, *Judge* Wythe. And in addressing George Washington, it was always *Your Excellency*. A wonderful anecdote recounted that Hamilton and some friends made a wager with Gouverneur Morris that he, Morris, would not dare to lay a hand casually on Washington's shoulder and address him as a personal friend. According to the tale, Morris took the dare one evening at the City Tavern, and for his pains received a glare so icily forbidding that he slunk from the great man's presence. Decorum had its value, though, especially when stakes were high and divisions deep.

The Convention's most remarkable rule was to conduct all proceedings in secret. To that end, the windows were kept tightly shut, sentries were posted at the doors and members were not allowed to copy from the daily journal. Benjamin Franklin, ever garrulous, was judged to be the number-one security risk, so delegates were careful to be at his side at all entertainments, steering the conversation away from sensitive topics. At one point, a set of notes was found on the floor, dropped there by one of the delegates in his haste. Washington treated the matter with such gravity that the notes were never claimed.

Secrecy played a crucial role. If all utterance was off the record, members would be free to speak their minds and change their minds. Nor would it be possible for news media to seize upon a scrap of information and whirl it into a major controversy. All the same, the hush-hush was disconcerting.

As veteran parliamentarians, the delegates knew all the special jargon and procedural devices of political assemblies. Among the latter was the ad hoc committee, which came in two varieties. Grand committees, usually composed of one delegate from each state, were appointed to work out a compromise when everything else had failed. Special committees were given particular tasks. The Committee of Detail, for example, took the broad understandings hammered out in general assembly and worked them into meticulous prose.

One committee was a legal fiction. The Committee of the Whole House, as it was called, was a parliamentary device enabling the General Assembly to reconstitute itself as a "committee." When it did so, Washington would step down from the dais and take his place at the Virginia table, and Nathaniel Gorham would replace him at the head of the room as committee chairman. Why the charade? In the Committee of the Whole House, votes could be taken again and again as members heard new arguments, rethought their positions and possibly changed their minds. In General Assembly votes were binding.

Voting was by states, as in the national Congress, not by individual delegates. As long as a state had at least two delegates residing in Philadelphia, its vote could be cast by any of them in attendance. This created an odd situation. If a state had, say, five delegates in residence and four happened to be indisposed, the sole member in the hall could cast the state's vote any way he chose. Suppose, on the other hand, two delegates were in attendance and they happened to disagree; they cancelled one another and the state's vote was nullified. Months of persuasion might come to naught if the right parties weren't present when a critical vote arrived.

The big question of the opening sessions was where everyone stood on the question of a stronger union. A majority of the delegates were nationalists, plainly enough, but there were all sorts of gradations among them—and some

Serious Business

In its first item of business, the Constitutional Convention wisely elected George Washington to be its presiding officer. Solemnly escorted to the dais, the General made a little speech of acceptance, confessing his want of qualification and calling upon God for help. After that, though a lively interest never left his face, he took no further part in the proceedings. But his presence on the dais, day after day, through the heat, the flies, the sometimes bitter debates, meant everything.

Washington was deeply concerned—sometimes painfully distressed—about the condition of the American Republic. It faced a host of difficulties and there was no promise that it would ever surmount them. Had the threats been military, the old general would have known precisely how to deal with them, but they were political, intellectual, even spiritual in nature; and Washington felt ill equipped in those areas. Accordingly, he did what he believed he could do best: make the delegates understand how serious a business this was.

Take the matter of secrecy. The delegates resolved early that their proceedings must be kept closely under wraps. For, if the public were looking over their shoulders, they could neither speak their minds freely nor work out delicate compromises.

How did Washington regard the secrecy rule? Early in the Convention, he was handed a paper dropped accidentally and left on the floor. That afternoon, just before adjournment, he rose from his seat. "Gentlemen!" he said, in a voice he might have used at the Battle of Germantown, "I am sorry to find that some one member of this body has been so neglectful of the secrets of the Convention as to drop in the State House a copy of their proceedings. . . . I know not whose paper it is, but there it is [throwing the paper down on the table], let him who owns it take it." William Pierce, alarmed, shot his hand into his own breast pocket to make sure he was not the culprit. "It is something remarkable," he penned in his memoirs, "that no person ever owned the paper."

One for whom seriousness came naturally was James Madison. He was the first to arrive in Philadelphia, almost two weeks before the Convention got under way, and he used the time to full advantage. He spent days and nights poring through hundreds of volumes, writing out lengthy notes and even penning an essay on comparative government. Small—"no bigger than half a piece of soap," someone said—slight of figure and so quietly spoken that he was repeatedly asked to speak up, Madison nevertheless dominated the proceedings. He sat on the front row and took notes far more complete than those of the Convention's paid scribe. For him, too, constitution writing was a serious business.

There were, of course, moments of pleasure. Everywhere, it seemed, there were teas, formal receptions and dazzling balls. If it was the hottest summer in Philadelphia's memory, it was also the most brilliant.

By day, however, the Convention was invariably back on task. And in its own perverse way, the heat may actually have helped out. Slatted blinds kept the sum from the Assembly chamber, but with the windows closed, the air inside grew lifeless and oppressive before midday. The New Englanders, who had come ill provided with woolen suits, stole envious glances at Washington, who seated on the dais in his light camlet coat and breeches, seemed imperturbable as a Gilbert Stuart portrait. But sitting through the suffocation, day after day, served as a reminder, if one were needed, that the American republic was in peril—and that the business of rescuing it was serious business indeed.

held their cards very close. Then, too, a small but determined minority were as far from nationalism as one could be. So who, precisely, was who?

• The Nationalists

No nationalist was more deeply committed than Alexander Hamilton. But the New York he represented was badly divided politically, and the other two delegates, John Lansing and Robert Yates, made sure to come down against Hamilton on every question—including nationalism.

It was the same way with Virginia. Madison was an ardent nationalist, but there were six other members of the state's delegation and none quite matched his zeal. Washington came close, perhaps, but the role of Convention President made it difficult for him to get down in the trenches. There were two other prominent Virginians, Edmund Randolph (the governor) and George Mason, but their nationalism wasn't always beyond question.

In the Pennsylvania delegation, James Wilson was as ardent a nationalist as Hamilton, and such was the force of his personality that he often carried the others along. But most weren't hard to carry. Gouverneur Morris believed in strong, can-do government and wasn't all that hostile to monarchy. And Benjamin Franklin could be described as nationalism's patriarch.

In the small states, nationalism depended on how individual delegates felt about their state going it alone. In the Deep South, for instance, with the Spanish down the coast and Indians on the frontier, going it alone was not an appealing prospect, so nationalist feeling was strong. Elsewhere some small-state delegates matched the strong union sentiments of a Madison or Hamilton—George Read of Delaware was willing to see the states "swallowed up entirely"—while others were more iffy. A few of the delegates converted to the nationalist cause in the course of the Convention. Rufus King of Massachusetts, for one, was rather skeptical at the outset, but as events moved along, he became an enthusiastic supporter.

> Washington believed that the Convention's president ought to be above politics. Subsequently, scholars have shown that various delegates believed he did not embrace a clear position.

• The Confederalists

Those who liked things the way they were—with the states fully sovereign and the Confederation weak—were generally termed "confederalists." Luther Martin of Maryland was the Alexander Hamilton of that persuasion. As far as he was concerned, American nationhood was a bad idea and the program advocated by the "monocrats" an ill-disguised attempt at empire. Martin frankly attended the Convention for the purpose of obstructing it, and believed that the best way to do so was by delivering long and ponderous harangues. It was not an effective approach.

Next to Maryland, the state most likely to opt out was New York. Both Lansing and Yates were cool to the idea of a strong union, and when the Convention began leaning that way, they pulled up stakes and left for good, promising to fight against any plan that ensued.

Beyond these firebrands, a number of other delegates were in sympathy with state sovereignty, even while they lamented the present situation. Randolph and Mason of Virginia, Paterson of New Jersey and Gerry of Massachusetts were among the deeply conflicted. They leaned first one way and then the other.

The confederalists reflected American thinking at the time far more accurately than the nationalists did. Most Americans were simply not ready for an American nation as such—indeed, they could scarcely conceive such a thing.

The Virginia Plan

Virginia Plan/Resolves:
see page 186.

When the day scheduled for the opening arrived, only two delegations had presented themselves. Those two, Pennsylvania and Virginia, began holding informal afternoon talks. What came out of these meetings was a set of fifteen resolves, mainly the work of Madison, constituting a general design of government. The Virginia Plan, as it would be called, moved boldly for an American union.

As soon as the Convention's preliminaries were out of the way, the Virginia Plan was officially presented to the General Assembly by handsome and debonair Edmund Randolph, who spoke for a full three hours. This wasn't at all what the delegates had expected—a full-dress proposal right off the bat. Nor could there be any doubt about the polity it proposed. There would be a national legislature elected on the basis of proportional representation, with larger states choosing more representatives and smaller states choosing fewer. The government, Randolph urged, must represent *the people*, not *the states*, and it must act upon them directly. Thus, everywhere there were, say, 40,000 voters within a contiguous space there would be an elected representative to the national assembly. Each district would have its own separate interests, and these would contend with one another for preference in the political arena. States as such would become irrelevant.

What must have turned in the minds of Randolph's listeners. A single government for the entire continent. Only people to be represented. States irrelevant. This was no minor revision of the Articles of Confederation—this was a revolutionary overthrow.

The Grand Convention was under way.

The Deliberative Process

By June, things had settled into a semblance of routine. The delegates met six days a week and generally took Sundays off. They convened around ten o'clock in the morning and continued until five or six in the afternoon. Not everyone attended all the sessions. On most days, there were no more than thirty members on the floor at a single time.

There were late arrivals and early departures too, some for political reasons and some for personal. By the time the New Hampshire delegation finally pulled in on July 22, the New Yorkers had all gone home, so there were never more than eleven states present. And by the end of August eleven of the original fifty-five delegates had left Philadelphia for good.

The proceedings were formal by our standards. Many of the speeches were written out beforehand and delivered rather stiffly. Where the discourse became interesting was in the more off-the-cuff exchanges, where the delegates batted theories and authorities back and forth like badminton birdies. On the whole, however, they worked out their own approach to the intellectual problem before them—an approach favoring their own experience. Never ask whether something *might* work but whether it has worked, does work or is likely to work, was the way they might have put it.

In this spirit, the Framers continually scrutinized their ideas by the light of human nature. And here they were often dismally pessimistic. Given the opportunity, almost everyone would lie, cheat, steal or try to beat the system—or so one might gather from listening to the debates. In this, of course, the Framers were laying out worst-case scenarios. If a mechanism seemed to function properly in the direst situation they could imagine, chances were it might function in the everyday world.

A 1799 engraving of George Washington presiding over the Constitutional Convention.
(Courtesy of the Free Library of Philadelphia.)

Decision making was despairingly tedious. The delegates would often decide an issue, place it on the shelf and return to it in a day or two, discovering that it had to be decided all over again. Resolving one knotty problem required no fewer than sixty separate ballots, while the wording of a single clause in Article III had to be reworked seven times. Typically, the moment a question was finally "settled," a new objection would pop up.

Participation was lopsided. Some twenty percent of the delegates accounted for eighty percent of the dialogue. Gouverneur Morris was heard most often with 173 speeches. James Madison was a close second with 161, and James Wilson and Roger Sherman were in third and fourth place respectively. On the other extreme, six delegates—Blount, Blair, Gilman, Bassett, Few and Ingersoll—never uttered a single word. Some of the disparity was due to a difference in political style. Morris' style was open, aggressive and forensic, whereas John Rutledge preferred to work behind the scenes. "Care not who reigns," he often cited, "care only who rules."

Core Framers

A careful study of the Convention's day-to-day process suggests that roughly fifteen of the fifty-five delegates—a quarter—were of truly commanding importance. These "Core Framers," as we will call them, made a variety of contributions. Some were good at crafting arguments or persuading the undecided. Others came up with creative innovations. Still others knew how to build a coalition or negotiate a compromise. In chapter 7 we will focus on the core delegates and see how they worked together to tackle a specific problem.

For now, our list of Core Framers, in three descending tiers of importance, looks something like this:

James Madison
James Wilson
Roger Sherman

Gouverneur Morris
Charles Pinckney
William Paterson
George Mason

John Dickinson
Edmund Randolph
Benjamin Franklin
Oliver Ellsworth
John Rutledge
William Samuel Johnson
Elbridge Gerry
Rufus King

The list is entirely subjective, of course, and it offers only a rough approximation, but few historians would probably quarrel with the general sense of it. Personality had a heavy impact on the Convention's outcome.

Conditions and Circumstances

Finally, we might keep in mind the physical conditions and social circumstances under which the delegates labored, for these too worked a subtle influence. The summer's Bengal heat, already mentioned, was accompanied by swarms of pestilent flies. These were a "veritable torture," as one visitor recalled, constantly "stinging everywhere and turning everything black [with their] filth." Mosquitoes were bad that year too and several members complained of bedbugs. And Philadelphia was anything but a model of cleanliness: hogs and chickens wandered the streets freely, and when the wind shifted, the stench of the slaughterhouse wafted in.

Orrery: A mechanical model of the solar system.

Yet Philadelphia was also America's showcase. But a few blocks from the State House the delegates could visit Charles Willson Peale's museum, with its fossil bones, stuffed animals and gleaming portraits of American heroes. Or they could pay a call on David Rittenhouse and see his famous orrery, or venture out to Bartram's Garden with its amazing botanical collection. Down along the riverfront one could wander along the miles of wharves and warehouses, and find shops selling everything from Chinese silk to French soap. There were bookstores and stationery shops and the Library Company at Carpenters' Hall, with its models of new-fangled machinery. There was even a College of Physicians, reputed to be on the cutting edge of medical science.

The message? This was no moribund society falling into tatters. America was going places.

Most of the delegates roomed within a few blocks of the State House. Madison took lodgings with Mrs. Mary House, celebrated for her hospitality, at the corner of Fifth and Market. Elbridge Gerry and his new bride rented a house on Spruce Street. Several Convention members checked into the Indian Queen, a hostelry on Fourth Street, where boarders sometimes crowded two to a room. Washington was a summerlong guest of Robert Morris, who despite his tottering financial empire lived as sumptuously as a European prince.

Morris was only one of those lavishing entertainment. He was joined by fellow Philadelphians (and fellow delegates) Jared Ingersoll, Thomas Mifflin and George Clymer. Dr. Franklin laid in a cask of porter for his own socials, which were noted for their conviviality, even though a glass or two made him dangerously voluble on Convention matters. Nor were the matrons of society to be outdone. They hosted an endless parade of afternoon teas and evening suppers, often provided with musical accompaniment, to the extent that some delegates began to feel a surfeit. Crusty George Mason, for one, complained of all the "etiquette and nonsense so fashionable in this city."

Charles Willson Peale welcoming Americans to his museum in Philadelphia.
(*The Artist in His Museum*, by Charles Willson Peale, 1822, courtesy of the Pennsylvania Academy of Fine Arts, Philadelphia. Oil on canvas, 103¾ × 79⅞ in. (263.5 × 202.9 cm). Gift of Mrs. Sarah Harrison (The Joseph Harrision, Jr. Collection). Acc. no. 1878.1.2.)

The entertainments, however, were often only extensions of Convention intercourse. Groups of delegates would gather nightly at the Indian Queen, the George, the Black Horse, the City Tavern or the London Coffee House to sip brandy, chat about current difficulties and, not infrequently, conduct back-channel negotiations. Indeed, the cozy, candlelit parlor of a comfortable inn provided an agreeable atmosphere for the Convention's spadework. Here it was not a matter of declamatory rhetoric but of engineering compromises, building coalitions and devising creative solutions.

For, first and foremost, the Founding needed to be a *political* undertaking—the forging of a common identity and sense of nationhood—and no document laying out a plan of government could perform that feat. Somehow the working politics of *patria* had to be assembled from the raw materials of discord.

An Assembly of Demigods?

Jefferson, writing from Paris, pronounced the Grand Convention "an assembly of demigods." Hyperbole aside, the Framers of the Constitution were exceptional by any standard. Several of them could be counted among the most brilliant men of their time. A dozen others might be described as first rank. And all were of conspicuous talent and achievement. Even more striking for such a gathering, they possessed an almost uncanny ability to reason together in ways that surpassed their reasoning as individuals. They were men of politics rather than politicians, the difference being that unlike our own world, their names would have been high on any list of the most admired. Some of them aspired to the highest renown possible for statesmanship—to be founders of a great nation. That aspiration would be sorely needed in the trials that lay ahead.

Suggestions for Further Reading

Douglass G. Adair, *Fame and the Founding Fathers*, ed. Trevor Colbourn (1974).

Lance Banning, *The Sacred Fire of Liberty: James Madison and the Founding of the Federal Republic* (1995).

Richard D. Brown, "The Founding Fathers of 1776 and 1787: A Collective View," *William & Mary Quarterly* (July 1976).

Stanley Elkins and Eric McKitrick, "The Founding Fathers: Young Men of the Revolution," *Political Science Quarterly* (June 1961).

Joseph J. Ellis, *The Founding Brothers: The Revolutionary Generation* (2000).

Arthur N. Holcombe, "The Role of Washington in the Framing of the Constitution," *Huntington Library Quarterly* (August 1956).

Adrienne Koch, *Power, Morals and the Founding Fathers: Essays in the Interpretation of the American Enlightenment* (1961).

Max M. Mintz, *Gouverneur Morris and the American Revolution* (1970).

Richard B. Morris, *Seven Who Shaped Our Destiny: The Founding Fathers as Revolutionaries* (1973).

John P. Roche, "The Founding Fathers: A Reform Caucus in Action," *American Political Science Review* (December 1961).

Geoffrey Seed, *James Wilson* (1978).

Thomas G. West, *Vindicating the Founders* (1997).

CHAPTER 6 STUDY AID ▬▬▬▬▬▬

(This aid is not all-inclusive and is not intended to be a substitute for thorough study of the material presented in the textbook.)

The Constitutional Convention I
The Framers

I. Overcoming Weaknesses

1. A new hope:
   - Social contract = conscious deliberation
   - Wisdom and reflection
   - Experience—tinkering with state constitutions
   - "Science"
   - Careful creativity

2. Nationalism:
   - Nationalists—America as a unified nation
   - American—large, powerful, stable, honorable and prosperous
   - Hamilton, Washington, Madison
   - Mount Vernon Conference (1785)

3. From Annapolis to Philadelphia:
   - Annapolis Convention (1786)—a question of commerce
   - Philadelphia (1787)—the question of the Confederation
   - Emergence of Madison
   - The drafting of Washington

II. Delegates

1. The gathering:
   - Madison first
   - Arrival of Washington
   - The very best (74 delegates appointed from 12 states; 55 attended)

2. Collective portrait:
   - Elites and statesmen
   - Lawyers, judges and landowners
   - Revolutionary experience

3. Intellectual Influences:
   - Classical education
   - Enlightenment influences—European (Hobbes, Locke, Voltaire, Rousseau, Montesquieu)
   - Enlightenment influences—Scottish (Smith, Ferguson, Hutchinson, Kames, Reid, Hume)

- Committed churchmen
4. "Interest:"
    - White, Protestant, male elites
    - Government securities
    - Property and slavery
    - How important?
5. "Ideology:"
    - Distrust of power
    - Upholding property
    - Republicans

III. Getting Started

1. The "Convention":
    - What was its "real" purpose?
    - Washington as president
    - Rules of order
    - Behind closed doors
2. Committees:
    - Grand
    - Special
    - Committee of the Whole
3. Voting by states, not delegates

IV. Nationalists and Confederalists

1. Nationalists:
    - Hamilton, Madison, etc.
    - Regional concerns
2. Confederalists:
    - Status quo (Luther Martin, Lansing, Yates, etc.)
    - State sovereignty (Randolph, Mason, Paterson, Gerry)
3. Virginia Plan/Resolves:
    - Madison
    - An American "Union"
    - National legislature—proportional representation
    - Representing people, not states
    - Favored larger states

V. The Process

1. In light of human nature:
   - Pessimistic outlook
   - Worst case scenarios
2. Deliberation:
   - Tedium
3. Participation:
   - Lopsided
4. Core framers:
   - Madison, etc.
   - Gouverneur Morris, etc.
   - John Dickinson, etc.
5. Conditions and circumstances:
   - Hot and uncomfortable
   - Philadelphia itself
   - Socializing
   - Demigods?

CHAPTER 6 REVIEW QUESTIONS ▬▬▬▬

NAME: _____   SECTION: _____

Key Terms

Nationalists

Alexander Hamilton

James Madison

Philadelphia

Constitutional Convention

Three Broad Commitments

Confederalists

Multiple Choice Questions

1. The Annapolis Convention of 1786 primarily dealt with:
   a. The colonial navy.
   b. Commercial issues and dissatisfaction with the government.
   c. Problems along the western frontier.
   d. The desire of some colonies to form regional alliances.

2. According to the collective portrait of the delegates at Philadelphia, what profession was most represented?
   a. Doctors.
   b. Professors.
   c. Lawyers.
   d. Clergymen.

3. Which of the following was not one of the Founders' Three Broad Commitments?
   a. Distrust of power.
   b. Commitment to republicanism.
   c. Respect for property.
   d. Desire for national sovereignty.

4. All of the following delegates were Confederalists except:
   a. Luther Martin.
   b. Elbridge Gerry.
   c. Gouverneur Morris.
   d. William Paterson.

Review Questions

1. What were the unifying ideals the Nationalists shared?

   _____

   _____

   _____

   _____

2. What impact did the Mount Vernon Conference and the Annapolis Convention have on the Constitutional Convention?

   _____

   _____

   _____

   _____

3. Why was James Madison such an ardent Nationalist?

   _____

   _____

   _____

   _____

4. Why was the Constitutional Convention held in Philadelphia? How did conditions and circumstances there shape the constitution-making process?

   _____

   _____

   _____

   _____

5. What was a Grand Committee? A Special Committee?

   _____

   _____

   _____

   _____

Review Exercises

1. Describe the implications of David Hume's quote, "What *is*, is as important as what *ought* to be." How did Hume's sentiment influence the Founders?

   _____

   _____

   _____

   _____

2. Briefly explain the concepts of ideology and interest according to Karl Marx. Why does the American Founding not fit into Marx's construct?

   _____

   _____

   _____

   _____

3. Explain why the Confederalists were more representative of the American people's thinking than the Nationalists.

   _____

   _____

   _____

   _____

Big Essay Question

Think about the circumstances the Convention delegates met in. Considering our modern media and technology, how might the Convention have turned out differently if it were held today? Be creative in your response, addressing differences within and without Independence Hall.

The Constitutional Convention II
Compromise and Creativity

(*The Ideas of the Constitutional Convention*, by Samuel Paul Baird, reprinted by permission of the artist.)

The Constitutional Convention was four long, sweltering months of politics. Members recalled the experience as exhausting, frustrating and often disheartening in the extreme. Ben Franklin, his gout-swollen legs propped on pillows, fanned himself continually and came out with sprightly one-liners about the ordeal of it all—it was virtually the only comic relief.

Politics meant compromise. Almost everything had to be compromised—not once but over and over again. There were so many interests, agendas, motives and points of view to consider that not infrequently resolution appeared to be hopeless. And as in all compromises, no one liked the result. Indeed, at summer's end, some delegates concluded that their work had been compromised to death.

Politics also meant creativity. This was a bit more mysterious. It is one thing to bargain or horse trade, and quite another to come up with constitutional mechanisms that really work. "A free government," John Adams observed, "is a complicated piece of machinery, the nice and exact adjustment of whose springs, wheels, and weights, is not yet well comprehended by the artists of the age, and still less by the people."

Opposing Forces

The story of the Constitutional Convention can be told in terms of two sets of opposing forces. What we might call the "centripetal" forces were the cohesive ones that tended to draw the states together to form a strong union. And the "centrifugal" forces were those that tended to drive the states apart.

Centripetal Forces

Had there been no cohesive forces drawing the states together, the project of union would have soon faltered. What were those "centripetal" forces?

- Impotence of the Confederation and the Threat of Anarchy

We have already seen something of the Confederation's impotence. It was much on the minds of the Philadelphia delegates. The problems went well beyond difficulties in obtaining public credit or the free-for-all in interstate commerce.

The Debate:
http://www.yale.edu/lawweb/
avalon/debates/debcont.htm

Centripetal forces:

183

Martial law had been declared in Georgia. A group in the New York legislature was allegedly negotiating with the Viceroy of Canada. And in Massachusetts, the worst case, Shays Rebellion seemed to confound the American Revolution itself.

Problems in the West may have been even worse. Spain had closed the lower Mississippi and was inciting Indian tribes to harass the frontier. The British were fostering similar intrigues in the Great Lakes. Some disgruntled westerners had begun to question affiliation with the East on any terms. "It will not be an easy matter to bring the Americans to act as a nation," gloated Lord Sheffield, adding, "They are not to be feared as such by us."

Anarchy was not an attractive prospect. Thirteen independent states, fighting and bickering among themselves, forming alliances and counteralliances, conspiring with foreign powers, using force to settle their disputes—was something like the nationalists' worst nightmare. "Look at the public countenance, from New Hampshire to Georgia!," cried Edmund Randolph. "Are we not on the eve of war, which is only prevented by the hopes from this Convention?"

- A Vision of American Nationhood

American nationalism was a by-product of the Revolution. It had sprouted in various places and for various reasons, but none was more important than in the ranks of the Continental Army, where young men had come together from all around the colonies to fight for a common purpose.

What the vision of an American nation looked like might be pasted together from scattered references. For some it was a peaceful, happy Arcadia stretching across the continent. For others it was a realm of promise and prosperity. Classical republicans described it as a people devoted to republican principles—justice, dignity, the rule of law—and to great human achievements. For the democratic republicans it was a place of equality, without rich or poor, where ordinary citizens counted. Virtually all the nationalists portrayed it as a power respected in the eyes of the world. Above all, it was a land of liberty.

That this was to become a compelling vision is an understatement. We have seen so many representations of it in patriotic songs and poetry, in election broadsides and celebratory posters, in symbols and effigies and Miss Liberty herself that we easily forget it was *created* not *revealed*.

- Strong Leadership and Esprit de Corps

While most of the delegates at Philadelphia leaned toward a stronger union, most Americans did not—at least not yet. Because they were swimming against the tide, the nationalists enjoyed unusually strong leadership. They were well organized, determined and politically savvy, and they had a knack for bringing things off. The battle they were now fighting was reminiscent of the battle they had once fought against the British. The mood in the Pennsylvania State House was often one of patriots called together at a time of crisis.

- George Washington

Washington may well have been the Convention's most important asset. Certainly he was a centripetal influence of the first order. He had become a symbol of the Revolution and a living embodiment of American nationhood. He was among the earliest and most energetic of the nationalists, writing poignant laments from Mount Vernon over the Confederation's sorry state. "Weak at home and disregarded abroad is our present condition, and contemptible enough it is," he fumed.

Our image of Washington as being above the fray of politics obscures how politically adept he was. The merest handful of US presidents can compare. He realized that his principal benefit to the Convention would be in his physical presence rather than positions he might take or theories he might expound. All the same, no one doubted where his heart lay. And when they saw him, day in and day out, anxiously engaged in the cause, all those images of the Revolution came back to mind. Washington held the Convention together and kept it on task as surely as he had done with the Continental Army.

Centrifugal Forces

The obstacles to be overcome were daunting, to say the least. They were not quirks in the minds of individual delegates but deeply rooted ideas, interests and opinions in American political society. The delegates only mirrored what was out there.

Centrifugal forces:

We must also remember that the American people had to ratify any proposal the delegates worked out. Surmounting difficulties among fifty-five men seated together in a room was one thing—winning the support of a diverse and often conflicted public opinion was quite another. The Framers worked, as it were, with skeptical constituents looking over their shoulders. If they gave away too much at the bargaining table, their work would surely come to naught.

In a manner of speaking, then, the story of the "centrifugal forces" and how they were overcome is the real story of the Constitution.

- The Confederation

Impotent though it was, the Confederation was recognized as America's legitimate government. It had won the war against Great Britain and proven itself capable of at least some governance. There were those who spoke of the Articles of Confederation with deepest respect, and several of the Philadelphia delegates had been among its authors.

The Confederation resolved the problem of territorial expansion by ceding all territorial claims to the central government.

Public opinion favored the idea of repairing the Confederation, shoring it up in crucial areas and plugging the main leaks, and most Americans seemed to think this was truly possible. Some historians have argued that the Confederation was not beyond hope and might indeed have been put into working order.

The moment the Philadelphia delegates went beyond their instructions to rehabilitate the Confederation, they entered a legal and ethical limbo. They had been sent by the states but under the authority of the Confederation to accomplish a prescribed task. Would the American public sustain their decision to toss a working government onto the trash heap? Doubts about this question dogged the Convention's heels from the beginning.

- The States

Unlike the Confederation, the American states were robust republican sovereignties. Each had its own identity, its own history, its own social structure and economic life, its own feeling of wholeness, its own culture and sense of style. And each was in the grip of powerful local interests who were not about to let go.

What the **Virginia Plan (Resolves)** proposed was essentially to put the states out of business. Under the strong national government envisioned by Madison, state governments would be reduced to administrative units, much like counties today, their sovereignty but a memory. Needless to say, not a single one of them contemplated such a step.

There was more than simple jealousy at work here. Political theory held that only a small, cohesive and culturally homogeneous society could exist as a republic. People had to know one another in order to exercise the responsibilities of citizenship, and they had to participate in a government close at hand. The convenient term for what the nationalists had in mind was not *republic* but *empire*.

Accordingly, many of the delegates had been sent to Philadelphia with explicit warnings not to tamper with the states. At the mere thought of such tampering, several delegates packed up and went home.

• The "Convention Breakers"

The last two centrifugal forces deserve a place of their own in this chapter. For these "convention breakers" very nearly did that—broke the Convention. One of them seemed odd and out of place. The other was only too predictable. How the delegates dealt with them takes us into the inner dynamics of how the Convention worked. These issues were, in turn, the question of large states versus small states, and the question of slavery.

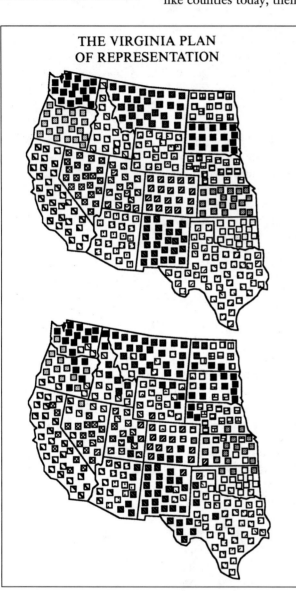

THE VIRGINIA PLAN OF REPRESENTATION

The Virginia Plan was to have representation in a national legislature based on the size of respective state populations. Small states feared that this would make for domination by large states (top). In practice, however, representatives were more likely to represent local or regional interests, which did not group within state lines (bottom). Actually, it would be the people of the United States, not individual states, that such a body would really represent.

Large States Versus Small

Going into the Convention, few delegates worried about a political difficulty in which a couple of large, populous states would be on one side and more numerous small states would be on the other. But just such a conflict awaited them. For there was a perception on the part of ten smaller states that Massachusetts, Pennsylvania and Virginia were bullies and troublemakers.

The charge was not wholly imaginary. The Big Three, as we might call them, were much larger and more populous than their neighbors.

Tyranny of the Majority

Were there actual situations in which people were simply voted to death? Indeed there were. In the French Revolution it occurred several times. The incident the world remembered best was the execution of the king.

In truth, Louis XVI posed a difficult problem for the Revolution. Now he would accept the new order and now he wouldn't. He was docile one moment and hostile the next. It occurred to the Jacobins that as long as Louis Capet was alive and dithering, he would be a rallying point for royalism within the country and intrigue without.

But how, exactly, to get rid of the king? Most of the deputies favored some sort of trial. After all, if law was really to govern the new republic, then bring Louis before a high court, charge him with treason, present evidence and carry out the sentence.

At that point, however, the constitutional scholars began scratching their heads. The new constitution specified "inviolability" for most of the king's actions. Besides, what were the specific crimes he could be charged with, and where was the evidence for his guilt?

But Robespierre, the leader of the Jacobins, cut through the tangles cleanly. Addressing the Assembly on December 3, 1792, he recast the issues in the most practical terms. "This is no question of a trial," he said, "Louis is not a defendant; you are not judges, but statesmen, and the representatives of the people. You have not to give a verdict for or against an individual, but to adopt a measure for public safety. . . .We talk of a republic, and Louis still lives!" The logic seemed convincing. Call it a trial if you will, and call the deputies judges, but don't worry about specific laws or details of evidence. Just vote.

On January 14, the voting began. The first question was whether Louis was guilty. (No crime was alleged, just guilt.) By a vote of 683 to 65, it was decided that he was. The second question was the choice of punishment. There, the vote was closer: 361 for immediate death, 72 for temporary reprieve and imprisonment, and 288 for imprisonment or exile. If the votes for reprieve and imprisonment were added together, they came to 360. Louis lost by a single vote.

The sentence was carried out in the Place de la Revolution on the morning of January 21, 1793. Like all affairs of the guillotine, it was short and simple. And at the end of it the people shouted: "*Le Roi est mort: Vive la nation!*"

One vote!

Their histories went back further, and they sometimes regarded sister colonies as offshoots or afterthoughts. They did indeed throw their weight around occasionally and believed they had a right to do so. And they wondered why it was that in the affairs of the Confederation, the vote of a single Rhode Islander was equal to that of eight or ten Virginians.

For Madison and the nationalists, this injustice simply had to be corrected. Any republic worthy of the name must represent the people *as* people, they said, and it must act upon them the same way. If a government gave equal representation to states, then it represented states and not people. By the same token, if it could not command (and of course punish) individuals, it could never be sovereign. If, for example, smugglers violated commercial laws in the sovereign-state sort of polity, the national government could never arrest and try them directly; it could only "request" that they be apprehended by some state—and perhaps be told to go to hell. For the nationalists, this was unacceptable.

The code word for their philosophy was *proportional representation*. That is, government must represent the people proportionally and act upon them as full citizens. The thinking may have been sound enough theoretically but it ignored that whole history of large-versus-small-state friction. So when the small state delegates looked over the Virginia Resolves, they saw something entirely different from the people being given a voice: they saw large states dominating the union—and small states getting shorted. That was not Madison's intention. What he envisioned was a withering of *all* states, small *and* large. Put another way, he imagined the American Republic as a single consolidated entity in which state boundaries were irrelevant and human beings were all that mattered.

But how did it look to the New Jersey delegation? It looked like going home and announcing that their state had become a colonial possession of dreaded Pennsylvania. Delegates from the small states saw themselves as fighting for their very existence.

James Madison was not often politically blind, but in this instance he came close to it. While he and the other nationalists kept insisting that the problem was artificial and would soon go away, quite the reverse was true. It got worse and worse. Given the fact that the small states outnumbered the large ones eight to three, and that the voting was equal among all eleven, it was remarkable that the nationalists were able to push the Virginia Plan toward tentative adoption. They were able to do so by building a coalition between the three largest states and the three southernmost ones—which believed they too would someday be populous. (At the time, Georgia had a smaller population than tiny Delaware.) It was a tribute to the political skills of Madison and his colleagues that they were able to keep this alliance together and operating.

New Jersey/Paterson Plan: Representation equal for each state regardless of population.

In the face of the large-state juggernaut, the small states, led by William Paterson of New Jersey, asked for time to regroup and come up with their own plan. Given the realities of the situation, the **Paterson**, or **New Jersey**, **Plan** was necessarily a moderate revision of the old Confederation. It would delegate to the national government some increased authority, but it stuck to the principle of equal representation of the states.

The New Jersey Plan was no more appealing to the nationalists than was the Virginia Plan to the confederalists. As long as representation was based on the states, sovereignty would remain fragmented and the American nation a chimera. In a series of speeches beginning on June 16, the New Jersey Plan was debated by the Committee of the Whole and more or less demolished. "We must remember the language with which we began the Revolution," pleaded James Wilson: "'Virginia is no more, Massachusetts is no more, Pennsylvania is no more. We are now one nation of brethren, we must bury all local interests and distinctions.'"

On June 19 the small state plan was voted down seven states to three, with Madison's coalition holding firm. But that was not the end. The small states would never sign onto the Virginia Resolves, they said, and if push came to shove they would leave the Convention. The question for the large states was, should they let the small states leave?

Not without a try at compromise, said Connecticut's Roger Sherman. He had been thinking about the problem since the beginning of the Convention, and he had worked out the only solution possible. If there was to be a two-house legislature, he submitted, let each side claim one house for its own. Proportional representation in the lower house would preserve popular sovereignty, and equal representation in the upper house would preserve state sovereignty.

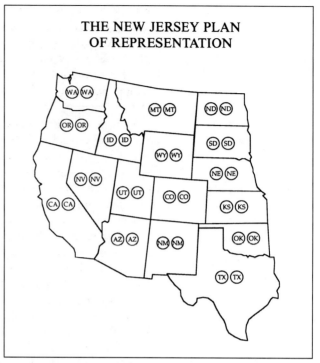

THE NEW JERSEY PLAN OF REPRESENTATION

The New Jersey Plan was to have equal representation of states within a national legislature. What was to be represented was the states, as sovereign bodies, not the people.

Because we take this solution for granted today, we overlook how bizarre it seemed at the time. Far from being a unified legislature representing the American people, Congress would be the strangest hybrid imaginable. And the rest of the country—would it be a single sovereignty (as indicated by the House) or multiple sovereignties (as indicated by the Senate)? The question seemed unfathomable.

For if political theory had one clear and settled idea, it was the idea of *sovereignty*. By its very definition, sovereignty could be vested only in a single authority. Accordingly, either the states must be sovereign, as they were in the present Confederation, or else the national government must. It was simply unimaginable that *both* could be sovereign at once.

However, this analysis missed an important point. Since any piece of legislation would have to pass *each* house independently, both principles could in fact be applied. A measure unacceptable to the American people would fail in the House, and a measure unacceptable to the American states would fail in the Senate. Perhaps it really *was* possible to have "parallel sovereignties" at work.

Lacking our hindsight, both sides saw Sherman's compromise as a defeat and dug in their heels. But the small states dug in less vigorously. Indeed, given the fact they were outvoted, small state delegates came to see the compromise as a rescue—the way a losing team might view the sudden hope of a tie—and reluctantly gave it support. They would vote for proportional representation in the lower house, they said, if Madison and his cohorts would vote for equal representation in the upper house.

But Madison balked. If states were the problem and union the solution, how else to view this ungainly proposal than as a disaster, he asked? And if the small states wanted to walk, let them do so. In the end they would have no choice but to come around.

So began the long, hot summer. It commenced with the two halves of Sherman's compromise framed as separate votes, and both taken on June 19. Proportional representation passed for the lower house. And equal representation *failed* for the upper. The nationalists had held their alliance together and their forces in line. The small state delegates cried betrayal. Then the Convention began slugging it out.

Day in and day out, the slugging continued. The large states threatened to unite on their own. The small states threatened to seek out foreign powers. The delegates grew weary. Tempers flared. "I . . . declare," shouted William Paterson, "that I will never consent to the present system. . . . Myself or my state will never submit to tyranny or despotism." James Wilson answered him icily. "The gentleman from New Jersey is candid in declaring his opinion," he said. "I commend him for it. I am equally so. I say again I never will confederate on his principles. If no state will part with any of its sovereignty it is in vain to talk of a national government." There was a great deal more.

As June wore into July, the deadlock continued. Neither side was willing to budge, for both saw too much at stake. The speeches grew tiring and repetitious. The heat made everything worse. Some delegates went back to their homes for a respite—several never to return. And hope for a settlement began to ebb away. It was, wrote William Few on June 28, "an awful and critical moment. If the Convention had then adjourned, the dissolution of the union . . . seemed inevitable."

While the dream of an American nation teetered on the abyss, the facilitators of compromise mustered their forces. Benjamin Franklin, for example. While he stood squarely with the nationalists, he also saw the need for a resolution. So, after listening to the umpteenth large-state-versus-small-state speech, he facetiously offered to chop Pennsylvania into small states if that would solve the problem. At other times he lectured like a schoolmaster. "When a broad table is to be made and the edges of planks do not fit," he intoned, "the artist takes a little from both, and makes a good joint. In like manner here both sides must part with some of their demands, in order that they may join in some accommodating proposition."

This was when "the doctor," as he was often called, made his historic plea for divine aid. He reminded the delegates that during the Revolutionary War the Continental Congress had often prayed for guidance in the very room where they now sat. "I firmly believe," he went on, "that without [God's] concurring aid we shall succeed in this political building no better than the builders of Babel. We shall be divided by our little partial local interests; our projects will be confounded and we ourselves shall become a reproach and bye word down to future ages."

Franklin's motion was not adopted, most likely for want of a chaplain, yet his plea may not have been without effect. They did stand at the judgment bar of history, some realized, and destiny did sit among them in this hall. And Franklin's appeal to a sense of the universal couldn't help but strike an American cord. God, he suggested, had favored their cause in order to favor that of mankind. "And what is worse," he added, "mankind may hereafter from this unfortunate instance despair of establishing government by human wisdom and leave it to chance, war, and conquest."

Whether by divine intervention or otherwise, events did take an unexpected turn. On July 2 the question of representation was voted on again—this time with a different result. Both Maryland and Georgia had been voting with the nationalist majority to produce a 7-to-3 result. This time, however, Maryland delegate Daniel of St. Thomas Jenifer was strangely absent when the vote was taken, and that swung the state's precarious delegation in favor of Sherman's compromise. Madison was still reeling from that blow when a second one fell. Abraham Baldwin of Georgia switched sides and nullified the Georgia vote entirely. The 7-to-3 majority was suddenly a 5-to-5 tie.

Now at a complete loss, the delegates appointed one of their Grand Committees (one member from each state) to try to work through the impasse. This group labored through the Fourth of July holiday to have a compromise proposal ready on the fifth—but the nationalists simply rejected it. They might not be able to go forward but they weren't going back either. That evening Luther Martin wrote that the Convention was on the verge of collapse.

And nine more days of stalemate still lay ahead. In the records, this period resolved itself into a wearisome blur. The summer heat was now record breaking. The flies buzzed and stung. The debates spun around and around. On July 10, Robert Yates and John Lansing Jr. departed for New York, promising to fight against any document the Convention might produce. Hamilton had already left. That a state as important as New York was now completely unrepresented further deepened the gloom. Washington wrote that he despaired of finding a way out—and regretted his own involvement.

On July 16 the heat wave finally broke. There were storms the night before, and with the dawn came cool breezes. The final vote was scheduled for the Connecticut Compromise and Madison, although bone weary, was confident that it would be rejected once and for all. But another surprise was in store for him. When the vote was taken, two of the Massachusetts delegates had unaccountably changed their minds—the vote split and Massachusetts was out. Maryland was back in the nationalist fold, a repentant

Philadelphia as the delegates saw it. Its Bengal heat, glittering society and bustling environment furnished a backdrop to the Constitutional Convention. (*Second Street, North from Market Street and Christ Church, Philadelphia,* by William Birch, courtesy of Independence National Historical Park, Philadelphia.)

Daniel Jenifer gazing birdlike over the rims of his bifocals—but now North Carolina defected. Madison's gasp was almost audible.

There was a climactic, mud-spattered entry by Alexander Hamilton, who had hastened back from New York for this very moment of truth. He dramatically cast the winning vote with the nationalists. But, alas, the rules of procedure forbade his participation. At least two delegates had to be in residence for a state to be officially represented, and the other New Yorkers had gone home.

Accordingly, the Connecticut Compromise passed, five states to four.

For those who consider the turn of cards in history, there was much to ponder. Daniel Jenifer's mysterious absence. Franklin's appeal to Providence. Abraham Baldwin's sudden change of mind. Votes switched at the very center of the nationalist coalition. The appearance of a procedural rule so obscure that the delegates had to stop and look it up. These small things had literally made an American nation possible.

Not least to ponder was the attitude of James Madison. He had watched his majority shrink, then falter, then die. He was numb with despair. When the small states had lost early on, they threatened to abandon the Convention. Madison made no such threat now. He returned to his lodgings and perhaps to his books. Later that evening, at the Lion Cafe, he still wasn't smiling, but he was grudgingly ready to propose a toast. This truly was a new kind of government, he allowed, one for which there was absolutely no precedent in history. It was on the one hand a government of the sovereign people of America, and on the other hand a government of the sovereign states. "Gentlemen," he said, "to the United *States* of America."

North, South and Slavery

The compromise over state sovereignty was an example of what we might call "constitutional serendipity," where an agreement forged in direst necessity was later revealed to be a source of great benefit. The Constitution eventually abounded in such windfalls. The compromise over slavery was not one of them, however. Quite the opposite.

Some scholars believe that agreements worked out over slavery at the Philadelphia Convention made the Civil War inevitable. At the very least it legitimized a practice far out of keeping with republican principles. The question becomes, then, why should such a "monstrous contradiction" be woven into the very fabric of the Constitution?

An answer of recent popularity holds that the Framers could not help but act out of ideological interest. After all, they were white Protestant males—and five of the Core Framers (not to mention George Washington) held slaves themselves. Hopefully we have learned to be wary of such tidiness. The real situation at the Convention was far more complex, far more ambiguous and in hindsight, far more tragic. It wasn't a simple case of master-class ideology.

Slavery, like state sovereignty, was a historical accident. It had made sense in colonial times, perhaps, but appreciably less sense now. By the end of the Revolution most Americans were at least mildly apologetic about it and some were downright hostile. Still, as David Hume had pointed out, what *is* established has its own validity, and slavery was established only too well.

Colonial slavery had been no one's particular fault—and at the same time everyone's. Labor was scarce. Conditions were harsh. And the wholesale kidnapping and selling of Africans had been a thriving enterprise for centuries. Oddly, as it seems to us now, most colonists never really thought about its moral implications one way or the other.

Eventually though, opposition to the practice did develop. It appeared first in Quaker Pennsylvania and from there spread to Puritan New England and elsewhere. By the time of the Revolution, slavery had more or less died out in most northern colonies. Its lack of economic viability was as important as moral repugnance in its demise—it simply didn't work very well. The Revolution also played a role. How, Americans asked, could someone be willing to fight and die for liberty if that person owned slaves?

At the same time, however, slavery got a second wind in the South. While the cotton gin had not yet been invented, tobacco, rice and indigo cultivation were all growth industries, and other forms of slave-driven enterprise were creating new promise. By the summer of 1787 slavery was not the "dying institution" it has sometimes been characterized.

We should also be clear about what was and wasn't conceded at the Philadelphia Convention. Literally none of the delegates imagined their mandate to include the possible elimination of slavery no matter how out of keeping it might be. Their task was to work out a better government—not work out a better society. Besides, they were already operating on the margins of what was politically possible, and taking on slavery would have put them far over the line. Whatever else it was, slavery was a system designed to insure white domination over an alien, stigmatized and resentful populace whose concentration in some areas inspired terror. For some whites it was a matter of self-preservation.

The real question dealt with the future. Many northerners (and some southerners) believed that slavery was on its way to eventual extinction, so why make a fuss over it? The answer in three words was: *the slave trade*. With a steady supply of new slaves, all sorts of eventual possibilities opened up. New kinds of crops might be cultivated. New uses for slave labor might be developed. And the new lands of the West were out there beckoning.

So, what about the slave trade? We recall that one of the Convention's central concerns was the regulation of commerce. It promised enormous benefits but was fraught with thorny side issues. The power to regulate commerce might become a weapon of destruction in the rivalry of the regions, for example. If one region gained control over the central government, it might seek to stifle another region's interests simply by burdening certain kinds of commerce— such as the slave trade.

Here was a possible scenario. The North gains control over Congress and immediately throttles slave imports. The effect, of course, would be to weaken the South, both economically and politically, which some northerners might

In parts of the Carolinas, the ratio of slaves to whites was as high as 50 to 1.

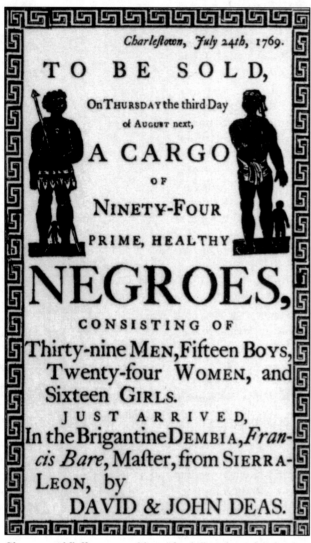

Charleſtown, July 24th, 1769.

TO BE SOLD,

On THURSDAY the third Day
of AUGUST next,

A CARGO

OF

NINETY-FOUR

PRIME, HEALTHY

NEGROES,

CONSISTING OF

**Thirty-nine MEN, Fifteen Boys,
Twenty-four WOMEN, and
Sixteen GIRLS.**

JUST ARRIVED,

In the Brigantine DEMBIA, *Francis Bare*, Maſter, from SIERRA-
LEON, by

DAVID & JOHN DEAS.

*Slavery, said Jefferson, was like a "fire bell in the night" for the
American Republic.*
(Courtesy of the American Antiquarian Society, Worcester,
Massachusetts.)

not particularly regret. At least there would be no further expansion of slavery nor contradiction in American ideals—for slavery really *would* be bound for extinction.

The question for the southern delegates, then, was whether they wanted to take such a chance? Some of course didn't; it was just too risky. Others did, though, and they had their reasons. Some of them harbored their own qualms about slavery. (George Mason of Virginia, for one, stood up in General Assembly and gave a rousing abolitionist speech.) Others saw the institution as a liability. Sooner or later, they knew, a slave-owning society was bound to experience servile insurrections, and these in turn could lead to foreign intermeddling and even worse complications. With slavery, they had a wolf by the ears, as Jefferson put it, and wondered if they ought not turn around and run.

There was potential here for a compromise and there were delegates capable of effecting it. Two of them were William Samuel Johnson of Connecticut and John Rutledge of South Carolina. They shared an important commonality. Both states were entirely dependent on exports for their income, and thus neither wanted to see taxes placed on exported goods. The Connecticut delegates were masterful politicians, too, and they spent much of their leisure time with the charming Carolinians.

Over port one evening, Johnson and Rutledge worked out the following agreement. Southerners would support the New England position on commercial regulation—that is, no power to tax exports, only imports—and New England would support the southern position on the slave trade. The Constitution would bar any interference with such trade for the next twenty years. That would give the South a hedge on the future.

This agreement touched only one aspect of the slavery problem. There were two others. The first was the question of how slaves should be counted, both for representation and taxation purposes. The southern position was clear if self-serving. Slaves ought to be counted as "persons" in calculating representation and as "property" in calculating taxes. In other words, let the slave population amplify the South's voice in Congress without increasing its tax liability. This the northern delegates couldn't abide. It would give the South a fixed and permanent political advantage, while at the same time boosting the traffic in slaves. One Yankee, Elbridge Gerry of Massachusetts, drily observed that slaves in the South were used to perform the labor of horses and mules in the North. Why not allow horses and mules representation? he asked.

This time compromise was proposed by James Wilson. Peering through the thick lenses that were always perched precariously on the end of his nose, Wilson dug up an old fraction used in the Articles of Confederation. Suppose the slave population were to be counted for three-fifths of the free population both for taxation and representation, he said. It was a shade better than half a loaf both ways. After a great deal more discussion, the southerners reluctantly agreed. Without the "federal ratio," Hamilton said later on, "no union could possibly have been formed." But there was another hidden cost. Now slavery was both recognized and protected in the Constitution—not for twenty years but forever.

The final element of the slavery compromise involved the recovery of fugitives. There were not a few northerners who would prove sympathetic to the cause of runaway slaves, as the Underground Railroad would someday show, and it would be easy for local governments to throw stumbling blocks in the way of recapture. The Constitution, said the southern delegates, must forbid such legislation absolutely.

Underground Railroad: Support system that assisted fugitive slaves.

Here was yet another painful dilemma. Northerners knew there would be opportunities for gross abuse, and indeed, literally tens of thousands of free blacks would be kidnapped into slavery under the terms of Article IV, Section 1. Yet one purpose of the national union was to protect property, all kinds of property, and the slaves sadly were that.

We can see these compromises as the requisite price of union. Yet we can also see them as a missed opportunity of tragic proportions. For while the abolition of slavery was beyond the Convention's capacity, closer limits on slave expansion might not have been. The South would not have been pleased by such limits, but it might well have accepted them.

As it was, in the twenty years of grace given to the slavetraders, more than a million *more* Africans would be imported into the South. The abundant supply would keep prices low, and low prices would fuel rapid expansion. Slavery would go on to accomplish everything the prophets of doom had foretold.

Creative Chemistry

So much for the politics of half a loaf. There was another kind of politics at work—a politics of innovation. On the surface, the two looked much the same. Both required haggling. Both entailed maneuvering and arm-twisting. Yet with the politics of innovation there was a different end in view: to come up with ideas that worked.

We have already seen that a group of some fifteen Core Delegates led out in the Convention's work. A useful way to understand how these central players interacted is to identify three separate roles they tended to play:

- Visionaries

We can think of the visionaries as political philosophers. They were the last-ditch nationalists like Madison, Hamilton, Wilson, the two Morrises and Charles Pinckney. They were "visionary" because they believed, without much proof, that a republic could be fashioned of imperial size and placed under a strong central government. Their role was to convince the others that it could really be done—and that *they* could figure out how.

- Innovators

If the visionaries were political philosophers, the innovators were political scientists. They were the ones who had to come up with the working dynamics of the new system. Sometimes they could draw upon the experience of the states for ideas, and sometimes they could borrow from Hume or Montesquieu. In a significant number of cases they had to figure things out for themselves.

The Convention's primary innovators were James Madison, James Wilson and Gouverneur Morris, with an important secondary in George Mason, Edmund Randolph, Oliver Ellsworth, Elbridge Gerry and Charles Pinckney. They worked together well, for the most part, and often in a characteristic pattern of interaction, as we shall soon observe.

- Facilitators

If the visionaries were political philosophers and the innovators were political scientists, the facilitators were old-fashioned politicians. It was their job to make sure that any idea the innovators came up with would be workable, practical and above all, acceptable to the people.

Some of the facilitators were masters of compromise. They could take antithetical positions and figure out a way to reconcile them. However, some of the facilitators performed the opposite function—steadfastly *refusing* to compromise. This too had a purpose, for if the Framers had compromised on some kinds of issues their work never would have been ratified. And there were other implements in the facilitators' toolbox. One was a knack for building alliances. Another was the art of persuasion. And a third might simply be called brokerage—the ability to work out political bargains.

Among the facilitators were Edmund Randolph of Virginia, Rufus King of Massachusetts, John Dickinson of Delaware and John Rutledge of South Carolina. Both Paterson of New Jersey and Madison of Virginia refused to compromise, famously so, when much was at stake, but on the other side, Benjamin Franklin spoke often and movingly of the need to accept half a loaf.

The best facilitator of all was Roger Sherman. The Connecticut delegation, of which Sherman was the leading member, was an engine of facilitation, with both William Samuel Johnson and Oliver Ellsworth playing roles similar to Sherman's. But Sherman handled the tough cases. He was one of the Convention's lowborn and self-made delegates, of a square-set, no-nonsense countenance. He was the only member who might be called a politician by profession, having served in one post or another for the whole of his adult life—and he truly was a pro.

Designing the Presidency

The chemistry of the Convention made some rather startling innovations possible. We might trace in detail how one of these was developed in order to gain a clearer picture of the Convention at work. The creation of the presidency is a good example. It shows how visionaries, innovators and facilitators interacted with one another in complex and sometimes surprising ways, and how together they created something entirely new.

(By Bill Mauldin, courtesy of Weston Bershoof.)

On the subject of the executive, the Framers began with nothing but questions. What is an executive? What do executives do? What constitutional mechanisms would promote appropriate executive behavior? Or *mis*behavior? There was a whole science to be learned.

As a beginning assumption, most of the Framers supposed that a weak executive—or executives, plural—would suit the American purpose best. This was the model used in several states and it had been proposed in the Virginia Resolves as well. The thinking was that since legislatures reflect the will of the people, executives ought simply to do the lawmakers' bidding.

When the issue was first taken up on June 1, however, one delegate had a markedly different idea. James Wilson proposed that the executive be a strong office, not a weak one, and be occupied by a single individual of "energy" and "dispatch." The motion received no second. "Energy" in an executive was no blessing, scolded Roger Sherman; it was a dangerous prelude to tyranny. Edmund Randolph agreed. A single executive was nothing but a "fetus of monarchy," he said.

But Wilson came back with a surprising argument. He had a skeptical, Socratic mind that cut like a razor through specious reasoning. He also had a strong bias toward democracy, which had something to do with the rugged, egalitarian world of his youth in the Scottish lowlands. Think about it, he began, a single executive, *if elected by the people*, might be just the opposite of the bugaboo tyrant—a safeguard *against* tyranny. Think about the dynamics involved. The single executive, with his own accountability, might provide a sort of counterweight to the legislature. If the latter got out of line—as it had in Wilson's own state—the executive might be inclined to resist it, for he would be mindful of the people who elected him. Wilson may have been pondering Adams' *Thoughts on Government* or the Massachusetts Model Constitution, both of which supported strong executives. Yet he was reasoning his way toward an entirely new constitutional idea.

The following day, two of the South Carolinians, John Rutledge and Charles Pinckney, declared themselves persuaded by Wilson's arguments and echoed his call for a single executive. But Randolph dissented yet again. There ought to be an executive committee of three, he insisted, whose members would be drawn from different parts of the country, and the three would have to work out agreement among themselves.

Executive Tyranny

With the benefit of hindsight, we see the Constitution today much as its supporters (the Federalists) did: as a preserver of republican freedom. But how did it look to the doubters? In a single word, threatening. Not benefiting form our hindsight, the Anti-Federalists could see only tyranny in the Constitution's provision for a strong and vigorous central government.

James Lincoln of South Carolina was typical: "From a well-digested, well-formed democratic you are at once rushing into an aristocratic government," he cried. Pennsylvania's James Warren agreed. "The Constitution will result in an immediate aristocratic tyranny," he said, "that from the difficulty, if not the impracticability of its operation, must soon terminate in the most uncontrolled despotism!" George Mason of Virginia had still another set of doubts. "The executive and the Senate form a combination that cannot be prevented by the representatives," he fretted. "The executive and legislation powers thus connected will destroy all balances."

The Anti-Federalists were missing a fine but nonetheless important point. A government with the right structure could be powerful without being tyrannical. Indeed, it must be powerful in order to maintain the rule of law. "A weak constitution," said Madison, "must necessarily terminate in dissolution. . . . Tyranny has perhaps oftener grown out of the assumptions of power [under] a defective constitution, than out of the full exercise of the largest constitutional authorities." That, as it turned out, was the view sanctioned by hindsight.

Wilson had an answer for that proposal too and he submitted it the next time the question came up. A three-man committee would simply bicker among itself and never decide anything, he said. Besides, single executives were found in several state governments, and *they* hadn't morphed into monarchs. Did Wilson's eye twinkle when he said this?—for the doubting Randolph happened to be one of them.

Roger Sherman, who the week before had scorned the idea of a single executive, now swung around and came on board himself. However, the executive ought to consult a council before acting, he added. Wilson demurred yet again. A council would *cover* malpractice, not *prevent* it, he argued. If something went wrong, the executive would blame the council and the council members would blame each other. All sense of accountability would be lost.

The Convention voted seven states to three in favor of a single executive and left the council question up in the air. Wilson was making headway. As discussion now switched to other features of the office, the delegates reflected again and again on the curious idea of a strong executive and strong legislature playing against one another to create balance. At least one of them, Gouverneur Morris, found the idea preposterous and spoke forcefully against it. But others began to come along. In the end, they voted to kill the council idea and go with a single executive.

Most of the delegates still favored his election by the legislature, however. There was a way to accomplish it, they thought, that would still let the executive function as a counterweight. If he were limited to a single term, for example, there would be no incentive for him to be the legislature's yes-man in order to insure his reelection. But, then, that single term would have to be a long one—maybe seven years or so—in order to keep from constantly changing executives, and with a seven-year term, what would keep him from straying into corruption? Well, there would have to be some mechanism of impeachment. The problem was getting a bit sticky.

Besides, Wilson still had his own idea. He had won the day on the question of single versus plural—perhaps he was feeling lucky. Why not, he urged, seriously consider election by the people instead of the legislature? The question must have been greeted by blank faces. Leaving aside the advisability of such a practice, how on earth could it be brought off? How could three million people scattered over a continent have the slightest idea how to nominate candidates, how to winnow them down to a manageable number, and how to make the final choice among them?

Wilson was undaunted. He volunteered to sit down and see if he could work something out. And the following day, July 2, he returned as promised with a set of concrete proposals. Let the states be divided into large districts, he said, and let the voters in each district cast ballots for electors. Let these electors then meet together in some designated place and elect the executive. Wilson's colleagues were not impressed with this contraption of springs and wires, and they voted it down forthwith. They opted instead to have the executive chosen by the Congress and be ineligible for reelection.

The matter was shelved for the time being and the Convention turned its attention elsewhere. When it took up the executive issue again, the Great Compromise between large and small states had been achieved, and it was clear that subtle balances had shifted. For one thing, several delegates had been pondering

Wilson's counterweight mechanism and its possible value. And now that the small states had a national government they could live with, their representatives viewed the strong executive concept more kindly. Gouverneur Morris was among those who had undergone a change of heart. Wilson was right, he said flatly: the executive ought to be chosen by the people.

Hard-headed Roger Sherman was still unpersuaded, however. The people would never be informed well enough to make a wise choice, he lectured, and even if they were, they could never muster a majority for any given candidate. So Wilson thought it all through once again. Maybe the popular vote wouldn't reach a majority, he allowed, but there was still a way to make the system work. In the absence of a majority, let the election be decided by the legislature, choosing among the strongest candidates. That way, the people would in effect do the nominating and the legislature would make the final pick.

Parties now emerged. Pinckney of South Carolina and Mason of Virginia led the fight against election by the people, while Wilson and Morris of Pennsylvania pressed it forward. The Convention listened to both sides and voted once again for election by the legislature. Only this time they struck out the ineligibility clause. If the executive was doing a good job, why shouldn't he be able to run again?

But that brought back the old problem of kowtowing to the legislature. James McClurg of Virginia, a delegate who had been sent to the Convention on short notice and had taken little part up to now, suddenly announced that he had the answer. Let the legislature elect the executive, he submitted, but let the executive *serve for life*. That way, there would be no need to curry favor with the lawmakers. Some delegates took the idea seriously. Gouverneur Morris, who had never shared the American disdain for monarchy, was so delighted with the election-for-life proposal that he switched sides once again.

Sherman, however, was unmoved. Monarchy is precisely what we would wind up with in an executive elected for life, he opined heatedly, and didn't we recently fight a war about that? Sherman had learned his lessons in the school of hard knocks and he could be as plain spoken as a drill sergeant. But the elegant Virginians agreed with him. The executive *needed* to be dependent on the legislature, Randolph and Mason both concurred, or yes, he might very well become a tyrant.

It was at this point that James Madison entered the fray. He hadn't thought much about executives before coming to the Convention, and his own plan had called for a weak one. But all the to-ing and fro-ing had gotten him into the library, as it were. He hauled out his copy of Montesquieu, and on its authority concluded that Wilson might well be right. Make the executive independent of the legislature and you might wind up controlling them both, he said. Each could be strong and vigorous. Each could do its own separate job. Each could be responsible to the people. And if either began stepping out of line, it would automatically behoove the other to resist. Madison even affixed a name to the idea: **separation of powers**.

The Convention voted McClurg's proposal down at this point but it still wasn't ready to adopt Wilson's. Indeed, the debate dragged on and on, and in the course of it the delegates changed their minds a dozen times more. How could they come up with a strong executive, they wondered, without making him too strong? The problem seemed unresolvable.

On July 26, George Mason took the Convention right back to the beginning with a proposal for election by the legislature, a seven-year term and ineligibility for reelection. The weary delegates approved the plan 6 to 3 and sent it off to the Committee for Detail for drafting.

Another month went by. On August 24, the delegates turned to the Committee for Detail's write-up of what they had reluctantly agreed to back in July. It still didn't sound right. Election "by the legislature" meant what, exactly? they asked. Election by the House? That would give an advantage to the large states. Election by the Senate? That would give advantage to the small states. John Rutledge moved for the two houses to vote together in one body, which might balance the advantage out. His amendment carried.

But the dogged Wilson wasn't beaten yet. He and Gouverneur Morris made one more attempt to secure the election of the executive by the people. It was voted down yet again but this time by only a single vote, six states to five. The Pennsylvanians were making headway.

On August 31, the delegates, who were sick and tired of the whole business, voted to turn it over to an ad hoc committee. This was their last resort. The committee they chose happened to be unusually vigorous, however, with Sherman, Morris and Madison among its members. Morris and Madison must have had an earnest little talk with Sherman—who had left skid marks throughout the entire process—for quite without warning the committee voted to abandon election by the legislature and switch to Wilson's "electoral college." Further tinkering was required with the operating mechanism, but at last they had it. It was a delicate compromise, so delicate that the Convention might have rejected it out of hand had they not tried everything else. But, alas, they had.

So it was that the Constitutional Convention came up with a single executive, elected by "the people," with a four-year term of office, eligibility for re-election and provision for impeachment. He would be stronger by far than any executive they had considered back in June, and with that in mind they now proceeded to limit his powers very carefully. Still, they wound up giving him entire charge of the military, entire charge of foreign affairs, extensive charge of appointments and the conditional veto of legislative acts. That was a great deal.

Serendipity

In the course of its slow evolution, the idea of the executive had been turned inside out. Instead of a glorified servant who "executes" the will of Congress, the executive had become a kind of elective

"Remember, gentlemen, we aren't here just to draft a constitution. We're here to draft the best damn constitution in the world."
(By Peter Steiner, courtesy of the Cartoon Bank.)

monarch, imparting energy and vigor to government. It was an extremely important innovation—one for which no single individual was responsible.

James Wilson had played the leading role, both as visionary and innovator. Sherman, Randolph, Rutledge, Mason, Charles Pinckney and Gouverneur Morris had hammered out the politics, backing and forthing many times. The delegates couldn't have reached a solution without all three roles being played—nor could they have reached it without an emerging theory, "separation of powers," expounded by Madison, to legitimize it. Many of them still suspected the theory and wondered whether it would actually work in practice. But somehow it felt right to them. A powerful executive might become a despot, true enough, but to do so he would have to cross swords with an equally powerful Congress.

This was the process. It was full of false starts and misdirection. But its tendency was to cut through layers of partisanship, prejudice and political myopia, and reach toward something like truth. For the American presidency, despite its newfangledness, became one of the signal achievements of modern-day political science. None of the participants had gotten what he set out for in the beginning. Each had played off against the others, had backed into corners, had temporized, compromised, returned to the drawing board for new ideas and together had groped for a deeper wisdom than any could call his own.

There was an odd kind of "synergy" in the outcome. A whole was created by the collective endeavor that was greater than the sum of its parts. And, as it turned out, there was an equally odd "serendipity." Things had just happily fallen into place.

Suggestions for Further Reading

Catherine Drinker Bowen, *Miracle at Philadelphia: The Story of the Constitutional Convention, May to September 1787* (1966).

Christopher Collier and James Lincoln Collier, *Decision in Philadelphia: The Constitutional Convention of 1787* (1986).

Joseph L. Davis, *Sectionalism in American Politics, 1774–1787* (1977).

Dinesh D'Souza, "We the Slaveholders" *Policy Review* (Fall 1995).

William W. Freehling, "The Founding Fathers and Slavery," *American Historical Review* (February 1972).

Calvin C. Jillson, "Constitution-Making: Alignment and Realignment in the Federal Convention of 1787," *American Political Science Review* (September 1981).

Calvin C. Jillson, "The Representation Question in the Federal Convention of 1787: Madison's Virginia Plan and Its Opponents," *Congressional Studies* (1981).

Charles L. Mee Jr., *The Genius of the People* (1987).

Peter S. Onuf, *The Origins of the Federal Republic: Jurisdictional Controversies in the United States* (1983).

Gordon Wood, *The Creation of the American Republic, 1776–1787* (1969).

CHAPTER 7 STUDY AID ━━━━━━

(This aid is not all-inclusive and is not intended to be a substitute for thorough study of the material presented in the textbook.)

The Constitutional Convention II
Compromise and Creativity

I. Opposing Forces (Centripetal)

1. Confederation = anarchy?
   - Problems of credit and commerce
   - Martial law in Georgia
   - Shays Rebellion in Massachusetts
2. Vision of nationhood:
   - By-product of Revolution
   - Peaceful Arcadia
   - Realm of promise and prosperity
   - Justice, dignity and rule of law
   - Equality and liberty
3. Strength of leadership:
   - Going against public opinion
   - Organization
4. George Washington:
   - Symbol of the Revolution
   - Embodiment of nationhood
   - Physical presence

II. Opposing Forces (Centrifugal)

1. Public opinion:
   - Favored decentralized government
2. Confederation:
   - Still the legitimate government
   - In need of repair not replacement
   - Consequences if Convention exceeded its authority?
3. The states:
   - Sovereign
   - Virginia Resolves
   - Political theory
4. Convention breakers:
   - Large versus small states
   - Slavery

III. Large versus Small States

1. The big three:
   - Massachusetts, Pennsylvania and Virginia
2. Proportional representation:
   - Representing people not states in theory
   - Favored states with larger populations
3. New Jersey Plan:
   - William Paterson
   - Equal representation of states regardless of size
   - Unacceptable to larger states
4. Connecticut Compromise:
   - Roger Sherman
   - Two-house legislature
   - Proportional and equal representation
   - Parallel sovereignty?
   - Initially unacceptable to all parties
   - After long, hot summer small states reconsider and promote compromise

IV. Slavery

1. Monstrous contradiction:
   - Slavery—a historical accident
   - The South's peculiar institution
   - Delegates limited mandate
2. Compromise #1—commerce and the slave trade:
   - Strange bedfellows
   - William Samuel Johnson—Connecticut
   - John Rutledge—South Carolina
   - Striking a bargain—no tax on exports in exchange for twenty more years of the slave trade
3. Compromise #2—representation of slaves:
   - Counting slaves for representation and taxation?
   - Persons versus property
   - James Wilson and the three-fifths compromise
4. Compromise #3—fugitive slaves:
   - Slaves to be property

V. Creative Chemistry:

1. Visionaries:
   - Political philosophers
   - Last-ditch nationalists
   - Madison, Hamilton, etc.
2. Innovators:
   - Political scientists
   - Working dynamics
   - Madison, Wilson, Gouverneur Morris, etc.
3. Facilitators:
   - Politicians
   - The art of the practical
   - Public opinion
   - Sherman, Randolph, King, etc.

VI. Serendipity and the American Presidency

1. Innovation:
   - James Wilson
   - Single, strong executive
   - Election by the people
   - Madison—separation of powers
2. Electoral College:
   - Districts and electors
3. Serendipity:
   - False starts and misdirection
   - Compromise
   - A new thing—the American presidency

CHAPTER 7 REVIEW QUESTIONS ━━━━━━

Key Terms

Virginia Plan

New Jersey Plan

Proportional Representation

Connecticut Compromise

Serendipity

Visionaries

Innovators

Facilitators

Multiple Choice Questions

1. Which of the following was a centrifugal force at the Convention?
   a. The Confederation.
   b. George Washington.
   c. Vision of American nationhood.
   d. Esprit de corps.

2. The "Big Three" included all of the following except:
   a. Pennsylvania.
   b. New York.
   c. Massachusetts.
   d. Virginia.

3. Which of the following was not a part of the slavery compromise at the Convention?
   a. The Three-Fifths Compromise.
   b. A fugitive slave law.
   c. Abolition of slavery in the North.
   d. Ending the slave trade in 20 years.

4. Which of the following Convention delegates does the text consider an innovator?
   a. James Madison.
   b. Alexander Hamilton.
   c. John Rutledge.
   d. Benjamin Franklin.

Review Questions

1. What were the main tenets of the New Jersey Plan? How was this plan received by the nationalists?

   _____

   _____

   _____

   _____

2. Aside from his political ideas, how did Benjamin Franklin benefit the Convention in Philadelphia?

   _____

   _____

   _____

   _____

3. How did the passing of the Connecticut Compromise exemplify serendipity?

   _____

   _____

   _____

   _____

4. How did visionaries, innovators and facilitators contribute to the creation of the presidency?

   _____

   _____

   _____

   _____

5. In what ways did the compromises discussed in this chapter exemplify synergy?

   _____

   _____

   _____

   _____

Review Exercises

1. In the context of this chapter, explain what is meant by centripetal and centrifugal forces.

   _____

   _____

   _____

   _____

2. Describe the vision of nationhood that the nationalists shared.

_____

_____

_____

_____

3. Explain the terms "republic" and "empire" as the confederalists understood them.

_____

_____

_____

_____

Big Essay Question

The time has come to grapple with the issue of slavery and the Constitution. Were the Founders wrong not to abolish slavery at the Convention? Were they untrue to their ideals? Keeping in mind the time period they lived in, write a thoughtful essay either defending or condoning the slavery compromise. Show an understanding of opposing viewpoints as well.

The Constitutional Convention III
Structure and Dynamics

(*Dawn*, by Katy Neale, reprinted by permission of the artist.)

After Edmund Randolph's presentation of the Virginia Resolves, the delegates to the Grand Convention came to realize that they were not repairing the Articles of Confederation but designing a new government—a new *idea* of government—from the ground up. Thereafter, every motion, every agreement, every compromise, every tactical maneuver had to have some bearing on the development of "the plan"—a working constitution.

The Confederation experience had underscored the difficulty of creating successful republican governments. We might better understand the nature of that difficulty if we cast it in schematic form. The Republican Problem, let us call it, is to design a government able to accomplish three separate ends. It must:

- Express the sovereignty of the people.
- Protect the rights of individuals.
- Seek the public good.

Just why the Republican Problem was so difficult can be seen in a few quick comparisons. The classical republics often expressed the sovereignty of the people well enough but they ignored minority rights—with tragic consequences—and failed the public good. Liberal republics, such as Georgian England, did better with minority rights but not as well with popular sovereignty, and served the public good only intermittently. Neither the American states nor the Confederation had much better track records, some erring one way and some another. For all of them, it was a little like a carnival game where you can knock down one bottle or possibly two but never all three.

Madison referred to the Republican Problem in *The Federalist* when he spoke of the "diseases" of republican government. The Framers must now seek out a "republican cure" for the diseases in question.

Fundamental Ideas and Conceptions

In order to fully understand the structure and dynamics of the Constitution, we must begin with some fundamentals. These are the foundation on which the edifice of government must be built.

English Bill of Rights:
http://www.yale.edu/
lawweb/avalon/england.htm

English Bill of Rights:
Gave civil and political
rights to the people and
political supremacy to
Parliament (1689).

Magna Carta: English
charter of liberties
asserting fundamental
rights and privileges
(1215).

Habeas Corpus: Writ
which requires reason
for arrest to be explained
to court of law.

Fundamental Law

Throughout the controversy with Great Britain, the colonists had constantly invoked *fundamental law*—law that stood above the ordinary acts passed by a legislature—which they code-named "the English constitution" or "the rights of Englishmen." Some scholars rejected the whole idea of fundamental law, as we will see in a later chapter, but Americans took it very seriously. Not many of them could have explained the concept very well. There was something in it of the law of nature—those basic ideas of right and wrong that most people accept—and something of historic agreements such as Magna Carta or the English Bill of Rights. There were even some common law precepts such as *habeas corpus*. Fundamental law came down to a belief that lawmakers couldn't do just any old thing they had a mind to—there were limits out there somewhere.

Over the long months of the summer, the Framers in Philadelphia thought a great deal about the document they were trying to work out. They referred to it as a "plan of government" but they realized it was more than just that. They came to understand that it was indeed a constitution—a set of fundamental laws created by the people themselves. A constitution exists prior to government and stands above the governing process. And government, in its turn, derives from the constitution and thus submits to the fundamental law.

These ideas had some important corollaries. First of all, constitutions could not be written by existing governments—that would be a case of the tail wagging the dog. And constitutions could not be adopted by governments either, only by the people themselves. Accordingly, it wasn't for the *states* to accept or reject the work of the Convention, nor was it for the Confederation to decide—it was for ordinary Americans. As the Framers finally worked it out, the people would call ratifying conventions within the various states and report their decision state by state, but the conventions themselves should have nothing at all to do with state governments.

This was truly uncharted water.

Written Constitutions

Writing out a constitution in black and white proved to be very different from the vague understandings of the English experience. With vague understandings there was always room for maneuver. With specific words on paper, by contrast, the wiggle room was much less.

Constitutional vagueness was usually dealt with by legal experts like Edward Coke or William Blackstone. When the provisions were written out and published, by contrast, they became public property. Anyone could haul out a copy of the Constitution and ask questions of those in power. Unsurprisingly, we find that written constitutions soon had a track record of rallying and focusing public opinion. They held government responsible in ways undreamed before.

Finally, by writing it all out on paper, the people gained a means of correcting constitutional drift—the very thing that had "gone wrong" with the English constitution. It was harder for the fundamental law to wander off track.

Edward Coke (pronounced "Cook"): A 17th-century English jurist instrumental in arguing that the king was subject to the law.

William Blackstone: Author of the "bible" on English jurisprudence.

Enumeration

Written constitutions changed the whole idea of authority. Heretofore, the powers exercised by a sovereign government were supposed to be unlimited. In ancient Rome, for example, there was a basic precept that *Caesar can do no wrong*—that literally any action willed by a Roman emperor was backed by the authority of law. Constitutionalism rejected this notion out of hand, of course, for what else was a constitution supposed to do but subject governmental power to certain limits?

But how to accomplish this in black and white? How to give Congress or the president the authority they need without giving them too much? One might say, for example, that Congress shall have the power to pass "all needful laws," only to discover that such broad and general wording posed no limits whatsoever. On the other extreme, one might stipulate that Congress shall have power "to regulate wagon traffic on national roads"—using concrete and specific language instead—only to learn that the lawmakers had no authority, later on, to regulate canal traffic, rail traffic or air traffic. It is a knotty little problem.

After much discussion, the Framers hit upon the idea of *enumeration*. Instead of trying to frame a grant of authority in general terms or trying to list out the multitude of possible particulars, they searched for a workable middle ground. They "enumerated" the powers of government, spelled them out, but did so in language that was neither too broad nor too specific. Enumeration reinforced the idea of limited government.

Republican Mechanisms

Republics did not necessarily require written constitutions or enumerated powers. But they did have essential requirements and the Framers had to think carefully about each of them.

Popular Sovereignty

The primary requirement was that the governance of a republic be for, if not always by, the people themselves. The power of government is always a benefit to *someone*. King, dictator, oligarch, plutocrat—there is always an interest to be served. In a republic the interest must be that of the *people as a whole*.

In order to achieve this benefit, the people as a whole must be "sovereign," which means they must consent to the laws that govern them. For John Locke (and many other political writers in the 1600s), consent was given tacitly rather than formally. People never sat around a table and negotiated an actual "social contract"; they agreed to the terms by remaining in a given political state, taking part in its activities, owning property and paying taxes.

With the American Constitution, the meaning of consent was dramatically altered. The social contract became overt and literal. Delegates to the Philadel-

Suffragettes demonstrating for the right to vote. Who should, and should not, give consent? (Courtesy of Brown Brothers.)

phia Convention were sent by almost all the states, and the document they worked out had to be ratified by the voters in every state that joined the union. There was nothing tacit about it.

There was another point. In the older view, it could be argued that once the social contract was worked out, the people had little further part to play. The American Framers had a different idea. They saw the Constitution not so much as a signed and sealed agreement as an ongoing grant of power from the sovereign people—"power on loan."

For convenience, then, consent in the American system may be broken down into two varieties:

Original Consent. The people work out a plan of government and formally adopt it—reenacting the social contract. Original consent is renewed each time a constitutional amendment is considered. If the people reject the proffered amendment, they in effect consent to carry on with the existing constitution. And if they accept the amendment, they consent to a new constitution.

Periodic Consent. The people, by means of the electoral process, give their periodic approval of the government's political behavior.

The Framers' view of popular sovereignty only mirrored the facts. Americans were independent minded, jealous of their personal freedom, spread across a continent and armed to the teeth: it would be impossible to rule them without their consent. Since the adoption of the Constitution, American voters have often brought their government up short on election day. And no administration has been able to advance policies very far that the people themselves oppose.

Representation

Representation was practiced in England, of course, where the Americans learned it firsthand, but it traced all the way back to ancient Greece. The idea was for a few elected individuals to represent the people as a whole, each acting in behalf of certain *constituents*. The process was two-way. The constituents, through their representatives, made their voice heard in government, and government, through those same representatives, got the constituents to approve unpleasant little matters like taxation.

With a bit of tinkering, the structure of representation could be designed to favor the rich, the poor, the intelligent, the powerful and so on. So abuses were common. In the so-called rotten boroughs of England, the only "constituents" represented were a handful of local peers.

There were also at least two different ideas of how the process ought to work:

Attorneyship Representation. The representative is conceived as a simple agent of his constituents, conveying their input to the legislative process without personal intervention. This was the kind of representation usually practiced in colonial governments. It was regarded as the more democratic form.

Virtual Representation. Here the representative is more of a free agent, bringing his own ideas into the legislative process. He may not speak exclusively for the interests of his own constituents but instead may represent the larger public good as he understands it.

Virtual representation got a bad name during the controversy with Britain. For Parliament claimed that colonial interests, while not directly represented, were "virtually" represented in that body, and thus that someone would always speak up for them. To American ears, this rang false to human nature. Virtual representatives didn't have to pay the taxes they were levying against the colonies, nor did they have to account to colonial constituents at election time. The most broad minded statesman in the world might never think twice about whom he was really "representing."

The Framers in Philadelphia discussed representation a great deal. George Mason favored attorneyship. "The representatives" he said, "should sympathize with their constituents, should think as they think and feel as they feel, and for these purposes should even be residents among them." Others opted for the virtual model. In the end, the delegates sought to incorporate both varieties into their constitutional architecture. They set up legislative districts in such a way as to compel the representation of specific interests—no rotten boroughs. Moreover, the representatives themselves would have to live under the

Constituents: People being represented.

Old Sarum is a notorious example of a rotten borough. It had no residents whatsoever.

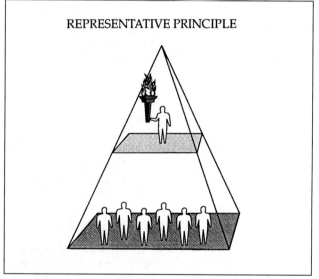

REPRESENTATIVE PRINCIPLE

Representatives, having passed the election process, would generally be more virtuous and wise than the ordinary citizen. Consequently they were expected to be leaders, refining and enlarging the views of their constituents, rather than acting upon them mechanically. The large republic provided the necessary distance between the representative and the whims and passions of his constituency, to make virtuous leadership possible.

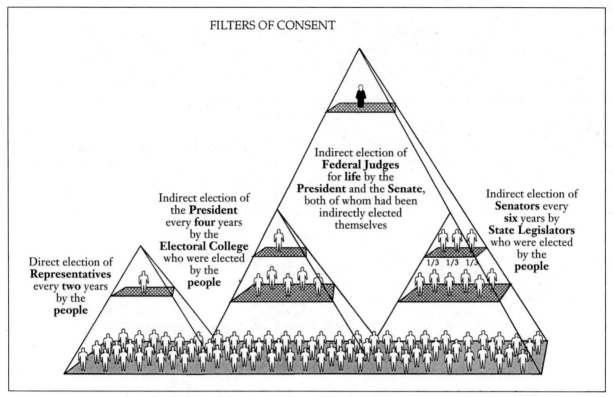

FILTERS OF CONSENT

Indirect election of
Federal Judges
for **life** by the
President and the **Senate**,
both of whom had been
indirectly elected
themselves

Indirect election of
the **President**
every **four** years
by the
Electoral College
who were elected
by the
people

Indirect election of
Senators every
six years by
State Legislators
who were elected
by the
people

Direct election of
Representatives
every **two** years
by the
people

1/3 1/3 1/3

To maintain a popular government while insuring against a democratic one, the Founders designed a complex system which would process the consent of the people through a set of filters. There were direct and indirect elections, staggered elections (in which one-third of the Senate would be up for election every two years) and overlapping terms of office (two, four, six, life).

Those with few filters between them and the people would necessarily be closer and more accountable to the often capricious passions of the people. Those with more filters between them and the people would be farther removed from the people, with greater opportunity for more cautious, reflective response to popular will.

rules—and pay the taxes—they voted for in Congress. Yet the Framers also expected representatives to be more than passive "attorneys" of their districts. They assumed that voters would choose representatives who were more virtuous and farsighted than the norm, and that the process would "enlarge and refine" public views.

Virtue Mechanisms

In the instance described above, representation becomes a kind of "virtue mechanism." That is, solely by means of structural design, a political system could be engineered to place the most virtuous people in positions of greatest public trust—using human nature as a design principle. In the above case, representatives tend to be more virtuous than those who elect them because, as it happens, even the most rascally of voters dislike putting rascals in office. (For example, think about the outrage against President Clinton on the part of those for whom sexual transgression is commonplace.) The Scottish philosopher David Hume had called attention to such mechanisms, arguing that human nature was predictable enough to make them work. Indirect election (representatives choosing representatives), he said, could select virtue from the general populace the way a sluice refined gold from river sand.

The Framers found other uses for Hume's machinery. In the operation of the electoral college, for instance, electors chosen in the various states would meet together to select the president. The president, in turn, would nominate justices to the Supreme Court. These would have to be confirmed by the Senate, whose members were chosen by state legislatures. Such indirect methods were partly to insulate the electoral process from popular passions, true, but they were also to give Hume's "refining effect" fullest scope.

A second set of virtue mechanisms was provided by the principle of "fame." According to Aristotle, a public person's concern for his reputation would, under certain conditions, operate as a strong restraint on his conduct. What conditions? The conduct must be open and visible to the body politic, and the responsibility for it must always be clear.

The Framers focused responsibility in several ways. After extensively debating a plural executive, they decided on a single executive instead, reasoning that in the latter case "fame" would be a much stronger deterrent. The principle of enumeration also helped to pin the blame where it belonged by spelling out who was in charge of what. And the Framers required that all proceedings of Congress be open to the public and published for all to read: a congressman's floor speeches or voting record were not to be hid under a bushel.

A final set of virtue mechanisms was found in the last clause of Article VI, where the Constitution stipulated: "No religious Test shall ever be required as a Qualification to any Office or public Trust under the United States."

While a few of the Framers were religious skeptics, most were committed churchmen—and even the skeptics appreciated religion's power to promote civic virtue. The question was, how to bring such power to bear? Some delegates argued for a mild religious test, requiring officeholders to embrace mainstream Christianity.

Experience had shown, however, that religious tests, however mild, had the effect of cementing an official tie between church and state. Several of the Framers regarded such a tie as desirable. No republican society, they argued, could succeed without *some* official religion. But most of the delegates took the opposite view. Official religion worked two kinds of mischief, they said. It opened the way for the official church to corrupt the political system, and conversely opened the way for the political system to corrupt the official church. Those delegates representing states where a religious establishment still persisted could testify to the baneful effects.

By prohibiting a religious test, the Framers aimed not to destroy the influence of religion on politics but to purify it. The theory went something like this. All believers, now lacking any official capacity, were welcome to exert their influence on government in any way they saw fit—just as any citizens were. And since no denomination stood to gain by way of patronage, the motives of all must be relatively pure. The only real message a church might have under the Constitution would be to urge integrity, responsibility and a sacralized civic virtue.

Most of the Framers had a strong confidence in the Constitution's virtue mechanisms. They believed that the national government would be more virtuous on the whole than the governments of the states, for it would draw upon the virtue of the entire nation.

The Constitution:
http://www.britannica.com/
eb/article?idxref=194987

http://www.jmu.edu/
madison/gpos225-madison2/
adopt.htm

Auxiliary Precautions

Yet the Framers were not willing to rely on republican mechanisms alone. Their view of human nature was rather skeptical, especially where politics was concerned, and they were not willing to assume the virtue of all public figures in all situations. "If men were angels," Madison wrote in an often quoted passage of *The Federalist*,

> no government would be necessary. If angels were to govern men, neither external nor internal controls on government would be necessary. In framing a government which is to be administered by men over men, the great difficulty lies in this: you must first enable the government to control the governed; and in the next place oblige it to control itself. A dependence on the people is, no doubt, the primary control on the government; but experience has taught mankind the necessity of auxiliary precautions.

The fundamental idea behind Madison's "auxiliary precautions" had emerged in the European Enlightenment. In simplest terms, it was that the power of self-interest could be utilized to control self-interest—control *itself*, in other words—the way the power of a steam engine could be utilized to brake a locomotive as well as drive it forward. The answer lay in structure once again.

The Framers termed their primary structural principle *counterpoise*. "Ambition must be made to counteract ambition," Madison explained. "The interest of the man must be connected with the constitutional rights of the place." What he meant was that through Hume-style structural engineering we saw above, it was possible to counterpose the self-interest of one player against that of another with the result that each would keep the other in line. "It may be a reflection on human nature that such devices should be necessary to control the abuses of government," Madison wrote, "But what is government itself but the greatest of all reflections on human nature?"

Runaway ambition was only half of the problem. The other half was what we might call group dynamics. Madison and several others had observed that a given group of individuals—say, an assembly of voters—could behave very differently in different circumstances. One "group personality," for example, might be hot and impetuous. The members could act with reckless abandon if their passions were stirred, if their condition was desperate or if someone stood to gain from inciting them to panic. And the other personality might be cool and reflective. The selfsame voters could act with great deliberation, avoiding haste, even regretting and nullifying earlier misadventures, if the situation were just a little different. Think of the movie scene in which the hero dramatically halts the lynch mob, delivers a scolding and sends everyone home feeling sheepish.

The Framers' constitutional engineering was thus twofold. First, they must make interest counter interest and ambition check ambition on the part of the political leadership. And second, they must incline toward the cool and deliberative side of popular judgment. Both ends could be accomplished through the careful design of structure.

James Harrington had suggested a first step. In his influential *Commonwealth of Oceana* (1656), Harrington had described a good structure for creating counterpoise. Two children have discovered a small cake. They fall to squabbling about the division of the prize between them, each contending for more than a fair share. Without some means of reining in their self-interest, the conflict is bound to go on and on. But an adult arrives on the scene with a structural solution. One child shall be allowed to cut the cake while the other is given first choice of the pieces. Observe the magical transformation, Harrington wrote. Self-interest, which formerly promoted injustice (and led to anarchy), now moves both cutter and chooser to behave equitably. The Framers thought carefully about "cutters" and "choosers" in the constitutional process.

They also considered means of separating the warm and cool sides of popular judgment. Longer terms in office, for instance, worked for the latter. An officeholder who could remember back when a particular episode, or something like it, had occurred before was less likely to react precipitously. The size of a political assemblage also affected its psychology. Large bodies numbering into the hundreds would stampede more easily than small ones of twenty or thirty, for with the latter there was always a way for the voice of reason to be heard.

The Framers' main strategy, however, was to make it possible for—and even incumbent upon—certain officials in the structure to throw on the brakes when events began moving too quickly. In so doing, they necessarily forced others to stop and think. This was why the Framers came to put so much faith in "separation of powers."

Separation of Powers Mechanisms

Government embraces a wide variety of human activities. Passing laws, building roads and pronouncing judgments in court are only three of the activities, but notice how dissimilar they are. In time, the various "powers," as they are called, were sorted into three general categories:

- *Legislative.* Enacting the laws that all must live by.
- *Executive.* Putting the laws into practical effect.
- *Judicial.* Applying the laws to specific cases and determining whether or not they have been violated.

In the classical republics, the legislative branch was held to be the most important of the three by far, for it was here that the sovereignty of the people became manifest. Stepping into the

Commonwealth of Oceana: Influential political work dealing with modern political ideas.

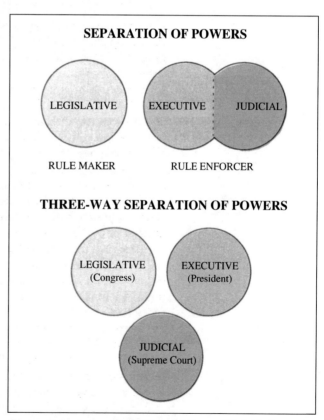

The traditional separation of Rule Maker and Rule Enforcer was modified by dividing the Rule Enforcer into two separate bodies (top) creating a three-way separation of powers (bottom).

classical frame of reference for a moment, let us try to imagine how the executive and judicial branches might be viewed through the eyes of the legislature:

The executive. This is the person charged with carrying out, or "executing," the legislature's will—a hired hand, so to speak. Suppose, for instance, that the legislative assembly decides to purchase new spears for the army. The executive goes out and negotiates contracts with the smithies. He inspects the finished products, pays for them and stows them away, returning to the legislature for further orders.

The judiciary. This is the person charged with hearing and deciding cases. He too takes orders from the legislature. If, let us suppose, the legislature determines there is too much shoplifting in the marketplace, judges may be instructed to tighten up on the rules of evidence, throw out sob stories and run up the sentences. They meekly obey.

Lest such thinking seem archaic, state governments commonly operated in this same manner before the Constitution was adopted, and some of them continued to do so afterward. It was considered to be very "republican."

It was this very system, however, that created much of the tyranny and anarchy of the ancient world—to say nothing of the American state governments—and for that reason Aristotle came up with an entirely different approach. We need to consider it too because it was equally influential when the Constitution was written. Aristotle associated the three departments of government with the three "estates" he found in most social hierarchies. Hence "the one," "the few" and "the many"—loosely connected with monarchic, aristocratic and democratic elements of society—could be equated with the executive, judicial and legislative branches respectively, and could be mixed in the structure of government in such a way as to check and balance one another. The one and the few, Aristotle supposed, would tug against the wishes of the many and vice versa, so that each would tend to hold the others in line. This was the origin of "counterpoise."

Aristotle's mixing and balancing of the estates became a central feature of English government. Crown and Lords checked one another, so the theory went, and in turn combined to check Commons. Several of the American Founders accepted this approach as a given. In some way, they believed, a republican government must be designed so as to play off class against class, and combine the psychology of the one, the few and the many into a dynamic working relationship.

The more modern idea of "separation of powers," which we encountered in chapters 5 and 7, seems outwardly similar to Aristotle's model, but it is actually quite different. It began as a critical insight. Observers of the English system noted that it did little good to mix and balance the various departments of government if one of them always proved to be stronger than the others and thus always succeeded in getting its way. One might as well go back to the all-powerful legislature ordering around its spear buyers and thief catchers, for in the end it came down to the same thing—as the American colonists had learned so well.

With this puzzle in mind, Montesquieu had begun to write about "separated powers." He supposed that if the various departments of government could somehow be separated from one another, such that none could directly control the others, the result might benefit the rule of law. But such separation would be tricky. How could a government coordinate its activities if each of its branches were a power unto itself? What would prevent the system from simply gridlocking? And how, in a practical sense, were the branches actually to be forced apart? Montesquieu had struggled with such questions. So did the Framers in Philadelphia.

Gradually, however, key delegates began to get hold of the idea. They had been trying to think of ways to make the government powerful enough to do the job required of it without making it too powerful for peace of mind. Separation might be the answer. If the legislative and executive branches could be pushed apart in some way without being driven to cross-purposes, each might become strong enough, and independent enough, to set up a working counterpoise. The executive would still carry out the laws passed by Congress, but he would not be just an errand boy. He would do his job blindly, as it were, without reference to any political purpose of the legislators. And vice versa. Once a law was passed, it would be out of Congress' hands entirely—so there was no point in shaping it so as to "get" someone.

But how to make the powers separate? State governments had struggled with the problem unsuccessfully, as we saw in chapter 5. Then the Massachusetts Model Constitution had come up with some answers. The key had proven to be the conditional veto, which John Adams had argued for in *Thoughts On Government*. Adams hadn't been keen on separation of powers. He had been thinking more along the lines of Aristotle's mixing and balancing approach. But strengthening the executive and giving him a negative on the legislature had indeed made separation possible.

The Framers were beginning to understand why. By enabling the executive to defend himself against aggressive legislators, the veto power allowed him to exercise an independent will. Yet it could never be *completely* independent because of the override provision. And, conversely, the legislature could protect its own integrity against an ambitious executive—simply by overriding his veto. So *its* will remained independent too.

Some Framers still weren't convinced. You *compromise* separation of powers by making the executive a kind of negative legislator—and that makes separation work? You hand an executive a timeworn instrument of blackmail and tyranny—and that creates freedom? It seemed like a parlor trick. At best, said the doubters, it would lead the executive and legislature to thumb their noses at each other and refuse to budge. But James Wilson didn't think so. With his portly bearing and cool self-assurance, Wilson always seemed to know

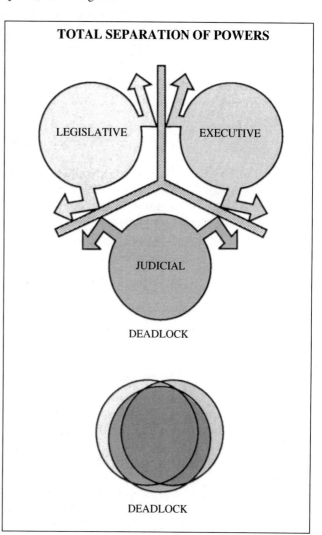

TOTAL SEPARATION OF POWERS

LEGISLATIVE

EXECUTIVE

JUDICIAL

DEADLOCK

DEADLOCK

With total separation of powers, there is a risk of deadlock (top) or that one of the powers will obtain total control (bottom).

The accumulation of all powers, legislative, executive, and judiciary, in the same hands, whether of one, a few, or many, and whether hereditary, self-appointed, or elective, may justly be pronounced the very definition of tyranny.

—*James Madison*

how a baffling system would *really* work, and the inclination here, he thought, would be not toward deadlock but compromise. In the next chapter, we will work through a hypothetical example of what Wilson meant.

Beyond the conditional veto, there were other things the Framers could (and did) do to make the separation of powers effective. They could allow each branch to determine the qualifications of its own members. They could enable each to lay down the rules of its own proceedings. They could make it possible for each branch to provide for its own funding, its own officers and support services, its own physical and institutional location. Not least, they could enumerate a specific list of powers for each, so that each would have its own separate sphere of authority.

There was another odd kink. When the design of the national government was complete, a number of "checks and balances" were added to the structure that required the sharing, rather than separating, of power. These too violated the separation doctrine, it would seem, but they really didn't. For they enhanced the *purpose* of separation. That purpose was to enable the branches of government to exercise an independent will, to check potential incursions into each other's domains, and to provide a functional counterpoise—*without working at cross-purposes*. It was, in Richard Neustadt's phrase, "separated institutions sharing power."

Separation of powers created a whole new approach to republican government. Instead of mixing and balancing the various estates of a hierarchical society, it became possible to base *all* branches of government on the people as a whole. In time, this breakthrough would have far-reaching, even transforming consequences.

Separation of Powers Design

Separation of powers enabled the Framers to produce a coherent structure of government. Each functional department became a separate branch, and each branch could be strong, independent and clearly defined. Given such a design, the government could be one of great "energy" without threatening personal liberty.

- Strong Legislature

Congress was granted the following enumerated powers by the new Constitution:

→ To lay and collect taxes, duties, imposts and excises.

→ To borrow money on the credit of the United States.

→ To regulate commerce with foreign nations and among the several states.

→ To establish uniform rules of naturalization and uniform laws of bankruptcy.

→ To coin money and regulate its value.

→ To fix the standard of weights and measures.

→ To provide for the punishment of counterfeiting.

→ To establish a postal system.

→ To provide patent and copyright protection.

→ To set up a federal court system inferior to the Supreme Court.

→ To define and punish felonies on the high seas.

→ To declare war.

➜ To raise and support armies and to provide and maintain a navy.

➜ To make rules for the government and regulation of military forces.

➜ To provide for militia forces when in service of the United States.

➜ To govern the District of Columbia.

When reviewing this list there are two things to keep in mind. First, it represented an enormous increase in the authority granted to the old Confederation. And second, it is extremely limited when compared to the powers commonly exercised by nation-states today. As the Framers saw it, there was power to do what had to be done—and hopefully not a great deal to spare.

And there was a catch. In addition to the enumerated powers, Congress was given the authority "to make all Laws which shall be necessary and proper for carrying into Execution the foregoing Powers. . . ." This clause turned out to be the Constitution's wild card and was destined to be played in many a tense hand of politics. Since no one knew what might be judged "necessary and proper," the way was open to argue for just about anything.

• Strong Executive

Under the Constitution, the president was responsible for executing, or carrying out, the laws passed by Congress. This activity, on a continental scale, would require the efforts of a vast number of functionaries, whom the chief executive could hire or fire at will. Moreover, think of all the suppliers of goods and services to government projects, the management of government properties, the handling of government assets. There was a treasure house of personal power here in the form of *patronage*.

Furthermore, the president was made commander in chief of all military forces and given charge of foreign affairs. Both arenas were of crucial importance and both, historically speaking, had been the proving grounds of the Caesars. The president, in other words, was to be much more than a mere "executive." His office had a vast potential for developing charismatic leadership, for molding public opinion, for embodying the will of the nation. The president could be a kind of king.

• Strong Judiciary

The separation of powers mechanisms worked differently for the judicial branch of government. By its very nature, the judiciary exercised no independent will. It could not advance its own aims, urge its own program, reward its friends or punish its enemies. It could not even enforce its own decrees. Yet the judiciary was of utmost importance to the rule of law. If the legislative branch was the essential rule maker, the court system was the ultimate rule enforcer, for it applied the law to specific cases and determined whether or not violators would be punished.

The Framers' objective here was to insulate the judicial system from all means by which the other branches had tampered with it in the past. Supreme Court justices were provided a life-

"And there are three branches of government, so that each branch has the other to blame everything on." (By Ralph Dunagin, courtesy of Tribune Media Services.)

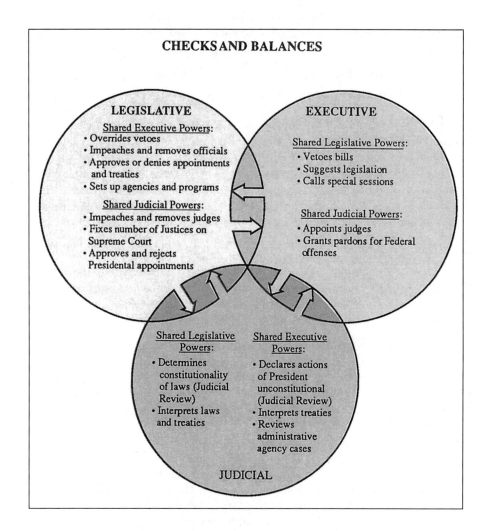

CHECKS AND BALANCES

Interesting Paradox: the same kind of powers must be shared to maintain separation of powers.

time tenure of office and a guarantee that their salaries would not be reduced. The penal system was placed under their supervision, and they were given charge of their own bureaucracy. The Constitution made it very difficult for politics to subvert justice.

The federal court system has proven to be as strong as the Framers hoped it would—and for some a good deal stronger. Isolating the justices from the political fray and faithfully (for the most part) carrying out their decisions created a situation in which the judiciary could truly play the role of referee.

Check and Balance Mechanisms

As the Framers began laying out the structure of government, they repeatedly asked themselves how a given constitutional device was likely to play upon human nature. For instance, in *Federalist* 51, Madison argued the case for separation of powers in these words: "The great security against a gradual concentration of the several powers in the same department consists in giving to those who administer each department the necessary constitutional means and personal motives to resist the encroachments of the others." We will soon see how those "constitutional means" and "personal motives" would intersect when the Constitution was put into practice—almost precisely as the innovators anticipated.

In the political psychology of separated powers, means and motives often led to wariness between the branches. All the threats to veto or to override could make the governing process, in Woodrow Wilson's words, "at war against itself." The political psychology of *checks and balances* was quite different. In most of these situations, power was shared between two different branches or two different authorities in the same branch: in order to perform a given function, both would have to agree. To be sure, a bit of the veto psychology also applied to these situations, for either branch could essentially veto a contemplated action by refusing to perform its part. To a much greater extent, though, the branches were induced to cooperate with each other, as we will see in the following chapter.

The Constitution's principal check and balance mechanisms are as follows:

- Bicameralism

Congress was divided into two separate chambers, the House of Representatives and the Senate. Such a division would have taken place even without the Great Compromise, for the Framers were strongly in favor of its value. John Adams had staked his career on bicameralism, and it had proven its worth in the Model Constitution.

The Framers assumed that the House of Representatives would embody the "mind or sense of the people at large," as James Wilson put it, and "be the most exact transcript of the whole society." Accordingly, it must be kept close to the average voter and designed to reflect his momentary hopes and fears.

Legislative districts of roughly 30,000 voters would each elect a single member to the House. Even though these districts lay within the boundaries of existing states, they were small enough with respect to most states (and would get progressively smaller as state populations increased) to focus upon discrete local interests. Thus, while a given member might represent a commercial constituency, his neighboring district might be industrial or agrarian. The interplay of these interests was expected to be lively. As various issues arose, the representatives would group together with little regard for state boundaries and have it out.

> Original size of districts in Constitution was 30,000 voters.

To keep the representatives in touch with public opinion, terms were kept short at two years—meaning that every congressman must account to the voters on a regular basis. Thus, as economic and political circumstances changed, the complexion of the House would change as well. There would always be something fleeting and transitory about the lower chamber, reflecting the emotional side of the body politic. In Madison's simile, it would be "hot."

The upper chamber, by contrast, had to be "cool"—the cream one poured into scalding coffee to make it drinkable. The psychology of the situation would be something like this. The people had their impulsive side, true, but they had their deliberative side as well. If the "cool" Senate caused them to pause and reconsider hasty measures, they might well change their minds. Put another way, the Senate might help the body politic to distinguish between apparent interest, short term, and genuine interest, long term.

But how could a constitution fill the upper chamber with such clear heads? It is easy to figure out ways of electing the tallest, the shortest, the smartest or whatever—but the *wisest*? The Framers struggled with this problem throughout the summer, and by September they were no nearer a solution than in May. In the end, they had to settle for an odd second best—wealth. By requiring senators to be elected by the various state legislatures, the Framers realized that wealth might well play a role in the outcome. And wealth wasn't wisdom. But at least the wealthy had a sizable stake in society, and for that reason would resist facile innovation. Furthermore, because the senators were one further tier from direct election, they would hopefully benefit from Hume's refining effect.

The lengthy (six-year) terms for the Senate had a similar effect, as did the comparatively small size of the body. Senators would know one another well and share a long institutional memory. If the system did not produce wisdom per se, it certainly did produce cool cream for the hot coffee. Historically, many measures of momentary popularity have sailed through the House of Representatives only to run aground in the Senate.

Bills could arise in either house, but to become law they had to be passed by both. The single exception was tax bills, which had to be initiated in the House. Since it was the people as a whole who had to pay the taxes, their representatives were given the right to settle on the amount required.

The two houses naturally checked and balanced one another. Sometimes they were thick as thieves and sometimes they were hardly on speaking terms. Whatever their relations, any piece of legislation that passed through both of them pretty well had the backing of the people.

- Power of Appointment

The appointment of many high-ranking officials—Supreme Court justices, ambassadors and ministers, Cabinet officers and the like—was to be made by the chief executive but subject to the "advice and consent" of the Senate. Advice and consent, especially the latter, altered the psychology of appointment considerably. The president would have a hard time installing mere cronies in high places if he must go before the Senate and explain each nomination.

Some of the Framers feared that extortion would result from this arrangement—that the Senate would blackmail the president into nominating people of its own choosing by refusing to confirm any others. This fear has proven as groundless as the obverse fear that the president would blackmail Congress with his veto power. In both cases, the players' personal motives are inclined by the structure toward a wary cooperation, for embarrassment afflicts both sides when a nomination fails—especially as a result of "political maneuvering."

- War Making and Foreign Policy

The Constitution gave the executive authority to send and receive ambassadors and ministers and to conclude treaties with foreign powers. These provisions placed American foreign policy squarely within the executive domain.

Since foreign war had spelled the downfall of many republics, the Framers were deeply concerned about these powers. Some feared that the president might be tempted to take bribes from alien governments—or even from certain states—so checks and balances were used here as well. While the executive could negotiate a foreign treaty on his own, it had to be ratified by a two-thirds majority of the

Senate. As for war making, Congress alone was given the authority to declare war, but once that was done it was the president who took charge of the fighting.

Personal motives could become frightening here. Some presidents have sought to avoid Congress (and hence the public) by conducting military operations without a declaration of war. Others have forced Congress' hand by placing US forces in harm's way. But Congress has fallen back on yet another check in the system—the power of the purse. By refusing to appropriate funds for a military operation, Congress can—and occasionally does—lodge a convincing negative.

- Powers of Investigation and Impeachment

While the Constitution did not specifically endow Congress with investigative power, such power inheres in the legislative process. For in order to frame a measure and debate its merits, the lawmakers must be able to consult experts, call in witnesses and examine relevant data.

This was yet another check and balance, complete with its own set of personal motivations. Individual congressmen have made—and occasionally broken—their political careers by conducting investigations. Whether specific action follows or not, the mere existence of an investigation serves to capture public attention—and puts public officials on notice.

The impeachment power illustrates how delicate the check and balance mechanisms can be. Three grounds for impeachment were included in the Constitution: treason, bribery and "other high crimes and misdemeanors." The first two were well understood. The third was intended as a catchall and was added only after long discussion.

But what, exactly, did the phrase "high crimes and misdemeanors" mean? One could argue that an executive who failed to execute the laws faithfully (Article II, Section 3) might well be in violation, yet if the executive simply marched in step with the legislature he would not be exercising an independent will. If Congress violated the Bill of Rights by, say, passing a law to silence critics, would a president be guilty of "high crimes and misdemeanors" for refusing to carry it out?

All the Constitution's check and balance mechanisms were ambiguous in some way. They required historical experience, established precedents and even adjudication in the courts before their operation would become settled. They also complicated political operations and encumbered the operators with all sorts of new calculations. Political novels such as *Advise and Consent* or *Clear and Present Danger* illustrate how entangled constitutional situations can become.

Critics have argued that so many "auxiliary precautions" make for a Constitution that is "all brakes and no engine." That may be true. It was not designed for efficiency, however, but effectiveness—against despotism. And in this purpose it has served us well.

Federal Mechanisms

The "federal" system of dividing government between sovereign states and an equally sovereign central authority was entirely a product of circumstances, as

Advise and Consent

For those who have not experienced it, the psychology of divided power is difficult to describe. It is a curious blend of hostility and friendliness, cooperation and obstruction. Allen Drury's 1959 novel, *Advise and Consent*, attempts to explore that psychology in detail. In the story, the US President, himself a rather doubtful character, has nominated the even more doubtful Robert Leffingwell to be Secretary of State. The novel goes on to probe the minds and hearts of the Senators who must now either confirm or oppose the nomination.

In the following excerpt, the President has just told Senator Orrin Knox that the Soviets have stolen a march on the United States and landed men on the moon:

"It is against that background," [the president] said quietly, "that I must ask you to permit Bob Leffingwell to be confirmed."

Senator Knox stared at him thoughtfully.

"How do I know you're telling me the truth?" he asked calmly, and the President looked at him in some disbelief.

"Do you think I would fabricate something as lurid as that?" he inquired dryly.

"You might," Orrin said. "But," he added quickly, "I don't think you are. I fail to see, however, why it should change my attitude about your nominee. If anything, I should think it would make me even more determined that he not be confirmed."

"I feel he is what we need in this situation," the President said with a quiet insistence. "It is inconceivable to me that you would stand in his way under the circumstances. I am asking you as a patriotic American to permit him to assume the office."

"Well, by God," Senator Knox said sharply, "so now it's patriotism, is it? Well, let me tell you, Mr. President. To me it's patriotic to do what I deem best in my own judgment for the country; it isn't to give in to you and let you ride roughshod over everything decent just because you claim it's patriotic and imply that those who oppose you are unpatriotic. What kind of damned slippery argument is that?"

"Senator," the President said, "do you have any conception of what I have just been telling you?"

"I have a conception," Senator Knox said shortly. "I also have a conception of what is decent and honorable and best for the country which I think is just as good on the moon as it is on earth or Venus or Mars or any other place we're going to go to. And my conception had no room for Bob Leffingwell and his wishy-washy attitudes toward the mortal enemies of the United States. Why, good Lord. You know as well as I do exactly what they're going to start doing tomorrow. They're going to start pressuring us as they never have before. And you want an obliging stooge like Bob Leffingwell to deal with *that*? What kind of conception do *you* have?"

In the end, of course, all is well for the United States. With all its bumps and abrasions, the system really does work.

we have seen. Doubters were not slow to point out that federalism was unplanned, unprecedented and almost unimaginable.

But not undefensible. James Wilson, who had fought to the bitter end against the Great Compromise (and thus against federalism), later came out with brilliant justifications for it. Federalism, he argued, offered nothing less than a whole *new* approach to the control of tyranny.

- Federal Separation of Powers, Checks and Balances

Just as there was a separation between legislative and executive branches in the national government, there was another separation between the powers enumerated in the Constitution and the powers reserved to the states. The states could no longer conduct diplomacy or field their own armies, true; but the central government could not license taverns or arrest thieves either.

Furthermore, the two levels of government operated as a check and balance against each other, sometimes pulling together and sometimes tugging apart. The states checked one another as well, by means of political activity in the Senate. If a certain state or a certain region became too strong, there was a more or less automatic movement in that body to counter the buildup. In the curious architecture of the Senate, small states could hold their own against large ones, and isolated states could band together against regional concentrations.

- Federalism and the National Interest

The checking of regional power worked against the formation of dangerous majorities. In the House, regional majorities formed regularly. Wherever there was a concentration of population—usually in the Northeast—voting in the House was likely to become lopsided, arousing fears of sectional dominance.

But in the Senate such a concentration was almost impossible. For example, when the Constitution was adopted, four populous northeastern states (Massachusetts, Connecticut, New York and Pennsylvania) could muster 27 votes out of the 65 possible in the House, perilously close to a majority, whereas in the Senate they could account for only 8 of 26. Any majority in the Senate had to be national rather than regional in character.

As soon as the various regions felt secure from a hostile majority, they could afford to relax. The protection of regional interest thus made it possible to articulate a purely national interest—something Americans had rarely felt under the Articles of Confederation. The people could rejoice in the peace of their greater republic and turn full attention to its promise.

Other Features of the Constitution

Beyond the Constitution's auxiliary precautions, there were other features of importance, and they too would exert a shaping influence. Before touching on a few of these, we should point out that the inclusion of a single phrase—even a single word in some cases—could (and did) have enormous consequences in the evolution of institutions.

Suffrage Qualifications

Virtually all of the states qualified the right to vote according to some standard of property ownership. For in the eighteenth century, "the people" didn't include *all* people by any stretch, only Aristotle's people of substance and account. In some states the requirements were quite restrictive, while in others they were comparatively liberal. The Framers discussed voting qualifications extensively. Democrats among them argued for liberal standards in the name of a more inclusive democracy. Others hung back. In the end, they settled for the same qualifications as the several states. That is, anyone able to vote for an assemblyman in, say, Massachusetts could also vote for a US representative in the same state.

Advocates of democracy have seen the suffrage clause as restrictive and "aristocratic." Yet it might have been precisely the opposite. Many state governments were substantially democratic already and growing ever more so. If the Framers wanted to use the Constitution as a bulwark against this trend, they forfeited an easy opportunity to do so by not imposing an independent federal standard.

Commercial Regulation

The felt need for commercial regulation was one of the driving forces behind union. Thus, the Constitution's famous commerce clause. It was short, vaguely worded and virtually without boundaries. It gave Congress the authority to "regulate Commerce with Foreign Nations, and among the several States, and with the Indian Tribes." Elsewhere, the states were enjoined from slapping their own tariffs on trade, as they had done in the Confederation.

With Congress taking charge of commercial regulation, the character of the regulation was bound be broad and general. It could not place a given state or group of states at a commercial disadvantage vis-à-vis their sisters, for to do so would run afoul of all that machinery outlined above. The effect was to create the largest—and eventually most prosperous—free-trade zone in the world.

Protection of Property

Historians have occasionally accused the Framers of devising a "backlash" plan of government expressly to protect property. Clearly the charge sticks and for reasons we ought to know well by now. For the Framers, *property* and *rights* were two sides of the same coin. A government unable to protect citizens' property could assuredly not protect their lives or liberties either, and come to that, one of life's greatest liberties was enjoying property to the full. Besides, a government based on ownership rested on people with something to lose.

The Constitution lodged the protection of property in several places. There were the implied limits on political participation described above. There was the protection of all minorities—including the wealthy—by means of the structural system. There was patent and copyright protection. There was even a specific prohibition against the states passing legal tender laws or impairing the obligation of contracts. And finally, there were the Constitution's notorious slavery clauses—which showed how far fifty-five property owners were willing to go.

Elasticity

One of the Framers' chief difficulties was that posed by the future. How to write a Constitution in 1787 that would still work in 1887 or 1987? While some regarded the task as impossible, others were more sanguine. If the Constitution's draftsmanship was kept reasonably brief and general, they thought, it might operate successfully for quite a while.

Accordingly, while the Framers pinned some things down very carefully, they left others vague and uncertain. Their strategy was to make the structure clear and concise while leaving powers and authority a little ambiguous.

They realized that sooner or later the Constitution would have to be amended. Just not frivolously. The process they set up required agreement by two-thirds of the Congress (both houses) *and* three-fourths of the states. Three-fourths is an exceptionally large fraction in politics. It required that the Constitution could only be altered by a substantial majority of the people nationally distributed. For every one of the twenty-seven amendments presently ratified, dozens have failed ignominiously, many for the lack of just one or two states.

At the same time, the Framers seem to have recognized that certain kinds of change—political, social, economic, technological—would probably require a subtler process of adaptation. The Constitution, in a word, would have to be stretchable.

The trick was to keep stretchability within limits. If the document proved to be too flexible, it wouldn't possess the detentive capacity necessary for constitutional government. And if it wasn't flexible enough, it would eventually have to be discarded. With such considerations in mind, the Framers appear to have included a discrete number of "**stretch-points**" in the constitutional text. These consisted of words or phrases so vague, general or ambiguous as to be subject to a variety of interpretations. What was "advice and consent"? "High crimes and misdemeanors"? "A republican form of government"?

Two of these stretch-points are particularly worth keeping in mind. The "necessary and proper clause," Article 1, Section 8, has already been mentioned. It would come up again and again in the course of American history. Similarly, the commerce clause, Article 1, Section 8, would fill the law books with adjudication as it was stretched first one way and then another by the Supreme Court.

Supremacy

The whole point of the Constitution, for the nationalists at least, was to provide a system of government able to counter the follies of the states. But how, exactly, to accomplish this? Within their own sphere of sovereignty, the states were still free to behave as they wished.

Articles of Confederation versus Constitution

GOVERNMENT UNDER THE ARTICLES OF CONFEDERATION:

1. States are sovereign.
2. No independent executive.
3. No federal courts—national laws are enforced by state courts.
4. No taxing power in Congress.
5. Congress has no power over interstate or foreign commerce.
6. Congress is an assembly of delegates chosen by state legislatures—delegates may be recalled at any time.
7. Articles may be amended only by the consent of all of the states.
8. Congress has only specific, delegated powers.
9. The central government cannot act directly upon the people.

GOVERNMENT UNDER THE CONSTITUTION:

1. People of the whole nation are sovereign—federal union divides exercise of sovereignty between central government and states.
2. Independent executive—chosen by electors.
3. Separate federal court system, with power to consider Constitutional questions and resolve disputes between states.
4. Congress may "lay and collect taxes, duties, imposts, and excises".
5. Congress has power to regulate commerce with foreign nations, among the several states and with Indian tribes.
6. Congress is composed of representatives who have definite tenure—House is chosen by popular vote, Senate by state legislatures.
7. Constitution may be amended with approval of three-fourths of the states.
8. Congress has implied as well as specific delegated powers.
9. The central government exercises its power directly upon the people, and concurrently with state governments.

For James Madison, the only solution was for the national government to have an absolute (as opposed to conditional) veto over all state laws. But this concept was troublesome. What became of state sovereignty, Madison's colleagues asked, if the national government could strike down state laws at will? And what happened to those delicate balances of federalism?

There were arguments on the other side as well. Of what possible use would the federal Constitution be if the states could simply ignore it? All the springs and pinions of the mechanism presupposed that national authority would have to be final.

The Framers struggled with this problem for months. Ultimately they had to settle for another compromise and more vague language. "This Constitution, and the Laws of the United States which shall be made in Pursuance thereof . . . shall be the supreme Law of the Land," it said, adding: "any Thing in the Constitution or Laws of any State to the Contrary notwithstanding."

As it turned out, the absolute and unqualified supremacy of the federal government was not established until the end of the Civil War—and then only on the battlefield.

The Constitution and the Republican Problem

We began this chapter with the Republican Problem. The first element of that problem, we recall, is to express the sovereignty of the people, as determined by numerical majorities. The Constitution clearly and consistently accomplished this end.

The second element is to protect the rights of minorities. Many of the Constitution's critics feared that it would never succeed at this decidedly more delicate task. Indeed, the movement for a bill of rights grew precisely out of that fear. It is worth noting, however, that the Framers, who were divided on so many issues, were virtually unanimous in believing that the constitutional mechanisms by themselves afforded ample protection to minorities. That was, after all, the whole point. And while it is true that the Constitution has not foiled every attempt at injustice, neither has the Bill of Rights. Together, they have foiled a very large number.

The third element of the Republican Problem is to act in behalf of the public good. Such good encompasses both majority *and* minority benefit, and thus can be extremely elusive. In short-run situations—where the public good is typically sacrificed—a republican government must be strong enough to resist the majority and wise enough to know when to do so. The American Constitution's rallying of virtue, together with its precautionary mechanisms, have often (though not always) made that strength-and-wisdom combination possible. As for long-run situations, exactly what the public good is and how it ought to be determined have provided the central text of our political drama from that time to this.

(By Mike Peters, courtesy of United Features Syndicate.)

The Sun Rising

On September 8, the Grand Convention's last ad hoc committee was appointed. The Committee of Style and Arrangement, as it was called, was given final charge of drafting the Constitution. The Framers were commonly referring to their work by that name now, a "constitution," not just a "plan" or a "proposal." Gouverneur Morris was the committee's guiding spirit. He would later boast that he had written every word of the finished document.

Which wasn't quite true. For no sooner had the "finished" document been submitted to the General Assembly on September 12, than the debate broke out anew. This word was wrong. That phrase needed fixing. There was a clause over here that might be misunderstood in light of another clause over there. And a few of the Framers still had pet projects—a canal over the mountains, a national university—that deserved one last try for inclusion. The pulling and hauling went on right up to the end.

Saturday, September 15, was the Convention's last working day, and like so many before it, it was filled with trauma. The bitterest enemies of nationalism—with the exception of Luther Martin—had long since departed for home. Those left were the Constitution's friends, or so they supposed. There were some nasty surprises in store.

Elbridge Gerry was the first of them. He stood up and recited an eleven-point critique of the Constitution. His real difficulty came down to fear of a peacetime army, which was too great a temptation, he said, for a republic to withstand. Reluctantly, Gerry declined to affix his signature.

While Gerry's demurrer was not completely unexpected, Edmund Randolph's was. Randolph had submitted the Virginia Resolves in the first place, and had stood with the nationalists ever since. Now, with heavy heart, he said, he must withhold his own support of the final product. The federal government was too strong, he feared, its powers too vague and indefinite, and it posed too great a threat to the states. Randolph was governor of Virginia and a man finely tuned to his constituents. He believed the Old Dominion would never ratify the Constitution as it stood—and would never forgive those who did.

There was a palpable heaviness in the hall when Randolph spoke, and it grew heavier still when he was followed by George Mason. The source of Mason's complaint was depressingly familiar—too much bending and crimping, too many lapses from republican purity. The government they had sketched out "would end either in monarchy or a tyrannical aristocracy," he concluded. Mason, like Gerry, had wanted contradictory things in the Constitution. He had wanted a national government so weak that it could never endanger the people's liberties—and he had wanted to trim a few of those liberties himself.

All three of these delegates had made strong contributions. They had served on the premier committees and taken part in the important debates. Madison was visibly shaken by their desertion. The Virginians had come to Philadelphia to create a strong national government, he supposed, and now, apart from the passive Judge Blair, only two of them would sign the final document—himself and George Washington.

George Mason favored laws to limit personal expenditures on fabrics, dress and furniture.

Ben Franklin sought to place the reversals in a broader context. He had prepared a little speech of his own, to be read by James Wilson the following Monday. This was the last day of the Convention, and most of it was to be ceremonial. Franklin began with reference to that pall of gloom which had accompanied Saturday's defections—the fear that the Constitution had compromised too much. "Mr. President," he began:

> I confess that there are several parts of this constitution which I do not at present approve. But I am not sure I shall never approve them. For having lived long, I have experienced many instances of being obliged by better information or fuller consideration, to change opinions even on important subjects, which I once thought right, but found to be otherwise. It is therefore that the older I grow, the more apt I am to doubt my own judgment, and to pay more respect to the judgment of others. . . .
>
> In these sentiments, Sir, I agree to this Constitution with all its faults, if they are such. . . . I consent, Sir, to this Constitution because I expect no better and because I am not sure that it is not the best.

Although nearing the end of his astonishing career, Benjamin Franklin contributed wit and wisdom to the Constitutional Convention. (By Charles Willson Peale (after David Martin), courtesy of the American Philosophical Society, Philadelphia.)

Franklin was equally appropriate off the cuff. "Whilst the last members were signing [the Constitution]," Madison penned in his now book-length notes:

> Doctr. Franklin looking towards the Presidents chair, at the back of which a rising sun happened to be painted, observed to a few members near him, that painters had found it difficult to distinguish in their art a rising from a setting sun. I have, said he, often and often in the course of the session, and the vicissitudes of my hopes and fears as to its issue, looked at that behind the President without being able to tell whether it was rising or setting: But now at length I have the happiness to know that it is a rising and not a setting sun.

The sentiment was light and charming. All the same, the old man wept when he signed the Constitution.

Suggestions for Further Reading

Douglass G. Adair, "Experience Must Be Our Only Guide: History, Democratic Theory, and the United States Constitution," in Ray A. Billington, ed., *The Reinterpretation of Early American History* (1966).

Douglass G. Adair, "That Politics May Be Reduced to a Science: David Hume, James Madison, and the Tenth Federalist," in Jack P. Green, ed., *The Reinterpretation of the American Revolution, 1763–1789* (1968).

George W. Carey, "Separation of Powers and the Madisonian Model: A Reply to the Critics," *American Political Science Review* (March 1978).

Rufus S. Davis, *The Federal Principle: A Journey Through Time in Quest of a Meaning* (1978).

Martin Diamond, "Democracy and The Federalist: A Reconsideration of the Framers' Intent," *American Political Science Review* (March 1959).

Richard Allen Epstein, ed., *Constitutional Protection of Private Property and Freedom of Contract* (2000).

Philip B. Kurland and Ralph Lerner, eds., *The Founders' Constitution* (1987).

Arthur O. Lovejoy, "The Theory of Human Nature in the American Constitution and the Method of Counterpoise," in *Reflections on Human Nature* (1961).

Broadus Mitchell and Louise Pearson Mitchell, *A Biography of the Constitution of the United States: Its Origin, Formation, Adoption and Interpretation* (1975).

Robert J. Morgan, "Madison's Analysis of the Sources of Political Authority," *American Political Science Review* (September 1981).

Sarah Baumgartner Thurow, ed., *To Secure the Blessings of Liberty* (1988).

CHAPTER 8 STUDY AID ▬▬▬▬▬

(This aid is not all-inclusive and is not intended to be a substitute for thorough study of the material presented in the textbook.)

The Constitutional Convention III
Structure and Dynamics

I. A New Idea of Government

1. The Republican Problem:
   - Express sovereignty of the people
   - Protect rights of individuals
   - Seek public good
2. Historical precedent:
   - Classical republics—ignored rights of minorities, failed to seek public good
   - Liberal republics—limited popular sovereignty, inconsistently sought public good
   - American states and the Confederation—very limited success
   - Republican diseases, republican cure

II. Fundamental Ideas and Conceptions

1. Fundamental law:
   - Above ordinary acts of legislation
   - English constitution
   - Stands prior to government and above the governing process
   - Created and ratified by the people
2. Written constitution:
   - Holds government responsible
   - Focuses public opinion
   - Checks constitutional drift
3. Enumeration of powers:
   - Limits government
   - Mix of broad and strict language

III. Republican Mechanisms

1. Popular sovereignty:
   - The people as a "whole"
   - Consent—"original" and "periodic"

2. Representation:
   - Attorneyship
   - Virtual
3. Virtue mechanisms:
   - Representative principle
   - Fame
   - Religion

IV. Auxiliary Precautions

1. Counterpoise:
   - One's self-interest versus another's self-interest
   - "Hot" versus "Cool"
2. Separation of powers:
   - Legislative, executive, judicial
   - Working counterpoise needed: total separation = deadlock
   - The executive and the veto
   - Qualification of members
   - Rules of proceedings
   - Enumeration of powers
   - Checks and balances

V. Separation of Powers Design

1. Strong legislature:
   - Taxation, commerce, mint money, court system, declare war, etc.
   - Correcting defects of Confederation
   - Retain limited government
2. Strong executive:
   - Executing the law
   - National administration
   - Commander in chief
   - Diplomacy
3. Strong judiciary:
   - No independent will
   - Rule enforcer
   - Referee
   - Isolated from politics as usual

VI. Checks and Balances

1. Shared powers:
   - Cooperation

- Compromise
- Independence

2. Bicameralism:
- House of Representatives—mind of the people—"Hot"
- Senate—deliberative—"Cool"

3. Power of appointment:
- President
- Senate—advise and consent

4. War and diplomacy:
- Negotiation and ratification of treaties
- War—Congress declares; president conducts

5. Investigation and impeachment:
- Investigation inherent in legislative function
- Impeachment—treason, bribery, high crimes and misdemeanors

VII. Federal Mechanisms

1. Federalism:
- Separation of powers with checks and balances between federal government and states

2. National interest:
- Dangerous majorities neutralized

3. Other features:
- Suffrage qualifications
- Commercial regulation
- Protection of property
- Elasticity
- Supremacy—national or state?

4. The republican problem—solved?
- Sovereignty of the people—yes
- Rights of minorities—yes and no
- Public good—always a work in progress

5. Rising sun:
- A constitution
- Final reckoning among the delegates
- Perhaps "the best possible"

CHAPTER 8 REVIEW QUESTIONS ———

NAME: _____   SECTION: _____

Key Terms

The Republican Problem

Enumeration

Popular Sovereignty

Virtue Mechanisms

Auxiliary Precautions

Counterpoise

Separation of Powers

Checks and Balances

Federalism

Multiple Choice Questions

1. Which of the following is not an example of periodic consent:
   a. An election.
   b. A law.
   c. A Constitutional amendment.
   d. An executive pardon.

2. State representatives voting on bills as they see fit is an example of:
   a. Virtual representation.
   b. Original consent.
   c. Attorneyship representation.
   d. Popular sovereignty.

3. All of the following are virtue mechanisms except:
   a. Fame.
   b. The Electoral College.
   c. Veto power.
   d. No religion tests.

4. Which of the following is not a power enumerated to the Legislative Branch:
   a. To set up the federal court system.
   b. To establish the postal service.
   c. To nominate justices to the Supreme Court.
   d. To coin money.

Review Questions

1. What benefits does a nation draw from having a written, as opposed to an unwritten, constitution?

   _____

   _____

   _____

   _____

2. Why does the text describe the Constitution's ban of religion tests as a virtue mechanism?

   _____

   _____

   _____

   _____

3. How did the Constitution create a "free trade zone" within the United States?

   _____

   _____

   _____

   _____

4. What does "elasticity" mean? What are some elastic clauses in the Constitution?

   _____

   _____

   _____

   _____

5. How did the Founders solve the three aspects of the Republican Problem?

   _____

   _____

   _____

   _____

Review Exercises

1. Define both original and periodic consent in your own words. How do we still exercise original consent?

   _____

   _____

   _____

   _____

2. Explain the concept of counterpoise as James Madison understood it.

_____

_____

_____

_____

3. Briefly explain the idea of federalism. What is it and how does it work?

_____

_____

_____

_____

Big Essay Question

Find a recent newspaper with a story about a current political issue or controversy. Describe the issue. Then explain it using concepts from this chapter such as counterpoise, fame and the other virtue mechanisms and auxiliary precautions. Be as thorough as possible.

The Meaning of the Constitution

(*The American Institution*, by Aimee Morgan, reprinted by permission of the artist.)

When it appeared that the ratification of the Constitution might come down to the pivotal state of New York, Alexander Hamilton began to pen a series of newspaper essays for fellow New Yorkers. He would describe how the proposed system would work and then go on to explain why it would work, why it would mobilize virtue and contain self-interest, would empower the people while protecting their rights—would make possible the Good Society.

Hamilton was soon joined in this effort by friend and colleague **John Jay**, and then by the indefatigable James Madison, who had learned so many of the answers the hard way. Indeed, before *The Federalist* was completed, Madison would be their principal author. As far as readers were concerned, however, all eight-five essays were written by a single disembodied intellect named "Publius."

The Federalist was the deepest and most searching inquiry into republican government that had ever been made, and for many scholars still the best. They chartered a tradition of constitutional analysis that still flourishes today, for Publius would eventually be joined by a distinguished company of historians, political scientists, legal theorists and assorted *philosophes*, all of them probing the mysteries of a single parchment.

What follows are but a few of the insights of Publius and his friends.

John Jay was a prominent New York statesman and first Chief Justice of the US Supreme Court. Wrote only 3 of the 85 essays in *The Federalist* due to ill health.

Federalist Papers:
http://www.yale.edu/lawweb/ avalon/federal/fed.htm

http://www.leftjustified.com/ leftjust/lib/sc/ht/fed/index .html

The Constitution and Human Nature

Even though the Framers did not write the Constitution for mankind as a whole, they believed it must be "true" to human nature. Had they gotten that wrong, as one historian observed, their project would have undoubtedly been short-lived. While they had no formal debates on human nature, their discussions touched on the subject over and over again. What kind of an animal was man, they asked, and how could his attributes be harnessed to the cause at hand?

Virtue or Self-Interest?

In chapter 1 we saw the ancients' answer to that question. Man, they held, was an animal in quest of virtue in all its forms, and political virtue most of all, for the *polis* was but the individual soul writ large. Thus, virtuous leaders were bound to seek justice, virtuous citizens must lose themselves in politics, and together they would honor the public good.

During the European Enlightenment, some thinkers—Machiavelli, Hobbes, the irrepressible David Hume—began to question the ancient wisdom, even though it had held sway for two millennia. These *realists*, as we might call them, questioned virtue from many angles. It was unstable, they argued, and could vanish overnight in trying circumstances. It was associated with visionary schemes, utopian projects, radical ideas and monkish otherworldliness. It could foment a conquer-the-world spirit of aggression. And it could prompt a society to purge itself of "undesirables."

The most telling indictment was that virtue did not truly reflect human nature. To be sure, *Homo sapiens* could be forced, under pressure, to rise above themselves in the name of *areté*, but there was always a great deal of back drag. It was, to borrow a phrase from Madison, like asking men to be angels.

The realists sought the Good Society in a different way. After carefully observing actual (as opposed to theoretical) human behavior, they concluded that most people were driven by self-interest more than virtue. They sought ways to increase their wealth, enhance their comfort and gratify their immediate desires. Self-interest did not necessarily incline them toward bad behavior even though it certainly might. It could also incline them toward creativity and cooperation, as in the marketplace. The trick was to observe self-interest and learn of its ways. Then, by designing an interest-driven—and interest-moderating—political structure, they could bring forth a Good Society that really worked.

Yet even with the realists in full cry, the older thinking still persisted. Advocates of virtue—we will call them the *idealists*—continued to insist that man could not abandon his moral sense, that self-interest could not answer human needs and that greed could never form the basis of a Good Society. They cited Montesquieu to this effect and the ever popular Rousseau.

Americans had a peculiar fascination with virtue, which they associated with their emerging identity. When they used the term, they imagined ideal characters, much like the action heroes of our own time, who fight on the side of right and never give a thought to reward. And the notion received a great deal of reinforcement. American founding myths—the Promised Land, the Chosen People—implied a special endowment of virtue. American churches, searching for common ground amid their differences, emphasized loving one's neighbor and living the Golden Rule. And not least, there was the commonwealth ideology with its creed of virtuous patriotism.

The Revolution proved that Americans were indeed willing to sacrifice for their country, and the virtue they spoke of was not empty prattle. But then came the postwar disillusionment. By the eve of the Constitutional Convention, it was unfashionable to speak of virtue in some quarters. Jefferson, for instance, who had once praised the ideals of his countrymen, now pedaled them softly. "The fantastical idea of virtue and the public good being a sufficient security of the state," he wrote to Edmund Pendleton, "I assure you was never mine."

As practical men, the Framers had to consider such realities. There was a sense among them that faith in American virtue must be amended. But *amended*, not *abandoned*. The centrality of virtue to a working republic was still accepted

The Problem of Sally's Two Dates

Sally Johnson would not see herself as a study in human nature. But Sally's dilemma presents some key issues of human nature in particularly convenient terms. Her difficulty is that she has two different dates for Saturday night.

It should be explained at the outset that Sally is a very nice person. She is radiant, wholesome and attractive. Along with a career in marketing, she wants to marry, raise a family, live in the suburbs and seek the Good Life. She is a good student at Wellesley College, is popular and well liked, is active in her church and an officer in her sorority. Toward other people she has been taught to behave with compassion and respect. She is the all-American girl.

But she has a problem. On Tuesday last, Fred Schultz called and asked her for a date on Saturday. Good old Fred. A date with him would unvaryingly include two lines of bowling at the student union, frozen yogurt, twenty minutes in the video arcade and a walk back to the dorm. Fred was, bless his heart, something of a nerd. But Sally wasn't doing anything on Saturday night, and so she accepted.

Then on Wednesday, who should telephone but Lance—*the* Lance. Lance W. Rockefeller IV. He had seen her at the Black and White Formal, he said, and would like to get to know her. On Friday he and some friends were going to take the Lear jet down to the Bahamas for the weekend. There would be swimming and tennis, a short cruise on the fam-

ily yacht, dinner at the Royal Poinciana and perhaps a stroll along the beach at sunset. Mom and Dad were staying at the villa themselves, so everything would be chaperoned and aboveboard. Would she like to come along?

Would she ever! But there is that problem of the other date—with Fred. Breaking it would be a simple enough matter. She could call Fred and make up an excuse. Of course, that would mean telling a lie. It would also mean breaching a commitment and violating a trust. Sally has been taught that trusts and commitments are matters of no small moment, and that lies are unthinkable.

What should she do? Here are the thoughts that flit through her mind while the decision is being made.

In the real world there is such a thing as a permissible lie. Indeed, the real world is quite patently founded on permissible lies. And lies aimed at averting hurt feelings are obviously permissible.

Lance Rockefeller, with all his millions, is probably not the marrying kind. Courtship with him—allowing the imagination to soar—might well prove tantalizing, frustrating, and in the end, disastrous. Fred, bless his heart, is the marrying kind and would probably make someone a good husband.

Suppose word got around that Sally Johnson broke dates, jettisoned commitments, jumped at the best opportunity. This might not be good for her reputation in the long run.

Actually, it might be wrong *not* to break the date. She could never marry Fred. She was just leading him on. To go with Fred and be hating him every minute *would not be fair to Fred*. For Fred's own good she should be up-front with him and let him find someone his own speed.

Who was this Lance, anyway, that she should compromise her integrity for him? What could a single date, no matter how glorious, have to compare with her idea of herself? "This above all, to thine own self be true. . . ."

On the other hand, why not do it to Fred? Fred would probably do it to her. Others had. Bad things happened in the world. It was a bad world.

Suppose she turned Lance down. Maybe he would call again. Indeed, maybe he would respect her the more for her honesty. Maybe forthrightness would give her the winning edge over competitors.

Then, again, suppose he never called again. Suppose this was her only chance. Suppose he took some other—less upright—girl to the Bahamas and would wind up marrying her. "The saddest words of tongue and pen. . . ."

Mrs. Lance W. Rockefeller IV. . .

There they are, the sentiments of mankind. Enlightened self-interest. Corrupt self-interest. Virtue for its own sake. Virtue by calculation. All of them occur to Sally as indeed they would occur to most of us in her situation.

The question is, which of them will determine the outcome?

by most of them. The question was not whether to forget about it entirely, but whether it could somehow be made to serve.

Virtuous Self-Interest

To begin with, they must squarely face virtue's limitations. It was unreasonable, for instance, to expect virtuous behavior all the time. Experience proved otherwise. There were stories in the Revolution of men standing rocklike in their battle lines—only to flee in terror on a subsequent engagement. Jefferson himself, to his lifelong shame, abandoned the Virginia governor's office at the approach of Lord Dunmore's troops and scuttled off to Monticello.

It was equally unreasonable to expect virtue in everyone. In the Revolution, the conduct of a comparative few had inspired others to what might be called situational virtue. On the night of the famous attack at Princeton, two of the three assaulting forces had encountered obstacles and turned back. The third force, commanded personally by Washington and inspired by his battlefield courage, overcame the obstacles and fought its way through.

Finally, few in the modern world could be expected to live by a code that was two thousand years out of date. Renounce one's private life and lose oneself in politics? View the political community as one's own soul writ large? Sacrifice personal interest for the public good? Not in the eighteenth century.

The Framers, then, agreed to subject virtue to fewer demands. After all, a commercial society did not require citizens to live in barracks, as they had in ancient Sparta, or walk barefoot in the snow to prove their hardihood. It required them to settle accounts, abide by contracts and be honest within reasonable limits. Nor were such behaviors altruistic, as *areté* might have been, or beyond the common range. Rather, they embodied what we might call *virtuous self-interest*, a milder and saner form of virtue that depended on horse sense to tame selfishness rather than zealotry to expunge it. With virtuous self-interest, citizens could lead ordinary lives and pursue their own happiness—subject mostly to the governance of the self.

Virtue and Structure

During the Confederation period, people like John Adams had thought a great deal about the possible use of structure to solve the virtue problem. It was an old concept, tracing all the way back to Aristotle, and it could be employed in a variety of ways. One of them was to provide a safety net in those instances when virtue—even among a virtuous people—might suddenly fail.

- Auxiliary Precautions

What Madison called "auxiliary precautions" were based on the realists' view of human nature rather than the idealists'. The guiding assumption was that in the best of societies some individuals would reach for power, some groups would ignore the public good, some voters would be easily manipulated and some players would never play by the rules.

So the Framers designed a structure of government according to the principle of "counterpoise," to the end that interest would counter interest and ambition thwart ambition. Auxiliary precautions were not, as some political scientists have contended, the center ring of the circus disguised as a sideshow. They really were, in the Framers' minds, "auxiliary." The center ring was to be the American people peacefully living their lives.

- Structure to Mobilize Virtue

The Framers also realized that structure might have a lot to do with the "situational virtue" mentioned above. In chapter 8 we saw how they employed specific structural devices—many of them borrowed from David Hume—to insure that the most virtuous wound up in stations of greatest trust.

They employed even subtler devices. They sought to make certain, wherever possible, that the wise leadership they hoped for could bring virtue to bear in concrete, practical ways. How, they asked, could a president rally the forces of justice in a dicey situation—the way Washington had rallied his troops at Princeton? The following represents a rough scenario (based on experience) of how the question might be answered.

The US Congress, fearful that a small religious group known as the Druids has become a public nuisance, passes a law to deprive all Druids of their civil and political rights. This measure violates the rule of law, for it singles out a specific group for punishment. It also violates the Constitution, which gives Congress no authority whatsoever in religious matters.

The president doesn't like Druids any more than Congress does, but he has taken an oath to defend the Constitution. Apart from that, he is worried about political fallout. He won the last election only narrowly, and the loss of the religious fringe might make all the difference next time. Besides, he is becoming seriously concerned about Congress. Victory on such a high-profile issue may tempt some muscle-flexing congressmen into who-knows-what foolishness.

For reasons of both virtue and self-interest, then, the president decides to veto the measure. He writes out a veto message and marshals every argument he can think of to give it weight. Some of his arguments appeal to political self-interest, others to a sense of civic virtue. The message is available for the public to read, so it is bound to raise a dust. And since the president's leadership is now on the line, he begins calling his friends in Congress and twisting their arms to help out.

Some congressmen are persuaded by the president's dialectics and others by his personal appeals. Still others, who may reject both, are moved to stop and think. Defeating the president on this kind of issue may come back to haunt them at election time. After all, did *they* want to answer for constitutional trespass?

The president doesn't have to persuade *all* the congressmen. A third of them plus one will suffice to block the override, and since a quarter of them voted against the measure in the first place, the president only has to change *one-twelfth* of the votes. He probably will.

How many of the altered votes are motivated by virtue and how many by self-interest? It doesn't really matter. The point is that in a situation where the worst in human nature had a tactical advantage, the constitutional structure began altering personal motives and rallying the forces of justice. Put simply, the Constitution operated to make virtuous conduct a matter of self-interest.

Idea of the Extended Republic

We know something of the objections raised by many Americans to what Madison and the nationalists called the *extended republic*. To some ears the term sounded like an oxymoron. Republics were supposed to build a sense of togetherness—a feeling of "commonwealth" and "public good." How could such a feeling be created across a sprawling continent? How could citizens maintain contact with one another and with the governing process? Worst of all, how could they withstand the turmoil of *so many* factions?

James Madison:
http://www.jmu.edu/
madison/

http://leftjustified.com/
leftjust/lib/sc/ht/fed/
index.html

Madison himself had been bothered by these questions, but in the course of his deliberations with fellow nationalists (and the study that occupied most of his evenings) he had come up with an answer. It was to become Madison's great contribution to political theory—and a cornerstone of the American Founding.

In his reading of the ever pertinent David Hume, Madison became intrigued with Hume's concept of political representation as a "refining" process. In each ascending tier of representation, we recall, the persons chosen were held to be ever broader in outlook and ever better known for their virtue. As Madison pondered this notion, it struck him that its implications were exactly the reverse of the small republic idea—for it meant that bigger was *better* not *worse*. The larger the territory the more tiers of representation required, and the more tiers of representation the more virtuous the government. Madison coupled this insight with an observation of his own. Factional turmoil was not rarer in smaller states than larger ones. If anything, just the opposite. In tiny Rhode Island, for example, not only was factionalism alive and well, one faction had an absolute chokehold on the government.

Suddenly it occurred to Madison that the conventional wisdom on factions might be all backward. It wasn't a case of the smaller the state the fewer the factions, as the ancients had supposed—but the smaller the state *the more risk of a factional takeover.* For in a small state, a single large faction might find itself with little or no opposition. All at once Madison saw the classical republics through new eyes. Their governments had always been plagued by factional conflict and its dire consequences. The malady had usually been blamed on democracy—on the unrestrained passions of the people. Perhaps the blame really rested on the *polis* itself and its diminutive size.

What if, thought Madison, a republic were to seek peace through the opposite strategy? Instead of urging citizens to overcome human nature and rise above self-interest, as the ancients had done, suppose the republic simply acknowledged self-interest and welcomed all factions to the fray. Each faction would have many competitors in the scramble for influence—and in the extended republic many, many competitors—and the probability that any single one of them could dominate all the others would reduce to zero. The large republic, then, must be stronger and more stable, not weaker and more faction-ridden, than the small republic. Bigger really was better.

Such a recasting of the problem and rethinking of the solution was little short of astonishing. Madison had taken two thousand years of unchallenged assumption and turned it upside down.

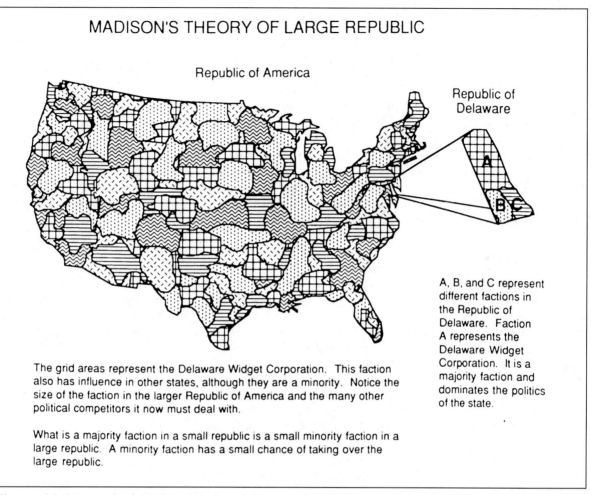

MADISON'S THEORY OF LARGE REPUBLIC

Republic of America

Republic of Delaware

A, B, and C represent different factions in the Republic of Delaware. Faction A represents the Delaware Widget Corporation. It is a majority faction and dominates the politics of the state.

The grid areas represent the Delaware Widget Corporation. This faction also has influence in other states, although they are a minority. Notice the size of the faction in the larger Republic of America and the many other political competitors it now must deal with.

What is a majority faction in a small republic is a small minority faction in a large republic. A minority faction has a small chance of taking over the large republic.

All at once Madison saw the classical republics through new eyes.

The Ambiguous Founding

The Founders' complex understanding of human nature led to a Founding which was ambiguous and multilayered. We have seen that all three kinds of republicanism—classical, liberal and democratic—derived meaning from the American Revolution. All three found fulfillment in the Constitution. As a result, the Constitution struck a balance between republican virtue and material self-interest—and redefined both. We have seen how virtue was redefined to reflect wisdom, prudence and common sense. Self-interest was redefined as well. It was the self-interest of a "moral and religious people" in John Adams' words—a self-interest of self-governance.

The Founding's ultimate reliance on virtue may point to a dark future, for our supply of moral energy might eventually run out. The Founders pinned their hopes on three possible sources of renewal. First, there was the religious

Factional Takeover: The Case of Grenada

We know it is difficult for single factions to take over large republics. Witness the United States. In small republics, by contrast, single factions can take charge much more easily. Witness Grenada.

In the spring of 1979, Grenada seemed anything but ripe for revolution. Life in the sleepy island had coursed along happily for more than twenty years under the uncontroversial Eric Matthew Gairy. True, there was some discontent. Youngsters unable to find work in the island's on-again, off-again economy idled about, filling their afternoons with fishing off the rust-colored reefs. When agents from Castro's Cuba came preaching an angry new gospel in the mid-1970s, some of these kids were ready to listen. So began the New Jewel Movement.

The movement's tactics were peaceful at first. Its presidential candidate, Maurice Bishop, sermonized about socialism and wrote blistering editorials in the *Torchlight*. Bishop was not content with constitutional politics, however, and his two lieutenants, Kendrick Radix and Bernard Coard, were even less so. With tactical and logistic support from Havana, they set about planning a coup.

The takeover proved to be absurdly easy. The NJM commandos merely waited until Gairy left the country, gathered up units of the People's Revolutionary Army and began battering their way into the country's clapboard police stations. By the end of the day, March 13, 1979, Grenada was their very own.

Of course, consolidating the NJM's rule, especially among a non-ideological and often unwilling populace, proved another matter. Gairy's entire government was jailed. His small defense force was rounded up and neutralized. Radio Free Grenada was set up to portray the former president as a fascist dictator, while the *Free West Indian* began inundating the island with Castroite propaganda. As for the *Torchlight*, which had earlier befriended the NJM, it was shut down completely. And when twenty-six leading citizens tried to launch a publication of their own, they were arrested and locked away in the Richmond Hill prison.

Meanwhile, Soviet "cruise liners" began putting into St. George's, and one of them unloaded three thousand AK47 automatic rifles for the People's Revolutionary Army. Popular uprisings were well and good, as Grenada's new masters understood— but they had to be kept under control.

influence. Once separated from the political process, churches would hopefully focus their attention on the making of citizens as well as the saving of souls. Second, there was education. So highly did the Founders regard this influence that several of them sought to provide for a national university in the Constitution. And finally there was the old Platonic hope that self-renewal might be generated by the Good Society itself—that good politics could forge good people. Of course all three propositions were iffy.

The Constitution and the Rule of Law

In chapter 5 we saw how the rule of law helped to explain shortcomings of both the Confederation and state governments. The Confederation was abandoned with the Constitution's adoption. Many of the state governments, learning from experience, reformed or completely rewrote their constitutions with the rule of law in mind.

The US Constitution was also written with the rule of law in mind. Using our earlier five principles as a guide, we can see some of the specific ways the Framers expressed rule of law concerns:

Generality. Congress was forbidden to create titles of nobility (which would impose different categories of citizenship) or to single out any person in a **bill of attainder**.

Prospectivity. Congress was prohibited from passing any *ex post facto* law.

Publicity. Congress was required to keep a journal of its proceedings and publish it to the people.

Consent. Suffrage was guaranteed to all who enjoyed that right in their respective states.

Due Process. Trial by jury was required in all federal cases, and Congress was forbidden to suspend *habeas corpus* under all but the most extreme circumstances.

But the way in which the rule of law figured into the Constitution was both broader and more subtle than these features indicate. The whole structure of the federal government was designed so that rule making and rule enforcement would be placed in different hands.

Congress was made the essential rule maker. The executive plays some role in the process—in his use of the veto, for example—but the *essential* rule maker is Congress. And the judicial system is the essential rule enforcer. Once again, the picture is muddied a little by the executive, who has certain enforcement functions as well—but the *essential* rule enforcer is the court system. For in the end, judges and juries must decide how, when, where and against whom the laws will take effect.

We have seen what happens when rule making and rule enforcement are not separated. In republican governments based on an all-powerful legislature, the outcome was often simple tyranny. For as with any Nero or Caligula, the

Bill of Attainder:
Legislative act in which an individual is simultaneously charged with a crime and found guilty.

The executive is in charge of arresting lawbreakers and bringing them to trial.

unchecked majority sought to have its way at all cost, victimizing outsiders, minorities, eccentrics, advocates of unpopular opinion or those who seemed ripe for plucking. In the notorious case of postwar Rhode Island, the debtor interest pushed laws through the legislature requiring creditors to accept depreciated paper currency in payment of loans—or go to jail. In contrast to the rule of law, this was the *rule of will*.

The Framers of the Constitution wanted no such tyranny. They took utmost pains to separate the judicial branch from both of the others and shelter it away from politics.

Rule of Law Politics

With this separation in place, the psychology of governance was all different. The rule maker, lacking enforcement ability, was obliged to operate blindly. He could no longer single out specific targets, for he couldn't be sure how his rules would be applied. Think about the "Druid" case once again. It would be useless for Congress to pass laws against the Druids, even without a presidential veto, for in the end, conscience-stricken judges could render such laws unenforceable.

So rule makers were obliged to change their ways. If they wanted to draft enforceable legislation, they must now try to frame their objectives as generally as possible. Instead of singling out the Druids by name, they might try legislating against a particular Druid practice such as, oh, jaywalking. The law now becomes more enforceable as far as the courts are concerned, but it also enjoins *everyone* from jaywalking, not just Druids. Judges like this kind of law. It is precise, morally defensible and amenable to adjudication. Unlike being a Druid, which is hard to prove and even harder to get juries riled up about, it is something the law can really sort out. Druids, of course, like anyone else, can avoid the law's sanctions simply by waiting for the light to change.

The Constitution not only protects Druids from Congress but also from the courts. Suppose the judicial branch loathed Druids and wished to lock them all up. They might nail the ones who jaywalk, true enough, but lacking the means to legislate, that is all the judges can do. They are as blind in their function as the lawmakers are. They can only address the general behavior of jaywalking.

Separating rule making and rule enforcement, then, brings the process of governance closer to the rule of law. The laws have an automatic tendency to become more general, more prospective and so on than they might otherwise.

What about checks and balances? These too can promote the rule of law, as yet another elaboration of our Druid story might illustrate. Suppose the original Druid measure passes through Congress and is vetoed by the president, as we saw above, and suppose the override fails. Congress is still out to get the Druids, but it has learned a hard lesson. And the jaywalking approach won't help either. At this point, congressional leaders may actually sit down with the president and say, *What sort of measure would you accept?*

This is an important question, one often asked in American politics. The president is likely to answer: *I would accept a measure closer in keeping with the rule of law*. Why? Because, being a canny politician, he has a sharp eye on the people. He knows they distrust laws that single out one group for punishment. He knows they realize that persecution of Druids today might lead to persecution of Mormons tomorrow and Libertarians the day after. And he knows the jay-walking subterfuge won't fool them. The people's virtue, knowledge and sophistication will weigh into the checks and balances of the system in large ways and small. So either the Druids (along with everyone else) must be held accountable to real laws or they must be let off the hook. If Druids rob banks or kidnap children, the laws can really put them out of business. Otherwise they (along with everyone else) are scot-free.

How the Rule of Law Creates Freedom

How, precisely, does the rule of law create freedom? For some people, freedom and law seem antithetical. How can anyone be free, they ask, if there are so many rules to obey? Others point out that some of the world's worst tyrannies have had the same machinery as democracies—i.e. legislatures, legal codes, court systems—so why didn't the law create freedom there? A third objection arises from the fact that majorities, often very slender ones, speak for everyone in the legislative process and often pass laws of dubious popularity. What "freedom" is there for the hapless minority?

The best way to see how rules create freedom is to visit a hot dog stand on a busy day. The hungry patrons automatically queue up into a line. The head of the line is served first. No crowding in. Places can be held by friends under prescribed restrictions. *No one has to have any of this explained.* Or think of a group of eight-year-olds hunkering down to a game of marbles. Before the play begins, they call out a set of rules for the match at hand. There isn't much

Fuel shortage in the 1970s. There were no rules posted or police to direct traffic, yet Americans queued up in an orderly way.
(Courtesy of Corbis Images.)

"legislation"—just quick agreement. In both cases we see the almost instinctive creation of rules to head off potential conflict. These rules don't constrain freedom—they make it possible.

Such unconscious rule making illustrates a central truth about the rule of law. For when the laws of society adhere to the rule of law, they function precisely like the examples given above—as facilitators of freedom. Put another way, the rule of law makes the laws of society work like the laws of nature. They become as steady and predictable as gravity, and living by them enables people to interact with mutual benefit. This fact underscores the difference between regimes of liberty and regimes of tyranny. The latter may have all the visible machinery of law, but because they lack the *rule* of law they don't resemble nature in the least. They are full of nasty surprises.

Consider the case of car theft. I see an automobile I have always wanted and discover an easy chance to steal it. Knowing the laws of society, I can assume that if I do steal the car, I will be caught and punished. Accordingly, under the rule of law, I alone determine what my fate will be—for I alone can decide whether or not to bring on the consequences. In a rule of will society, none of this may apply. I might decide to steal the car and, depending on my connections, may never go to jail at all. Conversely, I might decide not to steal the car and yet *still* wind up in the slammer—just because someone in power doesn't like me. Without the rule of law, I cannot govern my own destiny. With it, I can.

The rule of law also provides an answer to the slender majority problem. As long as the laws meet the tests outlined above, it doesn't really matter whether every single person approves of them. The important quality of law is predictability not popularity. Any law is bound to offend *someone*—work through some examples and see for yourself. So long as the laws satisfy the majority and are aimed at "bank robbers" rather than "Druids," they cannot pose a threat to freedom.

Law Versus "Administration"

There is an inherent tendency for all governments, not just tyrannical ones, to fudge here and there on the rule of law. Governments have to administer things—precisely in the way large corporations do. They must build roads, operate schools, collect garbage, care for the poor, maintain armies and navies and so on. They acquire large and complex bureaucracies to perform these tasks. And for most of the tasks, government need pay no attention whatsoever to the rule of law. *Administration* does not require it.

It is only *governance* that requires it. It is only when laying down the rules governing people's lives that the government must be careful about the rule of law. Consider any administrative situation and the difference soon becomes apparent. In building a road, let us say, a government can favor certain contractors, back out of agreements, ignore the public, conduct shoddy inspections and keep vital information secret. While these practices violate every principle of the rule of law (and certainly do the government no credit), they are not tyrannical. *For they don't govern people's lives.*

Whitehall: Administrative center for British Empire.

Some governments never distinguish between the two cases. They suppose they are *governing* their citizens when in fact they are *administering* them as they might administer highway construction. This is precisely what brought on the American Revolution. In order to reform their ramshackle empire, the bureaucrats in Whitehall began overhauling everything—forgetting that they were *altering the laws of society* in the process. What the American colonists reacted to was not the improvement of customs collection or the untangling of imperial authority—but the "administration" of their lives.

Behind the Constitution, then, there was a strong commitment to the rule of law. For as the Framers realized, that and that alone could create freedom.

The Constitution as a Moral Document

The American Constitution is sometimes said to lack a soul. It is not about truth or justice—those passions of the ancient republics—nor does it embody what philosophers call a moral theory. It is merely a design of government. So goes the critique anyway.

Those who hold this view go on to argue that the American people, faced with such emptiness, have had to turn to the Declaration of Independence or the Bill of Rights for the moral inspiration that a founding requires. Those documents bolster our liberal individualism, to be sure, and give us claims against society in the form of rights. But that is not quite a moral theory either. What of our claims *as* a society? What about our sense of nationhood and common purpose, our place in the world and the meaning of our national undertaking? What is there to say of the American people *as* a people?

For some, these questions are irrelevant. Americans, they say, are primarily understood as individuals, autonomous and independent, not as *a people.* The Founders seem not to have taken this view. They appear to have regarded the founding of the United States as just that—a *founding*, a full-fledged announcement of nationhood. And they regarded the Constitution not just as a plan for living together, but as a call to live by certain ideals. Why else would they be so concerned about virtue or the rule of law?

If this is true, why didn't the Founders come out and say so? They had their reasons. One of them was to get the Constitution adopted. They didn't want to antagonize the states (any more than they already had) with heady nationalist rhetoric. And they generally shied away from declamatory prose, which was often vague, usually sententious, and always a source of confusion. For them, the real truths were the "self-evident" ones.

The Dignity of Mankind

Let us consider the following case. Suppose that for the Founders, the moral theory of the Constitution was among those self-evident truths. It wasn't so much a point to argue as a given to assume. We should keep the Scottish Enlightenment in mind while exploring such a possibility, for thinkers like Francis Hutchinson had held that truth operated on the level of common sense and didn't require elaboration. And several of the Founders were among his disciples.

In order to see the world as the Founders did, we must glimpse their view of the past. They had recently fought a great war, which they saw as a war for all mankind, and against daunting odds they had won. They attributed their victory to civic virtue, and belief in that virtue both set them apart and bound them together. Moreover—and here is another crucial point—they widely understood the outcome in terms of divine favor.

At the same time Americans had proven the success of republicanism. They hadn't just *proclaimed* republican principles, they had *applied* them. They had come together as "the people" and created their own governments, and defects notwithstanding, the governments had actually worked.

Finally, and most importantly, the Founders identified both the Revolution and republican government with "the Laws of Nature and of Nature's God." In their minds, the reason for their double success was that they had acted in conformity with universal truth. For them there really *was* a moral law in the universe—and it made all the difference.

This aspect of the Founding is often glossed over. Yet it is difficult to make sense of the Founders' actions, and still less of their explanations, without weighing in these assumptions. Natural law, as we have seen, was understood to represent the higher law, the moral law, the law by which all human actions must be judged. Belief in such a code had a long and respectable history. The American Founders did not give lengthy disquisitions about it precisely because they more or less took it for granted.

It was according to natural law, as Charles Kesler points out, that the Declaration of Independence and its arguments for human equality, natural rights and government by consent held together and made sense. The Revolution worked, one might say, because the Laws of Nature were believed to operate for rather than against it.

And the same went for republican governance. The Founders recognized that most republican governments—indeed, practically all of them—had dismally failed. So why bother with republicanism at all? Why not just take the best features of the British system, elect a Parliament, find a worthy person to be crowned king and call the job done? This might well have been a useful course under the circumstances.

For an answer, we must read the Founders broadly, gauging assumption as well as opinion, and searching for a coherent center. Republicanism offered something that constitutional monarchy did not—a fundamental principle, embedded in the Laws of Nature and accepted by the Founders as true. To give it a name, we might try *the dignity of man*.

More a commonsense assumption than philosophical precept, the dignity of man meant that there was something distinctive about the human personality— something that no other life-form possessed. Mankind alone enjoyed the faculty of reason. Mankind alone spoke of right and wrong. Mankind alone had the ability to make free choices. Man wasn't just another animal.

The Moral Founding

Government had rarely acknowledged human dignity. Most government, in fact, was based on the opposite assumption, that some *Homo sapiens* were far superior to others, and it was these exalted beings—king, conqueror, dictator, true believer—who deserved to rule. As a result, most people on the planet had never thought about equality or rights or a voice in government. They were regarded as something like clever draft animals, suited only for exploitation.

Republican societies had attempted to swim against this tide. They had searched for every means imaginable to enable human beings as ordinary citizens to realize their full potential. In the process, they had taken every sort of wrong turn and wound up with tyranny, anarchy, dissolution or war, for the animal in question was extremely complex and its hopes seemed ever self-defeating.

The republican project, then, wasn't simply to devise regimes of justice but to figure out how human beings could live together in dignity. In this quest, the American Founders enjoyed a curious advantage. The thirteen states were like so many laboratories, each of them trying out various approaches to the common goal. Some results were pretty good while others were all but disastrous. Anyone could see, for example, that Pennsylvania was drifting into dangerous waters or that Massachusetts might go right over the falls. What was right or wrong with various constitutional strategies was being energetically debated all over the country.

The point wasn't that Americans had failed to get it right the first time—the point was that *they could get it wrong without giving up*. Such was their confidence in the republican idea that they could dare to tinker with the mechanisms for realizing it. We should think about what that meant. Thirteen independent sovereignties spread across a continent, and all of them convinced that republicanism was True. None had an entirely successful republican regime, nor could they find one *anywhere* they might use as a model. Yet they tinkered on. How on earth had such certainty made its way into so many minds?

This question points to the true Founding of America. We can think of it as a sea change, a "paradigm shift," in the consciousness of an entire populace, one that despite all particulars of locale and vagaries of circumstance rendered them into *a people*. It was the intuitive understanding that government had to be accountable to the dignity of mankind—and that there was a way to make it so.

This conception of the Founding helps to explain some of the "mysteries" of the Constitutional Convention. We asked how it was that key players could lose on crucial issues and still press forward. Or how the Framers could turn compromises into strokes of creativity. Or why they could forsake time-honored doctrines with such nonchalance. The answer was that they were held on task by a faith that transcended mere politics, and this faith gave them both strength and flexibility. They believed they could make all sorts of design adjustments and theory modifications without compromising the end in view—so long as they understood what that end truly was. They could avoid being doctrinaire because they were so certain of being right.

Faith in human dignity had some important corollaries for the Founding. One of these, as Lance Banning points out, was a belief that the people as a whole could be trusted. If the Constitution was skeptical about human nature, it was strangely sanguine about "the people." The entire citizenry, properly assembled, was not going to subvert the law or pervert democracy, the Framers thought. Individuals might try such things, yes, and factions surely would—that was human nature. But the people *as a whole*, acting constitutionally, must always be on the side of right.

A second corollary held that a constitution honoring the people's dignity could not fail to win their support. Thus, the Framers could sign their document, however unorthodox, and defend it with serene confidence. For when all was said and done, the people were not going to reject that which would give their lives fullest meaning.

The third and final corollary held that happy endings were embedded in the Constitution. Truth and justice may not win out in the short run—they hardly ever did—but they may well win out in the long. For once the people were empowered, truth and justice must surely be in their own interest. Given a sovereign choice, they would eventually, if not immediately, mend their errors and repent of their wrongs. They could muddle their way through the sorriest of difficulties if they believed that the cards were not stacked against them.

Much of the Constitution's structure was based on these assumptions. The principle of counterpoise, for example, was to insure that the people's considered wisdom, not their hasty impulses, would hold sway. And those fire walls between power and the populace were put in place not to rob the latter of decision making but to enlarge and refine the way they went about it. To borrow a phrase from Lincoln, the Constitution was written for "the better angels of our nature."

Faith in the dignity of man also shaped the way the Framers justified their work later on. In *Federalist* 43, for instance, Madison explained "good government" in precisely such terms. Good government must have energy, he said, must promote stability, must provide for the public safety and promote public happiness. It must comprehend the "character" of the people and speak for "the honor of mankind." It must "make possible a government informed by and fostering intelligence, virtue, and a dedication to greatness." The Constitution, in other words, emphatically *did* give an account of justice.

And it did something else. By seeking to embody the Laws of Nature—which

Principles embedded in the Constitution, such as the dignity of mankind, would eventually result in the rejection of slavery, even though the constitutional text protected it. (Courtesy of Stock Montage, Inc./Historical Pictures.)

Madison specifically mentioned in *Federalist* 43—the Constitution set up a supralegal standard for judging legislation and even for judging the popular will. Charles Kesler has argued that if the people themselves sought to demean human dignity, the Constitution in this larger moral sense would stand against *them*. Thus, even though the text of the document recognized slavery and the people themselves practiced it, the Founding as a whole condemned it, a fact which Lincoln saw clearly. For the dignity of man could never abide human servitude.

The idea of a moral founding puts a lot of things back together. It tells us that the Revolution wasn't one sort of phenomenon while events in Philadelphia were quite another. It links up the Declaration of Independence, the Constitution and the Bill of Rights, so that each becomes part of a larger whole. The laws of Nature and Nature's God mentioned in the Declaration's first paragraph are reconnected to the doctrines of equality, natural rights and government by consent mentioned in the second paragraph, and these in turn are embodied in a government capable of putting such principles into practice.

Thus, when we say the American Founding "worked," we don't mean that Americans became rich and powerful, or that they were able to keep their government reined in, or that they came to enjoy unprecedented personal freedom, though all of this may be true. We mean that the American Founding realized the republican project. It created a system of government that was accountable to the dignity of mankind.

The Constitutional Polity

The Constitution was more than an outline of government. It was also a blueprint for nationhood. Partly, of course, the nation in question was already in existence, but mostly it lay off in the future as a set of possibilities.

In examining such possibilities, we should keep in mind the ancient Greek connection between "polity" and "soul." The polity was thought by the ancients to be more than a collection of individuals—it was a higher embodiment of personhood. Thus, the capacity of the individual for moral thought or virtuous action was realized in the polity as justice. And, conversely, the just society was supposed to shape and guide the development of the individual soul.

Empire of Liberty

The Framers thought a great deal about the size and shape of that future nation, to say nothing of its character. It was principally the West that troubled them. There were not a few Americans who suspected the West of faltering in the march of human progress. How, they asked, could the institutions of civilization be left to the care of men wearing fringed buckskin and smelling of bear grease? Even scarier, maps showed that the West stood to become much larger and more populous than the East.

The problem of the West for America, then, was like the problem of the colonies for England. If its development got out of hand, there might be a terrible price to pay down the road. One could easily imagine a vast expanse of bailiwicks, fiefdoms and other jerrybuilt entities, most of them half-wild and semi-governed, quarreling and fighting with one another in a manner to shame the Balkans—and absolutely out of control.

Greed came into the picture too. Seven states had western land claims, and speculators had been busy figuring out how the various tracts could be turned into profitable ventures. However, in a remote backcountry, at the mercy of Indian attack and foreign intrigue, orderly settlement wasn't feasible without political institutions. But precisely *what* institutions? States? Territories? Protectorates? And by whom should these be governed? By existing states? By the national government? By themselves? Just how these questions were answered would determine the ultimate character of the United States.

Various statesmen suggested various solutions to the problem. John Jay had submitted a proposal to Congress that would have effectively closed the West to further settlement. Gouverneur Morris wouldn't go quite that far but he would make sure that the West always remained politically inferior to the East—a kind of imperial dominion. Elbridge Gerry would allow for the development of states in the West, but he would stipulate in the Constitution that those states could never outnumber the original thirteen. How else to hold them in line?

Agrarian republicanism: a romanticized view from the 1840s.
(*The Cornell Farm*, by Edward Hicks, 1848, courtesy of the National Gallery of Art, Washington, D.C. Oil on canvas, 36¾ × 49 in. (.933 × 1.244 m). Gift of Edgar William and Bernice Chrysler, 1964.23.4. Photograph copyright © 2001 by the Trustees of the National Gallery of Art.)

Thomas Jefferson disagreed with them all. He envisioned the West not as a barbarous outback but as an Arcadian idyll, a land of prosperous farms and self-reliant yeomen tilling their own soil. That vision would find expression in the lithographs of Currier and Ives a half century hence, and in the prose of modern writers like Willa Cather. If America was the chosen land, the West was to become the *heart*land.

Jefferson's solution to the western problem was an outgrowth of that famous passage he had written in the Declaration of Independence. Let the West create itself, he proposed. Let settlers build their own political societies, with a bit of supervision from the general government, and when those societies have reached a certain stage, let them take their place in the Union. Grant them full equality with the original thirteen and never think twice about their mounting numbers. The time may come when the entire Mississippi Valley would be divided into states, and who knew but what even Canada, Mexico and Cuba might eventually come aboard. Let America spread across the hemisphere, Jefferson rhapsodized, and become an "empire of liberty."

A scary thought? It was at the time. In retrospect, the scarier thought would have been the Morris or Gerry alternatives—holding the West in bondage. For that would have defined the United States in a far different way. And the likely result would have been not one secession movement (as in 1861) but a host of them, along with insurrections, filibustering adventures, plots, intrigues, tumults and, yes, civil wars. It would have been a case of the East trying desperately to hold on, as the British had tried before them, and in the end losing their grip.

These proposals were embodied in the famous Northwest Ordinance, a piece of legislation drafted by Jefferson himself and passed by Congress in New York while the Constitutional Convention was meeting in Philadelphia. The Framers discussed the measure at length. By committing all US territories to the supervision of the new federal Congress, they knew they were effectively making the Northwest Ordinance a part of the Constitution—and that the United States would grow to resemble Jefferson's "empire of liberty."

Northwest Ordinance:
A 1787 Congressional ordinance that established the coequal status of states created out of the Northwest Territory with the original states.

The Federal Republic

Just as no one had ever thought about "federalism" before, so no one had imagined what sort of polity a "federal republic" might be.

Federalism enabled the United States to realize Madison's extended republic with all its promised advantages. At the same time, it retained America's small "classical" republics—with all of *their* advantages. And it accomplished this double benefit while neutralizing the dangers of both. The large republic did not morph into a new Rome, nor did the small ones dissolve into anarchy and war. It brought the peace, stability and harmony of an Old World empire, together with the blessings of an imperial marketplace, and at the same time it brought the creative pluralism of the ancient Greek city-states, each with its own mark of distinction. And citizens were at once identified with a proud nation of consequence, and with close-to-home polities in which they could make a difference.

There was both toughness and flexibility in the combined system. It was tough because it was unified and strong. It was flexible because the constituent parts were free within limits to go their own way. The toughness never hardened into despotism, nor did the flexibility soften into chaos. Unseen balances seemed to play off one extreme against the other.

The Commercial Republic

Diversity was frowned upon in the classical republics. All members of a given class were expected to dress alike, act alike and pretty much think alike. Commerce was disparaged too. For all the buying and selling of the marketplace was thought to augment private interest at the expense of public. Together, in fact, commerce and diversity exerted a baneful effect on the ancient *polis*, or so it was believed. Goods for sale, especially luxury goods, implied that one citizen would have possessions different from another's, and this would strengthen the sense that both lived apart. And who knew but what the private life enjoyed by each might not eclipse the public life they shared.

Commerce led to an even deeper malady—"desire." A person who hankered after fine clothing or objects of art displayed a disturbing side of the personality, for desire was thought to be erotic in character and therefore ignoble. One reason for distrusting democracy was that the ordinary people, those lacking noble birth and high learning, were the ones most likely to be ensnared by desire. Let them have their "shiny things," sniffed the philosopher Zeno, while the virtuous meditate upon justice.

In the polity foreshadowed by the American Constitution, all this ancient wisdom would be turned inside out. For in the "commercial republic," as some were calling it, all interests, including the ignoble ones, would be placed on a par and given a political voice. No way of life would have a favored status and none would be disreputable. Public matters would be confined to a few discrete areas, carefully listed out, and the protection of property would leave individuals in control of their own lives.

What sort of world was implied here? First of all, it would be a world of diversity, even divergence. It would lack a single lifestyle or value system, just as it would lack a single religious truth. People would live differently in various parts of the country and there would be all sorts of pathways to success. The idea of *society* as an organic whole would eventually be replaced by *societies*, plural. These would exist not only as separate communities across the land but as separate groups, identities, interests and points of view within each.

Second, commerce and the things attending it would become as important as the traditional symbols of value, such as land. There would be an increased emphasis on business activity and the restless, mobile, open-ended way of life accompanying it. Old World standards based on heredity would give way to New World standards based on personal achievement. Money would talk.

There would be a new stress on innovation. Inventors would become folk heroes. Learning would emphasize science and technology and business would emphasize entrepreneurship. Americans would come to prize change, all kinds of change, and they would cheerfully call it progress.

Finally, the "pursuit of happiness" would expand in every direction, and it would be fueled wholly by "desire." As commercial activity delivered an ever greater abundance of goods and variety of choices, "happiness" would come to be defined as acquiring things.

The Inclusive Republic

Because the American Republic was so diverse, a traveler moving across it might seem to be moving through different worlds. Where communities were so unalike, there wasn't much chance for any one of them to become normative, so there would be no "right" America, just lots of variations on a general theme. And there would always be room for another community, a different idea or a new variation.

The Founding documents not only accepted such inclusiveness, they sanctioned it by their very wording. All men are created equal. No person shall be deprived. Representatives shall choose. There was nothing here about insiders and outsiders or "old settlers" and "new arrivals." The Founding was based on universals. No wonder it ushered forth a land of immigrants.

Inclusion would require the building of bridges. If you have to live with those who are different from yourself, you can't simply dismiss them as aliens. Sooner or later you must try to understand them and search out common ground. Toleration lay not solely in the national temper but in the national charter as well.

These were only a few attributes of the constitutional polity. History would reveal many more. What they all held in common was a taproot in that single sheet of parchment.

Inclusion would require the building of bridges across cultural differences.
(Courtesy of AP/Wide World Photos.)

The Inspired Constitution

At the turn of the twenty-first century, it is no longer common to assert that the US Constitution was divinely inspired. The notion savors too strongly of national chauvinism. It was popular a century ago, however, and not regarded as especially boastful. For the argument was that God had inspired the Constitution as a model for other regimes of liberty—much as the British Constitution had been a model before it.

Inspired or not, the Constitution certainly did become such an exemplar.

It was copied all over the world, with suitable variations, and whether by its own influence or some other, there are many regimes of liberty today. The belief in an inspired Constitution has not been without benefit.

Legitimacy

The government of the Confederation was discarded with the Constitution's adoption and is today all but forgotten. Nevertheless, it too was once regarded as an inspired document. There is a clear need, in other words, to look upon the fundamental law as beyond mere human agency. For if such law is of purely terrestrial origin, can it be completely "legitimate?" Will the people honor and venerate it sufficiently?

James Madison was concerned about such questions. The Constitution, he realized, could be no better than the public faith it inspired. If it seemed a frail and finite thing, it might lose its aura of mysterium and cease to hold sway. Having lost much of our innocence in the twentieth century, Americans have approached that very pass with the Constitution, as a number of recent commentaries suggest. Still, some good reasons may exist for the earlier view of an inspired Constitution. We might pause and consider a couple of them.

A Remarkable Generation

The success of the Constitutional Convention had a lot to do with human chemistry. It wasn't that the Framers were all brilliant, learned and forceful—although some of them certainly exhibited each quality. Fifty-five brilliant, learned and forceful men would never have succeeded as well as these did, for they would have recognized no leadership, brooked no compromises and braved no departures from the settled wisdom. Thus, "chemistry," in the sense used here, suggests that a peculiar mix of traits—brilliance *and* wisdom, forcefulness *and* flexibility—somehow fell into place in Philadelphia. But how did it fall into place? And why?

As a thought question, imagine trying to replicate such a mix today. It has been attempted, of course. Some of the best minds of the Western World came together to work out the League of Nations Covenant in 1919. And the League fizzled. Human chemistry can be very elusive.

Still more elusive is the character of an entire people. Yet it required a certain people to send those particular individuals to Philadelphia in the first place, and to fathom the significance of what they accomplished. The Convention delegates were in certain ways typical of their generation. In a James Madison, a James Wilson, a Roger Sherman, a Gouverneur Morris, we can see patterns of thought and approaches to life that appeared in some form all over the country.

One need only browse through *The Federalist* to feel the weight of this point. What is most remarkable about these essays is not their insight or sophistication but their intended readership. Who, one wonders, was supposed to curl up with such writings, assess their implications, appreciate their wisdom and be persuaded by their logic? And yet Americans did so, by the tens of thousands. Accordingly, whatever else we think about the Founding, it was the product of an extraordinary generation. We search in vain for another quite like it.

Appeal for Divine Aid

Benjamin Franklin's appeal for prayers at the Convention soon became famous. The important part of the story is that Franklin, like many others, literally did not know where else to turn. The "centrifugal" forces rending that assembly seemed all but irresistible, and time and again the outcome was in doubt.

It was mostly a fear of failure that drove the Framers on—that and a pretty good idea of failure's end result. They bolstered one another's flagging faith by alluding to the eyes of the world, which they imagined to be riveted on Philadelphia, and to the eyes of posterity—which would praise or blame them in epic measure according to how it all turned out. Such references might have been a kind of prayer in their own right. For in the Founders' world, meaning worked itself out in the long run, not the short, and one looked to history and to futurity for the shape of God's purposes.

Then, too, the vision before their eyes was an essentially spiritual one. It was Winthrop's city upon a hill—the New Jerusalem, the Promised Land. It had to be seen in large historical terms to be fully apprehended. Americans had come this far and with this sense of purpose, they told one another. They had uncovered the old within the new—rediscovered the secrets of the ages. It was unthinkable that they should falter now.

A Lucky Roll?

The breakup of the Convention was one possibility. Another might have been a constitution that didn't quite work—like the Articles of Confederation. Given the swirl of politics among them, the Framers might easily have created a system in which forces were out of balance, controls ineffective and powers dangerously askew.

If this seems beyond imagining, consider the following. The electoral college did not operate remotely as the Founders had anticipated. The election of president and vice president quickly proved to be unworkable, even hazardous, and required a short-order constitutional amendment. The document was not without its surprises.

With surprises in mind, here is one way to think about the outcome. If two dice can be rolled to produce one of eleven numbers (that is, numbers 2 through 12), we might imagine ten of the eleven as representing the possibilities for a constitution with fatal, debilitating flaws, of the kind we have seen so often. Only one of the eleven numbers represents that rare combination of qualities necessary for long-term success. The Framers had only a single roll of the dice—and they *had* to come up with a "seven."

In Retrospect

More than two centuries later, the US Constitution has come to seem inevitable, even foreordained. Moreover, it has become the admiration of that world of futurity the Framers imagined.

Yet when the Convention came to a close, the draft document wasn't admired by anyone. The Framers had debated every line of its text, not once but repeatedly, and had wound up compromising even the compromises. In the process, there was no philosophy, no authority, no conventional wisdom they hadn't more or less hashed up. To a few of them, it seemed best to confess failure and call for another convention.

If the Constitution had a prayer of ratification, however, the Framers must return to their states and represent it as the "the most brilliant document struck off by the hand of man"—to anticipate Gladstone's praise. That didn't look easy. Yet as they rose to speak in the various ratifying conventions, the Framers began to see their work in a different light. The most accomplished of them led the way—Wilson at the Pennsylvania convention, Hamilton at the New York and Madison at the Virginia. As it would have been impolitic to speak of compromises, they instead subtly reshaped political theory to account for the way things had come out—as though the compromises had been bold strokes of creativity. And in the process, oddly enough, they actually *became* bold strokes of creativity.

Take federalism, for example. While the delegates had been working it out at swords' points, federalism appeared to be a hopeless mishmash of concessions. In retrospect, however, it took on an aura that was almost cosmic. "Let our government be like the solar system," John Dickinson rhapsodized. "Let the general government be like that of the sun and the states the planets, repelled yet attracted, and the whole moving regularly and harmoniously in their several orbits."

The Constitution was filled with such serendipity. From small features opened worlds of fresh meaning. And in action it was not just a new form of government but a new way of governing. Congress scuffled with itself and bickered with the president. Each made up its mind and changed its mind and had its mind changed by the other. The people watched them both and talked incessantly of approving or disapproving their actions. Every once in a while they became mad as hornets and turned the rascals out. The process seems so normal today that we forget how astonishing it is—and how it seemed to pop up out of nowhere.

So it was that the Constitution began to look more like a revelation than a workpiece. And so it was that Americans began alluding to it as the hand of God in history. For in operation, it seemed to be bigger than any of its authors—or all of them combined.

Ultimately it is the people themselves who accept or reject the Constitution, then as well as now.
(Courtesy of The Granger Collection, New York.)

Suggestions for Further Reading

Joyce Oldham Appleby, Forrest McDonald and Joseph Cropsey, *Understanding the United States Constitution, 1787–1987: Three Bicentennial Lectures* (1988).

Herman Belz, *A Living Constitution or Fundamental Law?: American Constitutionalism in Historical Perspective* (1998).

Paul Eidelberg, *The Philosophy of the American Constitution: A Reinterpretation of the Intentions of the Founding Fathers* (1968).

Suzette Henberger, *Creatures of the Constitution: The Federalist Constitution and the Shaping of American Politics* (1994).

Louis Hartz, *The Liberal Tradition in America: An Interpretation of American Political Thought since the Revolution* (1955).

Charles R. Kesler, ed., *Saving the Revolution: The Federalist Papers and the American Founding* (1987).

Forrest McDonald, *Novus Ordo Seclorum: The Intellectual Origins of the Consitution* (1985).

Sarah Baumgartner Thurow, ed., *Constitutionalism in Perspective: The United States Constitution in Twentieth Century Politics* (1988).

Richard Vetterli and Gary Bryner, *In Search of the Republic: Public Virtue and the Roots of American Government* (1996).

Neil L. York, ed., *Toward a More Perfect Union: Six Essays on the Constitution* (1988).

CHAPTER 9 STUDY AID ━━━━━━━━

(This aid is not all-inclusive and is not intended to be a substitute for thorough study of the material presented in the textbook.)

The Meaning of the Constitution

I. The Constitution and Human Nature

1. Virtue and self-interest:
   - The realists—virtue does not reflect human nature
   - Self-interest dominates
   - The idealists—virtue essential to man's moral sense
2. Virtue amended—virtuous self-interest
   - Virtue's limitations
   - A less demanding form of virtue
3. The uses of structure:
   - A safety net
   - Auxiliary precautions
   - Mobilization of virtue
4. An extended republic:
   - Madison—reading Hume
   - Representation as a "refining" process
   - Bigger can be better
   - Tiers of representation
   - Increasing factions diminishes the threat of factionalism
5. Multi-layered founding:
   - Classical, liberal, democratic
   - Republican virtue and material self-interest
   - Virtue = wisdom, prudence, common sense
   - Self-interest as self-governance
   - Renewal of virtue—church, education, the Good Society itself

II. Rule of Law

1. In the Constitution:
   - Generality—no nobility or bills of attainder
   - Prospectivity—no *ex post facto*
   - Publicity—record and publish proceedings
   - Consent—suffrage
   - Due Process—trial by jury
   - Separation of powers

2. Politics:
- Rule makers
- Rule enforcers
- Checks and balances

3. Freedom:
- Rules do not constrain freedom; they make it possible
- Predictability—no nasty surprises

4. Administration:
- Does not require rule of law

III. Moral Document

1. Dignity of mankind:
- Success of Revolution attributed to civic virtue
- Divine favor
- Implementing republicanism
- Laws of nature and nature's God
- Man more than an animal

2. Moral Founding:
- Thirteen experiments
- A "people"
- The "whole" to be trusted
- Truth and justice in the long run

IV. Constitutional Polity

1. Empire of liberty:
- The West—barbarous outback or Arcadian idyll?
- West left to create itself

2. The federal republic:
- Advantages—toughness and flexibility

3. Commercial republic:
- Diversity
- Money talks
- Innovation
- Pursuit of happiness

4. Inclusive republic:
- Variations
- Bridge building

V. Inspired Constitution

1. Legitimacy:
   - Fundamental law
   - Public faith
2. Remarkable generation:
   - Human chemistry
   - Character of the people
3. Providence:
   - A spiritual vision—a City upon a Hill
4. Luck:
   - A rare combination of qualities
5. Inevitability?
   - Product of compromise
   - Ratification
   - Serendipity
   - The hand of God

CHAPTER 9 REVIEW QUESTIONS ━━━━━

NAME: _____   SECTION: _____

Key Terms

Virtuous Self-Interest

Extended Republic

Factions

Administration

Governance

Dignity of Man

Empire of Liberty

Inclusive Republic

Multiple Choice Questions

1. Which of the following groups best represents the idea of a faction?
   a. Hispanic Americans.
   b. Women.
   c. Senior citizens.
   d. The National Rifle Association.

2. Which of the following is not among the sources of renewal of virtue relied upon by the Founders?
   a. Religion.
   b. Education.
   c. The media.
   d. The Good Society.

3. All of the following are aspects of the Founders' faith in human dignity except:
   a. Happy endings were embedded in the Constitution.
   b. People would support the Constitution because it honored their dignity.
   c. The people can be trusted.
   d. In the Good Society people would always be happy.

4. What is meant by the Greek term "polity"?
   a. The soul of the people.
   b. Citizens who could vote.
   c. Property owners.
   d. The upper crust of society.

Review Questions

1. How does virtuous self-interest differ from the notion of *areté*?

   _____

   _____

   _____

   _____

2. Why did Madison's idea of an extended republic seem farcical to many of his contemporaries?

   _____

   _____

   _____

   _____

3. How does Madison's extended republic theory help solve the problem of factionalism?

   _____

   _____

   _____

   _____

4. What are some of the blessings and curses of living in a commercial republic?

   _____

   _____

   _____

   _____

5. What basic fear motivated the Founders? Was this fear legitimate? Explain.

   _____

   _____

   _____

   _____

Review Exercises

1. Explain how the Rule of Law creates freedom. What kind of freedom does it create?

   _____

   _____

   _____

   _____

2. Briefly outline the differences between administration and governance.

_____

_____

_____

_____

3. Explain how provisions in the Constitution led to America becoming a land of immigrants.

_____

_____

_____

_____

Big Essay Question

By now in the text we have seen George Washington in a number of different roles. From what you have read so far, and drawing on material in chapter 12, what was George Washington's significance to the American Founding?

The Ratification Campaign

Commemoration of the Constitution, *by Amos Doolittle (1789). All thirteen original states are displayed with their population and number of delegates to Congress.*
(Courtesy of the John Carter Brown Library, Brown University, Providence, Rhode Island.)

Many Americans believe that the adoption of the proposal written in Philadelphia was all but a foregone conclusion. Actually, the ratification of the Constitution was the product of a lengthy and highly contentious debate, and the outcome was anything but certain.

At the debate's beginning, most Americans clearly opposed the new Constitution. After all, they knew nothing about it, had not participated in its creation, and at the very least could suspect it on grounds of "innovation." This meant that the "Federalists"—those who favored adoption—had a colossal selling job to perform. And the buyers had a job of their own. They must examine the Constitution in minute detail and ask every tough question they could think of.

It is in this task that the people themselves assumed a role in the founding process, and a demanding role at that. Public debate in America had never been on such a high level—and might never be again. It was, observed John Adams, "the greatest single effort of national deliberation that the world has ever seen."

The fact that the ratification battle was vigorously and closely fought alters the nature of the Founding. For one thing, we can dismiss allegations (once quite common) that the Constitution resulted from an "elitist conspiracy," a "counterrevolution" or any other such coup-by-cabal. There is simply no way that a small group could have accomplished what had to be in order to get the Constitution adopted.

The ratification battle not only broadened participation in the Founding, it altered the terms. Where the Philadelphia Convention had been a deliberation among a small homogeneous group, the adoption campaign involved a very large number, and their backgrounds were as diverse as their thinking. There would be a winning side and a losing side, and thousands of Americans would have to make an up-or-down choice between alternatives. And no compromise was possible, only the most diligent kind of soul-searching. Americans had to ask themselves the tough questions:

What was the true meaning of the American Revolution?

What was the true essence of republican government?

What was the true destiny of the United States?

What had come out of the Philadelphia Convention was a mere proposal. What came out of the ratification debate was a binding commitment, pledging both present and future. And it was that commitment alone that rendered the Constitution legitimate.

The Ratification Process

Like everything else, the Framers in Philadelphia had debated every facet of the ratification process. Some had assumed that the existing state governments would ratify. Edmund Randolph, however, pointed out that if the question were put to state governments, many local politicos fearful of losing their places would either vote against it or else find some subtle way to bring about its defeat.

And there was a deeper issue. Both Madison and Wilson strongly argued for ratification by the people rather than the states, for the people alone were the source of political authority. Gouverneur Morris certainly agreed. In the Constitution's preamble, he opened with words that were certain to raise the ire of state governments: "**We the People** of the United States . . . "

Not everyone went along, however. Elbridge Gerry, still nervous about Shays Rebellion, submitted that the people had "the wildest ideas of government in the world." And several other delegates concurred. Would the people be able to follow the nuances and subtleties of constitutional deliberation? they asked. Did "the people" even exist? Nevertheless, the democrats had their way. Ratification would take place in the several states but by means of special conventions called independently of state government—and representing *the people*.

The Framers also hotly debated the question of how many states must ratify before the Constitution would go into effect. Any number less than thirteen would underscore the proposal's revolutionary nature. After more to-ing and fro-ing, they settled on nine as the magic number. But could they get that many? Rhode Island must be written off immediately. Maryland was almost as doubtful and so was New York. North Carolina was becoming questionable and would in fact be among the last to ratify. Subtracting those four, *only nine states were left.*

The document itself was sent off to Congress in New York. A bare eight days after receiving it, Congress dispatched printed copies to the several states and recommended that they call ratifying conventions.

The Federalists

The "Federalists" were not just the thirty-nine signers of the parchment drafted in Philadelphia. They were a kind of political party that gusted into being as soon as the Constitution was distributed.

Federalists:
http://members.tripod.com/
~dzierba/index-50.html

Political parties are complex organisms compounded of ideology and interest. To be successful, they must find a way to recruit dynamic leaders and industrious workers. Even more important, they must find a way to engage the hearts and minds of ordinary citizens at the "grass roots." All this was accomplished at fast-forward in the fall of 1787—without telephones, telegraphs or television. The sheer energy of the task was enormous.

It is one thing to ask why an Alexander Hamilton or James Wilson would put aside business affairs and attend to high matters of state. It is quite another to ask why an ordinary citizen would interrupt his farming or shipbuilding and begin writing letters to old comrades in the regiment. What did *he* expect to gain from constitutional politics?

We should keep the Founders' analysis of human nature in mind as we consider the possible answers. Many kinds of interest—often local in character—were clearly at play in the ratification campaign. But such interests were at play on *both* sides. If a certain farmer in upstate New York supported the Constitution in the hope of gaining a better market for his corn, we can be sure that at least one of his neighbors was ready to oppose it for some equally self-interested reason. We can't explain the ratification of the Constitution, nor the opposition to it, solely in terms of bread and butter.

Ideas can be powerful motivators as well, and it is on this level that the ratification debates fall into patterns that make sense. Federalists and Anti-Federalists alike were urged along by a set of fundamental assumptions, or "founding ideas," and it is these that need to bear the weight of our scrutiny. We already know something of the Federalists' ideas, for these had dominated the Philadelphia Convention. They included the vision of a strong and united nation-state, the promise of a dazzling national prosperity, and a belief that America was destined somehow to become that City upon a Hill.

These were compelling ideas. They appealed to younger men, to optimists and to those of high personal vitality. Indeed, where the Federalists distinguished themselves was in the sheer assertiveness of their campaign. They seized the initiative early on and refused to let go. They were well organized, capably led and determined to the point of doggedness. The campaign, some said, called back the glory days of the Revolution.

But knowing the Federalists tells us only half of the story. Voters had to consider the arguments of the *Anti*-Federalists as well, and lacking our hindsight, they didn't know but what the latter had the stronger case.

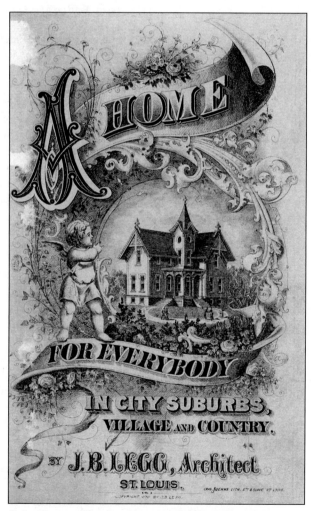

Federalists envisioned an America of unlimited possibilities. They were the forerunners of modern advertising.
(Courtesy of the Library of Congress.)

A few Anti-Federalists had attended the Philadelphia Convention themselves and could attest to the bargains and compromises behind the scenes—and to the personal motives of some delegates. Of course they too had personal motives. Some were men of prominence in the state governments and their fortunes were bound up with their circumstances. Others feared the interference of a strong national government in various local enterprises. Yet once again, most Anti-Federalists were men of principle and were every bit as high-minded as their adversaries. The story of the ratification struggle is not a tale of personal pique or thwarted ambition.

Anti-Federalists:
http://www.pinzler.com/
ushistory/argantfedsupp
.html

The Anti-Federalists

Anti-Federalists have been identified with both classical republicanism and democracy. Accordingly, their opposition has been taken to imply that the Constitution was dangerously deficient in one of two respects: either it violated ancient republican principles or else it placed power in the hands of an aristocratic elite. Anti-Federalists have also been identified with the "true" spirit of the Revolution. They were the Revolution's authentic heirs, so the argument goes, while the Federalists were its interloping stepchildren.

Whatever may be said for such arguments, it is certainly true that many Anti-Federalists *saw* themselves in this way. Thus, understanding the Anti-Federalists helps us to better understand the Founding. To be precise, why did the Founding take one fork of the road and not the other?

For most present-day Americans, the Anti-Federalists have suffered the fate of all historical "losers"—to be ignored, misunderstood or regarded as irrelevant. They are often associated with the Confederation, a government with few friends today, or with the corruptions of errant states. They ought to have known, we say, that theirs was a lost cause.

In the fall of 1787, however, the Anti-Federalists had a great deal going for them. They better reflected American public opinion than their opponents did. They held the upper hand in crucial states. Their spokesmen were among the famous orators of the country. Their objections to the Constitution were both real and substantive—and wherever they went toe-to-toe with the Federalists, they landed heavy punches. As late as May of 1788, only four states out of thirteen had ratified the Constitution while two others had considered and rejected it. In Massachusetts, one of the four, the vote had been nail-biting close. And in both Virginia and New York, which promised to be crucial, the tide seemed to be running the other way.

Why, then, did the Anti-Federalists lose? They were not, on the whole, as well organized as the Federalists or as capably led. They took too long in mustering their forces to full strength. And they allowed themselves to be outmaneuvered in two semantic particulars. First, they became the "anti's"—those who were against something rather than for it. This made them seem carping and negative. And second, they lost control of the key term in the debate—"federal." What they stood for was the old meaning of the word *federal*—to disperse power and authority—

while their opponents stood for a new meaning which oddly enough signified just the opposite. What the Constitution's supporters wanted was consolidation. But how do you argue against consolidation when it is called "federation" instead?

Below these difficulties lay something deeper. The Anti-Federalists' arguments, however meritorious, began to ring hollow upon the patient, steady thumping of Federalist persuasion. In critical numbers, Americans came to believe that the Anti-Federalists were not just ineffective but actually wrong. The strange story of the Anti-Federalists is that being as prestigious, as knowledgeable and as strategically well placed as they were, they still managed to lose. Or, put another way, if you really do stand for republicanism, democracy and the American Revolution, how can you possibly fail?

Our task, then, is to figure out why the Anti-Federalists' idea of the Founding wasn't the "right" one.

The Anti-Federalist Indictment

The Anti-Federalists spun a lengthy bill of particulars against the proposed Constitution. The president had no council to stay his hand. A vice president seemed unnecessary and dangerous. The West was sure to be sold out. There would be a peacetime national army at the beck and call of any tyrant. There would be a "federal city" off in the boondocks somewhere, a cross between Rome and Babylon, where power would multiply and debauchery fester. "The greatness of the powers given, and the multitude of places to be created," declaimed Richard Henry Lee, "produce a coalition of monarchy men, military men, aristocrats and drones, whose noise, impudence and zeal exceed all belief." And don't forget, it was all hatched in secrecy. "The evil genius of darkness presided at the Constitution's birth. It came forth under a veil of mystery."

Analyzing Anti-Federalisms' most effective arguments, we find a five-point indictment:

1. *The Constitution would create a government violating most if not all of republicanism's classical precepts.* Republics require a cohesive, homogeneous citizenry. They require a polity small enough to insure the citizen's direct participation. They require the denial of self-interest and the creation of civic virtue, and so they must look askance at commerce with its wealth and luxury. They must eschew concentrations of power, especially executive power, for such is the fodder of tyranny. And finally, republics must depend on the sovereignty of the people, and therefore must trust the will of the majority. The proposed plan of government would accomplish none of the above—on the contrary, their very opposites.

2. *The Constitution would reestablish the hated British forms and thus nullify the Revolution.* The powerful executive would become a "fetus of monarchy"—the phrase still ringing from Independence Hall. The representatives, so small in number, would open the way to aristocracy. The bicameral legislature would

The simple yeoman farmer: a vision dear to the Anti-Federalists. (Symbol for The Philadelphia Society for Promoting Agriculture, courtesy of the Library of Congress.)

look suspiciously like Parliament with its upper and lower chambers, and the elitist Senate would transmogrify into an American House of Lords.

3. *The Constitution would separate the people from the governing process and subject them to arbitrary restrictions.* Look at the long terms of office. Look at the blocks against direct election. Look at the smug and aloof judiciary with its lifetime tenure. And look at Madison's "counterpoise"—what was it but the defeat of popular sovereignty?

4. *Federalism in practice would amount to "splendid empire," for the residual sovereignty of the states would prove but a dream.* Note all those loosely worded clauses in the Constitution—they would never bind anyone. The powers enumerated in Article I, Section 8, while seeming to be limited, were in fact made infinitely stretchable by the "necessary and proper" clause—which Alexander Hamilton had already interpreted to mean "anything." And if one didn't like Hamilton's interpretation, there was always that standing army to back it up.

5. *There was no bill of rights.* Nor was the omission of such guarantees a mere oversight. Delegates to the Philadelphia Convention had thoroughly discussed the possibility of a bill of rights—and unanimously rejected it.

This was an impressive list. But the Anti-Federalists were not just "anti." They had their own vision of America and it was quite as compelling as that of the Federalists. It emphasized, in the first instance, a healthy diversity. Anti-Federalist America would be a patchwork of local cultures, each of them colorful and distinctive, and none of them answerable to national norms. It emphasized, in the second instance, the old republican idea of virtue. Americans would live a pastoral life close to the soil and close to the primary verities, a life of republican plainness and simplicity. Finally, in the third instance, Americans would exercise power themselves, not pass it along to some distant capital. Theirs would be an energetic, town-meeting style of governance, and as a result, government would remain under the guidance of decent, ordinary, God-fearing citizens. We need only think of the murals of John Steuart Curry or the movies of Frank Capra to appreciate how "American" this idyll was. If the Federalists' vision of America was a City upon a Hill, that of the Anti-Federalists was something more like *Our Town.*

Our Town: Play by Thornton Wilder dealing with everyday life in small New England town.

Ratification of the Constitution: http://www.nara.gov/exhall/charters/constitution/conhist.html

Anti-Federalist Strategy

Not only did the Anti-Federalists have an alluring vision and solid arguments, they had a promising political strategy. They would press hard on the bill of rights issue, where the voters might feel most vulnerable, and use this to force the calling of a new convention. The Anti-Federalists well knew that the Constitution was compounded of delicate compromises and hairspring understandings. If a new convention were called, everything would undoubtedly come unstuck.

But why indeed was there no bill of rights? Surely if Americans felt vulnerable without one, the Framers would have been savvy enough to include it. Yet they hadn't. And they had thought carefully about their reasons. In the first place, under the Constitution the people themselves were sovereign, so there was no authority beyond their own, which must be hedged about with restrictions. In the second place, by limiting powers which were not granted in the constitutional text, a way might be opened to claim the existence of such powers—a boomerang if there ever was one. And finally, with no means of enforcing the rights in question, such rights might go the way of all parchment barriers, to be ignored and forgotten. "No bill of rights," wrote Roger Sherman, "ever yet bound the supreme power longer than the honeymoon of a new married couple, unless the rulers were interested in preserving the rights."

These were worthy arguments. But the Anti-Federalists had equally worthy replies to them. Take the first one, for instance, that the people did not need a bill of rights against themselves. Was that really true? Anti-Federalists asked. Were the people any better guarantors of rights than kings were? In particular, were factional majorities apt to respect the rights of their foes? Madison himself had stewed about that.

Or take the second argument, that there was no need to limit powers not given. If there was no such need, the Anti-Federalists countered, then why had the Framers included clauses guaranteeing trial by jury and *habeas corpus* or prohibiting bills of attainder? In all of its enumerated powers did the Constitution even hint at such authority?

Or the third argument, that bills of rights were unenforceable. The point granted, the Anti-Federalists said, that had never stopped anyone in the past. A bill of rights was not supposed to be *enforced*—it was supposed to be a rallying point for public opinion. Whoever "enforced" the *English* Bill of Rights?

These were sobering responses, especially the last one, and not without effect. Score one for the Anti-Federalists. What they didn't count on, however, was the rapid deployment of a counterstrategy, and precisely that soon followed. Rather than continue denying the need for a bill of rights, Federalists pulled themselves up, conceded the point gracefully, and then urged that the Constitution be ratified anyway since it included all the machinery for adding a bill of rights by amendment. Such a reply was typical of the Federalists. It promised, in effect, that voters could have their cake and eat it too. They could have the Constitution with all its advantages *and* their bill of rights.

Federalists knew the American people well.

The Federalist Defense

The Anti-Federalists realized that the game would be won or lost in the big states: Pennsylvania, Massachusetts and Virginia. Without those states, the Union couldn't possibly succeed—nor could the Confederation possibly survive. And in any case, nine states had to ratify before the Constitution took effect.

As the battle took shape, it became clear that the Framers themselves would be the frontline defenders of their work. They were well equipped for the task. And so we see them outside the stuffy hall with its heat and flies, where they could speak their minds openly at last. There were the Pinckneys down in Charleston, drawling softly as they outlined the Constitution's advantages to fellow planters. There was Hamilton in New York, intense, obsessive, fairly bursting with energy, anxious to face down his nemesis Melancton Smith. There was Oliver Ellsworth in Connecticut, his clothing dusted with snuff, citing scripture to the state delegates—eighty of whom had names out of the Old Testament.

Clearly too, all stops would be pulled out and all authorities pulled in. The two most important authorities were John Adams, serving as minister in London, and Thomas Jefferson, similarly stationed in Paris. Adams was pleased with the Constitution—he pronounced it "the greatest exertion of human understanding"—though he couldn't help noting that it simply copied his own thinking. Jefferson, on the other hand, had his doubts. He didn't like the idea of the executive succeeding himself over and over and he wondered about that missing bill of rights. But after an urgent letter or two from his friend Madison, he was ready to say: "The Constitution . . . is unquestionably the wisest ever presented to men."

Thus primed, Federalists took the first hand. Delaware ratified unanimously on December 6. New Jersey followed on December 16, also unanimously. Georgia ratified on January 2, 1788, and Connecticut came through a few days later with a heavily lopsided vote. Four states were in the bag—but they were all small.

Pennsylvania was the first large state and the Constitution's first major test. Three of the Core Framers—Wilson, Morris and Franklin—were Pennsylvanians of high standing. Still, the state's politics was a donnybrook under the best of circumstances, with partisan bushwhacking, mass demonstrations, even the occasional riot, and the constitutional question promised to be an especially lively one.

Federalists had a comfortable majority in the Assembly. Their foes, however, had the ear of the democratic electorate and were prepared to make the most of it. If they could somehow delay the vote for a ratifying convention, they had every chance of electing a friendly majority in the Assembly and Anti-Federalist delegates to the convention later on. It soon came down to bare-knuckle tactics. The Federalists pushed for an immediate vote. The Anti-Federalists sought to block the vote by keeping their own members away and preventing a quorum. Mob action ensued. Bully boys broke through a door, roughed up two of the Anti-Federalist truants and bodily carried them to the State House, where they were held in their seats for the roll call. The resolution for a ratifying convention passed 45 to 2.

Nor was the convention itself much quieter. Many of the delegates knew little of the proposed Constitution and there were some who didn't want them to learn. As Davie of North Carolina said, "It is much easier to alarm the people than to inform them." But James Wilson delivered a masterful performance. His head held high to keep the thick glasses balanced on his nose, Wilson patiently answered objection after objection, his Scottish burr trilling out the "r's." It proved to be an experience in democratic politics to cheer the most jaded skeptic.

The convention sat for a respectable five weeks and then ratified the Constitution by a vote of 46 to 23. Wilson's reward was to be mugged by a band of ruffians while he was out celebrating. He was severely beaten and might well have been killed.

The next test came with Massachusetts. This was the largest of the conventions, with 355 delegates. They gathered at the Brattle Street Church in Boston, amid a storm of controversy in the press. As in Pennsylvania, local politics played a manifest role in the proceeding as backcountry farmers rattled into town to express themselves on the subject of seaboard merchants and their political shenanigans. Massachusetts, said the pundits, would never ratify.

But once again an odd chemistry took effect. Elbridge Gerry, the Massachusetts Framer who had refused to sign in Philadelphia, expected to dominate the proceeding with his eleven-point critique but the mayhem in Brattle Street was too much for him and he departed in a huff. After that, the accomplished trio of Rufus King, Nathaniel Gorham and Josiah Strong—the remaining Massachusetts delegates—held sway. Following Wilson's path in Pennsylvania, they explained the Constitution's fine points with a calming self-possession and fielded question after question from the floor.

The other distinguishing feature of the Massachusetts battle was the role played by ordinary citizens. One of them, a rough-hewn and self-taught farmer named Amos Singletry, discoursed at length on the Constitution's evils:

> Does not this constitution . . . take away all we have—all our property? Does it not lay all taxes, duties, imposts, and excises . . . ? These lawyers and men of learning, and moneyed men that talk so finely, and gloss over matters so smoothly, to make us poor illiterate people swallow down the pill, expect to get into Congress themselves. They expect to be the managers of this Constitution, and get all the power and all the money into their own hands. And then they will swallow up us little fellows. . . .

Federalists replied in kind. One of them was also a farmer, also unlearned, and also down-to-earth eloquent. "Mr. President," said Jonathan Smith,

> when I saw this Constitution, I . . . got a copy of it, and read it over and over. I had been a member of the convention to form our own state constitution, and had learnt something of the checks and balances of power, and I found them all there. . . . My honorable old daddy there [referring to Singletry] won't think that I expect to be a Congress-man, and swallow up the liberties of the people. I never had any post, nor do I want one. But I don't think worse of the Constitution because lawyers, and men of learning, and moneyed men, are fond of it. . . . These lawyers, these moneyed men, these men of learning, are all embarked in the same cause with us, and we must all swim or sink together. . . . We sowed our seed when we sent men to the Federal Convention. Now is the harvest. Now is the time to reap the fruit of our labor. And if we don't do it now, I am afraid we shall never have another opportunity.

It was a telling performance. Equally telling was Sam Adams' dramatic swing from opposition to support for the Constitution and Gov. John Hancock's own bellwether endorsement. Anti-Federalist ranks broke on February 5 and Massachusetts ratified 187 to 168. Had ten votes gone the other way, the Union would have undoubtedly died stillborn then and there.

Anti-Federalists took heart from this fact. If they could block ratification in New York and Virginia, both of which were due to convene in June, the Constitution might be defeated yet. But Maryland, one of the doubtfuls, ratified in April and South Carolina followed in May. That made eight states, one short of the nine necessary, and New Hampshire was leaning toward a scrape-by affirmative vote. Still, without Virginia and New York on board, it was hard to see an American nation setting sail.

If Massachusetts' had been the largest of the state conventions, Virginia's was the ablest. The Assembly Hall of the House of Burgesses was packed with members of the tidewater elite. Madison was there of course, and so was George Washington, but white-haired and blue-blooded Hugh Grigsby, a shrewd observer of the Old Dominion aristocracy, submitted that neither of those two Founding Fathers "stood in the estimation of Virginia on the same platform with Patrick Henry and George Mason as statesmen." Henry had boycotted the Philadelphia Convention when he "smelt a rat." And Mason had sat through every hour of it and denounced the outcome.

Henry showcased the Anti-Federalist approach to constitutional debate at its most passionate. "Whither is the spirit of America gone?" he asked in lamentation:

> Whither is the genius of America fled? . . . We drew the spirit of liberty from our British ancestors. But now, Sir, the American spirit, assisted by the ropes and chains of consolidation, is about to convert this country into a powerful and mighty empire. . . . There will be no checks, no real balances, in this government. What can avail your specious, imaginary balances, your rope-dancing, chain-rattling, ridiculous ideal of checks and contrivances?"

Against such a performance, James Madison must have felt puny indeed. He stood before the delegates beggarlike, his hat in his hand (and his notes in his hat), his voice so frail that those in the rear had to strain to hear him. And in the way of most Federalists, he simply plodded along with the dull, prosaic facts of the matter, answering questions, allaying concerns, parrying Henry's oratorical thrusts.

The real star of the show was Edmund Randolph. He too had been at the Philadelphia Convention and had refused to sign the Constitution. However, unlike his friend George Mason, who now hurled thunderbolts against the document, the stage-handsome governor had undergone a change of heart worthy of Damascus Road. Not only was he now in favor of ratification, he was in favor of it heart, soul and pocketbook. When Madison became so exhausted that he had to take to his bed, Randolph rallied the flagging Federalists and took command. It was, said Catherine Drinker Bowen, the political performance of his life.

The Virginia convention made its decision on June 25. The Constitution won by a slender ten votes. When news of the victory reached Poughkeepsie on July 2, the New York delegates had been convened there for two weeks. It was another case of tenpins wobbling precariously before knocking each other down. For if ratification had failed in the Old Dominion, it would surely have failed in New York as well, but as matters now stood, Virginia was in the Union (along with dithering New Hampshire) and the Constitution had sprung into life. If New Yorkers opted out now they would be literally on their own.

All the same, the New York convention brought forth its own Federalist hero. Alexander Hamilton, who had been abandoned in Philadelphia by his New

York colleagues, battled for the Constitution like a Roman gladiator and won almost single-handedly. "He is," observed Jefferson in another context, "a host within himself." The vote, taken on July 25, saw ratification squeak through 30 to 27.

As the New York debates had heated up after the Federal Convention, Hamilton and his friend John Jay, supposing that their badly splintered state might prove pivotal in the ratification contest, had teamed up with James Madison in what would prove to be the most famous collaboration in American political writing. *The Federalist* was a series of eighty-five newspaper essays about the Constitution. Under the pen name "Publius," they appeared first in New York papers and were then reprinted throughout the country. They were written in great haste, of course, and many of them made for a ponderous read. But in terms of sheer insight, there is nothing to compare with *The Federalist*, then or since.

Hamilton and Madison (Jay, whose health was poor, participated in only three of the papers) undertook a searching inquiry into the nature of republics and the effort paid off handsomely. For whatever else *The Federalist* accomplished, it pointed up the Federalists' cardinal strength. Having debated every line of the Constitution in Philadelphia and having learned principles through painstaking research, the authors didn't need rhetorical fireworks because they could use real dynamite.

"Publius" was particularly adept at justifying the Constitution's many compromises. Accordingly, what might be depicted by Anti-Federalists as a sellout (or even a washout) took on brilliance and sagacity in *The Federalist* essays. There was Madison's theory of factional behavior in a large republic. There was Wilson's theory of sovereignty as "power on loan." There was the idea of the president as representative at large. There was separation of powers. These weren't just clever apologies—they were breakthroughs in political thought.

It has been pointed out that *The Federalist*'s profundity was largely wasted. For the essays were not widely read by their intended audience and it can't be shown that they changed a single vote in Poughkeepsie. This critique misses a salient point. *The Federalist* was but an example, though an inspired one, of the Federalists' entire approach. What the essays accomplished in formal prose was also taking place on street corners, in city taverns and in public meetinghouses throughout the country. The Federalist style of calm, steady, rational argument, emphasizing cognitive depth rather than rhetorical display, triumphed in the ratification campaign. It remains a force in US politics to this day.

There were two areas in particular where the Federalists could go for the jugular. The first was the order and stability argument. With the Confederation

THE

FEDERALIST:

A COLLECTION

OF

ESSAYS,

WRITTEN IN FAVOUR OF THE

NEW CONSTITUTION,

AS AGREED UPON BY THE FEDERAL CONVENTION, SEPTEMBER 17, 1787.

IN TWO VOLUMES.

VOL. I.

NEW-YORK:

PRINTED AND SOLD BY J. AND A. McLEAN, No. 41, HANOVER-SQUARE. M, DCC, LXXXVIII.

To this day, The Federalist Papers *remain a fountain of wisdom on the Constitution.*
(Courtesy of The Granger Collection, New York.)

clearly failing, the only alternative to a stronger union seemed to be no union at all, and that would mean continuing trade wars, political frictions, boundary disputes, contested land claims and all the other baleful offspring of anarchy. Americans didn't want that.

Equally troublesome for Anti-Federalists was the human nature argument. Most Americans realized that human beings respond to their selfish desires rather than some abstract public good and that this fact explained the failure of ancient republicanism. Madison's spread-eagle nation-state with its candid avowal of self-interest brilliantly solved this problem. Interests could conflict and collide, Madison promised, and the outcome would automatically redound to the public good. People could serve the public interest by serving their own.

In both of these assertions, the Federalists were once again promising it both ways. State sovereignty would preserve all the vitality of localism—while union would bring the blessings of empire. And Americans could gain all the benefits of virtue without repressing their human appetites. Such arguments were simply unbeatable.

Capitulation

In the end, the ratification campaign turned into a rout. For as soon as key states had ratified, the Confederation lost all viability. At that point, the only alternative for the holdouts was going it alone, and even feisty Rhode Island wasn't up

George Washington: the indispensable man would become the indispensable president.

(*Washington's Triumphal Entry into New York City in 1783*, courtesy of the Abby Aldrich Rockefeller Folk Art Center, Williamsburg, Virginia.)

to that. Together with equally reluctant North Carolina, the tiny polity eventually threw in the towel.

Another kind of capitulation occurred on the floors of state conventions after the deciding vote. There were a few diehards who stormed back to their domiciles in disgust, but for the most part, winners and losers alike offered apologies and reconciliation.

Celebrations in the various states were something to behold. In one of them, held in Philadelphia, there was a "Grand Procession" a mile and a half long winding through the city, its centerpiece a float of the "Grand Federal Edifice," drawn by ten white horses. Harking back to the ancient world, this temple of American nationhood was supported by thirteen Corinthian columns, and upon its dome, bearing a cornucopia, stood the figure of *Plenty*. The symbolism seemed right.

Even grander celebrations were held in April of the following year when President Washington took the oath of office. He had performed his own quiet heroism in the ratification campaign, writing to Federalists and Anti-Federalists alike, urging, chiding, cajoling and dolefully lamenting as the skirmishes were fought. We don't think of Washington as a politician, but he truly was one of the best.

Why Federalism Won

The politics of the ratification campaign and the swinging of the balances were only visible manifestations of a much deeper phenomenon. The American people as a whole were making a decision, irrespective of local situations, and that decision was clearly *for* the Constitution.

Every once in a while, one of them sat down and wrote out his thinking on the matter, as in the case of Jonathan Smith described above. For thousands of others, we can only make guesses based on fragmentary evidence. But the general picture seems reasonably clear.

To begin with, Americans were more apt to side with faith and hope than with doubt and fear. Thus, where Anti-Federalists decried "commercialism," most Americans tended to think of prosperity instead, and where Anti-Federalists denounced "empire," their countrymen envisioned that City upon a Hill. Their optimism was bolstered by the Constitution's amendability. The document may not be perfect, they knew, but its flaws could eventually be ferreted out and repaired.

Then, too, as children of the New World, Americans truly believed in having it both ways. They were less interested in theoretical purity—as in, say, classical republican doctrine—than they were in practical outcome. So when the Federalists promised them all the benefits of the ancient republics and none of the costs, they replied: "Sounds good."

As a third point, Americans began to see that the Federalists were every bit as devoted to republicanism as their adversaries—they just weren't shackled to it. For the Anti-Federalists, republicanism was a kind of civil religion, and one had to accept its doctrines as a confession of faith. Federalists were more pragmatic. For them, classical republicanism with its rigid moral demands was no more valid or compelling than the liberal or democratic strains of republican thought, and it was far less relevant to American life. In consequence, they were

Anti-Federalist Fears Founded?

One of the main concerns of the Anti-Federalists was the specter of empire that the Constitution raised. In their arguments, they cried over and over again that the concept of parallel sovereignty was no more than a pipe dream and would lead to a large, tyrannical national government. While we all like to laugh at the seemingly unfounded worries of the Anti-Federalists today, some of their ideas have played out in American history. Ever since the signing of the Constitution, states' rights have been continually eroded. The tension between national and state sovereignty was played out most dramatically in the Civil War, but the issue still has not been fully resolved. Even in the twentieth century the fears of the Anti-Federalists have been recalled by event after event.

Consider, for example, the made-for-a-textbook case of Little Rock, Arkansas, in 1957. In the fall of that year, a number of the community's citizens, angered by the prospect of school desegregation, decided to defy a federal court order and simply refuse to integrate. They knew, of course, about the supremacy clause of the Constitution, but they sup-posed that states had their rights too, and that somehow, such rights could be enforced independent of the federal judiciary.

On the first day of school, nine black children appeared at Central High ready for class. There was trouble. A venomous crowd was milling about on the front steps and growling angrily about a lynching. Hesitantly, school authorities appealed to the Little Rock police department, and from there to the mayor's office, where it was decided to close the school. But the mayor of Little Rock was not sovereign, and so the decision was appealed still higher. The governor of the state, Orval Faubus, also decided against integration and called out the state militia to support the local police. However, since a federal court order was also at stake, the issue had to go higher still. Ultimately, it wound up on the desk of Dwight Eisenhower, president of the United States, who decided that the court order should be upheld. This is exactly the kind of scenario the Anti-Federalists predicted would occur. And what happened next was also what the Anti-Federalists knew would happen.

Eisenhower won out. To prove his point and establish the supremacy of the federal government, he nationalized the Arkansas state militia—meaning that Faubus lost command of his own troops—and sent in the 101st Airborne for good measure. The division's crack 327th Battle Group lined up outside Central High with fixed bayonets. Then the soldiers slowly advanced on the shouting throng of obstructionists. One stout soul had to approach within six inches of a gleaming bayonet before fully comprehending where ultimate sovereignty was now vested.

Still the question of whether or not sovereignty can reside in parallel entities continues to haunt the nation. Consider the outcome of the 2000 presidential election. Who finally determined the final vote count in Florida? True, the federal courts became involved on several levels, but in the end the state of Florida was still responsible for certifying its election results. And the nation was bound by that outcome.

willing to jury-rig a system from component parts, some classical, some liberal and some democratic, mixed and matched to their own situation. What was important to them was not adhering to a particular doctrine but pursuing a general spirit—one familiar to all Americans. *This thing doesn't work*, they said in effect, *so let's figure out how to fix it.*

Finally, Americans became persuaded that union was necessary to complete the American Revolution and endow their national experience with a true "founding." The Constitution's ultimate promise was that Americans, as a people, would be able to live a stable, secure and happy republican life. Nothing short of that promise could make their history add up. If all those terms—freedom, justice, opportunity, virtue—were to have real and practical value, then Americans, who had risked so much already, had to take that final historic chance.

In sum, each side had offered a solution to the Republican Problem. The Anti-Federalists' solution was familiar but problematic. The Federalists' solution was bold and risky but not unreasonable. There was something decidedly "American" in leaning toward the second alternative.

From Ratification to Politics

Anti-Federalism collapsed so quickly that the ratification controversy came to seem chimerical. It was not. Anti-Federalists had raised a number of issues that were not only not chimerical, they would never go away. We could rummage through the debate and pick out some questions that were destined to cast long shadows into the American future:

Was the grant of power to the federal government indeed too broad and loosely worded?

This question would dog the heels of the Washington and Adams administrations, and culminate in the dramatic election campaign of 1800. Themes of big government, busy government, distant government and unresponsive government have run through American politics ever since.

Could sovereignty truly be vested in parallel entities, or was it unitary by nature, as the Anti-Federalists claimed?

Questions of states' rights have been around as long as questions of curbing the government. Even in the early days, when the states seemed of much greater consequence than the Union, there was a steady erosion of power from the periphery to the center. The American Civil War resulted from the inability of states to assert themselves against a determined national government. When push came to shove—as the Anti-Federalists had prophesied—one kind of sovereignty or the other had to be decided on the battlefield.

Was republican society compatible with "imperial" nationhood, as the Federalists argued, or were the two hopelessly at odds?

America lived up to every detail of Hamilton's dream, becoming a nation to reckon with, even to fear, in the eyes of the world. For the most part, its international influence has been salutary, as republican idealism would require. But there have been some gray areas. The US wrested large chunks of the continent from neighbors to the north and south, then became a player in the global power game. As for its relations with native inhabitants, there is little or no defense for them. Anti-Federalists had their point about the choice between republic and empire.

Was a real "public good" to be found among contending private interests, as Madison claimed, or was that promise simply too good to be true?

Pork Barrel: Government projects or appropriations allocated on the basis of patronage.

Unquestionably, the extended republic delivered the strength and stability that Madison promised. The "public good," on the other hand, has proven more elusive. The way the federal system operates, representatives frequently seek measures of benefit to the folks back home without considering anyone else. The result has often been government by pork barrel. The Anti-Federalists may have been right when they argued that public good can only be achieved through civic virtue.

Finally, was republican society compatible with "commercial" values, as the Federalists maintained, or were the two destined to be forever at odds?

PACs: Political action committees formed to lobby for specific issues.

Commerce run amok has become yet another American theme. From the "trusts" of Rockefeller's day, to the "malefactors of great wealth" denounced by Franklin Roosevelt, to the corporate-sponsored PACs of the present day, "big business" has repeatedly been cast as the bogeyman. And in a different way, so has bourgeois materialism. What good is it to gain the world and lose one's own soul? the poets have asked of our pleasure- and gadget-loving society. And the main thrust of the counterculture has been against our enslavement to possessions.

These were only a few of the questions tumbling out of that first face-off, between supporters and detractors of the Constitution, and every one of them was to wind its way through US history. All of which suggests that the ratification debate was but a rough draft of American politics.

The fact that the choices were not simple or the outcome foregone establishes the adoption of the Constitution as the central event of the Founding. The American people decided to cast their lot with a strange form of government, man-made, oddly shaped and without historical precedent. For all they knew, that decision truly was the great mistake of their time—as the Anti-Federalists might have put it—and the downfall of the American Revolution. Whatever happened from that point forward, for good or ill, it would trace back to the moment the ninth state voted to ratify.

In the end, it was the American people who cast their lot with an untried form of government and brought the United States of America into being. (*Philadelphia Election Day*, by John L. Krimmel, courtesy of the Winterthur Museum, Winterthur, Delaware.)

Suggestions for Further Reading

Christopher M. Duncan, *The Anti-Federalists and Early American Political Thought* (1995).

Michael Allen Gillespie and Michael Lienesch, eds., *Ratifying the Constitution* (1989).

Cecelia M. Kenyon, "Men of Little Faith: The Anti-Federalists on the Nature of Representative Government," *William & Mary Quarterly* (January 1955).

Forrest McDonald, *We the People: The Economic Origins of the Constitution* (1992).

Jackson Turner Main, *The Anti-Federalists: Critics of the Constitution, 1781–1788* (1961).

Richard B. Morris, *Witness at the Creation: Hamilton, Madison, Jay and the Constitution* (1985).

Peter S. Onuf, ed., *Ratifying, Amending, and Interpreting the Constitution* (1991).

Josephine F. Pacheco, ed., *Antifederalism: The Legacy of George Mason* (1992).

Garry Wills, *Explaining America: The Federalist* (1981).

CHAPTER 10 STUDY AID ━━━━━━

(This aid is not all-inclusive and is not intended to be a substitute for thorough study of the material presented in the textbook.)

The Ratification Campaign

I. The Constitution

1. Issues and questions:
   - Innovation
   - Behind closed doors
   - Elitism and self-interest
   - The nature of the ratification debate
   - What did the Revolution mean?
   - What is republican government?
   - What is/are the United States?

II. The Process of Ratification

1. How to ratify?
   - State governments
   - The people
   - How many states needed?
2. Solution:
   - The people of each state
   - Special state conventions
   - Representatives chosen by the people
   - By a majority of the states

III. Federalists and Anti-Federalists

1. Federalists:
   - Almost a political party—ideology, leadership, rank and file, grass-roots appeal
   - Advocate strong national government
   - Rule of law
   - Commercial republic
   - Preferred liberal republican government
   - Vision—City upon a Hill
2. Anti-Federalists:
   - Not quite a political party
   - Backed by public opinion

- Controlled key states
- Opposed strong national government
- Feared loss of authority and influence
- Preferred blend of classical and democratic republicanism
- Constitution seen as liberal and elitist
- Saw themselves as true heirs of the Revolution

3. Anti-Federalist arguments and strategies:
   - Constitution violates classical republican precepts
   - Constitution mimics corrupt British forms
   - Constitution separates people from the government
   - Constitution means empire, not republic
   - Contains no bill of rights
   - Anti-Federalists vision of America—diversity, virtue, self-government
   - Strategy—demand bill of rights to protect people from their own excesses
   - Strategy—demand new convention, enumerated powers insufficient

4. Federalist strategies:
   - Yield on bill of rights
   - Focus on three most dominant states
   - Obtain endorsements of Adams and Jefferson
   - Argue for order, stability and security in union of states
   - Argue that structure needed as a precaution against human nature

IV.   Ratification

1. The vote:
   - Delaware, New Jersey, Georgia, Connecticut
   - Pennsylvania (dirty tricks), Massachusetts (very close)
   - Maryland and South Carolina make eight
   - Virginia (also close) is ninth, New Hampshire
   - New York: *The Federalist Papers*

2. Why?
   - Bandwagon
   - Will of the people
   - Vision of a City upon a Hill
   - Having it both ways—theory and practice
   - The spirit rather than the letter of republicanism
   - Necessity—promise of a stable, secure, happy republican life seemed to fulfill the promise of the Revolution
   - Then and now Americans tend to be Anti-Federalists at heart but Federalists in mind and purse—the tendency is to vote the latter

3. The outcome:
  - Big government fears not unfounded
  - States' rights diminished, everything tends to be a federal case
  - Imperial nationalism, imperialism, imperial presidency
  - Public good versus pork barrel, virtue versus self-interest
  - Commercialization—the business of America is business
  - Where do we stand on the question of the Constitution today—would we undo it or keep it?

CHAPTER 10 REVIEW QUESTIONS ———

NAME: _____   SECTION: _____

Key Terms

Ratification

Federalists

Anti-Federalists

The Federalist Papers

"Publius"

Multiple Choice Questions

1. All of the following were aspects of the ratification process except:
   a. Citizens within the states must call for the ratifying convention.
   b. The ratifying vote need only encompass a simple majority.
   c. The Constitution had to be approved by all state legislatures.
   d. Once ratified by nine states, the Constitution became the law of the land.

2. Which of the following was not one of the Anti-Federalist indictments against the Constitution?
   a. It lacked a bill of rights.
   b. The national government would be too far removed from the people.
   c. States would lose sovereignty.
   d. The ratification process was not legitimate.

3. Which of the following Founders was not an author of *The Federalist Papers*?
   a. Alexander Hamilton.
   b. Thomas Jefferson.
   c. John Jay.
   d. James Madison.

4. Which was the fourth state to ratify the Constitution?
   a. Delaware.
   b. Connecticut.
   c. New Jersey.
   d. Georgia.

Review Questions

1. According to the text, how did the ratification process alter the meaning of the Founding?

   _____

   _____

   _____

   _____

2. What did the Anti-Federalists have going for them? The Federalists?

   _____

   _____

   _____

   _____

3. Why were the Anti-Federalists so interested in including a bill of rights in the Constitution?

   _____

   _____

   _____

   _____

4. Why did the Anti-Federalists feel that the Constitution violated republican principles?

   _____

   _____

   _____

   _____

5. What is meant by the notion that public good can only be achieved through civic virtue? Did the Anti-Federalists violate this principle? Explain.

   _____

   _____

   _____

   _____

Review Exercises

1. Briefly describe the Anti-Federalist vision of America.

   _____

   _____

   _____

   _____

2. Summarize the arguments made in Massachusetts by Amos Singletry and Jonathan Smith. What were their main points of disagreement?

_____

_____

_____

_____

3. Describe the Federalist approach to endorsing the Constitution, as exemplified by *The Federalist Papers*.

_____

_____

_____

_____

Big Essay Question

In the previous question you described the Federalist approach to endorsing the Constitution. How might the Federalists alter their tactics if the ratification campaign was going on right now? What would they do differently, or the same, to "sell" the Constitution? Be thoughtful and creative.

The Bill
of Rights

(*We the People*, by Merrilee Allred, reprinted by permission of the artist.)

When the Bill of Rights became part of the Constitution in 1791, it was added by way of the amending process spelled out in Article V. Its enumerated items, arranged in clusters, became Amendments One through Ten.

Placing the Bill of Rights at the Constitution's end underscored its importance. As an addendum, it has occasionally threatened to overshadow the document it was meant to complement.

The Constitution and the Bill of Rights

Where the Constitution (like most blueprints) made for dry reading, the Bill of Rights had a ringing, rhetorical quality—as if asserting the cause of all mankind. There was another contrast. For those who saw the Constitution solely in terms of power, the Bill of Rights changed the subject, as it were, to freedom and dignity.

Modern-day political culture has sometimes gone even further and imagined a contradiction between the Constitution and the Bill of Rights—as if they were written by two different groups bound in opposite directions. Yet James Madison, the Constitution's primary Framer, also drafted the Bill of Rights. And he saw the two not in contradiction but in consonance—twin cornerstones of the Founding. He even suggested placing the Bill of Rights within the body of the Constitution rather than at the tail as a series of amendments.

For us to appreciate Madison's point of view, we must retrace the history of the Bill of Rights and take a closer look at its key ideas.

Bill of Rights:

http://www.nara.gov/exhall/ charters/billrights/billmain .html

http://www.aclu.org/library/ pbp9.html

The Demand for a Bill of Rights

When Washington had invited fellow delegates to sign the completed Constitution, George Mason had stunned them all by refusing to comply. The Constitution, he pronounced, was sadly and unforgivably wanting a bill of rights.

The term was not unfamiliar. After all, the English Bill of Rights (1689) was a landmark of America's constitutional heritage. And the Revolution itself had been propelled by rights-conscious slogans like: "No taxation without representation!" "From the beginning," write Kurland and Lerner, "the language of America has been the language of rights." More broadly, bills of rights were commonly discussed throughout the western world in the eighteenth century and here and there they actually materialized. In the US, no fewer than eight state constitutions had bills of rights attached to them. That of Virginia, which was often a model for the others, had been drafted by George Mason himself.

In order to understand what a bill of rights was and what it was intended to accomplish, we must recall that most governments at the time were monarchies and their powers were the prerogative powers of kings. Limiting such powers had proven to be a difficult task. A monarch might grant concessions of one kind or another in a time of crisis, but little by little he usually gained back the lost ground—and even added a few acres. Accordingly, the function of a bill of rights was twofold. First, the king's subjects got a chance to assert their rights in black and white. And second, the words on paper served to remind both parties, king and subjects, that the assertion had been made. As John Dickinson argued in an influential newspaper essay, a bill of rights would establish "in the minds of the people truths and principles which they might never otherwise have thought of, or soon forgot."

The rights asserted in such bills were almost always derived from natural rights, which like natural law were held to be universal in character and comprehensible to everyone. But because natural rights were vague and open-ended—the right to live, the right to be free—it was thought necessary to draw up a list of particulars to bring the rights down to earth. Some bill of rights documents were rather lengthy, listing out scores of specific items. Most, however, were fairly short, numbering between ten and twenty. Brevity added rhetorical punch.

At their most effective, bills of rights took the general concept of rights and shaped it into what might be called *Great Oughts*. Whenever you have suffered an injustice, a voice within often cries something like: *A person ought to be allowed to* _____ (fill in the blank). Think of the Great Oughts as the most profound and fundamental utterances of that voice. And when other people hear them, they can become banners to rally around.

The language of rights is not the language of supplication. Indeed, asserting a right is in effect a claim coupled with a threat. And yet, paradoxically, rights by their very nature are virtually unenforceable, which may be one reason why we get so upset when they are violated. Still, in the general way of eighteenth-century politics, bills of rights did serve to remind the king and his ministers that they might be treading on shaky ground.

Tanks called in to crush the Tiananmen Square protest in 1989: "Rights" guaranteed by the Chinese constitution proved to be quite illusory. (By Jeff Widener, courtesy of AP/Wide World Photos.)

At the time of the Founding, some Americans were downright skeptical about bills of rights. For one thing, the whole concept was easily misunderstood. "Rights," if they existed at all, were necessarily limited by the rule of reason, by political and economic circumstances and by the logic of governance. Those who failed to grasp such limits could set up a clamor for their rights that might easily lead to anarchy. Nor did rights enhance the spirit of community. The rights of the people *as a people* were one thing; the rights of individuals were quite another. For individuals must always assert rights *against* society.

Then, too, listing rights out always posed a problem. Why was this right to be included in a given catalogue and not that one? What happened to the rights that were excluded—did they cease to exist? And who got to decide?

James Iredell, an early Supreme Court Justice, pointed out that the language of a bill of rights could easily be reduced to mere babble, and Noah Webster provided a handy illustration. On his list of rights, he said, he would include stipulations "that Congress shall never restrain any inhabitant of America from eating and drinking, at seasonable times, or prevent his lying on his left side, in a long winter's night, or even on his back, when he is fatigued by lying on his right."

Tacking a bill of rights onto a *republican* constitution was especially troublesome. Unlike royal prerogative, the powers of republican government were those of the people themselves, and it seemed absurd for the people to curtail *their own* sovereignty. On the other hand, the *difficulties* posed by bills of rights could afflict a republican government quite as much as any other.

Even more so. The Framers in Philadelphia were particularly troubled by the notion of mixing bills of rights with enumerated powers. For the strategy of enumeration to work, there had to be a binding assumption that the government could act only in the enumerated areas and no other, yet any mention of rights was bound to suggest otherwise. For example, stating that the government could not abridge religious freedom implied that it had such authority in the first place, even though that authority was never enumerated.

Most important, for the Framers in Philadelphia, the Constitution was its own bill of rights. By enabling the people to live republican lives under a government they themselves controlled, it secured for them all the blessings that a bill of rights could ever hope to. Accordingly, as George Mason well knew, the Framers had carefully considered his arguments for a bill of rights and rejected them 10 to 0.

The Bill of Rights in the Ratification Debate

Anti-Federalists, as we know, saw an important opportunity in this situation. If opposition to the Constitution could be mustered on the grounds of its lacking a bill of rights, they might be able to force the calling of another constitutional convention—which would presumably deal with their *real* objections. Many Federalists were angered by what they saw as a cynical use of the bill of rights issue. It was a political red herring, they steamed, and deserved to go unheeded.

Red Herring: Something that distracts from the real issues.

Yet as the ratification debate unfolded, thoughtful Anti-Federalists made penetrating forays into the bill of rights issue. Suppose, they submitted, that the

Constitution's "necessary and proper" clause were interpreted the way that Alexander Hamilton had advocated. The government had the enumerated power to coin money and regulate currency, which meant that it also had the power to punish counterfeiting. What was to stop a go-for-broke Congress from declaring counterfeiting subject to general warrants, secret trials and punishment by drawing and quartering? In other words, a bill of rights clearly *could* apply to republican governance.

Federalists responded to this challenge just as thoughtfully—and with even more cunning. Perhaps there *was* merit in the Anti-Federalists' complaint, they conceded. But since the draft Constitution had been provided with an amending process, why not ratify it first and then, if the American people truly wanted a bill of rights, well, they knew how to get one. Few Federalists were sincere in making this offer. After all, once the Constitution was ratified, why would they have to bother? The Anti-Federalists had used a red herring—they could use one too.

James Madison, as usual, was out ahead of everyone. He considered the arguments for a bill of rights, and concluded that whatever the motives behind them, they might well be valid. Besides, such a mechanism could be made part of the Constitution's structural interplay, checking the government against the people themselves. And, as a newspaper commentator added, a bill of rights could be made "to secure the minority against the usurpation and tyranny of the majority," and defend "the sober and industrious part of the community . . . from the rapacity and violence of the vicious and idle."

But there must be some provisos. First of all, the rights listed in any bill would have to be framed with great care so as to not conflict with the Constitution proper or interfere with its other mechanisms. Second, they must be framed as *civil* rights, not *natural* rights, meaning that they must be concretely described, carefully limited and made to address real-life situations. Finally, they must be enforceable. The only sense it made for including a bill of rights in a republican constitution was to allow individuals, when their rights were violated, to seek actual redress in the courts.

Madison, in other words, was not primarily interested in Great Oughts. He wanted a bill of rights that was less a matter of ringing declarations and more a matter of nuts-and-bolts constitutional protections. But those protections, he believed, could be of inestimable value.

And so it was that James Madison almost single-handedly kept the bill of rights issue alive in Congress after it was politically dead. When the Constitution was ratified, Federalists and Anti-Federalists alike were willing to forget about the promised amendments. Not Madison. He had become a believer.

Drafting the Bill of Rights

It was easy for Madison—now *Congressman* Madison—to secure appointment to the appropriate congressional committee, which then solicited suggestions from the states. (Send us your favorite right.) These arrived in a farrago of natural rights, civil rights, historic privileges and pious declarations. Madison sifted through hundreds of items and winnowed them down to a discrete few.

Then he turned to the problem of draftsmanship.

Legal draftsmanship must always choose between two general approaches to the casting of an idea into prose:

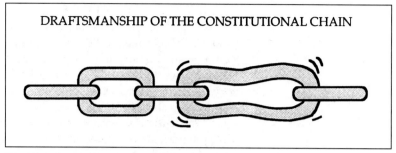

DRAFTSMANSHIP OF THE CONSTITUTIONAL CHAIN

The Founders drafted some clauses with the rigor of a steel link (left); and other clauses with the flexibility of a rubber link (right).

Broad and abstract language. Here the terms are vague and open-ended: "All people have a right to justice." In attempting to apply such language to specific cases—as a court would have to do—a variety of possible meanings and innumerable exceptions are always likely to come up, and the courts wind up with carte blanche in sorting them out. Yet this type of language has pronounced rhetorical value. It makes the right being stated sound like a Great Ought.

Narrow and concrete language. Here the terms are precise, legalistic and freighted with qualifiers. "All members of the XYZ Club, in good standing, with dues paid up, shall have the privilege of using the club swimming pool during the hours of 9:00 A.M. to 5:00 P.M. on Tuesdays and Thursdays, holidays excepted." Courts are far more restricted in the interpretation of such language, so it is far easier to apply it to specific cases. On the other hand, it has little or no rhetorical value.

Any draftsman wishing to assert a natural right would undoubtedly use the first alternative, or wishing to grant a legal privilege would use the second. But what about the sort of thing Madison had in mind—civil rights, subject to adjudication? There were arguments for leaning either way. Yet for the most part, Madison leaned toward the narrow alternative, for if you really mean the rights in your bill to appear in court, you must frame them as specifically as possible.

Accordingly, we can see a number of places where Madison consciously employed the narrow and concrete drafting strategy. Take the Third Amendment, for example:

No Soldier shall, in time of peace be quartered in any house, without the consent of the Owner, nor in time of war, but in a manner to be prescribed by law.

The wording is full of concrete terms such as *soldier*, *house* and *quartered*, and replete with qualifiers like *in time of peace*, *in time of war* and *without the consent of the Owner*. "Shorthand" words and phrases are also used. While these may sound vague—*in a manner to be prescribed by law*—they actually refer to well-established procedures.

Clearly, then, Madison intended the Third Amendment to appear in court. True, attorneys might still quibble over the meaning of some terms. They might argue that the alleged quartering was actually in a "barn" rather than a "house," or that the "soldier" was really a "sailor." Yet the courts would have little difficulty applying this kind of language to real-life situations.

Madison could have drafted the Third Amendment the other way, in which case it would go something like: "Government shall not interfere with private property." But think of the implications. Such broad and abstract wording would prohibit quartering, all right, but it might also prohibit much else. And the courts would have a field day deciding what the words *interfere*, *private* and *property* did or did not include. In the end, the legitimate work of government, which must always include *some* interference with property, could easily be undermined. Madison understood this irony. Simply by stating a right that most Americans strongly believed in, the Constitution could seriously be crippled—while the right itself remained unprotected.

This explains why many of the rights listed in the proposed amendments were drafted narrowly and concretely, and the situations they addressed were not general woes of humanity but difficulties Americans had encountered before:

Second Amendment: The right to keep and bear arms.

Third Amendment: The conditional right to be free from quartering.

Fourth Amendment: Security from unreasonable searches and seizures.

Fifth Amendment: Security from the expropriation of property without just compensation.

In the Fifth through the Eighth Amendments Madison included a list of procedural guarantees for persons accused of crimes. Since virtually all of these protections were found in the English common law, they could be described by "shorthand" references:

Double Jeopardy:
Putting a person on trial for an offense for which he or she has previously been tried.

Fifth Amendment: Grand jury indictment required for serious crimes.

No double jeopardy.

No self-incrimination.

Sixth Amendment: Speedy and public trial.

Trial by jury.

The accused to be informed of the nature and cause of the accusation.

The accused to be confronted with witnesses.

Compulsory process for obtaining favorable witnesses.

Assistance of counsel.

Seventh Amendment: Jury trial for civil suits.

Common law to govern appeals.

Eighth Amendment: Reasonable bail.

Reasonable fines.

No cruel or unusual punishment.

Even though the meanings of these terms were well established, some of them would be subject to the same difficulties outlined above. For example, the meaning of the phrase "cruel and unusual punishment" was rather different in the eighteenth century than it would be in the twenty-first. Some present-day Americans regard capital punishment as "cruel and unusual."

More problematic still was the inclusion of the following words in the Fifth Amendment: ". . . nor shall any person . . . be deprived of life, liberty, or property, without due process of law. . . ." The phrase *due process of law* was yet another shorthand expression familiar to the legal fraternity. It meant that accused persons should not be punished unless all the safeguards of the common law had scrupulously been applied to their case. By connecting this phrase with *life, liberty, or property*, however, an odd situation was created. The words *could* be interpreted to mean that legislative acts must never deprive people of life, liberty or property *at all*—that such ends can only be accomplished by courts. Once again, consider the effect on government. Most government regulations have the effect of curtailing liberty. If I am commanded by the law to provide brakes for my automobile, I lose a part of my "natural" freedom to drive any way I choose. So, does the Fifth Amendment mean that government may not require me to have brakes? And if so, is it still a real government?

The due process clause illustrated what dangers could befall a bill of rights. Meanings that were clear and unambiguous in the minds of the authors could develop all sorts of ambiguity when considered by subsequent generations. The words *due process of law*, once divorced from their traditionally accepted meaning, were so vague that they could be taken to mean almost anything.

The Great Oughts

There are three items in the Bill of Rights that were not drafted narrowly and concretely. They are often taken to be the most important rights of all—the ones that come to mind when the Bill of Rights is mentioned. Clearly Madison did not approach them in the way he approached the others. They are much more in the character of natural rights and thus fully qualify as Great Oughts. They are:

Freedom of conscience. Found in two separate clauses of the First Amendment.

Freedom of expression. Found in four clauses of the First Amendment.

Right to privacy. Implied by language of the First, Third and Fourth Amendments.

An obvious first question is why, when Madison took pains to draft most of the rights so narrowly, did he leave these three vague and general? One part of the answer is that there is simply no way to define religion, expression or privacy in narrow and concrete terms—words literally fail. Another part is that the subjects themselves are of overarching importance. Freedom of conscience, freedom of expression and freedom to live one's own life may be considered the fundamental ends of republican government—the "happiness" that free people seek. In other words, these truly are *Great Oughts*.

Freedom of Conscience

The First Amendment begins with these words: "Congress shall make no law respecting an establishment of religion, or prohibiting the free exercise thereof. . . ." Matters of worship, in other words, are beyond the reach of the federal government.

Religious Test: See page 227 for discussion.

In drafting the Constitution, the Framers had forbidden religious tests for officeholding. This was considered a bold step toward religious freedom, and it was taken only after agonized debate. But the First Amendment went further still. Not only must there be no religious test in politics, there must be no religious anything where the state was concerned.

In framing these clauses, Madison drew upon his own experience in Virginia. At the time of the Revolution, he and Jefferson had authored the bill that disestablished the Anglican Church as the "official" religion of the colony and proclaimed religious liberty. That too had been a momentous step, for it had cut a tie that many in the western world took to be essential.

Take the English case, for example. England itself enjoyed a kind of religious freedom. All churches were at liberty to preach their doctrines and practice their faith as long as they obeyed the law. There remained the established Anglican Church, however, and it was supported by public tithes. Granted, the church had an inordinate and occasionally untoward influence in politics, as its critics tirelessly maintained, but it also made an important contribution, something we might call "divine legitimacy." If an Anglican Archbishop was present at occasions of state, giving his benediction with grand ceremony, it must mean—and for many did mean—that God backed the government.

In America, as we have seen, the presence of an even greater number of contending faiths pointed toward a certain logic: that all be allowed to preach their own gospels and that none be accorded special favor. Some of the Founders believed that this approach would enhance civic virtue, as we saw in chapter 8. But others believed that a degree of religious influence still needed to be officially recognized, as it was in England, in order for the state to enjoy that legitimizing sense of mysterium.

The First Amendment cut through that debate like a butcher knife. Religion was a private affair, it said. Citizens of the Republic ought to be free to accept or reject whatever faith they chose, subject only to their own conscience. Church and state must remain separate and apart.

Freedom of Expression

Just as it was thought daring to separate church and state, it was thought daring to allow freedom of expression in politics. England had pointed the way there as well—and it was a way fraught with obstacles.

In *Leviathan* (1651), Thomas Hobbes' famous dissertation on political philosophy, Englishmen were presented with an argument for the complete annihilation of free speech. It came down to the simple fact that speech could be extremely dangerous. Hobbes had his supporters too, many of them in high places. In one notable case, a critic of the Stuart monarchy had had his books burned, his property confiscated, his tongue cut out and his person thrown into a dungeon for life.

Part of the problem was conceptual. When the head of the state actually embodies the state in some mystical way and serves at the pleasure of God—which is precisely what the Stuart monarchs believed—there can be no concept of "loyal opposition" such as we have today, for dissenters cannot possibly be loyal: they are quarreling with the state and with God. The English skirted this difficulty by aiming their complaints at the king's "evil counselors" rather than the king himself. In separating king from counselors, they were trying to separate state from government so that opposition to the one would not mean disloyalty to the other. (After all, the king could always get different counselors.) Counselors, however, were powerful men in their own right, and they took criticism no better than most kings. On the contrary, they hid behind the king's robes and labeled all critics as rebels.

Yet in time even the most hidebound came to see that there must be *some* political expression. Here and there, under varying restrictions, members of Parliament were allowed a degree of freedom to take issue with government policies. But only a degree. There was always the occasional backlash and offending MPs were sent to the tower. Free speech was in no way guaranteed.

And there was another problem. In alleging certain kinds of wrongdoing, such as bribery or corruption, a critic could also be charged with libel, for impugning the character of a public official was viewed no differently from slandering one's neighbor down the street. Here again, though, common sense eventually came to the rescue. It became plain to see that making public officials immune to corruption charges only invited worse corruption, and slapping vigilant citizens with lawsuits only killed off public virtue.

Freedom of speech involved both of these—opposing government policies and pointing out official corruption—and both took root in the American colonies. (One of the landmark legal cases involving free speech took place in New York City in 1734–35.) Both helped bring on the Revolution too. Those who opposed a given policy—such as the Stamp Act—alleged personal corruption on the part of the officials connected with it, and personal corruption—as in, say, the taking of bribes by customs officials—often led to a broader kind of political dissent. Both types of criticism were damaging to the royal government, and both were squelched whenever possible.

As a result, republican fervor became strongly identified with free speech. Virtue must be at liberty to speak its mind. Moreover, with the king and his evil counselors out of the picture, the concept of free speech became clearer. Since republican government served no one but the people (there were no references to "divine right" or God's pleasure), the people had a right to scrutinize it down to the smallest detail. A citizen could oppose any or all of its policies *without being disloyal*.

Freedom of speech, then, was often prominently listed in bills of rights. And it was expanded to include freedom of the press, freedom of assembly and freedom to petition the government for redress of grievances. Free expression was held to be nothing less than a republic's lifeblood.

In the trial of editor John Peter Zenger for libel, lawyer Andrew Hamilton argued that the truth of the allegation constituted a sufficient defense. The jury agreed.

The Right to Privacy

Nowhere in the Bill of Rights is there mention of the right to privacy. Moreover, the courts began to use that phrase only quite recently in US constitutional history. Some critics have denied that a "right to privacy" even exists.

Which brings us to the doctrine of *implied rights*. Those who contend that the right to privacy truly does exist must argue by implication. Their case goes like this. Freedom of religion implies that the private conscience ought not be intruded upon by government. Freedom of expression implies that people ought to make up their own minds and not be told what to think. The quartering amendment implies that the government ought to leave people alone in their own homes, and so does the search and seizure amendment. From all four it is possible to abstract an implied right to privacy. Furthermore, since the Ninth Amendment specifically states "The enumeration in the Constitution, of certain rights, shall not be construed to deny or disparage others retained by the people," the case for implied rights is arguably quite strong.

This still leaves the question of exactly what "privacy" is. Of course that question would be no different if an amendment actually stated: "Congress shall make no law abridging the privacy of individuals." The root idea is a very old one, found in some of the earliest common law cases. It is simply that there ought to be a sphere of life in which government cannot tread. For example, in medieval England there were instances where a fugitive was declared "home free" once he crossed his own threshold, and the pursuing sheriff had to give up the chase—a man's home being quite literally his castle.

It is possible to formulate a conception of privacy that is in keeping with other ideals of the Founding. It would go something like this. The rule of law is itself a means of securing privacy. For if government cannot use the laws to manage the lives of citizens, the laws create a private sphere in which citizens act solely on their own. Privacy, in other words, is only another word for freedom.

Described in this way, the Great Oughts form a conceptual whole, one that reinforces the American Founding. We have seen that the moral text of the Constitution was all about individual dignity and responsibility. The Great Oughts underscore this point. They affirm that one's mind, one's conscience, one's understanding and values, one's volition, one's expression and one's personal life belong to the individual alone—and that the individual must hold himself accountable for them.

So it was that the Constitution acquired its famous amendments. The articles submitted by Madison's committee were approved by Congress in the fall of 1790 and submitted to the states for ratification. It is of passing interest to note that Madison drafted several amendments that were not ratified. One of these—his own personal favorite—would have applied the Bill of Rights to the states. *They* needed it, he thought, more than the federal government did.

The Bill of Rights and the Supreme Court

After the advent of **judicial review**, it was up to the Supreme Court to interpret the Bill of Rights and apply it to specific cases. While the details of judicial review will be covered in a later chapter, one aspect of the interpretive process concerns us here.

Constitutional interpretation came to focus on those areas of the text where the broadest and most elastic wording was found, such as the commerce clause or the necessary and proper clause. The Bill of Rights amendments increased the Constitution's elasticity by perhaps a factor of three. This, of course, was largely due to the Great Oughts, which had to be drafted in the vaguest of language.

Even before the Court began to practice judicial review, it became obvious that the Bill of Rights would alter the way the constitutional system worked. Consider a couple of examples. With reporters poking into government operations, it became clear that every contemplated action must now be weighed according to how it would play in the press—and as a result governance by gentlemen behind closed doors would soon be a thing of the past. Or this. With that same freedom of the press, scurrilous attacks on public officials were bound to multiply and respect for government was bound to diminish. Where the imagery of republicanism always supposed government by virtuous statesmen, America's began to look like government by politicians.

The US Supreme Court has firmly asserted its own authority to define the scope of American rights.
(Courtesy of the Library of Congress.)

With the Bill of Rights assuming an ever more important role, it was only natural that the Supreme Court would pay ever greater attention to puzzling out its meaning. In countless specific cases, the Justices found themselves obliged to define "speech," characterize "religion," stake boundaries around the terms "abridge" or "deprive"—translate the Bill of Rights into constitutional law.

In the process, the Bill of Rights began to change. The reason why had to do with the way courts work. In theory, the Supreme Court, like any Anglo-American court, was bound by its own prior decisions, its *precedents*, in adjudicating a case at hand. If in an early decision the Court defined the phrase "freedom of speech" as referring only to *political* speech, then all subsequent decisions must respect this definition. In fact, it was impossible to hold the Justices to this rule, for their decisions could not be appealed, and thus they often departed from precedent to lasso new ideas. As a result, there was a built-in tendency for constitutional terms to become ever broader, more abstract and more inclusive each time a given word or phrase was adjudicated.

Take freedom of expression, for instance. What was clearly limited to *political* expression in the minds of the Framers gradually grew to include all kinds of expression. Everything from pornography in magazines to vulgarity in the movies to obscenity on the stage came to claim the protection of the First Amendment—and this was but a single avenue of development.

Judicial Review:
http://www.constitutioncenter
.org/sections/basics/basic_1d
.asa

How Free Should Free Speech Be? The Daniel Schorr Case

At sixty, CBS news correspondent Daniel Schorr, silver haired and distinguished looking, cut a figure of journalistic responsibility second only to Walter Cronkite. In truth, however, he was not quite the same benign uncle. For, in the fall of 1976, amid the passions of the presidential election, Schorr suddenly stunned the country by releasing to a New York newspaper the text of an extremely sensitive government report. The Pike Report, resulting from an extensive investigation of US intelligence activities, was so damaging to the pride and prestige of the CIA—which was faulted (among other things) for plotting the murder of foreign dignitaries—that the House had voted to suppress it. Schorr, moreover, was wholly unrepentant. He would not answer questions of the House Ethics Committee; he would not produce a copy of the re-

port; and he would most certainly not reveal the source by which he obtained it.

There had been pirated documents before, the most famous of being the Pentagon Papers of the Vietnam era. But there was a difference in the two situations. Because the Pentagon Papers had shed light on a war that was already intensely unpopular, there was a clear sense that the public interest had been served by their publication. Here, by contrast, many Americans were uneasy. Some of Schorr's most ardent defenders worried about the impact of the Pike Report on the intelligence community's morale. National interests were at stake on both sides.

For his part, Schorr saw only one of those interests: free speech. At issue, he complained, "was not my right to report, but the public's right to know." The national security in-

terest Schorr waved aside. Others in the journalistic community weren't so sure. An editorial in the *New York Times* condemned Schorr for "selling secrets." At the annual Gridiron Dinner, the correspondent found himself not a roast*er* but a roast*ee*. And CBS, after agonizing over the situation, finally decided to suspend him from its news staff. He subsequently resigned.

Where did the public come down? Ditheringly in the middle. When the House Ethics Committee moved toward a confrontation with Schorr (with the possibility of jail for contempt), the public rallied to his defense. Yet polls showed that Americans also feared the power of the press, power that in this case might have caused real injury. In the end, it came down to a question of whom was mistrusted most, the government or the media.

Daniel Schorr: How free should free speech be?
(Courtesy of Corbis Images.)

Many Americans came to deplore what they saw as the perversion of the Bill of Rights. The words of the first ten amendments ought to mean only what the Framers originally intended, they complained. But there was another side to consider. When the Bill of Rights was drafted, electronic surveillance or mind-altering drugs had not yet been invented. Should the protection we hope for at the turn of the twenty-first century apply only to the quartering of soldiers?

The double-sidedness of the question illuminates an important fact of republican life. Where fundamentals are concerned, the people cannot afford to crouch behind parchment barricades. No constitutional wording, however carefully composed or well intentioned, can prevent the deterioration of rights or the proliferation of license if the public itself lacks vigilance. Virtuous citizens, playing by the rules, are still the ultimate custodians of truth.

The Bill of Rights and American Freedom

There is a certain conception of freedom that emphasizes forward motion. It holds that democratic institutions are on a historical march from past to future, forging ever onward to mark the progress of mankind. This idea, rooted in the philosophy of Wilhelm Friedrich Hegel and others, has become popular among Americans. We have come to expect that each generation will be happier, more affluent and above all freer than its predecessor.

Against the backdrop of such thinking, the US Bill of Rights has come to play a role that few of its Framers would have imagined for it. By redefining and continually expanding rights, so the argument goes, a democratic people can continue to realize that promise of the future.

Viewed from this perspective, rights become identified with "justice" and "equality." After all, we never think of them as being attached to race or gender, nor to wealth or background or social class—but only to human beings *as* human beings. As a consequence, the scouting up of rights becomes a way of redressing whatever is wrong. When a group is found to be at a disadvantage, the problem can be corrected by giving that group its "rights." In this way the language of American politics has largely become the language of expanding rights. We speak of new rights for this group, that gender, some other ethnic or cultural identity, even for the disabled, the elderly, the young, the poor and those of varying sexual preference. If everyone has more and better rights, the argument goes, outsiders will eventually become insiders, inequality will vanish and justice will prevail.

In such a world, the rights that James Madison carefully narrowed down and "civilized" are often conceived in absolute terms—much like natural rights. And no matter how much they grant, it can never be quite enough. Thus, a wide latitude of self-expression in the arts needs to be widened still further, special facilities for the handicapped must be constantly improved, and "gender equality" in the workplace runs to nuances and subtleties beyond fathoming. Furthermore, by substituting the contemporary term *human* for the eighteenth-century term *natural*, this rights-oriented conception of life can be projected all over the

Technology Versus Rights

One argument for the existence of implied rights in the US Bill of Rights is that the Founders couldn't have imagined all the ways that later technology might be used to intrude upon rights. Electronic surveillance, for example. In James Madison's day there was no such thing, of course, but we have since raised it to a high art. In a world of satellite communications, eavesdropping antennae and computerized decoders, it is possible for us to listen in on telephone conversations around the world. Not coincidentally, the issue of privacy, which may not have seemed important in Madison's day, has suddenly become so.

Or consider some recent advances in chemistry. The perfection of sodium pentothal and other "truth serums" has made it possible to abridge rights in ways hitherto unimagined, for a single injection can make a victim spill everything. Other kinds of chemicals might conceivably be added to, say, a municipal water supply to create various dispositions—languor, hostility, euphoria—in the populace. Such dispositions might also be produced, perhaps more easily, by skillful manipulation of the mass media.

The list goes on and on. Nuclear power and nuclear weapons testing have created unimagined civil dangers, as has research into chemical and biological warfare. Genetic engineering raises the apocalyptic specter of man-made monsters. Recent forms of pollution—such as the toxic waste dumped into the Love Canal—give a whole new meaning to phrases in the Fifth Amendment.

If all of this sounds Orwellian, it was George Orwell who first called our attention to it. In *1984*, we recall, truth was continually victimized by the Thought Police, and Big Brother's TV cameras snooped everywhere. Science-fiction writers have taken it from there, inventing every imaginable invasion of rights from mass produced embryos (*Brave New World*), to emotional repression (*Fahrenheit 451*), to robotic tyranny (*Blade Runner*). Perhaps the ultimate derogation of rights was imagined in a story by Orson Scott Card, in which a victim was sentenced to die "by every means known to man." Each time he was executed, his existing consciousness—including the pain and horror of execution—would be taped and programmed into another mind, and the whole thing would be repeated.

There is, then, something truly to be said for a concept of human rights that transcends the Founders' own listing of them. After all, the worst thing they could imagine was an illegal tax on tea.

world, with the result that much of the world's tyranny, anarchy, poverty and exploitation can be explained simply as a want of rights.

Because this idea has important implications for republican governance, it might be worthwhile to make a few commonsense observations about it. First, rights are only "expandable" up to a point; beyond that point they rapidly come into conflict with each other. A customer's right to dine wherever he chooses necessarily conflicts with a restaurant owner's right to select his patrons. A woman's right to an abortion is at odds with her child's right to life. Tom's right to express himself through obscenity runs up against Dick's right to shape community standards and Harry's right to shield his children from smut. All rights cannot be respected for all people in all situations.

Second, dynamically expanding rights tend to become divorced from their accompanying responsibilities. In republican theory, rights and responsibilities were inseparable. The right to participate in the political process, for example, was also the responsibility to participate honestly and well. The right of free speech was also the responsibility of careful and thoughtful speech. When the expansion of rights is taken as a cure-all for social ills, responsibility is often left in the dust.

Finally, rights in conflict with and divorced from responsibility do not provide a recipe for social peace—or for the progress those rights are meant to facilitate. Quite the contrary. Groups see the expansion of other groups' rights as a threat to their own, fostering high anxiety. Casualties of the ensuing free-for-all tend to be: first, a sense of virtue in public affairs, and second, a conception of the public good as embracing everyone.

There is a subtler difficulty. If we lean too heavily on rights as a remedy, we may risk the "double jeopardy" described by political scientist Ralph A. Rossum. We discover that rights are not really enforceable by the courts at all, and thus that we have sought security behind a parchment barrier. At the same time, we ignore the fact that the Constitution is the *real* guarantor of our rights and we further weaken constitutional government.

These difficulties conceded, the Bill of Rights has not been without enormous good effect. No reasonable observer looking back over American history would say that those ten amendments were superfluous and unnecessary. Nor could one compare the fortunes of minorities in 1900 with those in 2000 and conclude that the Bill of Rights hasn't hastened the "march of freedom." If it has done nothing else, it has prodded Americans incessantly to live up to their founding ideals.

The Bill of Rights as a Moral Charter

What changed Madison's mind about the Bill of Rights was thinking about the Republican Problem. He had asked himself again and again how a republic could be designed so as to embody the will of people while at the same time protecting individuals and pursuing the public good. The Constitution's structure had been designed for that purpose. That it would operate successfully in most circumstances Madison and the other Framers were reasonably confident. They were less confident about unusual circumstances, and they had reason to be.

Virtually every system failure in republican history has occurred at a time of war, domestic upheaval, economic catastrophe or rapid social change. For in these situations, the perception of minorities is subject to drastic revision. Consider a few episodes. In the 1830s, during a time of rapid social change, Mormons and Masons were suddenly identified as bogeymen and targeted for persecution. In the 1890s, during a time of economic breakdown, "Jewish bankers" were accused of plotting to manipulate the money supply. In the 1940s, during a time of war, Japanese Americans were condemned as potential spies and locked up in prison camps. And in the 1950s, at the height of the Cold War, suspected Communists were investigated, deported, fired from their jobs, blacklisted and made to suffer appalling indignities. With every feature of the constitutional system in place and operating, majority opinion turned violently against these groups and the results were tragic.

In the last analysis, the Bill of Rights was written for them. That Congress "shall make no law . . . prohibiting the free exercise of religion" does not concern Catholics, Lutherans, Anglicans, Baptists, Methodists or Presbyterians. It concerns small sects with strange doctrines and disconcerting practices. Similarly, the First Amendment's freedom of speech is not for Republicans or Democrats. It is for Anarchists, Syndicalists, Communists, Radical Socialists, Skinhead Nazis and even less popular political faiths. And when the Bill of Rights promises privacy from intermeddling, it is not to protect the magazine-cover family in suburbia but motorcycle gangs, hippie communards and ragtag Bohemians. The overwhelming majority of Americans neither embrace nor sympathize with such alternatives—so why bother protecting them?

Part of the answer has to do with freedom. If one is free only to adhere to the norms, such freedom has little meaning. Not only do the unpopular minorities lose out, so does the majority itself, for its members act not out of choice but compulsion.

A second part of the answer has to do with justice. The justice delivered by real-life republics often falls short of perfection, as we have seen. David Hume argued that justice is not a fundamental passion. We seek it mostly for its utilitarian value, not its moral necessity, and that value is limited by all sorts of considerations. With the Bill of Rights, there is a kind of justice by fiat, moving beyond utilitarian value and extending equitable treatment to groups

The Bill of Rights as passed by Congress in 1789. Two of the original twelve articles would remain unratified.

(Courtesy of The Granger Collection, New York.)

The Price of Religious Freedom

Freedom of religion means more than having a Catholic cathedral on one corner, a Lutheran chapel on the next and a Jewish synagogue across the street. Where there is true religious freedom there will also be a vibrant, colorful and sometimes rowdy religious fringe. Americans know that well enough. They see Hare Krishna monks on the sidewalks, read ads on kiosks for Eckankar and peruse articles in the *National Enquirer* about swamis, gurus and fortune-tellers. It is entertaining to think that Los Angeles County has an official witch on the payroll, that San Francisco's Glide Church feature rock music and light shows, or that a group called "The Celestials" believes Mt. Shasta is an intergalactic UFO base.

Yet religion of the fringe poses painful dilemmas for democratic societies. There is, for instance, simple nuisance to think about. The Hare Krishnas can raise a frightful racket with their chants and drums. Other groups panhandle shoppers on the sidewalks or confront them with hellfire preaching. Among the beliefs of a Philadelphia cult called MOVE was the importance of depositing refuse on the street. But nothing compares with the nuisance created by a self-styled maharishi called Rajneesh Bhagwan Shree, whose followers moved in on the Oregon farming community of Antelope, registered as voters and proceeded to reshape the town in their own image.

Or there is the issue of fraud. Much of the astrological, fortune-telling and prophesying activities of the fringe religions—for which millions of dollars changes hands yearly—would be fair game for bunko squads in another setting. Many evangelical churches engage in high-pressure solicitation through their radio and television stations. Still others trade in miracles. A Portland woman recently sued the Church of Scientology for $39 million for falsely promising to alter her personality and raise her IQ.

A number of religious groups run afoul of fundamental mores. Polygamy, complex marriage and outright free love have eroded family values and created chaos in domestic relations. (When everyone is married to everyone else, who inherits what?) The use of drugs is claimed as necessary to some religious observances, and in the case of the Navaho Indians, drug laws have had to be altered accordingly. Some cultists have denied their children education, deprived them of medical attention or forbidden them to participate in citizenship.

The question of mind control raises another raft of issues. L. Ron Hubbard's practice of "dianetics"—a sort of do-it-yourself psychoanalysis—was in constant legal trouble and pronounced "a serious threat to health" by the American Medical Association, but after Scientology was converted to *The Church* of Scientology, its problems diminished. Followers of the Rev. Sun Myung Moon are widely accused of brainwashing recruits, but this is mild compared to the starvation, beatings and torture inflicted by other groups. Such was the degree of mind control achieved by Jim Jones over his followers in Guyana in 1978, that when he ordered them to commit suicide they willingly obeyed.

Churches, of course, get into politics too. This seems tolerable in the context of Republican versus Democrat or liberal versus conservative, but what about in the context of white versus black? Certain fundamentalist groups have encouraged racism among whites, while extremist black sects, such as Louis Farrakhan's in Chicago, have fostered the same sort of hatred in reverse. Then, too, Irish-American Catholics have gathered money for the IRA and Indian-American Sikhs have solicited funds for the Punjab—knowing full well that the result would be death and destruction.

And occasionally religions of the fringe have gone all the way. Anton LaVey's First Church of Satan may be harmless enough with its theatrical bohemianism, but some forms of devil worship indeed call for bloodletting. A teenager murdered his foster parents after claiming to have received satanic orders to do so, and in a spectacular Utah case, two self-proclaimed prophets embarked on a murder spree after God supposedly provided them with a hit list. In Idaho, a group calling itself "The Covenant, the Sword, and the Arm of the Lord" is wanted for multiple homicides.

Such difficulties are not experienced when there is no religious freedom. In Saudi Arabia, to name just one example, there exists near perfect religious harmony. Non-Muslims are welcome in the country, under carefully controlled circumstances, but their religion is not: all baggage is subject to inspection at the Rijadh Airport, and foreign religious items (such as family Bibles) are routinely confiscated. The only problem is that where there is no religious freedom—excesses and all—there is no other kind of freedom either.

who would otherwise be denied it. This is not perfect justice either—as witness the examples given above—but it could and did move American society in the right direction. One might say that the Bill of Rights helps *create* justice as an ideal.

A final part of the answer has to do with dignity. By affirming the legitimacy of the unpopular cause, the other point of view, the alternative lifestyle, we enhance respect for diversity and warrant that the choices we make have meaning and value. We affirm human dignity.

The Rights of Mankind

So understood, the Bill of Rights became an integral part of the Founding. In the Declaration of Independence, Americans submitted that government must protect the rights of its citizens. They went on to draft and approve a Constitution they thought capable of doing just that. The Bill of Rights reached back to the original founding document and reasserted its truths, then cast the Constitution's moral text into strong normative language. It tied the Founding together and made it a coherent whole.

The Bill of Rights reflects the "deeper wisdom" we have seen elsewhere. Like federalism, it was forced on the Framers by circumstances and then, slowly, embraced by them as its implications emerged. If they were slow to grasp its moral significance, it was because the moral significance of the Constitution was obvious to them and they saw no need for restatement. What they did not see was the view from two centuries hence, our own time, when the meanings of words had changed and public morality would need all the help it could get.

In 1948, the UN General Assembly proclaimed a Universal Declaration of Human Rights. It is to this document that we refer when we allege the violation of "human rights" today. The debt of the Universal Declaration to the US Bill of Rights is pretty clear. For example:

Article 18
Everyone has the right to freedom of thought, conscience and religion.

Article 19
Everyone has the right to freedom of opinion and expression.

Article 20
Everyone has the right to freedom of peaceful assembly and association.

We can think of such expressions in terms of Thomas Reid's "moral sense." What is it, asked Reid, that sets human beings apart and make them fully human? Their common intuition of right and wrong. Even where the content of that intuition may vary from culture to culture, the concept of *rights* can fuse it all together. True, we can't all agree that human beings have a right to financial success or happiness in marriage, but we can all agree that they deserve to live their own lives harmlessly or enjoy the fruits of their own labor. The American Founders' view of rights has largely become that of mankind.

Suggestions for Further Reading

Mortimer J. Adler, *We Hold These Truths: Understanding the Ideas and Ideals of the Constitution* (1987).

Akhil Reed Amar, *The Bill of Rights: Creation and Reconstruction* (1998).

Lance Banning, *The Sacred Fire of Liberty: James Madison and the Founding of the Federal Republic* (1995).

Irving Brant, *The Bill of Rights: Its Origin and Meaning* (1965).

Richard C. Cortner, *The Supreme Court and the Second Bill of Rights: The Fourteenth Amendment and the Nationalization of Civil Liberties* (1981).

Robert A. Goldwin, *From Parchment to Power: How James Madison Used the Bill of Rights to Save the Constitution* (1997).

Drew McCoy, *The Last of the Fathers: James Madison and the Republican Legacy* (1989).

Robert Allen Rutland, *The Birth of the Bill of Rights, 1776–1791* (1955).

Bernard Schwartz, *The Great Rights of Mankind: A History of the American Bill of Rights* (1977).

CHAPTER 11 STUDY AID ▬▬▬▬

(This aid is not all-inclusive and is not intended to be a substitute for thorough study of the material presented in the textbook.)

The Ratification Campaign

I. A Bill of Rights?

1. Federalists:
   - People already sovereign
   - Bill of Rights inherent in Constitution
   - A Pandora's box
   - Enforcement problematic
2. Anti-Federalists:
   - People need to be protected from each other
   - Check against enumerated powers
   - Rights need to be specified, not just implied
   - Symbolic value

II. Purposes of the Bill of Rights

1. Peoples' rights:
   - Assertion of rights
   - Reminders of rights
2. Specification:
   - Explicit expression of natural rights
   - The "Good"
   - Freedom not just assumed
3. Great Oughts:
   - Conscience
   - Expression
   - Privacy
4. Downside:
   - "Parchment barrier"
   - Individual versus society
   - Enumeration—what to include, what to leave out
   - Unseen implications or interpretations

III. James Madison

1. Bill of Rights:
   - Ensure minority rights
   - Does not contradict Constitution

- Civil rather than natural rights
- Enforceable in court of law

2. Draftsmanship:
- Broad versus narrow language
- Limit open-ended language
- Express "Great Oughts"
- Imply accountability

IV. Supreme Court

1. Judicial review:
- Constitutional interpretation
- Elasticity
- The meaning of words—"speech," "religion," etc.
- Intent versus application

VI. Bill of Rights and American Freedom

1. Expanded rights:
- Justice
- Equity

2. Civil rights to absolute rights:
- Duties
- Privileges

3. Conflicting rights:
- Abortion versus life
- Obscenity versus community standards

4. Other issues:
- Abrogating responsibility
- Loss of protection
- "Parchment barrier"
- Unenforceability

5. Moral character of rights:
- Protect those out of favor
- Affirm human dignity

6. Rights of mankind and the "Good":
- Integral part of Founding
- Tying the Founding together
- Deeper wisdom
- American Bill of Rights adopted by mankind

CHAPTER 11 REVIEW QUESTIONS ▬▬▬

Key Terms

Bill of Rights

Natural Rights

Great Oughts

Civil Rights

Draftsmanship

Conscience

Expression

Privacy

The Supreme Court

Multiple Choice Questions

1. Who authored the Bill of Rights?
   a. George Mason.
   b. Thomas Jefferson.
   c. James Madison.
   d. Gouverneur Morris.

2. Narrow draftsmanship is associated with which of the following words:
   a. Vague.
   b. Specific.
   c. Simple.
   d. General.

3. Which of the following is not a right protected by the Fifth Amendment?
   a. No double jeopardy.
   b. No self-incrimination.
   c. Trial by jury.
   d. Grand jury indictment for serious crimes.

4. The texts lists each of the following as Great Oughts except:
   a. Freedom of conscience.
   b. Freedom of religion.
   c. Right to privacy.
   d. Freedom of expression.

Review Questions

1. Why was a bill of rights not included as part of the original Constitution?

   _____

   _____

   _____

   _____

2. Why did the Founders fear that too much focus on individual rights might lead into the Human Predicament Cycle?

   _____

   _____

   _____

   _____

3. What are the inherent difficulties in drafting a bill of rights?

   _____

   _____

   _____

   _____

4. Why were certain rights drafted narrowly and others broadly? Why not draft them all one way or the other?

   _____

   _____

   _____

   _____

5. What role does the Supreme Court play in defining what the Bill of Rights means?

   _____

   _____

   _____

   _____

Review Exercises

1. Explain the relationship between natural rights and civil rights.

   _____

   _____

   _____

   _____

2. Explain the idea that natural rights are "unenforceable."

_____

_____

_____

_____

3. Briefly describe the interplay of rights and responsibilities as the Founders understood it.

_____

_____

_____

_____

Big Essay Question

Think philosophically about individual rights within a society. Does a community have rights the same way a citizen does? Are a group's rights paramount over individual rights? Create a scenario where an individual and a group each feel their rights are being violated by the other party. In a thoughtful essay resolve the dispute while addressing the issues raised above.

From the Constitution to the Republic

Jefferson, Hamilton, and Washington *by Constantino Brumidi (c. 1792)*. (Courtesy of Getty Images.)

On April 30, 1789, George Washington took the oath of office in New York City. His procession to the temporary capital sparkled with cheerful symbolism. He was given a public banquet in Philadelphia. He passed through a triumphal arch at Trenton. And he was rowed across the Hudson in a specially constructed barge with thirteen pilots at the oars. It was fitting that the new republicanism should make its debut amid fanfare. Beneath the celebration, however, deep currents swirled and eddied—as an end and a beginning came together.

Perils and Possibilities

In ratifying the Constitution, Americans had accepted a system with unprecedented power over their lives. Scarier still, the system was of their own creation—unknown and untried. Republican governments of the past had come to reveal all sorts of dangerous inclinations. Would the same thing hold true here?

Most statesmen could have dashed off a short list of challenges. There were disparate interests in political society—tidewater versus backcountry, North versus South, commerce versus agriculture. There was the divisiveness of local attachments. And there was nothing but the sovereignty of the people to bind Americans together—no king, no lords, no official church, no ivied ruins, no mystique of ancient nationhood.

On the other side, there was an empowering sense of adventure. The American people, *as* a people, had met their difficulties head on, adopted a plan to rectify them, and now stood willing to forge ahead. From antiquity they took a new sense of comfort. Where they had often spoken fretfully of the plight of Athens, they now began to emphasize the triumph of Rome. They were beginning to see themselves as modern-day heirs of the Roman Republic.

Ambiguity, Precedent and the General Constitution

Americans had lived under the British constitution long enough to know that their own founding document was but a rough sketch. What might be called the *general constitution* of any political society included many things that could never be reduced to parchment—traditions, precedents, established procedures, tacit understandings, behavioral codes and most important, working institutions of government. If all of this represented the living, breathing body politic, the document written in Philadelphia was only a skeleton. Everything else must now be filled in.

Much of the filling in would be accomplished by *precedent*. English culture had always been sensitive to tradition and Americans were inclined to follow suit. In consequence, many facets of the General Constitution would come to exist for no better reason than that's the way it was done way back when. Here was one of the great benefits of having George Washington as president. A person of lesser stature could not have established precedents as easily as Washington did, nor could he have made them as binding.

In seemingly small matters, there was large potential significance. Consider the manner of announcing the president. John Adams' suggestion of "His Majesty, President of the United States and Protector of Their Liberties" might have steered the executive office toward monarchy. Simpler forms were deemed more republican.

In some cases, the setting of precedents actually altered the way the Constitution worked. For example, the wording of Article II, Section 2 states that the president "shall have Power, by and with the Advice and Consent of the Senate, to make Treaties, provided two thirds of the Senators present concur." The clause seems to require the president to seek the "advice" of the Senate while treaty negotiations are in progress. The first time Washington did this he received more advice than he wanted, and much of it was confused and contradictory. He vowed never to bring the Senate to the negotiating table again, and his successors have remained as true to the vow as he did.

We have seen that the Constitution, while clear in most respects, was a study in ambiguity when it came to certain issues. The Framers could walk away from that little difficulty but the government couldn't. The president and his Cabinet had to decide for themselves how far the Constitution's "stretch-points" could be stretched, and when questions of interpretation arose—as surely they must—someone had to work out how and by whom they would be settled. Language could go only so far in creating a political society; beyond that it was up to reason, wisdom and virtue.

The Interplay of Personalities and Events

Republican theory required leadership to be *statesmanship*. The true statesman, in the thinking of the time, was one who always took the broader view and considered long-term consequences. He thought of the public good, not that of his friends or his "party," and thus stood above the fray of politics. He recog-

The Power of Precedent

How should citizens address the President of the United States? We know now, of course, but only with the benefit of hindsight. In 1789, when the first president took office, no one knew the answer and the question was vigorously debated. After all, in a seemingly small matter such as titles and forms of address, precedents could be established which might push the evolution of the president toward, say, monarchy. The question was not insignificant.

John Adams, for one, believed that the American president should possess as much dignity as any European monarch. "If the *state and pomp* essential to his great department are not, in good degree preserved," he wrote, "it will be vain for America to hope for consideration with foreign powers." Accordingly, Adams proposed that the president be addressed as: "His Majesty, President of the United States and Protector of Their Liberties."

That was a mouthful, especially to those who believed in republican simplicity. Indeed, after the Revolution it was quite fashionable for a time to dress without adornment, to avoid fancy speech and to build houses of dignified plainness. When the republican Mr. Jefferson heard about Adams' proposal in Paris, he repeated Ben Franklin's assessment of that worthy: "Always an honest man, often a great one, but sometimes absolutely mad."

The advocates of republican simplicity won the day. The chief executive was called simply "The President of the United States" and addressed even more simply as "Mr. President." For his part, Adams was injured by the affair, for it was now whispered that he secretly desired monarchy. If so, he must have disliked the title someone hung on *him*: "His Rotundity."

nized his own limitations as well as those of others, and was never so sure of his principles that he must advance them at gunpoint. Above all, he possessed those elusive qualities described by the word *areté*.

Events in the new republic were shaped by five personalities. All five had been frontline leaders in the Revolution, and three had been delegates to the Constitutional Convention while the remaining two had represented the United States abroad. While all five were staunch patriots, they embraced different strains of republicanism and in consequence had different ideas about the General Constitution. Thus, some would flesh out the bones of the Philadelphia document one way and some quite another. If any one of the five had been someone else, or if they had interacted differently, American history might well have been otherwise.

George Washington. "First in the hearts of his countrymen" did not say quite enough for him. By 1789 Washington was accepted as *the* Founding Father. His eager return to Mount Vernon after the war and his obvious reluctance to abandon it for public life only fortified the esteem in which he was held. While he was not a man of deep thought or wide learning, he was reasonably well read and held strong ideas. His support for independence from England and for the new federal Constitution had in all likelihood made both of these possible. He was no political fool either. He had had much to do with Congress during six years of war and knew its ways only too well. He realized that in order to maximize his effectiveness as president, he must remain above ordinary politics— while at the same time being very much a part of it.

Alexander Hamilton. His illegitimate birth in the West Indies may have been the great shaping force in his life, for it made Hamilton ever the outsider and lone wolf. He unabashedly admired English institutions, as he admired the aristocracy that supported them, and he envisioned some version of both for America. A man of personal charisma and intellectual vigor, Hamilton was not adept at politics. He was too brash and impetuous, too disdainful of lesser men and too scornful of ideas with which he disagreed. Once in a while his judgment failed him and he said and did incomprehensible things. For the most part, however, his vision was clear and his ideas exceptionally strong. He knew precisely what he wanted for the American Republic and precisely how to get it. "To confess my weaknesses," he wrote as a boy, "my ambition is prevalent."

Hamilton had an almost filial relationship to Washington, and he made the most of it. As aide-de-camp, he had been the general's right-hand man during the Revolution. Then, inexplicably, they had quarreled and Hamilton had severed all ties. The rift was not repaired until much later and Washington remained leery of Hamilton's volatility. Still, he made the young man his Secretary of the Treasury, the Cabinet post he deemed most important, and after that his support never wavered. Hamilton was portrayed by enemies as a cynical manipulator, spinning his webs out of flattery, but his influence with the President was far more substantial than that. The two men saw the world alike.

Thomas Jefferson. If Alexander Hamilton was one man of mystery, Thomas Jefferson was another. Through a combination of luck and skill, Jefferson had married well, acquired a fortune and worked his way into the dress circle of

Virginia society. Jefferson's mind ranged over broad expanses of the human experience, from art and architecture, to music and literature, to botany and zoology. History and political science were at the center of his attention, and he had studied law at William and Mary. He was by reputation, if not always by accomplishment, an eighteenth-century Renaissance man.

While still young, Jefferson had been catapulted into fame by his authorship of the Declaration of Independence. He failed to distinguish himself as Virginia's wartime governor, however, or as America's second minister to France. There was something deeply conflicted in his personality—a mind divided against itself—which made it difficult for him to execute effectively.

Jefferson's contribution to the new republic was that of visionary. He had articulated a rudimentary concept of democratic republicanism in the Declaration's opening paragraphs. Later on, while serving as Washington's secretary of state, he found himself embroiled in controversies which prompted an elaboration of that concept, and later still, as vice president, he continued to fill in the blank spaces. "Jeffersonianism," as it would be called, was part thought and part feeling, and if it wasn't quite a full-fledged political religion, millions of Americans would embrace it as such all the same.

James Madison. Both as "Father of the Constitution" and "Father of the Bill of Rights," Madison had already won fame enough for two Founders. During the Washington and Adams Presidencies he would achieve his third degree of glory as a "Father of American Politics." The friendship of Jefferson and Madison was of as great a moment in the new republic as that of Washington and Hamilton. Much of what would become known as "Jeffersonianism" would be worked out in an ongoing dialogue between them. It is a tribute to Madison's intellectual integrity that in the unfolding of real-world events he was able to rethink some of his key ideas and draw a different set of conclusions from them. Madison the Federalist was to become Madison the Democratic-Republican.

John Adams. Adams was every bit as capable as his fellow statesmen, but he lacked Hamilton's dash, Madison's depth and Jefferson's way with words. Accordingly, while they grew into marble heroes, "Honest John" never quite took his place beside them in the pantheon. That he was occasionally dismissed as "His Rotundity" tells us much about the inner man. No one had a deeper understanding of politics and government, history and law, human nature itself, yet Adams lacked some essential quality of leadership. "He is always a wise man, often a great one," Franklin said of him, "but sometimes he is absolutely mad." He was politically disadvantaged by his Yankee background and, as some would have it, Yankee character as well, for he could be brittle and obstinate in situations requiring finesse. Yet were it not for his personal integrity—and his ability to rise above partisanship—matters in the new republic may have turned out far worse than they did.

All five of these Founders knew the rough-and-tumble of politics. Yet all five may have been blinded into supposing that republican politics would somehow be different. They spoke wistfully of statesmanship as something over and above what they had experienced in the British Empire—as if the Revolution could somehow redeem them from the human condition. Events soon proved that to be wrong.

Alexander Hamilton:
http://xroads.virginia.edu/
~CAP/ham/hamilton/html

http://www.law.umkc.edu/
faculty/projects/ftrials/burr/
HamiltonBio.htm

Political-economy:
Social science dealing
with the interrelation-
ship of governmental
and economic processes.

Hamilton: Politics and Ideology

When President Washington appointed Alexander Hamilton to be his frontline economic officer, he knew that the new republic faced do-or-die challenges on precisely that front. It needed to establish foreign credit. It needed to work out favorable trade relations. It needed to put the government itself on a paying basis. It needed to establish a sense of legitimacy both at home and abroad. And it needed to untangle a skein of difficulties left over from the Revolution. For the British continued to occupy forts on US soil, pointing to the debts still owed London merchants, while Americans justified the debts by pointing to a want of trade. It was a barrow-full.

In Hamilton's mind, these problems were not isolated. They were tied together by what we saw in chapter 6 as an *ideology*. We recall from that discussion that coherent systems of ideas are often found in the political world. They bring order to otherwise chaotic situations—and they usually benefit a certain group or interest in society. Hamilton's ideology fit this description to a tee.

He had long been a student of British political-economy. The British had worked out their mercantile system over a period of some three hundred years and they had had ample opportunity to correct and fine-tune it. Hamilton had no doubt how the Lords of Trade in London would handle the Americans' present difficulties, and he proposed to handle them the same way. But first—or rather in the process—he must help to bring forth the sort of polity that would be capable of handling them. That was where ideology came in.

To begin with, Hamilton thought, America must become a fully sovereign nation: it must think and act like a unified commonwealth, not a gaggle of quarreling fiefs. It must develop its own identity, its own culture, its own traditions. And the integrity of the nation must be the prime consideration in determining policy. Individuals should be willing to sacrifice for the good of the whole.

Second, the various elites of society—the "rich and the wellborn"—must be weaned away from their local attachments and brought into partnership with the federal government. The quasi aristocracy that Hamilton had in mind would require certain modes of thinking and a certain style of governance. It would need ruffles and lace to awe the many and great projects to challenge the few. Only when aristocratic élan was infused to political leadership, Hamilton believed, could republicanism truly succeed.

These ends could all be achieved by a robust central government with extensive authority and ample revenue, a government able to command respect. But such a government was impossible to create under the Constitution with its carefully enumerated powers. At the Philadelphia Convention, Hamilton had argued for a general grant of legislative power, which he deemed absolutely essential for nationhood—and had been resoundingly outvoted. Yet he remained undaunted. By broadly interpreting constitutional language, Hamilton believed he could assemble the grant he needed from three enumerated sources: the taxing and spending clause, the general welfare clause and the necessary and proper clause.

The latter was the real key, for if its loose wording were construed broadly enough, the necessary and proper clause could tap power almost anywhere in the Constitution. Hamilton's strategy soon became evident. In a landmark memorandum interpreting the clause in question, he argued that the word *necessary* need not be limited to that which was absolutely indispensable. "Necessary often means no more than needful, requisite, incidental, useful, or conducive to. . . ." Congress, he urged, should not be hobbled as to its choice of means for a given legislative end—the means ought to be up to the discretion of the legislators. He went on to pronounce a soon-to-be-famous criterion: "This criterion is the *end*, to which the measure relates as a *mean*. If the *end* be clearly comprehended within any of the specified powers, and if the measure have an obvious relation to the end, and is not forbidden by any particular provision of the Constitution, it may safely be deemed to come within the compass of the national authority."

Hamilton's doctrine of *implied powers* became the basis of his entire legislative program, which emerged in a series of Treasury Department reports. The federal government should, Hamilton said:

1. Fund its entire debt at par value. Only thus would it acquire the good faith and credit of a sovereign nation.

2. Assume the debts of the states and pay them off as well.

3. Enact a tariff to protect certain domestic manufactures. This would create a balance among agriculture, commerce and industry, and would provide for a growing economy.

4. Negotiate a trade agreement with Great Britain, securing the best advantages possible.

5. Establish and operate a national bank, in cooperation with private financial interests, along the lines of the Bank of England. Such a bank would provide capital for economic expansion.

Hamilton's proposals were designed to address the problems described above. Yet they were also designed to advance his ideological agenda—and they fairly crackled with controversy:

1. The federal debt existed in the form of government notes—IOUs—dating from the Revolution. Most of these were no longer in the hands of their original owners (soldiers of the army, suppliers, et cetera) and were trading among speculators at a few cents on the dollar. If the government were to pay them off at par value, the speculators—many of whom had friends in high places—stood to make a stupendous killing.

2. Some of the states had already retired their revolutionary war debt, often at considerable sacrifice. These states, through general taxes, would now be required to fund the debts of those that had not paid off their obligations.

3. During the Constitutional Convention there had been stormy debates about tariffs. Agricultural states, especially in the South, feared retaliation against their own exports if the United States now began slapping tariffs on European manufactured goods. Besides, these goods would now be more expensive to buy—along with those of domestic manufacture. Hamilton was in effect dunning agriculture to subsidize industry—and consumers to profit producers.

4. Many Americans had grave reservations about seeking a trade agreement with Great Britain. They weren't sure that the new republic should cozy up to a power that was in the habit of exploiting it. Nor did they like the idea of

being drawn into European quarrels as a lackey of the British. The United States, they said, should establish trade relations with *all* countries and remain aloof from special attachments.

5. The proposed national bank drew the most fire of all. It contemplated an alliance between government and the "wellborn"—to the possible disadvantage of everyone else. It might prove to be the opening wedge of aristocracy. Worst of all, there was absolutely no constitutional authority for it. Any argument that would enable the government to establish and operate a bank would enable it to do virtually anything.

Washington knew that Hamilton's proposals would be hard to swallow. He also knew that their audacity would make it impossible for him to give them lukewarm support: he must either quash the entire program or back it to the limit. And he knew that a great deal depended on the outcome. Hamilton's proposals would begin fleshing out the Constitution in a certain way. They were, accordingly, as momentous as the Constitution itself.

The most troubling issue for the president was Hamilton's loose-jointed, free-wheeling **"broad construction"** of constitutional language. While the authority for most of the treasury secretary's program fell more or less within the Constitution's enumerated powers, the national bank clearly did not. And justifying it by means of Hamilton's "necessary and proper" argument left no logical stopping place, as critics were quick to point out. If a national bank was "necessary" to the coining of money and regulation of its value, why not a bank monopoly? Or state-operated gold mining? Or commodity price controls? A lot of things were arguably "necessary."

Washington solicited an opinion from Thomas Jefferson, his Secretary of State, knowing in advance that Jefferson would vehemently oppose Hamilton's position. Nor was he disappointed. For in his written opinion, Jefferson argued that the word "necessary" could only be defined one way—*that which was indispensable*. Congress, in other words, was limited to those means that were absolutely required for the performance of an enumerated task. Nothing in its constitutional role of coining money or regulating its value remotely required Congress to set up a bank.

Within the principles of **"narrow construction,"** as Jefferson's position soon became known, was the kernel of another political ideology—one almost diametrically opposed to that of Hamilton. And in the hothouse atmosphere of the new republic, that competing ideology was very soon to sprout. For the president, after much soul searching, decided to back Hamilton's program all the way.

Jefferson: Politics and Ideology

Like Hamilton, Jefferson had had little direct input into the Constitutional Convention. He was serving as US minister to France at the time. Nor was Jefferson's initial reaction to the document very favorable. He feared that there was too much power in the federal engine and too few brakes. It was only by means of his friendship with James Madison that he was eventually brought around to the Constitution's support.

If old-fashioned Toryism was the starting place for Hamilton's ideology, old-fashioned Whiggism was the starting place for Jefferson's. He truly, if a bit naively, believed in an lost golden age, a time of peace and plenty when sturdy English yeomen tilled their own soil and governed their own lives. Even the king in this mythical Saxon democracy was but an elected representative of the people.

Unsurprisingly, Jefferson subscribed to the "commonwealth ideology" discussed in chapter 3. Whigs believed that the ancient freedoms had been undermined, a little at a time, by the "court party," that cabal of would-be aristocrats always drawn to the center of power. And these must ever be resisted by the "country party," whose identification with and attachment to, the land is a source of sublime independence and great moral strength. If one would look for republican virtue, said the Whigs, look for it here.

Jefferson's own observance had deepened these ideas. His attachment to the soil was romantic, almost mystical, and in his *Notes on Virginia*, he had written enthusiastically about the natural world. Naturalism was one of the great themes of the time. Its underlying premise was that civilization corroded human character, and as a result the "natural man" was stronger, quicker, wiser, more alert and more wholesome than his city-bred counterpart. At the foot of the Blue Ridge Mountains, where Jefferson's Monticello looked out over a heart-stopping vista, he was convinced that he saw the corruptions of the centuries fading away and the natural man coming back into his own. For there stretched before him a vast expanse of rich land in moderate-sized freeholds, owned by families on the rise. The work ethic was strong in most of them, and their actions bespoke moral self-governance. Jefferson compared this highly idealized picture with the misery and squalor he had seen in France. Here, he thought, were the makings of a true republican society.

If this was not the first democratic vision of America, it was perhaps the most consequential. But its fruition depended on an approach to government that was almost exactly the opposite of Alexander Hamilton's. Power must be dispersed throughout society, not concentrated at its center. Politics must be local, not national, in character. And national authority, with its centralizing tendency, had to be rigorously curtailed by constitutional means—lest the "court party" resume its age-old machinations. Only the strictest possible construction of the Constitution would keep the government small, custodial and in its place.

Jefferson wrote his memorandum to the president with an acute sense of desperation. Strict construction was the fulcrum on which his vision of America turned. If he lost on that point, all else stood in peril. And when Jefferson did lose, he recognized the dreadful significance of it. Washington's adoption of the Hamilton program, given the precedent-setting circumstances, risked nothing less than a betrayal of the Revolution.

Foreign Intrigue

The rivalry between Jefferson and Hamilton on domestic policy may have turned out very differently at any other time in history. As it happened, while the two of them were squaring off, the calm world of the European Enlightenment came to an abrupt and shattering end.

Government by guillotine in Paris. The infant American Republic struggled to steer a steady course during the French Revolution.
(*Execution of King Louis XVI on January 21, 1793*, courtesy of Erich Lessing/Art Resource, New York.)

The French Revolution began in 1789, the year George Washington took office. It would continue to lurch and career through the entire decade of the 1790s—then erupt into a global war. Americans watched the unfolding of events with fascination. To many, it appeared that the French people had chosen to follow their own lead, hacking off the fetters of monarchy and stepping into a glorious republican future. But other readings were possible, especially after the execution of the king and the commencement of the Terror. Edmund Burke, a member of Parliament who had warmly supported the American cause, was among the first to point up the radical nature of the French Revolution, and suggest that it might not lead to a glorious anything.

By 1793 England and France were at war. The latter sent emissaries to the United States—the first of them being "Citizen Genêt"—and called on the American people to support the cause they themselves had inspired. While President Washington counseled strict neutrality—the last thing the US needed was a foreign war—Americans found such a feat impossible.

They divided on the French Question more or less as they were dividing over the issues posed by Hamilton's economic program. Hamilton's followers strongly identified with the British. England, they said, was fighting for the established order, political moderation and plain sanity. It was also fighting for a dominance of world trade that was more than incidental to Anglo-American relations. Jefferson's followers identified equally strongly with the French. Excesses notwithstanding, they said, the Revolution truly was about liberty, equality and fraternity. The revolutionary experience was bound to be a painful one because the French people had been downtrodden for centuries.

The situation would become ever more precarious for the American Republic. Every domestic issue would come to be seen in the light of the French Question and interpreted or misinterpreted accordingly. Foreign affairs are always capable of arousing strong passions and the present case was no exception.

The Emergence of Political Parties

Virtually none of the Founders expected political parties to develop in the American Republic. Despite the existence of Whigs and Tories in England, the modern concept of political parties simply did not exist in the 1790s. For it depended on another concept, also not yet fully in existence—that of *loyal opposition*.

The very words were an oxymoron. "Opposition" could not be "loyal," just as "rain" could not be "dry." The reason why had to do with the assumption, still flickering in the English mind, that monarchy had been anointed by God. Accordingly, the English common law had a doctrine known as *seditious libel*, holding that the state, in the person of the king, had a right to protect itself from sedition—that is, the desire to destroy or overthrow it—by punishing those who spoke against it with malice. The doctrine also came to protect the king's ministers, his officers and eventually even minor functionaries who acted in his name— the government in other words. Without being able to criticize the government, of course, politics as we know it could not exist, for that is what parties do.

That was only one obstacle. There was a deeper one rooted not in monarchies but republics, the concept of a public good. If you really believe in such a thing—and the American Founders did—it is almost impossible to believe in the sort of politics we practice today. For the public *as a whole* can have but a single good, not a multiplicity of them, and the political process ought to seek out that good alone. Any other will be the good of some group or party or class, not that of the entire body politic. If George Washington were asked if he represented Alexander Hamilton and his friends as opposed to some other interest, he would have been horrified. A president must represent *everyone*.

And there was yet another reason for being leery of political parties. In the Founders' minds, a "party" was merely a large and dangerous "faction." We recall that in *Federalist* 10, Madison had argued that factions would always exist when interests were in conflict. The trick was not to obliterate them or deny their existence, but to neutralize their effect through counterpoise. The more factions contending for power, the less likely it would be that any one of them could achieve hegemony. But for Madison, indeed for all the Founders, a *majority* faction—that is, a faction capable of dominating a legislative assembly— spelled the end. For, by definition, such a faction had won the political game and could enact its own will into law.

One might argue, then, that from the Founders' perspective, the Constitution had been designed to *prevent* the formation of political parties. In the operation of the electoral college, for example, we see the hope that the political game would be played by individuals and small groups, sometimes in contact with one another and sometimes not, acting out of self-interest perhaps but also acting out of civic virtue—and never acting as a "party." It seemed at least possible anyway.

Until Hamilton's program came along.

Hamiltonians

Any proposals as bold and controversial as Hamilton's would require skill to steer through Congress. Accordingly, Hamilton and a few close associates began meeting informally with senators and congressmen to discuss problems, plan strategy and cultivate political support. Of course these "Hamiltonians" had engaged in such kibitzing for years, now to seek one end and now to seek another. The objective here, however, was not just to achieve a single victory but to enact an entire legislative program and see to its implementation—to govern.

Hamilton's group enjoyed a number of advantages. It was organized around a coherent purpose and specific goals. It shared a vision of American nationhood that was steadily winning converts. And it had the support of George Washington. Clumsy at politics himself, Hamilton had the good sense to keep in the shadows and place other, more engaging personalities in the limelight. Since many of these had been supporters of the Constitution in the first place, it was only natural that they appropriate the name "Federalists."

It is important to remember that the Hamiltonians did not see themselves as "a party." They were "the government." They not only dominated Congress—a fact that became all too clear as the individual measures came up for passage—they wielded influence in the executive branch as well. For instance, recall that one of their objectives was to secure a trade agreement with Great Britain. In order to accomplish this aim, the Hamiltonians, working behind the scenes, succeeded in scuttling talks with the French and then proceeded to negotiate **Jay's Treaty** with Great Britain. Hamilton personally (and inappropriately) intruded into the negotiations. As a result, Jay's Treaty was more favorable to British interests than American.

> **Jay's Treaty:** Negotiated with Britain in 1794, US made major concessions to avert war over seizure of US ships. The terms were extremely unfavorable to US interests.

Public reaction was sharply divided. Those of pro-British sympathy applauded the treaty and soft-pedaled its controversial features. Many others, however, denounced the treaty with unwonted vehemence. "Damn Jay's Treaty and damn anyone who *won't* damn Jay's Treaty," they cried. John Jay was ubiquitously burned in effigy.

Equally disconcerting was the way Hamilton dealt with the so-called Whiskey Rebellion. To secure government revenue, Congress had passed an excise tax on the production and sale of whiskey. The effect of the tax in western Pennsylvania, where farmers reduced their grain to distilled spirits in order to transport it over the mountains to market, was to destroy the profitability of an entire industry. In 1794 some 3,000 farmers united in opposing the tax and disrupting its collection.

Hamilton had been waiting for just such an opportunity to flex the new government's muscles. He persuaded the president to call out the militia in four states and march on the rebels forthwith. Owing to Washington's ill health, Hamilton himself commanded the forces, some 15,000 strong, and saw to the capture of eighteen rebels. Even though only two of them were convicted (and both soon pardoned), the episode marked another bitter division. Farmers up and down the frontier denounced the "American Caesar."

Jeffersonians

Jefferson and Madison were only two of those who found these events appalling. There were many others. Some were former Anti-Federalists, still nursing their doubts about strong government. In their view, the double disaster of Jay's Treaty and the Whiskey Rebellion was but Act One of a drama written years before at the Constitutional Convention.

The old Anti-Federalists found allies among those who had favored the Constitution's adoption but were coming to have misgivings about Alexander Hamilton. Madison was one of these. He had been among the earliest and most energetic of the "nationalists," as we have seen, and at Philadelphia had been nothing less than Hamilton's co-conspirator. Now he saw the world through different eyes. Was this, he asked, what Hamilton's nationalism really meant?

The less self-assured might have been hard put to reexamine their assumptions. Not James Madison. His life could be described as an adventure of ideas and he followed wherever they led. His conception of a strong national government had been equipped with mechanisms to prevent what the Hamiltonians were now bringing to pass—or so he had believed. If there was a flaw in the conception, and evidently there had been, Madison would be the first to acknowledge it and start looking for possible remedies.

It was here that Madison's intellectual partnership with Jefferson came to the fore. The two had been friends from their old days in the Virginia House of Burgesses. They had remained in contact ever since, volleying ideas at one another in their correspondence and sorting out the world's experience. They had no trouble sorting this case. To anyone brought up in the commonwealth tradition, Hamilton's program represented all that virtue must guard against: elitism, patronage, favoritism, manipulation, corruption and ultimately tyranny. It was the "court party" at its worst.

Organizing opposition was almost second nature to them—they had been doing it since the days of the Stamp Act. Besides, the opposition was already organizing itself, grass-roots style, and seeking *them* out. After Jefferson resigned as Secretary of State in 1793, visitors made their way up the Blue Ridge hillside to Monticello, where the willowy Virginian was engaged in his lifelong pursuit of architectural renovation, to sound him out about the presidency. He had no appetite for office himself, he assured them, but he was not unwilling to hear their complaints, and somewhere in the back of his mind he did have such an appetite—if only to vindicate his idea of the *true* republic.

At no time did the "Jeffersonians," as they were beginning to call one another, see themselves as creating a political party. They were simply dealing with a problem and when the problem was solved that would end the matter. Still, the movement picked up speed. Jefferson and Madison provided it with inspiration as well as leadership. Jefferson, who was the better writer, penned hundreds of letters to encourage the faithful. Madison worked the halls of Congress. All were aware that President Washington would step down at the end of his second term in 1796, and Jefferson was mentioned ever more frequently as a worthy successor.

This left the Hamiltonians with a problem. Which of them ought to be put forward as their own candidate? Hamilton himself was out of the question. He was too cold and brittle for the campaign trail, and his well-known view of democracy—"Your people is a beast!"—did not commend him to ordinary voters. After a series of caucuses, the Hamiltonians came to agree that John Adams might fill the bill. While not precisely one of their number, Adams was a staunch supporter

Nestled in the Blue Ridge Mountains of Virginia, Jefferson's Monticello became the birthplace of the American party system.
(*Monticello*, courtesy of the Library of Congress.)

of the Constitution and he generally concurred with Hamilton's legislative program.

When the votes were counted in the electoral college, John Adams had the greatest number, by a very slender margin, and therefore was elected president. And as vice president? Thomas Jefferson of course.

Alien and Sedition Acts/Kentucky and Virginia Resolutions: http://www.yale.edu/lawweb/avalon/alsedact.htm

The Alien and Sedition Acts

The presidency of John Adams proved to be pivotal for the new republic. If George Washington was the first president, John Adams was the first ordinary president, the first who was truly elected (Washington had simply been acclaimed), and the first to be regarded as politically mortal. When Washington took a position, as he did on Hamilton's legislative program, opposition was obliged to be circumspect. When Adams took a position, it was just a position. With the Adams administration, political life settled into a bumpy normality.

Hamilton retained the allegiance of the Federalists and through them continued to influence the president. Hamilton also played his Washington card for a final, triumphant time in his drafting of the "Farewell Address." For anything that President Washington would say in benediction was bound to have scriptural effect.

The address spoke movingly against the "spirit of party." It affirmed the Founders' original assumption that political life in a republic need not and ought not be partisan. It also cautioned Americans against a too ardent attachment to foreign powers. The advice was unquestionably sound on both points—yet it was also unquestionably Hamiltonian. For by cautioning fellow Americans against the spirit of party, the retiring president was saying in effect that the Federalists were not a party at all but simply the government. And by warning them away from entangling alliances, he was not condemning trade relations with England, which were peaceful and commercial, only relations with firebrand France.

But the French Question would not be banished so easily. Indeed, it would return and return, like the proverbial bad penny, and eventually prove the undoing of Federalism in general, John Adams in particular, and all of the Founders' assumptions about politics.

It soon became clear to most Americans that right or wrong, the French Revolution was out of control. Nor did its partisans help things by mixing into US politics. Citizen Genêt, after meeting his cool reception from George Washington, tried circumventing the government and appealing directly to the people. At the same time, a number of French republican journalists, crossing the Atlantic to stir up sympathy, called upon Americans to support the French economically and militarily, as one republican people to another. Specifically, they urged, the US should honor the Treaty of Alliance dating back to its own Revolution, break all ties with Great Britain and throw the Federalists out of office.

Americans responded with ambivalence. Many of them did feel a sense of republican kinship. At the same time, they agreed with their president that foreign entanglement could prove their undoing. They regarded the old French alliance as a dead letter and Jay's Treaty, no matter how unpopular, as the law of the land. And increasing numbers of them viewed events in France with alarm. The Federalists capitalized on these doubts in fighting their own political battles. It was easy, for example, to suggest that Jeffersonians were nothing but an American version of Jacobins—wild-eyed and seditious.

Relations between the French government and the Adams administration continued to deteriorate. In addition to the frictions sketched above, there was a new one in 1797, caused by the resumption of Anglo-French hostilities. For this meant that US ships trading in the British West Indies were now subject to seizure. By 1798 war fever was sweeping the United States, and on the high seas Americans ships were engaged in armed conflict.

It would be difficult to imagine a more divisive set of circumstances. With American ships "under attack" by a foreign power, there was a strong inclination to rally around the flag and Hamiltonians exploited it to the limit. Jefferson's followers, on the other hand, viewed the hysteria as cold-blooded manipulation and said so. The temperature steadily mounted.

It was at this point that the partisan newspaper made its debut. It was a combination of local newsletter, serialized pamphlet, political broadside and town tattler. It specialized in purveying the inside dope—what was *really* going on—for which Americans have always had a peculiar

George Washington as president. Despite his heroic stature he was feared by some to be a tool of the Hamiltonians. (By Gilbert Stuart, courtesy of the White House Historical Association.)

weakness. Accordingly, the editors' free-swinging style, gross errors of fact and dark allegations of scandal were all submitted with greatest gusto.

There were papers on both sides. Those on the Hamiltonian side enjoyed the moral advantage of defending the government, while those on the Jeffersonian were attacking it. And the latter, remember, was sedition. It was openly criticizing elected authorities, subjecting them to malice, with the sole intention of undermining public confidence. George Washington, who caught the merest brush of tar, found the situation completely outrageous, while poor Adams came in for the entire bucket.

It was clear to Adams that the situation must somehow be defused. He dispatched emissaries to Paris with instructions to negotiate an end to the hostilities if at all possible, but Paris was swirling with its own dark passions and the time was anything but propitious. After the emissaries were solicited

XYZ Affair: Diplomatic incident in 1798 in which Americans were outraged over French demands of a bribe to negotiate with American diplomats.

for a bribe (the notorious XYZ affair), Franco-American relations seemed headed over the falls.

Hamilton and the Federalists responded with decisive action. War abroad and sedition at home posed dire threats to the republic, they concluded, and justified whatever means were at hand. Said Harrison Gray Otis: "Government has a right to preserve and defend itself against injuries and outrages which endanger its existence. . . ." The result, after a bitter debate in Congress, was passage of the infamous **Alien and Sedition Acts**.

The Alien Act authorized the president to deport any aliens he regarded as "dangerous to the peace and safety of the United States." Adams never availed himself of the authority the measure granted him, but not for a lack of urging on the part of Hamilton, who had fashioned it as a weapon against the foreign journalists. As for the domestic journalists, they were faced with the Sedition Act.

And this too was a weapon. It outlawed any and all "false, scandalous and malicious" writing against the government or its officers, including the president and members of Congress. By its terms, unfriendly journalists could be arrested, tried and subjected to heavy fines and jail time. And at the instigation of bitterly vindictive Federalists like Timothy Pickering, they were. Some fifteen editors were arraigned and tried, and ten of them found guilty. All of course were Jeffersonians.

Jefferson and other "Republicans," as they were beginning to call themselves, took vigorous exception to the Alien Act, which violated several provisions of the Bill of Rights. But their heavy fire was concentrated on the Sedition Act. Indeed, that piece of legislation would soon become the fulcrum about which issues of critical importance to the new republic would turn:

Constitutional Interpretation. We have already noted the divergence between Hamilton's loose construction and Jefferson's strict construction of constitutional wording. The Sedition Act brought that clash to a head.

With the adoption of the First Amendment, the federal government was supposedly bound by the injunction that "Congress shall make no law . . . abridging the freedom of speech, or of the press. . . ." If Federalist loose construction could slip around so clear and concise a prohibition as this, said the Jeffersonians, then surely all was lost. The Bill of Rights, the Constitution itself, were worth no more than the paper they were written on.

The Federalists had a reply. The Sedition Act, they explained, merely enacted into positive law the ancient common law of seditious libel. Since Great Britain had its own celebrated freedom of expression, and since the common law of seditious libel was not held to violate such freedom, what was wrong with enacting the ancient law into a federal statute?

The answer to this question would assume crucial importance in the American experience. According to the common law of seditious libel, there was to be no "prior restraint" on public utterance. That is to say, the government could not use licensing or some other procedure to determine who should and should not be allowed to publish facts and opinions in a newspaper. Once the facts and opinions were published, however, the newspaper became fully liable for all scurrilous remarks it made about government officials. The truth or falsehood of such remarks was beside the point. For the issue was not whether the official in question actually did what was alleged but whether the government was going to come out of it with a black eye.

The Federalist position on this question led to the second pivotal issue.

Political Opposition. Granting the old concept of seditious libel its due, said the Republicans (thinking out loud), perhaps it was out of date in the modern world. For in a republic, issues must be frankly and openly discussed, and the discussions must necessarily include the character of government officials, the policies they have adopted and the actions they have taken. The freedom to speak out couldn't just be freedom from prior restraint, it had to be complete freedom—freedom from consequences later on. Seditious libel, in other words, was unsuited to a republic.

Jefferson's followers weren't quite ready to push on to the final step in this logical process but the step was becoming clear. If citizens needed the freedom to speak against the government, then organized political opposition, on an ongoing basis, was as much a part of republican life as free speech was.

Truth and Falsehood in Politics. There was still the issue of truth to think about. If someone makes an allegation about a public official, it had darned well better be true—hadn't it? This seemingly simple question, when viewed closely, wasn't simple at all, for it disappeared into a labyrinth of unanswerables. Should the standards of the courtroom apply to political debate? Can questions of fact be neatly separated from questions of opinion? Are political slanders necessarily the same as personal slanders?

Out of the ensuing welter of discussion there emerged a whole new conception of political truth. Jefferson encapsulated it in his inaugural address:

> If there be any among us who would wish to dissolve this Union or to change its republican form, let them stand undisturbed as monuments of the safety with which error of opinion may be tolerated where reason is left free to combat it.

In other words, in republican politics, citizens must have the freedom to say pretty much anything—including "Let's dissolve the Union!"—and the voters must separate truth from falsehood themselves. In the end, Jefferson believed, truth would win out.

The Resolution of Constitutional Disputes. A fourth issue posed by the Alien and Sedition Acts had to do with constitutional disputes. Where two interpretations of the Constitution were at such odds as Hamilton's and Jefferson's, how could they possibly be reconciled?

The Republicans began thinking seriously about this problem. And the more they thought about it, the clearer it seemed that disputes must be resolved outside the federal government. After all, they reasoned, that government had been created by the sovereign states, not the other way around, so the *ultimate* sovereignty must lie with them. Besides, if constitutional interpretation were left up to some federal authority, state sovereignty could be kissed goodbye.

Accordingly, Jefferson and Madison approached state governments with what seemed to them a constitutionally sound idea. The states must take individual action to declare the Alien and Sedition Acts unconstitutional, they said. Only by such means could the federal government be kept in bounds.

The result was the **Kentucky and Virginia Resolutions**. Each of these states drew up and passed a resolution to the effect that the Alien and Sedition Acts were unconstitutional and therefore of no legal force within their respective jurisdictions. Each document also explained why this approach was the right way to resolve constitutional disputes. Jefferson, who drafted the Kentucky Resolution, and Madison, who drafted the Virginia, were coming down hard on the interpretation issue. It seemed fully capable of destroying the Union.

The Nature of the Union. The bedrock question underlying all of this had to do with the Union's ultimate character. Was it a union of sovereign states joined together by voluntary compact? Or was it a single sovereign entity in which the states played a local administrative role?

The Federalist, we recall, had argued for both alternatives at the same time, a position termed *divided sovereignty*. (That is, states remained sovereign in some areas while the United States assumed sovereignty in others.) Skeptics had argued that "divided sovereignty" was nonsense—an oxymoron—and predicted that sooner or later an issue would come along to prove their point. Well, here it was. And James Madison, who had come up with divided sovereignty in the first place, was turning to *the states* for a solution—rejecting his own doctrine!

The Kentucky Resolution, which was the more radical of the two, took the notion of ultimate state sovereignty a step further and for the first time invoked the "n" word. "Nullification" would cast a long shadow into the future. Yet under the press of the Alien and Sedition Acts it seemed the most logical term in the world. For if Congress did pass an unconstitutional law, shouldn't the sovereign states have the power to "nullify" that law within their own jurisdictions? The deeper question, unasked at the time, was that if a state had the power to nullify federal laws, didn't it also have the power to secede from the Union entirely?

For the time being, the difficulties posed by the Alien and Sedition Acts were resolved otherwise. Jefferson and his followers won the presidential election of 1800 and swept into power. And the notorious legislation lapsed into oblivion.

The laws had a "sunset provision" that would have let them automatically lapse if they were not renewed. Jefferson allowed them to lapse in 1801.

The "Second American Revolution"

The institutional effect of the Alien and Sedition Acts was to catalyze the formation of political parties. At some point along the way, it was no longer just a matter of writing letters, publishing newspapers or meeting together as alarmed citizens. The citizens organized themselves into clubs and societies, often using the words "Republican" or "Democratic" in their name. A sense of camaraderie burgeoned among them and they began to consult with one another. While there was no polite name for what was emerging, most people knew it was "party."

Some still shrank from the word—Thomas Jefferson among them. "If I could not go to heaven but with a party," he wrote scornfully, "I would not go there at all." It required mental gymnastics to make such a vow while building a party of his own, but as Joseph J. Ellis has noted, Jefferson "was psychologically up to the task." His ambivalence bespoke that of most Americans.

An important stage in the development process was political self-awareness. The Federalists came to think of themselves as supporters of the Constitution and defenders of sound government, while in their own mirror the Republicans saw the legitimate heirs of the Revolution. The latter also identified with those rough-hewn tillers of the soil Jefferson had written about, who alone knew the meaning of republican virtue. Soon they had hyphenated their name to "Democratic-Republicans."

Each party also drew an ever clearer picture of the other. As Jeffersonians studied Hamiltonians, they saw loose construction of the Constitution, a narrow conception of rights, a government of would-be aristocrats, a dim view of political opposition and the personal ambitions of an American Caesar. And as Hamiltonians swung the telescope around, they saw strict construction of the Constitution, a broad definition of rights, a government too weak to prevent anarchy, a rabble of self-styled democrats in sympathy with French radicals, a taste for seditious libel and the leadership of an avowed Deist. Both pictures were scary.

Brawl in Congress. *What had become of statesmanship?*
(Courtesy of the New-York Historical Society.)

Yet we should note that while the two parties demonized one another, they kept within certain limits. It was not a case, say, of one party being *for* the Revolution while the other was *against* it—as would often occur in European politics. They might resort to ridicule and name-calling but they wouldn't resort to the guillotine, for beneath their disagreements they had a common ground, or *consensus*, in the Founding itself. What they were disputing was how the Founding was to be understood and built upon. Consider the specific issues:

- Contrasting political ideologies.
- Contrasting ideas of constitutional construction.
- Contrasting notions of free expression and political opposition.
- Contrasting ways of understanding the Union.
- Contrasting visions of an American nation.

These issues have marked many of the paths crisscrossing American history, and every major political movement has come to bear some relationship to them. For each grows out of the Founding and seeks to define its true meaning.

The election of 1800 was a jarring contrast to the three preceding it and one of the most unruly in US history. Reckless charges flew back and forth between the candidates—and they really were *candidates* now—accompanied by

Election of 1800:
http://library.thinkquest
.org/12587/contents/
parties.html

http://library.thinkquest
.org/12587/contents/
timeline/index.html

The Election of 1800

Although there had been presidential elections before in the American republic—three of them to be exact—there had never been anything like this. If was fortunate, some said, that Washington had passed away the year before, for he would have abominated the very sight of it. He had repeatedly warned his countrymen against "the spirit of party" and now here it was in full flower.

There were plenty of issues to galvanize opposition to the ruling Federalists. Jay's Treaty with England, Hamilton's controversial financial program, the war scare with France, the specter of a standing army, and touchiest of all, the notorious Alien and Sedition Acts. These the Federalists had rammed through Congress expressly to silence political opposition—First Amendment or no First Amendment. As a result, for speaking "falsely and maliciously" against the government, twenty-five persons had been arrested, fourteen indicted and ten (including a U.S. Congressman) tried and convicted, all of them admirers of Thomas Jefferson.

Jefferson, as vice president, was oddly enough a part of the government himself. Before the Twelfth Amendment was passed, the vice president was the presidential candidate receiving the second highest number of electoral votes; thus, he naturally represented the opposition. And Jefferson had certainly done that. Every time the Federalists had

touched off a new controversy, the Virginian's facile pen had been set to framing objections. Soon everyone who was discontented, aggrieved or just politically ambitious came to see Jefferson as a rallying point.

The Federalists were amazed at how well Jefferson's Democratic-Republicans could organize. Almost overnight, it seemed, there were committees within committees, networks of correspondence, carefully coordinated propaganda campaigns. And the new party's agents were everywhere. "Every threshing floor, every husking, every work party on a house-frame or raising a building, the very funerals are infected with bawlers or whisperers against [the] government," complained Fisher Ames. In Congress, too, every debate turned into an election skirmish. The House, wrote one observer, was like "a conclave of cardinals, intriguing in the election of a Pope."

As the idea of political opposition was new to them, the Federalists were dumbfounded by it all. They fought back stridently, viciously, as though on the brink of Armageddon. If Jefferson were elected, shrilled Hamilton to Jay, it would "the OVERTHROW of the GOVERNMENT . . . a REVOLUTION, after the manner of BONAPARTE." Worse even than that, an anonymous pamphleteer moaned. "Murder, robbery, rape, adultery, and incest will be openly taught and practiced, the

air will be rent with cries of distress, the soil will be soaked with blood, and the nation black with crimes." But the Democratic-Republicans could sensationalize too. One editor referred to the President as, "old, querulous, bald, blind, crippled, toothless Adams."

There were other quirks in the campaign that might seem familiar today. When Jefferson dispatched his Philadelphia friend, Dr. Logan, to Paris to see if the French quarrel could be patched up, a poem in the Federalist press accused him of wanting to make time with Logan's wife. When Republican congressmen rose to speak against the Alien and Sedition Acts, Federalists in the House chamber were smitten with such a coughing fit that the speakers could not be heard. Elbridge Gerry, a prominent Massachusetts Federalist, dramatically switched parties and ran for governor. And a tunesmith knocked out the country's first political song:

> Rejoice, Columbia's sons, rejoice
> To tyrants never bend the knee
> But join with heart and soul and voice
> To Jefferson and Liberty.

Religion was hauled into it too. Jefferson, who had helped disestablish the Anglican church in Virginia, was depicted as an atheist, an infidel and a worshipper of the devil. The *Gazette of the United States* emblazoned an issue:

The Grand Question Stated

At the present solemn moment the only question to be asked by every American, laying his hand on his heart, is "Shall I continue allegiance to

God—and a Religious President;

or impiously declare for

Jefferson—and no god!!!"

Scare tactics or not, the Democratic-Republican juggernaut lumbered forward. Leaders in every state tirelessly plotted strategy and tallied up votes. In New York City, which would prove crucial, Aaron Burr swept the local elections with his own jerry-built political machine, and as a reward, was placed on the ticket as vice president. And almost daily, Jefferson himself, over dinner at the Francis Hotel in Philadelphia, held councils of war with Republican congressman. "A little patience," he assured them, "and we shall see the reign of witches pass over, their spells dissolved."

When the votes were counted, the Democratic-Republicans had won handily, and Thomas Jefferson became the third president of the United States. The Federalists were left in a daze. With the turn of the century, it seemed, a new world was dawning, at least in American politics, and if they were to be a part of it, they had better forget Washington's admonitions about the "spirit of party" and roll up their sleeves.

REPUBLICANS

Turn out, turn out and save your Country from ruin !

From an *Emperor*—from a *King*—from the iron grasp of a *British Tory Faction*—an unprincipled banditti of British speculators.   The hireling tools and emissaries of his majesty king George the 3d have thronged our city and diffused the poison of principles among us.

DOWN WITH THE TORIES, DOWN WITH THE BRITISH FACTION,

Before they have it in their power to enslave you, and reduce your families to distress by heavy taxation. Republicans want no Tribute-liars—they want no ship Ocean-liars—they want no Rufus King's for Lords —they want no Varick to lord it over them—they want no Jones for senator, who fought with the British against the Americans in time of the war.—But they want in their places such men as

Jefferson & Clinton,

who fought their Country's Battles in the year '76

The election of 1800: a second American Revolution?
(Courtesy of the New-York Historical Society.)

Thomas Jefferson and Aaron Burr each had the same number of electoral votes. The decision moved to the House of Representatives, with the potential for a constitutional crisis. After many attempts to the break the deadlock, a representative changed his vote and Jefferson won the presidency. The Twelfth Amendment was passed to avoid a repetition of this situation.

merciless lampooning in the press. A backdrop was provided by the naval war with France, which continued to flash and flare during the campaign. Several hundred US merchant vessels were seized by French privateers, but the American Navy, which had been expanded from three ships to fifty-five, acquitted itself well and bagged some eighty-five French prizes.

Federalists cashed in on the spiraling hysteria. Their campaign often took the form of marching, saluting and striking up the band. Congressman John Allen caught the spirit of it all and characterized his Republican foes as "an *insurrection* against the Government," while Senator James Lloyd expressed a wish "to lay hands on traitors." For the Republicans this was politics at gunpoint—using the emergency to "perpetuate [Federalists'] authority and preserve their present places."

When the votes were counted on election day, Jefferson had won, and his Democratic-Republicans had swept both houses of Congress. The result, said the new president-elect, was nothing less than the "Second American Revolution."

Constitutional Government

For a few of the surviving Founders, Jefferson's triumph marked the end of the American experiment. The "spirit of party" had prevailed after all. A hostile faction had not only swelled into a majority, it had captured control of the entire government. All of the Constitution's finely tuned mechanisms of counterpoise had apparently fizzled.

Yet the inauguration of Jefferson as president was not marked by the collapse of order or rioting in the streets—and still less of "majority tyranny." Life went on pretty much as it had. This remarkable anticlimax might well be one of the most significant events in American history, for it marked the first true experience of constitutional government. The party out of power became the party in power and vice versa. *Power changed hands peacefully*.

Only gradually did Americans sort out the full meaning of what they had witnessed. Among the dawning realizations were the following:

Constitutional Mechanisms. The mechanisms of counterpoise did do their job, but not precisely as the Framers had imagined. The theory had been to prevent any single group from gaining control, and that of course hadn't worked. Yet the mechanisms operated just as well in spite of the fact. Even when the Democratic-Republicans virtually monopolized the central government, the separations of power, the checks and balances, the federal-state dichotomy made it almost impossible to execute a tyrannical purpose.

For instance, there was enough disagreement among the Democratic-Republicans themselves—some of whom sought support from the Federalist minority—to make despotism unlikely. In consequence, Jefferson faced many of the same old obstacles that Adams had. Controversial ideas had a way of transforming into political dissent, and dissent made their progress very difficult.

Political Ideology. A second revelation was that being in power was rather different from being out of power, especially when it came to ideology. Jefferson's strict constructionism, which had made a great deal of sense when the Federalists were in charge, made less sense with the shoe on the other foot. For example, Jefferson soon found himself on the horns of an odd dilemma. Bonaparte, who had now declared himself emperor, suddenly found it expedient to unload the Louisiana Territory. Jefferson saw the opportunity to buy it—and thus nearly double the size of the United States—as a veritable godsend, but he lacked the constitutional authority to make such a purchase. Unless, of course, he could construe the Constitution more loosely than his ideology would allow. Ideology, Jefferson learned, must occasionally bow to practical matters. He bought Louisiana.

Loyal Opposition. A third revelation concerned political opposition. In his inaugural address, Jefferson uttered what was to become a famous line. "We are all Republicans," he said, "we are all Federalists." This statement is generally

"Of course, we must draw some sort of distinction between wishing to overthrow the government and not liking the present administration."
(By Helen Hokinson, courtesy of the Cartoon Bank.)

Swapping Issues

In the ideological world of European politics, it would be unthinkable for a party to embrace some position once held by its opponent. After all, parties are supposed to stand for something, yesterday, today and tomorrow.

Not so in American politics. Where the two parties are hard-headed, practical minded, and basically middle-of-the-road, it is comparatively easy for them to rummage through each other's garbage cans for usable issues. Indeed, it is almost as though they sometimes sat down and just swapped. A few memorable examples:

It was the Hamiltonians (forerunners of the modern-day Republicans) who started the tradition of loosely construing the Constitution in order to augment national power. The Jeffersonians (forerunners of the modern-day Democrats) believed in strict construction in order to curb national power. Today, those positions are reversed.

In the days of Andrew Jackson, Democrats were anything but big spenders: they were known as the party of small, lean, frugal government. Jackson himself went so far as to veto construction of a national highway through the Appalachian Mountains, believing it to be an unwarranted extension of federal power. Today, of course, the Democrats are blasted as the party of "tax and tax, spend and spend."

Throughout much of the nineteenth century, Democrats, not Republicans, were the hawks in foreign affairs. They were the ones, generally speaking, who wanted to fight Mexico and expand American territory into the West. In today's world, they are usually regarded as the doves.

Republicans got their start as the party of civil rights. The left-wingers of the 1860s were to a man Radical Republicans, some of whom embraced the idea of full and complete racial equality. Democrats, by contrast, had a reputation for racial prejudice.

Finally, many of today's Americans can recall a time when it was the Democrats, not the Republicans, who were famous for unbalancing the federal budget. Considering such historical flip-flops, it is little wonder that, say, Ronald Reagan could start out as a Democrat and convert to a Republican. "I didn't change," Reagan protested, "The Democratic Party did."

understood to mean not that Jefferson had accepted political opposition as legitimate but that he too rejected it. Like the Federalists before him, he believed that a government of the people ought not have to face organized dissent.

How did Jefferson square this belief with his *own* recent dissent? Simply by highlighting the special nature of the case. Hamilton and the Federalists were betraying the Revolution and running the country to ruin, Jefferson would have said, so desperate measures were called for. Now that the emergency was over, Americans could move forward once again. "We are all Republicans, we are all Federalists."

This sentiment did not diminish the opposition that Jefferson himself now faced from the defeated Federalists. Being turned out of office did not lessen their appetite for it, but only made them more determined to come back. Eventually the Federalists did fade away, but not without putting up a fight. They continued to battle the Democratic-Republicans on a local level through election after election, and they remained regionally strong in New England. Political opposition was here to stay.

Before the election, Republican Albert Gallatin, with sharp insight, had noted that "whoever dislikes the measures of Administration and of a temporary majority in congress" is believed by the government to be "an enemy, not of Administration, but of the Constitution." Gallatin was beginning to draw a distinction that few Americans, even in his own party, would have supported at the time: the "Administration" in power was *not* the same thing as the "Constitution." Clearly that was true. And coming to understand it thoroughly would make loyal opposition possible. If the Jeffersonians had been loyal opponents of the government before the election, then the ousted Federalists could be loyal opponents afterward.

Political Parties. A fourth dawning realization was that political parties might well have their own role to play in constitutional government. We will discuss that role in a subsequent chapter. For now, suffice it to note that parties did not behave at all in the way factions did.

Factions, as the Founders understood from antiquity, were groups in pursuit of a single narrow interest and oblivious to the public good. Neither criterion had fit the Jeffersonians. They reflected self-interest, true, but not a single one and certainly not a narrow one. And as for the public good, they believed that they and they alone represented it.

Political parties, then, were something new on the horizon. They were not "factions." They

"Old Ironsides," victorious in battle, gave a boost to American patria. (Courtesy of The Granger Collection, New York.)

were larger, fuzzier and far more complex. Indeed, in a manner not yet fully understood, they were manifestations of the public itself.

Popular Sovereignty. The transfer of power from Federalists to Republicans represented something which up to that point had existed only in theory—the sovereignty of the people. The fact was that for thousands of years the voice of the few was the only one that mattered, regardless of what the philosophers said. "The people" were seldom if ever heard.

Hamilton and the Federalists assumed that they spoke for the American people when they passed the Sedition Act and rigorously enforced it. But on sober reflection, the American people disagreed. Their election-day behavior sent a clear message. By changing the administration, peacefully and constitutionally, Americans were grasping the levers of true sovereignty. Virtually for the first time in history, the people were supervising the government.

American *Patria*

The naval war with France was America's first foreign conflict. Before its outbreak, Americans had regarded the United States as a kind of abstraction—like NATO or the UN today. The sight of US frigates returning to port with French prizes stirred deeper feelings—but so did the success of the Constitution. Unlike the old Confederation, the government of the Constitution had collected taxes, paid its bills and mounted a police action against would-be violators. Its credit had been restored by Hamilton's financial program and European merchants were willing to do business with it. It had negotiated a trade agreement with England which, however lopsided, gave it stature and credibility abroad. It had fought a foreign war and held its own.

We should credit more than the Constitution for these successes. Indeed, one might suggest that the ship of state had displayed questionable seaworthiness on its maiden voyage, and that seamanship alone had prevented the open seams and misaligned spars from sinking it. Something rather like Greek *areté*—a love of country that transcended ordinary limits—had shown itself to be as important to the Founding as structure or rights or the rule of law.

With the election of 1800, there was a sudden burst of confidence and stirrings of real patriotism. The system worked. The American Republic had arrived.

Suggestions for Further Reading

Albert H. Bowman, *The Struggle for Neutrality: Franco-American Diplomacy during the Federalist Era* (1974).

Richard Buel Jr., *Securing the Revolution: Ideology in American Politics, 1789–1815* (1972).

William N. Chambers, *Political Parties in a New Nation: The American Experience, 1776–1809* (1963).

Joseph J. Ellis, *American Sphinx: The Character of Thomas Jefferson* (1996).

Stanley Elkins and Eric McKitrick, *The Age of Federalism* (1993).

Ralph Ketcham, *Presidents above Party: The First American Presidency, 1789–1829* (1984).

Ralph Lerner, *The Thinking Revolutionary: Principle and Practice in the New Republic* (1987).

Glenn A. Phelps, *George Washington and American Constitutionalism* (1993).

Charles R. Ritcheson, *Aftermath of Revolution: British Policy toward the United States, 1783–1795* (1969).

James Roger Sharp, *American Politics in the Early Republic: The New Nation in Crisis* (1993).

Dan Sisson, *The American Revolution of 1800* (1974).

James M. Smith, *Freedom's Fetters: The Alien and Sedition Laws and American Civil Liberties* (1966).

Gerald Stourzh, *Alexander Hamilton and the Idea of Republican Government* (1970).

CHAPTER 12 STUDY AID ━━━━━━━

(This aid is not all-inclusive and is not intended to be a substitute for thorough study of the material presented in the textbook.)

From the Constitution to the Republic

I. Work in Progress

1. America:
   - North versus South
   - Town versus country
   - Commerce versus agriculture
2. General Constitution:
   - Rough sketch
   - Tradition, precedent, etc.
   - Filling in

II. Personalities

1. Statesmanship:
   - *Areté*
2. George Washington:
   - "Model" model
3. Alexander Hamilton:
   - Aristocratic
4. Thomas Jefferson:
   - Visionary
5. James Madison:
   - Architect of Constitution and Bill of Rights
6. John Adams:
   - Forgotten Founder?

III. Politics and Ideology

1. Hamilton:
   - Individuals to sacrifice for good of the whole
   - Aristocratic élan
   - Robust central government
   - Broad interpretation of Constitution—taxing and spending, general welfare, necessary and proper
   - Implied powers
   - Controversial proposals—assuming debt, tariffs, trade, national bank
   - Broad versus strict construction of Constitution

2. Jefferson:
   - Naturalism
   - The yeoman
   - The natural man
   - The land
   - Democratic vision
   - Decentralization of power
   - Strict construction of Constitution
3. Foreign intrigue:
   - Hamilton—Britain
   - Jefferson—France

IV. Emergence of Political Parties

1. Opposition:
   - Seditious libel
   - Public good
   - Factions
2. Hamiltonians:
   - Coherent purpose and specific goal
   - Vision of American nationhood
   - Support of George Washington
   - Federalists
   - "The" government
   - Jay's Treaty—favoring Great Britain
   - Whiskey Rebellion
3. Jeffersonians:
   - Madison
   - Organized opposition
4. Alien and Sedition Acts:
   - President John Adams
   - Citizen Genêt
   - The "press"
   - The "Acts"
   - Constitutional interpretation
   - Error of opinion—protected speech
   - Constitutional disputes
   - Kentucky and Virginia Resolves—the nature of the Union

V. Second American Revolution

1. Constitutional government:
   - Peaceful transfer of power
   - Constitutional mechanisms
   - Political ideology—flexible when in power
   - Loyal opposition—administration in power not the same as the Constitution
   - Parties
   - Popular sovereignty
2. American *Patria*:
   - America invented
   - Constitution implemented

CHAPTER 12 REVIEW QUESTIONS ▬▬▬▬

Key Terms

Statesmanship

Implied Powers

Broad Construction

Narrow Construction

Loyal Opposition

Hamiltonians

Jeffersonians

Alien and Sedition Acts

Multiple Choice Questions

1. The text describes the quality of statesmanship as possessing all of the
   following characteristics except:
   a. *Areté.*
   b. Politically savvy.
   c. Desire to fulfill the public good.
   d. Putting principle above party.

2. Which of the following was not included in Hamilton's agenda as
   Treasury Secretary?
   a. Establish a national bank.
   b. Enact tariffs.
   c. Pay off all existing consumer debts.
   d. Establish a trade agreement with England.

3. The Sedition Act was aimed at silencing:
   a. The French.
   b. Opposition newspapers.
   c. Traitors.
   d. The Anti-Federalists.

4. Who wrote the Kentucky Resolutions?
   a. Thomas Jefferson.
   b. James Madison.
   c. Alexander Hamilton.
   d. Elbridge Gerry.

Review Questions

1. What financial problems faced the nation as George Washington took office as president? How did Alexander Hamilton propose to solve them?

   _____

   _____

   _____

   _____

2. Why did Hamilton and Jefferson view the Constitution differently?

   _____

   _____

   _____

   _____

3. How did the French Revolution impact American politics?

   _____

   _____

   _____

   _____

4. Why weren't political parties a part of the British governmental system?

   _____

   _____

   _____

   _____

5. Why was Jefferson's election in 1800 dubbed "the Second American Revolution"?

   _____

   _____

   _____

   _____

Review Exercises

1. Briefly explain the causes and consequences of the Whiskey Rebellion of 1794.

   _____

   _____

   _____

2. Explain the main reasons for the passage of the Alien and
   Sedition Acts.

   _____

   _____

   _____

   _____

3. Explain why the English doctrine of seditious libel did not find a place in
   Constitutional America.

   _____

   _____

   _____

   _____

Big Essay Question

Many European democracies have dozens of political parties competing for
office. Yet America has remained basically a two-party country for over 200
years. Why? What are the advantages and disadvantages of our two-party system compared with multi-party governments in Europe? Be thorough.

Expounding the Constitution

The administration of the oath of office to the president by the chief justice of the Supreme Court symbolizes the equality of the branches of government. (By Bill Fitz-Patrick, courtesy of the White House Photo Office.)

If a constitution embodies the fundamental law, what happens when that law is violated? This can be an extremely troubling question—one that runs to the very marrow of republicanism. Constitutions always provide for the violation of ordinary law by describing police, court and penal apparatus. If the constitution *itself* is violated, however, there is no similar wherewithal to enforce compliance.

In the spring of 1861, charges were hurled between the North and the South that one of them or the other had "violated" the Constitution. The outcome of that controversy ought to give us sober pause. The American Revolution also began with such accusations. Over and over, colonial spokesmen alleged that Parliament, the court system, even the king himself were violating the "English constitution"—a charge vehemently denied. And as with the American Civil War, the issue had to be settled with fire and blood.

Questions of violating the Constitution fall into two categories. First, there is the possibility that someone in the government might knowingly, even deliberately, violate a constitutional provision to further some political purpose. And second, there is the possibility that various groups may simply differ in their understanding of constitutional language. Each category raises a tough question. In the case of willful violation, how is the violator to be identified—and thwarted? And in the case of semantic disagreement, how is a sound interpretation to be achieved?

Evidently, the Framers paid scant attention to such questions. But, as Christopher and James Lincoln Collier have pointed out, constitutional understanding and enforcement couldn't simply be left unattended—*somebody* had to do it.

Judicial Review

Judicial review was a term the Framers did discuss, if only in passing. It refers to the practice of submitting constitutional questions to the courts for resolution. In colonial days, if some local measure allegedly violated the colony's charter,

373

the matter would be submitted to the Privy Council, a body of high-ranking judicial authorities in London, which had a final say. Privy Council review established an important precedent.

With that precedent in mind, several state constitutions made use of judicial review. That is, when constitutional questions arose, they would be submitted to the state's highest court for resolution.

The theory behind judicial review went something like this. Since the judiciary has neither "energy" nor an "independent will," it will probably not abuse the review power in the way a legislature or executive might. The judiciary is also the most isolated and protected branch of government, making it difficult for interested parties to browbeat. It can't be a player, so make it an umpire.

Was judicial review supposed to apply to the federal Constitution as well? The question has two parts. The first dealt with state laws. Did the Framers intend federal judges to review laws passed by state governments and compel their compliance with the Constitution? If so, it was an extremely delicate matter. Think back to the tensions at the Philadelphia Convention between state and national authority. Madison had originally wished the national government to have a veto over *all* state laws—not just those in conflict with the Constitution—and to nullify them on any grounds it chose. But such a power would have effectively wiped out state sovereignty, and most of the delegates refused to consider it. A compromise of sorts was reached in the wording of the supremacy clause, stating that federal laws and treaties "shall be the supreme Law of the land; and the Judges in every State shall be bound thereby, any Thing in the Constitution or Laws of any State to the Contrary notwithstanding." (Article VI Number 2) The Framers' discussions of judicial review might have been limited to this passage. If some state law happened to conflict with the federal Constitution, and if the state's judges happened not to feel "bound thereby," it would probably fall to the US Supreme Court to strike it down.

But what about the other possibility? Suppose *Congress* violated the Constitution—what then? This was a contingency the Framers might not have considered. The reason why had to do with a certain legal doctrine of the time. Even though England did not have a written constitution, English jurists had long claimed the power to judge the constitutionality of parliamentary acts, as we have seen. Yet the popularity of that doctrine waned considerably after the Glorious Revolution. For if, as the argument went, Parliament truly spoke for the people, what sense did it make to allow a handful of judges, with no popular mandate whatever, to tell the people they were out of line? Accordingly, legal analysts such as Blackstone backed away from judicial review. And the American Founders? Their best legal mind, James Wilson, might well have wished to avoid a feature that was regarded as archaic or absurd.

Still, the Colliers' point remains: *somebody* had to police the Constitution. It seems inconceivable that the Framers would have ignored a need so obvious. Wilson, who was a very subtle man, might have reasoned that judicial review would come about anyway, with or without a formal provision, for circumstances would sooner or later require it. So argued *Federalist* 78, at any rate. If Congress passed a law violating the Constitution, Publius said, it would fall to the Supreme Court to throw it out.

Marbury v. Madison

In 1803 this was precisely what happened. The case, which has come to stand as a kind of addendum to the Constitution, was *Marbury v. Madison*. Its background facts are of utmost significance, not only to the establishment of judicial review but to its whole impact on constitutional law.

In 1803 the Supreme Court was fifteen years old. In the Chief Justice's carved oak chair sat the third individual to occupy that position, John Marshall. He was a Virginian with dark, wavy hair, courtly manners and a commanding presence. He was also a committed Federalist.

We saw in the previous chapter what that term meant. The Federalists had lost the election of 1800 and were turned out of office. Given the assumptions of the time, they regarded this cataclysm not so much as the people deciding against them but as the overthrow of government by a rabble. It was a view that justified any means they might employ to insure that "responsible" governance somehow continue in spite of everything.

Accordingly, the Federalists more or less barricaded themselves in the judiciary—something they still had the power to do. Adams nominated John Marshall to be Chief Justice of the Supreme Court. He also hurriedly appointed many lesser judges, staying up far into the night on his last day of office (according to folklore) to sign the necessary commissions. In the flush of their electoral triumph, the Democratic-Republicans would have none of this. They had beaten the Federalists fair and square, and they didn't have to sit still for any "midnight appointments." Jefferson decided to let them simply die on the vine. The commissions had been signed and sealed but they were not yet delivered, and the new secretary of state, James Madison, whose job it was to deliver them, agreed with the new president that delivery could not be compelled.

William Marbury, who was supposed to receive one of the appointments, decided to sue. In court, he requested a writ of mandamus, an old instrument in the common law used for compelling an officer to perform some task for which he has a legal responsibility. Such a writ, in this case, would require Madison to turn over the commissions whether he wanted to or not.

The question was, did the court that issued the writ have constitutional authority to do so? In truth, there was no simple answer. The Constitution had only sketched out the bare bones of a federal judiciary, specifying a Supreme Court and "such inferior Courts as the Congress may from time to time ordain and establish." In 1789, Congress had fleshed out the bones by means of the Judiciary Act, organizing circuit courts, an appellate process and a number of other particulars. Among these other particulars was the authority to issue writs of mandamus.

John Marshall:
http://odur.let.rug.nl/~usa/
B/jmarshall/marsh.htm

Chief Justice John Marshall. His shaping of the Supreme Court and Constitution places him among the Founders. (Engraving by Alonzo Chappell, courtesy of the Supreme Court of the United States.)

But did the Constitution authorize Congress to do this? Maybe, maybe not. The jurisdiction of the federal judiciary, which was carefully worded in the document, made no specific mention of mandamus, true, but it did mention categories of cases where mandamus might apply. It would have been reasonable to argue that the Constitution, in its brevity, couldn't be expected to list out every conceivable writ that might be necessary.

Instead, John Marshall, who heard the case in March of 1801, decided that Congress, in authorizing writs of mandamus, had exceeded its constitutional authority, and therefore that particular clause of the Judiciary Act of 1789 was null and void.

Marshall had chosen his case cunningly. By finding against Marbury he was finding against his own party. He was also trimming back the power of his own court by denying its mandamus authority. He figured that the Democratic-Republicans were unlikely to contest the decision—and he was right. Marshall sacrificed the battle in order to win the war, and win it he did. A precedent was now established for judicial review.

Marshall knew it would take more than shrewd politics to win over the doubters—after all, he was altering the Constitution himself. Accordingly, in his written opinion on the case, he laid out four separate arguments to justify his startling innovation. In essence, they were as follows:

1. A written constitution provides the fundamental law. If it should come into conflict with ordinary law, it possesses the inherent power to nullify the same.

2. Courts must determine what the law is before they can apply it. If there is a conflict between two laws, the courts must choose between them. If one of the two is the Constitution, they must always decide in its favor.

3. If the power of the courts extends to all cases under the Constitution, how could they operate without examining and interpreting it?

4. A law repugnant to the Constitution is not a law at all and cannot be enforced as such.

Scholars have not been entirely persuaded by Marshall's reasoning. None of his four arguments by itself or all of them together make an airtight case for judicial review. Indeed, in an irony that might have escaped Marshall, his logic for denying the mandamus power—namely that the Framers listed out certain powers and mandamus was not found among them—would also deny the power of judicial review.

By spelling out four separate arguments, each a little different, Marshall was also giving judicial review an extremely broad scope. For the courts to strike down clearly unconstitutional laws was one thing, but for them to expound and interpret the Constitution, as Marshall was suggesting, was a different matter entirely. The first had entered into all discussions of judicial review at the time, but the second had never been mentioned.

Marbury v. Madison thus opened a constitutional Pandora's box—one that two hundred years of history has afforded no way to close.

Judicial Review and the Constitution

Judicial review did more than keep laws in bounds. It altered the way the Constitution worked. Consider, for example, how it affected separation of powers.

As we have seen, separation of powers was so novel an idea that the Framers worried about how it would actually work. They realized that the branches of government couldn't be completely isolated from one another without causing confusion, yet they must operate more or less independently in order to deliver the promised benefit. Fine balances were set up among the structural mechanisms in order to achieve a precise equilibrium.

This was what made *Marbury v. Madison* a little scary. The Supreme Court was plunking itself down amidst the separation of powers and altering their working dynamics. Consider three questions:

1. Did Madison, as an officer in the executive branch, have a right to thwart the attempt of political rivals to establish themselves in the judiciary? Perhaps he did, according to separation of powers. But now it was up to the Supreme Court to decide.

2. Did Congress, representing the people, have a right to expand the court system's jurisdiction beyond what the Constitution spelled out? Possibly so. But it was now the Supreme Court's call, not Congress'.

3. Did the Supreme Court have the right to step into a quarrel between contending political parties? A wide-open question. But Marshall did not hesitate to answer it.

Judicial review, then, seemed capable of changing all the rules. The question was, would the rule changes strengthen and clarify the constitutional system, or weaken and confuse it?

Some historians have claimed there was a better alternative. The Framers, so the argument goes, intended *Congress* to answer constitutional questions. That is, when a point of interpretation arose, it should be up to elected representatives, rather than appointed judges, to rule on it. This is no simple solution either. For one thing, it would be like posting the fox to guard the henhouse—who else but *Congress* would be trespassing in the first place? And for another, think of the theory involved. It would amount to placing the people's representatives above the people themselves, for it was the latter who approved the Constitution.

Other answers to the review question are equally problematic. Jefferson supposed that each branch of the government ought to interpret the Constitution for itself, leaving the other two to agree or disagree as they chose. But this seems a recipe for anarchy. One could easily imagine the branches of government facing one another down defiantly, as when Andrew Jackson ignored a court order protecting the Cherokee Indians in Georgia and said, "Well, John Marshall has made his decision; let's see him enforce it."

Given such alternatives, judicial review made enough sense to enough people to become accepted as a valid constitutional principle. It was as though John Marshall had retroactively seated himself among the Framers in Independence Hall and added his own dimension to their work.

What, precisely, was that dimension? While there are no simple answers, it is fair to observe that judicial review would affect not just separation of powers but all the mechanisms of counterpoise. The Court now operated as a check against both the legislative and executive branches, which significantly complicated the balances. It also operated as an additional check against the states. All calculations of interplay among the branches, and between federal and state governments, had assumed the Court to be a neutral in the constitutional game. Now, not only was it a player itself, it was a player composed of a very few (six in the beginning, later nine) highly accomplished and strong-minded individuals—with no political accountability.

One could imagine the altered system going completely out of kilter. Corrupt bargains between Congress and the Justices might lead to abuses that no executive veto could check. Or on the other side, sweetheart judicial appointments might conceivably augment the power of the executive over Congress. Yet neither scenario has yet materialized. Most Justices have sensed that their role requires extremely high integrity. It is significant that in two hundred years of Supreme Court history not a single Justice has ever been impeached for corruption.

There was even better news. As history afforded an ever clearer perspective, it became apparent that key features of the Constitution operated as intended only *with* judicial review. Let us return to separation of powers for a moment. We noted above that it was unsettling to think what the Court's involvement might do to separation's delicate mechanisms. But what was happening without the Court's involvement? When Congress passed the Alien and Sedition Acts, Jefferson told voters that if elected he would refuse to enforce the laws as "unconstitutional." Then, in the Kentucky Resolution, he argued that states could nullify laws *they* thought were unconstitutional. This was government by face-off. No telling where it might have led.

With the Supreme Court in the mix, confrontation was replaced by calculation. We have already seen that Congress had to keep one eye on the possibility of an executive veto. Yet vetoes could be overridden by a two-thirds majority, and at election time they could even be appealed to the voters. Against the Supreme Court, however, there was no appeal whatever. Accordingly, Congress would have to think long and hard before passing a law that seriously risked violating the Constitution, and the president would have to think long and hard about a questionable executive action. The presence of an effective "umpire" worked to keep both legislative and executive powers in their separate channels.

And there was a broader significance. Once judicial review was added to the separation of powers mechanism, the entire Constitution was transformed, according to Charles R. Kesler. As drafted, Kesler argues, the Constitution was merely a plan of government. With the inclusion of judicial review, it became a wellspring of republican good. We will explore Kesler's ideas at the end of the chapter.

Justice Samuel Chase was impeached in 1804 but acquitted in a Senate trial in 1805. Charges were brought against him for political reasons rather than for corruption.

From Judicial Review to Constitutional Interpretation

A *Marbury*-style axing of federal law was not repeated for a long time. The power to nullify the will of the people, as it were, was obviously one to be used sparingly.

State laws, however, came up for review continually. It soon became apparent that *judicial review*—that is, testing specific legislation against the constitutional text—was hard to separate from *constitutional interpretation*. For as Marshall had argued in *Marbury*, in order to ascertain whether a given law violated the Constitution, one first had to determine what the Constitution actually said.

We have seen that in certain areas the latitude for such interpretation was rather wide. The Framers had buried some of their disagreements in deliberate ambiguity, and they had included stretch-points to make the boundaries of power flexible. When constitutional questions arose in these areas, interpretation became all-important.

Constitutional Interpretation

Among the stretch-points was the necessary and proper clause. Just how wide a stretch was possible with those three words? Alexander Hamilton had made them into veritable elastic bands ten years earlier, and he had convinced President Washington to go along with his interpretation. But the Federalists were out of office now, and Hamilton had been tragically killed in a duel. And it was no longer the President's call—but the Supreme Court's.

> In the most famous duel in US history, Vice President Aaron Burr challenged Alexander Hamilton for besmirching his reputation, and killed him in 1804 in New Jersey.

The Court addressed itself to the necessary and proper question in the 1819 case of *McCulloch v. Maryland*. The state of Maryland had passed a law that placed a tax on the issuance of bank notes. In addition to the various state bank notes involved, the state proposed to tax the notes of the Bank of the United States. This institution, recall, was that highly controversial element of Hamilton's financial program that had played such a role in creating the party system. It was still around, still doing a booming business and still setting Republicans' teeth on edge. Many of them would have gladly taxed its notes out of existence.

In settling the case, it became necessary to determine whether the Bank of the United States was itself constitutional. Did the federal government have authority under the Constitution to establish and operate a bank? We know that the Constitution made no mention of banks as such, though it did grant Congress the power to "coin money" and "regulate the Value thereof"—together with whatever authority was "necessary and proper" to carrying out that end. But was a federally owned bank *necessary* to coining money or regulating its value? Clearly not in any usual sense, for most nations performed those functions without the services of a bank.

But Marshall was undaunted. In writing the opinion of the Court, he employed Hamilton's rather singular definition of the word "necessary," quoting Hamilton almost verbatim. A bank, he said, while perhaps not essential to the government's monetary activities, was nevertheless convenient, useful and not inappropriate. And nowhere in the Constitution did it say Congress could *not* set one up. The Bank of the United States was constitutional, Marshall concluded. There was no appeal.

It requires little imagination to see how this decision affected the development of nationalism in America. Virtually the entire length and breadth of today's federal operations exist because of this "loose construction" of the Constitution—and because it is sanctioned by the Supreme Court.

CONSTITUTIONAL INTERPRETATION

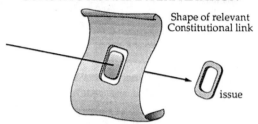

Shape of relevant
Constitutional link

issue

The Supreme Court has had to deal with a variety of
complex constitutional issues of different shapes
and sizes. Each issue is considered in relation to
some link(s) of the Constitution. If it reasonably
matches a constitutional link, it passes through as
constitutional (above); if it does not reasonably
match a link, it is rejected as unconstitutional
(below). On a practical level, the shape of
constitutional links are determined by the Court.
Consequently the Court, through reinterpretation,
has had the ability to modify the shapes of links,
thereby modifying those issues or actions which are
constitutionaly acceptable.

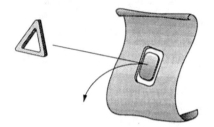

Reinterpretation

There was more than loose construction in store for the Constitution—there was also erratic construction. The Supreme Court demonstrated that it could overrule not just state or lower federal courts—it could overrule *itself*.

By established procedure, once a court in the Anglo-American legal tradition decides a case, that ruling becomes a binding precedent for the court's future action. That is, subsequent courts are obliged to resolve similar cases in a similar way. Otherwise the law lacks predictability. While the US Supreme Court generally respected this rule, it also proved capable of violating it. For with no appeal beyond the Court itself, there was no mechanism to *bind* the Justices to their own precedents.

Because the Constitution's stretch-points could be understood various ways, it was possible for the Court to produce different interpretations of a given clause at different times in history. Constitutional interpretation, in other words, led to constitutional *reinterpretation*.

A convenient example can be found in the history of the commerce clause. The Supreme Court, dominated by different personalities at different times and in different circumstances, produced widely varying interpretations of the commerce clause's meaning. While these were not precisely antithetical, they were indeed conflicting and they took the commerce clause down some very strange roads.

The deceptively simple wording of the commerce clause (Article I, Section 8) states, "Congress shall have the Power . . . to regulate Commerce with foreign Nations, and among the several States, and with the Indian tribes." As written, the wording contains three principal areas of ambiguity:

What is meant by the word "regulate?"

What is meant by the word "commerce?"

Is the word "power" to be understood as meaning *sole* power or only *some* power?

These questions would prove to be of inestimable importance. They would determine the reach of federal power, the boundaries between federal and state power, and even the particular venues into which federal power could extend. For the commerce clause was a wild card indeed.

With constitutional reinterpretation in mind, let us see how the scope of federal power could be extended or retracted, how the boundaries between federal and state power could be shifted one way or the other, and how the word "commerce" could bring all sorts of noncommercial things under federal control. We will consider four separate cases.

Gibbons v. Ogden

In 1824, John Marshall demonstrated how the wording of the commerce clause could be interpreted so as to maximize the scope of federal power while minimizing that of the states. Marshall was still Chief Justice, even though three presidents had come and gone, and he was still a stalwart Federalist. As such, he was committed to furthering Hamilton's nationalism and strengthening the federal government.

Gibbons v. Ogden concerned steamboat traffic on the Hudson River. One Aaron Ogden operated a ferry service between New York and New Jersey under a franchise granted to Robert Fulton, the inventor of the steamboat. Thomas Gibbons wanted to horn in. In court, Ogden pointed to his monopoly privilege issued by the state of New York. Gibbons pointed to the commerce clause. It wasn't for New York to regulate interstate traffic, he said, it was for Congress.

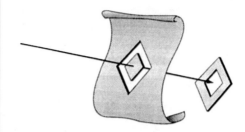

NATIONALISTIC INTERPRETATION:
Gibbons v. Ogden

The issue: Does Congress have the power to regulate navigation between two states? Here the Court determined that the shape of the commerce clause link was broad enough to mean this: While Congress did not have sole power to regulate commerce, it at least had a lot, especially from the perspective of that era.

In writing his opinion on the case, Marshall stressed the fact that there were no limitations or qualifiers in the commerce clause's language. He also gave those stretch-words the strongest tug possible. "Commerce," he said, included the articles of trade, the means of transportation and the routes employed, while the word "regulate" included fostering, inhibiting or protecting the commerce in question. With the whole field preempted by the federal government, Marshall concluded, state regulations had to give way.

As a result of this decision, federal power was enhanced significantly and not solely in commercial regulation. The word "federal," in fact, came to mean tough, competent and no-nonsense—as in "Don't mess with the feds!" Incidentally, the prestige of the Supreme Court was also given a hefty boost.

By liberally construing the word "commerce" in Gibbons v. Ogden, *the Supreme Court tightened federal control over trade.* (Robert Fulton's steamboat, Clermont, courtesy of The Granger Collection, New York. Lithograph, French, c. 1830–35.)

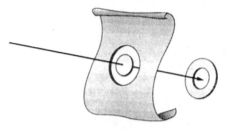

STATES' RIGHTS INTERPRETATION:
License Case

The Issue: Can states tax and license the sale of alcoholic liquors within their own borders. Here the Court said that the mere grant of some power to the national government, does not prohibit states from exercising power over the same thing.

The License Cases

In 1847, some twenty-three years later, a different Court under a different Chief Justice came up with a very different idea of the commerce clause. The 1840s was a time of states' rights sentiment, and Marshall's spread-eagle nationalism had come under a serious challenge. Inevitably, that challenge took aim at the commerce clause.

The question posed by a group of litigations known as the *License Cases* was whether states could tax and regulate the sale of liquors that had been shipped through interstate commerce. Then as now, domestic whiskey came almost wholly from Kentucky and Tennessee, to be carried far and wide along the river system. But most other states slapped imposts on the traffic, and required retail establishments to be licensed.

John Marshall might well have denied against the states, ruling that the commerce clause reserved all such regulation for Congress. But Chief Justice Roger Taney, a southerner and an ardent Jacksonian, read the commerce clause quite differently than Marshall had. He saw it less as a carte blanche for nationalism than as a charter for states' rights.

What Taney (pronounced "Tawney") picked out in the commerce clause was the absence of the adjective "sole" modifying the noun "power"—that Congress was not given the *sole* power to regulate interstate commerce, only *some* power. "It appears to me to be very clear," Taney wrote in the Court's opinion, "that the mere grant of power to the general government cannot, upon any just principles of construction, be construed to be an absolute prohibition on the exercise of any power over the same subject by the States." Thus, Taney reasoned, state regulations that did not conflict with those of the federal government also did not conflict with the commerce clause.

This decision gave a leg up to states' rights feeling—just as the earlier decision had to nationalism. In the politics of symbols, it came down for the Jacksonians.

U.S v. E.C. Knight

If it was possible to interpret the commerce clause both for and against nationalism, it was also possible to interpret it both for and against government power itself. We will soon see how it was used to extend the power of government. In *U.S. v. E.C. Knight* it was used to curtail it.

By 1895, a half-century after the *License Cases*, a great deal of history had slipped past and American opinion had undergone another sea change. So had the Supreme Court. It now reflected neither nationalism nor states' rights but a libertarian feeling that all government regulation was harmful. When Congress passed the Sherman

LIBERTARIAN INTERPRETATION:
U.S. v. E.C. Knight

The issue: Can Congress regulate monopolistic practices in manufacturing rather than transportation. Here the Court, interpreting the shape of the commerce link rigidly, said no. Interstate commerce meant only the physical transportation of goods across state lines.

Antitrust Act a few years earlier, many Americans, especially in the business community, had strong doubts about "trust-busting." Large corporations shouldn't be hauled before the bar of justice to explain their success, this view held, and they shouldn't be broken apart by meddling politicians.

The American Sugar Refining Company suffered just such a fate. It had monopolized no less than 95% of the American sugar market, selling its product in every state of the union. If there was ever a target made to order for the Sherman Act, this was it. But when the government's case came up to the Supreme Court on appeal, Chief Justice Melville Fuller couldn't follow the argument by which the Sherman Act claimed constitutional authority. The commerce clause, he said, dealt only with "commerce," which Fuller defined as the physical transit of goods across state lines. The issue here was "manufacturing"—a different matter entirely.

Fuller was doing precisely what John Marshall had done before him, only in reverse. Where Marshall had given the broadest definition possible to the word "commerce," Fuller was giving the narrowest. Congress could regulate the railroads that carried sugar from state to state, perhaps, but it couldn't regulate the company that loaded and unloaded the railroad cars—for that was not "commerce." Needless to say, *E.C. Knight* pretty well busted the trustbusters.

Katzenbach v. McClung

In the 1960s the Supreme Court found even greater elasticity in the commerce clause. By reversing Fuller's strategy of minimizing "commerce," it showed how the word could be stretched to cover just about any subject imaginable in which the government took an interest. The trick was twofold:

> Define "commerce" as broadly and inclusively as possible.

> Argue that "commerce" was affected in some way, however indirectly, by the activity in question.

For example, when Congress wanted to pass a Civil Rights Act in 1964, it was able to do so only on the authority of the commerce clause. (Scan through the powers listed in Article I, Section 8 and you will see why.) Civil rights may seem a long remove from commerce, but federal attorneys argued that there were "indirect effects" at work. Restaurants refusing to serve, say, black patrons traveling across the country would force them to go out of their way, alter their plans, perhaps forgo travel altogether. All this had an effect on commerce.

The case that finally made it to the Supreme Court sought to test how far this reasoning could be taken. Ollie's Barbecue in Birmingham, Alabama steadfastly refused to serve black customers (except at a small take-out window in the rear), and furthermore it didn't believe it could be forced to. Its attorneys argued that the establish-

SOCIO-POLITICAL INTERPRETATION:

Katzenbach v. McClung

The issue: May Congress use its commerce power to forbid racial discrimination by a restaurant on the sole basis that some of the food it serves originated from outside the state? Here the Court stretched the commerce clause link sufficiently to allow Congress regulatory authority over civil rights within the states.

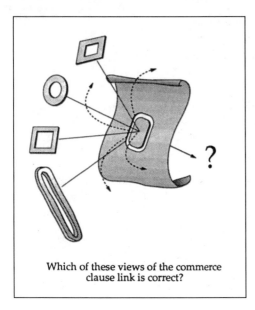

Which of these views of the commerce
clause link is correct?

ment was not near a bus terminal, a train station or a freeway
exit, and hence that its patrons had nothing to do with "interstate commerce." But the federal solicitors, realizing that the
Civil Rights Act hung in the balance, came back with a new
wrinkle. Some of the food served at Ollie's *did* pass through
interstate commerce, they argued, and on that account the law
could still be justified. Blacks turned away would consume less
food, less food would mean less commerce, and so forth.

The Supreme Court bought it. At the helm now was Earl
Warren, the Chief Justice responsible for *Brown v. Board of
Education*, the decision that ended school segregation, and he
was not one to quibble over details. Besides, he had a lovely
precedent. A 1940 case had held that a man who grew wheat on
his own farm and consumed it at his own table had an indirect
effect on interstate commerce. After all, the more wheat he grew
the less he had to buy on the interstate market!

We have civil rights in the United States today because of
the Warren Court, loose construction—and the commerce
clause.

These cases reveal not only the how of constitutional reinterpretation but
also the why. The motives fall into three general categories:

1. *Political.* Even though Justices could not be active partisans in their judicial
   role, their identification as nationalists, states' righters, libertarians, liberals
   and the like clearly influenced their interpretation of constitutional language.

2. *Intellectual.* Justices have also been attuned to the intellectual currents of
   their time, with a similar effect on constitutional reasoning.   Thus, the
   same Justice who might scorn "political" motives might not think twice
   about supporting a cause like civil rights.

3. *"Guardianship."* Some members of the
   Court have seen their role as surpassing
   ordinary jurisprudence and entering a
   realm of pure justice. That is, standing
   outside of time and circumstances (not
   to mention consequences), they might
   see themselves as able to work the kind
   of justice that politics—which is bound
   by those things—could not deliver on
   its own. They become like Plato's
   Guardians.

(By Dick Locher, courtesy of the Chicago Tribune/TMS.)

Ultimately, constitutional reinterpretation (especially of the guardianship variety) gestured toward rewriting the
Constitution itself—writing the Constitution as it *should* be. The implications of

Judicial Independence

The Founders, in their wisdom, made federal judges as independent as possible. How did this independence affect their behavior? A tantalizing clue is offered by the career of Earl Warren, US Chief Justice from 1953 to 1969, and one of the most influential jurists of all time.

Even in the beginning, Warren-watchers might have noted that beneath the man's political exterior resided a markedly different sort of individual. For instance, Warren the

Chief Justice Earl Warren.
(Courtesy of Harris & Ewing.)

politician, always going with the flow, had once been a virulent race-baiter. In the aftermath of Pearl Harbor, he had taken the lead in rounding up California's Japanese and sending them to concentration camps. After the hysteria died down, however, the other Earl Warren peeped out. "Whenever I thought of the innocent little children who were torn from home, school friends and congenial surroundings, I was conscience stricken," he wrote. At the end of the war, Warren suddenly emerged as a champion of Japanese-American civil rights.

In most matters, however, politics held Warren's inner man in check. As a young right-of-center district attorney he realized, for example, that it was impolitic to appear soft on communists, unionists or violent criminals, and in the famous *Point Lobos* case, he showed how hard he could be. He held the three defendants—all union men accused of murder—all night in his office, denied them counsel and later stacked the jury against them. He was widely accused of playing to the McCarthyite frenzy of the day.

But that was the political Warren, the eager young man on the make. What about Warren the Chief Justice—now well insulated from politics? In the strangely similar case of *Miranda v. Arizona* (1966), he turned loose a patently guilty Ernesto Miranda (along with other defendants) because:

> In each [case], the defendant . . . was cut off from the outside world. In none of these cases was the defendant given a full and effective warning of his rights at the outset of the interrogation process. In all cases, the questioning elicited oral admissions . . . which were admitted at their trials.

Judicial independence, then, turned Earl Warren inside out. The moment he was free from the constraints of electoral politics, the long-buried man of conscience began to come forth. Within a year of his appointment, the new Chief Justice had persuaded the Court to unanimously strike down school desegregation—and that was only the beginning.

Robert Bork:
http://www
.conservativeforum.org/
authquot.asp?ID=936

William Brennan:
http://www.law.harvard
.edu/alumni/bulletin/
backissues/fall97/
brennan.html

this desire have occasionally weighed upon members of the Court, prompting them to explain themselves philosophically. Their various positions can be arrayed between two theoretical extremes, each associated with a noted constitutional scholar:

Robert Bork. Justices may not rewrite the Constitution at all. Their interpretations of the text must be bound by the meaning of the words at the time they were written, and by the "original intentions" of the Framers.

William Brennan. The Constitution should not be an anchor tying us to antiquated values and archaic modes of thought. Justices ought to regard it as a "lodestar of our aspirations," and freely reinterpret it as those aspirations change.

In a critique of both extremes, political scientist Ralph C. Hancock has pointed out that the "original intentions" of the Framers were for a certain degree of growth and flexibility in the Constitution; otherwise they wouldn't have included such stretch-points as the commerce clause. As for Justice Brennan's "lodestar of aspirations" argument, the concept is so vague that it risks abandoning the Constitution entirely. Professor Hancock suggests that an acceptable mean might be found in the phrase "original aspirations." This idea will be explored below.

The Supreme Court and Politics

Once judicial review had been creaked open, the first question to slither out was that of politics. How would this strange new power affect the political process?

Dark scenarios took shape. What if the six (later nine) incumbents of the High Bench wound up deciding all the important questions themselves—without the aid of Congress? It was at least imaginable. The Constitution presupposed tension and conflict, so deadlock on tough issues was always possible. If judicial reinterpretation were given wide enough scope, the Justices might conceivably take such issues into their own hands under the guise of "consulting" the Constitution. There would be no further need of politics.

Originally there were six justices, but the number changed six times before 1869, when nine justices became the norm. That has been the number ever since.

John Marshall was aware of this possibility when he wrote the decision for *Marbury v. Madison* and he carefully steered the Court away from it. His opinion made it clear that Madison's *political* role as secretary of state was not under review—only his *administrative* role as a government functionary. The writ of mandamus applied solely to situations where the official had no personal discretion one way or the other but was supposed to act as a matter of course. From this and other precedents, the doctrine soon evolved that the Supreme Court was to keep hands off the political process. No believer in the rule of law wished to see government by judicial directorate.

Yet the tough questions seemed to gravitate toward the Supreme Court anyway—especially when the political process locked up. The idea of "nine old men" standing above the political fray and dispensing Platonic justice was not without its attractions. But a soon-to-be-famous case pointed up the possible dangers.

Dred Scott v. Sanford

The burning question of our antebellum history grew out of the spread of slavery into the West. All parties conceded slaveholding to be lawful in the original southern states and unlawful north of the Chesapeake. The question was, what about the *territories*?

In theory, the territories belonged to *all* Americans, and all were free to travel there, purchase property and take part in political life. But did that include slave owners? If so, there was nothing to stop them from going into the Missouri Territory, which was *north* of the Mason-Dixon Line, quite as much as the Alabama or Mississippi Territories to the south, and when they began doing just that, political hell broke loose.

In 1820, after a punishing debate, Congress managed to work out the Missouri Compromise, one of whose features was to draw a line across the map and stipulate that slavery must remain south of that line. Few at the time doubted Congress' authority to make such arrangements. All the same, the question of allowing slavery into the West continued to erupt periodically like a geyser. There were strong moral values, stark prejudices and important vested interests on both sides, and the political system proved utterly incapable of resolving it.

So the matter began drifting into constitutional waters. And dead ahead loomed an iceberg in the form of this question: did Congress have the constitu-

Dred Scott:
http://www.historyplace
.com/lincoln/dred.htm

http://odur.let.rug.nl/
~usa/E/dred_scottxx.htm

Mason-Dixon Line:
Boundary between Pennsylvania and Maryland established in 1767 and named for surveyors Charles Mason and Jeremiah Dixon; used to distinguish slave states from free states.

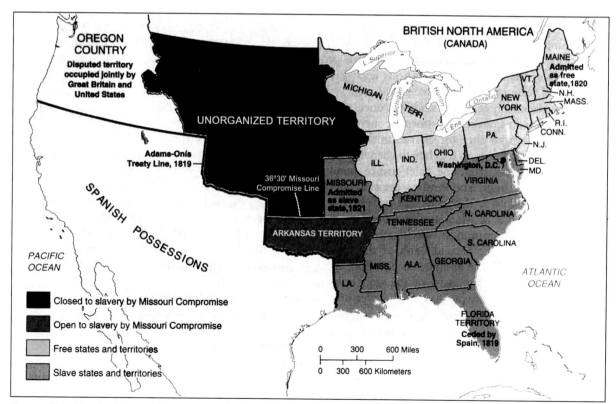

States affected by the Missouri Compromise of 1820. (Courtesy of D. C. Heath and Company.)

tional authority to forbid slavery in the territories—*any* territories—and to work out arrangements like the Missouri Compromise? Answered one way, it might demolish all opposition in the North. Answered another, it might throw brakes on the slave expansionists. But what was the answer?

A case was worked up to lay the question before the Supreme Court. It involved a slave owner, Sanford, transporting his slave, Dred Scott, into the territories north of the Missouri Compromise line. If Congress could legally draw such a line, it was supposed, then Dred Scott would become a free man the moment he stepped across it.

In 1857 the case was heard and decided by a Supreme Court packed with southerners. For all that, the reasoning behind the decision was neither reckless nor irresponsible (as it has sometimes been portrayed), given the assumptions of the time. Writing for the majority, Chief Justice Roger Taney held that Dred Scott had no standing to sue as a "person," for legally speaking he was an article of "property." Thus, the question came down to whether Congress could draw a line across a map and forbid citizens to cross that line at the risk of losing their property. The Court's answer was little in doubt.

Dred Scott v. Sanford may have been sound constitutional law but it was terrible politics. Southerners pounced on it gleefully, for it legalized slavery up and down the West, all the way to California. Northerners went ballistic. The dissonance illustrated the weakness of using constitutional interpretation to resolve intractable political issues. For, in the explosive situation it now faced, how could the Supreme Court enforce its ruling?

Instead of dousing the slavery issue, Taney and his fellow Justices had merely poured oil on the flames. Politicians friendly to the *Dred Scott* decision campaigned on the strength of its transcendent rightness, while those inimical to it began exploring how it could be legally undermined. And the nation edged closer to civil war.

The Switch In Time

Constitutional interpretation had other encounters with politics. During the Progressive Era, for example, the due process clause of the Fourteenth Amendment (to be discussed in a later chapter) was interpreted by the Supreme Court as invalidating many of the state regulatory practices enacted by Progressive reformers. States could not limit working hours or impose health and safety conditions in the workplace, the Court held, because these would have the effect of depriving employers of liberty and property "without due process of law."

Regulating business was almost as hot an issue at the time as slavery had been a century earlier. The reformers railed and fumed at the Supreme Court for its "biased" interpretations. And Justice Oliver Wendell Holmes Jr. came into fame for joining them in dissent. The Constitution, he argued, was not written on tablets of stone—it was "an experiment, as all of life is an experiment." Above all, the Constitution was a means of ascertaining the voice of the people. If the people wanted to regulate business practices they deemed harmful, it was not for nine appointed judges to stand in their way.

Tensions grew even tauter during the Great Depression. Franklin Roosevelt's New Deal sought to use the power of government in unprecedented ways to combat the Depression's worst effects. The Agricultural Adjustment

Act empowered the federal government to intervene massively in the market system by limiting supply, stimulating demand and supporting prices. The National Industrial Recovery Act commissioned cartel monopolies to readjust production and consumption. The problem was, how to find constitutional authority for such innovations? And the only possible answer was the commerce clause.

But there was a roadblock. When the Supreme Court looked back to its own interpretation of the commerce clause in *U.S. v. E.C. Knight*, it found nothing about economic experimentation. On the contrary, "commerce" had been defined so narrowly that it hardly encompassed commerce. Accordingly, in decision after decision, the Court struck down New Deal programs as unconstitutional. The Justices may not have seen themselves as entering the political struggle with these rulings, but that was precisely what they were doing. And dangerously. The demand for federal action was so great that the Court was essentially standing athwart an avalanche.

So the president decided to act. After his decisive election victory in 1936, he denounced the Supreme Court's "horse-and-buggy definition of interstate commerce." Then he proposed that the Court itself be dramatically overhauled and expanded—with his own appointees. The "nine old men" were overburdened, he offered glibly. It was an unparalleled intrusion into the judicial domain.

In the reaction that followed, the president received a jarring setback. It was clear that the American people, for better or worse, had come to accept judicial review as part of the system and were prepared to defend it as such. Their demand that the New Deal act decisively to fight the Depression did not mean—as Roosevelt supposed—that it act against the Supreme Court.

It was at this point that the Court members, recalling Marshall's earlier wisdom, decided it was best to avoid politics after all. Two Justices, Owen Roberts and Charles Evans Hughes, abruptly changed sides and began voting with the Court's New Deal liberals, tilting the balance the other way. Some wag called it "the switch in time that saved nine."

Judicial Legislation

Constitutional interpretation could affect the political process in yet another way. By interpreting the Constitution loosely enough and in a certain spirit, Supreme Court Justices could in effect take over the legislative process themselves.

The temptation to do so was frequently connected with the Bill of Rights, as we have seen. Since a number of the rights were framed broadly and abstractly, it was natural to ask what they amounted to in the context of daily life. What, for example, did the right of privacy actually include? Courts could say yea or nay to specific items as they came up for adjudication—but it was much simpler to spell out a comprehensive answer.

Protestors disputing Roe v. Wade. *The 1972 Supreme Court decision determined that abortion was protected by the Bill of Rights.* (Courtesy of AP/Wide World Photos.)

"Do you ever have one of those days when nothing seems constitutional?"
(Courtesy of Cartoon Features Syndicate.)

In the 1972 case of *Roe v. Wade*, the Supreme Court did just that. It not only placed abortion rights squarely within the privacy doctrine, it went on to detail the conditions under which abortion was and was not to be allowed. In other examples, the federal courts took charge of administering public school systems, staffing municipal fire departments and approving or disapproving a range of governmental policies. Some critics saw this as a usurpation of power. It is for the states to determine such matters by the democratic process, they argued, not for the Supreme Court to do so by fiat.

The dangers of **judicial legislation** are obvious. Supreme Court Justices are not elected by the people, even indirectly, nor are they accountable for their decisions. Conversely, while Court members may sincerely seek "pure" justice, they often also seek outside input. A handful of elite law school professors may have an untold impact on the outcome.

All constitutional interpretation—not just the runaway kind—takes a toll on the rule of law. While Justices can and often do act out of the highest motives, the fact remains that by reinterpreting the Constitution more or less at will, they are altering the fundamental law. And when that happens, expectations based on the stability and continuity of the law are simply left high and dry.

At its longest reach, constitutional interpretation became streaked with the arrogance that attends unchecked power. Americans occasionally heard Chief Justice Charles Evans Hughes' proclamation that "The Constitution is what the Supreme Court says it is." It was repeated in classrooms, lecture halls, textbooks, magazines and newspapers, and affirmed in a rough-and-ready way by each new batch of Supreme Court decisions. Political scientist Ralph C. Hancock points out that if the Constitution is what the Supreme Court says it is, Americans don't need a Constitution at all—just a Supreme Court.

The Constitution Behind the Constitution

A still more difficult question presents itself. Would it be possible *not* to interpret the Constitution? A moment's reflection must prompt us to say, "No." As long as the Constitution presents phrases like "necessary and proper" or "due process of law," *someone* has to interpret it. The question is not just *who?* It is also *how?* We have already seen some of the possibilities.

Is one of the possibilities "correct?" This rather metaphysical question asks us to consider that there might actually be a right way to interpret the Constitution—right according to some broader sense of constitutional truth. We might put the question this way: how would the Framers interpret the Constitution in *our* time?

In order to begin an answer, we must review the idea of natural law. As taught by Cicero, the natural law was the moral law, the law programmed in the

Judicial Legislation

Where does the Constitution say that school segregation is unlawful? Or that prayers may not be permitted in the classroom? Or that representation in state government must be apportioned on the basis of one person, one vote? The short answer is: nowhere. There is, however, a longer answer, which critics call *judicial legislation*. The classic example is the landmark Supreme Court case of *Roe v. Wade* (1973)—the abortion decision.

The case had an odd beginning. A girl represented in the court records as "Jane Roe" walked into a Texas counseling center in 1969 with a lurid tale of molestation by three drunken men on a lonely Georgia roadside. (It was later learned that the story was false.) The real trauma for her was learning that she was pregnant. Her former husband had once beaten her for conceiving, and the child had been taken away by her mother. She seemed a good candidate to challenge the Texas statute outlawing abortion.

Meanwhile, two young Dallas attorneys were looking for just such a candidate. Since graduating from law school at the University of Texas, classmates Sarah Weddington and Linda Coffee had remained active in the local pregnancy counseling center. Under Texas law, the center could not counsel abortion, and that fact severely limited its options. The only thing to do, concluded the two lawyers, was challenge the law in court. In March 1970, they learned of the existence of "Jane Roe."

The case itself was a labyrinth of applications, forms, hearings, appeals, briefs—and expenses. Though the original registration was only one hundred dollars, over the months the tab steadily mounted. Sarah Weddington wound up stumping the state for financial support and quitting her job to devote full time to preparation. But things were moving. From the Federal District Court in Dallas, the case steadily worked its way up the ladder of appeals. By December of 1971, Weddington, who had never yet argued in court, found herself standing before the highest bench in the land.

However well-crafted Weddington's arguments, the case turned in the end on Court politics. Five of the Justices—most of them liberals from the Warren Court—simply believed that abortion was right, and after re-argument the majority was raised to seven. Justice Harry Blackmun, who wrote the majority opinion, stood his justification on the implied right of privacy found in the First, Fourth and Fifth Amendments. And what about the right to life—something the Fourteenth Amendment stated very clearly? That, said Blackmun, who had spent a week of research in the Mayo Clinic library, posed no difficulty, for an unviable fetus was not technically alive.

All of this was not good enough for dissenting Justices Byron White and William Rehnquist, who saw it as an invasion by the courts into the domain of lawmaking. Said White: "In a sensitive area such as this, involving as it does issues over which reasonable men may easily and heatedly differ, I cannot accept the court's [determination]. This issue, for the most part, should be left with the people and to the political process." In other words, according to White, the Court was legislating.

Only much later did it come out that "Jane Roe" hadn't been raped at all. She had cooked up the story, ironically enough, in order to justify having an abortion.

human genes and thus accessible to everyone. It was the reference people had in mind when they used words like *justice*, *equity* and *fairness*. It was, furthermore, the law by which all positive law was to be judged and held accountable. If a legislature passed a law excusing robbery or murder, most human beings would find such a law morally repugnant.

As the English common law developed, it was always with some tacit reference to natural law. The rights of property, for example, or the sanctity of the home were not just arbitrary edicts handed down by judges—they were embodiments of natural law principles. The English constitution also came to reflect these principles. It consisted of documents (such as Magna Carta), traditions and practices, court decisions, legal doctrines, guarantees of rights (such as *habeas corpus*) and an evolved structure of political institutions. It worked as a whole not simply because it was established but also because it met rough-and-ready criteria of human justice.

When the conflict between Parliament and the Stuart monarchy began in the 1600s, jurists began thinking carefully about natural law and its significance. One of them, Sir Edward Coke (pronounced "Cook"), elaborated a set of legal doctrines that would be of importance to American judicial review. In order for judges to interpret the law correctly, Coke argued, they must understand *both* the constitution *and* the natural law. If an action by government, even by the king himself, were in violation of the constitution *or the natural law*, judges of the realm would be honor-bound not to enforce it. This doctrine (which was asserted far more often than actually practiced) explains how it was possible for the English to have constitutionalism without a constitution. For their natural law-based judicial review was able to garner a broad consensus of support.

Still, Coke's ideas eventually passed out of vogue. Parliament itself repudiated them in its drive toward political supremacy, and Blackstone's *Commentaries*—the Bible of the common law—asserted that legislative authority need answer only to itself. In this latter view, judges could not refuse to enforce "unconstitutional" or "immoral" laws, for judges too were bound by the will of Parliament.

Why? Because when judges became the arbiters of vague and amorphous natural law doctrines, an enormous discretionary power was placed in their hands. As nonelected officials, they did not represent the people, nor were they accountable to them. They were shielded from the bumps and abrasions of politics. It was all too easy for them to become legislators, constitution writers, even outright tyrants, all in the name of natural law.

Yet there was one group that refused to abandon Coke—the Americans. They were the last people in the world to suppose that Parliament need answer only to itself. As the great controversy of the Revolution heated up, Americans charged that Parliament was violating both the "constitution" and the "law of nature" when it attempted to tax them arbitrarily. And they kept that doctrine in mind when discussing judicial review later on. Indeed, the whole reason for including judicial review in state constitutions was that it enabled the law of nature to be used as a check on government.

So, why weren't the Americans fearful of judicial tyranny? Theirs wasn't quite the same situation as England's. Spelling out constitutional provisions in black and white—as opposed to England's constitution of tacit understandings—gave the judges far less leeway and thus fewer opportunities for abuse. In

Sir Edward Coke
http://www.thevickerage
.worldonline.co.uk/ecivil/
sir_edward_coke.htm

http://www.commonlaw
.com/Coke.html

the states where judicial review was allowed, judges were held to fairly narrow standards. They could strike down only those acts that clearly and obviously violated the constitution.

If the Framers in Philadelphia also accepted judicial review—and the weight of opinion suggests that they did—they most likely intended a similar standard. For example, *Federalist* 78 argued that Supreme Court Justices would strike down only those laws which violated the "manifest tenor" (i.e. actual wording) of the Constitution. In all other cases they ought to restrain themselves.

Yet, by the nature of things, there was nothing to hold the Justices to this or any other standard, as we have seen. Or was there? Thoughtful students of the Constitution began to consider this question in the context of natural law. If the *English* constitution was supposed to embody natural law in some way, might not the same be said for the *American* Constitution? Many Federalists evidently thought so. During the debate over a bill of rights, these Federalists came up with an intriguing argument. If you start listing out rights, they said, that might be regarded as a rejection of Coke's doctrine. Coke had maintained that the English constitution *already embodied* rights, even though they were not spelled out, because it embodied natural law. If the same could be said for the American Constitution, it was best not to enumerate rights separately—they were already there. Behind the Constitution, in other words, there was a larger, more shadowy constitution, written in the language of right and wrong.

If these observers were correct, then there might well be a philosophically cogent way to apply judicial review. That is, when a questionable passage is to be interpreted, we should always proceed in the light of natural law principles. But doesn't this land us right back in the old dilemma? Isn't natural law too vague and subjective to operate as a standard? The answer depends on *how* one thinks about natural law. If the law of nature is conceived simply as *do what is right* or *avoid doing what is wrong*, that is indeed pretty vague. On the other hand, if the law of nature were to be restated—and brought down to earth—as a coherent constitutional philosophy, the result may be entirely different.

Political scientist Charles Kesler has argued that the Framers in Philadelphia had a specific "moral theory" in mind when they wrote the Constitution, and that theory is crucially important to the practice of judicial review. "Interpreting the Constitution is not an act of will and not an act of discovering a past, particular will," Kesler writes, "but an act of inferring the meaning of particular provisions from the purposes of the Constitution as a whole." Once you understand the Constitution's moral theory, in other words, its ambiguous passages are easier to work out.

In an earlier chapter, we saw what James Madison had to say about the Constitution's moral theory in *Federalist* 43. The Constitution wasn't just a plan of government, he argued, but an embodiment of republicanism's "true principles." Its purpose was to promote "the common good of society" and "the happiness of the people." It comprehended "a due sense of national character" and contemplated "extensive and arduous enterprises for the public benefit." These phrases point to natural law principles. They remind us that the Constitution was regarded by its authors as a means for securing a larger end, one they all understood, one having to do with natural law, and as a consequence any vague or confusing language should always be viewed with that larger end in mind.

A Dramatic Turnabout

Linda Brown, age eleven, a bright-eyed youngster with a bashful smile, had always longed to attend Monroe Elementary with her white friends. Only five blocks from her home in Topeka, Kansas, the school stood like a citadel of forbidden desire. For Linda, like millions of other black children in 1954, was condemned to an all-black, racially segregated school far from home. So when lawyers for the NAACP came seeking plaintiffs for one of their school desegregation cases, Linda Brown gladly signed on.

In theory, *Brown v. The Board of Education of Topeka* had already been decided long ago. For the US Supreme Court, like other courts in the Anglo-American tradition, was supposed to be bound by its own precedents, and for the *Brown* case there was a clear one on the books. Back in 1896 the Court had considered a close cousin of school segregation, segregation in public transportation. And in that case, *Plessy v. Ferguson*, it clearly stated that "separate but equal facilities" for the two races did not violate the Fourteenth Amendment's requirement of equal protection of the laws.

Plessy v. Ferguson, too, had been a test case, and black leaders at the time had feared it as such. "It is of the utmost consequence that we should not have a decision against us," wrote Albion Tourgee to an associate, "as it is a matter of boast with the court that is has *never reversed itself on a constitu-*tional question." They were stunned when the decision came down.

By 1954, however, much had changed. The personnel of the Court had changed, of course, but more important, the world itself had changed. The *Plessy* decision had reflected the world of 1896. At that time most blacks endured a kind of twilight existence in American society. Since then there had been Jackie Robinson in baseball, Duke Ellington in jazz, Sidney Poitier in the movies and Joe Lewis in the ring. There had been *The Invisible Man, Black Like Me, Porgy and Bess, Ebony*. Most important, segregation had come to rub more and more Americans the wrong way.

Nothing better illustrated the new reality than the brilliant black attorneys who had joined the NAACP's legal staff: Charles Houston, James Nabrit, Spotswood Robinson III and Thurgood Marshall. Marshall combined the savvy of a winning trial lawyer with the touch of a down-home politician. He began laying the groundwork for a series of desegregation cases. For assistance, he reached out to the whole of the intellectual community, black and white—psychologists, sociologists, anthropologists, historians, constitutional lawyers—bring scores of them together for marathon brainstorming sessions.

Hearing the *Brown* case on the high bench were Justices Hugo Black, Robert Jackson, Frank Mur-phy and Wiley Rutledge, all of them appointed by Franklin Roosevelt. And sitting beside them were Felix Frankfurter and William O. Douglas, appointed more recently but with even stronger ties to liberal academe. Quite clearly, the sympathies of the Justices lay with the cause of the black plaintiffs.

Sympathetic or not, however, they still had to face the problem of *Plessy v. Ferguson*. In June of 1953, after six months of pondering, the Court called in counsel on both sides and handed them a long list of questions about the original purpose of the Fourteenth Amendment. What the Justices were really asking for was some valid rationale for reversing the *Plessy* decision.

A dramatic turnabout for Linda Brown. (Courtesy of Time Life Syndication. Copyright © 1953 by Time, Inc.)

But no clear rationale could be found. Marshall put no less than forty scholars to the task of researching the Fourteenth Amendment, and the results were at best uncertain. In all the debating back and forth, however, the members of the Court were convinced more than ever that segregation had to go. The new Chief Justice, Earl Warren, who had taken personal custody of the *Brown* case, was not overly concerned with narrow technicalities anyway. For him, the real questions of the law were: Is it right? Is it just? Is it fair?—and school desegregation flunked all three. Urged on by Warren's leadership, the Justices decided to simply overturn the *Plessy* decision, with or without a legal argument—and do it unanimously.

On May 17, 1954, in the Supreme Court's vaultlike chamber, the Chief Justice, in a quiet, emotionless voice, began reading the *Brown* decision to a packed and hushed audience. Before the first page was turned, reporters were racing to the telephones. "In the field of education," Warren said, "the doctrine of 'separate but equal' has no place. Separate educational facilities are inherently unequal. Therefore we hold that the plaintiffs are, by reason of the segregation complained of, deprived of the equal protection of the laws guaranteed by the Fourteenth Amendment." Linda Brown could go to Monroe Elementary at long last.

And *Plessy v. Ferguson*, the tried and true interpretation of the equal protection clause? It was simply tossed into the trash bin of history.

The question might be put this way: *How can the Constitution be interpreted so as to advance the republican cause?* Does a given interpretation enhance civic virtue, strengthen the rule of law, reinforce moral self-governance, promote opportunity? Does it burnish freedom? Expand choices? Facilitate human dignity? If so, chances are it reflects the Framers' "original aspirations."

Present-day judicial activism is often criticized for the want of such a moral theory. Kesler refers to it as "a kind of constitutionalism without the Constitution—natural law without nature." On the other extreme is the **legal positivism** of a Robert Bork, holding that Justices can only interpret the words as they plainly exist, and can only ascribe to them meanings which the Founders themselves specifically intended. This might be called a Constitution without constitutionalism.

With the two poles in mind, constitutional interpretation would seem to be an activity calling out for the Aristotelian mean. The Constitution must be flexible and adaptable to change—yet it must also serve the purpose for which it was originally written, the happiness of the people.

Legal Positivism: A philosophy of law holding that the meaning of the law must be confined to the wording of legal statutes and is not open to any moral considerations behind the law.

Judicial Review and the Founding

The reaction of the American public to Franklin Roosevelt's court-packing scheme underscores an important point. Whatever one may think of judicial review and constitutional interpretation, these have become integral parts of the American Founding.

When the Constitution was ratified, the federal judiciary was not a true coequal with the legislative and executive branches. It was, rather, a specialized court system designed to handle the troublesome litigations federalism would produce. Judicial review altered this situation dramatically and raised the Supreme Court to its own place in the firmament. After that, the Constitution's dynamics all worked differently, as we have seen.

Even in the Supreme Court's occasional arrogance of power, it is still playing the familiar constitutional game, checking, blocking, giving some other authority pause. Moreover, it has often interpreted the Constitution according to the Founders' own measure. Had it never expanded the Bill of Rights, millions would have forgone republican happiness. And had it never stretched the constitutional stretch-points, the federal

The US Supreme Court in 2002. (Courtesy of Consolidated News Photos, Inc.)

government couldn't have acted effectively in the modern world. Thus, John Marshall—"the great Chief Justice"—deserves to be ranked among the Founders themselves. A different hand at the helm in 1801 might well have resulted in a completely different constitutional world today.

It is worth pausing to consider once again the role of fortuity in the American Founding. Judicial review, like federalism and the Bill of Rights, might have been a historical accident, but from the standpoint of constitutional government, it was an extremely serendipitous one. Marshall's boldness and sagacity thus reflect that "deeper wisdom" we have encountered before. Those who look beyond human agency in the American Founding have an additional point to consider.

Suggestions for Further Reading

Leonard Baker, *John Marshall: A Life in Law* (1974).

Edward S. Corwin, *American Constitutional History: Essays by Edward S. Corwin* (1964).

Richard E. Ellis, *The Jeffersonian Crisis: Courts and Politics in the Young Republic* (1971).

Charles G. Haines, *The Role of the Supreme Court in American Government and Politics, 1789–1835* (1944).

Morton J. Horowitz, *The Transformation of American Law, 1780–1860* (1977).

Alfred H. Kelly, Winfred A. Harbison and Herman Belz, *The American Constitution: Its Origins and Development* (1983).

Forrest McDonald, *A Constitutional History of the United States* (1984).

Peter S. Onuf, ed., *Ratifying, Amending, and Interpreting the Constitution* (1991).

G. Edward White, *The Marshall Court and Cultural Change, 1815–1835*, abridged ed. (1991).

CHAPTER 13 STUDY AID

(This aid is not all-inclusive and is not intended to be a substitute for thorough study of the material presented in the textbook.)

Expounding The Constitution

I. Judicial Review

1. Courts to resolve constitutional questions:
   - Deliberate violations for political purposes
   - Different interpretations of Constitution's meaning

2. Judiciary without "energy" or "independent will":
   - Less likely to abuse power
   - Not a player but an umpire
   - Federal laws and treaties supreme law of the land
   - Somebody has to police the Constitution and Congress

3. *Marbury v. Madison* (1803):
   - John Marshall, Chief Justice and Federalist
   - President Adams' "midnight appointments"
   - James Madison's refusal to deliver commissions
   - Marbury and a "writ of mandamus"
   - Constitutional authority to issue such writs at issue
   - Marshall and the Court find portion of the Judiciary Act of 1789 unconstitutional
   - Judicial review established as a precedent—
     ▸ Constitution is fundamental law
     ▸ Courts determine what is law
     ▸ Courts examine and interpret Constitution
     ▸ Anything contrary to the Constitution cannot be law

4. Judicial review and the Constitution:
   - Altered constitutional balances and nature of separation of powers
   - Unsatisfactory alternatives—
     ▸ Congress to interpret Constitution
     ▸ Each branch of government to interpret Constitution
     ▸ States to interpret Constitution
   - Court a check on executive and legislative branches of federal government and states
   - Court has lived up to its assumed responsibilities
   - Constitution works as intended only with judicial review

5. From Judicial Review to Constitutional Interpretation:
   - Review of laws inevitably linked with interpretation of Constitution
   - Ambiguity and stretch-points gave latitude for interpretation
6. *McCulloch v. Maryland* (Bank of United States):
   - Necessary and proper clause
   - Necessary = convenient, useful, and not inappropriate
   - "Broad construction" sanctioned by Supreme Court

II. Reinterpretation

1. Erratic Interpretation:
   - Supreme Court could overrule itself
   - Supreme Court not bound by precedent
   - Interpretation of Constitutional stretch-points and ambiguity (such as the commerce clause) open to debate—more than a matter of semantics
2. *Gibbons v. Ogden* (1824):
   - State versus federal authority—steamboat traffic on the Hudson under the commerce clause
   - "Commerce" = articles of trade, means of transportation and routes employed. "Regulate" = fostering, inhibiting or protecting commerce
   - Enhanced federal power
3. License Cases (1847):
   - States' rights versus nationalism—taxing and regulating interstate sale of liquor
   - Congress not given "sole" power to regulate commerce, just "some" power
   - Enhanced states' power
4. *U.S. v. E.C. Knight* (1895):
   - Interpreting power of government to regulate—American Sugar Refining Co. and the Sherman Anti-Trust Act
   - "Commerce" not same as "manufacturing"
   - Curtailed power of government
5. *Katzenbach v. McClung* (1960s):
   - Extremely broad interpretation of "commerce"—Ollie's Barbeque
   - Indirect impact on commerce through racial discrimination
   - Expansion of federal government power
6. Reinterpretation's motivations:
   - Political—how do Justices perceive themselves—nationalists, states' righters, liberals, etc.
   - Intellectual—response to intellectual currents of the times

- Guardianship—seeking pure justice through judicial activism
- Robert Bork—Justices bound by Framers "original intentions"
- William Brennan—Justices should see Constitution as "lodestar of our aspiration"
- about "original aspirations?" (Professor Ralph C. Hancock)

III. The Supreme Court and Politics

1. *Dred Scott v. Sanford*:
   - The Missouri Compromise and slavery in the territories
   - Dred Scott found to be "property" rather than a legal "person"
   - Could Congress constitutionally place restrictions on use of such "property?" Supreme Court found that it could not
   - Decision intensified debate over slavery and fueled polarization prior to the Civil War

2. The Switch in Time:
   - Franklin D. Roosevelt and the New Deal—reform and the national government's power to regulate
   - What weight to give to the voice of the people in interpreting Constitution? (Note: Supreme Court overruled much of early New Deal even though New Deal initially enjoyed widespread public support.)
   - Roosevelt sought to alter the composition of the Supreme Court and appoint justices favorable to New Deal Roosevelt rebuffed by public opinion; Justices moderate opposition to New Deal

3. Judicial Legislation:
   - *Roe v. Wade* (1972)—interpreting the Bill of Rights.
   - Constitutional interpretation versus the rule of law—altering the fundamental law

IV. The Constitution Behind the Constitution

1. Practically speaking, interpretation cannot be avoided:
   - Who is to interpret?
   - How is Constitution to be interpreted?
   - How would Framers do so in our time?

2. The uses of "natural law":
   - Cicero—"natural law" was moral law
   - Constitutional law must be consistent with moral law
   - English "constitution" had foundation in "natural law"

3. An American view:
   - Coke's argument—constitution cannot stand in violation of "natural law"

- Natural law and natural rights seen as implicit in written constitution
- Written constitution overcomes ambiguity of appeal to "natural law" by limiting judiciary's discretion in reviewing constitutionality of legislative acts
- Can "natural law" be cogently defined as a moral theory and used as a foundation for judicial review?

V. Judicial Review and the Founding

1. Judicial review and constitutional interpretation have become part of the Founding

2. Supreme Court, through application of judicial review, has generally promoted republican ends

3. Judicial review has enabled government to adapt to changing times through evolution rather than revolution

CHAPTER 13 REVIEW QUESTIONS ▬▬▬▬

Key Terms

Judicial Review

John Marshall

Marbury v. Madison

Stretch-points

Commerce Clause

Original Aspirations

Dred Scott v. Sanford

Judicial Legislation

Multiple Choice Questions

1. In colonial days, if a measure approved by a state legislature violated a colony's royal charter, which British court would have jurisdiction over the matter?
   a. The Court of the Exchequer.
   b. The House of Lords.
   c. The Privy Council.
   d. The Court of Common Pleas.

2. The Supreme Court analyzing a congressional law to determine whether or not it comports with the Constitution is an example of:
   a. Judicial Legislation.
   b. Judicial Reinterpretation.
   c. Judicial Review.
   d. None of the above.

3. In which of the Supreme Court decisions discussed in the chapter did the Court use the commerce clause to limit the power of the government to regulate businesses?
   a. *Gibbons v. Ogden.*
   b. *U.S. v. E.C. Knight.*
   c. *Katzenbach v. McClung.*
   d. The License Cases.

4. Sir Edward Coke proposed that for judges to interpret laws correctly, they must understand both the nation's constitution and:
    a. Natural law.
    b. The people's civil rights.
    c. Previous judicial rulings.
    d. Political considerations.

Review Questions

1. What was the Judiciary Act of 1789 and how did it eventually lead to the practice of judicial review by the United States Supreme Court?

    _____

    _____

    _____

    _____

2. How does judicial review impact the way the separation of powers works in the United States government?

    _____

    _____

    _____

    _____

3. Why is the "necessary and proper" clause of Constitution considered a stretch-point? How did the Court interpret that clause in the 1819 case of *McCulloch v. Maryland*?

    _____

    _____

    _____

    _____

4. What were the License Cases about in the 1840s, and how did the Court use the commerce clause in deciding those cases?

    _____

    _____

    _____

    _____

5. Why did President Franklin D. Roosevelt fail in his attempt to diminish the Supreme Court's power of judicial review?

    _____

    _____

    _____

    _____

Review Exercises

1. Compare and contrast the notions of constitutional interpretation, reinterpretation, and judicial legislation.

   _____

   _____

   _____

   _____

2. Explain the notion of a judicial precedent. Does altering those precedents violate the Rule of Law?

   _____

   _____

   _____

   _____

3. Explain how the concept of interpreting the Constitution based on the Founders' original aspirations relates to Robert Bork and William Brennan's ideas discussed in the chapter.

   _____

   _____

   _____

   _____

Big Essay Question

Although it decides many types of cases, few get more attention than the Supreme Court's decisions in cases involving controversial moral issues (examples include burning the flag, prayer in school, terminating pregnancies through abortion, etc.). Which branch of government should make the decision regarding our country's national policy over such issues? Make a case for each of the three branches of government as the primary determiner over those issues, then describe how you think the national government should determine national policy on controversial moral issues.

A Republican People

Pledge of allegiance. (Courtesy of Photo Researchers, Inc.)

As we saw in chapter 1, a true founding not only brings forth a political system, it brings forth a body politic. And a republican founding must necessarily bring forth a republican people.

Did the American Founding create the American people or vice versa? The record suggests that each in its turn had an effect on the other, that the working out of successful republican institutions caused individuals to identify themselves with a common *patria*, and the identification of individuals with a common *patria* made it easier to work out successful institutions.

And what did it take to create a republican people? We have glimpsed some of the components already. It required a common value system, shared experience and a sense of mutual sacrifice. It required a working consensus on political fundamentals. And it required a host of subtle ingredients, everything from battlefield heroes to a national flag. There was place for a national literature, for an indigenous school of painting, for folklore figures, celebratory art, visual imagery, a style of architecture. And not least, it required a set of founding myths.

One might argue that for the Founding to really succeed, it must lead to the formation of an authentic "national character." This phrase appeared often in writings of the day. It may be taken to mean that political, economic and social institutions could take root only among coherent groups displaying common character traits, the belief being that a random collection of individuals, separated from one another and from all sense of community, could never constitute a republic, just as a collection of passersby on the street could never constitute a family.

Yet in a society that prized individual liberty, how were individuals to be forged together? What power was capable of imposing the uniformities that would make a republican community possible? Doubters looked at the Americans from across the Atlantic and predicted it would never come to pass. "Americans," said one, "are not a people, nor can they ever hope to be one. Their manners and morals divide them asunder and will continue to do so."

Complex processes were already at work to thwart that confident prediction. Americans, almost in spite of themselves, began to "Americanize" their world. Bounded roughly by the life span of the

409

founding generation, Americanization added to the Founding by elaborating a political system, an economic system and a society which were in distinctive ways both republican and American.

The American Good Society

In the Declaration of Independence, Jefferson sketched the outlines of an American Good Society:

> We hold these truths to be self-evident, that all men are created equal; that they are endowed by their Creator with certain unalienable Rights; that among these are Life, Liberty and the pursuit of Happiness.

With Jefferson's election to the presidency in 1800, Americans began to explore the meaning of this Founding Proposition and test it against the boundaries of reality. They accomplished this partly by living their own lives and seeking their own happiness, but they also attempted to fit their individual experience into a larger design.

To begin with, Americans began to see republican significance almost everywhere. There were those, for example, who consciously adopted simplicity of dress, speech and manners, as they believed would befit a republican people. There were others, in a similar spirit, who began employing classical forms in architectural design, invoking a republican past. Popular culture reflected the new spirit too. Heroes of the Revolution, in togas and garlands, found themselves in company with heroes of antiquity on everything from posters and pamphlets to book covers, lithographs, even Aunt Emma's tole painting.

As Americans became ever more conscious of classical parallels, they became ever more mindful of the role of civic virtue. A popular play of the time, Royall Tyler's *The Contrast*, juxtaposed satirical portraits of America's virtuous simplicity and England's decadent foppishness. The hero of the play, Colonel Manly, won the damsel's heart, as we might expect, precisely because he embodied true virtue.

Political sermons stressed the same point. Intoned Samuel Adams, the Boston rabble-rouser who had done much to bring on the Revolution:

> Neither the wisest constitution nor the wisest laws will secure liberty and happiness of a people whose manners are universally corrupt. If we are universally vicious and debauched in our

George Washington clad in a Roman toga. The desire to create heroes remains strong. (By Horatio Greenough, 1840, courtesy of the National Museum of American Art/Smithsonian Institution. Marble, 345.4 × 259.1 × 209.6 cm.)

manners, though the form of our Constitution carries the face of the most exalted freedom, we shall in reality be the most abject of slaves. Whether or not America will be able to enjoy its hard-won independence and freedom . . . depends on her virtue.

Accompanying virtue was "feeling." While Tyler's *Contrast* was packing theaters in New York, Henry Mackenzie's novel *The Man of Feeling* was at the top of the best-seller list. This too provided a clue to the way Americans were sorting out their republican identity. The man of feeling was one who eased the sufferings of others and reached out to the helpless and vulnerable. For a case in point, there was Joseph Warren, a promising young medical doctor who put aside his pacifist qualms and shouldered arms in the Battle of Bunker Hill. Warren became an American hero not because of his death in battle but because of his "sympathy." It was yet another term borrowed from David Hume, and its significance had to do with theories of the time about the nervous system. Sympathy was believed to be the agent conducting nerve impulses through the body. It also—and this was the real point—created moral sensitivity. Only those graced with true sympathy were fit to live republican lives and be trusted with political power. They alone could rise above the world—and change the world for the better.

Joseph Warren:
http://theamericanrevolution
.org/people/jwarren.asp

Europeans caught the sense of excitement. So many Enlightenment theories appeared to be taking on reality in the American Republic. Travelers began arriving for a firsthand look. Nicholas Cresswell, the Marquis de Barbé-Mabois and the Marquis de Chastellux were only three of those who toured extensively and took notes. What was the American Good Society really like? they asked.

Here is the sort of answer they came up with. Barbé-Mabois and a French companion, strolling through the Massachusetts countryside on an early autumn day, encountered a prosperous-looking farmer, to whom they put a series of questions. Who possessed the high and low justice in his district? What were the feudal rents and dues? Were the tithes heavy? Was the forced labor frequent and painful? What about the taxes, the prohibitions, the penalties? Who were the lords of the village and how did the farmer get on with them? Strangely enough, the man had no idea what they were talking about. "We could not make him understand at all what sort of beings lords of the village were," Barbé-Mabois reported, "and he could not distinguish the idea of superiority from that of magistracy." As for high and low justice, "He told us that justice was neither high nor low in America, but perfectly fair and equal for everyone."

Whether as description or prophecy, the Founding Proposition was beginning to have effect. An American Good Society was taking shape.

American Life

Colonial society had always been tied in some way to that of the mother country. But the Revolution had dramatically cut the tethers. In its aftermath, some Americans could no longer abide the drinking of tea—which they took to be a symbol of Englishness—and discovered a preference for coffee. Writers

Noah Webster:
http://m-w.com/about/
noah.htm

experienced a similar revulsion for Shakespeare and Milton, asking if there wasn't more interesting material to be found in the Hudson Valley or the New England town. One of these, Noah Webster, even set to work on a dictionary of the "American" language.

Americanization was viewed not simply as change but as transformation—even rejuvenation. Said Michel-Guillaume Jean de Crèvecœur, a Frenchman living in New York, "Every thing has tended to regenerate [the Americans]; new laws, a new mode of living, a new social system; here they are become men." As the travelers surveyed the American scene, what was it that caught their attention and prompted such exuberance?

The Family Farm

Most Americans were farmers. According to Jackson Turner Main's statistics for 1776, forty percent of them made their living by working their own farms, while thirty percent worked on farms owned by others. Another group, much smaller, owned large commercial plantations, the sort that would be romanticized in antebellum novels. The segment of the population (roughly ten percent) who were professionals, businessmen or urban artisans frequently owned modest farms as well, and even those townsmen who didn't might keep a cow, run a few chickens or tend a vegetable garden. Things of the earth were familiar to them.

The importance of farming was linked to the importance of family. The birthrate in America was near the biological maximum, and families were often extended—with aunts, uncles, cousins and grandparents, all under the same roof—rather than nuclear. Thirty-five percent of Americans lived in households of seven or more, and sixty-six percent in households of five or more. So many children made for a young population. In prewar Connecticut, thirty-two percent of the white inhabitants were under the age of ten, and more than half were under the age of twenty.

Owing to transportation difficulties, most farm families were isolated and on their own. Thus they had to be both self-contained and self-reliant. Everyone had to labor in the fields, especially in crucial times such as the harvest, women and children not excepted. And the latter always had assigned chores, such as milking the cows, which had to be done no matter what. Farm children learned responsibility.

They also learned to give and take. If the family was an economic unit, it was a social, cultural and educational unit as well. Older children minded the younger ones and taught them the ABCs. The arts of cooking, sewing, spinning, weaving, soap making, candle making, plowing, planting and the like were integrated into the family routine. It is significant that family portraits of the time show children as diminutive adults.

Children as miniature adults. A Puritan family portrait, 1670.
(*The Mason Children: David, Joanna, and Abigail*, courtesy of The Fine Arts Museums of San Francisco.)

As a practical matter, a single parent could not raise a family while also running the farm. Accordingly, escape from a tyrannical husband or pathological wife was extremely difficult, and separation other than by death was rare. Yet Alexis de Tocqueville, touring in the 1830s, noted that the American family was based on ties of affection far more than its European counterpart. There was less friction between the generations and less rivalry among siblings. On their own in a frontier world, family members needed one another to an extent we would have trouble imagining today. And perhaps they truly were "sympathetic."

Farm life was rustic, to be sure, but not without its own bucolic charm. It is significant that when Currier and Ives began mass-producing lithographs in the 1830s, most of their works portrayed idealized country life. Such depictions clearly reflected an American self-image.

The Plain-Style Home

For most Americans, life was of Arcadian simplicity. Dwellings consisted of a small wooden frame house covered with shingles or clapboard. The main floor was taken up by a living room with a large brick or stone fireplace at one end and a door at the other. All family activities were concentrated here. On a given evening, children might be playing, father dozing or reading before the fire, mother spinning or weaving, grandparents recounting stories of the good old days. The sense of togetherness we might find stifling was yet another of life's givens. It was a school for interpersonal skill development—not to say a school for the political arts.

While parents slept in the living room, children usually slept upstairs in the loft, accessed by a ladder. Plainness was once again the order of the day. Beds were of rope strung across a wooden frame and softened by a straw-filled mattress. Loft rooms were unheated, and on cold winter nights bed warmers, filled with coals from the fire, were a must. Sleeping three to a bed was not unusual.

All furnishings were simple. There would likely be a trestle table with benches, two or three plain wooden chairs and a single piece of furniture with pretense of style, generally a sideboard for the storage of utensils. Meat was roasted on spits over the open fire, turned gingerly by a child, while blackened iron kettles of beans or stew hung from nearby swivel hooks. There was often a beehive oven by the chimney for baking bread.

Beyond this, there wasn't a great deal. A spinning wheel perhaps, a crude loom, a rack over the fireplace for the family rifle—which was anything but a decoration—and pegs along the walls for hanging articles of clothing. Most eating utensils were wooden and well used. Windows were few, for even the waviest of glass was expensive. Most houses had oak floors covered with rag rugs. Any light not supplied by the fire came from tallow candles or whale-oil lamps.

Privies were located well away from the house. To answer the inconvenience of nocturnal trips—especially in winter—Americans made use of chamber pots fashioned of heavy crockery. And with family members sleeping together in a single room, privacy as we know it was simply unimagined. For the weekly bath, which typically took place on a Saturday night, water had to be heated on the hearth and poured into a wooden tub. The soap used was homemade and high-powered, and to conserve both it and the heated water, family members bathed serially—the last of them stepping into a blue-gray slurry.

Simplicity did not mean impoverishment. Americans ate better than most people today. They consumed an extraordinary amount of meat, roughly half a pound per person per day, and all sorts of fresh fruits and vegetables in season. While meat was generally smoked or salted for preservation, fresh meat was not a rarity, and out on the frontier hunting and fishing made a contribution of their own. Bread was home baked and reported to be delicious. Fresh milk, fresh butter, fresh eggs and homemade cheese rounded out the meal.

Along with the heavy consumption of food was a heavy consumption of alcohol. It too was often homemade—apple cider, peach brandy, home-brewed beer—and was said to pack a wallop. With few outside activities available, it enlivened many a long winter's evening. Americans, moreover, held their liquor well. Drunkenness was considered to be in bad taste.

To appreciate what this level of consumption signified, we must remember how meager, by contrast, was the diet of most Europeans. Indeed, Americans had the highest standard of living in the world. Their longevity, around thirty-five years, may not seem impressive by present-day standards, but the numbers were skewed by infant mortality. Most parents could expect to lose one or two children in the early years of life, and there were families who lost four and five. If one made it to adulthood, however, the statistics improved markedly and became much like those of the present.

Education was rudimentary by our standards, and except for New England, where public schools were well established, there was no systematic attempt to spread learning. Still, Americans had a high degree of literacy. Some of it was a product of the log schoolhouse, to be sure, but much of it came from the family hearthside once again. Older children taught the younger ones. Mothers bore a hand. Itinerant teachers were employed by local families for a few weeks at a time in exchange for room and board.

Such was the life of Jefferson's tillers of the soil. Its relevance to republicanism ought to be clear. Nor was it mere happenstance that rural Americans commonly regarded themselves as better than their urban counterparts—and much better than their European forebears. Living close to the land meant living in accordance with Nature, and that in turn meant living in accordance with Truth.

City and Town Life

A mere ten percent of Americans lived in towns or cities. And of the latter, only five—Philadelphia, New York, Boston, Newport and Charleston—had populations over 25,000 at the time of the Revolution. For all that, they had well-developed urban cultures. Indeed, Carl Bridenbaugh found them to surpass all English cities except London.

The world of the cities was markedly different from that of the countryside. Where life on the farm was simple and spartan, that of the city was complex and affluent. American cities were centers of sophistication. Their social structure was variegated and stratified. The city's thriving commercial life gave rise to conspicuous consumption and an equally conspicuous distance between rich and poor. Where the countryside looked back to a European past, the cities looked forward to an American future.

Boston, for example, was far advanced in the development of urban amenities. It had a good police force, subterranean sewer lines and the very latest in fire-fighting technology. Its medical establishment was on the cutting edge too. In the use of vaccination for the prevention of smallpox or in developing the newest treatments for scarlet fever, the city enjoyed international renown. As a publishing center, Boston was right behind London—and Philadelphia was right behind Boston. Bostonians contributed more scholarly papers to the Royal Society than the ten leading provincial cities of the British Empire.

The cities were places of economic specialization. There were rope mills and ironmongeries and a variety of manufacturing establishments. Boston was home to a robust marine insurance industry, while Charleston specialized in factoring agricultural commodities. The Philadelphia College of Physicians was something like the Mayo Clinic of its day—the place to send the hard cases—and New York was a shipbuilding center. Newport, alas, was the North Atlantic headquarters of the slave trade.

Rochester, New York after the completion of the Erie Canal. Market centers became bustling metropolises.
(Courtesy of the New-York Historical Society.)

American cities were equally well graced with amusements. Puritan Boston frowned on the theater, to be sure, but New York and Philadelphia soon had several excellent ones. In the South, when the scorching heat of summer drove the rice and indigo planters to their cool Charleston townhouses, cotillions began to flower. Philadelphia was the home of poets and painters, a couple of them known throughout Europe, and all American cities had good libraries. New York led the way in cosmopolitanism: its inhabitants spoke more than twenty-five different languages.

On the other side, American cities were beginning to show forth their own difficulties. They harbored illicit gambling, gangland racketeering and back-alley prostitution, to say nothing of Tammany-style corruption. Tenement slums were beginning to encroach on respectable neighborhoods. There were indigents and vagrants in the streets, and in certain neighborhoods a high incidence of crime. In Philadelphia, the city jail, some four stories high, was right across the street from the State House, and as delegates to the Constitutional Convention strolled past, they could see the prisoners holding their caps out on long beggars' poles and hear their pleading and cursing.

The world of the cities was not only different from that of the countryside, it was strangely fascinating. The palatial townhouses, the ornate carriages, the fashionably dressed women, the sparkling social gaiety exerted an almost hypnotic appeal. If it was to be lamented that a Robert Morris could wind up in the Prune Street debtors' prison, it was not to be forgotten that his mansion overlooking the Schuylkill boasted of an icehouse, a hothouse and a stable for twelve horses, and that a French visitor had declared its luxury superior to that of "any commercial voluptuary of London."

The city had played an important role in the American Revolution. It brought power and leadership together and concentrated urban sophistication in critical mass. It was in the city that protests against British policy had begun and Americans had taken their first measures against it. City life—buzzing, restless, often in disequilibrium—provided ready-made dissatisfactions, and in the American Republic it would continue to do so.

But even more relevant to the future was the city's dynamic pluralism. The city was a place not of one truth but many, each of them jostling for favor. To the extent that modern republicanism would require creative solutions, cross-fertilized from many contending ideas, the city was where it would happen.

Small towns were far more numerous than large cities. They ranged from a few hundred people to a few thousand. Sometimes the towns were tightly packed settlements on the order of the New England village. More often they were townships—that is, subdivisions of counties with a rudimentary structure of government.

These polities were equally important to Americans. Most people identified with their towns second only to their families, and they eagerly took part in local politics. The community at hand was often of more interest than the distant, glittering metropolis, for its schools, churches and business enterprises were the ones that really mattered.

Transportation, in the world of the Founding, was both difficult and dangerous. Overland travelers averaged no more than fifty miles a day, and they were miles full of hardship. Many Americans rarely left their own township. And with no mass media (other than newspapers), contact across the state was not extensive. Accordingly, there was little chance for cultural uniformities to develop.

America became a veritable patchwork of variety. There was much in the way of local color and distinctiveness. Habits, customs, folklore, patterns of speech and perceptions of other locales all reflected the patchwork effect. Even so, Americans of the most disparate backgrounds came to feel themselves bound together. That the Founding had worked, had proven itself and had introduced the sort of peace the Founders had promised tied one community to another, one state to another and, increasingly, one region to another.

And the Founding, in turn, was supported by those selfsame elements of happiness. The simplicity of farm life. The widespread ownership of property. The diffusion of initiative and responsibility. The localization of power. The sophistication of the city. And a conviction that the way it all fit together was unique.

An Emerging National Character

As far as Alexis de Tocqueville was concerned, Americans of the early 1830s did not yet possess a true national character. Yet many of his own observations attested just the opposite. At the very least, such a character was in the process of emerging, and Tocqueville, along with others, studied it with absorbed fascination. Americans as a people tended to be:

Optimistic. They looked to the future with confidence, trusting that tomorrow would be better than today. "America," an observer noted, "is the only country on earth that could be born in perfection and yet aspire to progress." Indeed, Progress—with a capital "P"—became an American cult. Believers accepted that the lives of individuals would continue to improve, that per capita income would steadily rise, that science and technology would surmount all human difficulties, and that American institutions would prosper the cause of truth.

Self-Reliant. Americans saw themselves as a can-do, go-ahead sort of people. They viewed life as a series of challenges and it was up to each person to meet those challenges as they came. Their speech was full of homey aphorisms—"If at first you don't succeed, try, try again"—and their popular literature full of tips for self-help. If you failed at one venture, you were supposed to try another. If you couldn't make a go of it here, you packed up and went somewhere else. Self-reliance was entrepreneurial by definition. Americans were ever and always in search of what they called the "main chance."

Innovative. New lands, observed Tocqueville, were more hospitable to new ideas. In America, where there were few established traditions and still fewer accepted orthodoxies, there was more room for innovation and creativity. This was particularly evident in the American taste for mechanical innovation. One side effect of the Founding was a spurt—and then a surge—of progress in the "mechanical arts."

Here are three quick examples. The rifle, with its absurdly long barrel and corkscrew "rifling," violated every tenet of ordnance design, yet it proved to be chillingly effective in battle. Interchangeable-parts manufacturing, pioneered by Eli Whitney, would soon have a revolutionary effect on all industrial processes, for instead of hand fitting each part to every other, artisans could assemble muskets or tackle blocks from randomly selected components. And finally, the cotton gin, another of Whitney's brainchildren, would comb sticky seeds from cotton fiber and usher forth a world-shaping new industry.

"Yankee ingenuity" was not limited to mechanical innovation. Americans searched for new avenues of commercial activity, new types of business organization, new entrepreneurial ideas, new products and services and much else.

Eli Whitney/Cotton Gin:
http://www.geocities.com/
Heartland/Pointe/3048/bio/
WHITNEY/eliwhitney.html

Practical-Minded. Americans had little taste for aristocratic learning. They did not excel in scientific inquiry, speculative philosophy or high literature. They often renounced theory in favor of practice.

On the other hand, they had few equals at down-to-earth problem solving. Applied science and mathematics, engineering, experimental agriculture and the like were precisely their cup of tea. They distinguished themselves in machine technology, bridge building, ship design, mining techniques, industrial processes and scientific farming.

Practical emphasis led to a mode of thinking that would eventually be called "pragmatism." Philosophically, pragmatists cared less about doctrinal purity than working result. They focused on clear understanding and effective outcome—the "how" rather than the "why" questions. Pragmatism was well suited to the Progress that Americans looked for. It was less well suited to their moral idealism.

Restless. Americans were never quite satisfied with the world. They always wanted more and better. And when they got it, they seemed to feel an inner emptiness rather than a sense of fulfillment. Restlessness led them to change directions abruptly. They sold the farm and moved to town. They switched jobs. They joined various organizations, tried different churches, took up hobbies. When there were rumors of a gold strike somewhere, they trooped off *en masse*.

Restlessness drove Americans toward geographic mobility, moving from place to place in order to improve their fortunes in the world. It also promoted social mobility. With changes in circumstance, Americans frequently moved from the working class into the owning class—and back again. There was a rapid circulation of property.

Ultimately, restlessness had to do with self-creation. Immigration itself was a self-creative act, a pulling up of Old World roots and their transplantation abroad. And once the immigrants got to America, the process of pulling up and putting down had a way of continuing. American jobs, American schools, American social climbing all had forms of self-creation in view—exercises for the none too complacent. "You are," said Americans, "what you make of yourself."

Immigrant family: following the American Dream.
(Courtesy of the Library of Congress.)

Materialistic. Americans often viewed the world in terms of wealth, convenience and creature comforts. They strongly valued economic prosperity and general well-being. As the log or clapboard house of the Revolutionary era gave way to more refined circumstances, Americans became preoccupied with housing, furnishings, conveyance, personal raiment and a proliferating variety of gadgets.

Material objects were not only valued in their own right but as symbols of success and social worth. Historian Richard Bushman has pointed out that the acquisition of certain goods denoted genteel status. As a result, Americans strained their incomes to acquire a piano, lace curtains or heavy brocade draperies, a cupboard full of china, a collection of leather-bound books.

Materialism could and did lead to aggressive behavior. Unfriendly observers called Americans "the most grasping people on earth."

Idealistic. Out of keeping with their materialism, Americans also continued to be highly—some would say naively—idealistic. Their public discourse was full of allusions to justice, honor, duty and the like—the language of classical virtue. American patriotism employed this language with particular emphasis.

Americans also focused on what might be called applied Christianity. Honesty and integrity, concern for the less fortunate, the tenets of common decency often made their way into everyday speech. America became what historian

The Inventor as Popular Hero

Although he declared that genius was 99 percent perspiration and only 1 percent inspiration, Thomas Alva Edison himself had some mighty inspirational strokes. One day in 1878, he sat down at his desk with a pencil and paper and worked up a sketch of a contraption. His assistant, John Kruesi, who was good at translating such sketches into actual working models, took the drawing, which looked rather like a doodle, and went to work. A week later, the two of them adjusted levers and screws and turning the crank, began

Thomas Edison, inventor. (Courtesy of Art Resource.)

speaking into a mouthpiece. "Mary had a little lamb, its fleece was white as snow. . . ." And lo and behold, the machine talked back.

The phonograph was only one of Edison's masterstrokes. He also invented the automatic telegraph, the quadruplex telegraph system, the improved stock ticker, the carbon telephone transmitter, the iron-alkaline storage battery, the movie camera and projector, the electric power plant and its entire transmission system, synthetic rubber, and a host of other things, eventually holding more than 1,300 patents. Oh, yes, and the light bulb.

Around such an individual there necessarily swirled a certain amount of folklore. Tellers of after-dinner stories loved to recount how, on his wedding night, Edison excused himself from the reception to check on something out in his workshop, and how his new bride, after waiting hours for his return, ventured out to the shop and found him busily engaged with a project.

Most of the Edison stories had a certain point to make. Edison, it was said, was notoriously slow-witted as a child. He almost drowned while exploring a shipyard. Schoolteachers found him impossible to teach, dis-

missed him as "addled," and after three months asked him to leave. He was fired from the Grand Trunk Railroad, where he worked as a newsboy, after his chemical experiments started a fire in the baggage car.

This was the Edison people remembered. They did not remember the Edison who conducted lengthy and furious court battles over patent infringement, who established the General Electric Corporation and sought to make it into a giant monopoly, and who felt at home in the world of Carnegie, Rockefeller and Ford. For what was important in the popular conception of Thomas Edison was his very ordinariness. He was thought of as *an* American, *the* American, almost *any* American. He came from a common family and a humble background. He lacked the advantages of breeding and education. He had no connections, no mentors, no patrons. He pulled himself up by his own bootstraps and perfected his own God-given intelligence.

Had Horatio Alger Jr. chosen to make an inventor the protagonist of one of his stories, he could have hardly improved on the real-life career of Thomas Edison. For Edison was an authentic rags-to-riches hero.

Andrew Burstein has called a "sentimental democracy." "Transfixed on noble ideals of liberty and happiness," Burstein writes, "Revolutionary Americans fashioned the dictates of sensibility into a romantic image of themselves."

God-Fearing. Puritanism had not disappeared in America—it had diffused into society. And here and there it continued to pop up. Even in the cities, for example, it was wholly unacceptable for women to wear makeup or for men to utter forbidden words such as *garter, leg, knee, skirt*.

Most Americans expressed belief in a Calvinistic God. Such a Deity was noted for His power and majesty more than, say, love and kindliness. He saved and damned whom He would, without explanation. As a result, human life was full of sorrow and uncertainty and the human heart was inclined toward sin.

In the Puritan view, the average Christian could never be a saint and must content himself with mere mortality. The best one could hope for was to work hard, save wisely, invest with prudence and let one's modest human accomplishments glorify the name of the Lord.

This kind of piety easily transcended formal church affiliation. It also erupted, periodically, into passionate religious revivalism—with its overwhelming sense of guilt.

Suspicious. Paranoia was yet another legacy of the Puritans. If God was active in the world, so was Satan—and his many minions. The minions, unfortunately, took the unwelcome form of Catholicism—an old Puritan bugaboo—Freemasonry and anything strange, exotic or foreign. Americans had settled notions of middle-class propriety to go along with their middle-of-the-road politics. Their magazine heroes were always clean-cut, red-blooded and "wholesome." Anything too far out of the middle-class norm was downright suspect.

Emerging Social Patterns

These elements of national character gave rise to—and were reflected in—distinctive social patterns. And it was within such patterns that the growth and development of republican institutions was to take place.

Individualism

Americans were often seen to possess a rough-and-tumble individualism, occasionally bordering on anarchy. "This fierce spirit of liberty," Edmund Burke had said, "is stronger . . . probably than in any other people of the earth." It was especially pronounced in the backcountry, which after the Revolution opened into the expanding frontier. Rugged and raw, this land was viewed by Americans more or less as the West would someday be portrayed by Hollywood.

Just how individualism became American is something of a mystery, but we can identify at least some of its sources. One of these, surely, lay in the circumstances of immigration, for those who put home behind them were less attached to society as such. Then, too, there was property ownership and the personal independence it conveyed, along with the fact that social controls grew weaker as one approached the frontier. And finally, there was that American feeling of equality to think about. Americans rarely found themselves looking over their shoulders at elders, overseers, foremen or office managers. Often they saw nobody above them but God.

American individualism was tempered by a strong emphasis on moral self-governance—another aspect of the Puritan heritage—and by an equally strong respect for the law. It was curious, travelers observed, how Americans could be at once so individualistic and yet so orderly.

Tocqueville made some canny observations about this puzzling combination. He noted that in Europe "patriotism of place" was romantic and sentimental: those who cherished their community did so out of purely virtuous motives. In America, by contrast, there was a more calculated understanding that the well-being of one's community was bound up with the well-being of oneself. Thus, the most self-serving person imaginable might conclude that it paid to be socially aware. "Enlightened self-interest," Tocqueville termed it.

His second observation was more pessimistic. Americans, thought Tocqueville, might be led by their self-interest to a condition we would probably call *privatism*. That is, individuals might lose social interest altogether, in favor of their own little world:

> To physical gratifications, the heart, the imagination, and life itself are unreservedly given up till, in snatching at these lesser gifts, men lose sight of those more precious possessions which constitute the glory and greatness of mankind. By these means, a kind of virtuous materialism may ultimately be established in the world, which would not corrupt but dissipate the soul and noiselessly unbend its springs of action.

America's ever more consumption-driven society has not refuted this critique. For example, in his analysis of consumer advertising in the twentieth century, Sut Jhally argues that Americans have never become "a people" as such, only a collection of individuals. Jhally points to the seductions of advertising as a constant reinforcement of American privatism. What counts is my life, my dreams, my ambitions, my desires—nothing else.

Egalitarianism

The distance between rich and poor was not nearly as great in America as it was in Europe. Virtually everyone owned property, and most of that was in small farms rather than large seigniorial estates. At the time of the Revolution, 95% of the land was in the hands of the common people.

Cheap land made it relatively easy to acquire a farm. It also kept wages high, for as soon as laborers got ahead, they began to think about setting out on their own. As a result, most permanent laborers were skilled artisans and relatively well paid.

Enjoying a rough equality of circumstances and exact equality before the law, Americans came to believe that all said and done, one person was more or

Ragged Dick and the American Dream

Richard Hunter, age fourteen, lived the life of a bootblack in the streets of New York. He had been orphaned as a small child and was quite on his own. He was not a model boy. He smoked, gambled and sometimes even swore. He was careless with extra earnings, too, spending frivolously for plays at the Old Bowery Theater and liberally treating friends to oyster stews. But he was manly and self-reliant, and wholly above doing anything dishonorable. He slept in the streets wherever a nook was available and dressed pretty much in rags. Indeed, he went by the nickname "Ragged Dick."

On the street one day, Dick spied a well-dressed boy about his own age talking to an older man. Overhearing the conversation, he gathered that the strangers were en route to Connecticut where the boy was to be enrolled at a boarding school. Further, the boy could use a guide and chaperon for the day while his uncle conducted some business. So Dick offered his services. It proved to be the turning point in his life.

For the boy, Frank, and his uncle turned out to be quite unlike anyone Dick had ever known. They had a purpose in life, knew exactly what they were doing, and from the beginning sought to make Dick think of better things. "A good many distinguished men have once been poor boys," Frank lectured earnestly. "There's hope for you, Dick, if you'll try."

Dick was completely taken back. "Nobody ever talked to me so be-fore," he said. "They just called me Ragged Dick, and told me I'd grow up to be a vagabond . . . and come to the gallows."

"Telling you so won't make it turn out so," Frank replied. "If you'll try to be somebody, and grow up into a respectable member of society, you will. You may not become rich—it isn't everybody that becomes rich, you know—but you can obtain a good position, and be respected."

What must he do? The advice poured forth in a torrent. He must stop smoking, stop gambling, stop sleeping in the streets, stop going to the theater and stop wasting his money on oyster stew. He must be honest, faithful, kind and moral in all things. He must work hard, learn thrift, invest wisely and, above all, find a way to gain an education. Frank and his uncle even set him on the path with five dollars and a suit of Frank's old clothes.

"Thank you for your advice," said Dick at the end of the day. "There ain't many that take an interest in Ragged Dick."

With that, Dick Hunter under-took to change his life. He gave up his bad habits, took a room at a boarding house, opened a savings account at the bank. Seen no more at the Old Bowery Theater, he went to bed early, slept well and arose in the morning to eat a good hearty breakfast. Getting educated was a little more difficult but not much. Dick discovered that a fel-low bootblack, Fosdick, was quite well learned—he had been or-phaned by a genteel family—so the two of them worked out an arrangement whereby Fosdick could share Dick's room free of charge in exchange for tutoring him in the basics.

In the meantime, there were a host of adventures in Ragged Dick's life. His bankbook was stolen by a fellow boarder, and by turns he solved the mystery. He outsmarted a pair of swindlers. He roundly drubbed a bully who ridiculed him for "puttin' on airs." And he met Ida, a nine-year-old with a silvery laugh, whose well-to-do parents, seeing the transformation in Dick's life, invited him out to their stately home for Sunday dinner.

Ragged Dick was first published in 1867. (Courtesy of Corbis Images.)

We encounter Dick Hunter again a year later—and what a change had come over him! He could read. He could write. He mastered some grammar, a little geography and the fundamentals of arithmetic. And with markedly improved speech and manners, he radiated an air of self-confidence. That quality came in handy the day Ragged Dick got his big break.

He was on a ferryboat at the time, seated near the rail. A child slipped and fell into the water, and it appeared that he would drown. But Dick, who could "swim like a top," dove in straightaway and pulled the boy out. At that point, the lad's grateful father, who was as impressed with Dick's bearing as with his presence of mind, promptly offered him a job in his countinghouse—for triple the going wages. Dick accepted, of course, for ever since that encounter with Frank and his uncle, he knew he was destined to succeed.

"Here ends the story of Ragged Dick," explained his creator, Horatio Alger Jr. "He is Ragged Dick no longer. He has taken a step upward, and is determined to mount still higher."

Mere kitsch? Far from it. The story of Ragged Dick, told over and over with different titles and characters, was quite possibly the most important piece of literature in nineteenth-century America. For Ragged Dick was everyman: every lean and hungry immigrant, every discontented farm boy, every homeless urchin in the crowded city streets. And America was his oyster. In Italy, in Serbia, in Ireland or the Ukraine, the poor were condemned to their poverty; but in the United States of Andrew Carnegie and John D. Rockefeller, poor boys—or at least so the story held—could make it to the top. "From rags to riches" was how it was put. It was called the American Dream.

less as good as another. Manifest inequalities in wealth, intelligence, social skills and the like tended to be compensated for in other categories, Americans believed, so that instead of a hierarchy of excellence, as in aristocratic societies, their world was a patchwork of acceptable differences. John Adams spoke of the "equality of knowledge, wealth, and power."

In an egalitarian society, ability and accomplishment were more important than family name, social rank or formal status. And there was a new emphasis on the tearing away of artificial barriers. Ethnic identity, national origins, religious affiliation, educational attainment—important standards of the past—lost much of their force in the new republic. Within limits, good people were where you found them.

Substantial equality made for markedly increased opportunity. For the obstacles that barred Europeans from such opportunity had much to do with aristocratic modes of thinking. In Europe, children were supposed to take the place their parents had occupied in a stable, hierarchical society. In America, by contrast, there were no places to take. Egalitarianism pointed toward a fluid, dynamic society, where everything was in constant motion and competition determined who got what.

Open channels of communication increased opportunity too. The person with the better idea was far more likely to win a hearing for it in America. (Many innovations in machine design came from the operators themselves, able to make their voices heard in the front office.) Opportunity was further enhanced by cheap land, open spaces, high mobility and innovative ways of thinking and doing. To a large extent, people were responsible for creating their own chances in the world.

In such a society, it was virtually impossible for aristocracy to gain a foothold. The wealthy enjoyed some of the amenities of the aristocratic life but they could never establish themselves as a permanent class apart. In the end, the differences between the classes came down to wealth alone—and wealth could be a very unstable commodity.

Egalitarianism produced its own set of myths. One of these might be called the Cult of the Common Man. Americans began to celebrate the Common Man as a kind of romantic ideal. It was the Common Man, with his storied combination of integrity and horse sense, who gave American society its dynamic creativity and rugged strength—or at least so the myth held. It was the Common Man who was breaking new lands to the plow, tinkering with new forms of machinery, trying out new kinds of entrepreneurship—improving the world as he improved his own fortunes. We can recognize the Common Man as a classical character type—one that combined the best features of republicanism and democracy.

A second egalitarian myth would eventually be called the American Dream. In America, this myth held, a poor boy (often portrayed as an immigrant) could go from rags to riches. As celebrated in the tales of **Horatio Alger Jr.**, the American Dream depended only on moral virtues—hard work, frugality, fortitude, self-reliance—which could be cultivated by anyone. God intervened in the process, generally in the form of astounding luck, because God favored the plucky. But the real benefactor was America.

Equality of opportunity, the American version of egalitarianism, wished all to be wealthy and powerful—in contrast to equality of result, which wished all to be poor and humble. It drew force from nearly every facet of the American character.

Community

The picture of a dynamic society composed of self-interested individuals needs to be counterbalanced by a strong emphasis on community. For that too was intrinsically American.

Families were communities in their own right. So were towns and townships, crossroad villages, rural counties, southern plantations and individual states. All of these had strong claims upon the identity and affections of Americans.

Community was more than a simple collection of neighbors. In some ways it was family writ large. The "soul" of the community included such things as religious congregations, clubs, lodges, schools and a clearly articulated social structure. Communities had their hometown heroes, their stalwart citizens, their first families and their beloved eccentrics. And they came equipped with their own folklore. American writers such as Nathaniel Hawthorne, Bret Harte and Mark Twain drew inspiration from such sources.

In America, as Tocqueville noted, communities were fountains of social energy. Political groups debated issues of the day. Business groups schemed to widen Main Street or bring in the new railroad. Religious groups united to care for the poor, eradicate vice and raise the spiritual tone. Circles and societies sponsored everything from Chautauqua lectures to barn dances to county fairs.

Travelers marveled at the gusto with which Americans threw themselves into community affairs. They were brimming with ideas and projects—some of them a bit elliptical—for enhancing prosperity, promoting growth and "boosting" the local advantages. Volunteerism was a way of thinking, not just acting, and Americans indulged in it heavily.

Community was not an unmixed blessing. It could and often did subject its members to powerful conformist pressures. In aristocratic societies, people took their cues from social superiors; in egalitarian societies, they took them from one another. Accordingly, in matters of taste, deportment and public opinion, Americans began to exhibit a high degree of orthodoxy. In politics, this meant a propensity to jump on the bandwagon. Later on, it would mean an inordinate reverence for opinion polls. Conformism was not limited to politics, however. It was manifest in virtually every aspect of community life.

Conformism led to a low tolerance for otherness. Mavericks were often labeled as misfits. Alternative social, political or religious ideas tended to be ridiculed. Immigrant groups found themselves victimized by *nativism*. Tocqueville saw that conformism created dangers of its own. In a land incapable of tyrannical government, he noted, tyrannical opinion could be every bit as damaging.

Pluralism

While the idea of community tends to be inherently exclusive, community in America displayed the opposite tendency. The reason why may have had to do with available space. That is, a given town or parish might have a sense of itself as a separate, integrated unit, but the town over the hill or the parish across the river might well be claimed by "others," and so had an equal right to full legitimacy.

Chautauqua Movement: Begun in 1873, a popular program of adult education throughout the US, with lectures, concerts and plays often presented outdoors or in tents.

Nativism:
http://history.acusd.edu/gen/civilwar/04/nativism.html

Nativism: Outlook favoring native-born inhabitants over immigrants.

An Alger Hero in Real Life

Horatio Alger Jr. might not have sold half as many books were it not for Andrew Carnegie. For, anyone who lacked faith in the American Dream had only to look to him. Though it was true he did not start out literally in rags, he started out pretty close, and he quite visibly wound up in riches.

In the little town of Dunfermline, Scotland, the Carnegie family was respectably poor. Hard times in the Lowlands drove them to America in 1848, and they settled in the Pennsylvania boomtown of Pittsburgh. Everyone, including thirteen-year old Andy, the family whiz kid, had to work in order to make ends meet.

Andrew Carnegie (1835-1919).
(Courtesy of Getty Images.)

Andy started as a bobbin boy in a cotton mill for $1.20 a week, and moved on a to become a telegraph messenger. Telegraphy fascinated him and he quickly got the hang of sending and receiving messages. In his spare time, like any Alger hero, he plugged away on an education, learning double-entry bookkeeping.

The big break came in 1853. Carnegie came to the attention of Thomas A. Scott, a rising power in the Pennsylvania Railroad, who made the young man his personal telegrapher and then his private secretary. Soon he knew the business so well that Scott could send him off to Europe to market the company securities, and on the commissions he earned (plus some shrewd investing on his own) he was making fifty thousand dollars a year.

At that point he began investing in earnest. Steel seemed to be the up-and-coming thing, especially for the expanding railroad industry, so Carnegie plunged headlong into the building of a single giant plant, which, in honor of the Pennsylvania Railroad's president, he named the J. Edgar Thompson Steel Works. Not surprisingly, Mr. Thompson was soon buying all of his rails from Carnegie.

That was how his whole career went. It wasn't so much that he knew about steel, it was that he knew about people. He had the knack of picking geniuses to work for him and then finding ways to make them outdo themselves. For example, Charles Schwab, one of his managers, noted how many heats of steel were being turned out by a rival furnace, and simply scrawled the figure in chalk on the plant floor one day. When the workers figured out what the number meant, they were determined to beat it. Almost daily the number kept going up, for Carnegie's "Lucy" furnace was now pitted in a go-for-broke contest with the competitor's "Isabella." Within a few weeks, Lucy's production had quadrupled.

Carnegie was always beating the competition, every which way, and his empire burgeoned accordingly. Eventually his own ships carried ore from his own mines to his own ports and over his own railroads to his own mills, and after the ore was turned into steel, his subsidiaries processed it into finished products.

By 1901, when Carnegie sold out, the firm was clearing $40 million a year—which was a lot of money in those days. But the man himself remained Algeresque to the end. In his book *The Gospel of Wealth*, he argued that it was a sin to die rich, for great wealth imposed great responsibilities. And taking his own advice, he retired to the castle he had purchased in Scotland and began giving it all away. The fact that every little town came to have its Carnegie-endowed library seemed a tribute not only to Andrew Carnegie but also to Ragged Dick.

To some extent, this pattern grew out of the Founding. After all, the founding documents were all about universals—"that all men are created equal"—not specific social, cultural or ethnic groups. Moreover, with no official religion, the United States was no longer culture specific. It could in theory welcome all comers.

As a result, the American notion of community was easily pluralized into communi*ties*. And within the plural form was the idea that communities could get along with each other, no matter how disparate they might be. In a community of communities, difference became more acceptable.

All the same, American inclusiveness would be sorely tested in the early republic. A large influx of dispossessed Rhinelanders in the 1840s and 1850s, followed by an even larger influx of Irish famine victims, brought more than a million impoverished immigrants to American shores. The newcomers had little education, few vocational skills, and in the German case, a language barrier. Moreover, they were almost exclusively Catholic. Many became victims of nativism in one form or another. Yet the hostility remained informal for the most part, and rarely hardened into official discrimination. As ragged as some of these immigrant communities were, they found themselves invigorated by the same combination of economic opportunity and social egalitarianism we have seen elsewhere. And eventually they were bidden to participate in the same up-by-the-bootstraps processes as everyone else.

American Exceptionalism

Growing out of the social milieu of the new republic were a number of ideas, values and attitudes that were self-consciously distinctive. While some of these had little effect on the development of American institutions, others had a great deal.

In particular, we might sketch out a set of concepts that historians have loosely termed "American exceptionalism."

Naturalism

With most Americans tied to agrarian pursuits, the natural world made its presence strongly felt. The rhythms of the earth—spring plowing, morning milking, the autumn harvest—were part and parcel of daily life.

Enlightenment writers such as Rousseau had romanticized the "natural man"—of whom the archetype was the American Indian—as opposed to the "artificial" product of civilization. The strengths of the natural man, so the argument went, were old-fashioned horse sense, the capacity to adapt and survive, and, not least, a God-given sense of the good. Whatever the truth of this theory, many Americans behaved as if they believed it. They explained the Common Man largely in terms of his contact with the natural world. And Jefferson, as we know, explained it best of all:

> Those who labour in the earth are the chosen people of God, if ever he had a chosen people, whose breasts he has made his peculiar deposit for substantial and genuine virtue.

The common man taming the wilderness.
(*The Hunter's Return* by Thomas Cole, courtesy of the Amon Carter Museum.)

Such ideas soon found literary expression in the figure of James Fenimore Cooper's "Leatherstocking." He was not an exile from civilization, precisely, but he was never quite a part of it either, and he always feared its seductions. His was the natural world of wide horizons and clean air, and his virtue was the elementary choice of right over wrong. He gave freely of himself to help others and rigorously adhered to the moral law. But the sound of a neighbor's ax always sent him farther into the wilderness.

Other expressions of American naturalism were found in the Hudson River school of painting, with its romantic interweaving of plowed land and wilderness, in the philosophical transcendentalism of Ralph Waldo Emerson and Henry David Thoreau, and eventually in Teddy Roosevelt's rough-and-ready "strenuous life." Many are still a part of our world today.

The Meaning of America

What Americans took to be the meaning of America progressed through several stages, beginning with the Puritans' report of a "hellish wilderness." We might think of the final stage as American nationhood. The successful Founding of the Republic—and the high idealism attributed to it—cast America in a far different light from the hellish wilderness. It became known by such affections as "sweet land of liberty."

That Providence might somehow have been behind the process—a proposition that many Americans took seriously—brought religious metaphors to mind. The three that came up most often were:

The Myth of the Garden. America represented a symbolic return to Eden. Its national experience was destined to revert to first principles and rediscover eternal truths.

The Myth of the Promised Land. America also represented an exodus from the corruption and folly of the Old World. And, by extension, those who came to America were God's chosen people.

The Myth of the New Jerusalem. Americans were destined to alter the course of human history and bring God's eternal purposes to pass. In America, all things would be made new again in preparation for the Millennium.

Expressions of these myths were not far to seek. They appeared in sermons, in political orations, in patriotic songs, even in the symbolism of public monuments. The uncapped pyramid and all-seeing eye found on the Great Seal, together with its mystical *Novus Ordo Seclorum*, gave their own subtle hint that America had been arranged by the gods.

Novus Ordo Seclorum:
http://www.greatseal.com/
mottoes/seclorum.html

America and the World

Early in their national career, Americans came to believe that their ideas and institutions were suitable, indeed desirable, for all mankind. This was particularly true of Europe, which was viewed by many Americans as far gone in moral decay. But it would be a blessing for *any* nation state to experience an "American" revolution.

It was as yet unclear what the phrase "sweet land of liberty" did and didn't encompass in the Americas. Expansionists wondered, as they pored over maps, whether the United States wasn't somehow meant to fill out the whole hemisphere. The phrase *Manifest Destiny* crept into political discourse.

The American Revolution had taken place amid a worldwide struggle between Britain and France. Shortly after the Constitution's adoption, that conflict entered its next phase, as we have seen. Americans, in danger of being caught in the middle, shied away from political involvement. Why should they risk being drawn into European quarrels? they asked.

More generally, many Americans came to believe that the United States should never conduct its foreign relations in the manner of Old World diplomacy. Republican statesmen—as opposed to monarchical power brokers—should have no interest in diplomatic machinations or *realpolitik*. On the contrary, they should further the cause of truth and justice among nations and teach by the power of example. America should be a light unto the world.

Manifest Destiny: Phrase first used in 1845 which came to mean that the United States was destined by Providence to spread across the continent.

Realpolitik: Literally "actual politics," politics based on practical considerations rather than theory or ethics.

Divine Purpose

If the hand of God was to be seen so clearly in the Founding, it stood to reason that God was vitally interested in America's success. Thus, Providence sanctioned American patriotism in a unique way: the cause of America was the cause of all mankind.

With those biblical metaphors in mind, Americans looked upon their fledgling republic as a final chance to redeem the human race. In the New World it might be possible to mend the errors and follies of the Old—to step outside of time and elude its inexorable decay.

Thus, Americans truly saw their country as "the world's last best hope." Its destiny, which had been anything but clear in the dark days of the Revolution, became steadily more so in the eyes of the Founding generation. "Our pure, virtuous, federated republic," wrote John Adams to Thomas Jefferson when both of them had mended their political quarrels and were growing gracefully old, "will last forever, govern the globe, and introduce the perfection of man."

America the Beautiful

As these notions began coming together, the American experience furnished a modern exemplar of Plato's connection between "city" and "soul." Americans devoutly wished for a Good Society. That wish had led them to overthrow British tyranny, to create contemporary republics and finally, to devise a new sort of polity, one of continental scale and, in their eyes, grand purpose. And in the process, they imagined themselves to be transformed. As colonists, they had been but pale lineaments of what destiny had in mind for them. As citizens of the American Republic, they saw themselves as historic fulfillment. No wonder they began to wax oratorical.

While the oratory abounded, the best single example of it would be found in a hymn composed at the end of the nineteenth century. *America the Beautiful* was written in 1893 by a Wellesley professor of English literature named Katherine Lee Bates. She might have polled Jefferson's contemporaries for the elements of her romantic idyll: spacious skies, amber waves of grain, purple mountain majesties above the fruited plain. The text included plenty of spiritual metaphors too: pilgrim feet, patriot dreams, a thoroughfare of freedom, and of course God mending every flaw. As for republican virtue, consider this line: "Confirm thy soul in self-control, Thy liberty in law." The imagery of "America the Beautiful" is an idealized and deeply symbolic self-portrait—America as Americans eventually came to see it.

This Good Society grew out of successful institutions, to be sure, but it also grew out of the imagination of the people. For them, the America of contingent possibility had metamorphosed into America as an eternal given.

Suggestions for Further Reading

John Boles, *The Great Revival, 1787–1805: The Origins of the Southern Evangelical Mind* (1972).

Richard L. Bushman, *The Refinement of America: Persons, Houses, Cities* (1992).

J. Hector St. John Crèvecoeur, *Letters from an American Farmer and Sketches of Eighteenth-Century America*, ed. Albert E. Stone (1986).

Joseph J. Ellis, *After the Revolution: Profiles of Early American Culture* (1979).

Jack P. Greene, *Pursuits of Happiness: The Social Development of Early Modern British Colonies and the Formation of American Culture* (1986).

Reginald Horseman, *The Frontier in the Formative Years, 1783–1815* (1970).

Jackson Turner Main, *The Social Structure of Revolutionary America* (1965).

Jean V. Matthews, *Toward a New Society: American Thought and Culture, 1800–1830* (1991).

Kenneth Silverman, *A Cultural History of the American Revolution* (1976).

K. Alan Synder, *Defining Noah Webster: Mind and Morals in the Early Republic* (1990).

David Waldstreicher, *In the Midst of Perpetual Fetes: The Making of American Nationalism, 1776–1820* (1997).

Robert H. Wiebe, *The Opening of American Society: From the Adoption of the Constitution to the Eve of Disunion* (1984).

CHAPTER 14 STUDY AID

(This aid is not all-inclusive and is not intended to be a substitute for thorough study of the material presented in the textbook.)

A Republican People

I. A Republican Founding

1. Identity:
   - Institutions and *patria*—an interactive process
   - Values in common, shared experiences, mutual sacrifice, working consensus, heroes and myths, arts and culture
2. Authentic national character:
   - Coherence rather than atomization
   - "Americanization"

II. The American Good Society

1. Declaration of Independence:
   - Self-evident truths and inalienable rights—equality, life, liberty, happiness
2. Republican significance:
   - Simplicity
   - Classical forms
   - Republican virtue, feelings and sympathy
3. Foreign perspectives:
   - European interest and insights

III. American Life

1. Americanization:
   - Rejection of things British
   - Regeneration
   - "New" ways
2. The family farm:
   - Farming predominates—extended families, self-sufficiency, true affection, bucolic charm
3. The plain-style home:
   - Simplicity, abundance, literacy, living close to nature
4. City and town life:
   - The city—sophistication, complexity; affluence, specialization, amusements, vice and corruption
   - The town—many towns and townships, community, diversity

IV. An Emerging Nation

1. Emerging national character:
   - Optimistic—inevitability of "Progress"
   - Self-reliant
   - Innovative—mechanical arts
   - Practical-minded—"pragmatism"
   - Restless—mobility and self-creation
   - Materialistic—symbols of success and social worth
   - Idealistic—"Sentimental Democracy"
   - "God-fearing"—Puritan legacy
   - Suspicious—paranoia

2. Social patterns:
   - Individualism—"fierce spirit of liberty"—
     - Immigration
     - Property ownership
     - Moral self-governance and respect for the law
     - Enlightened self-interest
     - Privatism
   - Egalitarianism—
     - Cheap land
     - Equality before the law
     - Opportunity
     - Open channels of communication
     - Cult of the common man
     - American Dream
   - Community—
     - "Fountains of social energy"
     - Conformist pressures
   - Pluralism = communities

V. American Exceptionalism

1. Naturalism:
   - The natural man
   - The common man

2. The meaning of America:
   - "Sweet land of liberty"
   - The myth of the garden
   - The myth of the promised land
   - The myth of the New Jerusalem

3. America and the world:
- A universal founding
- Manifest Destiny
- Statesmanship

4. Divine purpose:
- Divine Providence
- "The world's last best hope"

VI. The American Experience

1. America the Beautiful:
- Seeking the Good Society
- The imagination of the people
- Metamorphosis

CHAPTER 14 REVIEW QUESTIONS ▬▬▬▬

NAME: _____   SECTION: _____

Key Terms

National Character

American Good Society

Sympathy

Progress

Cult of the Common Man

American Dream

Pluralism

American Exceptionalism

Multiple Choice Questions

1. According to the text, where did Thomas Jefferson sketch his outline of the American Good Society?
   a. In the Virginia Statute of Religious Freedom.
   b In a letter to John Adams.
   c. In the Preamble to the Constitution.
   d. In the Declaration of Independence.

2. Who wrote the novel *The Man of Feeling*?
   a. Joseph Warren.
   b. Royall Tyler.
   c. Henry Mackenzie.
   d. Nicholas Cresswell.

3. Alexis de Tocqueville warned that American individualism may lead into what potentially dangerous condition:
   a. Republicanism.
   b. Privatism.
   c. Egalitarianism.
   d. Idealism.

4. Which of following is not an attribute of the common man listed in the text?
   a. Integrity.
   b. Rugged strength.
   c. Cautious timidity.
   d. Dynamic creativity.

Review Questions

1. Why did some argue that in order for the Founding to succeed it must lead to the formation of an authentic "national character"?

   _____

   _____

   _____

   _____

2. What was the traditional family farm's relevance to the development of early American republicanism?

   _____

   _____

   _____

   _____

3. What role did the "city" play in the American Revolution?

   _____

   _____

   _____

   _____

4. What is egalitarianism? How did egalitarianism influence the development of the American character?

   _____

   _____

   _____

   _____

5. What does it mean to live in a "plural" society? How did American pluralism grow out of the American Founding?

   _____

   _____

   _____

   _____

Review Exercises

1. Explain the early American notion of "sympathy." How did this attribute lead to the creation of civic virtue?

   _____

   _____

   _____

   _____

2. Explain why the text includes restlessness as an American character trait. Where did Americans' restlessness come from?

_____

_____

_____

_____

3. Briefly summarize the Myth of the Garden. What is this myth's place in describing the meaning of America?

_____

_____

_____

_____

Big Essay Question

This chapter makes the argument that many of the basic conditions of American life at the time of Founding helped form a republican people. Life in America has changed greatly since then. In a short essay, explain your understanding of what it means to be a "republican people." Explain what factors fostered the development of early American republicanism and how those factors have changed over time. Are Americans still a republican people?

CHAPTER 15

The Democratic Republic

(Courtesy of AP/Wide World Photos.)

As it turned out, the American Founding included a political system. But what kind of system? Designed by whom? To operate by what rules? And to what general purpose? Who decreed, for example, that it would be a system of two parties and two only, that the parties would represent goals and aspirations within the Founding, and that the dialogue between them would be of a certain character? There was no Philadelphia Convention for American politics, only the amorphous forces of history.

For most Americans, the election of 1800 was thought to be the end of party politics. The contest between Federalists and Democratic-Republicans had not been about establishing a party system but about defining the meaning of the Revolution—an issue that could be settled once and for all. And indeed, after their dramatic sweep from office, the Federalists gradually faded away. The Jeffersonians dominated politics so completely that politics itself lost meaning. To the extent that political contests remained, they tended to be within the victorious party.

What has been termed the Era of Good Feelings was the result. While in truth "good feelings" rarely prevailed, the presidencies of Jefferson, Madison, Monroe and John Quincy Adams *were* marked by the assumption that party politics, as such, would be the exception in the American experience, not the rule.

It was a bad assumption.

Politics of Consensus

What the Era of Good Feelings illustrated was the phenomenon of political consensus. *Consensus* means that there is substantial agreement on fundamentals—that politics divides over essentially peripheral matters.

Many historians believe that consensus is the distinguishing characteristic of American politics. If so (and other historians dispute it), American politics is unlike that of virtually every other democracy. Clearly Americans do enjoy a considerable degree of consensus—just how much is the point in dispute—and it provides a starting point for understanding the US political system.

The American consensus grew out of the Founding. Because Americans generally believed that the Founding's "self-evident truths" really were universal,

Era of Good Feelings:
http://www
.americanpresident.org/
kotrain/courses/JMO/
JMO_In_Brief.htm

http://www.nv.cc.va.us/
home/nvsageh/Hist121/
Part3/MonroeJQAdams.htm

there was nothing fundamental to squabble about. Consensus was further strengthened by the egalitarian, middle-class nature of American society. Where European society was often fragmented into well-defined and mutually hostile social classes, most Americans belonged to the same middling class of yeoman farmers, mechanics, artisans, shopkeepers and the like. As a result, there were no battles to fight between, say, aristocratic overlords and landless peasants.

The American consensus encompassed such essentials as the nature and purpose of government. Jefferson's contemporaries generally agreed, for example, that political process ought to have "good government" as its primary objective, and that "good" meant efficient, frugal, responsible and honest. Given such beliefs, campaign issues were ready-made. Smith promised to be more efficient than Jones. Johnson pledged to be more frugal than Jensen. Williams alleged corruption and mismanagement in the administration of Rogers. And so on. Even today, such election themes have a familiar ring.

By the same token, Americans shied away from deeply troubling or divisive issues. And when such issues did appear—as inevitably they must—voters had the devil's own time with them. Debates ran off the scale. Compromise became impossible. And the voters subjected themselves to an agony of moralistic introspection. Where basic issues of right and wrong were concerned, Americans had to abandon consensus.

The Two-Party Political System

Two Party System:
http://www.usatoday.com/
NEWS/COMMENT/columists/
neuharth/neu057.htm

http://www.realdemocracy
.com/no2party.htm

Thirty years later it was clear that the disagreement between Federalists and Democratic-Republicans at the beginning of the century had been only Act One of a lengthy drama. Consensus had not spelled the end of party politics after all. Indeed, party politics was back with a vengeance—and apparently back to stay.

But what kind of party politics? Conflicts during the administration of John Quincy Adams (1824-1828) seemed to indicate that several parties might eventually arise to challenge one another for preferment. Soon, however, the pattern shifted back to a two-way contest. The strong personality and single-minded outlook of Andrew Jackson, who was elected president in 1828, attracted a broad farrago of political interests and beliefs. Jackson's supporters proudly began calling themselves "Jacksonians."

By a sort of Newton's Law of Politics, an equally broad collection of interests and beliefs began assembling together in opposition. These adversaries of "King Andrew I" called themselves Whigs. The sobriquet was playful at first, but it eventually became the name by which the Whig party was known.

The Whigs did not challenge their Jacksonian rivals over bedrock issues such as the Founding, but they did challenge them on issues that mattered. We can think of the Whigs as political descendants of the old Federalists, for they had several beliefs of Federalist ancestry. They believed, for example, that government ought to be energetic, forging a muscular economic policy and building useful public works. They also inherited the Federalists' conception of the body politic, regarding it not as a collection of individuals but as an organic whole. And they had a more aristocratic idea of governance, believing that those of elite background and superior education ought to be kept in charge. If we reverse all three of these positions, we are in company with the Jacksonians—who traced their lineage back to Jefferson.

So much for philosophical differences. When it came to bare-knuckle combat, the parties proved they could work up quite a sweat. Take the famous "bank war" for example. It focused on the Bank of the United States, Hamilton's bank, the one that had caused such a furor back in Washington's time. It was still around, still going strong and still heavily laden with symbolism. When the bank's charter came up for renewal in 1836, Jackson was persuaded by his followers to take a stand in opposition and slay the "monster" then and there. According to the Jacksonians' view of the

Andrew Jackson slaying the Bank Monster in the name of democratic republicanism. (Courtesy of the New-York Historical Society.)

world, the Bank of the US savored too strongly of aristocracy, favoritism and proactive government. That it also played a role in economic development was of consequence to the Whigs, for that was the way *they* saw the world, but irrelevant to the Jacksonians. Before the bank breathed its last, the parties had to slug it out toe-to-toe in what became the conflict of the decade. Old Hickory likened it to the Battle of New Orleans.

There were shades here of the old ratification quarrel or the tumultuous 1790s. In other words, the dispute between the parties, like those earlier disputes, essentially grew out of the Founding. It wasn't a case of one party accepting the Founding while the other party rejected it, but a case of each party finding different implications in the Founding or building upon it in different ways. It was disagreement *within* the consensus.

Whigs and Democrats (as the Jacksonians were more formally known) fought skirmishes on local, state and national levels from the 1832 election to the mid-1850s, when the controversy over slavery finally did in the Whigs. In the realignment process that followed, another two-party system emerged, this time pitting Democrats against Republicans. By this time, it was more or less accepted that the United States would have a political system resting on two broad, nationally based parties.

Two-party politics was not really new. Whig and Tory, terms that had surfaced at the time of the Stamp Act, ran back in English history to the Glorious Revolution. The Tory party traditionally played a conservative role and supported crown and aristocracy in the face of liberal reforms, while the Whig party saw itself as a guardian of those reforms and a herald of the future. Even so, the idea of political opposition was new and to some rather frightening, as

Jackson/Democrats:
http://www.whitehouse.gov/
WH/glimpse/presidents/html/
aj7.html

http://odur.let.rug.nl/~usa/
E/bankwar.bankwarxx.htm

Whigs:
http://odur.let.rug.nl/~usa/
E/uswhig/whigsxx.htm

we have seen. How, Englishmen asked, could dissent against lawful authority be considered legitimate?

Edmund Burke, philosopher, essayist and Member of Parliament, did much to change popular thinking on the subject. In a series of influential essays, he pointed out that political disagreement was an accomplished fact, whether it was thought to be "legitimate" or not. Indeed, Burke insisted, political parties were the only way a democratic assembly could function—without them, it would be reduced to chaos.

There was a subtler point to make too. With the gradual shift away from "divine right" authority and toward popular sovereignty, those who disagreed with government policies could no longer be seen as "opposing God"; they were merely citizens with a different idea. Logically speaking, they had as much right to *their* notion of political rectitude as the government did.

All of this helps us to see why parties could emerge. But why specifically two parties? Why not three or four or twenty? Much of the answer lies in the Founding, once again, and in those two general views of it we have associated with Hamilton and Jefferson respectively. Beyond this, however, the Founding had two-party implications in its very architecture, some of them constitutional and some extraconstitutional. Let's consider three of these:

Each congressional district in a state elects a single representative, but an entire state becomes a single-member district for each senator as a senate seat comes up for election.

• Large, Single-Member Voting Districts

In other emerging democracies, voting districts were often designed to elect not just one but several members to the legislative assembly, distributing the popular vote among all contending parties. Thus Party A, let us say, with 30% of the vote, would gain 30% of the seats from that district. If the district in question filled ten seats in the assembly, Party A would be awarded three of them. Party B, with 50% or 60% of the vote, would be awarded five or six seats. Party C might come in with a single seat, reflecting only 10% of the vote. And so on.

This system, usually called "proportional representation," had much to be said for it. It was fair and democratic, and it gave voice to every shade of opinion in the spectrum. But it also encouraged the proliferation of parties, for every minimally worthy contender was paid off with at least some political power and a modicum of influence.

By arranging for US voting districts to elect only a single member to Congress, the Constitution had just the opposite effect. For in the large, single-member district, the party that won the most votes got to represent the *entire* district. Rather than small parties rewarded with small pieces of the pie, the American system tended to give the whole pie to a single contender.

HOW VOTES ARE COUNTED IN THE AMERICAN SYSTEM

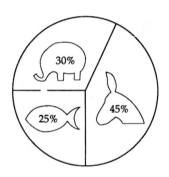

If the Donkey party gets a plurality of the vote, how much influence does the Elephant party have?

WINNER TAKE ALL

If the Donkey party consistently gets a plurality of the vote, the only way for the Elephant and Catfish parties to beat the Donkey party is to band together. At the end of the process, there will be two parties vying for majorities rather than multiple parties vying for pluralities.

• "Winner Take All"

The "winner take all" principle, illustrated by single-member voting districts, was found elsewhere in US politics. Sometimes it was extraconstitutional.

In the operation of the electoral college, for example, it was assumed by the Framers that the electoral votes of any given state, especially a large state, would be divided among several candidates, as in the proportional representation model. Actual practice proved otherwise. States tallied up the popular vote, determined which candidate had the most and awarded that person *the entire block* of electoral votes.

With such ground rules in force, small parties had very little chance. They could gain perhaps 10% or 20% of the popular vote, but that was rarely enough to win. If a party didn't have a good shot at gaining a plurality (that is, the largest single block of votes cast), it might as well cash in. The corollary to winner take all was loser take nothing.

With this logic in mind, we can see that the aim for pluralities soon became an aim for majorities (that is, more than half of all votes cast). If there were, say, three parties in the field and one of them could poll 40% of the vote, one could poll 30% and one could poll 20%, the latter two, gaining nothing for their efforts, would be strongly inclined to band together, enabling the combined party to poll 50%, and win. This logic would inevitably produce two parties, each within hailing distance of a majority, so that with a little help from independent voters, one or the other could win decisively.

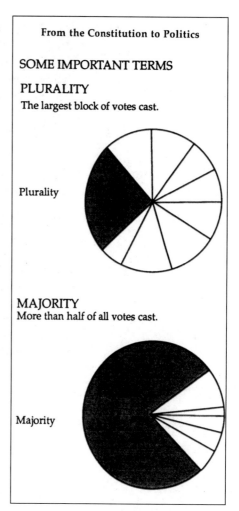

From the Constitution to Politics

SOME IMPORTANT TERMS

PLURALITY
The largest block of votes cast.

Plurality

MAJORITY
More than half of all votes cast.

Majority

• The Congressional Committee System

Once again by tradition, American legislative practice vested much of the power of Congress in the various committees of the House and Senate. The theory of the committee system went like this. Since all members of the legislative body couldn't pay equal attention to every matter under consideration, a committee on, say, transportation would look carefully into any proposal for highway legislation. The membership of the committee would roughly reflect the membership of the whole house, so if the committee members approved the proposed highway bill, there would be a disposition (but not a requirement) of the whole house to do the same.

Committee majorities became all powerful. They were able to elect the chair, govern procedure and strongly influence the deliberations. Accordingly, the same logic that drove voting districts to produce two broad-gauge parties drove the committee system to do the same. A party with only a single member on a twenty-person committee had little or no influence on the outcome.

One further aspect of the committee system came into play. The chairmanship came to be determined by seniority—that is, the member of the majority party who had been there the longest was automatically elected chair. To hold onto this powerful position, a party must be able to return its members to Congress over and over again. Only a broadly based, majority party could accomplish that.

Dynamics of the Two-Party System

When the Jeffersonians first banded together, the word *party* was still anathema. Yet thoughtful observers could see that both the Democratic-Republicans and their Federalist rivals were performing useful functions.

One of these, clearly, was to ascertain the popular will. In a large republic, as Madison had pointed out, there were innumerable competing interests, none of them able to exert much direct influence on government. There had to be some way to sort among these interests, combine them into coherent packages, or *platforms*, and mobilize support for them. Parties could do that.

A second purpose was coordination. Hamilton and the Federalists originally came together to coordinate a legislative program. The Constitution's structural devices—especially the separation of powers—made such coordination difficult. But with a party structure in place, there was a regular forum for discussing policy, working out differences, planning strategy and the like.

Finally, parties provided a useful refinement of the representation process. Without parties, representatives were often flying blind. They might meet with a few groups of constituents in their district, gather some general ideas and then make the arduous journey to Washington. If events there moved swiftly—as they often did—there was no real opportunity for the representative to check back with the voters and apprise them of developments. If we factor party into the equation, however, the situation changes dramatically. Instead of an isolated representative groping in the dark, there would be a broader organization, some general principles and an opportunity for the voters to wield constant influence. Parties, moreover, could offer the voters comprehensive choices. This approach or that one. This outlook or that one. This set of values or that one.

By the time of Andrew Jackson's election, party dynamics were much better understood. Martin Van Buren, who was Jackson's secretary of state and anointed political heir, made some canny observations about the benefits parties conveyed. Among these were the following:

- **Legitimacy**. The strong majorities a party could muster imparted a sense of legitimacy to the political process. Candidates elected by such majorities could feel they truly had a mandate from the people.
- **Moderation**. With a vigorous organization behind them, party leaders exercised a measure of control over local candidates, dissuading them from taking extreme positions or agitating dicey issues.
- **Predictability**. Tied to the party, candidates were less likely to pursue idiosyncratic aims, for they must observe a general set of principles. As a result, voters could vote for the party, whose principles were known to them, rather than for the question-mark candidate.
- **Responsibility**. With a given party in power, there would be a focus of responsibility. If things went awry, officeholders would not be able to point fingers somewhere else.

All four of Van Buren's principles illustrate something important about a two-party system: its moderating influence. We can see the nature of that influence in the way the system works. Consider for a moment just how different

> At a convention, party members argue over and then decide on the party platform, which becomes the formal declaration of party principles for that election.

two-party dynamics are from those of proportional representation.

In proportional representation systems with their numerous small contenders, there is a tendency to create ideological parties more or less along the lines of factions. And they *behave* like factions. They care exclusively for their own good, which they see with crystal clarity, and are not much concerned with that of the general public.

Since none of these parties could command a majority on its own, they must combine into *coalitions* in order to organize a government. We often hear of the "ruling coalition" in France or Italy, consisting of four or five partners, of whom at least one seems perennially dissatisfied. There is a reason for that. When a ruling coalition is being assembled, it is tricky to inveigle small parties to join. They may have only a seat or two in the legislative assembly but that seat or two could give the coalition its majority and make the whole thing work. So the splinter parties play a game we might call "coalition blackmail"—demanding exorbitant political payoffs for their participation. And at the first sign of difficulty, these fair-weather friends often become disaffected, pull out of the coalition and send the government sprawling. Then new elections must be called and the whole process begun again. Proportional representation systems are characteristically wobbly, then. What's more, they empower the very groups most likely to be narrow-minded and self-absorbed.

"MY FORMER OPPONENT IS SUPPORTING ME IN THE GENERAL ELECTION. PLEASE DISREGARD ALL THE THINGS I HAVE SAID ABOUT HIM IN THE PRIMARY."

(By Ralph Dunagin, courtesy of Tribune Media Services.)

Now, for contrast, compare the dynamics of the two-party system. Where only two parties exist, each with a potential majority of the voters, they necessarily bring together all kinds of interests, all shades of opinion and all styles of behavior. These differences must be factored down into common agreement if the party is to prevail. Thus, accommodation is practiced first and foremost *within* the party. Those who refuse to compromise with the otherwise-minded will simply drive them from the party's ranks and weaken its chances at the polls. This is why come election time we always see Senator Liberal and Congressman Conservative, who have been sniping at each other ever since the last election, suddenly arm in arm, smiling into the cameras. *They have to do this if they want their party to win.*

There is more. Two broadly based parties competing for the electoral majority will wind up appealing to many of the *same* voters. And those middle-of-the-roaders being appealed to will lean a bit to the left in one election and a bit to the right in another, but for the most part they care little about ideological issues—theirs is the politics of problem solving. This circumstance has occasionally made party platforms so similar that the voters have no real sense of choice. Dull campaigns and voter apathy are two possible outcomes. But closely fought elections in which candidates are discouraged from taking strong positions (for fear of alienating members of their own party) can also lead to issue dodging, mudslinging and other misbehavior.

Uneasy Bedfellows

The election of 2000 was a time of compromise for the Republican Party. In an effort to gain a crucial majority, Republicans all over the spectrum realized they must bed down together, however they might personally feel about certain issues. However, by May 22, 2001 the honeymoon was over. That was when Vermont Sen. Jim Jeffords, a Republican of the moderate—that is, liberal—persuasion, announced he would be leaving the party. The news was devastating to the GOP. It meant they would forfeit their razor-thin majority in the Senate.

Some of Jeffords' former colleagues put down his defection to quirkiness, flakiness or personal ambition. "Not everyone gets to wake up one morning and decide an inner voice has told him to overturn the results of a national election, an unprecedented legal struggle and a decisive Supreme Court decision to form a government," blasted a scathing editorial in the *Wall Street Journal*. Yet those closest to Jeffords said this was all wide of the mark. Jeffords was an independent-minded senator speaking for an independent-minded state: he called the issues as he saw them, not as he was told to see them by the party bosses. The real question was not why Jeffords had left the Republican Party—but why he had been a member in the first place.

The answer was that he saw himself as an old Teddy Roosevelt-style Republican, a "Progressive," who combined respect for traditional principles with sympathy for the poor and disadvantaged, especially among schoolchildren. Along with other moderates like John McCain and Olympia Snowe, Jeffords stuck with the party through thick and thin, suffering serial defeats on issues of great importance to him, because he knew that without banding together with his fellows he could achieve nothing at all. And so he compromised. When President Bush sought a $1.6 trillion tax cut after taking office, Jeffords agreed to support the measure, even though privately deploring it, as long as the Republican leadership agreed to trim off $300 billion for enhanced educational support. It was only when that $300 billion subsequently vanished that Jeffords finally bailed.

Question: was Jeffords' apostasy a good thing or a bad thing for the Republican Party? It was a good thing, replied conservative ideologues, for it got rid of one more "RINO"—Republican In Name Only—and thus purified party ranks. It was a bad thing, replied the practical politicians, for it loosened the party's hold on the Senate. Here is a third answer. Jeffords' exit will require the Republican leadership to be much nicer to the remaining RINOs, and the Republican president to move back toward the political center, from which, unlike his father, he might well be re-elected. Now, is *that* good or bad?

On the other hand, no political system is better at effecting compromise. With little of the intensely controversial in either party's platform, the issues of the moment can usually be negotiated. Better to settle for half a loaf, the politicos conclude, than none at all.

Accordingly, two-party politics soon established itself as a politics of practical outcome rather than a politics of ideological purity. The point was not to be true to a finely tuned faith but rather to solve problems and stay in office. It perfectly suited both the American temper and the national consensus.

It had a second effect, equally important. Once politicians had to come to terms with their opponents, they had to admit that their own view of the world wasn't God's truth, it was just a view. For all its election-time brashness, American politics was based on a humble conception of humankind. Bruisers could heckle the opposition but they couldn't lock them up or gun them down. Who knew but what the opposition wasn't right?

Above all, two-party politics was a stabilizing influence. Where multiparty systems knocked coalitions apart or burst into ideological fragments, the two-party system was all but shatterproof.

Consensus and Realignment

Critics of the two-party system have argued that its benefits are not worth the costs. In particular, they point to the lack of real and meaningful choice. Yet at certain points in American history, the system has shown it could offer alternatives, and significant ones at that. Just as in the election of 1800, it could facilitate a major change of direction.

This process of *political realignment* can be described in general terms. It begins with politics as usual. The consensus is being defined by the party in power, while the party out of power struggles to align itself with the same consensus as closely as possible.

Then an important new issue comes along. Its nature is such as to cut across the existing pattern of political alignment. The liberals in *both* parties, in other words, will take a similar position on it and so will both groups of conservatives. (Think about the abortion issue, for example.) At some point, there will be a knock-down-drag-out election—much like that of 1800. And in the campaign preceding it, one side or the other will often appeal to first principles—to the Founding, for example, or some other moral reference—which may well prove to be decisive.

The result of the election will be a new consensus, embodied in a new dominant party. The party formerly out of power, now reconstituted, becomes the party in power and vice versa. Perhaps an entirely new party may appear on the scene. In either case, the winner of the crucial election will probably dominate the two-party system for some time to come, leaving its rival in the "me-too" position.

Just such a turning point occurred in 1832. Andrew Jackson had been in office for four years, and his supporters had forged the Democratic Party into a formidable organization. As a result of the 1832 election, the Jacksonians put US politics on a new course—and dominated it for nearly thirty years.

The election of Abraham Lincoln in 1860 marked another critical watershed. Like Jackson before him, Lincoln spoke for a new party, the Republican, which had made its debut only a few years earlier, and addressed a new crosscutting issue—the expansion of slavery. As a result of the election and the tempest that followed, the Republican Party, and the new consensus it represented, ruled American politics until 1932.

That was the year Franklin Roosevelt and his New Deal swept into power. They represented a dramatic renunciation of the free-market, pro-business consensus of the past, which many Americans blamed for the Great Depression. In a historic landslide, Roosevelt overwhelmed his Republican opponent, who was identified with the old ways, and as a result Democrats held an edge in US politics until the election of Ronald Reagan.

Thus, the two-party system provides a balance between change and continuity. In periods of normalcy, it defines consensus, strengthens constitutional government and generally enhances stability. In periods of crisis, it helps change direction and search out a new consensus.

The March of Democracy

Andrew Jackson's followers called themselves Jacksonian *Democrats*. The appellation betokened one of the most consequential revolutions of all time. For the years between the election of Jefferson in 1800 and the re-election of Jackson in 1832 marked the transformation to what we today call *democracy*.

The term does not mean—as it did in ancient Athens—that all citizens take part in the governing process. All the same, suffrage in America has become almost universal, limited only by age, mental incapacity, lack of citizenship or a felony conviction. And political participation is indeed very broad.

Democracy, as we know, was not an avowed aim of the Founders. On the contrary, it was often their worst nightmare. Yet voting requirements had always been liberal by comparative standards, and throughout the colonial period most American males could participate in some way. What was it, then, that the Founders had feared?

The answer lies in history. The fate of the Athenian democracy, where factionalism and mob rule led to the downfall of free government, seemed to teach a poignant lesson. Accordingly, the Founders drew an important distinction between what they called "popular government" and what they called "democracy." Popular government recognized the sovereignty of the people and strove to reflect their will, but it placed the governing process in the hands of gentlemen. So, what happened?

The Democratic Revolution

The roots of American democracy run deep. Townspeople were choosing their own selectmen in colonial New England, and planters were sending their own representatives to the Virginia House of Burgesses. Democratic pressures of one kind or another were shoving politics this way and that in the years preceding the Revolution, as we have seen, and for many Americans the Revolution was not only about home rule but who would rule at home.

Nor did the Framers in Philadelphia universally abhor democracy—though most of them mistrusted it. There was, as they knew, no clear line to be drawn between "popular government" and "democracy," and thus there was nothing to stop the one from gradually mutating into the other.

The Framers considered this possibility when they discussed restrictions on voting rights. Most of them favored some kind of limitation, generally based on property ownership. Yet the final draft of the Constitution required only that "Electors in each State shall have the Qualifications requisite for Electors in the most numerous Branch of the State Legislature." Accordingly, if the states liberalized political participation, the national government would have no choice but to follow suit.

So, why didn't the Framers build higher barriers? The probable answer is that they believed so strongly in the sovereignty of the people they left the door of democracy unlocked. If the people chose to go through it, they had the right to do so.

Two-party politics, which was not necessarily democratic in itself, creaked the door open ever wider. In states where the two parties were most evenly matched, there was an incentive to liberalize voting requirements on the assumption that the new voters would gratefully vote for the party that admitted them to the polls. Closely fought election campaigns also reached for new sources of voter enthusiasm. If the outcome was in doubt, it behooved both parties to stir up as many participants as possible.

A number of politicos turned out to be highly gifted political engineers. They were not democratic theorists, necessarily, but their instincts led them to make democratic innovations—generally in the interest of winning. There was Melancton Smith of New York, for example, who both as an opponent of the Constitution and then as a supporter of Thomas Jefferson argued for a number of liberalizing innovations. Later on, fellow New Yorker Martin Van Buren also took up the democratic torch. Not only did he think farsightedly about parties, Van Buren became the father of the political alliance. If New York were to strike up a partnership with the South, he believed, their combined forces could dominate the national scene indefinitely. But Van Buren's most important contributions had to do with popular participation. The more of it the better, he said, and he got specific. He discovered, for example, that presidential elections, though they rarely affected most Americans, had the capacity to stir grass-roots enthusiasm as nothing else—and *that* stood to benefit the party. He was thinking his way through the practice of democracy.

Within a twenty-year period, the political engineers came up with a panoply of devices for enlisting and inspiring a growing army. Among their inventions:

- **The political convention**. In the old days, candidates were nominated by the party's officeholders, meeting in what was called a caucus. Conventions were much more fun. They featured carnival-style hoopla and shirtsleeve participation. And at the convention's end, amid cheering and singing and the playing of steam calliopes, the party had its candidate.

- **The party newspaper**. A new kind of journalism came forth. Its function was to disseminate information, encourage the faithful, give out the party's point of view, enlist new voters and make everyone feel they were a part of something worthwhile.

- **Party organization**. It was no longer sufficient to have "members"—the party had to be organized down to the lowest echelons. This meant that in each ward of a city, party representatives (or "ward heelers") would call regularly on the voters and make sure their voice was being heard. On election day, there would be a sweep of the city to get out the vote.

- **Ballyhoo.** The American democracy produced some of the best stump speakers in the world. It also produced some crowd-pleasing gimmicks, ranging all the way from fireworks to barbecues to torchlight parades. Election day became as exciting as the circus.

- **Symbols and slogans**. Democratic electioneering constantly sought ways to catch the public fancy. When Democrats accused the Whig nominee of being an aristocrat, Old Tippecanoe, as William Henry Harrison was known, replied that he would be glad to retire to a log cabin someday and drink hard cider. Thereafter Whigs trundled log cabins through the streets and passed out free cider. Slogans were roughly on the same level: "Tippecanoe and Tyler too!"

The farthest-reaching development was the so-called "spoils system." When a party came into power, there was an ever increasing expectation that it would avail itself of the opportunities provided by government patronage. Offices with sparse responsibilities and steady incomes could be awarded to party wheelhorses. Contracts for government business could go to politically friendly firms. "Pork barrel" projects—such as building roads and dredging harbors—could be concentrated in the home districts of powerful officeholders. The spoils system made it possible to enlist and "pay" dedicated armies of mercenaries. It made political participation a matter of self-interest as well as virtue.

Democratization changed all the rules of politics. As ever greater numbers became involved in the electoral process, the sophisticated deliberations of the Founders gave way to sloganeering, shibboleths and unabashed banality. Politicians were driven by new exigencies, such as funding their spread-eagle campaigns. And a high-voltage excitement seized the voters. Politics was becoming the country's prime-time sport.

By 1840, Joel Silby concludes in *Political Nation*, "parties had become communities—the sense of loyalty to them as to a family, a tribe, a religion, or a nation, had overwhelmed all else."

Log cabin as political symbol in the election of 1840.
(Courtesy of The Granger Collection, New York.)

Democratic Thought

We have learned something about the "how" of American democracy, but what about the "why?" What was it that possessed millions of Americans to become absorbed in the affairs of government?

Historians have long been curious about such questions. Where were the seeds of democracy first planted? they have asked. Was it something to do with the English heritage? Was it something rooted in the American character? Or was it something found in the American experience?

Answers have been traced to all three. Democratic notions were clearly in the baggage—not to say the prayer books—of the earliest settlers. And the American character had democratic impulses of its own. Self-reliance, for example. Those who must look to their own resources only naturally wanted to manage their own governance. As for the broader American experience, we should pause and consider the **Turner Thesis**.

Frederick Jackson Turner was an American historian writing at the turn of the century. In 1893 he wrote a landmark paper proposing that the best explanation for American democracy lay not in crowded cities or the halls of government—but out on the sparsely settled frontier. It was free land, said Turner, which made free government a working reality. For if members of the working class—those who in Europe would be condemned to a life of poverty—could but travel to the frontier and secure a quarter-section freehold, how many other things in their lives would change? They would become property owners. They would control their own livelihood. They would be reckoned as people of account. Their opinions would matter. Their self-worth would increase. Their outlook would broaden. Their opportunities would expand. The list went on.

Turner:
http://avery.med.virginia.edu/~mwk2c/turner/turner.html

Frontier Life:
http://www.pbs.org/wnet/frontierhouse/frontierlife/essay5.html

Critics of the Turner Thesis have pointed out that none of these effects would automatically result from securing a homestead unless there was a body of thought tying a lot of things together and making them into a whole. That's where the Founding comes in. And specifically, that's where Thomas Jefferson comes in. The single most important impetus toward democracy may well have been "Jeffersonianism."

Jefferson himself was not precisely a democrat. He shared many of the other Founders' qualms about the *demos*. As in other matters, however, Jefferson was conflicted, and he hid parts of his mind even from himself. His political life may be read as a gradual realization that "pure republicanism"—a term he often used—actually amounted to *democratic* republicanism. "In truth," he said, looking back at the Revolution in his old age, "the abuses of monarchy had so filled all the space of political contemplation that we imagined everything republican which was not monarchy." Subsequent events revealed "the mother principle, that 'governments are republican only in proportion as they embody the will of the people, and execute it.'"

Jefferson was not referring to mere "popular government" here. As Joseph Ellis has noted of Jefferson's correspondence with Adams in 1816:

Without fully realizing it at the time, [Jefferson] and his fellow revolutionaries in 1776 had launched a political movement whose full implications were only now seeping into conscious articulation. Here, for the

The Turner Thesis

(From Frederick Jackson Turner, *The Significance of the Frontier in American History*, 1893.)

To the frontier the American intellect owes its striking characteristics. That coarseness and strength combined with acuteness and inquisitiveness; that practical, inventive turn of mind, quick to find expedients; that masterful grasp of material things, lacking in the artistic but powerful to effect great ends; that restless, nervous energy; that dominant individualism, working for good and for evil, and withal that buoyancy and exuberance which comes with freedom—these are traits of the frontier, or traits called elsewhere because of the existence of the frontier. Since the days when the fleet of Columbus sailed into the waters of the New World, America has been another name for opportunity, and the people of the United States have taken their tone from incessant expansion which has not only been open but has even been forced upon them. He would be a rash prophet who should assert that the expansive character of American life has now entirely ceased. Movement has been its dominant fact, and, unless this training has no effect upon a people, the American energy will continually demand a wider field for its exercise. But never again will such gifts of free land offer themselves.

Turner saw America as another name for opportunity.
(*The Great West*, by Currier and Ives, 1870, courtesy of Christie's Images.)

first time, Jefferson embraced the idea that would eventually and then everlastingly be associated with his name. What he had always called "pure republicanism" was really "democracy," and what he had actually done in "the revolution of 1800" was to restore the democratic impulse of the American Revolution after its betrayal by the Federalists.

Even before Jefferson himself was fully on board, Jeffersonianism-as-democracy began to seize the American imagination. Partly this was due to the Declaration. Partly it was due to Jefferson's other writings and pronouncements over the years. Mostly it was due to his alluring vision of the American Good Society.

In the first place, it was a vision based on a kindly reading of human nature, emphasizing virtue and perfectibility. (Jefferson had been exposed to the Scottish Enlightenment early on.) It was also based on American exceptionalism, particularly in its agrarian dimension—"Those who labour in the earth are the chosen people of God"—which had been reinforced by Jefferson's travels abroad. American yeomen, he believed, were the world's last best hope.

It was, in the second place, a vision that emphasized the West, for which Jefferson came to have an almost mystical attachment. For him, history was not about integrating the West into the existing Union—but about the West transforming the existing Union into a new and dynamic America. It was a vision that emphasized the role of spontaneity and creativity in politics, even of borderline chaos. Where Madison's idea of the republic had centered upon order and stability, Jefferson's centered upon liberation. For him, the war against Great Britain was only a first step. Human freedom must now be unshackled from all its other bonds.

Finally, it was a vision that underscored politics as an end in itself—a good. Jefferson came to believe those who exercised political power, even in modest dosage, were ennobled by the experience. The democratic "city" enlarged the democratic "soul."

Correspondingly, Jefferson's vision of the Good Society de-emphasized some things. Materialism, for one, and privatism, for another. Even though the man himself spent his life building a dream in brick and mortar at Monticello—exemplifying both materialism *and* privatism—he spoke of the larger dignity conferred by the political life. His was, in some respects, an authentic classical republicanism.

And Jefferson was good at selling it to fellow Americans. He used the presidency as a bully pulpit. At the same time, he worked to dismantle as much of the Hamiltonian establishment as he safely could, and to make the government spare and frugal. He placed these actions in the larger context of history. "The same political parties which now agitate the U.S. have existed thro' all time," he wrote to Adams. "Whether the power of the people, or that of the *aristoi* should prevail, were questions which kept the states of Greece and Rome in eternal convulsions. . . ."

It is not difficult to see why Americans responded. From what we learned of their manners in the previous chapter, we can see how they would resonate with Jefferson's conception of the world. Their self-understanding tended to validate American benevolence. Their memories of the Revolution tended to validate liberation. Their optimistic, problem-solving character, together with their experience of personal sovereignty, validated politics as a good. And their strong sense of community gave democracy an immediate relevance. Jefferson was preaching to the choir.

The Democratic Soul

Nothing quite grasped the American imagination like the new politics. The sight of silk-stockinged Whigs trundling a log cabin through the streets to establish the common-man credentials of their candidate was strong evidence that democracy had truly arrived.

Critics of that democracy often portrayed it as a corruption of the Founding—the Athenian road to ruin. Yet Alexis de Tocqueville, who visited America in the early 1830s and focused on just such concerns, found anything but anarchy or mob rule. Under democracy, he observed, Americans were the happiest and best-behaved people on earth.

The primary purpose for Tocqueville's visit was to assess inner qualities of the democratic soul, which he thought destined to become the soul of the world. He found some impressive strengths, to be sure, but he also found glaring weaknesses.

Democratic Weaknesses

If there was a general weakness, it ran all the way back to Aristotle, whose observations convinced him that people fell into two natural categories—rulers and ruled. Rulers were hardwired as it were to exercise reason, cultivate virtue and make decisions. And the ruled—women, children, slaves, foreigners, persons of inferior capacity—were designed to do what they were told. Accordingly, the question posed by democracy was this: if a polity allows the "ruled part" a role in the governing process, what are bound to be the consequences?

Critics of America's budding democracy found several:

Leadership. The traditional notion of statesmanship, often associated with aristocracy, was an early casualty. Personal honor, a sense of decorum, classical learning and much else that was identified with the Founders soon passed out of style.

In the new democracy, operators often worked behind the scenes, leaving it for others to shake hands and make speeches. By extension, the concern for civic virtue was often trumped by the ways of power—which made virtue seem irrelevant. The politics of democracy, alas, could be the politics of the smoke-filled room.

There was a deeper difficulty. In a democracy, Tocqueville observed, leadership must always be weak, for it must always curry and flatter the masses. If the people themselves did not want to make hard choices, or risk present sacrifice for future benefit, or undertake the "great works of mankind"—no leader could inspire them to do so.

Manipulation. Much of what seemed spontaneous in the new politics was actually scripted. And behind the outpouring of grass-roots enthusiasm often lay cold manipulation.

Officeholders themselves took orders. If they owed their election to the party, they were ill advised to pursue an independent course. Where in Jefferson's day elected representatives had come together to plot strategy and ham-

Politics of the Smoke-filled Room

O How often is democratic politics stage-managed from some smoke-filled room, as legend always seems to have it? Probably not often, but it does happen. The Republican nomination of Warren G. Harding for president in 1920 has become an American political classic, and for some people at least, it proved the truth of the legend.

Harding was not a complete dark horse: he had been mentioned as a possibility early on. Yet almost no one looked on him as presidential timber. He was an affable, easygoing man, much given to front-porch gossip and backroom poker, precisely the sort of politician one would expect to come out of a small Ohio town. His real advantage was that he was a party regular and seemed easy to control. And everyone agreed that he looked like a president.

Just as Harding's manager, Harry Daugherty, had confidently predicted, the Chicago convention deadlocked at the outset. The three strong contenders—former Army Chief of Staff Leonard Wood, Illinois Gov. Frank Lowden and California Sen. Hiram Johnson—stalemated one another through ballot after ballot on the first day, until Senator Lodge finally recessed the convention. Late that night, in an assuredly smoke-filled room in the Blackstone Hotel, a group of Republican leaders, mostly senators, debated how to cut the knot. At long last they settled on the senator from Ohio. "This man Harding is no world beater," they later told reporters, "but we think he is the best of the bunch."

At that point, the candidate-to-be, who was asleep in an adjoining suite, was awakened and, still somewhat groggy, led into the room, where he was asked if there was any reason why he shouldn't be nominated. He thought it over but couldn't come up with one. When he went back to bed, it was with the knowledge that he would be the next president of the United States. "Well," he said, "we drew to a pair of deuces and filled."

Not by accident, the Harding administration would go down in history as one riddled with corruption, and the man himself would die, possibly of anguish and disappointment, before its third year. As just one ex-

Warren G. Harding, "the best of the bunch." (Courtesy of Getty Images.)

ample, campaign manager Daugherty, who would become attorney general, would be found running a well-lubricated graft ring from his combination brothel and speakeasy on K Street. The man who had cannily predicted that the nominee would be chosen by "fifteen or twenty men, somewhat weary" at "about eleven minutes after two o'-clock on Friday morning," forgot to predict what else was sure to follow.

mer out agreement, now it was often the party bosses who did that—passing the word down the line. Consider, for example, the instructions given to candidate William Henry Harrison by his Whig strategist. "Let him say not one single word about his principles. Let no committee, no convention, no town meeting ever extract a single word about what he thinks now or will do hereafter."

Others were manipulated as well. Crowds showed up on cue, bearing their placards and chanting their slogans. When candidates were nominated at the conventions, managers in the wings literally timed the audience's cheering on their watches, motioning with hand signals when it was permissible to stop.

Trivialization. Democratic politics occasionally crossed over into pure entertainment, since that was what some voters really wanted. The desire could be indulged in harmless ways, to be sure, but trivializing serious issues could exact a high price.

As a result, what appeared to be engagement in the political process might actually be disengagement from it. Instead of taking part in a decision they would have to live with, the voters were sometimes relegated to the sidelines—and the decision was made by others.

Yet this was by no means a general rule. Recent studies have shown that Jackson-era voters were highly active and well informed. Manipulated or not, they demanded that the party address their needs and aspirations.

Bigotry. In playing to the crowds, democratic politicos sometimes played to the worst in human nature. For if the voters could not be animated by dry issues of state, they could always be fired up by suspicion, fear and hatred—especially of outsiders.

Thus, racism, nativism, xenophobia and religious intolerance were surefire winners on the political stump. We have seen these elements in the American psychological makeup. They could be played up or played down, depending on the circumstance. Democracy couldn't resist the occasional temptation to play them up.

Self-Interest. While any political behavior could be self-interested, democratic self-interest came with a special kind of peril. For the *demos* always outnumbered everyone else. Madison's worst nightmare was the tyranny of the majority, and it wasn't mere theory.

For the most part, the Constitution's control mechanisms held democratic majorities in line. Every once in a while, however, certain interests banded together, usually during hard times, and demanded fundamental change. That farmers "ought to raise less corn and more hell," for example, became a battle cry of the depressed 1890s—and it countenanced some fairly radical measures.

Mandarins were famous in China as supercompetent civil servants, raising administration to a high art.

Corruption. Like self-interest, corruption is always possible in politics no matter what the system. Democratic politics, however, opened up new avenues for it.

With political appointees shuffling on and off the public payroll, there was little hope to cultivate a mandarin-like civil service. With power being exercised behind the scenes, accountability was often hard to nail down. With elections

Of Politics and Pop Culture

The following essay was written by a historian of modern America. Although it is deliberately unkind to both politics and popular culture, its basic thesis—that democratic politicians must appeal to a "pop culture mentality"—is worth thinking about.

Americans, who watch something like four hours of television every day, often seem not to know where popular culture leaves off and serious politics begins. This is because many politicians, in trying to reach the masses, have learned to appeal to the pop-culture mentality. A few particulars:

Popular culture has taught voters to look for, identify with and respond to *images*. I switch to Marlboros because I see myself (or would like to) as that suave, ruggedly handsome cowboy who is always squinting into the sunset. Unsurprisingly, then, politicians build images too. There are plenty of Marlboro Cowboys running for office every year, and their managers know just how to pose them in the light of the setting sun. The classic case, of course, was John Kennedy, who, after his debate with Richard Nixon on television, reminded many voters of the forthright young sheriff they saw every week on *Gunsmoke*. (Kennedy's opponent, with his shifty eyes and five o'clock shadow, reminded them of a "shady railroad lawyer.")

Popular culture has taught voters to love sports. They follow the home team passionately, keep track of box scores and spend Monday nights with the NFL. Politicians trade on this too. They make use of athletic metaphors—running, fighting, winning—and conduct their campaigns like athletic events. Everyone wants to be the come-from-behind candidate, like the team from Podunk who beats Nebraska in the Cotton Bowl, because they know the voters have a soft spot for the fighting underdog. The "fans," of course, are expected to root and cheer and even curse the umpire. And after the votes are counted, they are expected to go home and forget all about it. After all, it's only a game.

Popular culture has given voters a taste for scandal. Magazines like *True Confessions* and *Hollywood Tattler* ply their readers with salacious gossip while soap operas spin out an endless tapestry of intrigue. Politicians make good use of this taste. They know that allegations of scandal—especially juicy scandal—are surefire attention-getters, and on election day can be translated into votes. Bill Clinton should have thought of that when he first met Monica Lewinsky.

Popular culture has taught voters to love melodrama. Familiar heroes and villains permeate our dramatic entertainment, and familiar things happen to them in the end. The politicians know this too. That is why political issues are so often sensationalized and complex situations reduced to caricature. To many Americans Saddam Hussein and Osama bin Laden are not real people at all—just typical foils for *Mission Impossible*.

Popular culture has taught voters to love fantasy, and sometimes to blur its distinction with reality. Boat-eating sharks, a loveable extraterrestrial, a bespectacled boy wizard are not part of the real world. But neither is environmental protection without a heavy price tag, or resolving the Middle East conflict without substantial concessions. Do the voters really understand the difference between "Star Wars" the antiballistic missile system, and *Star Wars* the movie? Some don't.

Popular culture has taught voters to respond to advertising. Peering into the hamburger bun, the little old lady asks "Where's the beef?" and Wendy's doubles its sales. Only naturally, then, Walter Mondale could ask the same question of Gary Hart and wind up with a similar bonanza. (That episode clearly marked the turning point of the 1984 Democratic nomination.) Precisely like advertising, political slogans have long since become bumper-sticker clichés.

Popular culture has taught voters to respond to fads and fashions. Hemlines go up and down. Hairstyles are in and out. Preppy turns punk and punk turns Goth. Similar dynamics govern the fortunes of the politicians. In the 1960s rebellious youth rallied to George McGovern—in the 1980s they switched to Ronald Reagan. Each new cause in democratic politics is presented as the latest bandwagon, with the hope that fashion-minded voters will jump aboard. And, according to the polls, many of them do.

Why are there so many similarities between pop culture and democratic politics? Because both must please the common fancy. If popular culture doesn't give the people exactly what they want, they don't buy it. Politicians live by the same rule.

determined by large numbers, it was fairly simple to buy votes—sometimes on the open market. And with voting affected by crowd behavior, there were all kinds of opportunities for influencing the outcome—everything from ballot-box trickery to intimidation by hired brawlers.

Democracy's weaknesses gave rise to a troubling phenomenon—the political machine. These emerged in most large cities, especially cities housing immigrants, and several of them grasped to control state governments as well.

The most infamous of the political machines was Tammany Hall in New York. It began as one of several Tammany societies founded after the Revolution. It was named after Tamanend, a Delaware Indian chief, and like many other lodges, was replete with pseudo-Indian high signs and watchwords. In the beginning, its activities were merely social and patriotic, but with the advent of democracy it lost its childhood innocence. When the Jeffersonians first challenged the Federalists, Tammany, now under the leadership of Aaron Burr, became the powerhouse of the New York Democratic-Republicans. And with New York as a crucial state in national elections, Tammany came to have an even wider influence.

Tammany Hall backed Andrew Jackson and strongly promoted all the Jacksonian innovations. At the same time, it became New York City's primary welfare agency, helping thousands of Irish immigrants to find jobs, get out of legal scrapes and hold their own against the world. The newcomers were quickly naturalized and easily persuaded to support Tammany's candidates for office. Few of them minded the hints of Tammany Hall corruption now and then surfacing in the press.

Such corruption was anything but negligible. By the reign of Boss Tweed after the Civil War, Tammany was systematically stealing millions from the New York City treasury in the form of padded accounts, kickbacks, fraudulent construction contracts and other forms of graft. Tweed eventually went to jail, but Tammany was virtually unstoppable as a political force. It was not until the 1930s—when the New Deal took on public welfare—that the machine lost its choke hold on New York.

Political machines provided a devastating commentary on the condition of democracy's soul. In one especially notorious case, a mob incited by the Tammany machine of New York clashed with its Whig counterpart in the election of 1834, and three days of rioting was the result. Such scenes might have been all too familiar in ancient Athens—and a chilling reminder of a point made by Plato. He argued that the regime of justice tended to corrupt in stages, each of which worsened the condition of the soul. In the penultimate stage—which was democracy—everyone would pursue desires of the moment, and there would be a great confusion as groups pulled this way and that to gratify their indulgences.

Democratic Strengths

Defenders of American democracy—and their numbers steadily grew—were not slow in making the other side of the case. For every weakness, they said, there was at least one corresponding strength and perhaps several more:

The Tweed Ring

When the New York County auditor was killed in a sleighing accident in March of 1871, his replacement, William Copeland, found that some of the Manhattan Borough ledgers were kept locked away. Curious, he contrived to steal a look at them one day. To his utter amazement, they contained, in neatly penned figures, the untold story of the Tweed Ring. It made for pretty lively reading.

The story began when William Marcy Tweed, a sometime chairmaker, saddler, bookkeeper and fireman, at last found his true calling in politics, and in 1851 became a member of the New York Board of Alderman. Among the "Forty Thieves," as the board was sometimes called, he learned fast. By 1863,when he was made Grand Sachem of Tammany Hall—the granddaddy of American political machines—he was ready to apply his knowledge.

First, Tweed had to get the right few people into the right few slots in New York City government. His control of Tammany Hall helped a great deal, for with Tammany's enormous voting power, he could deploy officeholders like pawns on a chessboard. Eventually he saw to it that Peter "Brains" Sweeny was made city chamberlain, Richard B. "Slippery Dick" Connolly was installed as comptroller, and A. Oakley "O.K." Hall was elected mayor. With himself as president of the Board of Alderman and commissioner of public works, things were finally in the proper alignment.

Now came the payoff. Any contractor who wanted to do city business understood at the outset that he must come up with a 65 percent bribe. However, he could recoup this investment after the contract was awarded by submitting a 65 percent overcharge, which the city would faithfully honor. By such means, the cost of the county courthouse exceeded the architect's $250,000 estimate by a stupefying $12 million. (Itemized, the bill looked even crazier: one carpenter's work for one month cost the city $360,747.61) In five years Tweed and his friends stole $200 million.

Could they be stopped? Not very easily. With $200 million jangling in their pockets, the Ring was capable of unexampled bribery. Legislators were in their pay. Judges were in their pay. Law enforcement officers were in their pay. (When Copeland showed the secret ledger to Sheriff James O'Brien, the latter concluded that his cut hadn't been large enough, and tried to shake down Tweed for more.) And of the newspapers, some eighty-nine locals were directly controlled by Tweed through the use of city advertising.

Besides, New Yorkers rather liked Tweed. He was large—three hundred pounds—soft-spoken, plain

(Courtesy of the Library of Congress.)

mannered, clean living, sanctimonious and unctuously polite. He made sizable donations to every charity in the state. He held some forty public offices, including state senator, and appeared to be a very busy man. He had what we would today call a good public image.

And he had Tammany Hall. The Irishmen of New York did not know about Tweed's shenanigans, and they did not care to learn. They knew only that the Boss liked them, spoke their language, came to their celebrations, marched in their parades, supervised their naturalization as American citizens (150 in a batch, with no questions asked), fixed up their legal troubles and staunchly defended their causes. When election time rolled around,

they sent the Tammany ticket back into office again and again, regardless of what was rumored about graft and corruption. "As long as I count the votes," Tweed said to detractors, "what are you going to do about it?"

What indeed? Tweed and his Ring carried on briskly with their massive larceny. The Boss, a little tastelessly, bought himself a $15,500 diamond stickpin to wear in his cravat. He acquired a handsome house. And when his eldest daughter married, he threw a wedding bash to rival that of royalty. (Someone figured out that the money spent on gifts would have literally purchased the crown jewels of England.) And still the four of them won continual re-election, though some voters wondered how

they could live so well on their meager salaries.

Ultimately, Tweed had bigger plans. If he could control the Democratic Party in New York state, why couldn't he control it in the rest of the country as well, and make himself president? In 1869 he made a serious, and nearly successful, attempt to do just that. If only he could keep those nasty reformers from snapping at his heels. Every time one of them would allege some new wrongdoing on the part of the Ring, Mayor Hall was cued to reply: "It will all blow over." He even repeated the phrase after the secret ledger came to light. "The gusts of reform are wind and clatter," he intoned. "Next year we shall be in Washington."

The Public Good. Democracy imparted new energy to American idealism. Notions of inclusiveness, equal opportunity and individual worth steadily gained ground in the democratic revolution, for the new participants strongly supported them.

Something else was at work. When elites controlled the political process, many groups were simply ignored. But when the common people took charge, there was a much greater concern for the marginalized. Some examples: Immigrants who suffered discrimination could make use of democratic power to redress their grievances. Disadvantaged groups—such as the poor or disabled—could pry opportunity open by advancing their own candidates. Those exposed to unfair labor practices, hazardous working conditions or rank exploitation were often heard by the lawmakers when no one else cared to listen. The secret weapon in all three cases was the ballot box.

While no political system is equitable to everyone, democracy pushed to expand the pale of justice and drive politics toward a true search for the public good. This was the point that Jefferson had finally grasped. The public good lay at the very heart of republican theory, and yet nothing had proved to be more elusive in practice. Democracy made the quest for the public good a practical reality.

Creativity. Democracy had a way of mobilizing human creativity and bringing it to bear. For it came equipped with both a heightened awareness of problems and a widespread appeal for solutions.

As a consequence, Jacksonian America was alive with experiment and innovation. Tocqueville was amazed to see how many projects were afoot for the improvement of communities and the betterment of human life. Even though some of these undertakings were a bit doubtful, they represented a sincere, even devout, wish to make the world better.

In an aristocratic society, new ideas came from specific institutions—such as universities. In a democratic society, innovation bubbled up everywhere. The workers back in the shop did not wait for the front office to make suggestions for improvement—a sense of power and mastery was as common as the suffrage.

Wisdom and Virtue. Arguments against democracy held that wisdom and virtue were inherently aristocratic. The opposite case was equally plausible.

Lacking sophistication, the common people also lacked cynicism and jadedness. If they saw life in simpler terms, there was much to be said for their clarity of vision. The Scottish Enlightenment, as we know, argued for the innate wisdom of ordinary people. The truths that counted, so the argument went, often eluded the trained intellect and were apprehended in nonrational ways. In America, the common people could and did elect both fools and knaves to office, but in critical circumstances they had a way of coming up with an Abraham Lincoln.

The conscience of the common people also played a role. Back when the United States was run by gentlemen, slavery was tolerated in the South and accommodated to American values. With the emergence of democracy, slavery grew into a moral dilemma and finally into a moral outrage.

Redemption. Democracy appeared to have a built-in drive toward reform. Its emergence in Jacksonian America coincided with a veritable outpouring of reform activity—covering everything from temperance to abolitionism.

When politics became based on the common people, it tapped into some urge within human nature to set the world right. Tocqueville saw religion as the source of that urge, noting that those who took their faith most seriously were often in the forefront of the new activism. And it was not accidental that both religious revivalism and religious innovation—as in Mormonism, Adventism, Christian Science, Spiritualism and the like—accompanied the reform impulse. Democracy may have animated American spiritual life as it animated politics.

If rioting in New York showed the new democracy at its worst, there were scenes all over America that cast it in a much fairer light. For if democracy accomplished nothing else, it brought the age-old quest for justice down to the level of the citizen. And despite all the banality and excess, voters who had a real sense of power also had a real sense of commitment. All said and done, they took democracy seriously, not just as a means but an end.

Among Jefferson's beliefs was one he might have borrowed from the Puritans. Truth, for him, did not exist in plural forms, as we often suppose today—it was both unified and universal. Accordingly, he didn't see Truth (with a capital "T") precisely as a matter for voting—as in your truth wins over mine by ten votes. Rather, he saw it as something real, almost tangible, something that would emerge in time from the welter of ideas and perspectives in a public debate. The foremost business of a republic, he believed, was to search for such Truth—and it was every citizen's duty to take part.

The notorious Five Points district of New York, scene of the worst election rioting in US history. Had the Tories been right after all? (Courtesy of Brown Brothers.)

The Great Election Riot

The election of 1834—the first in which the mayor of New York was to be popularly chosen—terminated in mayhem. Campaign offices were attacked. Parades ended in fistfights. Partisans assaulted one another with brickbats, paving stones, knives, even guns. Scores were injured, many of them seriously, and one died. Here is the way a historian described it:

It began as a sort of naval engagement. For the Whigs had built a float-sized model of the *U.S.S. Constitution* and were trundling it through the streets, while the Democrats, in reply, had rigged up their own political boat, and the two vessels, pulled by horses and followed by brass bands, chased one another through Lower Manhattan.

It didn't get ugly until the Whigs towed their little frigate into Five Points, the Democratic stronghold—and New York's most squalid slum. Tammany Hall's Irish "bully b'hoys" brooked no nonsense from political rivals, especially on their own turf. So when one of the invaders taunted that "We should get along well enough if it were not for the low Irish," several fights broke out and swelled into a general melee. The Whigs beat a hasty retreat, but the dogs of war had been loosed. They next appeared at the Masonic Temple on Broadway, where Whig leaders had met to plot strategy. All at once Tammany brawlers rushed through the door and began laying about with shillelaghs and pick handles. That was April 8, the first day of the balloting. There was a great deal more to come.

The following morning, more than five thousand Whigs marched through the streets. They ventured into Five Points once again, flexing their muscles and shouting ethnic slurs. The Democrats retaliated by attacking Whig headquarters all over again. This time guns were drawn and shots fired on both sides, and there were appalling casualties. The Irish then headed to the Wall Street office of James Watson Webb, whose *Courier & Enquirer* had termed the earlier broil a "Reign of Terror." Webb and his men threw up a barricade of bundled papers and retired to the roof with an arsenal of weapons, vowing to shoot the first Jacksonian to come near. Eventually the crowd dispersed.

But on the election's third and final day, all hell broke loose. Once again the Whigs were out in the streets with their provocative little ship, and once again the Gaelic Democrats assaulted them. This time reinforcements streamed out of Whig headquarters and joined the fray, shifting the tide in their favor. But not for long. The Tammanyites summoned their own reserves and soon came charging back along Duane Street. Some fifteen hundred combatants fell upon one another with every weapon at hand—until the Whigs went for the really heavy artillery. They cleaned out the gun shops along Broadway and then headed for the state arsenal at Elm and Franklin, where they broke in and began passing out weapons.

As the crowd swelled to perhaps twenty thousand, Mayor Gideon Lee appeared on the scene with a company of watchmen. He held up his staff and commenced an impassioned plea for order—whereupon a rock sent his top hat spinning and the violence resumed. Lee was knocked to the pavement unconscious, and the watchmen scattered in a hail of stones. "We [are] in the midst of a revolution" cried the New York *Sun*, and not without reason. For the scene might have been out of Jacobin Paris: broken arms, bandaged heads, the fallen lying here and there and the city's chief magistrate—his battered hat now resting on his stomach—being carted off to hospital. His first act upon arriving there was to call out the army.

When the dust finally settled, the Democratic candidate had won the mayoralty by a whisker-thin margin, but the Whigs had captured the Common Council. "My boy," exulted one of them to a comrade, "we have created a truly new party!"

Looking back, we can see the great election riot as an aberration. But what must it have looked like to those who lived through it—and saw in America's new democracy a confirmation of ancient fears.

In democratic America, as Sidney Mead has shown, people often acted on that belief. Clearly they didn't always get the right answer in their quest for Truth and occasionally they got spectacularly wrong ones. But they kept trying. Was it right to put a sign in the window that read: "No dogs or Irishmen allowed"? Was it just to torch the Ursaline Convent in Boston because of alleged Catholic wickedness? Wasn't there something amiss with sending debtors to prison? Shouldn't women be able to control their own property? And what about the right and wrong of slavery?

Democracy, in other words, didn't *exclusively* work corruptions on the soul. For every hired brawler in the Five Points there were many honest seekers of the Good Society. But in contrast to Plato's world, these weren't found exclusively among philosopher kings—they were found among the ordinary. The true state of the democratic soul still awaited its proving.

Suggestions for Further Reading

John Ashworth, *Agrarians and Aristocrats: Party Ideology in the United States, 1837–1846* (1983).

Lance Banning, *The Jeffersonian Persuasion: Evolution of a Party Ideology* (1978).

Donald B. Cole, *Martin Van Buren and the American Political System* (1984).

Alexis de Tocqueville, *Democracy in America*, 2 vols., ed. Phillips Bradley (1945).

Daniel Feller, *The Jacksonian Promise: America 1815–1840* (1995).

Richard Hofstadter, *The Idea of a Party System, 1780–1840* (1969).

Lawrence F. Kohl, *The Politics of Individualism: Parties and the American Character in the Jacksonian Era* (1989).

Shaw Livermore, *The Twilight of Federalism: The Disintegration of the Federalist Party, 1815–1830* (1962).

Richard P. McCormick, *The Second American Party System: Party Formation in the Jacksonian Era* (1966).

Drew McCoy, *The Last of the Fathers: James Madison and the Republican Legacy* (1989).

Robert V. Remini, *Andrew Jackson and the Source of American Freedom* (1981).

Joel H. Sibley, *The Partisan Imperative: The Dynamics of American Politics before the Civil War* (1985).

Harry L. Watson, *Liberty and Power: The Politics of Jacksonian America* (1990).

CHAPTER 15 STUDY AID

(This aid is not all-inclusive and is not intended to be a substitute for thorough study of the material presented in the textbook.)

The Democratic Republic

I. **The Party System**

    1. Federalists v. Democratic-Republicans:
- The election of 1800
- The end of political parties?
- The "Era of Good Feelings"

    2. Political consensus:
- Agreement on fundamentals
- Division over peripheral issues
- "Self-evident truths"
- Limited class distinctions
- "Good government"
- Tendency to avoid or postpone divisive issues

    3. The emergence of the two-party system:
- Jacksonians versus Whigs
- Whigs resemble Federalists
- Jacksonian Democrats resemble Jeffersonians
- Viewing the Founding through different lens—The Bank of the United States controversy
- The legitimacy of dissent

    4. Why two parties:
- Large, single-member voting districts
- "Winner take all"
- Congressional committee system

II. **Dynamics of the Two-Party System**

    1. Parties reflect popular will:
- Platforms

    2. Coordination:
- Extra-constitutional forum
- Overcome structural impediments to coordination

    3. Representative process:
- A broader organization
- General principles

- Influence
- Comprehensive choices for voters

4. Benefits:
- Legitimacy—large majorities = mandate from the people
- Moderation—control of candidates
- Predictability—party represents general principles
- Responsibility

5. Proportional representation versus two-party system:
- Proportional representation encourages ideological parties that behave like factions
  - ▸ Encourages unstable coalitions
- The two-party system encourages accommodation within a party
  - ▸ Encourages competition for non-ideological middle-of-the-road voters
  - ▸ Encourages compromise
  - ▸ Focuses on practicality rather than ideology

6. Consensus and realignment—response to controversial issues that cut across party lines:
- Liberals versus conservatives
- New consensus may yield new political party
- Examples: Jackson, Lincoln, FDR

III. The March of Democracy

1. Fear of democracy:
- Factionalism and mob rule
- Popular government not same as democracy

2. The Democratic revolution:
- Roots of American democracy
- Two-party system and liberalized voting requirements
- Popular participation—political conventions, party newspapers, party organization, ballyhoo, symbols and slogans

3. The "spoils system"—patronage and pork

4. Parties as communities

IV. Democratic Thought

1. Why democracy?
- English heritage
- American character
- American experience

2. Frontier experience—free land

3. Jeffersonianism:
  - From "pure republicanism" to "democratic republicanism"
  - The American "Good Society"—perfectibility, exceptionalism, the "West," politics
  - De-emphasized—materialism and privatism
  - American benevolence
  - Liberation
  - Personal sovereignty
  - Sense of community

V. The Democratic Soul

1. Democratic weaknesses:
  - Leadership—behind the scenes
  - Manipulation—party bosses
  - Trivialization—politics as entertainment
  - Bigotry—use of suspicion, fear and hatred
  - Self-interest—tyranny of the majority
  - Corruption—political machines

2. Democratic strengths:
  - The public good—inclusiveness
  - Creativity—experiment and innovation
  - Wisdom and virtue—the common people
  - Redemption—reform and justice

CHAPTER 15 REVIEW QUESTIONS ━━━━━

NAME: _____   SECTION: _____

Key Terms

Era of Good Feelings

Jacksonians

Two-Party System

Coalitions

Political Realignment

Frederick Jackson Turner

Democratic Weaknesses

Democratic Strengths

Multiple Choice Questions

1. The Whig Party arose in opposition to which president?
   a. John Quincy Adams.
   b. James Madison.
   c. Andrew Jackson.
   d. James K. Polk.

2. Which of the following was not one of the benefits of the two-party system listed in the text?
   a. Legitimacy.
   b. Plurality.
   c. Responsibility.
   d. Moderation.

3. All of the following are methods used by early political parties to gain support except:
   a. Ballyhoo.
   b. Symbols and slogans.
   c. Party newspapers.
   d. Television commercials.

4. Which of the following is not an aspect of democratic creativity discussed in the chapter?
   a. Heightened awareness of social problems.
   b. Experiment and innovation.
   c. Clarity of vision.
   d. Widespread appeal for solutions to problems.

Review Questions

1. Why is consensus such an important part of American politics? How did the drive for consensus grow out of the Founding?

   _____

   _____

   _____

   _____

2. In what ways did the development of a two-party system alter the meaning of the American Founding?

   _____

   _____

   _____

   _____

3. How does the Congressional committee system discourage the proliferation of third parties in American politics?

   _____

   _____

   _____

   _____

4. What is the "spoils system"? How did the spoils system influence the spread of democracy in 19th century America?

   _____

   _____

   _____

   _____

5. Why does democratic politics occasionally lead to trivialization? What are the implications of this trivialization of politics?

   _____

   _____

   _____

   _____

Review Exercises

1. Explain why Andrew Jackson disliked the Bank of the United States. Why did the Whigs want to keep the Bank?

   _____

   _____

   _____

   _____

2. Explain the idea of political realignment. How is the notion of consensus involved in the realignment process?

_____

_____

_____

_____

3. Describe the Turner Thesis. How do Jeffersonian ideas complement Turner's thinking?

_____

_____

_____

_____

Big Essay Question

The chapter discusses Thomas Jefferson's ideal that democracy is really a quest for Truth. Is this just an ideal or can the political process really lead to Truth? In a brief essay explain the notion of Truth in the realm of politics as Jefferson understood it. Then discuss whether or not modern American politics is still engaged in the search for Truth, and if not, what can be done about it.

The Economic Founding

Maiden Lane in New York City. Bustling wharves and a booming economy. (Courtesy of the New-York Historical Society.)

American democracy evolved from the Founding. The same may be said of America's market-based economy. And like democracy, the market system could point to no specific chapter or verse in the Founding documents—only to the fact that Americans increasingly favored market approaches. In this chapter, we want to find out why.

Politics and Property

The ancients acknowledged a close tie between politics and property, but they differed about its meaning. For Plato, property was the root of privatism—it took the mind off politics. Accordingly, when designing his utopia, Plato forbade his Guardians to become property owners. They could never develop the virtue their station called for, he said, if they were distracted by possessions.

Aristotle emphatically disagreed. By his own observations—which for him took precedence over theories—those who owned property were not the problem but the solution. It was *because* they loved their treasure, Aristotle insisted, that property owners cared about society's well-being, for they had a tangible stake in it. Ownership encouraged family values too. The regard for possessions was not unlike the regard for one's own children, Aristotle submitted, and the ability to pass an inheritance from one generation to another boosted family solidarity. Property even applied to justice. How could a man help his neighbor or do a kindness to his community, Aristotle asked, if he lived in abject poverty?

Property owners would rarely be drawn to radical measures, Aristotle reasoned, for such might weaken the state and imperil their holdings. They would most likely be rational and calculating, for such qualities were necessary to successful ownership. And the virtues they would cultivate would not be the extreme ones advocated by Plato but those of moderation. Yet property owners would still be drawn to the political process—for wealth would confer power on them in subtle ways.

For Aristotle, however, more was not necessarily better. A superabundance of property could breed arrogance, insensitivity and a contempt for others. Indeed, a person of stupendous wealth might come to regard the state as his own private possession. Thus, Aristotle preferred the middle class in economic life, as he preferred the middle of the road in politics.

Both Aristotle's hopes and Plato's fears played a role in the American Founding. Recall that Whig property owners had preached the old commonwealth ideology, tying ownership to civic virtue. Recall that spokesmen of a propertied elite had convened in Philadelphia to draft the Constitution. Recall Hamilton's desire to wed the new federal government to the rich and the wellborn.

Finally, recall the commercial republic. It troubled the Founders with yet a new concern. Granted its economic advantages, what was to prevent it from creating great disparities of wealth and poverty? And if it did so, what then? Jefferson's sojourn abroad had shown him cities teeming with a rank, forlorn and resentful underclass. Could a republic abide such a thing? Or survive it?

Two Kinds of Economic Systems

Were we to visit Jacksonian America and ask what people might want of an economic system, their answers would probably emphasize three things:

Freedom. That is, individuals would be hampered by a minimum of economic restriction.

Opportunity. That is, the economy would provide a robust labor market and openings for entrepreneurial endeavor.

Growth. That is, the economy would be capable of improving its per capita performance and increasing society's aggregate wealth.

While these characteristics are often associated with a market economy, they are rarely associated with the mercantilist economy Americans had known as colonists. And in that simple fact lies a fundamental tension: How to change from one way of dealing with the world to its diametrical opposite?

The Political-Economic Problem

One day back in the 1960s, Jerry Rubin, founder of a radical political sect called the Yippies, made his way to the balcony of the New York Stock Exchange and sent a shower of paper dollars cascading down onto the trading floor. He wanted to see the capitalists scramble for them, he told reporters. He was not disappointed.

As a point of fact, human beings will scramble for virtually any scarce goods. Scarcity appears to trigger something primal in our brains, probably because we have lived with it for so long. It has dogged our existence for thousands of years—and continues to do so in times of plenty. For, oddly enough, our wants, which we often regard as needs, appear to be absolutely endless. Those who are comfortable want to be affluent. Those who are affluent want to be wealthy. And those who are wealthy want to be drop-dead rich. Most of Rubin's stock traders were already millionaires, yet they still hustled to pick up the free bucks.

The place to begin any discussion of economics, then, is with the abiding fact of scarcity. That, together with the turmoil Rubin caused, tells us a

Jerry Rubin and Abbie Hoffman: hijinks at the stock exchange. (Courtesy of AP/Wide World Photos.)

basic fact about the human condition: *scarcity causes conflict*. We don't need to be historians to know that most invasions, most revolutions, most out-and-out wars have had something to do with scarcity. Nor need we be philosophers to realize that these cataclysms could not have been prevented in the past—or avoided in the future—simply by improving industrial output. For scarcity will *always* exist.

Conflict is only one of scarcity's handiworks. Another, equally grim, is the merciless, grinding poverty that has typified so much of human existence. Just as most human beings have had to put up with a choice between tyranny and anarchy, most have had to live in circumstances beyond imagining: Constant hunger. Lack of shelter. Little or no medical care. Seventy-hour workweeks. Scant opportunities for enjoyment. No chance for education. No hedge against catastrophe.

(By John Agee, courtesy of the Cartoon Bank.)

When such circumstances prevail, one cannot really speak of political goods at all. Take freedom for example. The best-designed system imaginable can't secure freedom in a world of complete squalor. If, as in the Middle Ages, people find themselves impoverished, tied down, denied any and all opportunity and under the thumb of lord and priest, why should they worry about being free?

Economists have a way of looking at this difficulty. It sounds a bit cold until you think about the reality it describes. How, they ask, can society's scarce goods and services be distributed in such a way as to maximize cooperative behavior and minimize conflict? That in a nutshell is the *Political-Economic Problem*.

In all of history, only three general solutions to the Political-Economic Problem have emerged. And in the modern world, the contest among the three has been essentially narrowed to two:

> *Market systems*. Where prices, profits and other economic "laws" determine the alloca.tion of scarce goods and services.

> *Command systems*. Where the power of government determines the allocation of scarce goods and services.

The third solution was tradition-based systems, where scarce goods and services are allocated according to customary rules.

Old-time British mercantilism was an example of the command alternative.

Mercantilism

In Shakespeare's England, some aspects of economic life were governed by market forces, but virtually everything having to do with national industries or foreign trade was based on mercantilist logic.

Mercantilism's basic goal was to promote economic self-sufficiency and a favorable balance of trade. By carefully managing economic activity through a system of franchises, subsidies and tariffs, the government had to figure out how to import as little as possible, export as much as possible and keep gold moving into, rather than out of, the country's coffers.

Colonies were the centerpiece of the mercantilist system. For rather than having to purchase, say, tobacco from Spain or Portugal (and pay out valuable gold in exchange for it), England could import its own tobacco from Virginia, keep its merchant marine busy with the carrying trade, and hopefully sell the surplus *to* Spain and Portugal!

Mercantilism did not depend on the efficiency of its producers, the prices paid by its consumers, the quality of its products or the profits it generated for investors. It depended, rather, on personal relations among high-ranking officials, government bureaucrats, corporate executives and the controllers of liquid capital, such as the Bank of England. Think of it as the economic side of *patronage*.

We already know something of the difficulties mercantilism created for the American colonists. Their interests were sometimes looked after and sometimes ignored, depending on the politics of the moment, and toward the end, when politics turned nasty, their interests were wholly set aside. For example, that business of the tea. It all came about because the British East India Company—mercantilism in its purest form—was facing bankruptcy, and the politicians in Whitehall had to find a way to bail it out. Yet we shouldn't be too hard on Whitehall. Mercantilism was a given practically everywhere.

That sense of givenness helps us make sense of Hamilton's economic program. What it came down to was the prevailing mercantilist doctrine. Considering the needs of the entire nation—and mercantilism always did that—Hamilton proposed that manufacturing be promoted by means of a protective tariff; that a system of franchises be utilized to develop beneficial industries and internal improvements; and finally, that a bank be set up to supply needed capital. In all these matters, there would be a working partnership between the federal government and Americans of greatest consequence. Political aristocracy and economic command systems often went hand in glove.

Hamilton's ideas, while controversial, were by no means unpopular. Many Americans, and certainly many Federalists, accepted mercantilism as a given. Indeed, it is *still* a given in much of the present-day world. In Asia, for example, most economic systems are conceived in terms of the collective good, not an individual one, and operate according to a "national economic policy." Individuals are expected to subordinate personal desires to the larger goals.

Still, an increasing number of Hamilton's contemporaries were growing impatient with the mercantilist approach. They didn't like its aristocratic tone. They didn't like the complacency, corruption and cronyism that so often accompanied it. And they certainly didn't like its restrictions. If a young man had a better idea for making widgets, the last thing he wanted to hear was that widget making was a licensed monopoly.

The Market System

While mercantilism was still in its heyday, attention began turning toward a wholly different approach to economics. Though we often refer to this alternative as "capitalism," economists prefer the term "market system."

Unlike mercantilism, which requires meticulous planning, the market system operates more or less on its own. The actions of the players are not governed by any set policy at all, but by the players themselves—workers, managers, investors, consumers—each responding to economic forces.

The market system has been around since the Stone Age—its complex interactions performed unconsciously and therefore little noticed. The tribe's "flintwright" was practicing a crude form of it when he bartered his arrowheads for corn. And in the England of high-flying mercantilism, market economics was flourishing in every little hamlet, especially on market day. To appreciate the vitality of market exchange, one need only stand in the town square and watch the shoes and aprons and pitchforks made by the townsfolk being traded for wheat and potatoes and ale brought in from the countryside.

While the market system was taken for granted at the village level, it was considered inappropriate beyond that. After all, market exchange wasn't subject to political authority nor could it respond to some conception of the public good—it was simply individuals gratifying their desires. Yet these curiously rational and self-interested actions began coming to the attention of Enlightenment thinkers, the same ones who found importance in political self-interest. The emerging science of man obviously had economic as well as political dimensions, and the two appeared closely related.

Adam Smith, a prominent figure in the Scottish Enlightenment, became the best known of the new inquirers. Smith set aside conventional wisdom and conducted his own examination of economic behavior. The more he studied and thought, the more clearly he could see that the market system had profound implications for society. Indeed, Smith concluded, if his observations were correct, mercantilism was not only wrong but wrongheaded—defeating the very aims it professed to promote.

Significantly, Smith's book, which would shake the mercantilist world to its foundations, was published in 1776. It was also significantly titled. *An Inquiry into the Nature and Causes of* the *Wealth of Nations* was precisely what mercantilism claimed to have special knowledge of, and if that knowledge was in error, a very great deal was on the line.

For openers, the whole business of securing, maintaining, defending and ruling colonies—which was poignantly at issue just then—might be a stupendous mistake. For Smith compellingly argued that the "wealth of nations" was not created by economic policy at all but by the unfettered workings of the market system.

Town market. Buying, selling and bartering are among the oldest of human activities.
(Courtesy of the Colonial Williamsburg Foundation.)

Adam Smith

Adam Smith, the father of economics, was born in 1723 in Kirkcaldy, Scotland. Smith was the quintessential nerd. He was pale and skinny, had poor vision and never married. Smith was chronically absentminded, and it was said that he was often "absent in the company of friends and sociable when alone." He was frequently seen wandering the beaches of Kirkcaldy muttering to himself.

Despite his peculiarities, Smith's influence on the two hundred years that have followed him cannot be overstated. His book, *An Inquiry into the Nature and Causes of the Wealth of Nations*, published in 1776, has dominated economic thought like no other book has ever ruled over a discipline. The *Wealth of Nations* is nine-hundred sometimes laborious pages of history, sociology, politics, philosophy and economics, and could be subtitled "Everything There Is to Know about Anything in the Eighteenth Century." But more important, the book articulates the principles and identifies the issues that still color our economy today. *The Wealth of Nations* describes how markets work, belittles government intervention in the affairs of men, sings praises to free trade, chides free public education and explains how public virtue and self-interest work together to provide for the betterment of all men, both princes and paupers.

To appreciate *The Wealth of Nations*, it is helpful to understand Smith. He began formal higher education at Glasgow University at the age of fourteen. Three years later he received a scholarship to study at Oxford. Smith loved Glasgow and hated Oxford, for reasons that would after greatly affect his thinking. At Glasgow, teachers were paid according to their skills. Lecturers had a profit motive. At Oxford, teachers were paid a standard with no incentives, and their lectures were stale and uninspiring. Smith would later write that governments should pay for school buildings, and students should pay for teachers. The importance of incentive was forever impressed upon him.

After leaving Oxford, Smith spent two years looking for employment, finally receiving a post as a lecturer in Edinburgh. Soon thereafter, he was invited to join the faculty at Glasgow, where he would spend eleven years. During that time he published his first book, *The Theory of Moral Sentiments*. Smith's critics who claim that he was nothing more than a friend of the rich and an advocate of "survival of the fittest" surely have not read *Moral Sentiments*. The book is about good old-fashioned kindness and paints a picture of men who care as much for others as for themselves. The book was so popular that busts of Smith soon appeared in Glasgow bookstores.

In 1764, Smith was invited to tutor the young Duke of Buccleuch and to travel with him through Europe. This post had two significant effects. First, it gave Smith the opportunity

Adam Smith: Eccentricity and unparalleled brilliance.
(Courtesy of Corbis Images.)

to meet with the best minds of the continent and share ideas with them. Second, Smith was paid three hundred pounds a year for life, an extravagant sum that would allow him to spend time in Kirkcaldy writing *The Wealth of Nations*. It took Smith thirteen years to write the book. Ironically, it was published in 1776, and like *Moral Sentiments*, it was an instant success. He rode the wave of its popularity to the position of commissioner of customs in Scotland, even though the job required him to collect the tariffs that he lambasted in his book. Smith held the job until almost the time of his death, in 1790.

The stories of the man's odd nature and absentmindedness are both legion and legendary. Two stories are especially illustrative. At a dinner one evening, Smith broke into a tirade against a prominent politician and statesman of the day, criticizing both his policies and his character. He quickly recanted, however, when he remembered that one of the statesman's closest relatives was his dinner partner. And as commissioner of customs, Smith would often forge the signature of a prior commissioner when handed official documents. His clerks would then remind him that he had been made the commissioner several months before and had the authority to sign for himself.

But it was his brilliance and not his forgetfulness that made him famous. The economic policies Smith advocated over two hundred years ago are still argued today, and the opinions of most economists of today descend from him. Smith explained how self-interest, if left unfettered by the government, could work to increase the wealth of all men:

It is not from the benevolence of the butcher, the brewer or the baker that we expect our dinner, but from regard of their own interest. We address ourselves, not to their humanity, but to their self-love, and never talk to them of our necessities but of their advantages. . . . Every individual is led by an invisible hand to promote an end which was no part of his intention. By pursuing his own interest he frequently promotes that of the society more effectually than when he really intends to promote it.

Of government planning and intervention, Smith said "Great nations are never impoverished by private (but) by public prodigality and misconduct. For kings and ministers are themselves always, and without exception, the greatest spendthrifts in society." Smith advocated a limited yet important role for government that included national defense, police protection and public works. It did not include meddling with prices and profits. "To prohibit a great people from making all that they can of every part of their own produce, or from employing their stocks and industry in a way that they judge most advantageous to themselves is a manifest violation of the most sacred rights of mankind."

Smith's vision of markets, and the role played by competition in increasing a society's wealth, is continued today by many scholars. His epistles against protectionist tariffs and quotas are still cited in Congress. His writings on taxation, in which he advocated fairness, simplicity and restraint, have not lost any of their applicability. There are few men whose impact on academic thinking has been more pervasive.

—Contributed by Clayne L. Pope, Professor of Economics, Brigham Young University

How Markets Operate

Unlike mercantilism, which must be carefully thought out, the mechanisms of the market system are unplanned—even unconscious. If they come down to a single proposition, it is this: human beings, if free to do so, will act rationally in their own self-interest. It sounds simple but it can get very complicated.

Choice, Cost and Comparative Advantage

The place to begin is with scarcity. Since our wants are endless, scarcity will always rule. We confront this fact by prioritizing. We want the shiny red Porsche first, *then* the condo in Malibu. But even after ranking things in order, we still find ourselves facing choices. Helen says: I can afford to buy the blue dress or the red dress but not both. And every time a choice is made, something is given up. If Helen buys the blue dress, the red one will remain on the rack, and she will never know the joys that might have been hers in wearing it.

Economists define *opportunity cost* as the best alternative given up whenever a choice is made. It is not *every* alternative given up, nor all of them rolled into one, only the *best* alternative. If Helen would have otherwise chosen the red dress, then that becomes the cost of selecting the blue one.

Adam Smith began his analysis with the observation that every person, every group and every nation tends to specialize in producing those goods or services of which they are the low opportunity-cost producer. For example, colonial Virginians wound up specializing in the production of tobacco. They did so not because they were necessarily better at it than, say, London bankers, but because they found themselves in a situation where they gave up very little to grow tobacco, while London bankers would have had to give up their lucrative enterprises and much else in order to make tobacco culture work. Accordingly, Virginians could charge much less for tobacco than Londoners could. And the latter could charge much less for banking services.

This tendency, which operates independent of social, cultural or political factors, is called *the law of comparative advantage*. It is crucial for understanding how the market system works—and why its workings often seem to violate common sense. For common sense would hold that sophisticated London bankers ought to be better at tobacco farming than down-home provincials were, and therefore ought to be doing it themselves.

Smith noted that the law of comparative advantage had far-reaching consequences. If allowed to operate freely, it could change the world. To begin with, it would always drive an economy toward the full employment of resources—something mercantilism never did. This is because the opportunity cost of an unemployed resource is zero. A worker who is out of a job and sitting in the park gives up nothing but her leisure to flip hamburgers—so, barring a free handout, she is disposed to go to work for McDonalds. Similarly, an empty store or an unused warehouse tends to attract new tenants—if only the local karate club—for the owner gives up nothing to put such facilities back into operation.

This example may seem strained, but in our own time we often suppose that the Japanese ought to produce everything since they are so good at it. The law of comparative advantage suggests that they cannot have an advantage in every product.

Second, there is a tendency to produce all goods and services at the lowest opportunity cost possible. The market becomes a sleuth searching the world over for those who will do a job for less because they have less to give up. This is why manufacturing tends to move "offshore." The market goes to a village in Indonesia, where people have nothing to give up but sloshing around in a rice paddy, and says: "How would you like to go to work making computer chips?" A dollar an hour sounds like a fortune to them. And just imagine what it does for the price of computers.

Finally, there is a tendency toward economic interdependency. Precisely because the market hunts down that low-cost producer anywhere and everywhere,

CORPORATE LEADERS GATHER IN A FIELD OUTSIDE DARIEN, CONNECTICUT, WHERE ONE OF THEM CLAIMS TO HAVE SEEN THE INVISIBLE HAND OF THE MARKETPLACE.

(By Dana Fradon, courtesy of the Cartoon Bank.)

we find ourselves at the mercy of anyone and everyone for the goods and services we enjoy. A simple wooden pencil comes from places all over the globe. If there is a strike in the Brazilian timber industry, no wood for the pencil. If there is an earthquake in Crete, no tin for the little brass clip that holds the eraser. If there is political turmoil in Zaire, no graphite for the pencil's "lead." The market system is a one-world proposition.

Prices, Profits and Competition

The law of comparative advantage makes it possible to specialize and exchange. Each producer of goods and services comes to the marketplace and offers to exchange his or her particular specialty for all others that may be desired, using money as a medium of exchange.

The terms of the exchange process are governed not by external controls but by what Smith called the "invisible hand" of prices and profits. These too were "laws," Smith explained, and they operated so predictably it could be plotted on a graph:

> *Law of Supply.* When the price of a good or service rises, suppliers will want to supply more of that good or service.

> *Law of Demand.* When the price of a good or service rises, consumers will want to consume less of that good or service.

At what economists call the *equilibrium price*, the amount that suppliers wish to supply exactly equals the amount that consumers demand, and there will be no further price movement until conditions change.

Another kind of equilibrium is created by profits. High profits in a given industry tend to attract investment and activity, so that more and more suppliers

Supply and Demand:
http://ecedweb.uomaha.edu/
Dem_Sup/demand.htm

http://ecedweb.uomaha.edu/
Dem_Sup/supply.htm

http://tfc-charts.w2d
.com/learning/
law_of_demand.html

http://tfc-charts.w2d
.com/learning/
law_of_supply.html

http://tfc-charts.w2d
.com/learning/
supply_and_demand.html

will soon participate. Low or negative profits have precisely the opposite effect. At some point, equilibrium is reached and profits are neither especially high nor especially low but "acceptable."

No single player in the economic game can control prices, profits or terms of exchange because, in what Smith thought of as the natural order of things, there is free competition among all buyers, sellers, producers, distributors and laborers. Everyone acts independently according to the price and profit signals they receive.

Implications of the Market System

Smith demonstrated how specialization and exchange create wealth. In a famous example, he described how a group of pin makers, each specializing in some particular facet of the manufacturing process, could turn out many times more pins than the same number of individuals working alone. And with the later development of the moving assembly line—as in, say, an automobile plant—the leverage went higher still.

What created "the wealth of nations," then, was not economic restriction, as mercantilists supposed, but precisely the opposite, economic *un*restriction. For the more the players freely specialized and exchanged, the lower they drove opportunity cost and the more goods and services they accounted for. If there were no artificial restraints—the kind mercantilism always imposed—markets would go right on searching out low-cost producers and multiplying the benefits of exchange. The process reached toward the entire globe.

We might think of this wealth-making magic as the market system's stated promise. There were several implied promises as well. The first of these was freedom. In a command system, government power determined the allocation of resources, the terms of employment and sometimes even the prices of fin-

Assembly line. What specialization did for pin making, Henry Ford did for the automobile.
(Courtesy of Ford Motor Company, Dearborn, Michigan.)

ished goods. In a market system, all this was left to Smith's "invisible hand." Individuals, acting in their own self-interest, made the decisions that determined all outcomes, and no bureaucrats were on hand to say they must do this or must not do that. As a result, people not only felt freer, they actually were.

The second implied promise was opportunity. Command systems always restricted opportunity in one way or another. Production was limited to favored guilds. Distribution was awarded to specific franchises. Overseas trade was throttled with tariffs and quotas. But in a pure market system opportunity was wide open. Anyone with a new idea, a different approach or just a good deal of brass could break in.

A third implied promise was economic growth. All economic systems had inefficiencies that hampered optimal performance.

Henry Ford: A Case Study in Creating Wealth

Henry Ford provides a handy example of how specialization and exchange can create wealth. Before Ford came along, automobile production was a slow, expensive undertaking. A team of highly skilled artisans would build a car essentially from the ground up, fabricating parts as they went, then roll it out the door and build another one. The opportunity cost of such workers was extremely high, for they could always go down the street and build cars for someone else. As a result, automobile prices were very high. Motorcars were playthings for the rich.

All of this changed dramatically in the early 1910s. In an upstairs room of Ford's Highland Park, Michigan factory, a group of his workers were assembling magnetos (part of the Model T's ignition system) when someone got an idea. Instead of putting the magnetos together one at a time, why not try lining the workers up behind a long table and sliding the assemblies along it, each person performing a single task in the process? They were astonished to see how much more efficient things suddenly became. The same number of producers could more than triple their output without expending any more effort. But it had all been foretold by Adam Smith long ago—his parable of the pin makers carried to its logical conclusion.

By the end of 1912, Ford was developing a whole new approach to manufacturing, one that combined interchangeable parts, a meticulous division of labor and a continuous moving assembly line. The Ford factory became a great river of production, with small tributaries flowing into larger streams, and the streams joining the main waterway. Engines swung along overhead conveyors and dropped down into place. Doors and fenders were lifted from moving belts and bolted onto moving frames. Painters sprayed on the color (always black) as auto bodies bumped along in front of them. And every sixty seconds another Model T rolled out onto the loading dock. By 1913, Ford's volume had reached an inconceivable 75,000 units.

Mass production slashed the cost of Ford's vehicles. From a price per unit of around $1,200 in 1909—which even then was competitive—the figure spiraled steadily downward through the ensuing decade to an unheard of $225! The descent was so singular that Ford felt he had to account for it to his customers. "We have no apology to make for this price," a brochure explained, "but it is only fair that in explanation we assure you that the price is simply the result of the Ford Quantity System of Production."

Ford was creating wealth, all right, enormous wealth—some $64 million in annual profits—and he might have created even more. For the new workers were no longer high cost automotive technicians but ordinary laborers, and Ford could have paid them appreciably less. However, he had another flash of insight. He realized that if they were paid a decent wage, his workers could afford to purchase the vehicles they were making. Suddenly a vision of the future opened before him: it wasn't going to be a world of haves and have-nots any longer, but a world of generalized ownership. Accordingly, in a move so bold that it left the country gasping, Ford decided to *double* his employees' wages. He had come to see them as potential customers, and believed that if industrial practice followed his lead, there would soon be millions of others like them, buying the Tin Lizzies he could turn out like hotcakes.

Henry Ford became the prophet of the consumer society.

The particular inefficiencies of command systems stemmed from the inability of government planners to give the "right" production signals. As a result, producers were forever knocking out too many goods, too few goods, the wrong kind of goods, or goods of shabby quality—enormous inefficiencies. In a market system, by contrast, the power of self-interest was harnessed to efficient performance, for prices and profits unerringly delivered the "right" signals. Accordingly, market systems often experienced more or less steady growth—that is, greater per capita output—over an extended period of time. In a market system, there was a tendency for everyone, rich and poor alike, to grow richer.

Americans and the Market System

In England and much of Europe, the market system had to make its way slowly, often painfully, meeting dogged resistance from entrenched interests, old ways of thinking and the force of tradition. With every reform there were voices warning against "dangerous innovation."

In America circumstances were different. Interests were less entrenched. Ways of thinking were more supple. And while some traditions carried over from the Old World, tradition itself had a far looser grip. And since Americans favored the freedom, opportunity and material prosperity that markets promised to deliver, they resonated with market-style behavior.

The Founding made a difference too. For its ideas and ideals were often as relevant to the economic world as they were to the political. We might think of the Founding as inspiring, accelerating, perhaps even instigating the market revolution. The Declaration of Independence divorced past from future and cleared the way for change. The Constitution established the commercial republic—and the largest free market in history.

Between Washington's inauguration and Jackson's farewell a half-century later, virtually all the infrastructure required by the market system was laid in place. Its elements included the following:

An initial deposit in a bank can legally be multiplied several times. For example, $500 on deposit could ultimately be lent out as $5000.

Corporation: A legal term in which a group of individuals is considered a single entity for the purpose of limiting their personal liability in financial undertakings.

Flexible currency. Hamilton's fiscal plan secured a stable currency and confidence in government bonds. At the same time, inflationary policies in state governments fueled a surge of borrowing and investment.

A banking system. The Bank of the United States and its expanding branches provided the beginnings of a national banking system. Other banks, chartered by individual states, filled in the blank spaces. Banks contributed their share toward a stable yet flexible currency. Moreover, they pulled money out of thin air and made it available for investment.

Corporations. The concept of the corporation was shorn of its connection to the public good—a connection that had held corporations down—and restrictions on incorporation were gradually lifted. Furthermore, as the idea of limited liability caught on, Americans were encouraged to take bigger risks.

Transportation systems. Beginning with the first "turnpike" toll roads, Americans entered upon a century-long transportation revolution. The turnpike phase was soon followed by the canal phase and that by the steamboat phase. By mid-century the nation boasted enough railroad mileage to encircle the globe, and one railroad was being planned to span the continent. Each new phase of the transportation revolution expanded the scope of profitable exchange.

Industrialization. In filling a large order for government firearms, gunsmith Eli Whitney had found a way to manufacture the various components to exact specifications, with the result that each hammer, each trigger, each barrel could be fitted to any gun. Interchangeable parts made mass production possible. It also helped rationalize the production process, making each element so simple that unskilled laborers could be substituted for high-priced artisans.

Technological breakthroughs. Interchangeable parts were only the first of many far-reaching innovations. Americans made stunning breakthroughs in steam-engine technology, in sailing vessel design and in the proliferation of laborsaving machinery. Some inventions, moreover, made whole new industries possible. Whitney's cotton gin gave rise to the plantation South. Glidden's barbed wire opened the way for cattle ranching. And Colt's repeating revolver led to the conquest of the Great Plains.

Powerhouse industries. A few key industries made many others possible. Steel, for example, or coal, both of which were necessary for further industrial development, sputtered into life in Jacksonian America. Cotton growing led to cotton milling, then fabric weaving, and ultimately to the apparel industry. Spin-offs made ever wider circles.

Consumerism. A democratized idea of gentility promoted consumerism. Ordinary people began wanting symbols of the good life, and to get them they created mass markets for everything from knickknacks to fine china. It took a while to free Americans from the old Puritan notion of consumption as an evil. This was accomplished in large part by consumer advertising, which learned how make words and pictures represent middle-class dreams.

Legal support. The legal foundations of the market economy consisted of new legislation favoring commerce, pro-business interpretations of the common law and several landmark Supreme Court decisions. One of the latter, *Dartmouth College v. Woodward*, upheld the sanctity of contracts. Another, the *Charles River Bridge* case, came down for innovation over prerogative. More subtly, courts began to interpret rights by the light of liberal individualism rather than community interest.

Sears, Roebuck catalogue. The consumer society meant advertising. (Courtesy of Corbis Images.)

Ladies' luncheon at Delmonico's in New York City, 1902.
Consumption would beget conspicuous consumption.
(Courtesy of the Museum of the City of New York.)

None of these factors would have had much effect without a dynamic spirit of creativity. One felt it everywhere. When US trade was stymied after the Revolution, merchants headed off to such exotic places as China, Chile and Madagascar. When timber supplies dwindled beyond the Appalachians, builders worked out a novel form of construction called the "balloon frame," requiring less material. And while inventors were tinkering with wood-turning lathes and steam-engine valves, entrepreneurs were developing new kinds of business organization, new accounting methods, new product ideas, new marketing techniques.

The Founding quietly fostered such innovativeness, mostly by recasting public attitudes. Before the Revolution, the prevailing strain of republicanism was often the classical one, marked by a consciousness of virtue and a spirit of self-denial. The Founding turned backward-looking into forward-looking, and asceticism into modest indulgence. Americans whose parents and grandparents had lived in a two-room cabin began thinking about lace curtains for the bedrooms and a piano for the parlor. They spoke less about the Roman Republic and more about their own future. Classical republicanism took a back seat to the liberal and democratic varieties.

As a result, *liberal democracy*, as Americans would come to call it, was not solely about political participation. It was about adding onto the house, starting up a business, tinkering with the mowing machine to make it cut closer. It was about pressuring the mayor's office to lure the new railroad hither, about sending your son (even your daughter!) to college, about loading a clipper ship with ice from the local millpond and sending it off to India. Ultimately it was about re-creating oneself.

Commercial Mentality

Even in America, many of the changes catalyzed by the market system were painful. For commerce came equipped with a new set of values, a new logic, a new view of the world. While we have come to take such things for granted today, they were still a bit scary in Jackson's time. In a recent book on the subject, Charles Sellers has argued that many of the political battles fought during Jackson's presidency were really about the implications of market economics.

These larger difficulties were encountered on two levels, that of the individual and that of the nation. We should consider them one at a time.

Commerce and Character

Commerce affected virtually every aspect of the tidy, homespun world we associate with the American Revolution. More than anything else, it affected the way people thought.

For thousands of years, institutions rested on conceptions of human nature that focused on pride, glory, self-admiration, utopian perfectionism, religious fanaticism, quixotic adventurism and the like. In the world of the market system, such conceptions no longer seemed valid. On the contrary, people seemed far more interested in comfort, security, wealth and individual accomplishment—all of them personal rather than social ambitions. As Ralph Lerner has observed:

> Where the ancient polity, Christianity, and the feudal aristocracy, each in its own fashion, sought to conceal, deny, or thwart most of the common passions for private gratification and physical comfort, the commercial republic built on those passions.

Adam Smith argued that the market analysis of human nature was the more accurate one. Accordingly, Jacksonian Americans in their more advanced commercial society were bound to be happier and better adjusted than those living in colonial times. And that was only the beginning.

In a commercial society, prosperity depended on the widest possible compass of human interaction. Thus, there was a built-in tendency to seek peace among nations, to tolerate cultural differences and to promote human understanding. There was a parallel tendency toward stability. When market mechanisms balanced one person's interest against another's, the result was equilibrium, much as in Madison's large republic, and self-interest stayed in bounds. Commerce took much of the burden off governance.

There was more. Since commerce favored productivity, a commercial society preferred productive values to the more traditional ones. Thus, raw ability counted more than inherited rank or status did, and hard work, thrift, prudential behavior and the deferral of gratification were all held in regard. A different sort of person tended to get to the top.

In a commercial society, there was much emphasis on equality of opportunity but little on equality of result. On the contrary, it was often assumed that those of conspicuous talent and energy would wind up with great wealth and political power too. Aristotle had deplored the latter situation but Adam Smith took it in stride. When the best people were running things, he said, things would be better run. It was only when titled incompetents were put in charge that there was trouble.

Finally, commercial society had the effect of making the common people ambitious and enterprising, unlocking a vast storehouse of creativity. For there was nothing to compare with the power of human self-interest.

Not all attributes of the commercial personality were positive. As commerce reshaped society, practical ways of thinking and doing took on ever greater importance and left little room for art, beauty or grace. The aristocratic quest for excel-

EQUALITY OF OPPORTUNITY

Each participant in the economy should have an equal chance of economic success or failure. All should start the race at the same place and run under the same conditions with outcomes depending on individual performance.

EQUALITY OF RESULTS

Each participant in the economy should receive the same economic rewards regardless of performance.

lence was replaced, sighed Tocqueville, by "standards of prudent and conscious mediocrity." There was an economic explanation for this. The market system always sought out the low-cost producer, never the "best." As a result, mediocrity flourished everywhere.

There was also a tendency for organic wholeness in a society to dissolve into mere commercial relations, and for human beings to become no more than contracting parties. Affection could degrade into calculation, leaving people cut off from one another, while competition sorted them into winners and losers. And commerce promoted a desire for luxury and extravagance—a desire forever unfilled. "Restlessness goaded these people on," wrote Ralph Lerner, "and the prospect of happiness, like the horizon, beckoned and receded before them."

With its multiplying gratifications, the commercial world lured some away from public duties as well, just as Tocqueville predicted. It could also dampen ordinary decency, and on occasion turn the soul into flint. Those in pursuit of gain might become unkind and mean-spirited, even downright predatory, believing that everything had its price.

Finally, the market-driven world was one of contingency and impermanence. In contrast to the old agrarian ways, commercial America was constantly changing as innovators came up with a better this, a faster that, a newfangled something else. The pace became bewildering.

Commerce, then, loosened many of the old moorings. The result was often constructive, to be sure, but not universally so.

Commerce and Nationhood

While market economics was coming to the fore, observers on both sides of the Atlantic were thinking about its long-range implications. If Adam Smith was one key question-asker, another was a German economist named **Friedrich List**. List wrote a generation after Smith but focused on many of the same issues. And he arrived at markedly different conclusions.

The debate between List and Smith was roughly analogous to that between Hamilton and Jefferson, and was thus ultimately about the idea of nationhood. Unlike Alexander Hamilton, List wrote out his philosophy in detail and carefully argued each point, as had Adam Smith in *The Wealth of Nations*. The dialogue between them is instructive for us because Americans, in establishing an economic founding, had to make a choice between List's and Smith's conceptions of political-economy.

• Listian Political-Economy

Where Adam Smith was concerned about the well-being of individuals, Friedrich List was concerned about the well-being of nation-states. What is best for the country as a whole? he asked, and why should that be the paramount question? Then he spelled out his answers.

The Entrepreneurs

They come in all shapes, sizes and ages. You can't pick them out of your high school yearbook. Some are financial wizards; others can't balance their checkbook. Some dress in three-piece suits and carry sharkskin briefcases; others wear jeans and cowboy boots. Some sit in the back of 35-foot-long limos making deals over the telephone; others ride around in old pickups. They are the entrepreneurs—the few that make an economy grow and change. They destroy the old way of doing things—leaving insolvent companies, unemployment and shattered lives in their path. But they create the new way—building vibrant industries, generating new jobs, higher incomes and better living conditions for millions of people.

Sometimes we think entrepreneurs are distant figures form the past such as Edison trying different filaments for an electric light, or Andrew Carnegie shrewdly building a giant steel company out of nothing, or John D. Rockefeller combining all facets of the oil industry from exploration to the gasoline pump into Standard Oil, the mother company to a half-dozen *Fortune 500* companies today. But entrepreneurs flourish wherever markets exist and money can be made. They are with us today.

Any list of the richest Americans in the 1980s included a soft-spoken gentleman from Bentonville, Arkansas. Most mornings Sam Walton had a cup of coffee at the local diner and went off to manage his Walmart stores. Walton sensed that small-town rural America as well as the big cities could sustain discount stores. Through tight management controls and shrewd choices of location, he built a fortune out of merchandizing to the people in pickups like his. By 1989, the Walton family was estimated to be worth $9 billion.

Steven Jobs, along with his friend Stephen Wozniak, had the idea that a small computer could be tailored for the use of everyday consumers or employees doing dozen of different tasks. Wozniak, an employee of Intel, and Jobs, who worked for Atari video games, tinkered around Jobs' garage until they had built a working home computer that they sold to other computer freaks. Apple Computer was born when they got financial backing to market nationally. Soon the personal computer was under way. Steven Jobs was eventually forced out of Apple Computer, but you shouldn't feel sorry for him. He started a competing company and has an estimated fortune of $250 million. Many followed in his footsteps building fortunes off the personal computer. Most notably, Bill Gates, the founder of Microsoft, has a fortune estimated at nearly $60 billion.

The list could go on. But the point is clear. If money is to be made, entrepreneurs are there to make it, while the rest of us watch from the sidelines asking ourselves why we didn't think of that.

Friedrich List. Where Smith sought the well-being of individuals, List sought the well-being of nations.
(By Josef Kriehuber, courtesy of Presse-und Informatiosamt der Budnesregierung.)

In the first place, List said, a people can't afford to let economic freedom rule—for it is an unwise ruler. If, for example, the growth of major industries were simply left up to chance—as the market system does—such industries may develop in a haphazard way or not at all. (Some other low-cost producer, for instance, may wind up supplying steel or fossil fuel.) Well and good in time of peace, perhaps, but what about time of war? And what about placing oneself at the mercy of an economic rival?

Second, List argued that the people themselves were never good judges of how resources should be used, for they never gave a thought to *society's* interest. As a consequence, market choices could never create a true public benefit, much less a decent, moral way of life. Such ends could only be achieved, List thought, through strong government leadership.

Third, List argued that the test of an economy was what it could *produce*, not *consume*. Indeed, he lectured, if a society couldn't produce it couldn't consume either. Accordingly, government policies should always favor production over consumption, and should encourage the one and discourage the other.

Finally, List asserted that international trade was a rough-and-tumble game that the contestants must play to win. If a nation became strong in the right ways, it could dictate to others, building political mastery through commercial success. In such a struggle, List conceded, it was sometimes necessary to wring profits from one's own people through artificially high prices in order to build up a war chest for overseas competition. Thus, trade quotas, tariffs, monopolies and the like—all of which raised prices at home—could build up the industrial strength necessary to undersell rivals abroad.

Such arguments made sense to Americans because of their own experience with Great Britain—adept at Listian practices. The British mercantile system of monopolies, tariffs and protected markets had made it possible to lead out in the industrial revolution and rise to dominance in world trade.

Thus Hamiltonianism. In his *Report on Manufactures* (1791), Hamilton argued that the US couldn't hope to catch up with the British unless it was willing to subsidize its own industries and shelter them with tariffs. Indeed, added Albert Gallatin later on, so great was the British advantage, Americans might *never* pull astride. A "powerful obstacle" to American industry was "the vastly superior capital of Great Britain which enables her merchants to give very long term credits, to sell on small profits, and to make occasional sacrifices." Once out in front, moreover, the British found it possible to engage in commercial buccaneering. They could, for example, "dump" manufactured articles in a foreign market—that is, sell them at a loss—in order to drive local producers to the wall; then they could move in and take charge.

Even while Americans grudgingly admired British mercantilism, they recognized some of its dangers. Economics designed to benefit one nation-state at the expense of another did not promote peace and stability. The American Revolution had been among the bitter fruits of mercantilism, and it would not be the last. Trade wars, colonial rebellions and imperial showdowns would continue to ruffle the world throughout the nineteenth century—and shatter it in the twentieth.

• List versus Smith

Even as mercantilism marched forward, the thoughtful read Adam Smith with new understanding. The market approach presented new ideas about the world and these offered much to ponder. Was List right? Or was Smith?

Where List argued that the development of major industries could not be left up to chance, Smith would counter "Why not?" The laws of supply and demand, together with the economic function of profits, insured that money would end up where it did most people the most good. With the single exception of national defense—which might require certain vital industries—investment ought to be free to go where it would.

Where List held that market-based decisions could never define a true public good, Smith would come back with the same "Why not?" What "good" was out there beyond individuals' own perceived self-interest? Government could tell people in a paternal way that they *ought* to worry about one thing or another but it couldn't really change their minds—and especially in a political democracy. All it could do was hobble the economy in the name of some "ought."

Where List favored producers—who were always well connected—Smith favored consumers. What good is an economy, he asked, if it doesn't benefit *everyone*? If markets were allowed to operate freely, producers would make an honest profit (never an exorbitant one), laborers would make an honest wage (never an unfair one), and consumers would buy every good and service at the lowest possible cost. What was wrong with that?

Where List spoke of winners and losers in international trade, Smith spoke of *universal* benefit. To mercantilists that seemed downright bizarre. But Smith pointed out that every market exchange benefited *both* parties—buyer as well as seller, producer as well as consumer. There was no need to get the better of one's trading partners, for the market world was not one in which Britain's gain had to be Germany's loss. It was a world, rather, in which the size of the economic pie could be expanded through economic growth—and a bigger piece for Britain might mean a bigger piece for Germany as well.

Finally, where List condoned the gouging of one's own consumers in order to assault the economy of some rival, Smith shook his head in sorrow. Such tactics hurt everyone, he said. In economic warfare there were no victors, only victims.

At bottom, the respective doctrines of Adam Smith and Friedrich List represented two different views of the human condition. In List's world, the nation was the important thing, and its welfare justified individual sacrifice. It was a philosophy tinged with xenophobia. It suggested that all peoples ought to consider themselves at odds with all other peoples on the planet, and they were justified in doing whatever they must in order to prevail. Economics, said List, was about power and purpose, not about right and wrong.

In Smith's world, individuals were the important thing. It was for him to imagine a "national interest" apart from that of a nation's people. Indeed, as

Adam Smith:
http://socserv2socsci
.mcmaster.ca/~econ/ugcm/
3113/smith/farrar.html

http://iisd/iisd.ca/pcdf/
corprule/betrayal.htm

Friedrich List:
http://socsci.mcmaster.ca/
~econ/ugcm/3113/list

http://www.geocities.com/
Athens/Academy/1223/
krnkn_list_f.html

Smith talked of supply and demand and exchange, national boundaries tended to fade from the picture entirely. The low-cost producer of a given good or service might reside in this country or that one—or on the other side of the world.

The Tilt of the Economic Founding

From what we have sketched above, one can see that Adam Smith's ideas about the market system had a special relevance for the American Founding. Politics and economics truly were bedfellows.

For example, the message of liberal democracy, reduced to simplest terms, was that individuals were important. The message of the market system was identical. A similar parallel applied to opportunity. Command systems, such as that defended by List, depended on the same sort of privilege as aristocracy did, restricting this, barring that, placing something else in a favored position. The market system, by contrast, declared all opportunity to be wide open.

By stressing the collectivity, List and his colleagues sorted among groups, including some and excluding others, forging a world of insiders and outsiders. By stressing the individual, Adam Smith seconded the motion that all human beings were born equal and endowed with the same rights.

They differed about human nature too. Listians drew upon Plato and supposed that people would work hard, endure sacrifice and postpone gratification for the sake of civic virtue. Smithians preferred Aristotle. They believed that hard work and sacrifice were more likely to be undertaken for the good of the self than for the good of the nation.

Finally, the two systems required different governance. List's neomercantilism needed a powerful and officious government, able to get its way against grass-roots opposition. Smith's market capitalism allowed people to behave more or less as they thought they should, and it worked in tandem with constitutional mechanisms to balance interest against interest. Thus it pointed toward personal liberty.

So, was the choice between these alternatives a no-brainer? Anything but. For a variety of reasons, many Americans actually preferred List's philosophy, and not only back in the early days but right down to the present. Others, of course, were drawn to the thinking of Adam Smith. If there was a subtext to the American economic drama, it was double-mindedness over this fundamental choice. The Economic Founding was like a balance beam, now tilting this way and now tilting that.

The trouble was that economic theory never completely fit real-world circumstances. Take free trade, for example. Americans noted that the British could now afford to extol its virtues not solely because they had been converted by Adam Smith but also because they had built up a commanding lead over their rivals. For the rivals, though, things weren't so simple—they were like start-ups competing with Microsoft. Consequently, in their drive to catch up with the British, Americans did many of the same things the old-time mercantilists had done. They placed high tariffs on manufactured goods to protect local markets.

Listian Economics in James Michener's Alaska

When novelist James A. Michener wrote his fictionalized history of Alaska, he focused special attention on the manner by which Seattle merchants had conspired to hold Alaska in imperialistic bondage. It was a twentieth-century phenomenon, to be sure, but its mechanisms were those advocated by Friedrich List a century before, and its costs were enormous. Although the characters are fictitious, the effect of the Jones Act presented by Michener is accurate:

The Jones Act of 1920 passed with its three essential provisions in place: no ship of foreign ownership and registry could carry American goods from one American port to another; only ships owned and manned by Americans could do that; the ship itself, even if it was American-owned, had to have been built in the United States by American labor. The future of Seattle was ensured.

The effect of the Jones Act could best be illustrated by what happened to a modest grocery store in Anchorage. Sylvester Rowntree had invested his savings in a new store half again as big as the old one, and by the year 1923 it had again doubled, so that the owner could have profitably ordered, from suppliers across the United States, his goods in cargo lots. . . . But now the provisions of the Jones Act came into play: to use the Seattle docks for shipment to Alaska cost almost twice what the same dock services cost for a shipment, say, to Japan. And when the R&R [Ross & Raglan] ship was loaded, the cost-per-mile of goods to Alaska was much higher than the cost of the same goods being shipped to

other American ports by other lines. R&R had a monopoly which exacted a fifty-percent or better surcharge on every item freighted into Alaska, and the territory had no escape from this imposition, for there were no other avenues by which goods could get in: no highways, no railroads, and as yet no airplanes.

"That damned Jones Act is strangling us," Sylvester Rowntree wailed, and he was right, for the Act exercised its tyranny in the most unexpected ways. The forests of Alaska could have provided wooden boxes for the Alaskan salmon canneries, but the cost of bringing in American sawmill equipment was kept so excessive that it was much cheaper to buy the wood from Oregon than to use trees which stood fifty feet from a cannery, and tariffs kept out non-American.

In the years following passage of the Act, a dozen profitable extractive industries went out of business because of the exorbitant costs imposed by the new rules, and this happened even though scores of Canadian ships stood ready to bring heavy equipment in at reasonable cost and take finished products out at rates that ensured a good profit.

Such discrepancies were explained away by Marvin Hoxey, defending in public the Act which he had engineered, as "inescapable minor dislocations which can be easily corrected." When no attempt was made to rectify them, he told Congress: "These are nothing more than the minor costs which a remote territory like Alaska must expect to bear if it is to enjoy the privileges of life within

the American system." In his old age Hoxey had converted himself into a revered oracle, forever prepared to justify the indecencies to which Alaska was subjected.

What infuriated Alaskans like grocer Rowntree was not the pomposity of Hoxey and the self-serving statements of Thomas Venn, president of Ross & Raglan, but the fact that Hawaii, much farther from San Francisco than Alaska was from Seattle, received its goods at substantially cheaper rates. Rowntree's seventeen-year-old son, Oliver, figured: "Pop, if a grocer in Honolulu places a hundred-dollar order at the same time you do with a wholesaler in New York, by the time the two orders reach the West Coast docks, his has a total cost of $126, but yours is $147. Dockage fees being so different, by the time his goods get aboard they cost $137, but yours are $163. And now comes the rotten part. Because R&R rates are the highest in the world, by the time his goods reach Honolulu, they cost $152, while your goods landed in Anchorage cost us $191."

Defenders of the Jones Act came back with their own arguments, of course. They pointed out that the legislation boosted the nation's commerce, kept its merchant marine healthy and held the wages of US workers well above those of foreign competitors. These were all valid Listian points. But they did little to mollify outraged Alaskans, who paid some of the highest consumer prices in the world, or keep Sylvester Rowntree in business. Eventually he threw in the towel and called it quits.

They set up partnerships between government and private industry. They dabbled in economic planning. And later on, they even got into colonialism and began building their own empire.

On the local level, too, there was systematic intervention into the economy, generally in the name of community supervision. Certain markets were monitored and regulated, while others, such as gambling and prostitution, were shut down completely. City planning gave rise to meticulous zoning ordinances. Age limits, curfews, Sunday closing laws and a host of gender-specific regulations hobbled exchange in a variety of ways. Like Friedrich List, Americans did not trust the marketplace to make prime decisions.

Yet at the same time, Americans departed from the Listian faith. They sought out new markets, as we have seen, hunting whales in the far Pacific and hauling Russian pelts to China. They negotiated tariff reductions with some trading partners. And they asserted commercial rights so aggressively during the Napoleonic Wars that they were eventually drawn into the conflict themselves.

As their industry began to burgeon, Americans came to see advantages of their own in free trade. It would be nice, they said, to sell their own surplus manufactures overseas. Besides, foodstuff production was fast outpacing local demand, and cotton was rising to worldwide importance. The United States was achieving the same sort of dominance enjoyed by Great Britain.

Thus, by mid-century, Americans were coming to appreciate both the logic and broader vision of Adam Smith. They took the lead in opening Japan to foreign intercourse. And later on, in embracing their "open door policy" in China, they took a momentous step toward the new thinking. All countries ought to be free to trade with China, they maintained, and the US would fight if it must to defend that principle.

Open Door Policy: US policy of seeking equal trade and commercial opportunities in foreign nations and regions.

A FAIR FIELD AND NO FAVOR.
UNCLE SAM: "I'm out for commerce, not conquest."

(Courtesy of Stock Montage, Inc.)

On the other hand, the Listian side of their thinking drove Americans to take economic advantage of poorer, weaker countries, especially in the Western Hemisphere. In Mexico, Cuba and much of Central America, they pursued what was called *Yanqui imperialismo*, fortifying their commercial strength with gunboats. And some Americans—such as William Jennings Bryan—eloquently deplored that pursuit. Was it for us of all people to mimic the Old World and its ways? Bryan cried. What a betrayal of our ideals!

Americans were beginning to see what the market system implied for the world community. Just as they viewed their own Revolution as a herald of political freedom, they were coming to view the market revolution as a herald of the economic. Yet it was hard for them to defend either variety—and call down the Hitlers and Stalins of the world—in the face of their own high-handedness. Much of their Vietnam-era soul-searching was based on just such confusion.

In present-day America, the market system has achieved an almost religious orthodoxy and Adam Smith has become a secular saint. But the ghost of Friedrich List

The Race to the Bottom

Is Listian economics out of date? Anything but. It is a going concern in the modern world and continues to have clout in America. The latest installment, dated 2001, is by Alan Tonelson, a research fellow at the US Business and Industry Council. It is titled *The Race to the Bottom: Why a Worldwide Worker Surplus and Uncontrolled Free Trade Are Sinking American Living Standards*. For those who fear that Adam Smith's promises may amount to pie in the sky, the book is worth a read.

How, asks Tonelson, can Americans continue to believe in "neoliberal" economics in light of its failure in Russia, the Asian financial crisis and the recent bursting of the technology bubble? His prime arguments have to do with low-wage labor. The effect of globalization is to enlarge the available pool of such labor, for markets relentlessly search out the low-cost producer. While this does put people to work, it does not do so at high wage levels, especially in the poorest countries. And even in advanced countries wages often fall, for the high-paying jobs in manufacturing tend to move off-shore, while low-paying jobs in the service sector attract ever more applicants. Add a huge immigrant labor force to the equation and you wind up with twenty-first century America—a first-world economy with a third-world underclass.

Tonelson's solution? Play the game the way others do, placing the nation's needs first. He notes that developing countries like China and Korea require US multinationals "to transfer technology, to provide investment capital for other parts of the buyer's economy, or to purchase goods completely unrelated to the original transaction." America could press similar demands. It could also stem the tide of immigration and make it much tougher for companies to let those high-paying jobs go south.

Tonelson does not address the upside of the situation he describes—full employment, low inflation and a high rate of growth—nor does he discuss the living standards made possible by inexpensive consumer goods. That would require another book, written by someone else. Which is another way of saying that the debate between Friedrich List and Adam Smith continues to rattle on.

still haunts. When we fret about the environment, or pollution, or hazards in the workplace, or economic justice, or those dizzying cycles of boom and bust, we acknowledge that markets can't fix everything.

The American Economic Founding, in other words, is still in dynamic equilibrium. It tilts both ways.

Suggestions for Further Reading

Joyce Appleby, *Capitalism and a New Social Order: The Republican Vision of the 1790s* (1984).

W. Eliot Brownlee, *Dynamics of Ascent: A History of the American Economy* (1979).

James Fallows, "How the World Works," *Atlantic Monthly* (December 1993).

James Fallows, "What Is an Economy For?" *Atlantic Monthly* (January 1994).

Paul W. Gates, *The Farmer's Age: Agriculture, 1815–1860* (1966).

Carter Goodrich, *Government Promotion of American Canals and Railroads, 1800–1890* (1960).

Brooke Hindle and Steven Lubar, *Engines of Change: The American Industrial Revolution, 1790–1860* (1986).

Jack Larkin, *The Reshaping of Everyday Life, 1790–1840* (1988).

William J. Novak, *The People's Welfare: Law and Regulation in Nineteenth-Century America* (1996).

David M. Potter, *People of Plenty: Economic Abundance and the American Character* (1954).

Charles Sellers, *The Market Revolution: Jacksonian America, 1815–1846* (1991).

George Rogers Taylor, *The Transportation Revolution, 1815–1860* (1951).

CHAPTER 16 STUDY AID ▬▬▬▬▬

(This aid is not all-inclusive and is not intended to be a substitute for thorough study of the material presented in the textbook.)

The Economic Founding

I. Politics and Property

1. Plato—property = privatism:
   - Distracts from politics
   - "Guardians" not to own property
2. Aristotle—self-interest generates concern for society's well-being:
   - Font of family values and solidarity
   - Source of quest for justice
   - Source of moderation
   - Power draws one towards politics
   - Middle class most balanced influence
3. The American Founding—ownership and civic virtue (commonwealth ideology):
   - Constitutional convention = propertied elites
   - Commercial republic = economic class divisions

II. Two Economic Systems

1. The idealized American vision:
   - Freedom—minimum economic restriction
   - Opportunity—entrepreneurial
   - Growth—economic expansion
2. The political-economic problem:
   - Scarcity—wants cannot be satisfied—
     - ► Causes conflict
     - ► Will always exist
     - ► Related to poverty
   - How can scarce goods and services be distributed to maximize cooperation and minimize conflict?
     - ► Market systems
     - ► Command systems
3. Mercantilism (a command system):
   - Economic self-sufficiency
   - Favorable balance of trade
   - Colonialism
   - Economic "patronage"

- The way things are—Hamiltonian mercantilism—
  - ► Tariffs
  - ► Franchises
  - ► National bank
  - ► Convergence of government and economic interests in the hands of an elite
  - ► Pursuit of a collective "good"
  - ► Limited individual economic liberty
4. The market system:
   - Capitalism by another name
   - Adam Smith
5. The operation of markets:
   - Choice, cost, and comparative advantage—
     - ► Opportunity cost—the best alternative given up
     - ► Law of comparative advantage results in low opportunity cost producers
     - ► Specialization
     - ► Full employment of resources
     - ► Producers seek lowest opportunity cost possible
     - ► Economic interdependency
   - Prices, profits and competition—
     - ► Unseen hand
     - ► Law of supply = price rises, supply increases
     - ► Law of demand = price rises, consumption falls
     - ► Equilibrium price = supply and demand in balance
     - ► Free competition
6. Implications of market system:
   - Specialization and exchange create wealth
   - Freedom
   - Opportunity
   - Economic growth

III. America and the Market System

1. America and the market system:
   - Flexible currency
   - Banking system
   - Corporations
   - Transportation system
   - Industrialization

- Technological breakthroughs
- Powerhouse industries
- Consumerism
- Legal support

2. Spirit of creativity:
   - Innovation
   - Forward-looking
   - Liberal democracy

IV. Commercial Mentality

1. Commerce and character (commerce affects the way people think and interact):
   - Positive aspects—
     - More advanced commercial societies should be happier (more in tune with human nature)
     - Commercial societies would tend to seek peace, tolerance and understanding (better for business)
     - Tend to promote stability
     - Favor ability above status
     - Favor prudence and deferred gratification
     - Unlock creativity
   - Negative aspects—
     - Displace art, beauty, and peace
     - Encourage mediocrity
     - Human relations reduced to commercial transactions
     - Calculation rather than affection
     - Competition
     - Materialism
     - Restlessness
     - Privatism
     - Impermanence

2. Commerce and nationhood:
   - Friedrich List—
     - Well-being of nation-states paramount, not individuals
     - Economic freedom not in best interest of the state
     - Government must lead
     - Production more important than consumption
     - Mastery of international trade essential
   - Hamiltonianism—
     - Response to British mercantilism

- List versus Adam Smith—
  - ▶ Command economy versus supply and demand
  - ▶ Government "oughts" versus self-interest
  - ▶ Producers versus consumers
  - ▶ Winners and losers versus universal benefits
  - ▶ Economic welfare versus invisible hand
  - ▶ Nation versus the individual
- Factors influencing an economic founding—
  - ▶ Liberal democracy emphasizes liberty of individual, market economy also does so, while command economy emphasizes collective rather than individual opportunity
  - ▶ Market economy fosters unlimited opportunity
  - ▶ List favors Plato's insights
  - ▶ Adam Smith favors Aristotle's insights
  - ▶ Neomercantilism (Hamilton) favors strong government
  - ▶ Market capitalism favors personal liberty
- America's economic founding—
  - ▶ Double-mindedness
  - ▶ External and internal intervention in the market
  - ▶ Extols virtues of free trade
  - ▶ *Yanqui imperialismo*
  - ▶ Dynamic equilibrium between command and free market elements

NAME: _____   SECTION: _____

Key Terms

Property

Scarcity

Market System

Command System

Mercantilism

Adam Smith

Opportunity Cost

Friedrich List

Multiple Choice Questions

1. All of the following were what people wanted out of their economic system at the time of Andrew Jackson except:
   a. Freedom.
   b. Opportunity.
   c. Equality.
   d. Growth.

2. Who wrote *An Inquiry Into the Wealth of Nations* in 1776?
   a. Friedrich List.
   b. Thomas Jefferson.
   c. Alexander Hamilton.
   d. Adam Smith.

3. The idea that when prices rise producers will want to make more of a good or service is called:
   a. The law of supply.
   b. The law of demand.
   c. Opportunity cost.
   d. Comparative advantage.

4. Adam Smith favored all of the following except:
   a. Consumers.
   b. Lack of government intervention in the market.
   c. Taking advantage of weaker trading partners.
   d. Individuals.

Review Questions

1. What were Aristotle's views on the role of owning property in a political system?

   _____

   _____

   _____

   _____

2. In what ways does mercantilism exemplify the idea of a command system economy?

   _____

   _____

   _____

   _____

3. According to Adam Smith, how is the "wealth of nations" created?

   _____

   _____

   _____

   _____

4. How did technological innovations encourage the development of a market economy in America in the early to mid-1800s?

   _____

   _____

   _____

   _____

5. What was Friedrich List's economic philosophy? Have Americans totally rejected his ideas?

   _____

   _____

   _____

   _____

Review Exercises

1. Explain the law of comparative advantage. What role does this principle play in a market economy?

   _____

   _____

   _____

   _____

2. Explain the law of demand. How does the law of demand interact with the law of supply to create an equilibrium price?

_____

_____

_____

_____

3. Briefly describe the role of economic factors in the idea of liberal democracy in America.

_____

_____

_____

_____

Big Essay Question

This chapter discusses the political-economic problem and various approaches countries have adopted to solve it. In a thoughtful essay explain what the political-economic problem is, and whether or not you think either a command or a market economic approach is capable of solving it. Are there other alternative economic systems that would better solve the problem of scarcity? Explain.

CHAPTER 17

A New Birth of Freedom

(Courtesy of PhotoDisc, Inc.)

Despite the growing enthusiasm of most Americans, there were early signs that the American Founding had its weaknesses. Here and there disgruntled groups groused about their ill fortunes in the Union, and during the War of 1812 New Englanders met at Hartford, Connecticut to consider pulling out altogether. Two decades later, South Carolina "nullified" a piece of federal legislation and advanced arguments for lawful secession. And in 1836 a Boston editor, calling the Constitution "an agreement with hell," publicly burned a copy of it while his followers intoned a solemn "Amen." If these were only straws in the wind, it was a wind that seemed ominous.

Forgotten Americans

Much of the difficulty was rooted, oddly enough, in the Declaration of Independence. As Americans looked back, they increasingly identified that document as the Founding's spiritual centerpiece. Its opening paragraphs came to be accepted as holy writ and their significance pondered accordingly. What did it mean, Americans asked, that "all men are created equal," that "they are endowed by their Creator with certain unalienable rights," that they may not be governed without their consent? Were these principles to be taken as literally true? And if so, how well did they account for everyday realities? The answer, of course, was: not very well.

Native Americans

The presence in the New World of Native Americans—or "Indians" as Columbus hopefully christened them—proved to be endlessly complicating and hopelessly tragic.

Europeans had been struggling with "otherness" for centuries, and like most groups on the planet, had made little headway in accepting it. At first, they viewed the New World as Paradise Found, and its native inhabitants as God's favored children. But when the latter's use of torture and cannibalism convinced voyagers that the original assessment had been dead wrong, the Indian was quickly demoted to "daemon," "devill" and "childe of hell."

These biblical epithets fit nicely into the Puritans' conception of the New World. The American continent was an either/or place for them: if it was not the Promised Land, it was the hellish wilderness. And when it truly was hellish—and the perfidy of the Indians made it more so—Puritan perceptions became set in stone. In the Pequot War (1636), Massachusetts Bay settlers ruthlessly butchered men, women and children, putting entire villages to the torch and gunning down the survivors. They justified such conduct by the scriptures.

Even where White-Indian relations were not inspired by the Old Testament, the "Indian as other" proved to be cause enough for calamity. Frictions were always occurring out on the frontier. Promises were broken. Communication failed. Animals were stolen or simply wandered off. Chance encounters provoked violence. And European practice suggested that the most effective way of dealing with such incidents was to employ the strategy of "massive retaliation"—hit them back so hard that they will never try it again.

Sooner or later, brushfire conflicts almost always gave way to a general war, as the hard-pressed and often brutally battered natives would mount a go-for-broke effort to push the invaders out for good. And the inevitable failure of these attempts would shape the direction of all future intercourse.

The pattern went something like this. A war would be fought and the Indians would lose. They would be driven toward the west, to occupy lands regarded as worthless. White settlers would then push into the borders of those lands and a whole new set of frictions would arise. Tensions would build up on both sides and eventually touch off another war.

White-Indian relations were further complicated, if possible, by the European struggle for empire. Both the French in the north and the Spanish in the south made use of Indians as scouts, allies and proxies, sending them to attack English frontier settlements. During the Revolutionary War, Britain adopted similar tactics. The result was that hostility continued to simmer on the frontier long after the peace was signed.

At the close of the war, the Ohio Valley was thrown open to settlement and American pioneers marched in to occupy Indian territory. In dealing with the inhabitants, whites made use of a number of devices developed over the colonial period, including intimidation, fraudulent purchase and the never quite fair negotiated treaty. They justified the taking of Indian lands by appealing to biblical precepts, such as the notion that God reserved the earth for those who minded its tillage.

While the Indians were being exploited and defrauded, a few Americans struggled to include them in the constitutional polity in some way. But how? Their culture was so unlike that of the transplanted Europeans that they could hardly be regarded as citizens. Still, Puritan missionaries such as John Eliot had preached to the Indians and realized fair success, and life in the "praying towns" proved that Native Americans were far more adaptable than whites were. In the end, however, most such attempts were doomed. The converted Indians found themselves caught between opposing forces and ground to dust.

African Americans

The earliest voyages of discovery ran not westward to the New World but southward along the coast of Africa. The indigenous peoples thus encountered were neither understood nor appreciated—as Marco Polo had appreciated the Chinese—but were pitied, disdained or regarded as repellant. After all, they were black.

These "blackamoors," as they were called, had been hunted down and enslaved for a thousand years. Indeed, between the seventh and nineteenth centuries, Arab slavers are estimated to have transported more than fourteen million African captives across the Sahara and the Red Sea. Europeans now muscled into the trade themselves.

Slavery is not only an ancient practice, it is arguably part of the human condition. Before the nineteenth century, unfree labor in the form of serfdom, peonage, indenture, debt bondage and chattel slavery was all but universal. It was also taken for granted in the ancient world, where philosophers not only justified it but republicanized it, arguing that slave labor provided citizens the leisure for politics.

The American continent, with its rich potential and vast "empty" lands, was a perfect setting for slavery, and the imported "black-amoors" seemed perfect for the tasks at hand. As an institution, servitude ranged all the way from unspeakable harshness—generally characteristic of Latin America and the Caribbean—to somewhat milder forms. Markets, not morality, made

Slave ship. Opposition to slavery led America toward the Civil War. (Courtesy of the Library of Congress.)

the difference. Where slaves were expensive, they were treated with the care one would provide any costly investment. And they were expensive in the American South.

Nowhere was slavery questioned before the mid-1700s—a fact we might find astonishing today. But stop and think: for slavery to be doubted there must first exist a clear and compelling concept of freedom and such was simply not to be found. Throughout Latin America, which was ruled by absolute monarchs, slavery was accepted as a matter of course. And even where ideas of freedom were sprouting, in the English colonies, they were not associated with the laboring class, which was regarded as base and degraded. For most Americans there was little difference between a slave and an indentured servant.

The earliest stirrings of antislavery came from Quaker Pennsylvania and were based on a theological argument. For the choice between good and evil to have meaning, it had to be freely made, so spiritual freedom required personal freedom—and there must be something wrong with slavery. Abolitionist pioneers such as John Woolman began preaching this gospel to any and all who would listen.

But it was the ideas of the American Revolution that sowed the serious misgivings. If human beings were free and equal as a matter of nature, it made no sense for an island to rule a continent, as the revolutionists kept saying, but neither did it make sense for a white boss to rule a slave gang. The trouble was that slavery was now firmly established in the American colonies, and in the South, where it supported a thriving economy of tobacco, rice and indigo production, it had proven that it could pay handsomely. And beyond simple greed there were other considerations. Most whites regarded Africans as unfit for freedom, and their hostility toward free blacks bespoke the tip of a dangerous iceberg. Without slavery, gargantuan difficulties loomed.

Slavery/Abolition:
http://lcweb.loc.gov/exhibits/
african/afam001.html

http://lcweb.loc.gov/exhibits/
african/afam005.html

http://afgen.com/slave.1
.html

http://lcweb2.loc.gov/
ammem/aaohtm/exhibit/
aointro.html

http://lcweb2.loc.gov/
ammem/aaohtm/exhibit/
aopart1.html

Woolman preached
against slavery in the
1750s and 1760s.

John Woolman:
http://www.mindspring
.com/~strecorsoc/jwoolman/
title.html

In order to maintain the "peculiar institution" in the face of growing uneasiness, it was necessary to deny the slave's humanity, portraying him as infantile, irresponsible, even feeble minded. Yet such arguments proved hard to sustain. The accomplishments of Phillis Wheatley as a poet, Benjamin Banneker as a scholar and mathematician and Frederick Douglass as an orator and statesman had a decidedly unsettling effect. The only real hope was that slavery would somehow just die out.

We have already seen that the acceptance of slavery was the necessary price of union. While the Framers at Philadelphia would be roundly rebuked for paying that price, political scientist Dinesh D'Souza has given a more thoughtful analysis of the choice they had to make. It was not a compromise between principle and practice, D'Souza writes, but between "antislavery and majority consent." The Framers knew full well that slavery contravened the premises of popular government, but they also knew that most Americans accepted the practice. To outlaw slavery without the consent of the majority would *also* destroy popular government.

As a result of this paradox, D'Souza concludes, the Framers produced a Constitution in which slavery was tolerated, in deference to consent, but nowhere given moral approval. The Framers refused to recognize racial distinctions—avoiding the words *slave* or *Negro*—and their use of the word *persons* slyly acknowledged the slaves' natural rights. And if they protected the slave trade for a period of twenty years, they also condemned it by implication, tacitly admitting that it *ought* to be eliminated.

Abraham Lincoln, who was a profound student of the Founding, had a similar view of what the Founders had intended. Of the Declaration of Independence he wrote:

> They did not mean to assert the obvious untruth, that all were then actually enjoying that equality, nor yet, that they were about to confer it immediately upon them. . . .They meant simply to declare the *right*, so that the *enforcement* of it might follow as fast as circumstances should permit.

In sum, as historian Gordon Wood points out, "Before the revolution, Americans like every other people took slavery for granted. But slavery came under indictment as a result of the same principles that produced the American Founding. In this sense, the prospect of the Civil War is implicitly contained in the Declaration of Independence."

Slavery did die out north of Maryland, partly for economic reasons but mostly owing to its dissonance with the Founding. Elsewhere, however, it took a new lease on life with the advent of the cotton gin, with the opening of rich lands to the west, and with the flowering of optimism in the new republic.

American Women

The condition of women in the American colonies was little better than elsewhere. Typically, women were under the thumb of fathers, husbands, even their own male children.

In early America, women and children labored beside men.
(*Fields of Onions At Wethersfield*, courtesy of the Wethersfield Historical Society.)

Married women could not make contracts, control wealth or own real property. Their rights of inheritance and the guardianship of their children were severely limited. Even their wages were generally handed over.

Beyond these constraints, women's lives were subject to high-pressure drudgery, to boredom and loneliness, to marital relationships based on obedience and to careful training in psychological dependency. They were saddled with household duties (cooking, cleaning, mending, weaving, wood chopping, candle making, and a variety of farm chores), childrearing (six to eight) and operating associated family enterprises. They had a plateful.

Women's lot was justified by the "natural order" of the world, which declared them "the weaker vessel." They were also regarded as irrational, sensual, prone to luxury and inclined to sin. Moreover, the organic nature of Christian society, which was described in II Corinthians, required some members of the community to be the hands and some to be the feet. Women, of course, were the womb.

Women were held down by ministers as well as husbands and fathers, who saw to it that any spare energy was channeled into piety rather than politics. Nor did they get much help from intellectuals. Rousseau, for example, taught that women took up serious matters at the forfeit of their sexual identity—an idea dogging feminism to this day.

It is no accident that a Boston firebrand should have been the first to connect the plight of women to the Revolution. "Are not women born as free as men?" asked James Otis. "Would it not be infamous to assert that the ladies are all slaves by nature?" John Adams began to wonder himself. He concluded that although women weren't precisely slaves, they *were* dependent and therefore unsuited to republican freedom.

Other revolutionists came to different conclusions. Benjamin Rush, for one, took up the improvement of women's education in the new republic, arguing that the Revolution mandated change in all aspects of society—including gender roles. "[L]et the ladies of a country be educated properly, and they will not only make and administer its laws, but form its manners and character," he prophesied.

The Revolution also put women on the firing line in modest ways. They became participants, occasionally even leaders, in the boycott movement, demonstrating that, contrary to their "nature," they could turn away from self-indulgence as well as any man. They served the army as nurses, cooks and spies, occasionally even as soldiers. And thousands of them shouldered the burden of the family farm or business enterprise while the men were off fighting. Even this limited liberation had psychological effects, and from time to time we catch glimpses of them. Molly Pitcher's colorful comment when a British cannonball zipped between her legs couldn't have been made by a shrinking violet.

The Revolution suspended some of the old taboos too. Wives, for example, took to discussing political matters with their husbands. Proto-feminists Abigail

"Occupation?"
"Woman."

(By Chon Day, courtesy of the Cartoon Bank.)

Women's Movement:
http://www.umkc.edu/imc/adamsa.htm

http://chnm.gmu.edu/courses/zagarri/hist499/students/farish.html

That remark was made by Mary Ludwig Hays, who took her wounded husband's place on a cannon crew. She was the first woman to receive a military pension from Congress. "Molly Pitcher" was a nickname for several courageous women who helped American forces.

Hannah Fayerweather: Political astuteness among the "frail sex." (By John Singleton Copley, courtesy of Corbis Images.)

Adams, Mercy Otis Warren and Hannah Fayerweather often reported such conversations with an awakening enthusiasm. Adams was an especially good learner. Appropriating one of her husband's favorite adages, she declared: "All *men* would be tyrants if they could."

And there was the occasional place where theory and practice might actually coincide. In the concept of "republican motherhood," for instance, women could argue that they had a political role to play even through it was limited and indirect. The republican mother could teach civic virtue to her sons, they said, and thus watch over the revolutionary ethos. "Liberty is never sure, 'till Virtue reigns triumphant," wrote Benjamin Rush. "While you [women] thus keep our country virtuous, you maintain its independence."

It was probably inevitable that the Revolution sooner or later address the plight of women. Yet it was also probably inevitable that the time must wait for a new generation to come forth—one raised republican.

Jacksonian Reform

Accompanying the Jacksonian revolution was the first great reform period in US history. While democracy itself does not automatically generate reform, the American democracy, as we have seen, was deeply suffused with Puritan ideas and values and these worked a leavening for political betterment.

A key element of the Puritan legacy was the idea of the godly community. It held that righteousness was a matter for everyone's concern, not just pious churchgoers, for God might visit the wayward with fire, flood or marauding pirates. We use the term *soul-searching* to describe the process whereby an individual asks difficult, introspective questions, such as whether his life is in keeping with professed ideals. Sidney Mead has argued that precisely such soul-searching, Puritan inspired, became a driving force in American democracy.

Other streams fed into the reform-mindedness. Republican virtue was broadened out and enlisted. Religious revivalism made reformers out of many burgeoning new sects. And the Founding itself made a contribution. It gave Americans enormous self-confidence and made them conscious of setting an example.

Jacksonian reform took on a panoply of ills. It redesigned prisons, improved orphanages and humanized insane asylums. It set up public schools, founded scores of colleges, laid out park lands and beautified cities. It devised better police systems and more effective weapons against vice. And it mounted a spirited temperance crusade. But the reformers focused their main efforts where founding ideals were at stake. The forgotten Americans had begun to trouble them.

Native Americans

American treatment of the Indians, for instance, became increasingly bothersome to the reform conscience. Intellectuals began asking who the Indians were, what they symbolized and what value might be found in their culture. They even began wondering how Native Americans might fit into a more inclusive conception of nationhood.

They still encountered opposition, however. Indian wars continued to punctuate American life and political capital continued to be made from them. American folk heroes from Daniel Boone to Davy Crockett earned their stripes as Indian fighters. And where tribes continued to occupy promising lands, there were always plenty of covetous white settlers. This was particularly true in the Georgia backcountry, where the Cherokees and Chickasaws had settled down to an agrarian way of life. The problem wasn't so much that they were heathens—but that they were in the way.

Indian wars and "removals" nevertheless troubled the thoughtful. How could a nation founded upon justice behave so cynically? reformers asked. Jackson's cold-blooded exile of the Cherokees—attended by unspeakable horror—bothered some Americans quite as much as it did Alexis de Tocqueville. Just what were "American principles" anyway?

Native Americans:
http://falcon.jmu.edu/
~ramseyil/native.htm

http://www.yale.edu/
lawweb/avalon/ntreaty.htm

http://ngeorgia.com/
history/nghisttt.html

Trail of Tears: In 1838 the US government used the military to force Cherokees to march from their Georgia homelands to the Indian territory in the West. Thousands died along the way.

Trail of Tears. *Robert Lindneux's painting depicts the expulsion of the Cherokees.*
(Courtesy of Corbis Images.)

Andrew Jackson's "Benevolent" Indian Policy

General Andrew Jackson was the hero of the Battle of New Orleans and a noted Indian fighter against the Creeks and Seminoles before being elected president in 1828. The following excerpts from his second annual message to Congress in 1830 reflects his defense of the government's Indian removal policy:

It gives me pleasure to announce to Congress that the benevolent policy of the government, steadily pursued for nearly thirty years, in relation to the removal of the Indians beyond the white settlements is approaching to a happy consummation. Two important tribes have accepted the provision made for their removal at the last session of Congress, and it is believed that their example will induce the remaining tribes to seek the same obvious advantages.

The consequences of a speedy removal will be important to the United States, to individual States, and to the Indians themselves. . . . It will place a dense and civilized population in large tracts of country now occupied by a few savage hunters. . . . It will separate the Indians from immediate contact with settlements of whites; free them from the power of the States; enable them to pursue happiness in their own way and under their own rude institutions; will retard the progress of decay, which is lessening their numbers, and perhaps cause them gradually, under the protection of the Government and through the influence of good counsels, to cast off their savage habits and become an interesting, civilized, and Christian community. . . .

Toward the aborigines of the country no one can indulge a more friendly feeling than myself, or would go further in attempting to reclaim them from their wandering habits and make them a happy, prosperous people. . . . What good man would prefer a country covered with forests and ranged by a few thousand savages to our extensive Republic, studded with cities, towns and prosperous farms, embellished with all the improvements which art can devise and industry execute, occupied by more than twelve million happy people, and filled with all the blessings of liberty, civilization and religion? . . .

The waves of population and civilization are rolling to the westward, and we now propose to acquire the countries occupied by the red men of the South and West by a fair exchange, and, at the expense of the United States, to send them to a land where their existence may be prolonged and perhaps made perpetual. Doubtless it will be painful to leave the graves of their fathers; but what do they more than our ancestors did or than our children are now doing? . . .

Can it be cruel in this Government when, by events which it can not control, the Indian is made discontented in his ancient home to purchase his lands, to give him a new and extensive territory, to pay the expense of his removal, and support him a year in his new abode? How many thousands of our own people would gladly embrace the opportunity of removing to the West on such conditions! If the offers made to the Indians were extended to them, they would be hailed with gratitude and joy.

And is it supposed that the wandering savage has a stronger attachment to his home than the settled, civilized Christian? Is it more afflicting to him to leave the graves of his fathers than it is to our brothers and children? Rightly considered, the policy of the General government toward the red man is not only liberal, but generous. He is unwilling to submit to the laws of the States and mingle with their population. To save him from this alternative, or perhaps utter annihilation, the General Government kindly offers him a new home, and proposes to pay the whole expense of his removal and settlement.

Women's Liberation

Certain aspects of women's lives were improved, at least marginally, in the early republic. Commercial prosperity and a rising middle class rescued some women from nonstop drudgery. Greater opportunities for education were afforded by the women's college movement. More women had time and energy for activities outside the home.

Women coming together, if only at the parish bake sale, spread awareness of their common grievances. It also opened a door for them into the reform movement. They began as the movement's handmaidens—their all-too-familiar role—and thus humbly took orders from the clergy. But Abolitionist William Lloyd Garrison changed all that. One didn't need to consult Parson So-and-So, he told his female followers, to make sure one was in line. *Be your own person.*

Garrison pursued the logic of the Founding remorselessly. For him, personhood was all that counted. Black or white, male or female, bond or free—all were created equal, all were endowed with rights, all were given reason and moral conscience and all must be held accountable. It was time for practice to catch up with theory.

The notion had come up before. As early as 1801, a pamphleteer known only as "The Female Advocate" had argued for the full integration of women into politics. And Judith Sargent Murray had written:

> *The idea of the incapability* of women, is, we conceive, in this *enlightened age*, totally *inadmissible*; and we have concluded, that establishing the expediency of admitting them to share the blessings of equality, will remove every obstacle to their advancement.

But Garrison added a new wrinkle: the importance of making a fuss. He cut *The Liberator*, his abolitionist newspaper, away from the genteel concept of civil discourse and made it bold and demanding. It wasn't enough to be right, he told followers, one had to get the public's attention. His female adherents listened and learned.

And so began American feminism. It was a timid, uncertain beginning—but it would pick up confidence as it picked up steam. Women were not experienced politicians, and as humorous incidents illustrated, they were not used to taking charge. But from their hands-on experience with antislavery, they began to gain a clear idea of what they wanted.

Their first goal was to redress specific wrongs. Women must be allowed to execute contracts, hold property and control their own wages. They must be given equitable rights of inheritance and joint custody of children. The essential point of these demands was simple justice: how could a woman protect herself if all means of doing so were denied her? Most men could understand this argument well enough, and by 1860 some fourteen states had reformed their laws accordingly.

It was the second goal that raised the dust. Feminists demanded full rights of citizenship and full participation in politics. At this skeptics fired a salvo of hostile questions. If women supposed themselves equal to men, what was in store for society as a whole? What would happen to customs, traditions, manners, morals? And if women were politically autonomous, what, exactly, was their "interest?" Identical to that of husbands and fathers? Compatible?

"Declaration of Sentiments" from the Seneca Falls Convention (1848)

In 1848, Lucretia Mott and Elizabeth Cady Stanton organized the first convention in history devoted to women's rights. Held in upstate New York, the Seneca Falls Convention issued a "Declaration of Sentiments" modeled after the Declaration of Independence. The Declaration was written and presented by Stanton, and signed by sixty-eight women and thirty-two men.

The history of mankind is a history of repeated injuries and usurpations on the part of man toward woman, having in direct object the establishment of an absolute tyranny over her. To prove this, let facts be submitted to a candid world.

He has never permitted her to exercise her inalienable right to the elective franchise.

He has compelled her to submit to laws, in the formation of which she had no voice.

He has withheld from her rights which are given to the most ignorant and degraded men—both natives and foreigners.

Having deprived her of this first right of a citizen, the elective franchise, thereby leaving her without representation in the halls of legislature, he has oppressed her on all sides.

He has made her, if married, in the eye of the law, civilly dead.

He has taken from her all right in property, even to the wages she earns.

He has made her, morally, an irresponsible being, as she can commit many crimes with impunity, provided they be done in the presence of her husband. In the covenant of marriage, she is compelled to promise obedience to her husband, he becoming, to all intents and purposes, her master—the law giving him power to deprive her of her liberty, and to administer chastisement.

He has so framed the laws of divorce, as to what shall be the proper causes, and in case of separation, to whom the guardianship of the children shall be given, as to be wholly regardless of the happiness of women—the law, in all cases, going upon a false supposition of the supremacy of man, and giving all power into his hands.

After depriving her of all rights as a married woman, if single, and the owner of property, he has taxed her to support a government which recognizes her only when her property can be made profitable to it.

He has monopolized nearly all profitable employments, and from those she is permitted to follow, she receives but a scanty remuneration. He closes against her all the avenues to wealth and distinction which he considers most honorable to himself. As a teacher of theology, medicine, or law, she is not known.

He has denied her the facilities for obtaining a thorough education, all colleges being closed against her.

He allows her in church, as well as state, but a subordinate position, claiming apostolic authority for her exclusion from the ministry, and with some exceptions, from any public participation in the affairs of the church.

He has created a false public sentiment by giving to the world a different code of morals for men and women, by which moral delinquencies which exclude women from society, are not only tolerated, but deemed of little account in man.

Elizabeth Cady Stanton delivers her "Declaration of Sentiments" at the Seneca Falls Convention.

(Courtesy of Corbis Images.)

He has usurped the prerogative of Jehovah himself, claiming it as his right to assign for her a sphere of action, when that belongs to her conscience and to her God.

He has endeavored, in every way that he could, to destroy her confidence in her own powers, to lessen her self-respect, and to make her willing to lead a dependent and abject life.

Now, in view of this entire disfranchisement of one-half the people of this country, their social and religious degradation—in view of the unjust laws above mentioned, and because women do feel themselves aggrieved, oppressed, and fraudulently deprived of their most sacred rights, we insist that they have immediate admission to all the rights and privileges which belong to them as citizens of the United States.

Inimical? Finally, did equality in politics imply equality at home—and if so, what would become of "home" in the process?

Feminists came up with a quintessentially American answer to such taunts. Consider the American Revolution, they said, with its logic of independence. If human beings were truly created equal, endowed with rights and governable only by their own consent, what difference did it make if they were male or female? Why *shouldn't* women stand on their own legs and pursue their own happiness?

Feminism developed its own concept of civic virtue too. Its simple thesis was that women were better exemplars of such virtue than men were. They were by nature more humane, more giving and more committed to the common good. They couldn't fail to improve politics.

Antislavery

Like other Jacksonian reforms, antislavery grew out of religious revivalism, democratic soul-searching and the American Founding. Ever since the days of John Woolman, small but energetic groups had questioned the institution of slavery, and in the North at least to good effect.

Those who were most troubled by the "peculiar institution" took comfort in the hope that it must eventually die out. Some historians doubt the "eventual extinction" thesis. Slavery was often profitable even before the advent of the cotton gin, they point out, and afterward it was a gold mine.

The other disturbing fact about slavery was its need to expand westward. Cotton cultivation exhausted the soil. So low-yield plantations on the Atlantic seaboard went up for sale, while rich bottomlands in the Mississippi Valley saw a heavy new influx. No politically literate American could ignore the implications. Slavery had been the prickliest interest in the Union to accommodate, even when it was supposed to be dying; could its accommodation continue if it suddenly took a new lease on life?

Probably not. Since population growth was more rapid in the Northwest than the Southwest, slavery would soon be outvoted in the House of Representatives. That left the Senate. By tacit agreement, new states were admitted to the Union in pairs, one slave and one free, in order to keep the Senate balance on par.

And when that strategy failed, there was the Missouri Compromise, hammered out in 1820 after a bone-chilling North-South confrontation. Missouri was admitted to the Union as a slaveholding state and Maine as a non-slaveholding state. Then Congress drew a line westward from Missouri's southern boundary and proclaimed that slavery must keep south of that line.

These difficulties made the American people increasingly uneasy. In the South, a distinctive way of life had begun to emerge—its imagery the stuff of romance. Southerners who identified with moonlight and magnolias became anxious and then fearful about the prospect of slavery's eventual containment, for they recognized that it was slavery, more than anything else, which made the southern lifestyle possible. Northerners had their own worries. For many of them, the expansion of a revitalized slaveholding system cast dark shadows over the republic's future.

A slave auction in Virginia. Dark shadows over the republic's future.
(Courtesy of AP/Wide World Photos.)

It was into this situation that the Abolitionists made their appearance. Unlike earlier opponents of slavery, they had no truck with "eventual extinction" arguments, which they saw as political sophistry. Slavery was no dying institution, they pointed out—it had never been more alive. It must be ended here and now.

William Lloyd Garrison and his newspaper *The Liberator* made their debut in Boston in 1831. Garrison's was a strident and uncompromising voice, one that echoed Puritan self-certainty. "I am in earnest," he announced. "I will not equivocate—I will not excuse—I will not retreat a single inch—and *I will be heard.*" He immediately organized the New-England Anti-Slavery Society and two years later the American Anti-Slavery Society. He became, as he foretold, a force to be reckoned with.

Crisis of the House Divided

The complex causes of the American Civil War are beyond our scope here. The march toward Fort Sumter spanned a long human life, and most of it lay beyond the realm of the Founding. What *is* important to include is the way the Founding played into a few key developments.

Matters between the North and South reached their first real crisis over the acquisition of Texas in 1845. What was regarded by many northerners as the cynical exploitation of Mexico on the part of Texas settlers gave rise to whispers

A Call for Immediate Emancipation (1833)

William Lloyd Garrison founded the New-England Anti-Slavery Society in Boston in 1832. In these excerpts from its annual report in 1833, the Society firmly expounds the need for and benefits of immediate emancipation:

The New-England Anti-Slavery Society maintains that the slaves ought instantly to be emancipated from their fetters. It acknowledges no claims upon their persons by their masters. It regards the holders of slaves as guilty of a heinous sin. . . . It says to every individual— "Let the principle be clearly and firmly established in your mind that there is, and can be, no such thing as *property in man*, and you cannot, as a patriot, a philanthropist, or a disciple of Christ, oppose the immediate liberation of the slaves—you cannot but demand that liberation—you cannot be satisfied with any thing short of an immediate liberation.". . .

The Board of Managers are satisfied that the doctrine of immediate abolition is opposed by many, not because they really mean to justify crime, but simply through ignorance and misapprehension of its nature. . . .

What, then, is meant by IMMEDIATE ABOLITION?

It means, in the first place, that all title of property in the slaves shall instantly cease, because their Creator has never relinquished his claim of ownership, and because none have a right to sell their own bodies or buy those of their own species as cattle. Is there any thing terrific in this arrangement?

It means, secondly, that every husband shall have his own wife, and every wife her own husband, both being united in wedlock according to its proper forms, and placed under the protection of law. Is this unreasonable?

It means, thirdly, that parents shall have the control and government of their own children, and that the children shall belong to their parents. What is there sanguinary in this concession?

It means, fourthly, that all trade in human beings shall be regarded as felony, and entitled to the highest punishment. Can this be productive of evil?

It means, fifthly, that the tremendous power which is now vested in every slaveholder to punish his slaves without trial, and to a savage extent, shall at once be taken away. Is this undesirable?

It means, sixthly, that all those laws which now prohibit the instruction of the slaves, shall instantly be repealed, and others enacted, providing schools and instruction for their intellectual illumination. Would this prove a calamity?

It means, seventhly, that the planters shall employ their slaves as free laborers, and pay them just wages. Would this recompense infuriate them?

It means, eighthly, that the slaves, instead of being forced to labor for the exclusive benefit of others by cruel drivers, and the application of the lash upon their bodies, shall be encouraged to toil for the mutual profit of themselves and their employers, by the infusion of new motives into their hearts, growing out of their recognition and reward as men. Is this diabolical?

It means, finally, that right shall take the supremacy over wrong, principle over brute force, humanity over cruelty, honesty over theft, purity over lust, honor over baseness, love over hatred, and religion over heathenism. Is this wrong?

This is our meaning of Immediate Abolition.

Having thus briefly defined the extent of immediate abolition, it may be useful to state some of its probable, nay, certain benefits.

It will remove the cause of bloodshed and insurrection. No patrols at night, no standing army, will be needed to keep the slaves in awe. The planters may dismiss their fears, and sleep soundly; for by one act, they will have transformed their enemies into grateful friends and servants.

of a "slave power conspiracy"—to steal more land for slavery. The ensuing war with Mexico and conquest of even more southwestern territory brought the federal government skidding to a halt. One last accommodation was painfully worked out, but that was all the political system could withstand. After the Compromise of 1850, the United States was venturing into *terra incognita*.

Three events in the turbulent decade that followed marked out the limits of the Constitution to deal with this most intractable of difficulties.

Compromise of 1850:
A combination of provisions attempting to stop the expansion of slavery in some areas while guaranteeing its continued existence in others. It was hoped it would be the final solution regarding the question of slavery in the US; of course it was not.

- The Kansas-Nebraska Act

In 1852, Illinois Senator Stephen A. Douglas, seeking to extend statehood on the western frontier, presented Congress with a bill that for political reasons nullified the old Missouri Compromise. Douglas should have known better. But he assumed that slavery was ill suited for either of the proposed territories and thus that there was no cause for concern. Why insult the South by forbidding slaves into Kansas and Nebraska, thought he, especially when southern support for their organization was vital?

In the brouhaha that followed, southerners raised the most perplexing question yet. If the territories belonged to everyone, they asked, how could Congress forbid *some* from taking their property (in the form of slaves) *anywhere*? What sort of republic could draw lines on a map and deny certain citizens the rights enjoyed by others? The tragic flaw of federalism now became manifest, for neither the states nor the national government seemed able to resolve such an issue. The expansion of slavery was posing questions for which there were literally no answers.

In the end, so dreadful was the fallout from the Kansas-Nebraska Act controversy that the Whig party simply broke into fragments and perished—an exceptionally bad omen.

- Popular Sovereignty

Douglas defended the Kansas-Nebraska Act by invoking a fundamental principle. Americans shouldn't ponder the imponderable, he said. They should keep their minds focused on the simple and clear idea of *popular sovereignty*. If the citizens of a given state wished to allow (or disallow) the institution of slavery, they had an unquestioned right to do so; the same ought to hold true for a given territory. Accordingly, when the territorial population reached a certain number—say, 60,000—let the settlers hold a referendum and decide the slavery issue for themselves.

"Bleeding Kansas:"
Nickname for the Kansas Territory following violence over the expansion of slavery there in 1855–56.

Douglas didn't think about the idea's practical consequences. In the bare-knuckle world of the frontier, popular sovereignty was an open invitation to filibustering, ballot-box stuffing, bushwhacking and brushfire civil war—all of which eventually stained "Bleeding Kansas." For both pro- and antislavery activists took Douglas at his word and resolved to settle the issue for themselves.

Douglas didn't consider the moral implications either. Voting up or down on the question of slavery seemed uncomfortably like voting up or down on right and wrong. Wasn't popular sovereignty limited by certain things, such as natural rights? people asked. Come to that, did Americans truly *believe* in natural rights? Events in "Bleeding Kansas" left room for doubt.

- The Dred Scott Case

In 1857, the case of *Dred Scott v. Sanford* was cooked up to put the issue of slavery expansion before the Supreme Court and settle it once and for all. Here again lay the assumption that the constitutional system somehow held the key.

While the facts of the case were complicated, the principal issue was quite simple. Dred Scott, a slave, was taken by his master into a "free" territory, then returned to the South. Scott then sued his master on grounds that his sojourn north of the line had set him free. The question behind the question was whether or not Congress could legally create free territory in the first place, as it had with the Missouri Compromise.

The case was actually decided on narrow jurisdictional grounds, as we saw in chapter 13. But in a lengthy *obitur dictum*—that is, an opinion unrelated to the Court's finding—Chief Justice Roger B. Taney put his ideas on the record anyway. And the long and short of it was that the Missouri Compromise was unconstitutional.

The *Dred Scott* decision was a bombshell. Far from laying the question of slavery expansion to rest, it demonstrated how utterly incapable the constitutional system was of resolving it. Northern opinion, which was by now highly inflamed, ascribed the decision to the "slave power conspiracy." Northern politicians, moreover, openly discussed ways of subverting the *Dred Scott* decision. Others told the voters they would ignore it.

The House Divided and the Founding

In theory, the constitutional system could have averted the ultimate crisis. David Donald has pointed out that even with the election of a "Black Republican" president in 1860, constitutional mechanisms would have prevented him from appointing a rural postmaster, much less harming slavery, without the concurrence of the South. But affairs had reached the point where rational discourse was no longer possible.

Abraham Lincoln was one of the few who understood why. Beneath the surface difficulties between North and South there was a deep underlying problem, as Lincoln knew, and as long as that problem remained, there would always be something to upset the equilibrium—political issues, economic issues, cultural issues, it didn't matter. The underlying problem was this:

Democracy absolutely and necessarily depended on the principles set forth in the Declaration of Independence. If legal equality and inalienable rights were not accepted as a given, the sovereignty of the people made no sense. Slavery, by contrast, absolutely and necessarily depended on the exact opposite of those principles. Legal *in*equality and *privileges for the few* had to be its fundamental assumption. How else could one justify enslaving other human beings?

Lincoln saw this. He saw that slavery undermined the very ideas that made America work. And he saw the necessary corollary: that if Americans continued to hold slaves, they would sooner or later lose faith in their own Founding. For example, what else but a loss of such faith could give rise to the Douglas solution? If you allow people to vote up or down on slavery, you must think that human rights can be decided by referendum. You cannot believe in this approach and *also* believe in the American Founding.

Lincoln's "House Divided" Speech

In 1858 the Illinois State Republican Convention nominated Abraham Lincoln to run against Stephen A. Douglas for the US Senate. In accepting the nomination, Lincoln delivered a speech he had been preparing for months. When some criticized it as too radical, Lincoln responded, "You will see the day when you will consider it the wisest thing I ever said." Here are some of his prophetic words:

If we could first know where we are, and whither we are tending, we could better judge what to do, and how to do it. We are now far into the fifth year since a policy was initiated [Kansas-Nebraska Act] with the avowed object and confident promise of putting an end to slavery agitation. Under the operation of that policy, that agitation has not only not ceased but has constantly augmented. In my opinion, it will not cease until a crisis shall have been reached and passed. "A house divided against itself cannot stand." I believe this government cannot endure permanently half slave and half free. I do not expect the Union to be dissolved—I do not expect the house to fall—but I do expect it will cease to be divided. It will become all one thing, or all the other. Either the opponents of slavery will arrest the further spread of it, and place it where the public mind shall rest in the belief that it is in the course of ultimate extinction; or its advocates will push it forward till it shall become alike lawful in all the states, old as well as new, North as well as South.

Have we no tendency to the latter condition?

Let any one who doubts carefully contemplate that now almost complete legal combination—piece of machinery, so to speak—compounded of the Nebraska doctrine and the Dred Scott decision. Let him consider not only what work the machinery is adapted to do, and how well adapted; but also let him study the history of the construction, and trace, if he can, or rather fail, if he can, to trace the evidences of design and concert of action among its chief architects, from the beginning. . . .

The result is not doubtful. We shall not fail—if we stand firm, we shall not fail. Wise counsels may accelerate or mistakes delay it, but, sooner or later, the victory is sure to come.

This was what Lincoln meant when he said: "A house divided against itself cannot stand." The house was not just divided in disagreement; it was divided *against itself*—built upon contradictory principles. Accordingly, Lincoln prophesied, "It will become all the one thing or all the other."

At least one other clear-sighted American agreed. Alexander Stephens, upon his election as vice president of the Confederacy, said:

> Our new government is founded on the opposite idea of the equality of the races. Its cornerstone rests upon this great truth: that the Negro is no equal to the white man. This government is the first in the history of the world based upon this great moral truth.

Unlike Lincoln's house, Stephens' would not be divided. It would rest securely on a foundation designed to support the "peculiar institution."

Soul-Searching

When Lincoln issued the Emancipation Proclamation in September of 1862, it was a curious document indeed. It freed all the slaves beyond the President's control—that is, those in the rebellious southern states—and none of the slaves within his control, in the four marginally loyal border states. Lincoln, said the cynics, was so desperate to gain favorable opinion that he had sunk to playing games.

The man himself lent credence to that suspicion. Born and raised in Kentucky, Lincoln was a more or less typical southerner, and had never espoused racial equality. He confessed at one point that preserving the Union was his real end—freeing the slaves was only a means. But such utterances did not reflect the innermost Lincoln, whom Richard N. Current called "the Lincoln nobody knows." That Lincoln was a dour, often morose but deeply thoughtful man, who proved himself capable of astonishing moral growth.

Lincoln searched his soul about slavery and found it abominable. He also searched his soul about freeing four million slaves and crashed headlong into Jefferson's obstacles. What on earth would America do with so many blacks? he wondered. How could owners be compensated for their loss? How could the freedmen be protected from angry and resentful whites? How could white society be protected from *them*? He found no answers.

It would seem clear that only suffering and loss on an unimagined scale could have steeled Lincoln and fellow northerners to take such a step. Without the horrific carnage at Shiloh, Antietam and a score of other battles, the controversy over secession might have remained only that—a disagreement settled by arms. As it was, the scale of the slaughter soon far outpaced anyone's expectations. Americans could not but ask why.

North and South had squabbled about policy issues, about capital investment, about constitutional interpretation and about theories of American nationhood. They had pointed fingers at each other's styles of living, ideals of honor, even notions of pleasure. None of these things nor all of them together seemed sufficient to justify the fields of bloated corpses being photographed by Matthew Brady. The war simply *had* to have a higher meaning.

Most northern soldiers, according to their letters home, saw it as a war to preserve the Union. The proposition was that this of all nations must not have been created in vain. But why not? Lots of human enterprises were created in vain. Corporations declared bankruptcy. Marriages went bust. Towns with high hopes saw the railroad pass them by. And after all, the United States, with its incessant sectional quarreling, had not been a model of harmony. So, why not just let the southerners depart in peace?

It was this question that appeared to lie at the heart of northern soul-searching. Letting the South go would be so easy. The two nations might even reach an accommodation afterward or, better yet, find a way of getting back together. So what justified the present agony?

Lincoln's extraordinary powers of expression enabled him to put the soul-searching into words that struck strong resonance:

> Fourscore and seven years ago our fathers brought forth upon this continent a new nation, conceived in liberty, and dedicated to the proposition that all men are created equal.
>
> Now we are engaged in a great civil war, testing whether that nation, or any nation so conceived and so dedicated, can long endure.

The nub of the matter might have come down to three inconspicuous words: *or any nation*. The question in Lincoln's mind was simply whether American principles would work. Anywhere. Anytime. The whole point of the American Founding had been a conviction born of rational thought and human experience that a Good Society was truly possible. The question, alas, was still open.

Civil war carnage: "The last full measure of devotion." (Courtesy of Corbis Images.)

Lincoln ended the Gettysburg Address by vowing that "from these honored dead we take increased devotion," that "we here highly resolve that these dead shall not have died in vain," and finally "that this nation, under God, shall have a new birth of freedom." Disguising with poetry, the President was in fact critiquing what he had come to praise. The war, he was saying, was itself a product of the Founding—a "birth of freedom" that had somehow gone awry. If the great bloodletting was to make any sense at all, it must result in a *new* birth of freedom. Americans must take this painful opportunity to get it right.

Had these been only the sentiments of a single gifted orator, they would not have packed the wallop they did. But there were many others who shared them, in the halls of Congress, in statehouses and courthouses, in church congregations and barbershops and general stores across America. Most importantly, fellow believers were found in the military. One of them was Joshua Lawrence Chamberlain. A professor of rhetoric at Bowdoin College in Maine, Chamberlain requested a leave of absence to join the Union Army. When it was denied, he applied for a sabbatical in Europe, then headed for the governor's office and signed up with the Twentieth Maine regiment.

Chamberlain's first action was at Fredericksburg, where he spent a long night piling up corpses to shield himself from enemy bullets. Only a fragment of his regiment survived the battle. Chamberlain was placed in command of the survivors and for "reinforcements" was given 120 mutineers from another Maine outfit. He talked the mutineers into taking back their muskets and returning to the fight.

Chamberlain made both himself and the Twentieth Maine famous at the Battle of Gettysburg. They were placed at the base of Little Round Top on Cemetery Ridge and ordered to hold the Union flank at all costs. After beating back several assaults by Law's hard-fighting Texans and Alabamians, Chamberlain was informed that the regiment—or what remained of it—was out of ammunition. He was fearful to give way lest the flank be turned (and quite possibly the war lost), so he gave the order to fix bayonets and charge. The sight of these doughty Maine men whooping down the hill into the teeth of the Confederate attack so unnerved their adversaries that the latter threw down their arms and surrendered.

The action at Gettysburg proved to be only the beginning for Chamberlain. He went on to fight in every major battle in the East, was wounded a total of six times, and was cited for bravery on four separate occasions. The curious thing about his military career—apart from the fact that he survived it—was his willingness to put himself in harm's way not just once but over and over again. Chamberlain was not driven by hatred of the South or a lust for glory. Why, then, his almost manic devotion to the Union cause?

A clue might be found in some things he said after the war, when he was asked to explain what the conflict was all about:

> It seems we might spend an hour thinking . . . whether anything has been won to recompense the sacrifice, whether there was any righteous cause there, so that these deaths and loses may enter into an immortal life—anything to look forward to, into which we also, the living, may build our lives. . . . The pressing question before us was whether we had

a Country; whether we were a people, or only a populace; whether we were a mere chance partnership holding only by human will, or a Nation, constituted in the purpose and calling of Divine Providence. . . . All the great ruling sentiments which have their vital source in this idea—patriotism, loyalty, self-devotion for the sake of others . . . these were the prize for which we wrestled in that terrible arena. . . . We fought for the worth of manhood; for law and liberty, which mean freedom for every man to make the most of himself . . . without oppression or depression.

Fighting for "the worth of mankind," in this context, meant fighting for human dignity. Chamberlain realized that if there were slaves anywhere in a supposedly free society, there might as well be slaves everywhere, for it meant that freedom was not a right but a privilege. True liberty could never rest on such a foundation.

In assessing the relative military strength of North and South, historians have concluded that the two sections were actually quite well matched. The North had more of this advantage and the South had more of that one. Given that rough parity, the war came down in the end to a question of raw attrition—which side could abide the slaughter the longest. It is here that our hero from Maine comes into full significance. He was certainly not everyman in the North, not even a numerical majority, but there were enough Joshua Lawrence Chamberlains in the Union ranks to prosecute the war almost indefinitely. When one was killed, another stood ready to take his place. They became the soul of the northern army.

In the spring of 1865, Lee's warriors, for all their courage and prowess, ran out of fighting resolve. They had fought for home and loved ones and their own way of life—all-powerful motivators. But they had also fought to perpetuate human slavery and to destroy the Union on which their own freedom rested. Did they *really* prefer to base that freedom on racial superiority, as Stephens claimed? Or did a voice occasionally whisper that if all weren't free and equal as a matter of right, it followed that none were equal and none were really free? There were passages in private diaries suggesting that some southerners were assailed by precisely such doubts.

Although severely wounded in 1864, Chamberlain continued his military service through Appomattox and then served four terms as governor of Maine and was president of Bowdoin College. Recipient of the Medal of Honor, he was active in veteran affairs and lived until 1914.

The New Constitution

When the war ended, no one knew quite how to put the United States back together. Lincoln appeared to have a conciliatory attitude toward the South, but that became moot after his assassination. Radical Republicans—whom we might think of as spiritual heirs of the Abolitionists—had their own ideas about reconstruction. Many of them thought the South should be treated like a "conquered province" and rebuilt from scratch.

If fate hadn't placed Andrew Johnson, a Democrat and a Southerner, in the White House at precisely this juncture, Reconstruction might have gone far differently than it did. As it was, Radical Republicans came to believe that the outcome of the war depended on making sweeping changes—over any and all

Lee surrendered at Appomattox on April 9, 1865 and Lincoln was shot just five days later on April 14, 1865. He died the following morning.

opposition. They searched for a transcendent meaning in the war's ghastly toll and concluded, with Lincoln, that there must be a "new birth of freedom." For them, however, the new birth wasn't rhetorical but real. They set about to rewrite the Constitution.

There were two objectives driving the effort. First, slavery must be ended, both in name and in fact, and the freedmen must be given some sort of opportunity for a life. And second, secession must be eliminated once and for all as a political contingency. The Union itself must be redefined—even refounded.

Ending Slavery

Given the circumstances under which the Emancipation Proclamation had been issued, slavery was by no means legally abolished. Its perpetuation in some form was at least as imaginable as sudden and total freedom for some four million slaves.

But in northern minds, the war to preserve the Union had become a war to end slavery. In that sense Lincoln's bold action in issuing the proclamation truly had been catalytic—and the slaughter truly had achieved a higher meaning. Accordingly, the Thirteenth Amendment, constitutionally terminating slavery, soon emerged as the centerpiece of Reconstruction. Its ratification sailed through the North and moved swiftly through the South at gunpoint.

The more difficult question was whether some other form of slavery, or quasi slavery, might take the peculiar institution's place. And here northern opinion was less adamant. Much of the world still practiced watered-down servitude, often under the guise of indebtedness, and with a bit of legerdemain the South might well do the same. Besides, complete equality of the races—given widespread discrimination in the North—was simply beyond imagining. Black voters at the polling place? Black children in white schools? Black constables and jurors and justices of the peace?

In order to preclude such nightmares, southerners would presumably resort to desperate measures, such as single-party voting, which could break the Republican monopoly in Washington. So the Radicals began thinking about an artificial political system for the South—one *they* could control. If the freedmen were truly to be free, went the argument, "carpetbag" regimes would have to be installed in the conquered states and maintained with bayonets.

Accordingly, a series of Reconstruction Acts were passed by Congress, vetoed by President Johnson, and then re-passed over his veto. These measures carved the South into military districts, enfranchised the freedmen, clamped down an ironfisted rule and set about to reconfigure the Confederacy. Then the Radicals considered a second constitutional amendment. This, they hoped, would place Reconstruction permanently beyond the reach of politics.

Carpetbagger: A disparaging term for a northerner who came to the South after the Civil War seeking economic or political gain.

Redefining the Union

In retrospect, the American Union appeared to have a fatal defect. Just as slavery had undermined the Declaration of Independence, federalism had undermined the Constitution. For federalism, with its dual sovereignty, left open the question of whether the nation had been created by sovereign states or the states had been created by a sovereign nation.

The ambiguity, to be sure, had made the Founding possible. For both nationalists and states' righters could draw a comforting picture of where the *real* sovereignty lay, and for the latter such a picture was vital. Indeed, in the famous Kentucky and Virginia Resolutions, Jefferson and Madison had even sketched out a theory whereby the states could block federal action, if need be, and thus save the Constitution. But what if *a state* violated the Constitution—who was to blow the whistle then?

In 1832, this issue was dramatically addressed. The South Carolina legislature declared a federal law null and void within its own jurisdiction—and dared the government to enforce it. This bold step was taken on the basis of arguments advanced by **John C. Calhoun**, the most renowned constitutional theorist of his time. Beginning with the Virginia and Kentucky Resolutions, Calhoun reasoned his way through an orderly process by which a state like South Carolina could nullify a federal law, interpose its own authority, and in the final extremity call a convention and secede from the Union. Even though a feisty President Jackson backed the Carolinians down in 1832, Calhoun's argument for constitutional secession remained alive and well in the South. In December of 1860 it was put to the test.

Not everyone bought Calhoun's view of the matter, especially in the North. Some, for instance, reasoned that the moment the ninth state ratified the Constitution, those nine states dissolved as separate entities and reconstituted themselves as a single sovereign nation—from which there was no voluntary exit. In the tense prelude to civil war, partisans grasped at such arguments with desperation. The fact of the matter remained that federalism was a muddy concept, and no amount of constitutional metaphysics could clarify it.

Accordingly, after the war, Radical Republicans came up with a second non-negotiable demand. Secession must be made legally, morally and constitutionally impossible—*it must never happen again.*

Fourteenth Amendment:
http://wwwaccess.gpo.gov/
congress/senate/
constitution/amdt14.html

The Fourteenth Amendment

The Fourteenth Amendment was designed to meet both of these demands. It was supposed to make the freedmen truly free. And it was supposed to take secession off the board for good. But could it really accomplish either aim?

We have seen that constitutional wording could be problematic enough when all the parties agree. Here was a case of adding important language when the parties, North and South, did not agree in the least. Rough sailing lay ahead.

The Fourteenth Amendment began with a definition of national citizenship, one the southern states couldn't slip around. If a person was born on US soil, he or she was an American citizen and entitled to constitutional protection. Section 1 continued with these words: "No State shall make or enforce any law which shall abridge the privileges or immunities of citizens of the United States; nor shall any State deprive any person of life, liberty, or property, without due process of law; nor deny to any person within its jurisdiction the equal protection of the laws."

The intention of all this verbiage was to prevent the southern states from re-enslaving the freedmen. The message was that laws which protected whites must protect blacks as well—when applied to one American must apply to all.

But *intention* is never enough. Courts must interpret specific words and try to implement their meaning. And here was where the Fourteenth Amendment was not so simple.

To begin with, all three clauses were vaguely and abstractly worded, and thus open to various interpretations. In all three, moreover, the same general concept was repeated in slightly different ways. The hope, of course, was that each clause would cover loopholes that might appear in the other two. It was a difficult and awkward strategy, but it might have worked if northern opinion had solidly backed the intended purpose—equal rights for the freedmen. Unfortunately, such unanimity was absent, and the courts were left free to make of the Fourteenth Amendment what they would. Clever lawyers were soon diligently undermining it.

In areas of the South where the Union Army and carpetbag governments were firmly in control, a more or less effective reconstruction effort was begun, and some of the liberated slaves truly tasted the wine of freedom. Time, however, was not on their side. Neither the Union Army nor northern officeholders could remain in the South indefinitely.

The Fourteenth Amendment became a kind of constitutional time bomb. Its wording imprecise and its purpose irrelevant, it imposed unspecified limitations on the states—and thus potentially redefined federalism. However the courts of the time interpreted its meaning, the addendum remained there nonetheless, ticking away. At any time, future courts might endow it with momentous new significance.

Let's consider a single instance of what was to happen later on. We know that the Bill of Rights applied only to the federal government, not the states. The latter remained perfectly free to restrain speech, set up an official church or confiscate private property—all of which various states did. Enter the Fourteenth Amendment with its ambiguous prohibitions. The courts might suddenly remember that the phrase "due process of law" referred to the law of nature, which the Bill of Rights was supposed to embody in some way, and that its inclusion in the new amendment must mean that the Bill of Rights now applied to the states. Indeed, the Supreme Court eventually did just that.

Now think how such a development might alter the way federalism worked. In the old antebellum Constitution, the national government had very little to do with ordinary citizens. It could draft them in time of war or tax them, usually indirectly, but beyond that people simply didn't "hear" from Washington very much. But if the states were now bound by the Bill of Rights, who else but a muscular and officious federal government would play the enforcer?

The same held true for any of the Fourteenth Amendment's clauses. If and when the courts saw fit to grace them with power, Americans must look to Washington for enforcement. When it came to "privileges and immunities,"

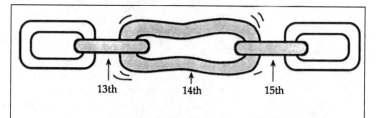

Three new links were added to the Constitutional chain following the Civil War. The Fourteenth Amendment constituted a significant new stretch-point for constitutional interpretation.

"equal protection of the laws" or "due process," the federal government would be required to take the part of citizens *against their own states*.

So Reconstruction failed, but only in the short run. In the long run, it nurtured the seeds of a transformation that would be all but revolutionary.

The Second Founding

As the dust settled from the Civil War, it was clear that some things had changed substantially. Slavery was out of the political arena at last. Race relations would remain troubled and unjust, especially in the South but to some extent everywhere. Some forms of quasi peonage would still be practiced, principally in the guise of sharecropping and convict labor, but the acceptance of lawful servitude was a thing of the past.

Secession was washed up as well. Even without the Fourteenth Amendment, Calhoun's constitutional arguments wound up on the junk pile of history. And democracy turned an important corner. It was still about power and interest, to be sure, and a binge of corruption during the Grant administration would underscore that fact. But it was also about right and wrong. The voice of the Abolitionists would continue to echo in American politics. Wrong was something that had to be battled against and overcome—no matter if it had an imposing constituency.

For instance, in Helen Hunt Jackson's two best-sellers, *A Century of Dishonor* (1881) and *Ramona* (1884), this child of the abolitionists would set forth a case against the continued betrayal of Native Americans almost as effective as Harriet Beecher Stowe's case against slavery in *Uncle Tom's Cabin* (1852). It would elicit an outpouring of sympathy.

Feminism would rekindle itself in the suffragette movement. Not only were women suitable for politics, they would argue, they were *more* suitable than men, because they were more attentive to those right and wrong issues. Women would receive full political rights with the adoption of the Nineteenth Amendment in 1920. But real, operative gender equality would still lie off in the future.

Anti-suffrage headquarters. Notions of women's political inferiority challenged the American Founding.
(Courtesy of Instructional Resources Corporation.)

With the Dawes Act in 1887, the federal government would abandon its war making against the Indian tribes in favor of accommodation. (Even so, the Wounded Knee tragedy was yet to come.) Indians would be offered homestead lands on the same terms as whites, and national citizenship into the bargain. Even though lawmakers would later regret this approach and attempt to salvage what they could of tribal culture, it demonstrated a willingness to give Native Americas full legal rights.

Other victims of discrimination would fight similar battles. Chinese and Japanese on the

West Coast, Hispanics along the Mexican border, Mormons in the Utah Territory and a host of other smaller groups would contend for freedom and legal equality. Eventually all of them would win substantial if not total victories.

The black experience in America would be blighted by segregation and lynch law. Its tragic course would not improve substantially until after World War II, and then only by means of a sea change in social attitudes. But such a change had to come about sooner or later. For when Martin Luther King said "Thank God, we are free at last!" he was reaching back not only to the Civil War with its battle cry of liberation, but to the Founding with its battle cry of liberty.

So what, precisely, was the new birth of freedom? Before the Civil War, republican thought always assumed, with Aristotle, that nature fitted some to be rulers and some to be ruled. Indians, women and African slaves were only three of the latter. We can think of this as the "chosen" model of society, as when God chose Abraham and his posterity for special blessings. Chosenness, thanks to the Puritans, became an American hallmark.

And then there was that other model of society, the one embodied in the Declaration of Independence. Also referencing nature, it drew no distinctions between those fitted to be rulers and those fitted to rule. No one was chosen in advance. Everyone was self-selected by their own ability and exertions.

Historian Shelby Foote has referred to the American Civil War as the centerpiece of American history. We will live with its implications as long as we remain a nation-state, he said. And chiefmost of those implications was that the American people, as a people, finally made a choice between the two models of society. Lincoln's new birth of freedom was the choice they made. The government of the people, by the people and for the people, not perishing from the earth, resolved to become in fact what it was in theory.

The Founding, in a way, was complete.

Suggestions for Further Reading

Michael Kent Curtis, *No State Shall Abridge: The Fourteenth Amendment and the Bill of Rights* (1990).

David Brion Davis, *The Problem of Slavery in the Age of Revolution, 1770–1823* (1975).

David Donald, *Lincoln* (1995).

Eric Foner, *Reconstruction: America's Unfinished Revolution, 1863–1877* (1988).

Reginald Horseman, *Expansion and American Indian Policy, 1783–1812* (1967).

Julie Roy Jeffrey, *The Great Silent Army of Abolitionism: Ordinary Women in the Antislavery Movement* (1988).

Dorothy Jones, *License for Empire: Colonialism by Treaty in Early America* (1982).

Linda Kerber, *Women of the Republic: Intellect and Ideology in Revolutionary America* (1980).

Gary B. Nash, *Red, White, and Black: The Peoples of Early America* (1991).

James M. McPherson, *Battle Cry of Freedom: The Civil War Era* (1982).

David M. Potter, *The Impending Crisis, 1848–1861* (1976).

Richard Slotkin, *Regeneration through Violence: The Mythology of the American Frontier* (1973).

James Brewer Stewart, *Holy Warriors: The Abolitionists and American Slavery* (1976).

Rosemarie Zagarri, *A Woman's Dilemma: Mercy Otis Warren and the American Revolution* (1995).

CHAPTER 17 STUDY AID ▬▬▬▬▬

(This aid is not all-inclusive and is not intended to be a substitute for thorough study of the material presented in the textbook.)

A New Birth of Freedom

I. Forgotten America

1. Declaration of Independence:
   - Founding's spiritual centerpiece
   - "All men are created equal"
   - "Endowed by their Creator with unalienable rights"
   - Government by consent

2. Native Americans:
   - Issues of "otherness"
   - Native inhabitants—"God's favored children" or "childe of hell"?
   - Frontier frictions
   - Massive retaliations
   - Struggle for empire
   - Biblical precepts

3. African Americans:
   - Slavery and the human condition
   - Markets and morality
   - Antislavery stirrings
   - The "peculiar institution"
   - The price of union—popular government and consent of the majority
   - Tolerance, not moral approval
   - The promise of the Declaration of Independence

4. American Women:
   - Limitations and constraints
   - The "natural order" and the "weaker vessel"
   - A revolution within the Revolution—the beginnings of a republican generation

II. Jacksonian Reform

1. The reform impetus:
   - Puritan antecedents—the godly community
   - Republican virtue

- Religious revivalism
- The Founding itself

2. Native Americans:
- Inclusive nationhood?
- Wars and removals
- American principles?

3. Women's liberation:
- The rising middle class
- Personhood
- Association
- Redress of wrongs
- Citizenship and politics
- The logic of the Revolution

4. Antislavery:
- Eventual extinction versus westward expansion
- Political balance and the Missouri Compromise
- Abolitionists—William Lloyd Garrison

III. Crisis of the House Divided

1. Prelude:
- Texas
- Mexican War
- Compromise of 1850

2. The Kansas-Nebraska Act:
- Senator Stephen A. Douglas
- Nullifying the Missouri Compromise
- Expansion of slavery
- End of the Whig Party

3. Popular Sovereignty:
- Slavery in the territories
- "Bleeding Kansas"
- Popular sovereignty versus natural rights

4. The Dred Scot case:
- Seeking a constitutional solution
- Could Congress create free territory?
- Missouri Compromise unconstitutional
- A question beyond the scope of the Constitution

IV. The House Divided and the Founding

1. Inherent premises:
   - Democracy—sovereignty rests on legal equality and inalienable rights
   - Slavery—premised on legal inequality and privileges for the few
   - Slavery undermined faith in the Founding
   - "A house divided against itself"
2. Soul-searching:
   - Emancipation Proclamation
   - Search for a "higher meaning"
   - Preservation of the Union
   - Gettysburg Address—"A new birth of freedom"
   - Joshua Lawrence Chamberlain

V. The New Constitution

1. Re-uniting the nation:
   - Re-founding the Union
2. Ending slavery:
   - Thirteenth Amendment
   - Carpetbag regimes
   - Reconstruction Acts
3. Redefining the Union:
   - The defects of federalism
   - The Fourteenth Amendment—citizenship, due process, equal protection
4. The Second Founding:
   - The end of slavery
   - An end to secession
   - Challenging discrimination
   - Theory becoming practice

CHAPTER 17 REVIEW QUESTIONS ━━━━━

Key Terms

Forgotten Americans

Massive Retaliation

"Blackamoors"

Peculiar Institution

Republican Motherhood

Abraham Lincoln

The Fourteenth Amendment

New Birth of Freedom

Multiple Choice Questions

1. All of the following were advocates of women's rights discussed in the chapter except:
   a. James Otis.
   b. Benjamin Rush.
   c. Hannah Fayerweather.
   d. James Madison.

2. Which of the following was not a factor the text listed as spawning the antislavery movement?
   a. Religious revivalism.
   b. Popular sovereignty.
   c. The Founding.
   d. Democratic soul-searching.

3. Which of the following was not mentioned as a factor leading to the crisis of a "house divided"?
   a. The Kansas-Nebraska Act.
   b. The Dred Scott Case.
   c. Separation of Powers.
   d. Popular Sovereignty.

4. What state was Abraham Lincoln born in?
   a. Illinois.
   b. Tennessee.
   c. Kentucky.
   d. Vermont.

Review Questions

1. In what ways did the failure of federalism in America lead to the Civil War?

   _____

   _____

   _____

   _____

2. Why did Stephen Douglas' proposal to let the citizens in each new state vote on whether or not to allow slavery in that state fail to prevent impending conflict?

   _____

   _____

   _____

   _____

3. What was the Dred Scott case about? What impact did this Supreme Court decision have on the abolitionist and pro-slavery movements?

   _____

   _____

   _____

   _____

4. What reasons did Joshua Chamberlain give for his involvement in the Civil War? How did men like him eventually lead to the Northern victory?

   _____

   _____

   _____

   _____

5. Briefly, what were the purposes of the Fourteenth Amendment?

   _____

   _____

   _____

   _____

Review Exercises

1. Describe the plight of Native Americans before and after the Jacksonian reform era. How were Native Americans perceived by Puritans? Did treatment of Native Americans change during the reform era?

   _____

   _____

   _____

   _____

2. Describe societal notions of women's proper role before the Jacksonian reform era. Briefly, why did these notions change?

_____

_____

_____

_____

3. Explain the origins of African slavery. Why does the text describe slavery as arguably a part of the human condition? Why did these ancient notions about slavery change in America?

_____

_____

_____

_____

Big Essay Question

The Civil War and its aftermath have been described by many historians as a "Second" Founding. In a thoughtful essay, explain what the Civil War changed about the Founding. How were these changes accomplished? Did the Second Founding nullify or enhance the original Founding?

Unveiling the Statue of Liberty by Edward Moran (1886).
(Courtesy of the Museum of the City of New York.)

In their old age, after the passions of politics had cooled, Thomas Jefferson and John Adams not only managed to rekindle their old friendship—interrupted when they ran against each other for president—they also began sorting out the meaning of the American experiment. Their decade-long correspondence sparkles with thoughtfulness and illumination.

Jefferson/Adams: http://etext.virginia.edu/ toc/modeng/public/JefLett .html

Yet it also demonstrates that these two battle-scarred veterans could agree on very little. Why had the colonists opposed British rule? How did the Revolution and the Constitution fit together? What was the American Republic really all about? When it came to deep questions about the Founding, the Founders themselves had disparate answers.

So the Founding didn't come equipped with simple, clean and packaged explanations. But most Americans didn't mind. They had come to accept it as a marvelous event nonetheless, quite beyond the wit of man. "After our Constitution got fairly into working order," wrote James Russell Lowell in 1888, "it really seemed as if we had invented a machine that would go of itself." Which brings us back full circle to those college students mentioned in the introduction, who both accept the Founding as a cosmic given and remain blissfully ignorant of its nature. Hopefully, our study has moved us beyond that.

While Jefferson and Adams had only fifty years of perspective, our view is much longer. For the purpose of a final accounting, let's try to imagine what the two of them might conclude if they could look back from our vantage point.

Intentionality

Much of what went into the Founding was either accidental or circumstantial. There was the situation of thirteen colonies, each different from the others in background and character, and a rebellion separating them from their parent. There were influences pulling the liberated polities toward federation and influences driving them apart. There were ideas of the European Enlightenment, many of them curiously relevant to the New World, and there was the legacy of English Puritanism, mellowed but still potent. And don't forget the seismic and portentous presence of slavery. These were all factors that no one could have planned for—or avoided.

Other elements of the Founding might be called innovative. These too were unplanned but they were not lacking in conscious intention. A politician approaches an old problem in a new way, perhaps, or a constitution writer draws upon his own experience to modify an existing point of doctrine. By such means, tradition was subtly recast into new forms.

Finally, there were those aspects of the Founding that involved more or less pure theory—such as the separation of powers or the concept of the large republic. Here forethought was of the utmost importance and innovation boldly broke new ground. These elements remind us that the Founding really was a *founding*—a product of conscious intention.

And they call to mind the Founders' frequent allusions to the ancient world. For the ideas and ideals—not to mention the lessons—of antiquity provided inspiration to those for whom the Founding was an act of deliberation. We have seen what some of those ideas and ideals were, and the role they came to play. There was Plato's belief in the Good Society. There was the broader Greek emphasis on virtue, and the Roman emphasis on law. There was Aristotle's political science, with its focus on structure and counterpoise, and his insistence on the mean, which in politics meant middle of the road and in economics middle class. Finally, there was the assumption that politics was the individual soul writ large and conversely, that such moral qualities as justice and honor could only be created in a political setting.

For all that, the American Founding was not lifted out of antiquity. Its substance was not ancient but modern, and not Greek or Roman but Anglo-American. What *was* borrowed from the ancient world was conscious purpose—the creation of political society by "wisdom and forethought." The notion of citizens designing the government that would order their own lives lay at the heart of classical republican thought. And the American Founders were ever conscious of the parallel.

The Founding Myth

We have seen that myths too were central to a founding. Some American myths tumbled out of the Puritan experience, as we have also seen, or later on out of the frontier experience. The Chosen People, the City Upon a Hill, the American Dream all might lay claim to mythic status. But if there was *a* Founding Myth, it was probably none of the above. It was, rather, that short legal brief penned by Thomas Jefferson in 1776.

At the time of its writing, the Declaration of Independence did not mean anything like what it has come to mean today. It was what its name asserted, an announcement of colonial separation. While Jefferson was tinkering with its prose, most members of Congress regarded independence as an accomplished fact and were thinking far ahead. Their focus, moreover, was on the individual states, not the United States as a whole. Thus, the Declaration of Independence was not supposed to lay down basic principles, proclaim a creed or establish American nationhood. It was only supposed to declare independence.

With these facts in mind, we shouldn't be surprised that the draftsmanship of the document was handed over to a mere cub, or that the other members of the committee (Franklin and Adams) hardly bothered to check on its progress. Jefferson sat down at his little writing table and began to work something up. He had drafted documents for the Congress before and he freely borrowed themes and phrases from earlier efforts. He had his political reference works at hand too but never had to consult them, for he was, as he said, simply distilling into concise language what Americans had been talking about for a long time.

The remarkable thing about the Declaration of Independence, then, is not how it was written but that it was able to encapsulate in some fifty-eight words a vision, a sense of the world, that Americans would come to find so compelling. After the war was over, the Constitution adopted and a working republic in place, Americans looked back on those fifty-eight words and saw much more than Jefferson had meant to say when writing them.

For the words had come reveal that Founding Myth. Americans seized upon them and said in effect, yes, this is who we are and what we're all about. Jefferson, it seemed, had tapped into what Carl Jung would call the collective unconscious of his countrymen.

When we examined the Declaration of Independence in chapter 4, we noted that Jefferson made two separate claims, one highlighting the role of the

Carl Jung (1875-1961): A prominent Swiss psychologists and one of the founders of psycho-analysis. Believed that a primary symbol called an archetype formed the basis of human consciousness.

Grant Wood's Stone City, Iowa: *The rolling hills of a mythic agrarian republic.*
(Courtesy of Joslyn Art Museum.)

individual in the natural order, his freedom and equality with his fellows, and the other promising that individuals liberated from artificial restrictions would interact harmoniously to maximize human happiness. That this was a full-fledged vision and not just cheerful rhetoric would be born out in the murals of John Steuart Curry or Thomas Hart Benton or Grant Wood, whose vistas of the Jeffersonian Good Society present rolling panoramas of field and farm populated by well-mannered, purposeful citizens.

Yet John Adams did not find the vision so appealing. In his correspondence with Jefferson, he pointed out that the Declaration of Independence did not begin to describe the real world. If government did nothing but protect life, liberty and the pursuit of happiness, there would be personal freedom, to be sure, but precious little else. Justice would be feeble, for the strong would have their way. Equality would be shortchanged, for the talented and energetic would pace far ahead. Order would be iffy because governance would be hamstrung. And security would simply fall by the wayside. Reality was messy.

Is it any wonder, then, that Jefferson himself, when asked about his own slaveholding in light of the Declaration, could give no satisfactory answer, or that Jefferson's countrymen were unable to defend things like nativism or racial discrimination? They had a Founding Myth all right, but they hadn't begun to work through its implications.

The remarkable thing is that in the face of life's messiness Americans didn't simply forget about the Declaration. The reason they didn't is that it had come to symbolize the Founding itself, and could be ignored only at peril. For example, when Abraham Lincoln was asked how slavery could be reconciled with American ideals, he replied: "I would rather be assassinated on this spot than surrender the idea of equality embodied in the Declaration of Independence." Eerily, he got his wish.

The Declaration, then, became a window on the American soul. The view it afforded was one of future possibility, not present reality, of aspiration more than accomplishment—a nation devoted to the natural order of things and to the highest in human potential.

It thus sparked an odd sense of *patria*. Once, back in Andrew Jackson's day, an American diplomat rose at a state dinner and offered the following toast: "Our country, may it always be right. But right or wrong, our country!" He was expressing the two sides of American patriotism. For some, patriotic sentiment could only mean "Our country, right or wrong." For others, it had to be "Our country, may it always be right." The first alternative was like the patriotism of other nation-states, while the second was uniquely American. For if Jefferson's vision was correct, there could never be a legitimate case of America versus the world, only America versus tyranny, America versus aggression, America versus inhumanity. In consequence, American patriotism came to have universal implications—and all of humankind ought to share in it.

Americans also came to believe that their ideals could repair any difficulty at hand. All would be well, so the argument went, if we could put this dithering aside and get back to founding principles—which generally meant picking out a single theme and expounding it as holy writ. For some it was the rule of law. For others it was the sovereignty of the people. For still others it was personal rights or the primacy of the individual. And yet others looked back to classical republicanism and high moral conduct.

But almost all joined hands in Jefferson's fifty-eight-word poem, for it seemed to encompass everything. It gave the Founding both a center of gravity and a sense of divine approval. This, it said, is who we are and what we stand for—what America is all about.

Such is the power of myth.

The Unified Founding

Constitution:
http://press-pubs.uchicago
.edu/founders/tocs/toc
.html

While myth was one unifying element in the Founding, there were others. The Constitution itself supplied an important one. It was designed, as we have seen, to unite theory and practice. By making the sovereignty of the people an operating reality—not just a philosophical abstraction—the Constitution made it possible for Americans to put their ideals into practice. By reconciling personal liberty with civic order, the Constitution gave real substance to the notion of rights. And by making federalism effective, the Constitution made it possible for Americans to enjoy two different kinds of freedom. They gained what has been called negative freedom—freedom *from* government—by obliging the government to control itself, and they gained positive freedom—freedom *in* government—through participation in state and local politics.

To appreciate what a unified Founding means, we might consider a couple of parallels between politics and economics. In politics, we have spoken of popular sovereignty. It means that the people themselves are really in charge. Individual voters may not feel the weight of popular sovereignty but politicians do. Come election time, they know they will stand or fall according to whether or not they have pleased the electorate.

The economic counterpart of popular sovereignty is consumer sovereignty, and it works precisely the same way. In command economies—the kind advocated by Friedrich List—it is producers, not consumers, who have power and you can feel that power in the air. Magazine articles feature production. Tour guides beam with pride as they show you the latest dam or powerhouse. And consumers make do with whatever the system provides. The reverse is true in a market economy. There it is consumers, not producers, who have the power and once again you can feel the difference. Stores go out of their way to be helpful. Advertisers lay out fortunes. And companies who fail to please their customers wind up in the same trash bin as out-of-tune politicians.

Or consider opportunity. Is it a political phenomenon or an economic one? Actually it is both. The opportunity to participate politically—to vote and run for office and join interest groups—not only parallels economic opportunity, the two are connected. In theory, a market system provides opportunity for everyone, based solely on raw ability. In fact, as we know too well, society short-circuits market mechanisms and curtails opportunity out of fear or jealousy or prejudice. Thus, it was not the market system that opened up restaurants and law schools to black patrons; it was the Civil Rights Act of 1964. When African

Americans became participants in the democratic process, the gates of economic opportunity creaked open for them.

A unified founding, then, permeates the entire fabric of life and makes such parallels possible. It affects politics and economics and a good many other things. Ultimately it affects the way people see the world.

The America Question

If the United States regards itself as the world's nation, then it stands to reason that the Founding marked a turning point in human history. The argument goes something like this:

Political society has never quite suited the human animal, for most polities have been filled with tyranny, anarchy, artificial barriers and lopsided benefits. In the Good Society, by contrast, human beings blossom, their creative energies are liberated and they strive to fulfill some sort of larger destiny. Such a development, no matter how local in the beginning, will eventually affect the entire world—by influence, by example, by political interaction and a score of other mechanisms. The renewal of the human self must lead to the redemption of all society.

But do such things really happen? Has the appearance of the United States of America catalyzed anything like such a world makeover? Many Americans affirm that it has, pointing to things like constitutional government, political democracy, economic prosperity, industrial power, military prowess and a whole raft of achievements in science and technology. Superpower status, they say, must surely count for *something*.

Before venturing my own opinion—and the question can be answered with nothing else—we should pause to consider the counter case, which goes something like this:

Human nature is not full of glorious possibilities—human nature is the problem. The reason that life is so fraught with pain and suffering is that there is something truly wrong with our genes. *Homo sapiens* will to power. They will to selfishness. They delight in causing discomfort. And as a consequence, every society, no matter how well intentioned, will sooner or later sink into corruption, depravity, stupidity, aggression or what have you. It is no accident that the Good Societies of antiquity survived but a few fleeting years.

Based on *these* assumptions, the American Founding looks a lot different. We might see it less as the turning of a corner in history than as a sudden quick-step in history's plodding march—a brief deviation from the norm. The Founders themselves were well aware of this possibility and in their darker moments they alluded to it. If their work lasted only a generation or two, perhaps that was all they could expect.

Such, to give it a name, is the **America Question**. Did the American experiment permanently alter the course of human events in some fundamental way? Or was it just another experiment, like the English Commonwealth or the communist utopia, and in the end but a noble failure? The question is still open, of course, but it does seem worth asking. Indeed, it might be one of the important questions of our time.

The Sacred Fire of Liberty

Suppose the America Question could be answered affirmatively. The Founding has truly altered the course of history. But what, specifically, is altered? You might think about your own answer before reading mine.

Living as we do in the world of modern liberalism, it is hard for us to imagine the world that went before. Throughout the length and breadth of it, the only human beings who really mattered were Aristotle's few. They were the ones who made the decisions, controlled the wealth, monopolized the power and set the tone of society. All others constituted a gray mass of toilers and plodders whose lot in life was to work and suffer.

This helps us to understand why slavery wasn't considered so exceptional. The plight of the slave simply exaggerated the plight of the ordinary. Most people lived out their lives in dank hovels, clapboard shacks or communal barracks, and were worked to exhaustion paving roads, draining swamps, rowing galleys or tilling the lands of others, as sorry and expendable as draft animals. It did not seem an unjust situation. It was just the way the world was.

Of all historic advances of the human mind, perhaps the single most extraordinary was the sudden perception—within the space of a few decades—that this way of the world was wrong. All at once, significant numbers in the transatlantic community concluded that society should be seen as a collection of individuals rather than as a single corporate entity, and thus that the old assumptions were outmoded. No ten-year-old, they said, should waste away in a tin mine simply by the luck of the draw. No ox-girl should be condemned to a life of hopelessness merely to meet a social need. No person should be told what to think, what to believe, how to pray or what their lot in life must be, just because the powerful wished to arrange it so. Human beings were *not* draft animals.

The new proposition was that people counted as people, not just the few but everyone. Their potential was individual, not collective, and thus each must be free to develop his or her own personhood. The word *freedom* had had a political meaning up to that point, signifying the legal ability to vote. The new freedom was something else entirely, a freedom *from* society, not *in* society, and it was better described by the word *liberty*. It was the freedom of the person, the individual, the self—the freedom to be oneself, to find oneself, to think one's own thoughts and strive for one's own chances, to live in a manner completely different from one's neighbor. In the world's long history, there had never been anything quite like it.

The breakthrough wasn't simply John Locke's doing, nor that of a few Enlightenment theorists. It resulted from a rare combination of ideas, circumstances, political accidents and economic developments. It was, however, the classic case of the genie out of the bottle, and it was abroad in the world for better or worse. And the bottle from which the genie escaped was unquestionably the American Founding.

The battle cry of *Liberty!*, then, wasn't solely against the British Empire—it was also against history. And what the Founders proposed was that history could change—the world could be different. Accordingly, what Lance Banning has called "the sacred fire of liberty" ties the Founding together and gives it coherence. It links the Declaration of Independence to the Constitution, the Constitution to the Bill of Rights and the events of Washington's time to those of Lincoln's. It defines the American character too, and still colors American life. Do Americans contend with violence in their schools, decay in their cities and "road rage" on their highways? Has their culture become a "culture war," while their politics divides so evenly that a single Senate vote tilts the balance? Blame liberal individualism.

But the sacred fire also accounts for American greatness. Millions of the world's downtrodden have found a decent life in the United States. Many born on the bottom rung have worked their way to the top. Americans have struggled against every sort of bigotry—much of it in their own midst—and advanced human dignity in countless ways. They have pioneered applied science, from the Model T Ford to the moon landings, while at the same time fostering a care for the underdog and a concern for the earth. And they have shown the world a Good Society that despite its faults really works.

The Founding and the Good

But why must they seek to remake the world in their own image? At the deepest level of the events we have described, we can glimpse an important answer.

At the core of the Founding lies a certain set of assumptions. The first of these is that there is such a thing as right and wrong in the world and that most people know the difference. As a result, it becomes possible for political societies to work out a consensus on fundamental issues.

A second assumption holds that the consensus in question can form the basis of a Good Society. That is, human beings, through reason and persuasion, can reach agreement on such basic values as personal freedom, legal equality and essential rights, regardless of their individual interests. To borrow a phrase from Plato, we could call this trinity of goods *the* Good.

Moon landing, 1969. The energy released by the American Founding has yet to reach its limit. (Courtesy of NASA Headquarters.)

Which leads to the third assumption. Once the Good is made the moral foundation of a society, that society can liberate the individual with a certain confidence. For once individuals are made free, they will labor not only for their own interest but that of the group as well, within the framework of the consensus. Things like justice, decency and the rule of law become possible. Popular government becomes possible. A better world becomes possible.

For a kind of civic virtue comes into being that is *not* like the virtue of old. It connects to human nature in an entirely different way. In place of the citizen-soldier whose life has been consecrated to his comrades, we can have the middle-class accountant who polishes her Volvo with pride but who also volunteers for service at the homeless shelter. She believes, somehow, that her own well-being is bound up with that of others.

A new kind of self-interest comes forth as well. Instead of trading in the pain or misfortune of others, this enlightened version seeks to serve others in a curious, left-handed way. Consider Bill Gates, for example. In another time and place, Gates might well have built his empire by plundering towns or bullying peons—his methods have earned him that image—but in present-day America he must do it by providing better software at a lower price. His well-being is tied to the community too.

The world has not run this way for long. Much of it doesn't run this way still. At the beginning of the twenty-first century, we can point to many societies that would question each and every assumption listed above. They would disagree about right and wrong, and assert that the values embraced by Americans are nothing but cultural artifacts. They would disagree about anchoring human happiness in a moral consensus, and assert that it must be anchored in some political or religious orthodoxy. And they would disagree that human beings, once freed from restraint, would naturally do the "right" thing—asserting that they would most assuredly lapse into wrong.

To truly understand the American Founding, then, we must see it in this context. For it continues to gainsay the world's experience. In much of the world, for instance, race still matters a great deal, and because race is identified with political boundaries, people think of themselves as belonging to a sort of national family. In politics, in economics, issues come down to a question of our family as against all others. Americans simply don't think that way. They see the world in terms of the individual, the human being, the person of whatever race or background, and the question they ask is: what can such a person do with a fair chance?

That is why the American nation points beyond nationhood. Why it could become a sanctuary for the dispossessed. Why it instinctively opposes tyrants. Why its economics move toward globalization. Why its citizens obsess over human rights. "The force that motivates [America]," writes James Fallows, "is a vision of people always in motion, able to make something different of themselves, ready for second chances until the day they die." And so, to the extent that America continues to press its case against history, the sacred fire of liberty may well burn all the brighter.

The dialogue between Jefferson and Adams went on for years and remains a fertile source on the Founding. Even though they disagreed about much and remembered things differently, it was clear to both of them that the Founding had been a remarkable achievement.

They came to appreciate that America was first and foremost an idea, and that the idea had universal implications. Other nation-states had evolved into being over the centuries, and their institutions reflected the hit-and-miss vagaries of time. The United States, by contrast, had been thought up, "invented," and its institutions reflected conscious deliberation. It embodied, in some way, the age-old desire for a Good Society.

They also came to realize that the desire would never quite be fulfilled. So America too would reinvent itself, reforming this, tinkering with that, rethinking something else—and always flailing itself with criticism. For, in truth, its

Aftermath of 9/11: Americans still draw upon their Founding for the strength to face challenges. (Courtesy of Corbis Images.)

ideals *were* unattainable, as Adams could see. Life, liberty and the pursuit of happiness—for *everyone*? Liberty and justice—for *all*? Americans were doomed to eternal frustration.

They died on the same day, Jefferson and Adams, and it just happened to be July 4, 1826, precisely half a century after the Declaration of Independence. If further proof were needed that America had been arranged by the gods, there it was. But for most Americans no further proof was necessary. Theirs was the world's nation. And even though living up to its own principles was still a long way off, the principles were in place and their meaning was clear. The rest was up to history.

Suggestions for Further Reading

James Fallows, *More Like Us: Making America Great Again* (1997).

Michael G. Kammen, *A Machine That Would Go of Itself : The Constitution in American Culture* (1986).

Michael G. Kammen, *People of Paradox: An Inquiry Concerning the Origins of American Civilization* (1972).

Max Lerner, *America as a Civilization*, 2 vols. (1957).

Seymour Martin Lipset, *The First New Nation: The United States in Historical and Comparative Perspective* (1963).

Pauline Maier, *American Scripture: Making the Declaration of Independence* (1997).

Garry Wills, *Inventing America: Jefferson's Declaration of Independence* (1979).

CONCLUSION STUDY AID━━━━━

(This aid is not all-inclusive and is not intended to be a substitute for thorough study of the material presented in the textbook.)

Conclusion

I. Intentionality

1. Jefferson and Adams:
   - The Founding—disparate answers
   - "A machine that would go of itself"
2. Accident and circumstances
3. Innovation
4. Republican theory:
   - Ancient and contemporary

II. The Founding Myth

1. Declaration of Independence:
   - The individual
   - Republican cooperation
   - Implications
   - Window on the American soul
2. The unified Founding:
   - The Constitution
   - Popular sovereignty
   - Consumer sovereignty
   - Opportunity
3. The America Question:
   - A turning point?
   - An aberration?
4. The sacred fire of liberty:
   - Has anything really changed in the world?
   - Justice
   - Individual, not collective, potential
   - Liberty
5. The Founding and the Good:
   - Fundamental axioms
   - Civic virtue
   - Self-interest
   - American perspective
   - America—an idea

The Declaration of Independence

When in the course of human events it becomes necessary for one people to dissolve the political bands which have connected them with another and to assume, among the powers of the earth, the separate and equal station to which the laws of nature and of nature's God entitle them, a decent respect to the opinions of mankind requires that they should declare the causes which impel them to the separation.

We hold these truths to be self-evident, that all men are created equal; that they are endowed by their Creator with certain unalienable rights; that among these are life, liberty, and the pursuit of happiness. That, to secure these rights, governments are instituted among men, deriving their just powers from the consent of the governed; that, whenever any form of government becomes destructive of these ends, it is the right of the people to alter or to abolish it, and to institute a new government, laying its foundation on such principles, and organizing its powers in such form, as to them shall seem most likely to effect their safety and happiness. Prudence, indeed, will dictate that governments long established should not be changed for light and transient causes; and, accordingly, all experience hath shown that mankind are more disposed to suffer, while evils are sufferable, than to right themselves by abolishing the forms to which they are accustomed. But when a long train of abuses and usurpations, pursuing invariably the same object, evinces a design to reduce them under absolute despotism, it is their right, it is their duty, to throw off such government and to provide new guards for their future security. Such has been the patient sufferance of these colonies, and such is now the necessity which constrains them to alter their former systems of government. The history of the present King of Great Britain is a history of repeated injuries and usurpations, all having, in direct object, the establishment of an absolute tyranny over these States. To prove this, let facts be submitted to a candid world:

He has refused his assent to laws the most wholesome and necessary for the public good.

He has forbidden his governors to pass laws of immediate and pressing importance, unless suspended in their operation till his assent should be obtained; and, when so suspended, he has utterly neglected to attend to them.

He has refused to pass other laws for the accommodation of large districts of people, unless those people would relinquish the right of representation in the legislature, a right inestimable to them and formidable to tyrants only.

He has called together legislative bodies at places unusual, uncomfortable, and distant from the depository of their public records, for the sole purpose of fatiguing them into compliance with his measures.

He has dissolved representative houses, repeatedly for opposing, with manly firmness, his invasions on the rights of the people.

He has refused, for a long time after such dissolutions, to cause others to be elected; whereby the legislative powers, incapable of annihilation, have returned to the people at large for their exercise; the state remaining, in the meantime, exposed to all the danger of invasion from without and convulsions within.

He has endeavored to prevent the population of these States; for that purpose, obstructing the laws for naturalization of foreigners, refusing to pass others to encourage their migration hither, and raising the conditions of new appropriations of lands.

He has obstructed the administration of justice by refusing his assent to laws for establishing judiciary powers.

He has made judges dependent on is will alone for the tenure of their offices and the amount and payment of their salaries.

He has erected a multitude of new offices and sent hither swarms of officers to harass our people and eat out their substance.

He has kept among us, in time of peace, standing armies, without the consent of our legislatures.

He has affected to render the military independent of, and superior to, the civil power.

He has combined with others to subject us to a jurisdiction foreign to our Constitution and unacknowledged by our laws, giving his assent to their acts of pretended legislation—

For quartering large bodies of armed troops among us;

For protecting them by a mock trail from punishment for any murders which they should commit on the inhabitants of these States;

For cutting off our trade with all parts of the world;

For imposing taxes on us without our consent;

For depriving us, in many cases, of the benefit of trial by jury;

For transporting us beyond seas to be tried for pretended offenses;

For abolishing the free system of English laws in a neighboring province, establishing therein an arbitrary government, and enlarging its boundaries, so as to render it at once an example and fit instrument for introducing the same absolute rule into these colonies;

For taking away our charters, abolishing our most valuable laws, and altering, fundamentally, the powers of our governments.

For suspending our own legislatures and declaring themselves invested with power to legislate for us in all cases whatsoever.

He has abdicated government here by declaring us out of his protection and waging war against us.

He has plundered our seas, ravaged our coasts, burnt our towns, and destroyed the lives of our people.

He is, at this time, transporting large armies of foreign mercenaries to complete the works of death, desolation, and tyranny already begun with circumstances of cruelty and perfidy scarcely paralleled in the most barbarous ages, and totally unworthy the head of a civilized nation.

He has constrained our fellow citizens, taken captive on the high seas, to bear arms against their country, to become the executioners of their friends and brethren, or to fall themselves by their hands.

He has excited domestic insurrections amongst us and has endeavored to bring on the inhabitants of our frontiers, the merciless Indian savages, whose known rule of warfare is an undistinguished destruction of all ages, sexes, and conditions.

In every stage of these oppressions, we have petitioned for redress in the most humble terms; our repeated petitions have been answered only by repeated injury. A prince whose character is thus marked by every act which may define a tyrant is unfit to be the ruler of a free people.

Nor have we been wanting in attention to our British brethren. We have warned them, from time to time, of attempts made by their legislature to extend an unwarrantable jurisdiction over us. We have reminded them of the circumstances of our emigration and settlement here. We have appealed to their native justice and magnanimity, and we have conjured them, by the ties of our common kindred, to disavow these usurpations, which would inevitably interrupt our connections and correspondence. They, too, have been deaf to the voice of justice and consanguinity. We must, therefore, acquiesce in the necessity which denounces our separation, and hold them, as we hold the rest of mankind, enemies in war, in peace, friends.

We, therefore, the representatives of the United States of America, in general Congress assembled, appealing to the Supreme Judge of the world for the rectitude of our intentions, do, in the name and by the authority of the good people of these colonies, solemnly publish and declare, that these united colonies are, and of right ought to be, free and independent states: that they are absolved from all allegiance to the British Crown, and that all political connection between them and the state of Great Britain is, and ought to be, totally dissolved; and that, as free and independent states, they have full power to levy war, conclude peace, contract alliances, establish commerce, and to do all other acts and things which independent states may of right do. And, for the support of this declaration, with a firm reliance on the protection of Divine Providence, we mutually pledge to each other our lives, our fortunes, and our sacred honor.

The Constitution of the United States of America

We the people of the United States, in order to form a more perfect union, establish justice, insure domestic tranquillity, provide for the common defense, promote the general welfare, and secure the blessings of liberty to ourselves and our posterity, do ordain and establish this Constitution for the United States of America.

Article I

Section 1.

All legislative powers herein granted shall be vested in a Congress of the United States, which shall consist of a Senate and House of Representatives.

Section 2.

1. The House of Representatives shall be composed of members chosen every second year by the people of the several States, and the electors in each State shall have the qualifications requisite for electors of the most numerous branch of the State legislature.

2. No person shall be a representative who shall not have attained to the age of twenty-five years, and been seven years a citizen of the United States, and who shall not, when elected, be an inhabitant of that State in which he shall be chosen.

3. Representatives and direct taxes[1] shall be apportioned among the several States which may be included within this Union, according to their respective numbers, which shall be determined by adding to the whole number of free persons, including those bound to service for a term of years, and excluding Indians not taxed, three fifths of all other persons.[2] The actual enumeration shall be made within three years after the first meeting of the Congress of the United States, and within every subsequent term of ten years, in such manner as they shall by law direct. The number of representatives shall not exceed one for every thirty thousand, but each State shall have at least one representative; and until such enumeration shall be made, the State of New Hampshire shall be entitled to choose three, Massachusetts eight, Rhode Island and Providence Plantations one, Connecticut five,

New York six, New Jersey four, Pennsylvania eight, Delaware one, Maryland six, Virginia ten, North Carolina five, South Carolina five, and Georgia three.

4. When vacancies happen in the representation from any State, the executive authority thereof shall issue writs of election to fill such vacancies.

5. The House of Representatives shall choose their speaker and other officers; and shall have the sole power of impeachment.

Section 3.

1. The Senate of the United States shall be composed of two senators from each State, chosen by the legislature thereof,[3] for six years; and each senator shall have one vote.

2. Immediately after they shall be assembled in consequence of the first election, they shall be divided as equally as may be into three classes. The seals of the senators of the first class shall be vacated at the expiration of the second year, of the second class at the expiration of the fourth year, and of the third class at the expiration of the sixth year, so that one third may be chosen every second year; and if vacancies happen by resignation, or otherwise, during the recess of the legislature of any State, the executive thereof may make temporary appointments until the next meeting of the legislature, which shall then fill such vacancies[4].

3. No person shall be a senator who shall not have attained to the age of thirty years, and been nine years a citizen of the United States, and who shall not, when elected, be an inhabitant of that State for which he shall be chosen.

4. The Vice President of the United States shall be President of the Senate, but shall have no vote, unless they be equally divided.

5. The Senate shall choose their other officers, and also a president pro tempore, in the absence of the Vice President, or when he shall exercise the office of the President of the United States.

6. The Senate shall have the sole power to try all impeachments. When sitting for that purpose, they shall be on oath or affirmation. When the President of the United States is tried, the chief justice shall preside: and no person shall be convicted without the concurrence of two thirds of the members present.

7. Judgment in cases of impeachment shall not extend further than to removal from office, and disqualification to hold and enjoy any office of honor, trust or profit under the United States: but the party convicted shall nevertheless be liable and subject to indictment, trial, judgment and punishment, according to law.

Section 4.

1. The times, places, and manner of holding elections for senators and representatives, shall be prescribed in each State by the legislature thereof; but the Congress may at any time by law make or alter such regulations, except as to the places of choosing senators.

2. The Congress shall assemble at least once in every year, and such meeting shall be on the first Monday in December, unless they shall by law appoint a different day.

Section 5.

1. Each House shall be the judge of the elections, returns and qualifications of its own members, and a majority of each shall constitute a quorum to do business; from day to day, and may be authorized to compel the attendance of absent members, in such manner, and under such penalties as each House may provide.

2. Each House may determine the rules of its proceedings, punish its members for disorderly behavior, and, with the concurrence of two thirds, expel a member.

3. Each House shall keep a journal of its proceedings, and from time to time publish the same, excepting such parts as may in their judgment require secrecy; and the yeas and nays of the members of either House on any question shall, at the desire of one fifth of those present, be entered on the journal.

4. Neither House, during the session of Congress, shall, without the consent of the other, adjourn for more than three days, nor to any other place than that in which the two Houses shall be sitting.

Section 6.

1. The senators and representatives shall receive a compensation for their services, to be ascertained by law, and paid out of the Treasury of the United States. They shall in all cases, except treason, felony, and breach of the peace, be privileged from arrest during their attendance at the session of their respective Houses, and in going to and returning from the same; and for any speech or debate in either House, they shall not be questioned in any other place.

2. No senator or representative shall, during the time for which he was elected, be appointed to any civil office under the authority of the United States, which shall have been created, or the emoluments whereof shall have been increased, during such time; and no person holding any office under the United States shall be a member of either House during his continuance in office.

Section 7.

1. All bills for raising revenue shall originate in the House of Representatives; but the Senate may propose or concur with amendments as on other bills.

2. Every bill which shall have passed the House of Representatives and the Senate, shall, before it become a law, be presented to the President of the United States; If he approves he shall sign it, but if not he shall return it, with his objections, to that House in which it shall have originated, who shall enter the objections at large on their journal, and proceed to reconsider it. If after such reconsideration two thirds of that House shall agree to

pass the bill, it shall be sent, together with the objections, to the other House, by which it shall likewise be reconsidered, and if approved by two thirds of that House shall agree to pass the bill, it shall be sent, together with the objections, to the other House, by which it shall likewise be reconsidered, and if approved by two thirds of that House, it shall become a law. But in all such cases the votes of both Houses shall be determined by yeas and nays, and the names of the persons voting for and against the bill shall be entered on the journal of each House respectively. If any bill shall not be returned by the President within ten days (Sundays excepted) after it shall have been presented to him, the same shall be a law, in like manner as if he had signed it, unless the Congress by their adjournment prevent its return, in which case it shall not be a law.

3. Every order, resolution, or vote to which the concurrence of the Senate and the House of Representatives may be necessary (except on a question of adjournment) shall be presented to the President of the United States; and before the same shall take effect, shall be approved by him, or being disapproved by him, shall be repassed by two thirds of the Senate and House of Representatives, according to the rules and limitations prescribed in the case of a bill.

Section 8.

The Congress shall have the power

1. To lay and collect taxes, duties, imposts, and excises, to pay the debts and provide for the common defense and general welfare of the United States; but all duties, imposts, and excises shall be uniform throughout the United States.

2. To borrow money on the credit of the United States;

3. To regulate commerce with foreign nations, and among the several States, and with the Indian tribes;

4. To establish a uniform rule of naturalization, and uniform laws on the subject of bankruptcies throughout the United States;

5. To coin money, regulate the value thereof, and of foreign coin, and fix the standard of weights and measures;

6. To provide for the punishment of counterfeiting the securities and current coin of the United States;

7. To establish post offices and post roads;

8. To promote the progress of science and useful arts, by securing for limited times to authors and inventors the exclusive right to their respective writings and discoveries;

9. To constitute tribunals inferior to the Supreme Court;

10. To define and punish piracies and felonies committed on the high seas, and offenses against the law of nations;

11. To declare war, grant letters of marque and reprisal, and make rules concerning captures on land and water;

12. To raise and support armies, but no appropriation of money to that use shall be for a longer term than two years;

13. To provide and maintain a navy;

14. To make rules for the government and regulation of the land and naval forces;

15. To provide for calling forth the militia to execute the laws of the Union, suppress insurrections and repel invasions;

16. To provide for organizing, arming, and disciplining the militia, and for governing such part of them as may be employed in the service of the United States, reserving to the States respectively, the appointment of the officers, and the authority of training the militia according to the discipline prescribed by Congress;

17. To exercise exclusive legislation in all cases whatsoever, over such district (not exceeding ten miles square) as may, by cession of particular States, and the acceptance of Congress, become the seat of the government of the United States, and to exercise like authority over all places purchased by the consent of the legislature of the State in which the same shall be, for the erection of forts, magazines, arsenals, dockyards, and other needful buildings; and

18. To make all laws which shall be necessary and proper for carrying into execution the foregoing powers, and all other powers vested by this Constitution in the government of the United States, or any department or officer thereof.

Section 9.

1. The migration or importation of such persons as any of the States now existing shall think proper to admit, shall not be prohibited by the Congress prior to the year one thousand eight hundred and eight, but a tax or duty may be imposed on such importation, not exceeding ten dollars for each person.

2. The privilege of the writ of habeas corpus shall not be suspended, unless when in cases of rebellion or invasion the public safety may require it.

3. No bill of attainder or ex post facto law shall be passed.

4. No capitation, or other direct, tax shall be laid, unless in proportion to the census or enumeration hereinbefore directed to be taken.[5]

5. No tax or duty shall be laid on articles exported from any State.

6. No preference shall be given by any regulation of commerce or revenue to the ports of one State over those of another: nor shall vessels bound to, or from, one State be obliged to enter, clear, or pay duties in another.

7. No money shall be drawn from the treasury, but in consequence of appropriations made by law; and a regular statement and account of the receipts and expenditures of all public money shall be published from time to time.

8. No title of nobility shall be granted by the United States: and no person holding any office of profit or trust under them, shall, without the consent of the Congress, accept of any present, emolument, office, or title, of any kind whatever, from any king, prince, or foreign State.

Section 10.

1. No State shall enter into any treaty, alliance, or confederation; grant letters of marque and reprisal; coin money; emit bills of credit; make any thing but gold and silver coin a tender in payment of debts; pass any bill of attainder, ex post facto law, or law impairing the obligation of contracts, or grant, any title of nobility.

2. No State shall, without the consent of the Congress, lay any imposts or duties on imports or exports, except what may be absolutely necessary for executing its inspection laws: and the net produce of all duties and imposts laid by any State on imports or exports, shall be for the use of the treasury of the United States; and all such laws shall be subject to the revision and control of the Congress.

3. No state shall, without the consent of the Congress, lay any duty of tonnage, keep troops, or ships of war in time of peace, enter into any agreement or compact with another State, or with a foreign power, or engage in war, unless actually invaded, or in such imminent danger as will not admit or delay.

Article II

Section 1.

1. The executive power shall be vested in a President of the United States of America. He shall hold his office during the term of four years, and, together with the Vice President, chosen for the same term, be elected, as follows:

2. Each State shall appoint, in such manner as the legislature thereof may direct, a number of electors, equal to the whole number of senators and representatives to which the State may be entitled in the Congress: but no senator or representative, or person holding any office of trust or profit under the United States, shall be appointed an elector.

    The electors shall meet in their respective States, and vote by ballot for two persons, of whom one at least shall not be an inhabitant of the same State with themselves. And they shall make a list of all the persons voted for, and of the number of votes for each; which list they shall sign and certify, and transmit sealed to the seat of the government of the United States, directed to the president of the Senate. The president of the Senate shall, in the presence of the Senate and House of Representatives, open all the certificates, and the votes shall then be counted. The person having the greatest number of votes shall be the President, if such number be a majority of the whole number of electors appointed; and if there be more than one who have such majority, and have an equal number of votes, then the House of Representatives shall immediately choose by ballot one of them for President; and if no person have a majority, then from the five highest on the list the said House shall in choosing the President, the votes shall be taken by

States, the representation from each State having one vote; a quorum for this purpose shall consist of a member or members from two thirds of the States, and a majority of all the States shall be necessary to a choice. In every case after the choice of the President, the person having the greatest number of votes of the electors shall be the Vice President. But if there should remain two or more who have equal votes, the Senate shall choose from them by ballot the Vice President.[6]

3.   The Congress may determine the time of choosing the electors, and the day on which they shall give their votes; which day shall be the same throughout the United States.

4.   No person except a natural born citizen, or a citizen of the United States, at the time of the adoption of this Constitution, shall be eligible to the office of President; neither shall any person be eligible to the office who shall not have attained to the age of thirty-five years, and been fourteen years a resident within the United States.

5.   In case of the removal of the President from office, or of his death, resignation, or inability to discharge the powers and duties of the said office, the same shall devolve on the Vice President, and the congress may by law provide for the case of removal, death, resignation or inability, both of the President and Vice President, declaring what officer shall then act as President, and such officer shall act accordingly until the disability be removed, or a President shall be elected.

6.   The President shall, at stated times, receive for his services a compensation which shall neither be increased nor diminished during the period for which he shall have been elected, and he shall not receive within that period any other emolument from the United States, or any of them.

7.   Before he enter on the execution of his office, he shall take the following oath or affirmation:—"I do solemnly swear (or affirm) that I will faithfully execute the office of President of the United States, and will to the best of my ability, preserve, protect and defend the Constitution of the United States."

Section 2.

1.   The President shall be commander in chief of the army and navy of the United States, and of the militia of the several States, when called into the actual service of the United States; he may require the opinion in writing, of the principal officer in each of the executive departments, upon any subject relating to the duties of their respective offices, and he shall have power to grant reprieves and pardons for offenses against the United States, except in cases of impeachment.

2.   He shall have power, by and with the advice and consent of the Senate, to make treaties, provided two thirds of the senators present concur; and he shall nominate, and by and with the advice and consent of the Senate, shall appoint ambassadors, other public ministers and consuls, judges of the Supreme Court, and all other officers of the United States, whose appointments are not herein otherwise provided for, and which shall be established

by law; but the Congress may by law vest the appointment of such inferior officers, as they think proper, in the President alone, in the courts of laws, or in the heads of departments.

3. The President shall have power to fill up all vacancies that may happen during the recess of the Senate, by granting commissions which shall expire at the end of their next session.

Section 3.

He shall from time to time give to the Congress information of the state of the Union, and recommend to their consideration such measures as he shall judge necessary and expedient; he may, on extraordinary occasions, convene both Houses, or either of them, and in case of disagreement between them with respect to the time of adjournment, he may adjourn them to such time as he shall think proper; he shall receive ambassadors and other public ministers; he shall take care that the laws be faithfully executed, and shall commission all the officers of the United States.

Section 4.

The President, Vice President, and all civil officers of the United States, shall be removed from office on impeachment for, and conviction of, treason, bribery, or other high crimes and misdemeanors.

Article III

Section 1.

The judicial power of the United States shall be vested in one Supreme Court, and in such inferior courts as the Congress may from time to time ordain and establish. The judges, both of the Supreme and inferior courts, shall hold their offices during good behavior, and shall, at stated times, receive for their services, a compensation, which shall not be diminished during their continuance in office.

Section 2.

1. The judicial power shall extend to all cases, in law and equity, arising under this Constitution, the laws of the United States, and treaties made, or which shall be made, under their authority;—to all cases of admiralty and maritime jurisdiction;—to controversies to which the United States shall be a party;[7]— to controversies between two or more States;—between a State and citizens of another State;—between citizens of different States;—between citizens of the same State claiming lands under grants of different States, and between a State, or the citizens thereof, and foreign States, citizens or subjects.

2. In all cases affecting ambassadors, other public ministers and consuls, and those in which a State shall be party, the Supreme Court shall have original

jurisdiction. In all the other cases before mentioned, the Supreme Court shall have appellate jurisdiction, both as to law and fact, with such exceptions, and under such regulations as the Congress shall make.

3. The trial of all crimes, except in cases of impeachment, shall be by jury; and such trial shall be held in the State where the said crimes shall have been committed; but when not committed within any State, the trial shall be such place or places as the congress may by law have directed.

Section 3.

1. Treason against the United States shall consist only in levying war against them, or in adhering to their enemies, giving them aid and comfort. No person shall be convicted of treason unless on the testimony of two witnesses to the same overt act, or on confession in open court.

2. The Congress shall have power to declare the punishment of treason, but no attainder of treason shall work corruption of blood, or forfeiture except during the life of the person attained.

Article IV

Section 1.

Full faith and credit shall be given in each State to the public acts, records, and judicial proceedings of every other State. And the Congress may by general laws prescribe the manner in which such acts, records and proceedings shall be proved, and the effect thereof.

Section 2.

1. The citizens of each State shall be entitled to all privileges and immunities of citizens in the several States.[8]

2. A person charged in any State with treason, felony, or other crime, who shall flee from justice, and be found in another State, shall on demand of the executive authority of the State from which he fled, be delivered up to be removed to the State having jurisdiction of the crime.

3. No person held to service or labor in one State under the laws thereof, escaping into another, shall, in consequence of any law or regulation therein, be discharged from such service or labor, but shall be delivered up on claim of the party to whom such service or labor may be due.[9]

Section 3.

1. New States may be admitted by the Congress into this Union; but no new State shall be formed or erected within the jurisdiction of any other State, nor any State be formed by the junction of two or more States, or parts of States, without the consent of the legislatures of the States concerned as well as of the Congress.

2. The Congress shall have power to dispose of and make all needful rules and regulations respecting the territory or other property belonging to the United States; and nothing in this Constitution shall be so construed as to prejudice any claims of the United States, or of any particular State.

Section 4.

The United States shall guarantee to every State in this Union a republican form of government, and shall protect each of them against invasion; and on application of the legislature, or of the executive (when the legislature cannot be convened) against domestic violence.

Article V

The Congress, whenever two thirds of both Houses shall deem it necessary, shall propose amendments to this Constitution, or, on the application of the legislatures of two thirds of the several States, shall call a convention for proposing amendments, which in either case shall be valid to all intents and purposes, as part of this Constitution, when ratified by the legislatures of three fourths of the several States, or by conventions in three fourths thereof, as the one or the other mode of ratification may be proposed by the Congress; Provided that no amendment which may be made prior to the year one thousand eight hundred and eight shall in any manner affect the first and fourth clauses in the ninth section of the first article; and that no State, without its consent, shall be deprived of its equal suffrage in the Senate.

Article VI

1. All debts contracted and engagements entered into, before the adoption of this Constitution, shall be as valid against the United States under this Constitution, as under the Confederation.[10]

2. This Constitution, and the laws of the United States which shall be made in pursuance thereof; and all treaties made, or which shall be made, under the authority of the United States, shall be the supreme law of the land; and the judges in every State shall be bound thereby, any thing in the Constitution or laws of any State to the contrary notwithstanding.

3. The senators and representatives before mentioned, and the members of the several State legislatures, and all executive and judicial officers, both on the United States and of the several States, shall be bound by oath or affirmation to support this Constitution; but no religious test shall ever be required as a qualification to any office or public trust under the United States.

Article VII

The ratification of the conventions of nine States shall be sufficient for the establishment of this Constitution between the States so ratifying the same.

Done in Convention by the unanimous consent of the States present the seventeenth day of September in the year of our Lord one thousand seven hundred and eighty-seven, and of the independence of the United States of America the twelfth. In witness whereof we have hereunto subscribed our names.

[Names omitted]

Articles in addition to, and amendment of, the Constitution of the United States of America, proposed by Congress, and ratified by the legislatures of the several States, pursuant to the fifth article of the original Constitution.

Amendment I

[First ten amendments ratified December 15, 1791]

Congress shall make no law respecting an establishment of religion, or prohibiting the free exercise thereof; or abridging the freedom of speech, or of the press; or the right of the people peaceably to assemble, and to petition the government for a redress of grievances.

Amendment II

A well regulated militia, being necessary to the security of a free State, the right of the people to keep and bear arms, shall not be infringed.

Amendment III

No soldier shall, in time of peace be quartered in any house, without the consent of the owner, nor in time of war, but in a manner to be prescribed by law.

Amendment IV

The right of the people to be secure in their persons, houses, papers, and effects, against unreasonable searches and seizures, shall not be violated, and no warrants shall issue, but upon probable cause, supported by oath or affirmation, and particularly describing the place to be searched, and the persons or things to be seized.

Amendment V

No person shall be held to answer for a capital or otherwise infamous crime, unless on a presentment or indictment of a grand jury, except in cases arising in the land or naval forces, or in the militia, when in actual service in time of war or public danger; nor shall any person be subject for the same offense to be twice put in jeopardy of life or limb; nor shall be compelled in any criminal case to be a witness against himself, nor be deprived of life, liberty, or property, without due process of law; nor shall private property be taken for public use, without just compensation.

Amendment VI

In all criminal prosecutions, the accused shall enjoy the right to a speedy and public trial, by an impartial jury of the State and district wherein the crime shall have been committed, which district shall have been previously ascertained by law, and to be informed of the nature and cause of the accusation; to be confronted with the witnesses against him; to have compulsory process for obtaining witnesses in his favor, and to have the assistance of counsel for his defense.

Amendment VII

In suits at common law, where the value in controversy shall exceed twenty dollars, the right of trial by jury shall be preserved, and no fact tried by a jury shall be otherwise reexamined in any court of the United States, than according to the rules of the common law.

Amendment VIII

Excessive bail shall not be required, nor excessive fines imposed, nor cruel and unusual punishments inflicted.

Amendment IX

The enumeration in the Constitution of certain rights shall not be construed to deny or disparage others retained by the people.

Amendment X

The powers not delegated to the United States by the Constitution, nor prohibited by it to the States, are reserved to the States respectively, or to the people.

Amendment XI

[January 8, 1798]

The judicial power of the United States shall not be construed to extend to any suit in law or equity, commended or prosecuted against one of the United States by citizens of another State, or by citizens or subjects of any foreign State.

Amendment XII

[September 25, 1804]

The electors shall meet in their respective States, and vote by ballot for President and Vice President, one of whom, at least, shall not be an inhabitant of the same State with themselves; they shall name in their ballots the person voted for as President, and in distinct ballots, the person voted for as Vice President, and they shall make distinct lists of all persons voted for as President and of all persons voted for as Vice President, and of the number of votes for each, which lists they shall sign and certify, and transmit sealed to the seat of the government of the United States, directed to the President of the Senate;—The President of the Senate shall, in the presence of the Senate and House of Representatives, open all the certificates and the votes shall then be counted;—The person having the greatest number of votes for President, shall be the President, if such number be a majority of the whole number of electors appointed; and if no person have such majority, then from the persons having the highest numbers not exceeding three on the list of those voted for as President, the House of Representatives shall choose immediately, by ballot, the President. But in choosing the President, the votes shall be taken by States, the representation from each State having one vote; a quorum for this purpose shall consist of a member or members from two thirds of the States, and a majority of all the States shall be necessary to a choice. And if the House of Representatives shall not choose a President whenever the right of choice shall devolve upon them, before the fourth day of March next following, then the Vice President shall act as President, as in the case of the death or other constitutional disability of the President. The person having the greatest number of votes as Vice President shall be the Vice President, if such number be a majority of the whole number of electors appointed, and if no person have a majority, then from the two highest numbers on the list, the Senate shall choose the Vice President; a quorum for the purpose shall consist of two thirds of the whole number of Senators, and a majority of the whole number shall be necessary to a choice. But no person constitutionally ineligible to the office of President shall be eligible to that of Vice President of the United States.

Amendment XIII

[December 18, 1865]

Section 1.

Neither slavery nor involuntary servitude, except as a punishment for crime whereof the party shall have been duly convicted, shall exist within the United States, or any place subject to their jurisdiction.

Section 2.

Congress shall have power to enforce this article by appropriate legislation.

Amendment XIV

[July 28, 1868]

Section 1.

All persons born or naturalized in the United States, and subject to the jurisdiction thereof, are citizens of the United States and of the State wherein they reside. No State shall make or enforce any law which shall abridge the privileges or immunities of citizens of the United States; nor shall any State deprive any person of life, liberty, or property, without due process of law; nor deny to any person within its jurisdiction the equal protection of the laws.

Section 2.

Representatives shall be apportioned among the several States according to their respective numbers, counting the whole number of persons in each State, excluding Indians not taxed. But when the right to vote at any election for the choice of electors for President and Vice President of the United States, representatives in Congress, the executive and judicial officers of a State, or the members of the legislature thereof, is denied to any of the male inhabitants of such State, being twenty-one years of age, and citizens of the United States, or in any way abridged, except for participating in rebellion, or other crime, the basis of representation there shall be reduced in the proportion which the number of such male citizens shall bear to the whole number of male citizens twenty-one years of age in such State.

Section 3.

No person shall be a senator or representative in Congress, or elector of President and Vice President, or hold any office, civil or military, under the United

States, or under any State, who having previously taken an oath, as a member of Congress, or as an officer of the United States, or as a member of any State legislature, or as an executive or judicial officer of any State, to support the Constitution of the United States, shall have engaged in insurrection or rebellion against the same, or given aid or comfort to the enemies thereof. But Congress may by a vote of two thirds of each House, remove such disability.

Section 4.

The validity of the public debt of the United States, authorized by law, including debts incurred for payment of pensions and bounties for services in suppressing insurrection or rebellion; shall not be questioned. But neither the United States nor any State shall assume or pay any debt or obligation incurred in aid of insurrection or rebellion against the United States, or any claim for the loss or emancipation of any slave; but all such debts, obligations, and claims shall be held illegal and void.

Section 5.

The Congress shall have the power to enforce, by appropriate legislation, the provisions of this article.

Amendment XV

[March 30, 1870]

Section 1.

The right of citizens of the United States to vote shall not be denied or abridged by the United States or by any State on account of race, color, or previous condition of servitude.

Section 2.

The Congress shall have power to enforce this article by appropriate legislation.

Amendment XVI

[February 25, 1913]

The Congress shall have power to lay and collect taxes on incomes, from whatever source derived, without apportionment among the several States, and without regard to any census or enumeration.

Amendment XVII
[May 31, 1913]

The Senate of the United States shall be composed of two senators from each State, elected by the people thereof, for six years; and each senator shall have one vote. The electors in each State shall have the qualifications requisite for electors of the most numerous branch of the State legislature.

When vacancies happen in the representation of any State in the Senate, the executive authority of such State shall issue writs of election to fill such vacancies: *Provided*, That the legislature of any State may empower the executive thereof to make temporary appointments until the people fill the vacancies by election as the legislature may direct.

This amendment shall not be so construed as to affect the election or term of any senator chosen before it becomes valid as part of the Constitution.

Amendment XVIII[11]
[January 29, 1919]

After one year from the ratification of this article, the manufacture, sale, or transportation of intoxicating liquors within, the importation thereof into, or the exportation thereof from the United States and all territory subject to the jurisdiction thereof for beverage purposes is thereby prohibited.

The Congress and the several States shall have concurrent power to enforce this article by appropriate legislation.

This article shall be inoperative unless it shall have been ratified as an amendment to the Constitution by the legislatures of the several States, as provided in the constitution, within seven years from the date of the submission hereof to the States by Congress.

Amendment XIX
[August 26, 1920]

The right of citizens of the United States to vote shall not be denied or abridged by the United States or by any State on account of sex.

Congress shall have the power to enforce this article by appropriate legislation.

Amendment XX

[January 23, 1933]

Section 1.

The terms of the President and Vice President shall end at noon on the 20th day of January and the terms of Senators and Representatives at noon on the 3rd day of January, of the years in which such terms would have ended if this article had not been ratified; and the terms of their successors shall then begin.

Section 2.

The Congress shall assemble at least once in every year, and such meeting shall begin at noon on the 3rd day of January, unless they shall by law appoint a different day.

Section 3.

If, at the time fixed for the beginning of the term of President, the President-elect shall have died, the Vice President-elect shall become President. If a President shall not have been chosen before the time fixed for the beginning of his term, or if the President-elect shall have failed to qualify, then the Vice President-elect shall act as President until a President shall have qualified; and the Congress may by law provide for the case wherein neither a President-elect nor a Vice President-elect shall have qualified, declaring who shall then act as President, or the manner in which one who is to act shall be selected, and such person shall act accordingly until a President or Vice President shall have qualified.

Section 4.

The Congress may by law provide for the case of the death of any of the persons from whom, the House of Representatives may choose a President whenever the right of choice shall have devolved upon them, and for the case of the death of any of the persons from whom the Senate may choose a Vice President whenever the right of choice shall have devolved upon them.

Section 5.

Sections 1 and 2 shall take effect on the 15th day of October following the ratification of this article.

Section 6.

This article shall be inoperative unless it shall have been ratified as an amendment to the Constitution by the legislatures of three-fourths of the several States within seven years from the date of its submission.

Amendment XXI

[December 5, 1933]

Section 1.

The Eighteenth Article of amendment to the Constitution of the United States is hereby repealed.

Section 2.

The transportation or importation into any State, Territory, or possession of the United States for delivery or use therein of intoxicating liquors in violation of the laws thereof, is hereby prohibited.

Section 3.

This article shall be inoperative unless it shall have been ratified as an amendment to the Constitution by conventions in the several States, as provided in the Constitution, within seven years from the date of the submission thereof to the States by the Congress.

Amendment XXII

[March 1, 1951]

No person shall be elected to the office of the President more than twice, and no person who has held the office of President, or acted as President, for more than two years of a term to which some other person was elected President shall be elected to the office of the President more than once.

But this article shall not apply to any person holding the office of President when this article was proposed by the Congress, and shall not prevent any person who may be holding the office of President, or acting as President during the term within which this article becomes operative from holding the office of President or acting as President during the remainder of such term.

This article shall be inoperative unless it shall have been ratified as an amendment to the Constitution by the legislatures of three-fourths of the several States within seven years from the date of its submission to the States by the Congress.

Amendment XXIII

[March 29, 1961]

Section 1.

The District constituting the seat of Government of the United States shall appoint in such manner as the Congress may direct.

A number of electors of President and Vice President equal to the whole number of Senators and Representatives in Congress to which the District would be entitled if it were a state, but in no event more than the least populous State; they shall be in addition to those appointed by the States, but they shall be considered, for the purposes of the election of President and Vice President, to be electors appointed by a State; and they shall meet in the District and perform such duties as provided by the twelfth article of amendment.

Section 2.

The Congress shall have power to enforce this article by appropriate legislation.

Amendment XXIV
[January 23, 1964]
Section 1.

The right of citizens of the United States to vote in any primary or other election for President or Vice President, for electors for President or Vice President or for Senator or Representative in Congress, shall not be denied or abridged by the United States or any State by reason of failure to pay any poll tax or other tax.

Section 2.

The Congress shall have power to enforce this article by appropriate legislation.

Amendment XXV
[February 10, 1967]
Section 1.

In case of the removal of the President from office or of his death or resignation, the Vice President shall become President.

Section 2.

Whenever there is a vacancy in the office of the Vice president, the President shall nominate a Vice President who shall take office upon confirmation by a majority of both Houses of Congress.

Section 3.

Whenever the President transmits to the President pro tempore of the Senate and the Speaker of the House of Representatives his written declaration that he is unable to discharge the powers and duties of his office, and until he transmits to them a written declaration to the contrary, such powers and duties shall be discharged by the Vice President as Acting President.

Section 4.

Whenever the Vice president and a majority of either the principal officers of the executive departments or of such other body as Congress may by law provide, transmit to the President pro tempore of the Senate and the Speaker of the House of Representatives their written declaration that the President is unable to discharge the powers and duties of his office, the Vice President shall immediately assume the powers and duties of the office as Acting President.

Thereafter, when the President transmits to the President pro tempore of the Senate and the Speaker of the House of Representatives his written declaration that no inability exists, he shall resume the powers and duties of his office unless the Vice President and a majority of either the principal officers of the executive departments or of such other body as Congress may by law provide, transmit within four days to the President pro tempore of the Senate and the Speaker of the House of Representatives their written declaration that the President is unable to discharge the powers and duties of his office. Thereupon Congress shall decide the issue, assembling within forty-eight hours for that purpose if not in session. If the Congress, within twenty-one days after receipt of the latter written declaration, or, if Congress is not in session, within twenty-one days after Congress is required to assemble, determines by two-thirds vote of both Houses that the President is unable to discharge the powers and duties of his office, the Vice President shall continue to discharge the same as Acting President otherwise, the President shall resume the powers and duties of his office.

Amendment XXVI

[June 30, 1971]

Section 1.

The right of citizens of the United States who are eighteen years of age or older to vote shall not be denied or abridged by the United States or by any State on account of age.

Section 2.

The Congress shall have power to enforce this article by appropriate legislation.

Notes

1. See the Sixteenth Amendment.
2. See the Fourteenth Amendment.
3. See the Seventeenth Amendment.
4. See the Seventeenth Amendment.

5. See the Sixteenth Amendment.
6. Superseded by the Twelfth Amendment.
7. See the Eleventh Amendment.
8. See the Fourteenth Amendment, Sec. 1.
9. See the Thirteenth Amendment.
10. See the Fourteenth Amendment, Sec. 4.
11. Repealed by the Twenty-first Amendment.

Federalist 10 (1787–1788)
James Madison

November 22, 1787
To the People of the State of New York

Among the numerous advantages promised by a well-constructed union, none deserves to be more accurately developed than its tendency to break and control the violence of faction. The friend of popular governments never finds himself so much alarmed for their character and fate as when he contemplates their propensity to this dangerous vice. He will not fail, therefore, to set a due value on any plan which, without violating the principles to which he is attached, provides a proper cure for it. The instability, injustice, and confusion introduced into the public councils have, in truth, been the mortal diseases under which popular governments have everywhere perished, as they continue to be the favorite and fruitful topics from which the adversaries to liberty derive their most specious declamations. The valuable improvements made by the American constitutions on the popular models, both ancient and modern, cannot certainly be too much admired; but it would be an unwarrantable partiality to contend that they have as effectually obviated the danger on this side, as was wished and expected. Complaints are everywhere heard from our most considerate and virtuous citizens, equally the friends of public and private faith and of public and personal liberty; that our governments are too unstable; that the public good is disregarded in the conflicts of rival parties; and that measures are too often decided not according to the rules of justice and the rights of the minor party, but by the superior force of an interested and overbearing majority. However anxiously we may wish that these complaints had no foundation, the evidence of known facts will not permit us to deny that they are in some degree true. It will be found, indeed, on a candid review of our situation, that some of the distresses under which we labor have been erroneously charged on the operation of our governments; but it will be found, at the same time, that other causes will not alone account for many of our heaviest misfortunes and, particularly, for that prevailing and increasing distrust of public engagements and alarm for private rights which are echoed from one end of the continent to the others. These must chiefly, if not wholly, effects of the unsteadiness and injustice with which a factious spirit has tainted our public administrations.

By a faction I understand a number of citizens, whether amounting to a majority or minority of the whole, who are united and actuated by some common impulse of passion, or of interest, adverse to the rights of other citizens, or to the permanent and aggregate interests of the community.

There are two methods of curing the mischiefs of faction: the one, by removing its causes; the other, by controlling its effects.

There are again two methods of removing the causes of faction: the one, by destroying the liberty which is essential to its existence; the other, by giving to every citizen the same opinions, the same passions, and the same interests.

It could never be more truly said than of the first remedy that it was worse than the disease. Liberty is to faction what air is to fire, an aliment without which it instantly expires. But it could not be a less folly to abolish liberty, which is essential to political life, because it nourishes faction than it would be to wish the annihilation of air, which is essential to animal life, because it imparts to fire its destructive agency.

The second expedient is as impracticable as the first would be unwise. As long as the reason of man continues fallible and he is at liberty to exercise it, different opinions will be formed. As long as the connection subsists between his reason and his self-love, his opinions and his passions will have a reciprocal influence on each other; and the former will be objects to which the latter will attach themselves. The diversity in the faculties of men, from which the rights of property originate, is not less an insuperable obstacle to a uniformity of interests. The protection of these faculties is the first object of government. From the protection of different and unequal faculties of acquiring property, the possession of different degrees and kinds of property immediately results; and from the influence of these on the sentiments and views of the respective proprietors ensues a division of the society into different interests and parties.

The latent causes of faction are thus sown in the nature of man; and we see them everywhere brought into different degrees of activity, according to the different circumstances of civil society. A zeal for different opinions concerning religion, concerning government and many other points, as well of speculation as of practice; an attachment to different leaders ambitiously contending for pre-eminence and power; or to persons of other descriptions whose fortunes have been interesting to the human passions, have, in turn, divided mankind into parties, inflamed them with mutual animosity, and rendered them much more disposed to vex and oppress each other than to co-operate for their common good. So strong is this propensity of mankind to fall into mutual animosities, that where no substantial occasion presents itself, the most frivolous and fanciful distinctions have been sufficient to kindle their unfriendly passions and excite their most violent conflicts. But the most common and durable source of factions has been the various and unequal distribution of property. Those who hold and those who are without property have ever formed distinct interests in society. Those who are creditors, and those who are debtors, fall under a like discrimination. A landed interest, a manufacturing interest, a mercantile interest, a moneyed interest, with many lesser interests, grow up of necessity in civilized nations and divide them into different classes, actuated by different sentiments and views. The regulation of these various and interfering interests forms the principal task of modern legislation and involves the spirit of party and faction in the necessary and ordinary operations of government.

No man is allowed to be a judge in his own cause, because his interest would certainly bias his judgment, and, not improbably, corrupt his integrity. With equal, nay with greater reason, a body of men are unfit to be both judges and parties at the same time; yet what are many of the most important acts of legislation but so many judicial determinations, not indeed concerning the rights of single persons, but concerning the rights of large bodies of citizens? And what are the different classes of legislators but advocates and parties to the causes which they determine? Is a law proposed concerning private debts? It is a question to which the creditors are parties on one side and the debtors on the other. Justice ought to hold the balance between them. Yet the parties are, and must be, themselves the judges; and the most numerous party, or in other words, the most powerful faction must be expected to prevail. Shall domestic manufacturers be encouraged, and in what degree, by restrictions on foreign manufacturers? are questions which would be differently decided by the landed and the manufacturing classes, and probably by neither with a sole regard to justice and the public good. The apportionment of taxes on the various descriptions of property is an act which seems to require the most exact impartiality; yet there is perhaps, no legislative act in which greater opportunity and temptation are given to a predominant party to trample on the rules of justice. Every shilling with which they over-burden the inferior number is a shilling saved to their own pockets.

It is in vain to say that enlightened statesmen will be able to adjust these clashing interests and render them all subservient to the public good. Enlightened statesmen will not always be at the helm. Nor, in many cases, can such an adjustment be made at all without taking into view indirect and remote considerations, which will rarely prevail over the immediate interest which one party may find in disregarding the rights of another or the good of the whole.

The inference to which we are brought is that the *causes* of faction cannot be removed and the relief is only to be sought in the means of controlling its *effects*.

If a faction consists of less than a majority, relief is supplied by the republican principle, which enables the majority to defeat its sinister views by regular vote. It many clog the administration, it may convulse the society; but it will be unable to execute and mask its violence under the forms of the Constitution. When a majority is included in a faction, the form of popular government, on the other hand, enables it to sacrifice to its ruling passion or interest, both the public good and the rights of other citizens. To secure the public good, and private rights against the danger of such a faction, and at the same time to preserve the spirit and the form of popular government, is then the great object to which our inquiries are directed. Let me add that it is the great desideratum by which alone this form of government can be rescued from the opprobrium under which it has so long labored and be recommended to the esteem and adoption of mankind.

By what means is this object attainable? Evidently by one of two only. Either the existence of the same passion or interest in a majority at the same time must be prevented, or the majority, having such coexistent passion or interest, must be rendered, by their number and local situation, unable to concert and carry into effect schemes of oppression. If the impulse and the opportunity be suffered to coincide, we well know that neither moral nor religious motives can be relied on as an adequate control. They are not found to be such on the injustice and violence of individuals, and lose their efficacy in proportion to the number combined together, that is, in proportion as their efficacy becomes needful.

From this view of the subject it may be concluded that a pure democracy, by which I mean a society consisting of a small number of citizens who assemble and administer the government in person, can admit of no cure for the mischiefs of faction. A common passion or interest will, in almost every case, be felt by a majority of the whole; a communication and concert results from the form of government itself; and there is nothing to check the inducements to sacrifice the weaker party or an obnoxious individual. Hence it is that such democracies have ever been spectacles of turbulence and contention; have ever been found incompatible with personal security or the rights of property; and have in general been as short in their lives as they have been violent in their deaths. Theoretic politicians, who have patronized this species of government, have erroneously supposed that by reducing mankind to a perfect equality in their political rights, they would at the same time be perfectly equalized and assimilated in their possessions, their opinions, and their passions.

A republic, by which I mean a government in which the scheme of representation takes place, opens a different prospect and promises the cure for which we are seeking. Let us examine the points in which it varies from pure democracy, and we shall comprehend both the nature of the cure and the efficacy which it must derive from the Union.

The two great points of difference between a democracy and a republic are: first, the delegation of the government, in the latter, to a small number of citizens elected by the rest; secondly, the greater number of citizens and greater sphere of country over which the latter may be extended.

The effect of the first difference is, on the one hand, to refine and enlarge the public views by passing them through the medium of a chosen body of citizens, whose wisdom may best discern the true interest of their country and whose patriotism and love of justice will be least likely to sacrifice it to temporary or partial considerations. Under such a regulation, it may well happen that the public voice, pronounced by the representatives of the people, will be more consonant to the public good than if pronounced by the people themselves, convened for that purpose. On the other hand, the effect may be inverted. Men of factious tempers, of local prejudices, or of sinister designs, may, by intrigue, by corruption, or by other means, first obtain the suffrages, and then betray the interests of the people. The question resulting is, whether small or extensive republics are most favorable to the election of proper guardians of the public weal; and it is clearly decided in favor of the latter by two obvious considerations.

In the first place it is to be remarked that however small the republic may be, the representatives must be raised to a certain number in order to guard against the cabals of a few; and that however large it may be, they must be limited to a certain number in order to guard against the confusion of a multitude. Hence, the number of representatives in the two cases not being in proportion to that of the constituents, and being proportionally greatest in the small republic, it follows that if the proportion of fit characters be not less in the large than in the small republic, the former will present a greater option, and consequently a greater probability of a fit choice.

In the next place, as each representative will be chosen by a greater number of citizens in the large than in the small republic, it will be more difficult for unworthy candidates to practice with success the vicious arts by which elections are too often carried; and the suffrages of the people being more free, will be more likely to center on men who possess the most attractive merit and the most diffusive and established characters.

It must be confessed that in this, as in most other cases, there is a mean, on both sides of which inconveniencies will be found to lie. By enlarging too much the number of electors, you render the representative too little acquainted with all their local circumstances and lesser interests; as by reducing it too much, you render him unduly attached to these, and too little fit to comprehend and pursue great and national objects. The federal Constitution forms a happy combination in this respect; the great and aggregate interests being referred to the national, the local and particular to the State legislatures.

The other point of difference is the greater number of citizens and extent of territory which may be brought within the compass of republican than of democratic government; and it is this circumstance principally which renders factious combinations less to be dreaded in the former than in the latter. The smaller the society, the fewer probably will be the distinct parties and interests composing it; the fewer the distinct parties and interests, the more frequently will a majority be found of the same party; and the smaller the number of individuals composing a majority, and the small the compass within which they are placed, the more easily will they concert and execute their plans of oppression. Extend the sphere and you take in a greater variety of parties and interests; you make it less probably that a majority of the whole will have a common motive to invade the rights of other citizens; or if such a common motive exists, it will be more difficult for all who feel it to discover their own strength and to act in unison with each other. Besides other impediments, it may be remarked that, where there is a consciousness of unjust or dishonorable purposes, communication is always checked by distrust in proportion to the number whose concurrence is necessary.

Hence, it clearly appears that the same advantage which a republic has over a democracy in controlling the effects of faction is enjoyed by a large over a small republic—is enjoyed by the Union over the States composing it. Does this advantage consist in the substitution of representatives whose enlightened views and virtuous sentiments render them superior to local prejudices and to schemes of injustice? It will not be denied that the representation of the Union will be most likely to possess these requisite endowments. Does it consist in the greater security afforded by a greater variety of parties, against the event of any one party being able to outnumber and oppress the rest? In an equal degree does the increased variety of parties comprised within the Union increase this security? Does it, in fine, consist in the greater obstacles opposed to the concert and accomplishment of the secret wishes of an unjust and interested majority? Here again the extent of the Union gives it the most palpable advantage.

The influence of factious leaders may kindle a flame within their particular States but will be unable to spread a general conflagration through the other States. A religious sect may degenerate into a political faction in a part of the Confederacy; but the variety of sects dispersed over the entire face of it must secure the national councils against any danger from that source. A rage for paper money, for an abolition of debts, for an equal division of property, or for any other improper or wicked project, will be less apt to pervade the whole body of the Union than a particular member of it; in the same proportion as such a malady is more likely to taint a particular county or district than an entire State.

In the extent and proper structure of the Union, therefore, we behold a republican remedy for the diseases most incident to republican government. And according to the degree of pleasure and pride we feel in being republicans ought to be our zeal in cherishing the spirit and supporting the character of federalists.

Federalist 51
James Madison

February 6, 1788
To the People of the State of New York

To what expedient, then, shall we finally resort for maintaining in practice the necessary partition of power among the several departments, as laid down in the Constitution? The only answer that can be given is that as all these exterior provisions are found to be inadequate, the defect must be supplied by so contriving the interior structure of the government as that its several constituent parts may, by their mutual relations, be the means of keeping each other in their proper places. Without presuming to undertake a full development of this important idea I will hazard a few general observations which may perhaps place it in a clearer light, and enable us to form a more correct judgment of the principles and structure of the government planned by the convention.

In order to lay a due foundation for that separate and distinct exercise of the different powers of government, which to a certain extent is admitted on all hands to be essential to the preservation of liberty, it is evident that each department should have a will of its own; and consequently should be so constituted that the members of each should have as little agency as possible in the appointment of the members of the others. Were this principle rigorously adhered to, it would require that all the appointments for the supreme executive, legislative, and judiciary magistracies should be drawn from the same fountain of authority, the people, through channels having no communication whatever with one another. Perhaps such a plan of constructing the several departments would be less difficult in practice than it may in contemplation appear. Some difficulties, however, and some additional expense would attend the execution of it. Some deviations, therefore, from the principle must be admitted. In the constitution of the judiciary department in particular, it might be inexpedient to insist rigorously on the principle first, because peculiar qualifications being essential in the members, the primary consideration ought to be to select that mode of choice which best secures these qualifications, second, because the permanent tenure by which the appointments are held in that department must soon destroy all sense of dependence on the authority conferring them.

It is equally evident that the members of each department should be as little dependent as possible on those of the others for the emoluments annexed to their offices. Were the executive magistrate, or the judges, not independent of the legislature in this particular, their independence in every other would be merely nominal.

But the great security against a gradual concentration of the several powers in the same department consists in giving to those who administer each department the necessary constitutional means and personal motives to resist encroachments of the others. The provision for defense must in this, as in all other cases, be made commensurate to the danger of attack. Ambition must be made to counteract ambition. The interest of the man must be connected with the constitutional rights of the place. It may be a reflection on human nature that such devices should be necessary to control the abuses of government. But what is government itself but the greatest of all reflections on human nature? If men were angels, no government would be necessary. If angels were to govern men, neither external nor internal controls on government would be necessary. In framing a government which is to be administered by men over men, the great difficulty lies in this: You must first enable the government to control the governed; and in the next place, oblige it to control itself. A dependence on the people is, no doubt, the primary control on the government; but experience has taught mankind the necessity of auxiliary precautions.

This policy of supplying, by opposite and rival interests, the defect of better motives, might be traced through the whole system of human affairs, private as well as public. We see it particularly displayed in all the subordinate distributions of power, where the constant aim is to divide and arrange the several offices in such a manner as that each may be a check on the other—that the private interest of every individual may be a sentinel over the public rights. These inventions of prudence cannot be less requisite in the distribution of the supreme powers of the State.

But it is not possible to give to each department an equal power of self defense. In republican government, the legislative authority necessarily predominates. The remedy for this inconveniency is to divide the legislature into different branches and to render them, by different modes of election and different principles of action, as little connected with each other as the nature of their common functions and their common dependence on the society will admit. It may even be necessary to guard against dangerous encroachments by still further precautions. As the weight of the legislative authority requires that it should be thus divided, the weakness of the executive may require, on the other hand, that it should be fortified. An absolute negative on the legislature appears, at first view, to be the natural defense with which the executive magistrate should be armed. But perhaps it would be neither altogether safe nor alone sufficient. On ordinary occasions it might not be exerted with the requisite firmness, and on extraordinary occasions it might be perfidiously abused. May not this defect of an absolute negative be supplied by some qualified connection between this weaker department and the weaker branch of the stronger department, by which the latter may be led to support the constitutional rights of the former, without being too much detached from the rights of its own department?

If the principles on which these observations are founded be just, as I persuade myself they are, and they be applied as a criterion to the several State constitutions, and to the federal Constitution, it will be found that if the latter does not perfectly correspond with them, the former are infinitely less able to bear such a test.

There are, moreover, two considerations particularly applicable to the federal system of America, which place that system in a very interesting point of view.

First. In a single republic, all the power surrendered by the people is submitted to the administration of a single government, and usurpations are guarded against by a division of the government into distinct and separate departments. In the compound republic of America, the power surrendered by the people is first divided between two distinct governments, and then the portion allotted to each subdivided among distinct and separate departments. Hence a double security arises to the rights of the people. The different governments will control each other, at the same time that each will be controlled by itself.

Second. It is of great importance in a republic not only to guard the society against the oppression of its rulers, but to guard one part of the society against the injustice of the other part. Different interests necessarily exist in different classes of citizens. If a majority be united by a common interest, the rights of the minority will be insecure. There are but two methods of providing against the evil: the one by creating a will in the community independent of the majority—that is, of the society itself; the other, by comprehending in the society so many separate descriptions of citizens as will render an unjust combination of a majority of the whole very improbable, if not impracticable. The first method prevails in all governments possessing an hereditary or self-appointed authority. This, at best, is but a precarious security; because a power independent of the society may as well espouse the unjust views of the major as the rightful interests of the minor party, and may possibly be turned against both parties. The second method will be exemplified in the federal republic of the United States. Whilst all authority in it will be derived from and dependent on the society, the society itself will be broken into so many parts, interests and classes of citizens, that the rights of individuals, or of the minority, will be in little danger from interested combinations of the majority. In a free government the security for civil rights must be the same as that for religious rights. It consists in the one case in the multiplicity of interests, and in the other in the multiplicity of sects. The degree of security in both cases will depend on the number of interests and sects; and this may be presumed to depend on the extent of country and number of people comprehended under the same government. This view of the subject must particularly recommend a proper federal system to all the sincere and considerate friends of republican government, since it shows that in exact proportion as the territory of the Union may be formed into more circumscribed Confederacies, or States, oppressive combinations of a majority will be facilitated; the best security, under the republican forms, for the rights of every class of citizen, will be diminished; and consequently the stability and independence of some member of the government, the only other security, must be proportionally increased. Justice is the end of government. It is the end of civil society. It ever has been and ever will be pursued until it be obtained, or until liberty be lost in the pursuit. In a society under the forms of which the stronger faction can readily unite and oppress the weaker, anarchy may as truly be said to reign as in a state of nature where the weaker individual is not secured against the violence of the stronger; and as, in the latter state, even the stronger individuals are prompted, by the uncertainty of their condition, to submit to a government which may protect the weak as well as themselves; so, in the former state, will be more powerful factions or parties be gradually induced, by the like motive, to wish for a government which will protect all parties, the weaker as well as the more powerful. It can be little doubted that if the State of Rhode Island was separated from the Confederacy and left to itself, the insecurity of rights under the popular form of government within such narrow limits would be displayed by such reiterated oppressions of factious majorities that some power altogether independent of the people would soon be called for by the voice of the very factions whose misrule had proved the necessity of it. In the extended republic of the United States, and among the great variety of interests, parties, and sects which it embraces, a coalition of a majority of the whole society could seldom take place on any other principles than those of justice and the general good; whilst there being thus less danger to a minor from the will of the major party, there must be less pretext, also, to provide for the security of the former, by introducing into the government a will not dependent on the latter, or, in other words, a will independent of the society itself. It is no less certain than it is important, notwithstanding the contrary opinions which have been entertained, that the larger the society, provided it lie within a practicable sphere, the more duly capable it will be of self-government. And happily for the *republican cause*, the practicable sphere may be carried for a very great extent by a judicious modification and mixture of the *federal principle*.

Publius

Gettysburg Address

Fourscore and seven years ago our fathers brought forth upon this continent a new nation, conceived in liberty, and dedicated to the proposition that all men are created equal.

Now we are engaged in a great civil war, testing whether that nation, or any nation so conceived and so dedicated, can long endure. We are met on a great battlefield of that war. We have come to dedicate a portion of that field, as a final resting-place for those who here gave their lives that that nation might live. It is altogether fitting and proper that we should do this.

But, in a larger sense, we cannot dedicate—we cannot consecrate—we cannot hallow—this ground. The brave men, living and dead, who struggled here have consecrated it, far above our poor power to add or detract. The world will little note, nor long remember what we say here, but it can never forget what they did here. It is for us the living, rather, to be dedicated here to the unfinished work they who fought here have thus far so nobly advanced. It is rather for us to be here dedicated to the great task remaining before us—that from these honored dead we take increased devotion to that cause for which they here gave the last full measure of devotion—that we here highly resolve that these dead shall not have died in vain—that this nation, under God, shall have a new birth of freedom—and that government of the people, by the people, and for the people, shall not perish from the earth.

GLOSSARY

Alger, Horatio Jr. (1832–1899): American writer of popular boys' stories whose heroes gain success by struggling valiantly against poverty and adversity. All stories also contain an element of luck.

Alien and Sedition Acts: Collective name given to four acts passed in 1798 by Congress that restricted freedom of speech and the liberty of foreigners living in the U.S.

American Exceptionalism: Attitude attributed to Americans suggesting that they are somehow unique or exceptional to other political societies. Allows them make their own set of rules that are not bound by convention or even world experience.

America Question: The US is a nation quite unlike any other, seeming to operate successfully on a set of principles different from any other nation. The America Question is: What has made those successes possible?

Anarchy: Literally "rule of no one." Mob rule. Chaotic lawlessness due to absence of governmental control.

Anti-Federalists: Opponents of a strong national government who opposed ratification of the Constitution.

Articles of Confederation: Document which set up a loose confederation of states that comprised the first national government of the US from 1781 to 1788.

Aristocracy: Rule by a small group of a society's "best" citizens, the selection of which may be based on birth, wealth, ability, social standing or ecclesiastical position.

Bill of Attainder: Legislative act that authorizes the detention of a person, declares them guilty and imposes a punishment without a judicial trial.

Broad Construction: A reading of the Constitution, originating with Alexander Hamilton, holding that the federal government possesses a wide range of implied powers necessary for the execution of its responsibilities.

Brown v. Board of Education of Topeka (1954): Supreme Court decision declaring that "separate but equal" schools for different races were unconstitutional.

Calhoun, John C. (1782–1850): South Carolina politician and US vice president (1825–1832); defender of states' rights, slavery and legality of secession.

Calling: A Puritan belief that by pursuing worldly careers virtuously, a person was in effect glorifying God.

Calvin, John (1509–1564): Wrote *Institutes of the Christian Religion* in which he advocated purification of the church. His theology was the foundation of the Puritan religion.

Civil Liberty: Also known as moral self-governance; the freedom to do what is right.

Common Law: Body of law developed in England by judicial decisions over time. Based on custom and precedent, it constitutes the basis of the English legal system.

Constitution: A written or otherwise recognized agreement within a polity setting forth principles and laws upon which a government will be structured and guaranteeing certain rights to the people.

Counterpoise: Control mechanism by which the self-interest of one group is balanced against that of another.

Covenant: A formal agreement among the members of a political or religious group which functions as a founding document.

Deists: Those who subscribe to a school of religious thought which emphasizes that a basic morality is inborn in every person which can be accessed by the use of reason and a belief in a Creator who is the rational architect of an ordered universe.

Demagogue: A leader who gains power by appealing to popular passions and prejudices, and by championing the cause of the common people.

Democracy: Governmental system in which ultimate political authority lies with the people, through direct participation.

Despotism: Oppressive rule by a single individual.

Divine Right of Kings: Theory that legitimized the power of kings over the people by holding that kings inherited their authority directly from God.

Dred Scott Decision (1857): Supreme Court ruling that slaves are not citizens and therefore cannot sue, and that Congress has no jurisdiction over slavery in the territories.

English Bill of Rights: Incorporated in 1689, gave civil and political rights to the people and political supremacy to Parliament.

English Enlightenment: Dawn of an era of new ideas and "light" in the seventeenth century; in English political philosophy, stressed application of the "laws of nature" by writers such as John Locke and Thomas Hobbes.

Equilibrium Price: In a free market, the price at which the quantity that consumers want to purchase equals the quantity that producers want to supply.

Ex Post Facto: Literal translation means "after the fact". When discussed in conjunction with law, refers to making something a crime and holding a person accountable to it after the action has already occurred.

Farewell Address: Given by George Washington in September, 1796. Influenced by Alexander Hamilton, it cautioned against political parties and foreign entanglements.

Federalism: The division of power between the national and state government. Both act directly upon the people, are supreme within their proper spheres of authority, and must consent to constitutional change.

The Federalist: Collection of eight-five essays written by James Madison, Alexander Hamilton and John Jay, published under the name "Publius." It was the deepest and most searching inquiry into republican government ever written.

Federalists: Supporters of a strong national government who favored ratification of the Constitution.

Founding Myth: Imparts a sense of legitimacy to a political society by identifying the founding as sanctioned by the gods, by nature, by truth and justice or by history.

Gibbons v. Ogden (1824): Supreme Court decision that only federal authorities can regulate interstate commerce.

Good Society: Escapes the human predicament by providing benefits for its citizens.

Great Oughts: Certain rights drafted into the Constitution in rhetorical rather than legal language. Meant to be shining standards of rights that people *ought to have*, and were to be used as rallying points for citizens. In the US Constitution they comprise freedom of expression, freedom of conscience and the right to privacy.

Implied Rights: Rights not specifically identified in the Constitution that have been inferred from stated rights.

Jay, John (1745–1829): Prominent New York statesman and first Chief Justice of the Supreme Court. His participation in writing the essays in *The Federalist* was limited because of ill health.

Jay's Treaty: Negotiated with Britain in 1794. The US made major concessions to avert a war over the seizure of US ships. The terms were extremely unfavorable to US interests.

Judicial Legislation: The result when a court crosses over the fine line between interpreting the law and making a law, in favor of making a law.

Judicial Review: Power of the court to declare laws or acts of the legislative or executive branches unconstitutional. The Constitution is supreme law, acts contrary to it are unconstitutional, and thus null and void.

Kentucky and Virginia Resolutions: Response sponsored by Thomas Jefferson and James Madison to the Alien and Sedition Acts. In 1798, they argued that the states created the federal union and retained the right to declare acts of the federal government null and void if not deemed beneficial or benevolent.

Lawgiver: One who divines the laws of society and sets them forth, endowing the law with a special sanctity.

Law of Comparative Advantage: Every individual, group or nation can produce at least one good or service at lower opportunity cost than others. To maximize their standard of living, they should specialize in the production of such goods or services.

Laws of Nature: Refers to the notion that there are laws that govern the entire universe giving it order and purpose. These laws are presumed to be accessible to all human beings, endowing them with certain unalienable rights. (See Natural Law.)

Legal Positivism: A philosophy of law holding that the meaning of the law must be confined to the wording of legal statutes and is not open to any moral considerations behind the law.

Libel: The publication of knowingly false or malicious statements that damage someone's reputation.

Liberalism: Philosophy emphasizing individual freedom from several forms of restraint, including government.

License Cases (1847): Supreme Court decision reinterpreting the commerce clause as not giving the federal government sole power to regulate trade; increased sovereignty of states.

List, Friedrich (1789–1845): German economist who advocated economic well-being of nation-states over that of individuals and the government's responsibility to foster production.

Locke, John (1632–1704): English philosopher and political theorist, influential in colonial times for ideas of "social contract" and the principles of the rule of law.

Loyal opposition: Philosophical stance citizens take when they oppose something the government has done or is doing, yet remain loyal to the form of government itself.

Manifest Destiny: Phrase first used in 1845 which came to mean that the United States was destined by Providence to spread across the continent.

Marbury v. Madison: Supreme Court decision of 1803 that created the precedent of "judicial review."

McCulloch v. Maryland (1819): Supreme Court decision determining that states cannot tax federal institutions; an exercise in broad construction.

Mercantilism: British economic system that sought the self-sufficiency of Great Britain through favorable balances of trade with colonies and other imperialist policies. (See study aid for chapter 4.)

Monarchy: Rule by one, usually a king or queen.

Narrow Construction: A reading of the Constitution, originating with Thomas Jefferson, holding that the federal government's powers are strictly defined and specifically delegated.

Nationalists: Not a recognized group, but a label applied by historians to supporters of a strong central government.

Natural Law: The notion that there are laws that govern the entire universe giving it order and purpose. Natural Laws are the moral equivalent to physical laws like gravity.

Natural Liberty: Freedom to do whatever one desires.

Nature: The transcendent entity that gives order to the universe.

New Jersey/Paterson Plan: The small states' rebuttal to the Virginia Plan in which states would retain sovereignty, and representation would be equal for each state regardless of population.

Oligarchy: Oppressive rule by an elite few.

Opportunity Cost: The cost of any choice is measured by the value of the best forgone alternative.

Particular Founding: Correct only at a given time, in a given place and for a given people. (See study aid for chapter 1.)

Patria: The concept of a fatherland that evokes patriotic feelings and that stands above a particular government or political organization of society.

Patronage: A system whereby one person in society is dependent upon some higher person—his patron—for many of the opportunities of life. Operates on the basis of favors and informal understandings.

Political-Economic Problem: Dilemma of how to distribute scarce goods and services to maximize benefit to society.

Polity: A group of people who organize themselves into a political society.

Popular Government: Based on the natural rights concept that ultimate power rests with the people who can create, alter or abolish government. Differs from a democracy in that popular government avoids direct contact with the people, opting instead for representative institutions operating as filters between the people and the government.

Predestination: Doctrine that God, in consequence of his foreknowledge of all events, infallibly guides those who are destined for salvation or damnation.

Puritanism: A religious movement and culture based on Calvinistic doctrine and characterized by simplicity and austere living. This was done in an effort to "purify" the Church of England. (See study aid for chapter 2.)

Representation: A system where selected leaders represent a larger group of citizens.

Republic: A government in which supreme power resides in a body of citizens entitled to vote, and which is exercised by elected representatives responsible to the citizens and who govern according to law.

Republicanism: A political philosophy derived from ideas associated with classical antiquity which recognized the ultimate political power of society as being vested in the "people" and which strove to balance the inherent interests within society in order to produce a stable and effective government.

Rule-mindedness: A characteristic need in humans to create order by making and obeying rules.

Rule of Law: In the private sphere of human activities, the government may not act except in the enforcement of a known, general rule. For the rule of law to exist, five elements must be present: Generality, Prospectivity, Publicity, Consent and Due Process.

Scarcity: Unlimited wants in the face of limited resources, meaning that there will not be enough goods and services to satisfy all wants.

Scholasticism: A mode of inquiry that employs human reason to reach conclusions about theological questions.

Scottish Enlightenment: Ideas advocated by Thomas Reid, David Hume, Lord Kames, Thomas Ferguson, Francis Hutchinson and Adam Smith, stressing the role of the common person and common sense in perceiving truth; intuitive truth is revealed to everyone.

Sedition: Actions or criticisms that incite rebellion or discontent against established government.

Seditious libel: Political doctrine which holds that the government had the right to punish those who speak against it with malice.

Separation of Powers: The structural design in government that places rule-making and rule-enforcing powers in separate hands. The officials of each branch are selected by different procedures, have different terms of office, and are independent of one another. Designed to prevent tyranny.

Smith, Adam (1723–1790): Scottish economist whose work, *The Wealth of Nations*, has been vastly influential; argued for personal freedom to pursue economic goals with little government intervention.

Sovereignty: The power to make final or ultimate decisions, especially in regards to government.

State of nature: Hypothetical existence in which all humans lived in perfect freedom without society or government. All had the same rights granted by Nature and therefore enjoyed a basic equality.

Statesmanship: A quality necessary to some degree for republican leaders. Characterized by virtue (*areté*) as exhibited by putting public interests above private, showing enormous personal integrity, and exercising wise, practical, far-sighted leadership.

Stretch-points: Portions of the Constitution written ambiguously so as to leave them open to various interpretations about how far the powers of the government would extend and into what areas.

Structure: An overall organizational system composed of structural controls, using the predominance of self-interest to channel human nature toward a desirable outcome.

Timocracy: Government in which love of honor is the ruling principle.

Tocqueville, Alexis de (1805–1859): French statesman and author. His two-volume work, *Democracy in America* (1835), makes detailed observations about American society and politics.

Tribalism: One aspect of human nature. Reflects human desire to be with their own kind. Creates a sense of community and common purpose.

Turner's Thesis (1893): Proposal by historian Frederick Jackson Turner that America's uniqueness was tied to the opportunities presented by a vast frontier of unsettled, free land.

Tyranny: Rule of will. The use of the power of government to further the ends of a person or group.

Universal Founding: Correct for all people at all times and in all situations.

***U.S. v. E.C. Knight* (1895):** Supreme Court decision which curtailed the power of the federal government to regulate commerce by narrowing the meaning of the word "commerce."

Utopia: A futuristic place of ideal perfection (especially in laws, government and social conditions).

Virginia Plan/Resolves: Plan backed by the nationalists and large states at the Constitutional Convention, which proposed creating one large, unified republic in which representation would be decided by population.

Winthrop, John (1588–1649): Leader of the first Puritan colony in America. His vision of the Puritan colony as a city upon a hill is fundamental to the American character.

Zoon Politikon: Man as a political animal that is naturally interested in government and society.

INDEX

Note: Page numbers followed by the letter *f* indicate figures.